MODERN CAPITALISM

The Royal Institute of International Affairs is an unofficial body which promotes the scientific study of international questions and does not express opinions of its own. The opinions expressed in this publication are the responsibility of the author.

The Institute gratefully acknowledges the comments and suggestions of the following who read the manuscript on behalf of the Research Committee: Professor Asa Briggs, Alan Bullock, Sir Robert Shone.

MODERN CAPITALISM

The Changing Balance of Public and Private Power

ANDREW SHONFIELD

OXFORD UNIVERSITY PRESS

LONDON   OXFORD   NEW YORK

OXFORD UNIVERSITY PRESS

Oxford   London   Glasgow

New York   Toronto   Melbourne   Wellington

Nairobi   Dar es Salaam   Cape Town

Kuala Lumpur   Singapore   Jakarta   Hong Kong   Tokyo

Delhi   Bombay   Calcutta   Madras   Karachi

To ALFRED HECHT
for several years of argument
and encouragement leading
to this book.

CONTENTS

Part 3

MARKET IDEOLOGIES

Part 4

Part 4—*continued*

AN ESSAY ON SOME POLITICAL IMPLICATIONS OF
ACTIVE GOVERNMENT—*continued*
Independent Official, 404; A Reversal of the Separation of
Powers, 408; Discretionary Power versus Judicial Authority,
411; Conseil d'État, 414; Development of French Administrative Law; 417; Emphasis on Procedure, 419; The Ombudsman,
421; A Cult of Bureaucratic Humanity, 425

APPENDICES

ABBREVIATIONS

AAA:	Agricultural Adjustment Administration.
AER:	*American Economic Review.*
BDI:	Bundesverband der Deutschen Industrie.
ECE, *Econ. Survey Europe :*	Economic Commission for Europe, *Economic Survey of Europe.*
ECSC:	European Coal and Steel Community.
EEC:	European Economic Community.
ENA:	Ecole Nationale d'Administration.
ENI:	Ente Nazionale Idrocarburi.
FCC:	Federal Communications Commission.
FDES:	Fonds de Développement Economique et Social.
ILO:	International Labour Organization.
IMF:	International Monetary Fund.
KW:	Kreditanstalt für Wiederaufbau.
LO:	Landsorganisationen (Swedish Federation of Trade Unions).
IRI:	Istituto per la Ricostruzione Industriale.
NEDC:	National Economic Development Council.
NIESR, *Econ. R.*:	National Institute of Economic and Social Research, *Economic Review.*
NRA:	National Recovery Administration.
OECD:	Organization for Economic Co-operation and Development.
RFC:	Reconstruction Finance Corporation.
SAF:	Svenska Arbetsgivareföreningen (Swedish Employers' Confederation).
SEC:	Securities and Exchange Commission.
SEDEIS:	Société d'Etudes et de Documentation Economiques, Industrielles et Sociales.
TCO:	Tjänstemännens Centralorganisation (Swedish Central Organization of Salaried Employees).
USIS:	US Information Service.

INTRODUCTION
TO THE PAPERBACK EDITION

THE text of this edition contains a number of small amendments which are intended to clarify the argument, correct errors, and remove certain ambiguities which have been pointed out to me. I have been particularly well served by my perceptive French translator and friend, Bernard Cazes, who has brought a number of new points to my attention. Occasionally, where some development traced in the original text up to 1964/5 has had a simple sequence which could be mentioned in a footnote, I have done so.

But I have not attempted to bring the whole story up to date. As I see it, a book of this sort has something in common with a snapshot taken with a wide-angle lens: its interest depends in great part on the fact that a large range of data is brought together at a single time. Of course it is not absolutely simultaneous; but it is my hope that it all belongs within a sufficiently short period to produce something of the wide-angle camera effect. The device helps because it poses sharply for the reader—as it did originally for the author—the question whether despite the variety of historical experience of the societies which figure in the analysis, there is something like a unifying theme in their recent behaviour. I use the qualifying phrase 'something like' advisedly because some commentators have suggested that I am trying to prove, on the basis of patchy evidence, a series of theoretical propositions about the inevitability of something called 'planning'. What I conceive myself to be doing is rather to tease out of a variegated mass of factual data some general indications of a *trend* in the institutional behaviour of the advanced industrial societies clustered around the North Atlantic area. If the conclusions that are suggested by this exercise lack the inevitability and force that they would have if they emerged from a systematic theoretical structure, that is one of the consequences of the method of investigation. This is a piece of contemporary history, not a description of an economic model.

On the other hand, it is not intended as an up-to-the-minute account of the way we live now. It is about trends and about the evidence for them. Some reviewers have complained that it was 'out of date', either before the writing of it was completed or, more kindly, that it had become so between writing and publication. I have no doubt that some of the illustrations that I have used, on the snapshot principle, could be bettered by taking data derived from a later period. I am particularly conscious that the experiments with 'incomes policies', which I discuss in Chapters VIII and IX, have gone further in the late 1960s. What I have tried to do is to capture some of the flavour of this endeavour as it originally developed and to identify some of the difficulties in the way of an incomes policy which, it could be seen from the start, would not easily be removed. Nothing which has happened in the past few years has made the exercise seem any easier.

It may not just be the data which lack some topicality; one may have picked out the wrong trends by generalizing from data which are subsequently found to be untypical. This is the view amiably expressed by Professor Charles Kindleberger, who said that with 'the era of European super-growth' now over 'one of the first victims of the change is this highly useful and stimulating book'.[1] In view of this comment it seems necessary to make it clear that it is no part of the thesis of this book that, as a result of the various devices of economic intervention which have been developed (and occasionally discarded) since the war, Western Europe has achieved 'super-growth' for ever. It is clear that the earlier rate of growth in the years immediately following the war was faster and could be sustained on the long haul. My contention is only that there is some evidence, particularly from experience of the early 1960s, that the more careful management of the economy, the improvement in the techniques of economic measurement, the increased awareness of the longer-term implications of day-to-day decisions, whether in the public or the private sector, and the attempt to eliminate contradictory assumptions behind decisions independently taken, together contribute to the likelihood that the average rate of growth in the Western industrial world will continue to be higher than that of even the most prosperous periods before the Second World War. Again, this is not a conclusion which emerges irresistibly from a new theory of growth: it is merely a reasonable probability, based ultimately on political judgement, which emerges from an examination of the way in which a number of countries have managed their affairs in the first couple of decades after the war.

Economists seem to be particularly given to misunderstanding each other's purposes. Economic theorists have some difficulty in believing that when one is trying to write a piece of contemporary history, designed to illuminate especially the political processes of government in the management of the economy, one is not really engaged in a clandestine attempt to inflict a new body of theory on an unsuspecting public. The first part of the book is a survey, necessarily brief and superficial, of the arguments of economists about the nature of the post-war experience of high and continuous economic growth. What I have tried to do here is to explain why I believe that, in spite of the prognostications of talented and erudite economists using the evidence of past long-term trends, a major set-back of Western economic growth seems on

---

[1] See Samuelson and others, eds., *Readings in Economics* (New York, 1967).

balance unlikely. I had hoped that my cheerfulness on this point would have broken through the discussion of gloomier interpretations of the future in Chapters II and III. But it seems that some professional colleagues were not sure: 'Suddenly, in Chapter IV,' remarked a writer in *The Economic Journal*,[2] 'Shonfield disowns the pessimistic view of the future long-term prospects for capitalism. . . .' To avoid the possibility of any further misunderstanding, I take this opportunity to explain that rather than adopt a fixed glad smile throughout the text, my aim has been to allow the reader to feel something of the ebb and flow of the argument, by summarizing sympathetically the views of those who differ from me.

February 1968 A. S.

[2] June 1966, p. 374.

INTRODUCTION

THE first thing to be explained by the author of a book such as this is by what stretch of arrogance he comes to embark on it. The subject-matter which it covers includes the evolution over a couple of decades since the war of the institutions of half a dozen countries: to do the job comprehensively would require more knowledge of a detailed and varied character than any single person is likely to accumulate. The obvious alternative is to collect a number of experts on the individual themes treated in this volume and get each of them to produce a considered piece on his own topic. I must confess that, as a reader, I find that this mode of treatment often leaves me with a faint, though unmistakable, sense of dissatisfaction. It is, when well done, a useful way of purveying a lot of information and ideas on a difficult or diffuse subject. But I have discovered that my preference as a reader is for the unitary, though partial, vision of a grand theme by a single pair of eyes, rather than for a series of minor, though definitive, variations on it. It is in this spirit that I have approached the writing of this book, knowing that in some sense the attempt will inevitably fall short of success—that at the very least certain important matters will be left out and that the proportions of others which are included will not always be quite right. I have confined myself in this description of modern capitalism in the West to the things that I know about; however much one tries to enlarge one's grip on the relevant data, that is bound to produce a somewhat biased sample of life.

There is perhaps some consolation in the fact that much of the material is itself hardly amenable to systematic analysis. Up-to-date and reliable documentary evidence on contemporary trends is often not obtainable, and when it is it frequently cannot be interpreted without the aid of experience depending on direct observation. This inevitably introduces an element of the impressionistic and the personal. A considerable amount of the data that I have used is derived from personal interviews. I have tried, wherever I could, to indicate the sources; but this has not always been possible.

Among the major countries which figure in my argument about the different styles of modern capitalism, there is one important absentee. That is Japan. The omission is deliberate. It seemed to me that Western capitalist society—that is broadly the countries located around the North Atlantic area—having a great deal of history in common, speaking languages closely related to one another, and sharing certain traditional conventions about political behaviour, would make a meaningful field of study. The behaviour of individual nations in the group can often be treated, without straining the facts, as variations on certain common historical themes. Japan's achievement in the postwar era is a phenomenon on its own: starting with an economy which was not yet fully developed, it has emerged with extraordinary speed as a leading industrial nation, having doubled its national product in a decade. It would be misleading to treat this as in any way typical of the performance of contemporary capitalism in developed economies.

I originally intended that my cut-off date for the study would be the autumn of 1964. It seemed a convenient moment to draw a line—with an election in the United States leading to an overwhelming Democratic majority on a scale not seen since the mid-1930s; a Labour Government in Britain for the first time in thirteen years; and the appearance of a new draft Four-Year Plan (the Vth) in France. But I found that in practice there was an unavoidable margin of historical spill-over on to later events. This proved to be especially difficult to manage in the British context, where the techniques of government in the economic sphere seemed to be changing in an interesting fashion during the first six months of Labour rule in 1964–5. It was impossible at the time of writing to make any firm judgements about the significance, still less the likely results, of the changes in the methods of planning which the Labour Government had begun to undertake at this stage. But it seemed wrong to ignore the experiment. What I have done is to try to indicate the range of fresh possibilities which it has opened up.

Another notable omission from this study is an analysis of the contribution of postwar international institutions to the new economic order. The book is primarily concerned with the domestic arrangements of states—though it does discuss some of the ways in which these impinge on external relations, e.g., in the sphere of international trade. The contribution made by the international organizations is an important one, and seems likely to become more so in the late 1960s and the 1970s. It is, for instance, clear that the continuing expansion of international trade—on which, I argue, much else in our postwar prosperity and more daring economic policies depends—will require positive international action. At this stage, in the mid-1960s, the unsolved problem of creating an efficient international currency system, which will allow world monetary liquidity to expand smoothly and automatically, as required for the finance of an increasing volume of trade, seems to present the most serious single hazard to the extended bout of prosperity that has been enjoyed by Western capitalism.

In a sense, what we have been witnessing is the beginning of an 'international society' in the field of social ideas. We are used to thinking of the exchange of patents and industrial licences, but less familiar with the effects of sharing our experiences on the behaviour of political and economic institutions. The tendency has been to regard these as *private* matters, peculiar to each nation, and no business of anyone else. The study of comparative government is still at a pretty elementary stage. The impetus for a bigger effort in this field, of which this book is an expression, comes in part from the recognition that any serious attempt to organize international relations on a more rational pattern, with a higher built-in safety factor, involves quite profound changes in established national habits of conducting domestic government. So the data collected in this book can also be regarded as being, in part, a prolegomenon to the study of what is required for a more effective international economic society.

The reader will surely detect in the pages which follow my strong feeling about the special nature of the period which we in the West have traversed in the past couple of decades. In a sense the book is an oblique record of my own conversion from one view of the world, a view with strong elements of the cataclysmic, to another and more hopeful standpoint. Starting most unpromisingly from an especially bestial and destructive war, after an interregnum of peace in which our societies seemed to be devoted to proving that they could not use private enterprise effectively in the general interest, the West embarked on a period of continuous economic growth remarkable alike for its dynamism and its orderliness. It would surely be very hard to argue that the societies in which we live are not vastly superior in human terms to those of a quarter of a century ago—superior specifically in the sense that the anxieties about dire poverty, the commonplace risk of total material deprivation which dominated the youth of myself and my contemporaries, barely touches the youth of today. They have other and more interesting things to bother about. Many people of my generation who, in the 1930s, had come to take for granted the ineradicable destructiveness of capitalism, have lived through a major personal experience in witnessing the metamorphosis of the system since the war. This book has been prompted in large measure by the desire to give the experience a personal expression.

Acknowledgements

My main debt of gratitude is to Zuzanna Shonfield, my wife, who took an active part in the research which went into several portions of the book; her contribution is especially marked in Chapters XI, XII, and XVI. In addition to her specific contributions, I am conscious of how much I have benefited throughout the time that I have been writing from her feeling for the substance and style of the whole text; it would have been a different *kind* of exercise without her continuous work on it. My other strong personal debt is to Philippa Gibson, who besides coping with the considerable physical chores of producing a series of versions of a complicated text, thought about the book and helped me to organize it into a manageable shape.

One of the valuable amenities that was given to me in the course of the study was the hospitality of the International Cultural Centre in Tunisia, and of the Center for the Study of Democratic Institutions, California, U.S.A. Both places in different ways provided the environment that I needed in order to push ahead with the particular phase of the work on which I was engaged.

I was assisted by a great many people in the course of my researches; it is hard at this stage to identify precisely which individual idea I owe to whom. But I can at least identify those who kindly read the various portions of the text, when it was in draft, and improved it by their comments. On Part I, 'Economic Trends', I had the benefit of criticism and comment from I. M. D. Little, Alfred Maizels, and Christopher McMahon. In the French chapters I have leaned heavily on Bernard Cazes, who took a close interest in the whole work as it progressed. Paolo Baffi of the Banca d'Italia read and commented on the Italian section; Wilhelmine Dreissig, Wilhelm Hankel, and Kurt Richebächer on the German chapters; William Diebold and Theodore Geiger on the American ones. I had the good fortune of being able to discuss various phases of the work with Alan Bullock, Chairman of the Research Committee of the Royal Institute of International Affairs, who took an active interest in the project right through. I was also helped by the friendly criticisms of the other two readers appointed by the Research Committee, Asa Briggs and Sir Robert Shone. The three readers are all extremely busy men and I much appreciate the trouble which they took over the text. Finally my thanks are due to three of my colleagues at Chatham House, Miriam Camps, Rosalyn Higgins, and Hermia Oliver.

April 1965

Part 1

ECONOMIC TRENDS

I

THE SIGNS OF CHANGE

WHAT was it that converted capitalism from the cataclysmic failure which it appeared to be in the 1930s into the great engine of prosperity of the postwar Western world? There is one simple answer which rests on a denial of the validity of the question itself. The economic order under which we now live and the social structure that goes with it are so different from what preceded them that it is misleading—so it is alleged—to use the word 'capitalism' to describe them.[1] Since a large part of my argument in this book is about the changes which have indeed taken place in the economic management of the modern societies of the Western world, I have some sympathy for this position. If in spite of that, I have decided to stick to the old-fashioned capitalist label, it is because I believe that our societies continue to possess many characteristics which are inextricably connected with their antecedents in the nineteenth and the first half of the twentieth centuries; the word helps to emphasize the continuity. There are, after all, still large areas of economic activity which are open to private venture capital, and in these areas its success or failure is determined by the familiar ingredients: the amount of liquid funds available, the efficiency with which they are manipulated, the personal initiative of the controllers of this private wealth and the enterprise of competing owners or managers of private capital. Moreover the prizes for individual success are still large, and they convey on those who win them considerable economic power. The popular idea of how to make good and realize one's private dreams has not altered much; and this no doubt reflects the fact that postwar parvenu millionaires have not been in noticeably shorter supply than in other periods in the past. There is one further justification for the continued use of the word 'capitalism', and that is that no one, not even its severest critics, has proposed a better word to put in its place.[2]

One of the reasons why people of my generation, brought up in the 1930s, have to argue their way through this semantic difficulty is that the performance of capitalism since the end of the Second World War has been so unexpectedly dazzling. It is hard for us to believe that the bleak and squalid system which we knew could, in so short a time, have adapted itself, without some covert process of total destruction and regeneration, to achieve so many desired objectives. In the early postwar period we were inclined to dismiss the high rates of economic growth in Western Europe as evidence of an effort

[1] See C. A. R. Crosland, *The Future of Socialism* (London, Cape, 1956), pp. 56 ff.
[2] Ibid., p. 67.

of reconstruction, which was bound soon to come to an end. Then there was the Korean war boom in 1951 and the recession which followed it in the year after. Things seemed to be moving back into a familiar pattern. If they did not do so quite at once, this could be explained by the delay in catching up on certain amenities and improvements in living standards, where progress had been held back by the wartime and postwar shortages. Thus in the years immediately following 1952 Europe experienced its first major boom in durable consumer goods, in the American style. So far it all had a highly precedented look.

However, the second half of the decade of the 1950s, when the transient impulse behind the prosperity ought surely to have run out, produced in the event a further sharp increase in West European output. Against the anticipated trend, the rate of advance slowed down most of all in the United States and Canada, where the exceptional activity engendered by the repair of wartime destruction and neglect had contributed least to the prosperity of the early 1950s. In Europe, several countries—Italy, Sweden, Denmark, and Switzerland—actually increased their output faster during the late 1950s and early 1960s than they had done between 1950 and 1955.[3] Even countries like Britain and Belgium, which lagged well behind the European average during the period 1956–61, showed no sign of any reversal of the upward trend: they still maintained a rate of growth which was quite respectable by historic standards. In Britain, for which these were years in which the economy was especially hindered by stop-go policies, national production nevertheless increased at an average annual rate of 2·1 per cent, which compares with an average rate of growth of 1·7 per cent a year between 1913 and 1950 and 2·2 per cent from 1870 to 1913.[4]

High European rates of growth, especially in the early 1950s, were stimulated by the great influx of labour into industrial employment. Hours of work also tended to be longer during the early reconstruction period; this was especially true of Germany. But in the second half of the 1950s output per man-hour in the twelve Western industrial countries[5] taken together increased slightly faster than during the period 1950–55. By historic standards the productivity increase achieved during the 1950s as a whole— an average for the twelve countries of 3·5 per cent a year—was quite exceptional: twice as much as the average for the whole of the period beginning just before the First World War, in 1913, until the conclusion of the main reconstruction phase after the Second World War in 1950.[6] Only the United States had achieved in its earlier history a sustained rise in productivity

[3] See Table A-2, p. 202, in Angus Maddison, *Economic Growth in the West* (London, Allen & Unwin, 1964). I have drawn liberally on this book for data in this chapter.
[4] Ibid., Table I-1, p. 28. The Belgian figures show a similar pattern.
[5] USA, UK, Germany, France, Italy, Sweden, Norway, Denmark, Belgium, Holland, Switzerland, Canada.   [6] See Maddison, Table I-7, p. 37.

comparable to that of the 1950s. Throughout Western Europe the rate of increase in output per man employed was well above that of any earlier period for which records are available. By the time that the decade ended, it had become clear that Western Europe was reaping the benefit of a significant change of trend, and that the change was not simply the reflection of a full employment policy which had put more people to work.

The extraordinarily rapid increase in output per worker was accompanied by a mounting demand for more labour. By the end of the 1950s it had become normal in several European countries for the number of vacant jobs advertised by employers looking for workers to exceed the total of available unemployed persons by a large margin. The spate of immigrant workers who poured across Western Europe in these years, first from Italy, and later, when this source began to dry up, from as far afield as Turkey, reflected something more than the European industrialists' search for stop-gaps during a period when profits were high and waiting to be made. In practice, the immigrants could only be brought in if the trade unions allowed it; and the trade unions allowed it only because they believed that the era of full employment had come to stay.

There were, of course, variations in the degree of confidence felt by organized labour in different countries. In Britain, for instance, there was a marked lack of enthusiasm for any positive immigration policy designed to fill specific gaps in employment. This was no doubt partly to be explained by the special circumstances of Britain's international position, and the official theory of the open door to all comers from anywhere in the Commonwealth. But it is hard to avoid the impression that the leaders of the British trade unions also felt less secure in their enjoyment of the new situation at home than, for example, the corresponding men in Germany. Perhaps the explanation is to be sought in the psychological effect of *uninterrupted* economic growth stretching over several years; this seems to be quite different from the mood of people who have experienced, as the British have, the occasional interruption of prosperity and the temporarily renewed fear of unemployment caused by their government's deflationary policy. The significant influence on the workers' view of full employment is evidently neither the size nor the duration of mass unemployment experienced in the more remote past;[7] rather the test that seems to be applied is the apparent steadiness and reliability of the new prosperity.

Perhaps more surprising is that full employment and the enhanced bargaining power of wage-earners have not resulted in the diversion of resources away from investment, which is heavily dependent on profits for its finance, and into personal consumption. In fact, the level of domestic investment, measured as a proportion of the gross national product, was notably higher in

[7] This was much lower at its peak in the early 1930s in Britain than in Germany.

the 1950s than in any comparable period in the first half of the twentieth century in all West European countries for which records exist.[8]   Once again, the United States is different: there the proportion of investment was lower than during the period before the First World War (1900–13).   Indeed, this simple contrast suggests the most obvious reason why the United States grew faster than Western Europe during the earlier period and more slowly in the later one.

Welfare and Savings

The success of the modern capitalist society in reversing the pressures making for high consumption at the expense of investment is one of its outstanding achievements.   For years it was common doctrine among many economists that the Soviet system had a decisive advantage over the West because it could, and would, compel a much higher level of investment than was within our compass.   No doubt it is true that in an emergency the Soviet rulers are able to squeeze that extra bit of savings out of their people.   But over the postwar period as a whole, the Soviet '25 per cent rule', whereby one-quarter of the national product is supposed to be devoted to new investment,[9] does not appear to have put the rate of capital accumulation in the USSR significantly ahead of the dynamic West European countries like Germany and the Netherlands.   Most of the others were at or near 20 per cent of GNP.[10]   Even the laggards of the 1950s, Britain and Belgium, have been moving up rapidly towards this level in the early 1960s.

How has this outburst of saving been brought off in these highly unpromising circumstances?   In part it has been the result of incentive taxation.   The high taxation inherited from the war and the immediate postwar period made the tax reliefs granted by governments, notably by way of generous allowances for industrial investment, an extremely powerful stimulus to plough back profits which would otherwise have gone into dividend distributions.   Then there is the 'forced saving' imposed by the state in the form of taxes, to finance the greatly increased share of investment for which it has become responsible.   The wage-earners have also found, as their earnings have risen, that they have to contribute a larger proportion of their incomes to the improved social insurance schemes that have been introduced in one country after another.   Several of these social insurance funds have accumulated large surpluses.   Finally, increasing numbers of workers year by year have engaged

[8] See Maddison, *Economic Growth*, App. I.
[9] See ECE, *Econ. Survey Europe 1955*, p. 198 (1956).   'New investment' is not directly comparable to any of the standard measures of investment used in the West.   It comprises all additions to capital, including stocks, after deductions for plant, etc., physically retired.   The ECE Survey suggests (p. 199) that for practical purposes the Russians in the mid-1950s probably treated gross investment as a 'satisfactory approximation' for measuring new investment.
[10] GNP at market prices; investment including housing.

themselves in contractual saving, often organized by their employers, to provide for extra pensions on retirement.

In human terms it is the welfare aspect of the new capitalism which is its most striking characteristic. Certainly, ambitious public welfare services are no novelty in advanced European countries like Germany and Sweden. These are the countries which have continued to lead in social experiment. But what is distinctive about the postwar period of improvement is not only its wide geographical spread throughout Western Europe, but also the speed with which the advance in national income has been translated into larger benefits for people unable to pre-empt a direct share of the prosperity through their own earnings. The duty to ensure that the non-earners did not lag any significant distance behind the earners was most clearly expressed in the German pensions reform of 1957. Under this all existing pensions, based on each individual's earnings and contributions to the scheme, were to be upgraded every two years in line with the growth of national product—unless there was some overriding economic consideration, judged to be so by a panel of experts independent of the Government, which demanded that the adjustment be delayed. This German break-through to a more advanced form of social equity has influenced thinking on social security problems throughout Europe and has given a further impulse to the movement of reform.

The increasing dependence on immigrant labour, which was a feature of the European prosperity of the late 1950s and early 1960s, is unlikely to be indefinitely extended. At a certain stage political and cultural objections to this economic convenience make themselves felt. If the pace of immigration had been slower, it might have taken longer before these objections asserted themselves. But where a country like Switzerland, admittedly the extreme case, raises the number of immigrant workers eightfold in the course of a decade, so that by the early 1960s one-third of its labour force consists of foreigners, the older inhabitants of the place are bound to feel anxious. Even the United States in the heyday of mass immigration did not change the composition of its society as rapidly as this. However, the interesting point to observe about the mood of resistance to labour immigration on the scale of the early 1960s, which has appeared in other European countries besides Switzerland, is that it is not primarily motivated by anxiety on the part of indigenous workers that the immigrants will undercut their wages and thus rob them of the fruits of full employment. No doubt this thought has been in the minds of individuals, but the important fact is that it has not been taken up by the leaders of organized labour, in spite of its attraction as a ready-made demagogic theme.

On the contrary, the fear of the more sophisticated trade union leaders has not been that wages would fail to go up fast enough—because immigrant labour or other causes acted as a brake—but that wage claims might be pushed up so high that either the stability of prices or economic expansion itself would be menaced. By the end of the 1950s they had become pretty confident that wage-earners, using the ordinary weapons of bargaining at their disposal, would be able to increase their wages each year in line with the growth of the national product. This has not, of course, been true everywhere in the West at all times since the war. Outstanding exceptions are Germany during the early 1950s, when the fruits of rising productivity were channelled into business profits rather than into wage incomes, and France during the late 1950s, after the advent of General de Gaulle, when real wages were successfully held down for a couple of years while the incomes of other groups moved ahead.

But taking the period as a whole the significant point is that prosperity has not depended, as it has done on some occasions in the past, on a shift in the distribution of incomes in favour of profits and against wages. In the short run, of course, there have been ups and downs in the relative rates of growth of real profits and real wages. There have also been longer-term shifts in the use of national resources for particular purposes, e.g. an increase in exports or a rise in the proportion of the national product going into investment, and during the period when such changes were occurring the rise in wage-earnings has lagged behind the growth of total national output. But it is observable that where wage-earners receive a disproportionately small share of the growth of national product during a period of years, as in Germany during most of the 1950s and in France in the closing years of the decade, this is followed by a period when wages tend to move up faster than the growth of national product, and there are widespread complaints that profits are being squeezed. They usually are.

Societies in which the innovating businessman has had such wide scope, and the rewards from risk capital skilfully deployed have been so high, have also usually been marked by the characteristic overtones of entrepreneurial arrogance. Woe to the unsuccessful! Even the charity which is doled out to them is tainted with moral condemnation. In a period of economic opportunity the poor man must be actively discouraged from finding a way of opting out; the rich man must restrain his generous impulse. Some of these sentiments are no doubt present, at least in latent form, in contemporary Western society; they come to expression most readily in the United States, where public welfare services are still not taken fully for granted. But elsewhere the concern about poverty has dominated the politics of the postwar generation; parties of the Right and Left have competed with one another in demanding action by the state, of an increasingly subtle and sophisticated kind, to mitigate sickness, penury or plain misfortune.

Full employment is not sufficient to explain the political phenomenon. Indeed, prosperous workers in well-paid jobs knowing that they can walk out of them and find others just as good are not generally in the mood to care over-much about the problems of the misfits or the unlucky. There is some further factor which has come into play here. In part it may be the momentum of a greatly enlarged public service actively engaged in thinking about the problems of social amelioration and looking for opportunities for innovation in this field too. The professionals in welfare have exercised an influence on the politicians. However, there are other influences too, more difficult to identify, which go with the atmosphere of the times.

In Western Europe, at any rate, the popular temper has surely been softened as a result of nearly two decades from which the experience of any serious economic disturbance has been absent. There have been business fluctuations in this period and moments when unemployment has temporarily risen. But it has rarely risen by more than an additional 1 per cent of the labour force, and the downturn in business profits has signalled no more than a short pause in the growth of national output. The 'bad' years for France, Italy, and Germany have been those in which the national product has grown by only 2–3 per cent.[11] In Britain and Sweden, which did on one or two occasions actually experience a reversal of the upward trend in output, the size of the drop from the previous peak to the deepest trough of recession was limited to $\frac{1}{2}$ per cent.[12] Belgium had the worst record in the 1950s, where the maximum downswing was 1·8 per cent. This was exceptional; no other West European country experienced a fall of more than 1 per cent in its GNP. It is true that industrial output fluctuated more widely than this: activity in manufacturing and building work has been subject to some erratic movements on one or two occasions since the war. National output as a whole was only sustained by the greatly increased weight of non-industrial service expenditures compared with prewar.

There were two periods of industrial strain, 1951–2 and 1957–8. In the first of these all the West European countries except Germany suffered a temporary decline in industrial output of several percentage points; most of them dropped between 5 and 10 per cent below the previous peak level. But the trouble righted itself fairly quickly and production began moving up again within a period varying from one year to about eighteen months from the original moment when the downturn started.[13] In 1957–8 the recession was much shallower (except for Belgium) and lasted a shorter time. Indeed for most of West European industry it was a levelling off rather than a

[11] Even the sharp deflation of 1964 in Italy produced no worse effect than this. It was not in any sense a business recession which 'happened' to the Italian economy; it was deliberately engineered as a short term (and remarkably effective) method of overcoming a major balance of payments deficit.

[12] Of GNP on a year to year basis. All figures in this paragraph are from Maddison, *Economic Growth*, ch. 2, Table II-3, p. 47, and App. A, and Banca Nazionale del Lavoro *Bulletin*, June 1960.

[13] The Swedish recession lasted 21 months. See M. Gilbert, 'The Post-War Business Cycle in Western Europe', *AER*, May 1962, on which the argument in the text is based.

downturn of the curve, and industrialists tended to act during the period of strain as if they were involved in a holding operation, not a crisis. Above all, the cumulative process set in motion by business recessions in the past—the drop in confidence and industrial orders leading to widespread dismissal of labour, this in turn causing a further drop of demand and more dismissals—did not occur.

Anatomy of Recession

To put this record into perspective it may be compared with the last previous period of Western prosperity of comparable length, from 1901 to 1913—still often referred to by people who lived through it on the continent of Europe as *la belle époque,* as if no further historical identification were necessary. It was a period of rapid growth with only short interruptions; by 1913 industrial production in the advanced countries of Western Europe had increased by about half above the level at which it stood at the start of the century.[14] If we take as a comparable starting-point the year 1950—when nearly all the West European countries had regained or surpassed their prewar level of output—twelve years later, in 1962, their aggregate industrial output had doubled.

Business also suffered from bigger ups and downs during the 1901–13 period—although by the historical standards of Western capitalism they were far from violent. A calculation by Maddison,[15] comparing the amplitude of industrial fluctuations in individual countries during the earlier period with the period following the Second World War, shows that there were one or two exceptional cases. France and Belgium achieved more even progress, interrupted by smaller industrial recessions, during the 1900s. In the other countries, the downswings in the poor business years of *la belle époque* were bigger. However, it is worth noting that the recessions themselves did not last significantly longer; recoveries seemed to get under way as quickly then as in our own time. What emerges from this broad comparison of the two eras of prosperity separated by forty years is that the relative performance of the dynamic countries who set the pace of economic growth in Western Europe—Germany, Italy, and France—was much better during the later period: they moved ahead a great deal faster in the good years and suffered from smaller fluctuations in the poor ones than a slow-growing country like Britain. But Britain itself, although lagging behind the others, also did better during the period after the Second World War than in the earlier phase of prosperity: in particular the downswings in British business recessions were very much milder than they had been during the Edwardian period of economic expansion.

[14] See OECD, *Industrial Statistics, 1900–1962.*
[15] Banca Nazionale del Lavoro *Bulletin,* June 1960.

The United States experience, however, cuts right across this pattern. First of all, it was able to keep up a significantly faster rate of industrial expansion throughout the 1901–13 period than the Europeans at that time, in spite of the fact that it suffered from more violent recessions. Secondly, comparing the US performance in the two periods of prosperity, the pace of industrial expansion was significantly slower during the years after the Second World War than it had been in the 1900s. Thirdly, the United States had more recessions than Western Europe during the postwar period and they cut output down much more sharply. For the United States, therefore, the economic trend since the end of the war is by no means exceptionally favourable. On the contrary, it has tended to be more prone to business fluctuations than in good times in the past and it has failed to regain the rate of industrial growth which it managed to sustain over many years before the First World War. There is little evidence of any fundamental change in the nature of capitalism here. And this in turn has led some Americans to argue that Western Europe's postwar economic success is little more than US experience repeating itself. 'Just wait until you reach our level of consumer saturation', they say. 'Then you too will find that business fluctuates more and industry does not increase its output over the years quite so fast'.

This argument will reappear later in another context. For the moment all that I want to say about it is that it lacks immediate plausibility, because there is plainly no scarcity of unsatisfied needs among the considerable body of the poor in America. If all that were necessary to raise the level of output were that the United States should contain a sufficient number of people lacking the goods and services which go to make a comfortable middle-class existence, the wheels of industry would have been steadily whirling round. A more convincing explanation for America's slow growth seems to be offered by a comparative study of the business cycles themselves in the United States and Europe. At any rate it seems likely that if the United States had had fewer business fluctuations and if its downswings had been limited to the European average, the rate of growth over these years would have been significantly higher than it was.

First of all, what were the causes of America's 'extra' recessions?[16] In Europe there were two occasions when industrial production fell: 1951–2 and 1957–8. The first was a straightforward reaction, following the violent boom set off by the Korean War. Commodity prices had been pushed up to dizzy levels; everyone was trying to accumulate stocks; and meanwhile the order books of one industry after another were over-filled by people desperately trying to spend their anticipated earnings in a hurry. When all this collapsed, an additional force was set in motion. Several countries ran into balance of payments troubles at a time when their currency reserves were at

[16] In the argument which follows I have leaned heavily on the analysis by Milton Gilbert, 'The Postwar Business Cycle in Western Europe', *AER*, May 1962.

an extremely low level, and promptly imposed import restrictions. These put a curb on the exporting industries of some of the major European industrial countries. However, the American economy meanwhile remained extremely buoyant; the country was in the middle of a great armaments boom which continued into 1953. This, together with the measures undertaken by several West European governments to stimulate business activity and raise the level of employment, halted the recession and produced an upturn by the end of 1952.

The second postwar recession in Europe, in 1957–8, was of a quite different order from the first. It was not set off by any external political shock like the Korean War. Rather it was the outcome of a series of deliberate measures of restraint introduced independently by a number of governments at about the same time, following a period of extremely rapid expansion. Their common fear, after five years of uninterrupted boom, was that rising costs, particularly wage costs, would get out of hand. Milton Gilbert[17] argues that the recession would have come earlier if it had not been for the short Suez war at the end of 1956, which pushed up world prices and gave business a lift. It is clear at any rate that the downturn of the business cycle in 1958 was not of the simple traditional type engendered by the spontaneous actions of businessmen, faced with markets which they judged had become over-supplied. The very speed with which these markets responded in 1959, as soon as some quite mild stimuli had been applied, suggests the contrary. Now that European currency reserves were in better shape and the governments themselves had become more firmly committed to policies of full employment, there was less hesitation than there had been in 1952 about giving a decisive boost to demand, once it was clear that industrial production was flagging. Again, as in the recovery from the earlier recession, a powerful expansion of international trade in 1959, deriving this time from the European Common Market as well as from the United States, put the finishing touches to an incipient boom.

Milton Gilbert sums up the experience of the two European postwar recessions as follows:

In neither case was there the typical sequence of expansion becoming a boom which itself created distortions that caused the recession. In the 1951–2 case there were distortions on the side of the balance of payments, but these came from a shock to the economy from the political sphere. In the 1957–8 case there was not much in the way of distortions in the economy ; restraining action was taken precisely to prevent their arising to a serious degree. . . . It is because the recessions followed from acts of policy that I think the term business cycle does not fit.[18]

He adds, I believe with justice: 'Had the idea of the business cycle not existed, it would hardly have been invented to describe the postwar fluctua-

[17] Ibid.   [18] Ibid., p. 100.

tions in Europe'. This is not merely a terminological point: it has some practical importance for the control of business recessions. The decay of what Gilbert calls 'the business cycle mentality' in Western Europe means that even small stimuli on the part of governments, when trade has turned down, are readily accepted and interpreted by business as the signal for the resumption of the normal, vigorous, secular expansion. In the United States the average businessman's expectation that he may have to run hard for cover once every two or three years if he is to avoid damage has the effect of exaggerating any stresses and strains on the economy.

However that would not of itself explain why there are more American recessions, only why when they occur they go deeper. The 'extra' US recessions occurred in 1948–9, in 1954, and again in 1960–1. Two of these are fairly readily explicable in terms of special circumstances which were present in the United States and not, at any rate in the same degree, elsewhere. The reversal of 1948–9 reflects the strains incidental to the postwar turn-round of a vast economic engine, which had been operating at full pressure on one set of tasks and suddenly had to find itself another. It was inadequately prepared for the event. And that was the more serious because the Americans could not fall back on the ready-made job of repairing war-damaged or neglected industries, which was urgently waiting to be done in Europe.[19] The war years themselves had been their period of reconstruction, after the epoch of rust and decay and neglect in the 1930s. The 1954 recession, too, may be seen as the reaction to an unusually abrupt change in political and military circumstances. As the Korean War ended, the United States cut back suddenly on what had been a rapidly expanding arms programme. In one year defence expenditure, which by then made up the greater part of the Federal Budget, fell back by 7 per cent. However, the house-building boom of 1954–5, which was directly stimulated by government financial measures, and the record motor car sales of 1955, also based partly on cheap credit, soon put the trouble right,

On the other hand, the 1960–1 recession does not seem to have been due to an exceptional set of economic circumstances visited on the United States alone. The contrast was indeed startling: the United States, which had for several years previously seen its output growing at a slower rate than that of Western Europe, now found its industries moving into reverse at a time when the rest of the Western world continued to enjoy a steady advance in industrial production. In this instance the damage done had all the appearance of a self-inflicted wound. US Government policies, reflected in the Federal Budget, positively put a brake on expansion before the recovery from the previous recession in 1958 had gathered full momentum. In the second quarter of 1960, when unemployment was already more than

[19] It is noteworthy that among the European countries only Switzerland, as unravaged as the US, suffered a recession of any magnitude at this time.

5 per cent, the Government went out of its way to produce a grotesquely large budget surplus. The OECD, commenting on the turn-round from a budget deficit of $11 billion in the middle of 1958 to a surplus of $4½ billion two years later, judged that this $15½ billion drop in the net demand made by the Government on available economic resources—equivalent to 3 per cent of the national product—'constituted a significant brake on the expansion'.[20]

Even by the end of 1960, when unemployment had climbed to nearly 6½ per cent, the Federal Government was still taking more money out of the economy than it was putting into it—with a budget surplus of $400 million. It is true that the central bank reacted to the situation more sensitively than the US Treasury on this occasion; however, interest rates were still kept relatively high, by comparison with the level to which they had been allowed to fall in previous recessions, and the instruments for bringing about an expansion of credit were not used decisively.[21] There is an air of sustained intellectual confusion about the whole affair. It would be wrong to regard this as a wholly typical performance. The United States happened at the time to be involved in the unusual experience of a crisis of confidence in its currency, and this undoubtedly contributed to the floundering in economic policy. For the first time the US authorities had to face the depressing problem of running an international reserve currency which the rest of the world no longer believed to be inevitably worth its official equivalent in gold. The anxiety induced by this shock and the desire to encourage the waverers among the foreign holders of dollars inhibited the use of cheap money policies; in particular, the authorities hesitated to cut the rate of interest, for fear that more dollar capital might be tempted to move abroad in search of a higher return.

It is perhaps significant that the only other country which suffered from a business recession during the early 1960s was Britain—the keeper of the other international reserve currency, which was also under pressure. The trouble here started in the second half of 1961 and lasted until early 1963; thus it was extended over a longer period than the American recession, though the actual drop in industrial production was much smaller. The British ailment was rather like a lingering bout of influenza treated by old-fashioned drugs; the American had the appearance of a violent but shorter attack of pneumonia. It is possible to argue that the British would have cured their troubles earlier, perhaps in the middle of 1962 when Mr Reginald Maudling took over as Chancellor of the Exchequer from Mr Selwyn Lloyd (the originator of the deflationary measures which had caused the recession), if the quality of economic information available to the British Government had been better—say as good as the information available to the Americans. It seems clear that one of the factors prolonging the British

[20] OECD, *Econ. Surveys, The United States*, 1961, p. 21.   [21] Ibid.

recession was a technical deficiency both in the factual material supplied to the Government and in its interpretation.[22] It was only when the effects of the business downturn became painfully obvious in the form of rising unemployment in the early winter of 1962 that the Government acted decisively to stimulate demand. Even so, the level of British unemployment at the trough of the recession was only a little over 2 per cent, whereas in the United States at the comparable stage it was almost 7 per cent. Adjusting the British figure to put it on the same basis as the American would raise it to 3 per cent,[23] so that the US level of unemployment was over twice as high.

It would be wrong to press the analogy between the American and the British recession of the early 1960s too hard. In the British case the Government's commitment to full employment—which had come to be accepted as meaning a ceiling of 2 per cent registered unemployed—was clear and absolute. As soon as it became apparent that the ceiling might be exceeded, the machinery of government for creating more demand, above all in the weak sector of investment in manufacturing industry, went promptly into action. It was only because the recession could be plausibly presented as no more than a temporary pause in the rising curve of industrial production that the remedies were delayed for so long. Indeed, it was not until the winter of 1962–3 that the downturn in industry, which had been clandestinely gathering force for some time, became fully visible.

What can be said about the behaviour of the British Government during the long period of stagnation from the middle of 1961 onwards is that it probably would have been ready to act more decisively, as well as earlier, if it had not been obsessed by the worry about international confidence in the value of the pound sterling. But at least it started off by being clear about its own objectives. The check to production imposed in the second half of 1961 was a deliberate act of policy. The British Government, starting from a position of very full employment, wanted to halt the rise in output and was prepared to risk an actual recession. This was not true of the United States. There the trouble originated in blunder. The only thing that can be said by way of mitigation is that the peculiar circumstances of the United States are such as to compound any such blunder and make it look worse than it would anywhere else.

US–Europe Contrasts

This brings us back to the question why American recessions seem to be deeper than those in Europe as well as more frequent. The most obvious

[22] See, for instance, Mr Maudling's speech at the Annual Bankers' Dinner, Mansion House, Oct. 1962, when he argued on the basis of the latest figures of the industrial production index that output was going ahead very satisfactorily, at a time when, as subsequent information showed, it was lagging badly.

[23] See NIESR, *Econ. R.*, Nov. 1962, p. 6.

factor is that the Americans started their recession from a less favourable position—viz. a slower rate of economic growth than the Europeans and with a bigger proportion of idle productive capacity, both labour and machines. A check to the advance imposed in such circumstances can easily tilt the economy past the critical horizontal position and point it downwards. These are not mere metaphors; they correspond to the realities of business psychology in an economy where there is a lot of visible slack when order books suddenly begin to empty. Add a scepticism about the ability, or willingness, of the government to act promptly to stimulate demand, and there is the complete recipe for the 'business cycle mentality'. Indeed, in circumstances such as those of the United States in the 1950s, those who have the mentality most highly developed are also likely to prove to be the fittest to survive. Thus the process of natural selection in the business community adds a further touch of reinforcement to the currents making for a more volatile economy.

Plainly the special difficulties of the United States in recessions are bound up with its relatively slow secular rate of economic growth. But it may also be that the slow rate of growth is itself largely caused by the incompetent handling of business cycles. If the bungling of the recovery following the 1958 slump is regarded as normal, and it turns out that *any* vigorous economic expansion is habitually aborted in the womb, then the feebleness of the American average performance during the second half of the 1950s and the early 1960s would be readily explicable. There is indeed one clearly identifiable factor which seems almost to be designed to interfere with economic growth during a business upswing, and that is the American tax system. Because the US Government draws such a high proportion of its revenue from direct taxes on individuals and businesses—about 70 per cent of total tax—the effect of a sharp rise in profits and other income during the early stages of a business expansion tends to be offset on a larger scale and more rapidly than in other countries. The rapidity is due to the efficiency of the American tax-gathering system which is very prompt in making its deductions from earnings. According to the US Commission on Money and Credit (which was set up by the Committee for Economic Development and reported in 1961), the category of tax payments which moves up or down most sharply in response to changes in the national income is corporate tax; next in order of sensitiveness is personal income tax, and after that sales taxes, excise, and other indirect imposts.[24] All told, the Commission estimated that these taxes together offset between 33 and 40 per cent of any rise or fall in the national product. An automatic stabilizer of this power is, of course, a boon during a business decline. It means that a government has some room for manoeuvre before the cumulative forces of an economic recession tighten their grip.

[24] See *Money and Credit* (New York, Prentice Hall, 1961), pp. 124–5.

But it also works in the opposite direction—to stabilize before stabilization is due, in a period of economic recovery. The tax relief proposals which President Kennedy pressed on a reluctant Congress just before his death in 1963, and which were finally passed with some modifications in 1964, were intended to undo the damage caused by this defective piece of fiscal machinery to US economic growth.

Postwar experience suggests that the existence of built-in economic stabilizers may have an unfortunate effect on the making of economic policy. They serve to reinforce a mood of quiescence at the point where government faces a choice between different courses of action. This is specially so in the United States with its popular tradition of shouting 'Hands off!' as soon as it looks as if the Federal Administration may be about to move in any-where with a positive policy. The only exception is when there is a manifest crisis, as in Franklin Roosevelt's 'hundred days' during 1933. Then the Government is allowed, indeed expected, to interfere everywhere. But that is only on the theory that the body of the nation is temporarily crippled. As soon as it recovers its faculties, the nursemaid in Washington is supposed to be sent away to her normal menial duties in the back part of the house. The theory has not prevented the Government from intervening with good effect in postwar American recessions. But it has created inhibitions which have affected the speed of the initial reaction, and have impeded the formu-lation of coherent economic policy at a single centre of power. It is not therefore a complete surprise to discover that the average American postwar recession has plummeted down to twice the depth of the European average before it has been arrested.[25]

However, there are other differences beyond the immediate conduct of business cycle policy by governments in the United States and Europe which are probably as important in explaining the contrast in the results to date. It should not be forgotten that government policy in recession has only been seriously tested once in Europe, in 1958; the Europeans were very largely pulled out of the trouble in 1952 by forces beyond their control. But if it is true, as I argued earlier, that recessions tend to go deeper if the decline starts from a position where there is a lot of slack in the economy, then one important area of inquiry is why the pressure of demand was kept up so successfully in Western Europe during the late 1950s and early 1960s—after the job of postwar reconstruction had been completed—while in the United States the natural push seemed to have gone out of the system. As Walter Salant said in a comment on the contrast between the American and European business cycles, 'Let us praise policy, but not mainly anti-cyclical policy in the usual and narrow sense. European countries have kept a good head of steam in the boiler at all times, whereas we in the United States have not'.

[25] Maddison, *Economic Growth*, Table II-4, p. 48. Belgium was the only European country which suffered recessions of comparable magnitude to the American ones.

And he goes on to suggest that the emphasis in any analysis ought to be on 'the long-run policies that put steam in the boiler and gave anti-cyclical policy the freedom of action it had'.[26] These long-term influences are the subject of the next two chapters.

---

[26] *AER*, May 1962, p. 121, discussion of Milton Gilbert's paper.

II

INTIMATIONS OF STABILITY:
BUILDING AND INTERNATIONAL TRADE

THERE is an alternative view of the high prosperity and rapid growth of postwar capitalism in the Western world which is far less hopeful than that outlined in the last chapter. On this view, instead of a break with our squalid past, what we have really been seeing is a continuation of its essential features muffled under a rather thicker disguise than usual. The extended period of prosperity since the war is, it is argued, no different in essence from the long economic upswings which have been observed on various occasions since the middle of the nineteenth century. The only thing that might be held to distinguish our period is that it shows a somewhat sharper upward displacement from the average long-term growth curve than was in evidence in comparable periods in the past. But nothing that has so far occurred indicates any alteration in the basic shape of the long-term curve, with its alternations of upswings and downswings, which has been built up on systematic information stretching back for more than a hundred years. What we have been enjoying in the past decade and a half, it is averred, is essentially the same thing as has happened often before, only rather more so. The most that is conceded by this school of thought is that we may be able, by the use of improved economic techniques, to make the downturn from our present economic prosperity less violent than it has been normally in the past. But that a downturn will occur, and will be both sharper and more prolonged than anything that has been experienced since the end of the Second World War, is taken for granted.

Since this is the view held by some of the outstanding economic historians of our time, e.g. Simon Kuznets and Arthur Lewis, who have added substantially to our knowledge of the long-term forces which have guided the development of our society over the past century and into the modern era, it demands careful consideration. Indeed, it is probably fair to say that the balance of opinion among economists whose authority is acknowledged in this field has been on the side of the pessimistic interpretation of the postwar story. By that I mean that they see some mitigation of the miseries caused by the alternation of periods of prosperity and depression, but no decisive let-up in the cycle itself. Moreover, the longer the present prosperity lasts, the higher the probability, on this reasoning, that the downturn will occur soon. Businessmen, on the other hand, seem to act as if they believed that the longer it has lasted the more likely it is to go on for ever. When questioned they may deny that this is what they really do believe. Scratch almost any small businessman, especially at a time when the stock market has fallen a few points, and you will find folk memories of some great historical slump stirring not far beneath his skin. The reason why he acts the way he does, in spite of his fears, is that he expects to gain less on balance during slumps, through having adopted a cautious investment policy, than he will certainly lose during the booms through being under-invested. In other words, it pays to bet on booms, because the downswings are confidently expected to be either shorter in time or shallower than the upswings, or both.

To this the sceptical economic historian is inclined to reply: 'Yes, that is exactly what always happens to business expectations during the upward phase of the long-term economic cycle.' In that phase it is quite difficult to make things go seriously wrong. The business recessions when they occur start from a high level of prosperity and any downturn is quickly and easily reversed. The situation is exactly the opposite of this during the downward phase of the long-term cycle. Then the recessions last longer and the periods of prosperity are both shorter and feebler.

The intellectual basis for this view of the steady alternation of the underlying economic forces was provided by Simon Kuznets.[1] He discovered, from a careful examination of American data stretching back to the third quarter of the nineteenth century, that in addition to the familiar boom-and-bust sequence which tended to recur every four to five years or so,[2] there was a pronounced rhythm with a longer beat lasting some eighteen to twenty years. This has come to be known as the 'Kuznets cycle', and I shall use this convenient label for it. A Kuznets cycle is divided round about the middle into two contrasting parts, corresponding to the upward and the downward phase mentioned earlier. Thus after the buoyant period of the late 1860s and early 1870s, there was a long bad patch which started with the economic crisis in 1873 and lasted until the trough of the depression in 1879. After a better, though by no means brilliant, period in the 1880s there was another period of depression running from the early 1890s until the end of the nineteenth century. This was followed by the long period of prosperity from 1901 until the outbreak of the First World War.[3] The Kuznets cycles continued, overlaid by other factors, in the war and the immediate postwar period, but only asserted themselves again plainly in the 1920s (upswing) and

[1] See *Capital in the American Economy* (Princeton UP, 1961)
[2] The so-called 'Kitchin cycle'.
[3] In fact the US ran into trouble in the years immediately before the First World War: the period from 1907 onwards when progress, although still rapid, was significantly slower than it had been in the early years of the twentieth century, is described as a period of 'stagnant growth' and is regarded by some American economists as being analogous to the cyclical slow-down experienced in the second half of the 1950s and early 1960s.

in the 1930s, when the expected downward movement was aggravated by a number of exceptionally powerful forces all pushing in the same direction.

On this showing the slow economic growth of the United States from 1953 onwards may be regarded as the natural sequence to the earlier upswing of the Kuznets cycle. That the West Europeans meanwhile enjoyed a longer, more vigorous, and less interrupted period of prosperity may be attributed simply to the fact that their normal cycles of prosperity and depression were distorted by an unusually destructive war, followed by an extremely active period of reconstruction. The theory which thus explains the contrast between US and European postwar behaviour is simply that the rhythm of the underlying economic cycles was out of phase on the two sides of the Atlantic—for reasons which have their origin in military and political causes. These, it is held, were sufficiently strong to distort normal economic trends in Western Europe until the effects of war and its aftermath had worked themselves out.

There is in any case no reason why these long-term business cycles in different countries should coincide. Indeed, there were wide variations between countries in the dates of the great crashes and booms of the second half of the nineteenth century.[4] Sometimes one country would stay fairly prosperous for long periods while the others were in the doldrums. This happened to Britain on several occasions.[5] What has been termed the 'echo

[4] See W. A. Lewis and P. J. O'Leary, 'Secular Swings in Production and Trade 1870–1913', *Manchester School of Social & Economic Studies*, May 1955.

[5] Lewis and O'Leary show that the building booms in Britain during the 1870s and again during the 1890s almost exactly coincided with protracted slumps in building in the US. Indeed, the whole investment cycle in the two countries moved in precisely opposite directions. They are unable to find a convincing reason for this marked deviation, and suggest at one point that it may have been 'an accident' resulting from a process set in motion as far back as the beginning of the nineteenth century: 'the different effects which the Napoleonic wars may have had upon the progress of residential building in the two countries'. Simon Kuznets and his followers believe that the engine chiefly responsible for these long swings of prosperity followed by depression is the progress of domestic building, above all the building of houses. Residential building has traditionally accounted for a high proportion of all investment, and if it is possible to show that there are independent identifiable factors, connected with the changing size and composition of the population, which cause marked changes in the demand for housing, this provides a plausible explanation for the initiation of these long cycles. Periodically, natural causes or migration or political and social influences result in a more rapid rate of increase in the population. Then at some later stage the exceptional rate of growth moderates; there is still an increase but it is no longer so fast. The drop in the *rate* at which demand for housing expands has a decisive effect on the prosperity of the building industry. In addition, Kuznets has shown that railway-building in the US has been subject to similar alternations of long booms and slumps, related to changes in the rate of population increase.

One of the reasons why the upswing lasts so long is a rising demand for houses and construction generally which cannot be met at once. That causes a backlog, which tends to last through the period when other forces, notably in manufacturing industries, give rise to independent cyclical recessions. It is because of this buoyant

effect' of population changes—i.e. the delayed response in the market for new houses a generation after a rise or fall in the number of new babies born, when the latter have grown up and are establishing their own homes—is very marked in the United States. An additional factor there, apart from changes in the birth rate, was, until the 1920s, the fluctuating waves of immigration. The combined results of these forces are clearly visible in the rising demand for houses in the early 1900s, and again in the 1920s and in the 1940s.[6] There ought to be another wave of rising demand in the late 1960s and 1970s, as the baby crop of the years of prosperity following the depression of the 1930s reaches maturity.

The trouble is, however, that the historical pattern of the American building cycle seems to have been completely disrupted in the 1950s. Then, against all that might have been predicted on the basis of population 'echo effects', which ought to have produced a downturn (reflecting the low birth rate of the depression years), housebuilding went ahead faster than ever before. This seems to have been the result of unprecedented postwar affluence, particularly of the very young, who formed their households at an earlier age than in the past and were able to buy their own homes. The complicated effects of this change in the structure of the American housing market, which may be viewed as an anticipation by one generation of growing adults of the demand that would normally be expected to come from the succeeding generation, have been analysed by Burnham Campbell.[7] His conclusion is that if past trends reassert themselves, there will be 'a considerable decline' in housebuilding in the United States during the late 1960s and early 1970s.

On this showing it seems that we may now be heading for serious trouble on two fronts at once. The phasing of the Kuznets cycle in the United States and in Western Europe looks as if it is about to coincide (as a result of the offbeat American housing spurt in the 1950s) just as we are due to move into the long downswing. That was the danger of which Professor Arthur Lewis, a devoted Kuznetsian, warned us back in the middle 1950s in the following terms:

It is disturbing to note that the alteration of building cycles which existed throughout the nineteenth century has probably now ended. The US, the UK, Germany and France are all four currently involved in great building booms and great home investment programmes . . . presumably all four will therefore have building slumps at about the same time. This has never happened in the past century. . . . What will happen round about 1960 (plus or minus one or two years) if the USA, the UK, Germany and France then all enter upon building downswings at the same time?[8]

---

pressure at the base that the smaller business recessions do not become cumulative and produce a series of disasters. That is just what tends to happen to them during the downswing of the Kuznets cycle.

[6] See B. O. Campbell 'Long Swings in Residential Construction', *AER*, May 1963.
[7] Ibid.   [8] Lewis and O'Leary, *Manchester School*, May 1955.

Declining Share of Primary Produce

Even this, however, is not the end of the catalogue of gloomy prospects which the modern economic historian, projecting forward the economic rhythms of the past century, sets before us. He has discovered another time-bomb ticking away inexorably, this one at the very centre of the international stage. World trade has also been behaving peculiarly in recent years—expanding faster, along different lines, and for longer periods of time than the observed rhythmic patterns of the past would suggest as normal. The most notorious divergence from the historic norm is the vast increase in trade between advanced industrial countries selling each other manufactured goods. There is little doubt that the vigour and dynamism of the export industries of Western countries have provided one of the major impulses for the sustained economic growth of the 1950s and 1960s. In the past such export successes in the industrial countries have depended on some exceptional increase in the buying power of the primary producing countries. This has usually been caused by a rise in the prices of primary produce and a worsening of the terms of trade for the industrial nations. The latter have sold more goods, enjoyed higher money profits and employed more people, but at the cost of getting less from abroad in return for each unit of production exported. That is what happened during this century in the 1900s and again in the prosperous years of the 1920s. On the other hand, periods of low commodity prices and favourable terms of trade for the industrial countries have been associated with poor business and high unemployment.[9]

But something quite different has occurred during the 1950s and early 1960s. Since the collapse of the Korean War boom the industrial countries have generally enjoyed the benefit of falling prices for the primary produce which they import and rising prices for the industrial goods which they export. They would, of course, have been ruined by this situation long ago, if they had depended for the prosperity of their export trade on the buying powers of the primary producers. Because industrial countries have learned how to replace some primary products with synthetics and to reduce their requirements of others by means of improved techniques both in manufacturing and in agriculture, they have become less dependent on the older channels of trade. They have had the opportunity of turning trade into other channels; and they have seized it. The result of the extraordinary increase in the volume of manufactured goods exchanged among the advanced countries is that the share of manufactures in world trade, in relation to foodstuffs and raw materials, has risen dramatically. This share had averaged 43 per cent of the total for more than half a century before the outbreak of the Second World War, and it had rarely deviated in any one year by more than a

[9] See Arthur Lewis, 'World Production, Prices and Trade, 1870–1960', *Manchester School*, May, 1952.

couple of percentage points from the average.[10]   After the war there were twelve years of steadily increasing deviation which brought the ratio by 1962 up to 55 per cent.[11]

Plainly this rate of displacement of primary produce as a proportion of international trade cannot continue indefinitely.   It is moreover to be observed that since it is calculated on the basis of value rather than volume, the displacement also reflects the declining prices of primary products in relation to industrial goods.   There is a school of thought among economists which sees this shift in the terms of trade in favour of the industrial countries, as well as their increased dependence on commercial exchanges with one another, as a temporary aberration from an established secular trend, which will reassert itself again fairly soon.   It follows, if they are right, that there will almost inevitably be a marked slow-down in the expansion of world trade in manufactured goods, while this large-scale adjustment is taking place.[12]

The most persuasive argument along these lines has been presented by Professor Arthur Lewis, an economic historian who has contributed to our understanding of long-term trends in international trade.   He contends that there is a high, if not overwhelming, probability that relationships between the main elements in international trade which have shown a marked statistical stability over three-quarters of a century, up to the Second World War, will continue to assert themselves.   His explanation of why they have not reasserted themselves before now is fully consistent with his view, which is essentially a philosophical one, on how the inner mechanism of economic history really works: he holds strongly that there is more in common between two periods separated by a hundred years, like the 1860s and the 1960s, than there are differences between them.[13]   In any secular struggle between constants and variables, as he sees it, the constants win out.   However, it requires a very close examination of the facts to identify what the secular constants truly are.   They are of two kinds.   There is firstly the relationship between the aggregate values of the main categories of merchandise which move in world trade (primary produce and manufactured goods), and secondly the relationship between world production of these goods and the amounts which are internationally traded.   Thus Lewis suggests that the reason why trade in manufactured goods between the advanced industrial countries, in Western Europe, North America, and Japan, has been going forward at an unprecedented pace for over a decade is that this trade is still making up the 'lost ground' of the 1930s.[14]   During the Great Depression and the period of

---

[10] See Arthur Lewis, *Economic Development and World Trade* (Vienna, Internat. Econ. Ass., 1952, mimeo).   [11] See GATT, *International Trade 1962.*
[12] It is conceivable that the old relationship between primary produce and manufactured goods might be re-established through a sharp swing in the terms of trade against the industrial countries, while the volume of trade was unaffected.
[13] A point made verbally by Professor Lewis to the author.
[14] *Economic Development.*

economic nationalism which followed it, international trade in manufactured goods, as a proportion of world output, fell steeply. Even when factory production in Western countries rose again in the late 1930s, exchanges of manufactured goods across national frontiers did not revive. World trade in manufactures as a proportion of total manufacturing output sank well below anything previously experienced in recorded economic history. No wonder, therefore, so the argument runs, that the rebound which occurred during the postwar period, when the conditions of international trade returned to something more like normal, was unusually vigorous.

There is clearly something in the argument that the flows of goods which had been artificially restricted between industrial countries by the autarkic policies of the 1930s were likely to go forward with an extra dash when the barriers were systematically dismantled from the late 1940s onwards. But the implications behind Lewis's historical arguments are much more portentous. International trade in primary produce as a proportion of total primary production also fell off during the 1930s. It has been regaining its lost ground more slowly in recent years. In view of the fact that trade in manufactured goods has moved ahead so much faster than primary produce since the war, there is reason to expect a pretty drastic adjustment in the present ratio between the two to bring them into line again. Unless the export sales of primary produce suddenly make an enormous spurt—or the terms of trade swing dramatically in favour of primary producers—the implication is that the rate of growth of international trade in manufactured goods will be drastically curtailed. Lewis calculates that world trade in primary produce as a proportion of world output will get back to its secular norm by about 1966.

It is quite feasible [he says] that when the exchange of manufactures against manufactures reaches what used to be its 'normal' level in relation to production, its rate of growth will decline. Since this will happen before the trade in primary products reaches its 'normal' level, it is then even possible that the share of manufactures in world trade may decline again, and stabilise at around 43 per cent. In the middle 1960s we shall be able to speculate more confidently about such matters, with the aid of additional hindsight.[15]

At this level of statistical sophistication, the right answers depend more than ever on the selection of the particular aggregates and relationships which are examined in the course of trying to determine the constants and the variables. Alfred Maizels, for example, in his monumental work, *Industrial Growth and World Trade*,[16] published after Lewis's analysis, identified a curious and interesting change of trend in the behaviour of imports of manufactured goods going into a group of the most important industrial countries.[17] From 1900 onwards the record showed that these countries, like all other

[15] Ibid.   [16] London, CUP, 1963, pp. 139–40 and Fig. 15, 1, p. 388.
[17] France, Italy, UK, W. Germany, Japan.

countries going through the process of industrialization, had depended more and more on their own domestic production for their supplies of manufactured goods and less and less on imports. But in the 1950s the trend sharply changed. Maizels goes on to argue that there is probably a difference between the behaviour of countries in the early stages of industrialization, when their dependence on foreign supplies of manufactures (as a proportion of their total consumption) tends to be drastically reduced, and the behaviour of advanced societies with very high living standards, seeking a much wider variety of products in conditions of unrestricted international trade. He finds some further supporting evidence for this hypothesis in the behaviour of imports into the smaller, rich countries of Western Europe, who are traditionally very heavily dependent on imports and have since the war increased their dependence further. The inference that he draws is dramatic: he foresees the likelihood that imports of manufactures into the large industrial countries during the 1960s and early 1970s will rise year by year one and a half times as fast as the annual increase in their real income. Since imports from the primary producing countries (other than oil imports which are a special case) have been increasing only about two-thirds as fast as the rise in real income per head in the industrial world—and the evidence suggests that this ratio is not likely to be altered, unless there is some quite drastic change in the needs of the industrial countries—there is no sign here that the pattern of international trade is going to be under any compulsion to return to some fixed secular norm.[18] Rather the contrary: manufactured goods will on this showing continue to move ahead faster and their share of total international trade will increase further. Finally—and this is the important practical conclusion—the continuing stimulus to rapid economic growth in the industrial West, imparted by the dynamic trade in manufactured goods, would be very powerful indeed.

Long Swings in Construction

On the opposite side, however, the gloomy prognosis is stubbornly maintained and further reinforced by a series of elaborate calculations drawn from a hundred years of economic history. These are dominated by the familiar alternation of extended building boom and extended slump associated with the Kuznets cycle.

Believers in the Kuznets cycle prophesied [Lewis said in 1962] that the 1950s would have only minor crises, but that around the year 1960 the major industrial countries would enter a period when unemployment was naggingly persistent and

---

[18] *Industrial Growth*, p. 389. Note that this calculation, as with the rest of Maizels's figures, is in volume terms. The 'large industrial countries' are US, Germany, Britain, France, Italy, and Japan. Imports of manufactures are assumed to rise at a rate of 6–7 per cent per annum, against an annual increase of just over 4 per cent in total real income. For imports of primary produce in relation to the growth of real income see ibid., p. 397.

the rate of growth of production below average. . . . We shall not have a great depression, like those of the '70s or the '90s or the '30s, because we understand these things much better than did our forefathers, but it will be at least another five years before we resume the carefree progress of a Kuznets upswing.[19]

That was written, it is fair to say, shortly after the stock market collapsed on Wall Street in the summer of 1962, at a time when the United States economy appeared to be slowing down again after moving out of a recession only the year before, while Britain was moving into another recession, all on its own. This book is being written at a time when the industrial countries of the West, led by the United States, have for several years been expanding fast, and the kind of question that people are asking (in their pessimistic moods) is whether it is reasonable to expect a continuation of quite the same tempo in the future. No doubt such circumstances as these are bound to colour one's commentary on a system as notoriously volatile in the gestures that it makes as capitalism has been ever since birth. But from the present vantage point it is hard to imagine anything much more 'carefree' than the mood of business and of international trade in 1963–4 which is not positively orgiastic.

In fact Lewis makes the whole process of the alternating economic swings which Kuznets first identified sound more uniform, unalterable, and long-standing than the available historical evidence will really warrant. As Kuznets himself points out,[20] the greater part of the twentieth century, from 1914 onwards, has been dominated by world war and its aftermaths: this has obscured the normal underlying pattern of economic events, so that his theory really depends on data drawn from the pre-1914 world, with no more than two long swings of twenty years each, going back to the 1870s, for which reasonably precise economic information exists. For the period before that, there is a paucity of exact data—although Kuznets believes that such indications as can be gleaned suggest that the basic rhythm which he has identified probably went back as far as the 1780s.[21] He may well be right about the long alternation between a run of good years and a run of bad, and yet the causal mechanism may have been very different. After all, Joseph predicted something similar to Pharaoh in Egypt, apparently with some success, on another basis altogether.

The second point to be observed is that the Kuznets thesis is founded on a detailed study of the experience of one country, the United States, which happened to be subject to unusually sharp fluctuations in population, as the waves of immigrants rose and fell during the forty years before the outbreak of the First World War. Some interesting work has been done which suggests that similar long swings took place in other countries;[22] but the same causal nexus, deriving from changes in the size of the population and

---

[19] *Economic Development.* [20] *Capital.*
[21] 'Swings in Population and Economic Growth', American Philosophical Soc. *Trans.*, vol. cii (1958). [22] See Lewis and O'Leary, *Manchester School*, May 1955.

building cycles induced by them, is not firmly established. Thirdly, there is even in the United States a very striking change of trend within the broad cyclical pattern identified by Kuznets from about 1920 onwards. Before 1920, as Kuznets points out, the upswings in what he calls the 'population sensitive' investment, i.e. residential building and railway construction, coincided with a low level of other forms of investment, chiefly for the production of consumer goods. And he notes that this latter form of investment moved up during the periods when constructional activity moved down. His explanation for this phenomenon is essentially that the pattern of output was determined by the shortage of total resources available for investment. In the early days of capitalism investment in consumer goods industries is held back during a construction boom because there is simply not enough to go round for both. The result is that although the alternations in building demand dominate the long swings up and down, the violence of these swings is cushioned by the opposite trend in other types of investment. But after 1920 the earlier limitations on the productive capacity of the United States, which had prevented two long booms from occurring in these different sectors of the economy at the same time, were no longer present.[23] They happened together. That also opened the way to the coalescence of two long slumps in the greatest depression of all time.

It follows, if Kuznets is right, that part of the essential machinery of long-term cyclical movement was all of a sudden profoundly changed. The change is profound because the amplitude and violence of these movements are determined by the coincidence of a number of different factors. The ups and downs of housebuilding become vastly more important after a certain date because the timing of *other* factors, largely independent of building, shifts in such a way that all types of investment now move in step. By the same token they could, of course, as a result of some new extraneous factor, e.g. massive government intervention in the finance of housing, be moved right out of step again. That is in fact what I believe has happened since the war.[24]

Equally important in any judgement about the likely persistence of the long cycles of rapid growth followed by stagnation are the changing size and power of the various factors which have been responsible for these sharp alterations in the past. For instance, the type of fixed capital investment which Kuznets identifies as 'population sensitive'—i.e. determined by changes in the rate of growth of population—is 40 per cent of total capital formation

---

[23] See Kuznets, *Capital*, p. 349.

[24] Lewis and O'Leary point to an interesting earlier example of offsetting economic movements in Britain during the last quarter of the 19th century, which made the effects of the business cycle much less fierce here than in the US. When British export trade was booming, domestic building activity was slack; and during periods when exports slumped, building at home rose to take up some of the resulting slack in the economy. This was certainly not planned and there was no similar compensating movement between the building and the export sectors in the US.

in the 1870s and drops to 25 per cent in the 1900s.[25]   It has fallen further since.   Moreover the composition of the investment responding to population changes has altered drastically.   In the past a large element in the total was railroad construction.   Railways were built to meet intermittent surges in the demand for transport as the Americans opened up the Middle and Far West; this demand is closely correlated with variations in the growth of the national population.   But whereas investment in the railways accounted for over one-third of all the 'population sensitive' capital in the 1870s, and for about one-quarter in the 1900s, it had fallen to a little more than one-eighth in the decade 1945–54.[26]

History begins to look a great deal less ineluctable when it is examined closer at hand.   The apparent constancy of some of the economic historian's aggregates loses its impressiveness when the identifiable constituent pieces change so radically.   Most striking of all, residential construction—the key factor in the argument—has become markedly less important in the economy: as a proportion of US national product it has fallen by one-third, from 4·5 per cent of the total in the 1900s and 1920s to 3 per cent in the 1950s.[27]   In view of this, and of the other changes already noted, it would indeed be very remarkable if the mechanisms which appeared to have generated the long economic swings in the past were still functioning in a comparably decisive fashion in the world economy today.

That we ought positively to expect something other than a continuation of past historical trends is suggested even more strongly when we turn our attention away from the factors which have dominated the economic landscape in the past and start to measure some of the other forces which nowadays exercise a large influence on the pace and direction of the economy. Still using the United States as our example—because it is here that the facts about the long economic swings have been most firmly established—the outstanding change is that the share of the Federal Government in the GNP has risen from 1·5 per cent in the 1920s to 9 per cent in the 1950s.[28]   Thus, as B. G. Hickman points out in his analysis of long swings in the American economy, while the power of the traditional market forces connected with building slumps and booms has been greatly reduced, the influence of changes in government spending and taxation has been 'enormously enhanced'.   And he concludes that it was the failure of the Federal Government to cut taxes when its military expenditure fell back abruptly after 1953 which was responsible for the check to American economic growth between then and 1960, rather than, as Kuznets suggests, the emergence of one of his ten-year economic downswings.[29]   The contrast between the two halves of the 1950s in the behaviour

[25] Amer. Philos. Soc. *Trans.*, 1958.   [26] Ibid.
[27] B. G. Hickman, 'Post-war retardation', *AER*, May 1963.   [28] Ibid.
[29] See *Capital*, p. 460.   'We may now [late 1950s] be in a downward phase of the long swing, reflecting the currently low rate of family formation and additions to the

of the Federal Government as a purchaser of goods and services is dramatic. From 1950 to 1955 its purchases rose by 101·4 per cent; from 1955 to 1960 they fell in real terms by 1·8 per cent.[30] This means that the Government put into the economy an extra annual $22 billion's worth of orders between the beginning and the end of the first period, while it took out of the economy nearly $1 billion annually between the beginning and end of the second period.[31] The consequences of this massive act of deflation would have been much more serious if state governments and local authorities had not continued to spend more and more each year on public services. The obsession with the achievement of a balanced budget at the centre was happily countered by the carefree mood at the periphery.

Will the Import Spree Last?

Nothing in the foregoing argument is intended to suggest that there are *no* special factors of an impermanent character which have contributed to the exceptional run of prosperity which the Western industrial nations experienced since the Second World War. The exceptional stimuli are particularly in evidence in international trade; and we have already noted that a dynamic export sector is a powerful engine of accelerated economic growth. There is little doubt that the politics of international trade have been unusually favourable in this period. From about 1950 onwards[32] the governments of the Western capitalist countries have been engaged in the deliberate reduction of barriers to imports. But it is not merely that a series of cuts in tariffs or the removal of import quota restrictions have created opportunities which lively exporters, out for a quick profit, have been able to seize. More important is the general atmosphere and mood created in the business community by an experience extended over a considerable period, which suggests that whatever the apparent deviations at any given moment of time—and there is rarely a moment when some country is not trying to slip in a little bit of extra trade protection somewhere—the tide of history is moving in the direction of more rather than less scope for international trade.

labour force resulting from the low birth rates of the 1930s.' Hickman, however, concludes that although the US ills cannot be explained in terms of an old-fashioned building cycle, the 'long swings' are still with us in another guise. 'Nothing in a century of experience with long swings suggests an economy capable of quick enough automatic adjustment to the elimination of backlogs or the deceleration of autonomous expenditure to prevent prolonged departures from a full employment growth path.' This gloomy opinion seems to correspond with the view of many of the economists who took part in the discussion at the American Economic Association meeting on the experience of the US since the war viewed in the historical perspective of long-term cycles, at which Mr. Hickman's paper was read. It is perhaps worth noting that the meeting took place before the US had the experience of its first extended period of uninterrupted expansion since the war, the Kennedy-Johnson boom of the 1960s (see *AER*, May 1963).

[30] OECD, *Econ. Surveys: United States*, 1961, p. 19.
[31] Values measured at constant 1954 prices.
[32] Starting with the OEEC trade liberalization programme.

To those who have come to take the trend for granted, it was no surprise that the construction of the first stage of the common external tariff of the European Common Market should be promptly followed by a negotiation under the aegis of the GATT—the 'Kennedy Round' of 1964—which aimed to cut the general level of tariffs in all the industrial countries by up to 50 per cent. It is worth making the point that the emergence of a powerful customs union like the European Common Market might just as easily, in other political circumstances, have led to the raising of tariffs all round. That it served instead to trigger off the most ambitious venture yet in multilateral tariff reduction is one more event that is likely to reinforce those attitudes in the business communities of the West which tend to promote a further expansion of international trade.

The point is that nowadays selling goods of any sophistication in a foreign market often requires a substantial investment. This can only be justified if there is a solid expectation of sales over a fairly long period. It is indeed the security of the tariff structure, the assurance that the individual import duties are firmly anchored, which is at least as important as the actual level of the tariffs themselves. The GATT was therefore wise to put so much of its effort into a series of agreements 'binding' existing tariffs. As a result of this there has been a significant decline in the familiar risk run by successful exporters selling to any country which is equipped with the usual political lobby devoted to keeping foreign goods out.

Perhaps the last time in history when there was a political movement of comparable force in international trade was in the middle of the nineteenth century.[33] In this case the impetus was given by one nation, Britain, which systematically dismantled her tariffs, having been convinced by the argument of British economists that this was in her own interest, from the early 1840s onwards. The example was enormously contagious because the British happened to be the outstandingly successful practitioners of the new industrial and commercial techniques. A certain intellectual leadership went with this position. Indeed, the exponents of the great English doctrine viewed their task of making converts abroad in something of the same spirit—and with equal fervour—as Jean Monnet and his group approached their objective of a United States of Europe a century later. The high point of the movement was probably the Anglo-French commercial treaty negotiated in 1860 by the leading philosopher of free trade, Cobden. At the time it was regarded as a political act of comparable magnitude to some of the decisions taken by the European Common Market under the Rome Treaty. France, for so long

[33] A. H. Imlah (*Economic Elements in the Pax Britannica*, Cambridge, Mass., Harvard UP (1958), p. 190) estimates that international trade from 1840 until the early 1870s increased in volume at a rate of no less than 13 per cent a year. This was nearly double the rate of expansion in the early 19th century, from 1800 to 1840.

the citadel of doctrinaire protectionism, had at last surrendered. Indeed, many French businessmen were incensed with Napoleon III for letting the English have their way; there was a violent protest from 1,400 manufacturers who went so far as to threaten reprisals by 'cannon fire'.[34] Politics certainly played an important part in the French Government's decision. As has happened not infrequently in the European Common Market and in the GATT, considerations which have nothing to do with commerce have sometimes had a decisive role in the politics of international trade. In this instance Napoleon III was engaged at the time in negotiating the annexation of Savoy and Nice after his successful Italian campaign.[35] The British on their side were so eager to spread the good doctrine of free trade, which was seen by its Cobdenite supporters as embodying forces of radical political change that were bound to affect any country embarking on it, that they gave to France far bigger tariff concessions than they received in return. A large number of French goods were allowed into Britain duty free, while the French in exchange merely removed their absolute prohibition on certain imports of British goods, with a promise to reduce the maximum tariff on them from 30 to 25 per cent at the end of a further five years.

The incident is worth recalling because of the way the story ended. The apparently irresistible wave of history which had been initiated by the British was found to be dependent on very tenuous political forces. When the political mood changed, during the era of unrestrained imperial rivalry after 1870, one country after another raised its tariff barriers against the foreigner—until Britain was left by the end of the century as the odd man out.

However, one does not have to postulate another great political reversal in the Western world in order to foresee a slowing down of the recent tempo of advance in international trade. There are factors of a more straightforward economic character which might produce the same result. The point is simply that while tariffs are actually in process of being reduced, at the same time as some of the other more subtle and less visible barriers to foreign trade, the growth of international trade from one year to another is given a series of extra fillips. Even if all the tariff cuts made from the late 1940s onwards are held and consolidated, there must come a time when the additional momentum, over and above the 'normal' expansion of world trade, disappears.

Any such check to the rate of growth of international trade could, if it were significant, produce multiplier effects which would slow down the economic expansion of the whole Western world. Governments which had happily allowed their exports to rise, in the confident expectation of buoyant markets abroad for their export industries, would become cautious. Those

---

[34] See S. B. Clough, *France: a History of National Economics, 1789–1939* (New York, Scribners, 1939).

[35] Lord Morley alleged that the conclusion of the Anglo-French commercial treaty removed a real threat of war with England over Napoleon's Italian annexations.

which felt that their currency reserves were only just adequate or that they needed to be systematically enlarged in line with the anticipated expansion of national output and trade,[36] would try to curb the growth of their imports. They would try to hedge their risks more than in the past, with the result that the bias would be towards a more deflationary policy than they would have adopted if export markets had looked more promising. That in turn would reduce the export opportunities open to their normal suppliers abroad; and some of these would then feel that they ought to protect their balance of payments in the same manner.

This depressing sequence might occur. But the actual outcome will plainly depend in large measure on the state of currency reserves and international payments at the time when the momentum of tariff cutting ceases. If, for example, the efforts that are currently being made to reform the world currency system were to succeed, and a continuous flow of additional monetary resources, acceptable to all nations, were provided for the finance of international trade, the mood of governments would be very different. The pressure would be taken off national currency reserves and external trade policies would not have to be conducted in a spirit of nervous anxiety. That indeed is precisely what has helped the trading relations of West European countries in the 1950s and early 1960s, when the requirements of increasing international liquidity were largely met by gold and dollars transferred to them from the United States. So long as the Americans remained in deficit and the dollar was treated as an international medium of exchange as good as gold, West European reserves went on rising and West European nations could afford to be extremely generous with one another. The great postwar movement of liberalization in international trade in the West can be regarded, in part, as a by-product of this curious, and necessarily impermanent, monetary relationship.

In 1965, when this book is being written, the prospect that the American balance of payments may be brought into equilibrium, causing a cessation of the outflow of dollars before any alternative currency resource has been created by international agreement, is in fact the chief menace to Western prosperity. But if this menace is overcome and a new system for the continuous reinforcement of international liquidity is established, there is no reason to expect that the subsequent disappearance of the extra stimulus of tariff-cutting, which we have enjoyed hitherto, will impose a check on the rate of economic growth in the West. So long as governments are not hemmed in by fears for their external reserves, they will presumably be ready to offset any loss of momentum that might occur in the export sector by raising the level of output elsewhere. For the present, however, exports still

[36] The view that national currency reserves also need a steady rate of growth is held by some small nations, e.g. Holland, with a heavy dependence on international trade.

play a crucial role in sustaining Western economic growth, and the forces making for the enlargement of international trade are therefore of especial importance.

In the first half of the 1960s the movement towards lower tariffs, both within groups of industrial nations, like the European Economic Community and the European Free Trade Association, and between them has been in full vigour. The consequences of what has already been agreed will continue to make themselves felt in the form of increasing opportunities for exports for several years to come. Underlying the calculation by Maizels, mentioned earlier, that imports of manufactured goods into the advanced industrial countries may rise at more than twice the rate of the annual increase in the real income per head of these countries, are two different assumptions.[37] His argument is not only that actual and prospective tariff reductions will expose a lot of additional customers to the export salesmen; it is also that the underlying market and technological forces are now more favourable to international trade than they have been in the past—and are likely to stay so. This is partly because of the effect of mass affluence on the buying habits of people. As personal incomes rise beyond a certain level where basic needs have been met, the volume of what the Americans call 'discretionary spending', and with it the range of goods bought, increases disproportionately. The goods also become more rapidly obsolescent, as fashions change or improvements in quality are introduced. Markets as responsive as this are a magnet to trade across national frontiers. The sheer diversity of demand for consumer goods—and also for consumer services, like tourism and travel—stimulates buying from abroad.

There is a further factor which has a profound effect on international trade, and that is the deliberate pursuit of full employment in the industrial countries.[38] The marginal elasticity of import demand (in relation to income) is high in such circumstances: a 1 per cent increase in income, starting from a situation in which available productive resources are for the moment fully employed, will give rise to an increase of imports of more than 1 per cent. Because it takes time to mobilize the additional domestic resources to produce what is required to meet the new demand, the gap is filled by buying abroad. Even assuming there were a country whose economic policies were so efficiently conducted—with the aid of 'incomes policies' and the like—that money expenditure always rose at exactly the same pace as the rise in the aggregate volume of production, it would still be remarkable if in each category of goods the supply could be made to coincide precisely with the demand. So long as most industries are working at or near full capacity, the probability is that the conjunction of full employment and rapid growth

[37] See *Industrial Growth*, pp. 140 and 416.
[38] I am indebted to Mr Nicholas Kaldor for this observation.

will result in constant calls being made on imported goods to meet a series of temporary bottlenecks.[39]

More fundamentally, it may be asked why we should attach quite so much importance to this kind of spill-over into international trade. Must we, in order to be happy and prosperous, be for ever taking in each other's washing? In theory it would be easy to organize our affairs in such a way as to secure economic growth without the special stimulus of export trade; if foreign markets were closed, the state would make good the deficiency in demand required for full employment by measures to raise domestic purchasing power. There are, however, some practical problems which would arise, and they could be awkward. Since full employment in a rapidly growing economy tends to result in a very high pressure of demand for imports, a government which adopted this course would want to make absolutely sure that the nation's economic frontiers were securely watertight. Imports would have to be closely planned and controlled. This is how the Soviet system works; there is no evidence that it puts a brake on the *volume* of production. Where such a system is deficient is in its failure to encourage rational and efficient use of domestic resources—i.e. the value of what is produced is less than it would be if trade were differently organized. It is indeed significant that the first moves towards a new economic policy in Eastern Europe during the early 1960s, specifically concerned with the husbanding of national resources and their employment in such a way as to produce a higher rate of return, were taken in the industries engaged in foreign trade. It was here that the Polish authorities, for instance, evidently felt that the potential for greater efficiency in production, by more selective industrial effort at home and more extensive buying abroad, could be most quickly realized. The planners made no secret of their intention that the new norms for calculating profit and loss in the export industries, and the methods adopted there to provide management with stronger incentives to efficiency, should serve as pilot projects for the rest of the economy. Similar steps were taken in Hungary.[40] There, and in Czechoslovakia too, the extensive development of foreign trade—for all the difficulties and uncertainties which this imparted

[39] It is also to be expected that the higher level of output resulting from the reduction of such bottlenecks, e.g. in advanced capital goods, will make it possible for any given country to increase the volume of its exports as well. The normal accidents of technological progress make it unlikely that these exchanges on the margin of full employment economies will all be one way. The essential point is that the matching of surplus and deficient productive capacity in different countries through international trade will raise the level of output all round. In any individual country it will be possible to maintain a given level of employment and pressure of home demand with a smaller degree of inflation than would occur with less international trade Or alternatively, if it is thought that there is a maximum acceptable degree of inflation which sets the limit to the employment of resources in a modern economy, it would follow that international trade would permit a lower level of unemployment.

[40] See ECE, *Econ. Survey Europe 1962* (1964).

to the process of domestic planning—was seen as the key to the more economical use of national resources, human as well as material. The growing importance which the Communist countries in the 1960s attached to the principle of comparative advantage in international trade is noteworthy. It is clear that their views on this matter were influenced by the evidence of the successful use of international trade as an engine of economic growth and efficiency in Western Europe.

For a Western capitalist society enjoying full employment, with all the additional pressure for imports which that tends to bring with it, a background of dynamic international trade with world markets increasing steadily from year to year is vital. Indeed, the assurance that the opportunity for increased exports will both be available and be seized may be the condition for the maintenance of a full employment, high-growth policy in certain countries. Unless national currency reserves are extremely large, running an economy at full stretch necessarily involves certain risks. If a country which possesses only modest reserves cannot plan ahead with a fair measure of assurance that its exports will rise, caution will suggest the need for something less than full employment in order to safeguard the balance of payments. British policies in the late 1950s and early 1960s serve as an illustration—in a very mild way—of how a country's external payments may influence its government's decision about the extent to which it will pursue a policy of full employment. With low reserves and a currency especially vulnerable to sudden fluctuations in international confidence, the British Government felt that it had to reinsure, more than other nations were doing at the time, against the possibility that imports would rise faster than exports. The simplest way of achieving this was to try to reduce the marginal elasticity of demand for imports by creating a larger margin of unemployed resources.

We have seen that the especially high elasticity of import demand in the modern world is partly due to the difficulty of matching the growth of demand at home quickly with domestic supplies, in a situation where domestic resources are fully employed. The problem is eased if the economy is operating with a surplus of factors of production. The practical question, which the British experience has left unanswered, is how big a surplus is required in order to make a significant difference to the outcome. In Britain what happened was that the unemployment level moved up from 1·5 per cent in 1960–1 to over 2·5 per cent in the course of the induced economic stagnation of the subsequent two years.[41] Whether it was the effect of the increased unemployment or of the halt in the growth of production from mid-1961 to mid-1963 which was responsible for the brake on imports, and

[41] The actual figures, seasonally adjusted, were 1·5 per cent in the first quarter of 1961 and 3 per cent in the same quarter of 1963, when however there was some exceptional unemployment as a result of abnormally bad weather (see NEDC, *The Growth of the British Economy* (Mar. 1964), p. 13).

hence for the improvement in the balance of payments, it is impossible to say. The experiment did not last long enough to discover what would have happened if Britain had been able to resume a steady rate of economic expansion with unemployment maintained at something over 2 per cent. There is nothing in the evidence available to show whether or not this would have reduced the growth of British imports significantly below the level of Germany and other European countries, where the rate of unemployment in the early 1960s was 1 per cent or less.

In using this British example—and in particular the incident of the 'wage pause' introduced by Mr. Selwyn Lloyd, the Chancellor of the Exchequer, during 1961–2—the intention is merely to illustrate the sort of thing that *could* happen, if governments once began to distrust their own ability to meet the cost of rising imports out of increased export earnings. There were in fact a variety of motives behind the British Government's action—and a variety of different explanations of it offered over the period of the 'wage-pause' experiment. The British Treasury contained some pure theorists of old-fashioned wage inflation, who believed that the chief consequence of a rise in unemployment would be to affect the price of labour, and therefore the cost of British exports. The import elasticity of demand at the margin did however still come into their calculations via another route. The evidence suggests that when imported manufactured goods are freely available in a competitive world market, quite small movements in domestic prices have a disproportionate effect on the volume of goods imported. In other words, the price elasticity of substitution of imports for domestic products is very high.[42] The argument was simply that if British wage inflation could be moderated so that the rise in wage costs was less than that of the countries normally supplying imported goods to Britain, the effect on the volume of imports would be disproportionately large.

The general point to observe is that so long as the elasticity of substitution, as it affects the manufactured goods exchanged between industrial countries competing with one another in international trade, is high, there is an additional risk in running a full employment economy with a rapid rate of growth. This is the risk that the rise in costs may proceed somewhat faster in one's own country than it is going to in those of one's competitors. If nations were to become obsessed by this danger, they would tend to hedge their risks in such a way as to err on the side of the probability of something less than full employment. Again, they would be induced to take this course more readily if they felt that international trade as a whole was not likely to expand fast enough to provide them with the opportunity for a rapid increase in export earnings.

[42] See Christopher Dow, *The Management of the British Economy 1945–60* (London, CUP, 1964), p. 391.

To sum up—if nations come to take the view that there is a probability that their exports will not rise significantly from one year to the next, they will be induced to embark on one of two courses. Either they will attempt to reinsure against trouble by trying to damp down import demand through a policy aimed at something less than full employment and possibly a slower rate of growth. Or they will use import restrictions as the instrument for pursuing a policy of full employment at home. The conclusion is that if the Western world is to avoid the slow-down in the rate of growth of real income which would result from either of these two courses,[43] it is necessary to ensure that international markets for industrial exports continue to expand rapidly.

There is one practical implication of the argument which is worth noting. In conditions where full employment has already been widely established, governments should be encouraged to make free use of the variety of incentives and aids to exporters, whenever a persistent adverse movement of their balance of payments suggests that an extra sales effort abroad is necessary. This is quite different from the beggar-your-neighbour policies pursued before the war, when several countries shaped their whole economic policy in such a way as to increase their export surplus at the cost of someone else's deficit. The datum line in the postwar world is full employment and the existence of policies aiming to maintain it. All that is being argued in this context is, first, that miscalculations of the proper balance of supply and demand required for full employment are inevitable in these circumstances; secondly, that it is essential for the common good of all nations trading with one another that national authorities should be encouraged to err on the side of excessive expansion rather than excessive contraction; and therefore, thirdly, that governments should deliberately adopt a liberal interpretation of the international trade rules governing assistance to exporters, whenever a country with a good full employment record can demonstrate the need to increase its foreign exchange earnings. The line between legitimate government help, for example in the form of trade intelligence services provided free of charge or subsidized market research, and straightforward export subsidies easily becomes blurred. No doubt businessmen who have to compete with a country whose exporters receive the benefit of a more liberal interpretation of the international rules will mobilize their members of parliament to protest against unfair trade practices and favouritism to foreigners. But resisting this kind of pressure is, after all, a small price for governments to pay for the sake of maintaining the overall bias, which now exists throughout the Western world, towards a steady and rapid expansion of international trade. Governments ought to be sufficiently confident about

[43] The second course would result in the loss of benefits from international specialization; in particular, it would tend to reduce the pace of technological change (see Ch. III).

this to base their domestic policies on the assumption of favourable external conditions for as far ahead as they can see. Once they are led to expect that the weather outside may at some stage turn foul, they will begin to build some dangerously efficient protective dykes. The techniques for doing so are by now highly developed.

III

INNOVATION SPEEDED UP

IT may be objected that the argument at the end of the last chapter is circular. Full employment, because it encourages the overspill of imports, is good for international trade. But expanding international trade is itself one of the major factors helping to sustain full employment. That works all right, so long as no other outside force intervenes. But say there were some powerful independent factor tending to slow down international trade over the coming years; the circle would then be broken. The spring, once released and uncoiled, would simply dangle: international trade grown sluggish would probably induce some nations to abandon full employment; that in turn would further reduce the tempo of international trade, and so on.

It is contended by some economists that they can already identify just such a long-term trend militating against the continued expansion of international trade at the pace which it has sustained in recent years. Thus Professor Austin Robinson argues that in the second half of the twentieth century it is reasonable to expect 'the ratio of exports to national income for some of the more mature countries to be declining'.[1] This would be a sharp departure from the trend of the 1950s and early 1960s when the exports of industrial countries as a whole, particularly their exports of manufactured goods, almost invariably increased as fast or faster than their national incomes. The cause of this change, according to Robinson, is essentially technological. He compares the situation today with conditions in the nineteenth century, when because the transmission of technology was relatively slow, a nation like Britain could enjoy for a long period decisive advantages in textiles and other industries. But nowadays 'differences of comparative advantage are becoming narrower and shorter lived'.[2] If this were so, the maintenance of the high prosperity and rapid economic growth which we have enjoyed in the Western world since the war would involve new problems and their solution would require new techniques. The happy result so far has been achieved, it is worth reiterating, in an extraordinarily favourable climate of international trade. The practices and economic policies that have been evolved during this period have been conditioned by

[1] 'Rethinking Foreign Trade Policy', *Three Banks Review*, Dec. 1963.
[2] There are other factors which Robinson foresees will make nations rely more heavily on domestic supplies and less on foreign trade than in the past—rising costs of certain imports of materials and the increasingly specialized needs of local markets. But the technological one is the most important.

this background. There is no clear evidence to date that they would continue to operate successfully if one of the major conditions changed.[3]

The technological factor, on which so much else depends, must therefore be more closely examined. It is perhaps easiest to do so by starting with a statement of my own hypothesis, which is roughly the opposite of Professor Robinson's. It is that the pace of technological advance has speeded up so much that a series of apparently small and relatively short-lived advantages by one country over another are likely to result, over an extended period, in a continuing and large increase of the export trade in advanced manufactured goods.

First, what is the evidence that such a speed-up in technological change has occurred? It must be admitted that there is no means of showing in any measurable sense how the pace of innovation in industry compares with what it was a century or a half century ago. At most, it is possible to demonstrate that for a selected number of important innovations the time interval between the appearance of the crucial idea and its development into a marketable product has been considerably shortened in recent years.[4] This is a result that might reasonably have been anticipated from having vastly more scientists and technologists working than ever before and incomparably better and more rapid communication among those with interests in common.[5] Evidence of a more direct kind, which can be tested, is provided by changes in business management practice in the amortization of new capital equipment. Again, comprehensive data are lacking, so that the change cannot be described in terms of the conduct of the average firm. But the managements of leading companies in a variety of industries confirm that they have reduced the calculated working life of newly installed plant and equipment—and increased the annual allowance for depreciation—because of their experience

[3] There is no inherent reason, as was shown in Chapter II, why full employment should not be achieved without the support of rapidly expanding international trade. But to maintain it in conditions where export sales were not increasing would require an extremely tight restriction of imports, because as we have seen the marginal elasticity of import demand is high under full employment in an advanced economy. And such a restrictive policy would certainly slow down the rate of economic growth through the delays which it would impose on the supply of new capital goods and other products of advanced technology (see below, pp. 44–45).

[4] Thus Professor D. E. Marlowe has estimated that it took 56 years (1820–76) for the development of the telephone; 35 years (1867–1902) for radio, and 14 years (1922–36) for television. His most recent example is the rapid absorption of transistors into industry within about five years of the launching of the idea in 1948 (see 'The Flow of Scientific Research Information to Industry', *OECD Observer*, Apr. 1964).

[5] Kuznets suggests that the improvement in communication between different scientific disciplines remote from each other has been a major factor in speeding up technological change. The methods and assumptions of one science have been absorbed and adapted and tested in another. Meanwhile the technical capacity to conduct experiments on the basis of new theory—and to do so quickly—has greatly increased (see *Capital*, p. 442).

that the plant becomes technically obsolescent much faster than it used to, certainly well before it is physically worn out.[6]

Turning now to the effect on trade in consumer goods, we have already seen that the affluent and highly organized modern mass market is a powerful magnet for international trade in this field. Here the technological factor operates by giving the large prizes to those manufacturers who are quick enough to supply constantly new or improved products to meet changing tastes. Of course such trade in manufactured consumer goods has always existed; the point is that the scope for it, especially in the markets of the advanced industrial countries, has now been greatly enlarged. More significant, however, is the evidence of what looks like a new trend in the import trade of advanced countries in the other main category of manufactures, capital goods.

Traditionally world trade in capital goods has been to a large extent a one-way street, with four big industrial countries—Britain, the United States, Germany, and France—supplying between them nine-tenths of all the world's exports while themselves importing a small fraction of the total.[7] Between 1899 and 1937, as Appendix I shows, when world trade in capital goods rose vigorously, only some 6 per cent of the total increase was absorbed by the big four.[8] The smaller industrial countries of Europe took rather more; but the overwhelming proportion went to the other regions of the world, largely to the primary producing countries. In the postwar period the proportions have changed drastically. Approximately one-third of the very large increase in world exports of capital goods which occurred in the 1950s was absorbed by the countries of Western Europe. And within Western Europe it was the most advanced big three—Britain, Germany, and France—whose imports went up fastest. Between 1950 and 1959 they absorbed between

[6] By way of illustration it is worth describing what has happened to the depreciation policy of the largest British manufacturing company, Imperial Chemical Industries. The large and dynamic firm, it is worth observing, is not to be treated as an exceptional case; rather it tends to set the fashion. The period of depreciation for equipment in ICI, which was commonly 20 years plus before the war, was reduced from 1950 onwards, when, according to the chairman, the company was 'beginning to think in terms of 15 years' for new projects. In the early 1960s this came down to 12–15 years; and more recently the average for new plant has come down to about 10 years. For certain kinds of investment, where the risks of technical obsolescence are thought to be high, the amortization period is down to 5–7 years. (Information supplied in 1964 by Sir Paul Chambers, chairman of ICI.)

[7] The source for these figures and for the argument which follows is Maizels, *Industrial Growth*. 'Capital goods' in this definition consists of machinery and transport equipment, other than passenger road vehicles. For a more detailed treatment of the figures see Appendix I, p. 428.

[8] 1937 is a convenient terminal date because it marks the high point of business activity in the 1930s. If one compares 1899 with the peak year in international trade during the inter-war period, in 1929, the increase absorbed by the big four was around 10 per cent of the total.

them 15 per cent of the total increase in world trade in capital goods. The comparable figure for the period between 1899 and 1937 was 5 per cent.

The same trend is observable in the United States, where the change is even more spectacular. From the start of the century until the Second World War, US imports of capital goods rose hardly at all: between 1899 and 1937 they accounted for 1 per cent of the total increase of world trade in these items. During the 1950s as much as 10 per cent of the increase in world exports of capital goods was absorbed by the American market.

Perhaps most striking of all is the way in which the recent growth of imports of capital goods into these advanced countries of Western Europe and North America seems to be reinforced as time goes on. One might have explained the burst of importing in the early postwar period as a catching-up operation: after years of war destruction and neglect of equipment, it would be reasonable to expect that the effort to reconstruct and modernize quickly would result in heavy buying abroad. But in fact imports of capital goods by the big industrial countries went on rising in the late 1950s; so did their proportionate share of the world market. In the United States, where the postwar reconstruction effort any time after 1950 can hardly have been a significant influence, the underlying trend can be clearly observed without the intrusion of other factors. Whereas during the first half of the decade US imports absorbed 7 per cent of the rise in world trade in capital goods, from 1955 to 1959 the proportion went up to 14 per cent. Indeed, taking the four biggest industrial countries of the Western world together—United States, Britain, Germany, and France— which have traditionally been thought of as almost completely 'self-sufficient' in meeting their capital equipment needs, their imports during the late 1950s amounted to slightly more than 30 per cent of all world trade in capital goods.

It is, of course, impossible to demonstrate the existence of a long-term trend from data relating to so short a period. However the indications which these facts provide suggest an unusually vigorous exchange, based on comparative technological advantage, among industrial countries. Perhaps the nature of the change that has occurred in the importing habits of these leading countries in world trade emerges most sharply when one looks at the share of capital goods in their total imports of manufactures at different periods of history. At the peak of inter-war prosperity in 1929, the big three countries in Western Europe devoted 18 per cent of their imports of manufactures to capital goods. Thirty years later, in 1959, with a vastly increased import bill, the proportion had risen by nearly half, to 26 per cent. In the United States over the same period, the corresponding proportion had more than doubled, from 6 per cent in 1929 to 13 per cent in 1959.[9]

[9] Maizels, *Industrial Growth*.

It is sometimes argued by economists that the great surge of trade in manufactured goods between the industrial countries, which has been a peculiar feature of the postwar world, is a species of Western folly—a characteristic phenomenon, some would go so far as to say, of a certain type of decadence associated with the excessive proliferation of marginal choices; or at best an eccentric foible which has produced little of real value beyond the pleasure of registering a large number of additional exports each year in the customs houses of the various countries. What has really been gained, it is asked, if a few more Englishmen buy Mercedes Benz cars instead of Jaguars, and a few more Germans buy Jaguars instead of Mercedes? It is of course impossible to say how much of the additional choice given to consumers as a result of the freer movement of goods across national frontiers is of this marginal kind. Personal experience suggests that standards of finish and reliability of performance, as well as the convenience of new gadgetry, vary considerably between the products of one country and another at any moment of time. Under the pressure of the competition from abroad, the process of innovation in domestic industries is often visibly speeded up. In the meanwhile enterprising people can go out and buy their extra consumer satisfactions from foreign suppliers, without having to wait until home producers deign to catch up with foreign standards. It may be that each single one of these additional satisfactions does not amount to much. But even on crude quantitative grounds, the fact that the process of innovation has been accelerated means that there are more of these satisfactions over any given period of time.

It is, however, in the field of capital goods that the influence of the factor of accelerated innovation can be seen in its clearest contemporary form. Out of the total increase in trade in manufactures between the industrial countries during the 1950s, more than a quarter consisted of capital goods. Again, the argument used by economists of the traditional school, who refuse to recognize the crucial change in the technological tempo of our times, is that nothing significant would be lost if such imports of capital goods by industrial countries were cut severely. The argument is based on the view that there cannot be many differences between the standards of performance of products turned out by advanced countries which time and a little patience will not repair. The comparative advantage in this type of trade is thought likely, as Austin Robinson says, to be 'narrow'—and to become narrower. However, say the innovator is himself always moving another step ahead, while the follower is catching up, the result must surely be that at any given moment of time the follower will be suffering from a permanent lag. If what nations sell in international trade is, to an increasing extent, the ability to innovate quickly—to produce more advanced designs, to absorb the latest improvements in technology into the servicing or replacement of machines more rapidly than the average—then the disadvantage of the supplier with even a small, though persistent, technological lag will widen rather than narrow.

This lag becomes a more important factor in determining a country's international competitive position in a period when machines are overtaken by technical obsolescence earlier in their lives than in the past. The point may be illustrated by a simplified arithmetical example. A firm which uses a standard machine with a working life of ten years is offered a new and greatly improved version of it. There is only one maker, and he has a three-year lead on the other producers. If the buying firm sticks to its old suppliers, it is liable to suffer on two counts. First, it has to wait three years before it gets the advantage of higher efficiency or better quality products from the new machine. Secondly, the new machine is itself subject to the pressures of accelerated technical obsolescence; as a result of the original delay in buying, the firm risks having to pay higher capital costs in the end. Suppose that after ten years from the machine's appearance on the market, when the first lot sold are due for physical replacement, another technical advance occurs. Then in order to take immediate advantage of it, the laggard firm must write off its machine over seven years (ten minus three), which will involve it in an annual capital charge some 40 per cent above that of its more advanced competitors.[10] The moral is clear: buy now. Besides, the tax system in most Western countries is designed to make it easy to pay later.

This tendency to import more capital goods in order to cheapen the process of investment in an era of rapidly advancing technology is not confined to the capitalist world. The same considerations figure largely in the minds of modern Soviet planners. I was once given a direct insight into their thinking on this subject in the course of a discussion during 1959 with senior technicians and managers in the Leningrad *Sovnarkhoz*. Two complete British factory installations, supplied by International Plastics Ltd, had been bought and set up in the Leningrad region. They were extremely advanced, automated factories for making chipboard, and their cost ran to something over £1 million. The question which we were discussing in 1959 was whether there was any prospect of further orders for British plants of the same type. The answer was yes—assuming this particular investment programme continued—up to perhaps two more; but if it was decided that the Soviet Union required additional plants beyond that, it would be worth while to set up their own production line for making the equipment. In the context of their

---

[10] On a straight line system of depreciation, the annual charge will be some 14 per cent of the capital sum instead of 10 per cent. No allowance is made for any offset from the second-hand sale of the partly used machine. The MAPI method of calculating return on investment, which has been developed in the United States, provides a systematic way of taking this and the other factors in the example into account.

own extensive investment needs, and the limited supplies of capital and skills, it would not pay them to put the resources of technology and specialized manpower into a project like this, unless they could see a fairly extended run of new chipboard plants coming out of it. If it seemed likely that only very few of these highly specialized and expensive machines would be needed, it would pay to import them.[11]

The fact that imports of this kind are 'capital-saving' is a potent factor making for their rapid expansion during a period in which fixed investment absorbs an unusually high proportion of the national income—in many countries of the West, as well as in Russia and Eastern Europe. Of course to the extent that a country imports its investment goods, it will, if it is paying for them, have to surrender the equivalent amount of resources in additional exports. (This assumes that it is not paying for the goods by surrendering part of its currency reserves; obviously such an alternative course cannot be pursued over a long period without the reserves running out.) The act of saving, or withholding of supplies, inflicted on consumers in order to finance the investment, cannot be evaded. The reason why a decision is made to import these products of advanced technology, rather than make them at home, is that in this way it is possible to economize on technological resources, the supply of which may be absolutely limited in the short or medium term. Another way of saying the same thing is that a country whose scientific manpower is already fully employed in an existing programme of research and development can only embark on an additional project by putting something else farther back in the queue.

The outcome is yet another illustration of the general principle, noted in Chapter II,[12] that full employment makes for a high marginal propensity to import. It is worth following the way in which the principle manifests itself in some detail because it serves to focus attention on the main point, which is that if the demand everywhere on the available technological resources were not so heavy, the appearance of new capital goods and production techniques in one country would not so readily be translated into imports by another. The second country would use its own 'technological surplus' instead. The accelerated pace of innovation in technology is an independent factor in determining the volume as well as the shape of world trade. The open question is whether in the long run the accelerated innovation may be matched by an even more rapidly increasing supply of scientific manpower— or whether there is an absolute limit on the human side, which will leave us in the present condition of shortage for as far ahead as it is possible to see.

---

[11] They also had to pay heavily to acquire the technique of operation. Memorably, a British works manager of the old school, lent to the Russians to help them to run in the new plants near Leningrad, remarked with some complacency over a cup of tea in his hotel: 'We got them to pay'—and he named an enormous sum—'for the *know-all* to go with that plant'. 'What was that?' I asked. 'The book of instructions', he said innocently.   [12] p. 34.

It is not by any means only in the sphere of capital goods that the acceleration of the technological tempo becomes visible. In some ways its effect on the growth of international trade in chemicals is even more dramatic.[13] Chemicals make up a much smaller share of world trade than capital goods; but in the 1950s their contribution to the expansion of international trade in manufactures was disproportionately large. The figures show that in 1950 chemicals accounted for less than 10 per cent of all trade in manufactured goods, but were responsible for 18 per cent of the vast increase in world exports of manufactures which occurred during the subsequent decade. Again, it was the export of chemicals from one industrial country to another which was the most dynamic element: it accounted for more than half of the increase in world trade in chemicals during the 1950s.

Typically, the traditional chemical products which have sustained the exports of the leading industrial countries to the more backward areas in the past—dyestuffs, explosives, and fertilizers—have not grown so fast. The non-industrial countries of yesterday are now making all of these things. The big advance occurred in the new chemical products developed (though not invented) since the war. The demand for such products as these comes just as strongly from the import markets of the advanced countries, which are dependent in turn on some piece of innovation starting up in one or the other of them, as from the more backward countries. By now the precise *relative* degree of industrial sophistication between countries seems to matter much less than in the past; unless a country has a very great chemical industry, covering the whole range of new products, with a research and development budget to match, it is likely to be a heavy importer.

It so happens that there is in any case a secular trend towards increasing emphasis on chemical manufacture as countries advance. The rate of growth of chemical output tends to be much faster than that of manufacturing industry as a whole. This has been true ever since the beginning of the century, and the trend has continued markedly since the war. It is plain that the mere transfer of the earlier harvest of technological progress in the advanced countries to the less developed ones would ensure a very rapid rise in chemical output in the latter. What is less familiar is the rapid succession of new products moving into international trade. Maizels calculates that by 1959 these products[14] accounted for one-quarter of world trade in chemicals. The case of plastic materials, which he has analysed in detail, serves as an illustration of the process. Exports of plastics have increased faster than any other chemical product: they rose sixfold during the 1950s.

[13] See Maizels, *Industrial Growth*, ch. 11, from which the figures in what follows are derived.
[14] He lists five categories as 'technically new products developed during or since the last war': antibiotics, sulphonamides and hormones; vitamins; anti-knock compounds (tetra-ethyl lead); synthetic detergents; plastic materials.

Two-thirds of this expansion took place in trade between the industrial countries, most of whom were manufacturing plastics and increasing their own output sharply during that time; and only one-third went to all the other markets of the world put together. The leading four industrial countries—United States, Britain, Germany, and France—which are responsible for 80 per cent of world exports of plastics, once again provided an important and expanding market for each other's specialities.[15]

Labour- and Capital-Saving Investment

Thus if it is true that the prosperity of the Western capitalist world is in some measure dependent on the rapid growth of international trade, it appears that the best assurance of the latter is provided by a continued high rate of technical innovation. Lest this be thought to be setting mankind an impossibly onerous task, we ought to observe that the same conclusion—about the central role of innovation—would be reached if there were no international trade at all. In Western Europe by the early 1960s the main sources of surplus labour which had fed the industrial working force on a Gargantuan scale in the 1950s, had dried up. It is a well attested fact that rapid rises in per capita incomes have generally been correlated with rapid increases in the employed labour force.[16] The reason for this is partly the obvious one that almost any new investment undertaken to make use of some existing surplus of labour, even if it purports to be a duplication of an existing plant, usually turns out to be the vehicle for technical improvements which raise productivity.

Equally important is the effect of a ready supply of additional labour on the overall economic strategy of a country. We saw earlier how once an economy has reached a state of full employment while pursuing the objective of a high rate of growth, it is likely to run into production bottlenecks.[17] Some of these can be overcome by drawing in more imported goods. However, a large portion of a modern economy depends for its motive power not on goods but on services, and many of these are difficult or impossible to import. The services sector in an advanced Western economy is as large or larger than the manufacturing sector, in terms of its contribution to the national product.[18] There is in addition the whole activity of building, whose end product cannot usually be imported. It is plain that a country which can rely on an ample supply of additional labour each year is less likely to

[15] App. II, p. 430, for a discussion of the time-lag in technological development and its effect on world trade in synthetic products.

[16] See ECE, *Econ. Survey Europe 1962*—'Some Factors in Economic Growth in Europe in the 1950s'. The one country which showed no correlation of this kind was France, where economic growth was rapid without any large increase in the numbers employed. [17] See pp. 34–35.

[18] In the US, where the expansion of the services sector has gone farthest, its share of the national product was approaching 40 per cent in the early 1960s, while the share of manufacturing was under 30 per cent.

be impeded in its general progress by production bottlenecks than one which cannot. The result as usual is that the well-placed country will drive the engine of economic growth much harder; it will be prepared to take risks which a country facing the prospect of labour shortages will be less prepared to contemplate. The case is exactly parallel to the problem faced by a country with a small currency reserve which hesitates to expand production and is always worried about getting into a boom, because it knows that this is likely to bring an importing spree in its train. The general conclusion appears to be that the nations which grow fastest are those which have to hedge their bets least.

In the changed conditions of the 1960s in Western Europe the emphasis is therefore more strongly than ever on labour-saving innovation as the means of continuing the rapid increase in incomes which has been enjoyed since the war. There is some hope too that future innovations may be capital-saving as well as labour-saving. If they are not, the new situation may place an additional burden on Western societies, in the form of a requirement to save more.[19]

[19] Assuming that capital-output ratios become less favourable. Kuznets (*Capital*, p. 445) argues that in the period ahead we are likely to see this happen, because he expects that there will be a revolution in power production and holds that, on past experience, such changes usually result in a rise in the capital-input without a commensurate return in output. He foresees a slowing down in the rate of economic growth unless an additional slice of incomes can be diverted into savings. I do not find this argument compelling. It depends on the unchanging behaviour of technological factors whose nature has altered profoundly compared with the past periods which Kuznets takes as his reference point. To take one example, the revolution in electric generator design, which in Britain raised the size of new generators installed from a standard 30,000 kw. around 1950 to something over ten times as large by the early 1960s, has brought down the capital cost per unit of electricity in a dramatic fashion. The following table shows the rate of progress achieved. It should be observed that the figures in the last column (of the investment necessary to produce an additional kilowatt of electricity) are measured in current money costs, and make no allowance for the general rise in capital goods prices over these years. If the 1963 costs were recalculated at constant 1950 prices, the capital cost of electricity sent out in 1963 would have been considerably lower than the figure shown in the last column.

Year of commissioning	Size of generating unit (Megawatts installed)	Capital cost of complete power station (£ per kw. sent out)
Early 1950s	30	67
1952	60	57
1956	100	58
1957	100	59
1958	120	53
1959	200	50
1962	275	43
1963	550	37

Source: Progress Review No. 52: 'Electrical Power Generation from Fossil Fuel', *J.Inst. of Fuel*, Mar. 1962.

More generally Kuznets's argument relies on the fact that investment in new forms of energy production occurs typically in very large indivisible blocks, with a long 'lead

Conclusive evidence that the current and future crop of technical innovation is likely to be capital-saving is impossible to find. But there are many favourable indications. Steel technology provides an interesting and suggestive example. The economies that have been achieved in the 1950s in the use of steel have already made a significant difference to the cost of such diverse pieces of capital equipment as bridges and motor vehicles. Two factors have combined to reduce the input of steel required per unit of new investment. One is the smaller relative importance of the traditional massive piece of capital equipment made wholly of steel—typified by the steam engine and the ocean-going ship—in the total of investment. The other influence is the improvement in quality, both of the design of equipment and of the steel used in it. Because, first of all, the tensile and other properties of steel are better understood and, secondly, because greater precision in the control of the steel production process allows products to be made to much closer specifications, designers have been able to tailor the use of their materials to the purpose which the finished product is to serve in a way that was not possible in the past. One result is that the average weight of steel going into a British car of standard performance was reduced by approximately 25 per cent in the course of a decade in the 1950s.[20]

Overall, the effect of technological advance—on consumer goods as well as capital goods—has been to reduce the amount of additional steel required for any given increase in industrial output. The economists of the British Iron & Steel Federation calculate that whereas before 1958 the requirements of additional steel consumption in relation to a given rise in industrial production as a whole, during peak periods of economic activity in the business cycle, were in the ratio of something over 1 : 1, they had dropped by the early 1960s to less than 1 : 1. Provisionally their estimate is that an advance of 10 per cent in the industrial production index is likely to induce an advance of 9·5 per cent in steel consumption.[21] The Iron and Steel Board (UK) in its long-term plan for the industry in 1961 related the fall in the amount of steel required for investment to the general improvement in capital-output ratios. It said: 'Although as a result of technical progress, individual machines may be replaced by larger, more complex and costly machines, it is common experience that through economies of scale or faster or more continuous

time' before they begin to produce their full rate of return. During the initial period therefore the yield per unit of capital tends to be low. However, the same considerations apply by now to many modern manufacturing industries where scale is a decisive factor in technology; and it is not apparent that their capital-output ratios have suffered in consequence. There is no reason to suppose that investment in power is as different from other forms of industrial investment as it has been in the past.

[20] Estimate of British Iron & Steel Research Ass. The steel used in 1960 was of higher quality and cost more, but on balance there was a significant economy in costs.

[21] Information supplied orally.

running, the increase in productive capacity is relatively greater than the increase in capital cost.'[22]

Another and equally striking form of capital-saving which has been opened up by the introduction of improved machinery is in the use of stocks. The total investment in stocks is large. In Britain, for example, the aggregate value of stocks held is equivalent in value to around 45 per cent of gross national product. Moreover any rise in the national product normally necessitates an increase in stocks, though fortunately not in the same ratio. It is impossible to say what the normal ratio is. But what is clear is that in a rapidly expanding economy, the cost of the annual addition to stocks makes up a significant portion of capital investment. Thus in Germany during the second half of the 1950s the cost during the years of vigorous expansion (i.e. all except 1958) was of the order of 10 per cent of total investment.[23] Sizeable reductions in the ratio of stocks to the volume of production or sales have been achieved in businesses which have introduced computer systems of control. This is the result of quicker and more accurate and frequent enumeration of stocks in warehouses and improved techniques of locating what is wanted at short notice. The saving in capital employed is sometimes very large indeed.

Some of the most dramatic results so far have been achieved by the United States Government in the Department of Defense. Mr Robert McNamara, the Secretary of Defense, deliberately set out to exploit the new techniques of stock control in the major cost-reduction programme on which he embarked in the early 1960s. A good example of what can be done by the determined employment of automatic methods and machines is contained in his 1963 Annual Statement on the cuts made in the stockpile of 'excess and long supplies'.[24] These are items for which there is no immediately foreseeable use or for which uses are expected to be found only after long delays; they amounted in value at the time of Mr McNamara's statement to some $13,000 million. There is no way of avoiding the accumulation of such stocks: they are generated as a result of the constant and rapid changes in weapons technology; materials and spare parts collected in anticipation of a

[22] *Development in the Iron and Steel Industry, Special Report* (London, HMSO, 1961), para. 75. The subsequent Special Report of the Iron and Steel Board, reviewing development plans for 1965–70 (HMSO, 1964), noted the further decline in steel requirements in the early 1960s, compared with its previous estimates based on the experience of the late 1950s, and suggested that this might be due in part to 'changes in the kind of goods produced by each industry, as well as actual savings in the weight of steel used to produce a particular product brought about by either improved design or the use of steel of improved properties'. The effect of substitution by aluminium, plastics and other new materials was estimated to be 'relatively small' (para. 67).

[23] OECD, *Statistics of National Accounts.*

[24] Statement before the House Armed Services Committee, 30 Jan. 1963, sect. XB. See also for more details Hearings of the Joint Economic Committee, 'Impact of Military Supply and Service Activities on the Economy', Mar./Apr. 1963.

given production programme are found not to be wanted, and the problem then is to prevent them from being wasted altogether. In fact the Department of Defense was managing in the early 1960s to find a use for approximately 8 per cent of this stock annually, that is for something around $1 billion's worth a year. The improved programmes of stock control were estimated to add to this annual off-take each year from 1961 onwards an amount rising to $435 million by the end of 1964–5. Thus the final effect of the operation would be a *recurring* saving on stocks of some 3·3 per cent a year (the annual off-take having been raised from 8 to 11·3 per cent). This is the kind of sustained capital-saving, with stocks costing progressively less year after year, which sounds like an accountant's private dream. No doubt the circumstances are unlikely to be repeated elsewhere on quite the same absolute scale. After all, stockpiles of $13 billion's worth of unwanted modern equipment are not expected in the ordinary course of business or nature—but the type of problem itself is probably not entirely remote from storage and warehousing operations conducted in many other places inside and outside the United States.

To argue that technological innovation is central to the development of modern capitalism is reminiscent of the theories of J. A. Schumpeter. It may be useful at this point to say a word about his position and how it relates to the view advanced here. Schumpeter believed that it is in the nature of traditional capitalism to be violent, to move forward by fits and starts, and that the reason for its uneven progress lies essentially in the discontinuous process of innovation and in the violent response of entrepreneurs to it. The upswing of investment associated with some piece of successful innovation—it need not always be technological: the innovator may simply have discovered a new market to be exploited—turns into a slump because at a certain stage the innovation becomes *too* fashionable. The path-breakers are followed after a lapse of time by a host of inferior men who temporarily glut the market, so that the profit on the original process is eliminated. The price comes down sharply; fortunes are lost; and the impulse which generated the boom is then brusquely reversed.

Because of the reversal of expectations among borrowers and lenders alike, the whole system of business calculation is temporarily awry. At this moment, even if there are fresh innovations in the pipeline, they are held back. The risks of failure in any new business enterprise, which necessarily relies on uncertain calculations about the future, are greatly increased at such times. A wise businessman therefore waits 'until things settle down' before embarking on any new venture.[25] Schumpeter insists that the process of

[25] See J. A. Schumpeter, *Business Cycles* (New York, McGraw Hill, 1939), p. 135. The later versions of Schumpeter's theory put the emphasis squarely on this factor of uncertainty in entrepreneurial calculations as the reason why a check to expansion leads to a period of depression. The point is not given quite the same stress in his

'creative destruction' in a slump—whereby the inefficient firms are bankrupted—is as essential to capitalist growth as the innovations themselves.[26] However, he does foresee the likelihood that as the capitalist system develops into more sophisticated forms and the individual units of enterprise become large and very powerful, the economic ups and downs which accompany innovations will be greatly reduced and may possibly be eliminated altogether. This he calls, with a certain characteristic verbal infelicity, the process of 'trustification'. At this stage innovations are introduced and developed in an orderly fashion—the entrepreneurs no longer 'swarm' back and forth in a violent manner, and the whole sequence is 'institutionalized'.

Schumpeter here points to one of the important factors which helps to explain the much more placid behaviour of the postwar business community in the advanced countries of the Western world. He generalized it by saying that at a certain stage economic development as a whole becomes increasingly 'a matter of calculation' *(Rechenstift)*.[27] What he did not quite foresee was the vast importance of the authoritative calculations made by postwar governments, whose activities as entrepreneurs have become much the most important single force in the whole system. The significance of the act of government 'planning'—even if it is no more than an attempt to set out a series of consistent intentions about the government's own investments in a form that is readily understandable by other businessmen—will be examined more closely in later parts of this book. At this stage I only wish to point to the connexion between Schumpeter's 'institutionalized innovation', with the consequent reduction of entrepreneurial uncertainty, and the phenomenon of accelerated innovation. For it will be recalled that what held back the advent of new products, on Schumpeter's theory, was not the lack of new ideas, but the recurrent enfeeblement of initiative caused by the confusion of business calculation during slumps. If Schumpeter himself saw this connexion, he certainly did not make it central to his theory. His warnings about the danger of soft public policies which would damp down the business cycle and mitigate the creative destruction of a slump suggest that he thought rather that capitalism in its new form would lose its earlier capacity for rapid growth. However, the emphasis in the exposition of his theory is not always the same, and there are besides occasional nuances in his long and complicated asides which escape even the attentive reader. This great man had a certain compulsive erudition which he deployed so richly in his work that one sometimes feels in going through it that one is tramping across land that is

earlier work. He quotes a remark by Professor Machlup to express his conclusion:—
'Entrepreneurial risk of failure is at a minimum in equilibrium and slowly rises as prosperity develops. Entrepreneurial activity stops at a point at which that risk is a maximum.'

[26] See *Capitalism, Socialism and Democracy* (London, Allen & Unwin, 1943).

[27] *The Theory of Economic Development*, trans. Redvers Opie (London, OUP, 1934), p. 253n.

soft from over-ploughing. The mind drags. But the significant facts in the economic history of our times rarely escaped him. Among other things, he is highly unusual among the analysts of the phenomenon of the economic cycle in believing that the object of his researches is not a permanent feature of the universe. 'Crises will disappear', he says, 'earlier than the capitalist system, whose children they are.'[28]

Recessions and Business Psychology

Once businessmen in general become convinced that they can safely ignore the risk of a serious recession during the productive life of some piece of capital in which they are thinking of investing, the whole tempo of an economy is likely to change. It moves forward then in the spirit of a driver who, arriving at a stretch of straight broad highway where he can see far ahead, slams his lever into top gear and lets out the throttle. Maddison[29] lists the urges to invest which will operate powerfully on the ordinary businessman in such circumstances. He will expect wage-rates to go up continuously and fast, and will be casting about for ways of saving labour. He will expect that price movements, when they occur, will generally be upwards; so that he will have an incentive to borrow in order to buy productive equipment early rather than late. 'He will in fact become concerned with the risks of not investing, i.e. lack of capacity to meet expanding demand with consequent loss of market share to competitors. . . .' Maddison goes on to argue that this preoccupation with the dangers of being under-invested in a rapidly expanding market may even change the standard rate of profit which a businessman thinks he has a right to expect. The reduction of the uncertainty of investment should in the long run make him content with less.

It should also influence other aspects of the psychology of investment. Anxiety about the possibility of business recessions and the associated uncertainties of the market not only makes a cautious entrepreneur look for a higher rate of return on the money that he sinks in an enterprise; it also means that he will try to cut down to a minimum the time that he has to wait before he gets the money put into his original investment back. Investigations in certain manufacturing industries in the United States and Britain have suggested that the 'pay-off period' which is looked for by businesses employing this criterion is commonly 5 years or less, and frequently as little as 3 years.[30] That may well mean that an entrepreneur will only look at a manufacturing project if the rate of profit that it promises is above the normal rate *to begin with*. However if the chances of sudden changes in the climate of business are greatly reduced, it is to be assumed that the average

---

[28] Ibid., p. 255. The 1st edition of this book was published in 1911 and the final big book on *Business Cycles* in 1939; his theory naturally evolved over a quarter of a century, though in its essentials it remained remarkably unchanged.

[29] *Economic Growth*, pp. 50 ff.

[30] See R. R. Neild, 'Replacement Policy', NIESR, *Econ. R.*, Nov. 1964.

businessman will tend to feel less vulnerable on this count too, and will risk his money on certain ventures which, although profitable and productive in the long run, he would have avoided in the past because of their unsatisfactory initial return.

All this helps to explain why the level of investment in the industrial countries of Western Europe has been sustained recently at so much higher a level than in the past. If investment is measured as a proportion of gross national product, the ratio during the 1950s was half as high again as that recorded in any previous comparable period of time.[31] The contrast with the United States is once again striking. There the investment ratio during the 1950s was—as shown in Chapter II—somewhat lower than it had been in the period of prosperity from the turn of the century until the outbreak of the First World War. Moreover, the trend of American investment rates during the 1950s was downward, while in Western Europe the share of investment in the national product tended to increase during the 1950s. It is not difficult to find reasons to explain why the American business community was evincing this unwonted timidity, while the European were being so bold. When thin order books keep the average manufacturer working well below capacity for an extended period of years, the desire to invest in new plant grows feeble. Add to this the risk that he may be caught short with his capital project completed just as the economy slides into yet another recession, and the incentive to hesitate is powerfully reinforced. Why should he hurry? His calculation of the return on new capital invested is a function of the probable extent to which the installed productive capacity will be used. Fluctuations in demand caused by frequent business cycles clearly reduce the average rate of profit over the life of a piece of capital. Indeed the cause of the exceptionally large increase of production in Western Europe is not only that investment has been higher than in the past, but that productive capacity has been more fully used.

The OECD, when it came to examine the prospects of achieving its target of a 50 per cent growth in output during the decade of the 1960s, in the light of the economic experience of the West since the war, emphasized above all the beneficent effect of a 'sustained pressure of demand on the productive resources of the economy'.[32] 'Some countries [it goes on] were much more successful than others in achieving and maintaining this pressure of demand and we believe that this is a fundamental reason why their growth rates were higher. . . . By contrast, the absence of a sufficiently strong pressure of demand in the United States in the second part of this period [i.e. of the 1950s] is the proximate explanation of the rather modest rate of growth

[31] See Maddison, *Economic Growth*, ch. 2 and App. I, for figures on this and the argument which follows.
[32] *Policies for Economic Growth*; *Report to the Economic Policy Committee*, Nov. 1962, p. 17.

achieved.' Raising the level of demand will not, however, by itself do the trick. It is only when businessmen are given the confidence that the increase in demand will be steadily maintained during a long period ahead that they respond by investing more. The British example shows what happens when they are suspicious—all too justifiably as it has turned out on several occasions since the war—that the rising curve of demand will be artificially flattened out. The essential message of this story is that rapid economic growth results from the expectation of steady growth.

The businessman's view of how his government is likely to act in the face of recession therefore becomes decisive. In the United States the experience of a series of postwar business cycles has created a recession psychology—typified in the fear that, as the US President's Council of Economic Advisers put it in their Annual Report at the beginning of 1964, 'simply because of its duration, the current expansion must be approaching its end'. This was after the recovery from the previous recession had been in progress for no more than thirty-three months. Historical memories took the business cycle analysts back to the longest boom of the 1950s, which had lasted forty months altogether in 1954–7, and they decided that the current prosperity was likely to come to a halt soon. The makers of policy in the United States, who have deliberately set themselves the aim, since the Kennedy Administration came to power in 1961, of matching European rates of economic growth, thus have a major psychological barrier to overcome. The longer any period of rising prosperity lasts, the more nervous the American business community becomes—and therefore the more liable to interpret any minor setback as the signal for setting an inventory recession in motion. When people are as trigger-happy as this, the burden on the public authorities is that much greater. The public sector in the United States therefore has to be more active, more powerful, and more decisive than its equivalent in Europe if it is to resist the pressures on the economy coming from the private sector. It so happens that the public authorities in America are less well equipped than those in Europe for such an endeavour.[33]

It was not, however, the lack of equipment which was chiefly responsible for the measures which positively held back growth and aggravated postwar business recessions in the United States. A propensity to cut Federal Government expenditure on the slightest provocation held back the advance of the economy towards full employment in the boom of 1954–7 and again in 1959–60. Part of the trouble, as Maddison points out, was the dependence on 'built-in stabilizers'—like the automatic changes in tax flows and in the ebb and flow of payments out of public funds for unemployment and relief, as business activities went up or down—to keep the economy on an even keel. Again, the existence of a comparatively weak public sector, especially in the area

[33] See Chs. XIII & XIV.

controlled by state governments, who are responsible, for example, for fixing the amount of unemployment pay, tended to make such stabilization measures less effective than they would have been in Western Europe. Briefly, the public treasury controlled by many of the state governments—the standard of relief and welfare services varies enormously from one to the other—is much less generous than in Europe. The whole approach to the use of the resources of government power in combating a business cycle was different from that of Western Europe.[34] As Maddison says, 'the main emphasis in Europe was on discretionary changes in policy and very little was heard of built-in stability'.[35] It is worth observing in passing that built-in stabilizers are the natural psychological successors to the old-fashioned 'invisible hand' of the market: the deep-seated desire of economists of the classical tradition to believe in the automaticity of economic processes has had an important influence on governments in the Anglo-American world. For the most part it has served to reinforce their instinct, which was already quite strong enough, not to intervene.

The early 1960s in both Britain and the United States brought signs of a change in public policy. The British problem was much the less serious of the two, in terms of its cyclical effects, since what had to be overcome was a set of business expectations based on the experience of 'stop-go' policies, which though they impeded a smooth and rapid process of growth fell far short of business recessions. In the United States the economic policy-makers of the Kennedy and the Johnson Administrations set themselves the task of convincing business that a period of uninterrupted steady economic expansion could be sustained for long enough to achieve full employment. An important advance in this direction came in the spring of 1964, when after three years of boom, a further considerable reinforcement of the 'pressure of demand' was assured through the cut in tax liabilities of some $11,000 million. The reinforcement was timely, because even after the sustained three years' recovery, business investment was still a lower proportion of GNP than it had been in the early 1950s and unemployment was still over $5\frac{1}{2}$ per cent. It seemed that the United States had at last embarked on long-term fiscal policies—first raising the level of government expenditure

[34] The nature of the problem and of the political obstacles in the way of a solution are indicated in the following exchange among members of the Commission on Money and Credit which reported in 1961. The majority report stated: 'Variations from state to state in eligibility, in the level and duration of benefits, in waiting periods, and in ceilings, weaken the stabilizing action of the system. Federal action should require that all states comply with at least uniform minimum standards'. But some members of the Commission dissented. 'Fred Lazarus, Jr.: "I am opposed to uniform federal minimum standards. These would greatly reduce the flexibility needed to meet the varying problems of each state and would be a large step towards complete federal control of these programs". Messrs Black and Schuman wish to be associated with Mr Lazarus' comment' (*Money and Credit*, p. 128).

[35] *Economic Growth*, p. 132.

in the early phases of the recovery (1961–3) and then following with a massive reduction in income and company tax—analogous to those which had helped to bring full employment to the rest of the Western world.

It is, however, only the first step. The OECD's warning on this matter is worth recalling:

> We think there is a danger, in the United States and also in some other countries where the problem of adequate demand may arise, that budgetary policies appropriate to their economic situation may be inhibited because public opinion mistrusts deficit financing which . . . leads to growth in the public debt. The mistrust may be the greater if widely differing views are held on the desirability of extending the scope of government. Such attitudes create political obstacles to government action. . . .[86]

Thus beyond the technical economic issues there are problems arising from the individual character of the political institutions of different countries and from practices which originate in historical experiences long since past, but which continue to exercise a potent influence on the management of economic affairs in the second half of the twentieth century. These form the main theme of the remainder of this book.

There is, however, one further argument about the relationship between technology and growth which suggests that some kind of American lag is inevitable, whatever the Americans may do to mend their political institutions and bring them into consonance with modern economic needs. This requires to be briefly examined. Maddison, for example, whose detailed examination of the factors responsible for postwar economic growth leads him to an optimistic assessment of the future, nevertheless sees a built-in disadvantage operating against the United States. Suggesting some figures, not for purposes of prediction but rather as broad indicators to use in assessing the future success or failure of economic policy, he says: 'There will probably be something wrong with policy if productivity grows less than 3 per cent a year in European countries, or 2·5 per cent in the United States.'[37]

Why the difference in capacity for growth? Maddison's argument is simply that the most advanced economy which operates closest to the frontiers of existing technology is at a certain disadvantage. The less advanced can apply year after year not only the techniques and equipment deriving from new inventions, but also some of the fruits of the old. Thus they should be able to gather in a larger annual crop of technological benefits. This is a specific application of the general argument advanced by Professor Gerschenkron about the advantages of 'backwardness' in general in the history of the industrial revolution in different countries. 'The more delayed the industrial development of a country', he says, 'the more explosive was the great spurt of its industrialization, if and when it came.' The generalization fits some of our experiences since the war rather well. Thus Western Europe as a whole grows faster than the United States; Italy, after the postwar reconstruction phase is over, grows faster than the West European average; Japan grows faster than Italy. If it is objected that India grows much more slowly and that other countries in Asia grow hardly at all, this merely serves to recall Gerschenkron's qualification about the whole process of industrialization—'if and when it came'.[38] There is nothing inevitable about it.

There are, of course, many other factors besides the sheer size of the technological gap which have influenced the speed of the rate of catch-up in different countries. Among the most important, on which Gerschenkron lays particular stress, is the marked divergence in the national institutions of the late-comers to industrial capitalism in the nineteenth and twentieth centuries from those of the pioneering Anglo-Saxon model. The faster rate of growth of Germany, for example, was due to the fact that industrialization tended to proceed 'under some organised direction'. The state acted as guide. In Britain it had never presumed to do so. The absence of state interference in Britain was itself a factor making for more rapid growth here than in the rest of Europe at an earlier stage.

The technological argument for expecting a slower rate of growth in the United States than in Europe, although plausible, is by no means overwhelming. First, there is no reason to expect a high degree of symmetry between the industrial revolutions of the past and the series of technological spurts that are foreshadowed in the rest of the twentieth century. It is already apparent that in the contemporary and forthcoming phase of industrial advance, the flexibility of different societies in establishing novel forms of industrial organization, in inculcating new habits of management and attitudes of mind among workers about the acceptable rate of change in conventional methods of production, will play a large part in determining the relative speed of advance. Gerschenkron's institutional and cultural factors may operate in quite different ways in a modern context. There is no reason to suppose that culture invariably works in favour of backwardness.

On the contrary, there are some strong reasons for supposing that in a period of accelerated technological change the advantages of 'forwardness' may be very great indeed. If the opportunities for raising productivity by means of new techniques continue to multiply and if they result in radical changes in the quality, or even the identity, of a large number of products, the big prizes, for example in export markets, will go to those who are habitually first. The consolation prizes to be won by those who set about exploiting technology of a somewhat older vintage, hoping to offset age by lower wage costs, will in that case be worth much less. The argument may be put rather more formally by saying that the transient monopolistic element

---

[38] *Economic Backwardness in Historical Perspective* (Cambridge, Mass., Harvard UP, 1962), p. 44.

in the new products may produce advantages for the innovator, both by shifting the terms of trade in his favour and by enlarging his export market opportunities. It is indeed most striking how these 'transient' technological leads perpetuate themselves. Hufbauer (see Appendix ii) has shown that the 'imitation lag' in synthetic products—i.e. the time between the first commercial manufacture of a synthetic in one country and its production somewhere else—runs to several years even in advanced industrial economies like Britain and France. Equally relevant is the evidence produced by Freeman[39] in a study of the effects of innovation in plastic materials, that a lead once established in one or more new products is remarkably persistent. The point is simply that the break-through which leads to the production of a new chemical, for example, is only the beginning of an extended process of innovation. The firm which gets ahead initially tends to go on making improvements both in the quality of the products and in the process of production. This explains how it is that Germany before the Second World War and the United States during the period after it managed to retain a stubborn lead in the production and export of certain plastics, in spite of the fact that there was no secret about the underlying technology required for their manufacture.

In sum, it is likely to be the habit of rapid and continuous innovation which will produce the greatest rewards, in an age in which scientific discovery is communicated faster and the opportunities for its exploitation in productive processes are uncovered more rapidly than in the past. The concept of higher returns from an increasing physical scale of capital is an old and familiar one; but perhaps equally important in present conditions are the returns related to the time-scale of new investment. The more the time-scale of innovation is compressed, the bigger the return. Innovation in this sense is not merely inventing a new product or process, but ensuring that the existing productive apparatus can be rapidly converted to meet new requirements and exploit the transient opportunities offered by the market. This is where the habitual acceptance of a certain tempo of change, by management and by labour, may well be decisive. There is nothing so far to show that the Americans will be less flexible in this regard than their European competitors, and some evidence which suggests that with their vast budgets of research and development, their more sophisticated institutions for the management of innovation, and the underlying cultural bias in favour of rapid change, the conditions for accelerated economic growth in the second half of the twentieth century may be especially in their favour.

[39] NIESR, *Econ. R.*, Nov. 1963. See also App. ii, p. 430.

IV

THE ARGUMENT IN BRIEF

THE advanced industrial countries of the Western world have during the 1950s and early 1960s enjoyed an extended period of prosperity for which it is impossible to find a precedent. Three major factors can be identified which are responsible for the distinctive economic flavour of the postwar period.

First, economic growth has been much steadier than in the past. It has not been completely even, but the recessions, when they have come, have been very mild and shallow by historical standards. In several countries they have resulted in nothing more than the temporary slowing down of a continuing advance. There has been no halt or reversal. In others, where production has fallen back in recessions, these interruptions have been short-lived and have had relatively little effect on the level of employment.

Secondly, the growth of production over the period has been extremely rapid. It is true that in the United States there have been periods in the past, notably from 1900 to 1913, when the average rate of economic growth was even higher than in the 1950s. But the American case was exceptional in the postwar Western world.[1] It was accompanied by many features which had no parallel elsewhere—notably a rising level of unemployment and a declining level of business investment, measured as a proportion of the national product. In Western Europe the pace of economic advance after the middle of the century was much faster, as well as being less interrupted, than in any known comparable period of peacetime history.

Thirdly, the benefits of the new prosperity were very widely diffused. In the conditions of full employment and rising demand for labour established in almost all areas of Western Europe during the 1950s, average wage earnings rose as fast as, or faster than, the national product. In the United States too consumption rose fairly steadily and the upward trend was barely interrupted even by business recessions. What distinguished Western Europe was the deliberate effort to widen the spread of consumer benefits, by means of welfare services and pension schemes, to those members of society who cannot rely on automatic gains as a result of the rise in wage-earnings.

It is noteworthy that this diffusion of rising incomes over the population as a whole has not reduced the flow of savings required to support a high level of investment. On the contrary, Western Europe has set aside a larger

---

[1] Canada is regarded for the purposes of this argument as part of the North American complex, inextricably linked with the US economy.

61

proportion of its resources for investment than ever before. Again the United States is different: there the rate of investment was somewhat lower than in the period of expansion immediately preceding the First World War. One of the aims of the Democratic Administration which took office in 1961 was to raise the level of American investment, with the help of fiscal incentives and the promise of sustained economic expansion uninterrupted by serious recessions.

The evidence suggests that a continuing 'recession psychology' in the United States has been a major reason for the contrast between American and West European economic experience in recent years. Analysis of the actual recessions which have occurred since the war suggests that they have been aggravated in the United States by government financial policies. There have been more recessions in the United States than in Western Europe, and they have been allowed to go further before the government intervened decisively to boost demand.

There is an alternative explanation of the postwar contrast between North America and Western Europe, which sees the latter as enjoying an exceptional and transient expansion while the former is closer to the long-term economic norm. An important school of economic historians argues on the basis of the experience of the past century that the favourable conditions from 1950 onwards reflected a 'long upswing' (of about ten years' duration) of a kind which has been seen regularly, alternating with downswings of about equal duration, in the past. On this view there has been no decisive change of trend in the Western capitalist world leading to a sustained high rate of economic growth. The reason why appearances suggest that there has been is that a number of extremely favourable conditions have fortuitously combined to accelerate the expansion of the 1950s; the lucky combination is unlikely to endure.

Two powerful economic forces have played a major part in raising the tempo of economic growth in the West. They are: (1) the sustained expansion of international trade, and (2) the great building boom of the 1950s. Some economists, among whom Simon Kuznets and Arthur Lewis are outstanding, maintain that these are transient phenomena; both residential building and international trade in manufactured goods are believed to have been subjected to a species of forced growth, which will be matched by a markedly slower rate of expansion later on.

The central thesis of this book is that there is no reason to suppose that the patterns of the past, which have been ingeniously unravelled by the historians of trade cycles, will reassert themselves in the future. To begin with, the advent of full employment, and its conscious pursuit in the advanced industrial countries as an act of policy, have added a new dimension to international trade. When countries are operating constantly at the margin of their available resources, their imports of manufactured goods tend to rise faster than their domestic output of manufactures. This tendency is particularly marked during a period of rapidly advancing technology.

The distinctive features of the new era of capitalism which has opened since the end of the Second World War are first, the conscious pursuit of full employment, and secondly, the accelerated pace of technological progress. The latter has made possible a high and steady increase from year to year in output per man-hour. This process will continue and may accelerate.

The rapid expansion of international trade is not a necessary condition for prosperity and full employment; but it makes it possible to achieve these ends in much greater comfort. Autarkic policies have awkward by-products, including an excessive amount of policing which generally goes with a system of tight economic controls. The level of prosperity, too, will tend to be higher when more trade flows. If imports are not impeded by quota restrictions or high tariffs, the very rapidity of the technological advance and the need to exploit transient opportunities before end-products or novel techniques become obsolescent will act as a powerful engine increasing the volume of international trade. At the same time, international trade in advanced capital goods and new products, like chemicals, will itself tend to accelerate the rise in productivity. And that will help to maintain the expansion of output in the advanced nations, even when labour for new jobs is short.

The early stages of the new capitalism were sustained in several countries with the help of ample supplies of additional labour moving into industry. The 1960s show a marked change in the trend. This has reinforced the emphasis on technological innovation in general and on higher education in particular.

Thus far the argument has tried to show only that continuing prosperity and uninterrupted growth on the scale of recent years are possible in the future. The underlying conditions in the second half of the twentieth century are more favourable than at any time in the history of capitalism. The more interesting question, however, is whether success is probable. The answer to this depends very largely on political will and skill: specifically on the management of the institutional apparatus which guides Western economic life. The body of this book is devoted to the examination of these institutions.

There is an alternative approach which sees this whole issue as a technical problem, and one that was solved some time ago as a result of the advance in economic techniques. Once Keynes showed how an economy should be handled when it produced the recurrent signs of debility, there was little more to it, it is averred, than following the instructions in the new guide book. You might find yourself with a little more inflation than you had bargained for, but you could always rely on having plenty of economic growth. Now the curious thing is that Keynes was remarkably uninterested in the process of growth. Indeed, he held the strange view that ordinary people's wants in the advanced Western societies were so near to being satiated that it would be necessary, after only a few years of full employment, to proceed to quite extraordinary devices—for example, establishing a rate of interest of zero per cent—in order to keep economic activity going.[2]

Keynes's view was limited by his essential preoccupation with the problem of how to provide employment for more people, using a given stock of productive assets. Additions to the stock were important in so far as the act of investment itself would employ additional labour. As Schumpeter put it, the theory was chiefly concerned with 'an analysis of the factors that determine the higher or lower degree of utilisation of an existing industrial apparatus'. That was natural enough, given the overwhelming human problem of mass unemployment in the depression years of the 1930s; but it resulted in some narrowing of the intellectual horizon. The problems of capitalism in the 1930s—how to bring a given production apparatus into full use—were not typical of the periods of capitalism which preceded or succeeded it. Schumpeter concludes: 'Those who look for the essence of capitalism in the phenomena that attend the incessant recreation of this apparatus and the incessant revolution that goes on within it must therefore be excused if they hold that Keynes's theory abstracts from the essence of the capitalist process.'[3]

This is not to deny that the control over the business cycle, which owes so much to Keynes's work, has been one of the decisive factors in establishing the dynamic and prosperous capitalism of the postwar era. Indeed, it is probably the single most important factor in this change. So many other developments flow from it, notably the reduction of business risks and the incentive to speed up the process of investment. My point is only that if the change from old-style capitalism to the new style had depended solely on a process of intellectual conversion to the system of economic doctrines developed by Keynes, it is unlikely that it would have got as far as it has. Moreover, the future would by now be looking highly uncertain. After all, there have been many occasions since the war when we have seen people in authority, who believe themselves to have penetrated the truths of Keynesian economics, being guided in an emergency by quite other, and often contradictory, policies.

What is characteristic of the postwar period is that a variety of independent forces have combined to increase the available powers of control over the economic system and at the same time to keep the volume of demand constantly at a very high level. Governments have therefore been given time to learn how to intervene with increasing skill, without causing disaster in the course of educating themselves.

There is indeed an element of paradox in the fact that the two nations

[2] *General Theory of Employment* (Macmillan, 1936), ch. 22.
[3] *History of Economic Analysis* (Allen & Unwin, 1961), p. 1175.

which had earliest and most readily absorbed the Keynesian message—Britain and the United States—were also the least successful among the Western capitalist countries in managing their economies after the Second World War. This contrast would itself be sufficient to suggest that the purely intellectual change, which is popularly labelled the 'Keynesian revolution', is not the decisive factor. Something more is evidently required than a knowledge of techniques. On the continent of Europe during the period immediately following the war, the Keynesian message was not generally accepted. Yet there were other more powerful factors which allowed these countries to avoid any serious cyclical fluctuations and to maintain a significantly higher rate of economic growth than either Britain or the United States.

This success of the continental Europeans was so glaring that by the early 1960s it had become a significant factor in both British and American domestic politics. At any rate both countries embarked on policies which were intended to mark a deliberate break with the past, while copying some feature, real or imagined, of the European experience. In Britain the effort was concentrated on avoiding 'stop-go' measures, which had interfered with an even rate of growth; the formula adopted was economic planning on the French model which, by making progress more even, would also, it was expected, make it more rapid. In the United States, after the Democratic Administration took office in 1961, following eight years of Republican rule, the whole focus of economic policy shifted: it came to concentrate on the objective of full employment, which was to be achieved by deliberately pushing up the demands on the country's productive apparatus.

It is worth noting that when the United States came to set itself its new objective, it did not turn to Britain for its model, despite the fact that the British had successfully maintained a state of full employment, without interruption, for two decades. It was the experience of continental Europe in the 1950s which beckoned to the Americans. What had been achieved there was the combination of full employment with a high rate of growth and international competitive power which had notably eluded the British.

In the chapters which follow I shall try to identify the characteristic institutional features of the economic order which has gradually emerged in postwar capitalism. There are big differences between the key institutions and economic methods of one country and another. The differences are often the subject of sharp ideological cleavages. Yet when the total picture is examined, there is a certain uniformity in the texture of these societies. In terms of what they do, rather than of what they say about it, and even more markedly in terms of the pattern of their behaviour over a period of years, the similarities are striking. This may be because nations exchange their experiences nowadays, including the intimate experiences of management both in the public sphere and in business, more actively than ever before.

That may also be one of the reasons why the design of the pattern has become clearer in the 1960s than it was in the 1950s.

Some of its outstanding features may be usefully listed at this stage:

1. There is the vastly increased influence of the public authorities on the management of the economic system. This operates through different mechanisms in different countries: in one the control of the banking system is decisive, in another it is the existence of a wide sector of publicly controlled enterprise. In all of them the government's expenditure has been enormously enlarged and determines directly a large segment of each nation's economic activities.

2. The preoccupation with social welfare leads to the use of public funds on a rising scale, most notably to support people who do not earn, either because they are young and being educated or old and retired. Public welfare policies, of course, have a long history in several European countries; what is, however, characteristic of the postwar period is the steady advance of social welfare measures over wide areas of the Western world. This is most obviously reflected in the fact that education and pensions together have been absorbing an increasing proportion of the national income of the advanced capitalist countries. (Again a proviso must be made about the United States in the 1950s.)

3. In the private sector the violence of the market has been tamed. Competition, although it continues to be active in a number of areas, tends to be increasingly regulated and controlled. The effort to secure an enlarged area of predictability for business management, in a period in which technological change is very rapid and individual business investments are both larger in size and take longer to mature, has encouraged long-range collaboration between firms. Governments in their anxiety to increase the area of the predictable for purposes of economic planning have encouraged firms within an industry to evolve agreed policies on the basis of their common long-range interests. The classical market of the textbooks in which firms struggle with one another and disregard any possible effect that their actions may have on the market as a whole has become more remote than ever.

4. It has now come to be taken for granted, both by governments and by the average person in the Western capitalist countries, that each year should bring a noticeable increase in the real income per head of the population. The accepted procedure of annual wage claims in most countries reflects this expectation. It is, in fact, capable of being fulfilled, at any rate for a long time to come, as a result of the accelerated pace of technological innovation in industry. But to secure the full benefits of the enlarged industrial potential requires new forms of organization, (a) in the sphere of research and development, and (b) for the training of workers and generally for the more efficient deployment of scarce resources of skilled manpower. A conscious effort has begun to be applied in both fields since the late 1950s. The purpose of (a)

is to reduce the time span from the inception of novel ideas to their development into usable models ready to be absorbed into the process of production; while (*b*) aims to reduce the bottlenecks caused by the shortage of trained labour capable of responding to new technology. There is increasing realization that in a full employment economy, rapid technical progress can be sustained only if there is an active public policy designed to speed up the transfer of people from jobs in which they are established to new forms of employment.

5. The characteristic attitude in large-scale economic management, both inside government and in the private sector, which has made itself increasingly felt during the postwar period, is the pursuit of intellectual coherence. Its most obvious manifestation is in long-range national planning. Lengthening the time horizon used in making economic decisions also means extending the range of data that have to be studied in the present; more current facts become relevant. Thus the framework of systematic analysis has to be extended in two dimensions. Techniques and institutions, different in the various countries and varying in efficiency, have been developed to meet the demand for both explicitness and coherence in those economic decisions which have a significant impact on national production or public welfare. Once again the motive is at least partly the desire, in the face of greatly accelerated change, to try to reduce the area of the unpredictable to a manageable series of clear alternatives.

Finally, it remains to consider how far the methods being adopted for the efficient management of the new capitalism are compatible with the ideas and practice of traditional parliamentary democracy. There are two main questions. In what ways are the national democratic styles in different countries being modified? How much of the original objective of government by popular consent can be sustained in a system in which the sphere of active government has been greatly enlarged, and is likely to become more so?

Part 2

THE APPROACH TO PLANNING

V

THE ETATIST TRADITION: FRANCE

THE features of the contemporary system listed towards the end of the last chapter—above all the predominant role of the public sector and the reduction of the power of the market—might seem to suggest that we were witnessing a return to some earlier, pre-capitalist, order. The historical analogy that most readily springs to mind is the period of the sixteenth and seventeenth centuries in Europe, after the nation-state had established itself and appeared to be about to make a take-over bid for the control of everything in sight, including religion and commerce. The truth, however, is more complex When the British went ahead in the eighteenth century to produce their own peculiar version of the new industrial society, this was falsely assumed to be *the* model for the capitalist system. There were others; but they somehow failed to achieve the doctrinal force and the proselytizing power of the British arrangement.

Classical economics, which was largely a British invention, converted the British experience—or rather what the British hoped would eventually emerge from the trend which they had detected in their own story—into something very like the Platonic idea of capitalism. Out of Ricardo's preference for 'strong cases' there came the picture of a perfect market, unimpeded by the influence of any public authority, with a vast multiplicity of small buyers and sellers, none of them strong enough to impose a desired direction on events. This was not too wildly unlike the conditions in the British textile industry or the London Stock Exchange to provoke ridicule. The chief characteristic of the system, and incidentally its great glory, was believed to be the impossibility of imposing any direction on it whatsoever—whether from inside the market, by the firms themselves, or from outside it by the authority of the government. The market place, the small independent trader, and the non-interventionist public authority were indissolubly associated with political freedom.

In the history of capitalism Britain and France supply the convenience of sustained polarity. It is remarkable how two nations, geographically so close, so interested in a neighbour's ways of doing things, so proud of their capacity to learn from outsiders, should yet have been so little influenced by each other's experiences. The sharp contrast in national style and practice is not noticeably modified over the centuries. The essential French view, which goes back to well before the Revolution of 1789, is that the effective conduct of a nation's economic life must depend on the concentration of power in

71

the hands of a small number of exceptionally able people, exercising foresight and judgement of a kind not possessed by the average successful man of business. The long view and the wide experience, systematically analysed by persons of authority, are the intellectual foundations of the system. The design and efficiency of the machine of government then determine the degree of practical success achieved.

There have been moments when the French appeared as if they might be about to embark on an Anglo-Saxon deviation from their own system. But such moves never attracted authentic national support. The most notable were directly associated with Franco-British commercial negotiations. It is as if the French felt that coming closer to the British in trade necessarily involved important doctrinal decisions. The two outstanding occasions are the Eden Treaty of 1786,[1] when French policy was temporarily dominated by the economic thinking of the Physiocrats, and the Cobden–Chevalier commercial treaty of 1860,[2] at a time when Napoleon III was consciously trying to liberate French economic enterprise from some of the controls which had impeded its progress. Neither attempt showed any staying power. The consensus of French opinion was that they were aberrations.

A hundred years after the Cobden–Chevalier treaty, the roles were reversed and the British were trying to learn the French formula of economic success. In the early 1960s the French way became, quite suddenly and probably for the first time in modern history, the object of widespread admiration in the Anglo-Saxon world. In Britain especially, but also in the United States, the makers of economic policy had become convinced that there were important elements in the French method which were worth imitating and adapting to their own uses. The British planning agency, the National Economic Development Council, set up in 1962, was designed after close and intensive study of the Commissariat du Plan in Paris. Whatever the actual arrangements made—and these will be the subject of more detailed analysis and comparison in a later chapter—the British planners at least *believed* themselves to be applying techniques which had been developed by the French. In the United States there was no comparable institutional imitation of an overt character. But the influence of the Gallic fashion on the thinking of the Kennedy Administration from 1961 onwards is clearly evident in the fervour with which it embraced the very un-American device of setting precise long-range targets for national economic growth. Indeed, it was the Americans who were most insistent at the meetings of the Organization for Economic Co-operation and Development in Paris in 1961 that the whole of the

---

[1] The Eden Treaty, in the last years of Louis XVI's Government, was especially unpopular in France; it was blamed for the economic depression of 1788–9 which preceded the Revolution; and was the subject of complaint in some of the *cahiers* submitted to the Estates General in 1789 (see Clough, *France*, pp. 38–9).

[2] See Ch. II, pp. 31–32.

Atlantic group should commit itself to the objective of a 50 per cent increase in production during the decade of the 1960s. This was a characteristic American political ploy—importing a foreign device for domestic use by way of an international pact, largely of American making. The British were at this stage not yet ready for the plunge; they raised objections in the OECD which the majority, led by the Americans, overcame. In the years that followed, the United States Government continued to use the OECD as a kind of intellectual springboard to project ideas on economic planning and allied topics into its home territory.[3]

The setting of economic growth targets implies, if they have any practical significance, a relationship between public authority and private enterprise which is quite different from the tradition of the Anglo-American world. It belongs to the very stuff of the French tradition, which has in turn shaped many of the working assumptions behind the management of economic policy on the continent of Europe. In the form in which it has developed today the French method is probably the most interesting and influential expression of capitalism in its new guise. Other countries may have improved on individual French institutions or techniques; but no other nation has so self-consciously fought to make a coherent system out of the devices which have been adopted more or less haphazardly elsewhere. And in no other is the new felt to fit so snugly into the old. It provides, therefore, some of the richest material for the analysis of modern capitalism.

The Record of Public Intervention

The turn-round in British and American thinking about France and its economic methods is dramatic. It is worth asking how and why it occurred. In the middle 1950s the verdict on French prospects was almost uniformly unfavourable. As late as 1958 an elaborate and comprehensive study of the French economy by the Rand Corporation, *The French Economy and the State* by Warren C. Baum,[4] concluded that there was little chance of the emergence of any dynamic impulse in an economy where everyone was after a 'quiet life' and matters were so organized as almost always to stultify the effect of market forces. It was the way in which the country was cushioned from the forces of the market place that was found to be the most serious and abiding weakness in the French system. The result, Baum argued, was bound to be that prices would be pushed up above the level which they

---

[3] Professor Walter W. Heller, the Chairman of the US President's Council of Economic Advisers, was one of the most active figures in this process, and the evidence suggests that President Kennedy himself was personally involved. It was on American urging that the OECD staff embarked on a series of close studies of the process of planning, and more generally of the influence of the public authorities on the economy in selected member countries—France, Germany, Britain, and Sweden. These studies in depth were intended to provide insights into the different techniques by which public action could influence the rate of economic growth. See *Growth and Economic Policy* (OECD, 1964) and reference below, p. 296.   [4] Princeton UP, 1958.

would reach in a properly functioning market economy, that the rate of technical progress would be slower, and that the volume of output would be lower.

As the Americans saw it then—and British observers did not disagree with them—the French were the most highly protected and most cartelized society among the advanced nations of the West. They were therefore the most feeble, for their economy was least sensitive to the beneficent pressures of the market and most subject to gross intervention by an incoherent yet over-weening state apparatus. To obtain the flavour of the change of attitude, it is worth recalling President Kennedy's comment a mere four years after the Rand Corporation study was published. Speaking at his press conference on 24 May 1962 about the problem of accelerating US economic expansion, he said that he had asked the Council of Economic Advisers 'to consider particularly the case of France which has had rather extraordinary economic vitality' in order to see whether this might suggest the reasons and the possible remedies for the slow growth of the American economy.[5]

One answer to the French puzzle which should be scotched straightaway is that there was a sudden change for the better in 1958 after the regime of General de Gaulle was installed in power. In fact the most rapid rise in French industrial efficiency occurred during the earlier years of the 1950s, and slowed down sharply after 1958. From 1955 to 1958 the increase in French productivity in manufacturing was 8 per cent per year, which was faster than in any other West European country.[6] During the subsequent three years the rate of increase dropped by more than half. This was the effect of the policy of deflation which de Gaulle's Government was strong enough to make effective. It was coupled with the devaluation of the franc in 1958 and reinforced by the damper on wage increases during that and the subsequent year. The result was to give France a decisive competitive advantage in international trade, and its exports benefited accordingly. In the following years, with the balance of payments extremely strong, the country was able to resume its rapid rate of economic expansion, which had been interrupted by this deflationary Gaullist interlude.

It is fair to say that there was no reason why the British and American observers in the 1950s should have anticipated that this time the French formula would work so brilliantly. After all, there was a record of a long series of failures.[7] The idea that guiding an economy on the basis of the long-term views of officials in Paris produced especially favourable results had not been borne out by the facts. There was the celebrated case of the French sailing ship subsidy in the late nineteenth century. Just at the time when steamships were taking over, the French Government, moved by faith

[5] USIS report.
[6] NIESR, *Econ. R.*, Aug. 1962.
[7] Not least, until 1958, the failure to form a stable government.

in the warlike virtues of old-fashioned seamen and their vessels, decided to provide a special bounty for sailing ships. The result was that in the thirty years from 1880 to 1910, when the British sailing fleet dropped from 4 to 1 million tons, French sail tonnage remained more or less constant. At the end of the period French sea transport was technically backward, with over 40 per cent of the merchant fleet still made up of sailing ships. While Britain's steamship tonnage had increased by $7\frac{1}{2}$ million tons during the thirty years to 1910, the French had only a half a million tons more than in 1880.[8]

This is not an isolated example. The efficient state-run canal system, perhaps the greatest of Louis XIV's public enterprises, was the object of a costly programme of improvements in the last quarter of the nineteeth century.[9] This was a time when the canals were being used less and less, as the railways took over. In Britain from the middle of the nineteenth century onwards the canal companies were in retreat. The most that they could hope for was a take-over bid by a railway company. No wonder then that the British were inclined to be contemptuous of the pretensions of French officials to a special kind of wisdom in the conduct of economic affairs. More generally, they observed that the excessive regulation of corporate enterprises—each limited company had to be licensed individually until the late 1860s—hampered the development of business and its ability to collect risk capital for new ventures. The result was to make private enterprise still more dependent on the goodwill of the public authorities.

But was the trouble simply, as the British critics of France averred, that officials were meddling in business, where their role could not of its nature be other than obstructive or, with luck, irrelevant? Or was it rather that the men in authority happened to be of inferior quality and made the wrong choices? A conservative bureaucracy in a period of revolutionary technological change like the nineteenth century would clearly slow down the rate of progress. In such circumstances a country like Britain or the United States would gain a decisive advantage by leaving the individual innovators to get on with it, neither curbing nor actively helping them. But once the apparatus of government is directed to the exploitation of technological change and the men in charge are attuned to the expectation that this change will proceed at a high tempo, the balance of advantage could shift in favour of those who try to organize for change well ahead, and away from those who merely suffer it to happen.

The English myth of the inevitable obtuseness of government officials has

---

[8] J. H. Clapham, *The Economic Development of France and Germany, 1815–1914* (London, CUP, 1955), ch. 10, p. 243. The French realized their error before this and by 1902 the subsidy was withdrawn; but the sailing tonnage went on increasing until 1906. The subsidized French ships were able to compete on long-distance routes, e.g. carrying English coal to Chile (see Clough, *France*, p. 242).

[9] Clapham, *Economic Development*, pp. 351 ff.

a long history. Adam Smith's celebrated criticism of Colbert—'a laborious and plodding man of business, who had been accustomed to regulate different departments of public offices and to establish the necessary checks and controls for confining each to its proper sphere'[10]—sets the tone. However, choosing particular industries and enterprises to receive state support and others to be subjected to special taxes was not in itself as mistaken a procedure as Adam Smith liked to suggest, especially as France in the second half of the seventeenth century had fallen behind both Britain and Holland in the development of certain manufactures. The subsequent history of French economic regulation gave it a bad name. By the eighteenth century, when individual business initiative was being released in Britain and was doing great things, economic progress in France was impeded more than ever by a meddlesome bureaucracy which contributed hardly anything of its own. But perhaps still more impressive in British eyes was the fact that even when the system was brought under the relatively efficient control of the Napoleonic régime, it was still unable to equip France with the necessary means to overcome the military challenge of a much smaller power. Britain had less than half the population of France at this time and far fewer natural resources. Yet it won. There is little doubt that in the minds of the subsequent generation the evidence of the victory in war helped to reinforce the British sense of superiority in the theory and practice of economic affairs. It came to seem obvious that the British system, deliberately reliant on invisible sources of personal initiative, must work much better than the carefully organized economic schemes of the French.

It must be conceded that the French were blatantly unwise in many of their economic policies during the post-Napoleonic period in the first half of the nineteenth century. This happened to be a period of unusual intellectual vigour as well as business enterprise in Britain. The 1840s and 1850s were the years in which the bold ideas underlying the system invented by the Utilitarians became fashionable dogma.[11] The sense of newly revealed truth comes through unmistakably in the arguments of the Corn Law abolitionists: free trade was not merely a piece of sensible economic policy, it was an integral part of a way of life. The English of this period were system-builders and proselytizers of the same quality as the French of the late eighteenth-century enlightenment or the founders of the American Constitution. Because violence and bloodshed were absent, this revolution is sometimes overlooked. The pragmatic air which the English affected does not deceive: their attachment was to a doctrine of universal application, marvellously usable. The conviction of the wrongness of the French system was readily consolidated then. It was part of the spiritual stock on which Britain lived for the subsequent century.

[10] *The Wealth of Nations*, Book IV, ch. 9.
[11] See for illustrations G. M. Young's *Victorian England* (London, OUP, 1953), ch. 8.

Yet France's historical performance was not as uniformly meagre and unsuccessful as the British liked to suggest. Going right back to Colbert, there were important economic gains which the master of seventeenth-century *dirigisme* had achieved. For example, his system of subsidies assuredly helped to stimulate French shipbuilding at a time when it was backward, and so enabled France to build up a merchant fleet on the model of the British and the Dutch. This in turn was probably a factor in the rapid increase in French overseas trade during the eighteenth century.[12] Equally, the deliberate effort to introduce new industrial processes from abroad, by the import of both machines and skilled labour to go with them, gave a fillip to French technological progress. Indeed, the evidence suggests that the period of very intensive state regulation of commerce and industry in the second half of the seventeenth century was one of unusually rapid advance. J. U. Nef estimates that during this period, from 1660 to 1685, 'at least one heavy industry, metallurgy, as well as almost all the luxury trades and the artistic crafts, were developing even more rapidly in France than in England'.[13]

It is arguable that what was wrong with the Colbertian system was not the selective subsidies or the interest-free loans in favoured industries or the inspectors sent out to see that products were produced in accordance with the methods laid down; rather it was the continued existence of powerful guilds of a medieval type, as well as a whole complex of local impediments to the free movement of trade. Certainly it was the fault of the French administration that the tax system helped to perpetuate these great obstacles to progress. But the point is that it was not excessive centralization, but on the whole the decentralized powers in the hands of people outside the King's government, which tended to impede economic enterprise. This is most obviously true of the local customs barriers (the *octrois*). Colbert had abolished these in the royal domains (the *Cinq Grosses Fermes*), but was unable to carry the process further owing to lack of funds. The right to collect local duties, as well as all other taxes in any given district, had been sold to tax-farmers, and the only way to abolish duties would have been to buy the rights back.[14] The same shortage of tax revenue was responsible for the reinforcement of the power of the guilds to impede the country's economic advance on another front. Having made membership of a guild compulsory for all practitioners of almost any trade, the state imposed various dues on them and then sold the right to collect to a tax-farmer. Part of the responsibility for this arrangement lies with Colbert himself in his

---

[12] See *New Cambridge Modern History*, vol. V, ch. 10, pp. 341–3.
[13] *Industry and Government in France and England, 1540–1640* (Ithaca, N.J., Cornell UP, 1957), p. 146.
[14] See Alfred Cobban, *A History of Modern France* (London, Penguin, 1961), i. 37 and 45.

capacity as Minister of Finance.[15]   By the eighteenth century these organizations not only controlled the right of entry into their trades, but also regulated the price of their products.   An ordinance was issued in 1751 prohibiting any 'notices announcing the sale of goods at cheap prices'.[16]

But when central control over some economic activity was exercised on behalf of the state by able men, the French system could occasionally achieve impressive results.   Perhaps the outstanding case was Lavoisier, the great chemist, who was put in charge of the state saltpetre monopoly, devoted to the manufacture of gunpowder, in the late eighteenth century and reorganized it.   The later successes of the French revolutionary armies in the 1790s owed a lot to his work.[17]   There were other technical achievements of French state enterprises, notably in the military field.   Where the French were notoriously weak was in controlling costs.   It was part of the Colbertian system of thinking, which continued to provide the guide-lines for much of French economic policy for a long time, that *quality* must always be the decisive factor in trade.   Competitiveness in price was regarded as a subsidiary matter.[18]

This is one of the abiding features of the French approach to economic activity.   It contrasts most sharply with an equally persistent British attitude. The British have seen themselves traditionally as traders above all, and have prided themselves chiefly on being able to offer the keenest prices.   A producer is thought of as being no more than the servant of a market, responding, just like a merchant, to a series of essentially transient opportunities.   The notion of the supplier with a long-term production policy, aiming at what economists nowadays call 'producer dominance'—i.e. a position in which he can, within limits, dictate prices to the market, because his product is distinctive and special and not immediately vulnerable to the challenge of near-substitutes—is not something which was readily absorbed into the thinking of British capitalism.   It has been suggested that the traditional French concentration on quality, at the expense of other market factors, is itself the result of the country's social structure back in the seventeenth century.   The customers for the products of the new manufactures in France were overwhelmingly the group of very rich people centred on the great court in Paris.   Admittedly the volume of production involved in this kind of work was a small proportion of the total output of the nation.   But it tended to absorb the energies of the most enterprising workshops.   In Britain at the same time a smaller share of this kind of 'discretionary spending', i.e. spending beyond what is necessary to secure subsistence or 'necessities'

---

[15] *New Cambridge Modern History*, v, ch. 10, 1, pp. 228–9.
[16] Cobban, *Modern France*, p. 42.
[17] Ibid., p. 103.   That did not however save him from the guillotine to which he was condemned as a tax-farmer.
[18] See G. N. Clark, *The Seventeenth Century* (Oxford Paperbacks, 1960), p. 71.

according to the conventions of the time, was almost certainly devoted to articles of the highest luxury, and rather more to articles of ordinary convenience, like textiles and window-glass.[19]

It is easy to see that if the guarantee of a high standard of quality is thought to be invariably more important than achieving a low price, the argument for state regulation of the productive process, even at the cost of some loss of competitive power, is compelling. But then it also comes as no surprise that during the early era of mass production, based on innovation with simple techniques and cheap labour, the French policy should have had so little success. The mass market was missed. Even in fields where regulation and standardization produce obvious economic benefits, notably in the organization of transport, the French never seemed to achieve any significant advantage over the disorderly British. The English canal system grew into a jumble of different dimensional standards—varying in depth and width, with locks of differing design[20]—and yet it was not noticeably less efficient than the unified French system in carrying goods about the country. On the railways, the British were prepared to deviate sufficiently from their principles to introduce a standard gauge.

It may be, however, that in a later phase of industrial development, such as that reached in the Western world by the middle of the twentieth century, the emphasis on 'quality' in its widest sense, rather than on price, begins to pay off in a way that it has not done in the past. Once again it is the factor of greatly accelerated technological change which is decisive. Especially in the field of capital goods, what matters most to the potential buyer is that a new machine or piece of equipment should be of the most advanced technical design. He wants to be assured that his competitors will not be able quickly to lay their hands on another machine which will produce goods that are better and more readily marketable than his own. No doubt if the supplier of the advanced machine hoists his price high enough, there is some point at which the potential customer will be put off. But this does not mean that the latter will go out and buy an inferior machine in the same class at a lower price. If he can possibly do so, he will hold off for a while and delay his investment in the hope that the price will come down. The general point is that the opportunities for 'producer dominance' are much greater in a market

[19] See Nef (*Industry and Government*, ch. 5), who possibly overstates the actual contrast between the structure of production in Britain and France in the 17th century itself. It is more that the bias in the two countries was tending in markedly different directions. France, having a more powerful and centralized administrative system than Britain, was able to tax a rather larger part of the notional surplus, beyond the minimum level of national subsistence. This must have exercised an important influence on the demand for products other than the simple necessities of life. No doubt, it was one of the factors which made 17th-century England distinctly provincial by comparison with France in all the arts other than literature.

[20] J. H. Clapham, *An Economic History of Modern Britain* (London, Macmillan, 1927), vol. i, pp. 83 ff.

for technically advanced products. In such a market the emphasis on guaranteed minimum standards, backed by a centralized research effort and a national programme of supervised industrial training, may provide a nation with a new competitive edge in world export markets.

Towards the Mixed Enterprise

In addition to its concern with quality, French economic policy has traditionally applied itself to extending the range of national production. The state has seen it as one of its obligations to ensure that the nation's industrial base should be as wide as possible. Again, the historical contrast with British economic policies is sharp. The British created a heroic role out of the posture of the intransigent shopkeeper: you buy wherever it is cheapest, regardless of who made the goods. For if you concentrate on trading efficiently it is firmly believed that production will look after itself. You will, above all, be prevented from wasting your resources in producing things which others can turn out more cheaply than you.

In nineteenth-century Europe, this was thought to be an extremely Machiavellian doctrine, deliberately propagated by the world's leading producer of manufactures in order to induce potential competitors to refrain from learning the business. It was clear that the only way to develop the necessary competitive power to match that of the established producer with a head start in the market was to build up industries beneath the shelter of tariffs. Tariff-cutting in the name of free trade was seen as Britain's secret weapon; the only way to counter it was to unmask the hypocrisy of those wielding it. Thus Friedrich List, the inventor of 'national economics', was warning all Europe in the 1840s against 'the crafty and spiteful commercial policy of England' which wished to deny to others the use of the instruments of state power and protectionism that had been responsible for establishing Britain's own commercial hegemony. List is scathing about classical English economics, which did not, he averred, look beyond the principles governing a short-term profitable bargain. 'The establishment of powers of production it leaves to chance, to nature, or to the providence of God (whichever you please), only the State must have nothing at all to do with it, nor must politics venture to meddle with the business of accumulating exchangeable values. It is resolved to buy wherever it can find the cheapest articles—that the home manufactories are ruined by their importation matters not to it'.[21] The real issue of economic policy is therefore evaded. It is how to build up a nation's productive power. This is, of course, exactly in line with the

---

[21] *The National System of Political Economy* (1844), Eng. ed. p. 350. The conflict between the two theories, presented in terms of short-term versus long-term objectives, is neatly expressed by the dictum of a French writer, Louis Say (the brother of the economist, J.-B. Say), which List quotes (p. 354): 'La richesse ne consiste pas dans les choses qui satisfont nos besoins ou nos goûts, mais dans le pouvoir d'en jouir annuellement'.

traditional French view: indeed List saw himself as an exponent of Colbert's 'industrial system', which he described aptly as 'a system which has solely in view the founding of a national industry . . . without regarding the temporary gains or losses of value in exchange'. He believed that the British doctrines concentrating on cost and price factors, combined with an apparent indifference to the problem of long-term investment, were part of an intellectual trick perpetrated by a satisfied industrial nation. He would have been surprised to find how seriously the British continued to take their theory long after their near-monopoly in world trade in manufactured goods had disappeared. In this matter the British were not hypocrites but crusaders.

The French, having been strikingly unsuccessful by comparison with their British rivals in the first couple of hundred years of industrial capitalism, found in the mid-twentieth century an economic climate more congenial to their system. Their administrative methods had to be improved if they were to take advantage of the opportunities offered. This was done outstandingly after the Second World War; and the intricate system of economic controls, incentives, and subtle moral pressures, operating under the guidance of the Commissariat du Plan, is its most sophisticated expression. But well before modern planning came into its own, the French had already provided a foretaste of the productive power of their traditional system when the conditions were favourable. This happened during the decade following the First World War.

It was little noticed at the time. France tended to be regarded as a relatively backward, war-devastated country in which progress was impeded by an exceptional political instability. In fact the popular picture of the country at this stage was not too dissimilar from the view of France held abroad during much of the 1950s. It was only with the appearance of 'strong government'—under M. Poincaré in 1926—that foreigners began to observe that something significant had been happening. (The analogy with General de Gaulle's régime, which many held to be responsible for France's economic success after 1958, suggests itself.) The Poincaré stabilization of the franc at a very low level, after it had been devalued, simply gave French industry a further fillip by making its exports inordinately cheap. The advance right through the period from 1920 until the peak of the boom in 1929 was impressive: during that time industrial production doubled. Industry in France was probably growing faster during the decade of the 1920s than anywhere else in Western Europe.[22] By 1929 France was producing more motor cars than any other European country, having overtaken Britain a couple of years before. Her steel output was as large as Britain's.

All this reflected a great investment effort, which owed a great deal to the impulse of the state. War reparations provided part of the public funds

[22] See OECD, *Industrial Statistics 1900–1962*.

which were used, for example in the steel industry, to re-equip and modernize plant—much as Marshall Aid funds provided the wherewithal after the Second World War to equip France with an enlarged up-to-date steel industry. But it was not simply a matter of providing subsidies. The state also intervened in a more active role, as manager and entrepreneur, in various sectors of the French economy.

It was during the period after the First World War that the so-called 'mixed enterprise', i.e. a partnership of private and public capital, made its début on a large scale.[23] This is a very characteristic French device; a natural development of traditional forms of economic intervention, it was used in the 1920s as part of an effort to extend the range of French industry in branches of production where private capital would not venture on its own. The older method employed by the French Government to this end was the grant of an exclusive concession to a chosen firm. The change that now took place was to reinforce the relationship by a closer contractual arrangement with the chosen instrument, giving the state joint ownership of the assets. The oil industry and the chemicals industry in particular were invaded by several joint enterprises of this type. Both were industries in which France was backward. Quite deliberately the French state formed, in the Compagnie Française des Pétroles, a fighting company which would involve the national prestige in a struggle for position with the established giants of the oil industry, American, British, and Dutch. It may appear that there was nothing new in the establishment of a 'mixed enterprise' in this sphere of business, since Winston Churchill had adopted precisely the same device when setting up the Anglo-Iranian Oil Company (later British Petroleum) with a 51 per cent government share of the equity before the First World War. The difference is that the British Government with a majority share-holding deliberately abdicated its management rights, while the French Government with a minority holding in CFP insisted on theirs.

In some instances the state had no equity investment at all in the mixed enterprise, and yet controlled the management. This was the formula adopted for the Crédit National, a bank established after the First World War to handle compensation payments and reconstruction credits to industry. The company was accorded certain privileges by the state—for example, it has the valuable right to raise money by public lottery—and in return for this, as well as the assurance of a great deal of government business, the state appoints the top management, the managing director and his two deputies. This powerful financial instrument has been used, particularly since the Second World War, to guide the direction of investment over a wide range of private industry which uses the Crédit National as its banker.[24]

---

[23] See A. Chazel and H. Poyet, *L'Économie mixte* (Paris, Presses Universitaires, 1963).
[24] See Ch. VII.

In addition to the joint undertakings in partnership with private enterprise, the French Government found itself immediately after the First World War in possession of a number of assets taken over from the Germans. There were the Saar coal mines, for example, and the Rhine Navigation Company. A British observer, Sir Robert Cahill, who wrote a big official report, *Economic Conditions in France*,[25] in the early 1930s, counted at that time altogether seventy-eight autonomous institutions of state character but 'with separate legal personality' and finances. He also comments on the 'marked extension' of state activity in French productive enterprise during the period from the end of the First World War onwards. This extension, it is to be observed, took place without any doctrinal bias in favour of nationalization. The short period of left-wing government after 1924 made little impact on the ownership of French industry. If enterprises fell into state hands or were taken under the state's partial control, it was for economic rather than political reasons. In this respect the Third Republic in the 1920s was only carrying on the same tradition which had led the French kings to establish the Gobelins and Sèvres factories in order to ensure that France would make tapestries and china of the highest quality.

It is interesting to observe—another foretaste of the 1950s—that this burst of state enterprise after the First World War was associated with a series of attempts to put the nation's investment effort into the single framework of a long-term plan. The National Economic Council, established in 1924, was a consultative body of representatives of the two sides of industry and of consumers, which set about making an economic survey of France. There were also plans for 'national equipment' (*Outillage National*) in 1926 and 1929. With the state involved not only in manufacturing industry but also in shipping and other forms of transport, in electricity and mines, it came naturally to French politicians of the Right as well as the Left[26] to think in terms of a national plan which would bring these multifarious initiatives into a single frame of reference.[27]

However, the relationship between modern French planning and the older French device of the mixed enterprise is both more subtle and reciprocal.

---

[25] London, HMSO, 1934. Cahill was Commercial Counsellor at the British Embassy in Paris from 1921 to 1939. His 1934 report is an extremely well informed and considered document.

[26] It was Tardieu who prepared the very ambitious *Outillage* programme in 1929 (see Clough, *France*, p. 342).

[27] Sir Robert Cahill's remark on the *non*-economic aspects of the *Outillage National* plans in his report for the British Government is worth quoting. He says that they 'go far beyond . . . undertakings of a merely productive character, and aim at general social, moral and intellectual welfare' (*Economic Conditions in France*, p. 570). The notion of a national plan which is somehow the expression of the 'general will', i.e. serves the deeper spiritual need of the community rather than merely making it more productive in turning out an undifferentiated mass of goods, fits readily into the mainstream of French thought—running right through from Jean-Jacques Rousseau to Pierre Massé, the head of the Commissariat du Plan in the 1960s.

The point has been well expressed by the authors of *L'Économie mixte*, an essay summing up the experience during the 1950s and early 1960s.[28] They say:

Si le Plan est une nécessité pour l'économie mixte, il faut dire réciproquement que l'économie mixte est une chance pour le Plan. On se demande parfois comment un Plan non autoritaire peut être exécuté, comment les entreprises et les administrations peuvent se solidariser sans être ligotés, et ce qu'il y a d'intermédiaire entre la bonne volonté et la contrainte. Ces 'mystères' de la planification française ne s'expliqueraient pas si le Commissariat du Plan n'était pas en quelque sorte *l'institution centrale* des relations d'économie mixte, car c'est d'elles qu'il tire ses principales forces. . . .[29]

In other words, what is called 'indicative planning', that is a system which relies on pointing out desirable ends rather than on giving orders to achieve them, can be relied upon to work effectively only in a situation where there is a central core of important enterprises which are more responsive to the desires of the state than the ordinary private firm. It should be noticed that these are not passive instruments of state power; that is not at all what is required for the tasks which they are designed to fulfil. They are supposed to show initiative, and they are not expected to be inhibited about making big profits. Of the four French firms which showed the largest net earnings in 1961, three were mixed enterprises engaged in the profitable oil business.[30] Rather, what is required of a mixed enterprise is that the management should be equipped with a special set of antennae which will be in contact with the centres of state authority, reacting with more than usual sensitiveness to any messages from them.

The story, however, is not one of a simple straight-line development from the mixed enterprises devised in the period after the First World War to the full-scale planning which emerged after the Second World War. There were a number of deviations and frustrations en route. For example there was

---

[28] Chazel & Poyet, p. 111.

[29] 'If it is true that the mixed economy needs the Plan, it is also true that the Plan for its part provides a favourable environment for the mixed economy. One sometimes wonders how a Plan which is not authoritarian can be made to work, by what means private enterprises and public administrative bodies coalesce in common purpose without being yoked together; is the secret to be found somewhere between the voluntary principle, based on good will, and compulsion? The key to these deep mysteries of French planning is that the Commissariat du Plan is, in some sense, the centre-piece of the institutional network of the mixed economy; and it is out of this system that it draws its main power.'

[30] Chazel & Poyet, *L'Économie mixte*, p. 46. The four companies in order of importance were:

		Net Profit (NF)
1.	Compagnie Française des Pétrôles	106·89 m.
2.	Rhône-Poulenc	79·67 m.
3.	Société Nationale des Pétroles d'Aquitaine	54·3 m.
4.	Compagnie Française de Raffinage	51·44 m.

The first, third, and fourth are mixed enterprises.

the swing towards full-scale nationalization, first of all under Léon Blum's Popular Front Government in the middle 1930s and again immediately following the Liberation in 1945–6. The left-wing parties believed, as it turned out mistakenly, that the Government could more easily get its wishes respected by an enterprise which was wholly owned by the state than by one whose management was merely dependent on its goodwill. It is curious that the French waited so long before they were able to make full use of the instrument which they had forged after the First World War. The chief cause of frustration, which held back progress for more than a decade after the great advance of the 1920s, was the failure to see that these instruments of public and semi-public economic enterprise could only function efficiently under the impulse of high and sustained demand for the products of French industry. The earlier success had occurred against the background of the steady inflation of the first half of the 1920s and was accompanied by a series of devaluations of the franc. When the inflation was brought to a halt in the latter part of the decade, French industry at first benefited from the high pressure of world demand for its exports, because the French franc was grossly undervalued. (The same thing happened again after 1958.) But later on, during the Great Depression of the 1930s, especially after Britain and the United States had devalued their currencies, the French franc, now become a symbol of stability in a world of uncertain values, was supported at its old par value by a policy of rigorous deflation.

Although French unemployment never rose to anything like the levels reached by the leading industrial countries of the West during the early years of the depression, over the whole period of the 1930s the French economy probably suffered far more serious permanent damage than that of any other country. The pressure of unemployment never became intolerable because there was a bolt-hole for labour dismissed from industry: immigrant workers, of whom there were large numbers in France, were sent back home, mainly to Poland, while many Frenchmen who lost their jobs returned to the family farms and added to the underemployment on the land.[31] The French, alone of the advanced industrial countries, did not regain the 1929 peak level of industrial production until some years after the Second World War.

Postwar French planning can be regarded as a device that mobilized a number of instruments of public enterprise and pressure, which had been lying around for some time, and pointed them all in the same direction.[32]

---

[31] Arthur Lewis, *Economic Survey 1919–39* (London, Allen & Unwin, 1949), p. 69.
[32] Charles P. Kindleberger in his suggestive study, *Economic Growth in France and Britain 1851–1950* (London, OUP, 1964), concedes that French planning represents 'an ancient tradition' which emerged in a novel form after the Second World War (p. 188); but goes on to argue that the distinctive feature of France's postwar economic performance was the changed state of mind of the people. 'When all are resolved to grow, however much they disagree on political issues, government policies will be conducive to growth' (p. 208). This does not seem a very satisfactory

But it also carried the evolution of these instruments themselves one stage farther. Just as there had been the earlier discovery that in order to push economic activity in a desired direction, it was not necessary for the state to take over an enterprise completely—a minority shareholding would do,[33]— so now it was found that in certain spheres the state could achieve its ends by means of a contractual relationship with private enterprise which did not involve any public ownership whatsoever. The planners developed an intricate network of commitments on the part of private firms—to invest in certain objects, to take their business to a certain region of the country, to adopt specific techniques of production, and so on—all in return for favours from the state. These favours have generally taken the form of tax reliefs or cheap loans. How widespread the latter are is shown by the calculation that 80 per cent of business borrowers in the early 1960s were servicing their loans at rates of interest below the market rate.[34]

On this showing the enterprises directly owned by the state, either wholly or in part, fulfil the role of pace-setters of the system. The state needs them in the same way that any manager needs an independent yardstick in order to decide the limits of the possible. But the foothold inside the business of production is important not only because it provides a vantage point for inspection. It also allows the state's representatives to claim a place on the side of management in the dialogue between planners and producers, and to do so as of right. The state as an entrepreneur is taken very seriously. There is no disposition in France to treat it, in the way that the British and Americans instinctively tend to do, as if it were bound to come off worst in any serious competitive encounter with proper businessmen. No doubt the French state is more adept at these things partly because it has been in active business, one way or another, two or three centuries longer than the British or American.

Herbert Luthy once described the French postwar economic system as

explanation; certainly no one noticed any marked national consensus around the 'resolve to grow' in the early and middle 1950s when France was successfully transforming its economy. Kindleberger's main point, that France did the trick by directing its investment towards industries with a high rate of innovation, which produced an extra technological dividend, is surely right; and he also shows how the initial impulse to embark on rapid technological change was concentrated in public and semi-public enterprise, and then spread to private industry. But he does not seem to give sufficient emphasis to the quality of the postwar public servants responsible for the new approach, and to the institutional background which allowed them to organize themselves to take the initiative—during a period when they were plagued by a succession of weak governments, costly wars, and a deeply divided society—in a manner which would have been barely conceivable in Britain.

[33] A law of 1958 lays down that where the nationalized holding is less than 30 per cent of the assets of a business, the management put in by the state is not even to be accountable to parliament. The executive thus has a freer hand if it owns less.

[34] Chazel & Poyet, *L'Économie mixte*, p. 102. The authors comment that the percentage provides a fairly good indication of the extent of the French state's activity as a banker in the country's business life.

'synthetic capitalism'. The phrase had a contemptuous intention, for, like almost everyone else, Luthy missed the dynamic potential of the system in the changed conditions of the early 1950s, when he was writing: he could see only a kind of *Ersatz* for the fully-fledged capitalism of the Anglo-Saxons. But he identified perceptively one distinctive feature of the postwar French economic method and its derivation from a family tree with its roots stuck in the seventeenth century. He says:

... there is in all this an ingrained mistrust of the natural play of forces of a free economy, and a profound conviction that it is better to produce synthetically, as in a laboratory, the theoretical conditions of a competitive market than to risk the shocks and hazards of real competition. . . . In the last resort, however, this synthetic capitalism with which it is desired to endow France is completely in the tradition of the French mercantilism which was inherited from the *ancien régime* and consists of protectionism and enlightened state intervention.[35]

[35] *The State of France*, trans. E. Mosbacher (New York, 1955), p. 455.

VI

BRITAIN IN THE POSTWAR WORLD: ARM'S LENGTH GOVERNMENT

IF the story of France since the war is the reassertion of an old tradition in a new and more favourable context, Britain's postwar experience provides another kind of illustration of the way in which a living tentacle reaches out of past history, loops itself round, and holds fast to a solid block of the present. The striking thing in the British case is the extraordinary tenacity of older attitudes towards the role of public power. Anything which smacked of a restless or over-energetic state, with ideas of guiding the nation on the basis of a long view of its collective economic interest, was instinctively the object of suspicion. It might have been thought that the advent of the Labour Government in the mid-1940s, and the revolutionary enlargement of the public sector which followed, marked the sharpest possible break with the whole trend of previous economic policy. Certainly it was thought so at the time. It is ironical to reflect that the first generation of French planners under M. Monnet, groping for a method of inflicting the long-term public interest on private enterprise, turned naturally to Labour Britain for their model. They found what they wanted in the industrial Working Parties, the precursors of the abortive Development Councils, established by Sir Stafford Cripps in the late 1940s.[1] When the French established the *commissions de modernisation* for their key industries and used them as the basis for constructing a nation-wide plan with a clear order of priorities, they believed themselves to be taking over an essentially British device, merely adapting it slightly to their own purposes.

By 1948 the basic elements of modern planning were present in Britain as in no other major Western country. In addition to the Development Councils, which seemed to offer the means for the systematic assertion of governmental influence in private industry, there was by then a large nationalized sector which was responsible for a substantial part of the country's investment. The nation's finances had also apparently been brought under tight central control. The Bank of England, now nationalized, could no longer claim the formal independence of government policy it had possessed previously, and, much more important, the introduction of modern budgeting methods provided the British Chancellor of the

---

[1] Information supplied by M. Étienne Hirsch, who was deputy to M. Monnet at the Commissariat du Plan (from 1949) and subsequently (1955) the head of the organization.

88

Exchequer with the means of exercising a sophisticated form of control over the economy as a whole. Again, British methods were several years in advance of most of the rest of Europe. Only the Swedes and the Dutch had achieved anything like this degree of mastery of the new techniques. Finally, the state in Britain had pushed ahead in the field of social welfare, above all through the National Health Service. All this added up to a formidable array of public power and influence.

Moreover the Labour Government appeared to be determined to exploit both. It talked constantly of 'planning'; there was to be an 'economic budget' which would match the detailed objectives of numerous individual industries with the resources available, bringing them into a coherent design determined by a set of national priorities. The Government's first annual *Economic Survey* in 1947 appeared to foreshadow the bodily transfer of central controls, hitherto used for military purposes, to a civilian production plan. No limit seemed to be recognized to the matters which could be subjected to this type of control; even the country's external trade and payments were apparently expected to respond to official decree. 'Certain peacetime problems, such as the control of balance of payments', the *Economic Survey* says, 'can be handled by much the same techniques as were used for allocating our resources of manpower, materials and shipping during the war.'[2] Why, after these promises, did the British socialists fail to set up even the rudimentary machinery for long-term planning of the kind which became commonplace in Western Europe during the subsequent decade and a half?

Plainly, the Labour Government of the 1940s never understood 'planning' in this sense. Certainly it allowed itself to be disappointed too easily when it discovered that its initial facile vision of limitless possibilities for the application of frictionless controls—the 1947 *Economic Survey* mood—did not correspond with the facts of economic or political life in peacetime Britain. But it never seems to have made any serious effort to adjust the techniques to these facts. The truth is that the whole operation of Labour planning, when it worked at all, was directed to strictly short-term objectives. The Government's policy in the late 1940s was dominated by two considerations— easing the physical shortages of materials and food, and improving the balance of payments. It was the former which provided the basis for 'planning'. Supplies of steel, timber, and a large number of other essential industrial materials were not available in sufficient quantities to meet current demands. Had they been offered freely for sale on the market, their price would have risen sharply and they would probably have been used for purposes which would have made no contribution either to the balance of payments or to the Government's chosen social welfare objectives, like public

[2] For a more detailed account of the curiously confident mood of this period, see my *British Economic Policy since the War*, 2nd ed. (London, Penguin, 1959), pp. 166 ff.

housing. It was therefore necessary to ration the right to buy these materials on the basis of a systematic view of the needs, resources, and potential of a variety of producers and consumers.

What is significant is that as soon as the pressure of particular shortages was removed, so the overall view of national economic objectives was discarded. The shortages were not, as Labour's political opponents angrily averred, an occasion which the Government had seized in order to carry out its policy of economic planning; they were its sole rationale and purpose. There is no evidence that as the controls over the distribution of scarce goods were progressively removed, the Government cast around for other means of making the economy move in the direction of its long-term objectives.

This attitude, which saw the central government's role as being almost exclusively concerned with short-term objectives, was not confined to the state's relations with private enterprise. Within its own sphere there was the same lack of interest in a long-term synoptic view of the pattern of the economic forces subject to public direction. There is no doubt that to establish this kind of synopsis would have required a considerable administrative and intellectual effort, at a time when there were many other pressing matters requiring the administrators' attention. But it is noteworthy that nowhere within the elaborate network of new governmental machinery established in the 1940s was room found for the systematic assertion of Britain's long-term economic interest. That was not attempted until the early 1960s. And it was a Tory Government which finally made the effort to bring the multifarious separate strands of public expenditure into a single coherent forecast.[3] Before that, loose ends had been left to trail independently and no attempt had been made to join them together in a single common design. Until this was done in the public sector, where around two-fifths of the nation's fixed capital investment was taking place, the machinery of modern planning could not begin to function.

In fact the ethos of the Labour Government during its period of rule in the immediately postwar period was curiously antipathetic to this type of activity. It was a strong government and it greatly reinforced the power of public authority; but it tended to treat such authority, except when there was a manifest and immediate emergency to be coped with, as essentially plural.

---

[3] *Public Expenditure in 1963–4 and 1967–8*, Cmnd 2235 (1963). The White Paper stated that the first long-term survey of this kind was undertaken inside the Treasury in 1961. What prompted it originally was traditional fiscal anxiety about a tendency for public expenditure to absorb an increasing share of national resources. But by the time that the Treasury brought itself, two years later, to make public its thoughts about the future, the focus of the whole exercise had shifted. The White Paper is oriented towards production and gets down to such grubby details as the problem of raising output per head in building, on the ground that a bottleneck at this particular point could impede the whole process of economic growth in the public sector.

Co-ordination was *ad hoc*; the longer-term policies of each department and agency of government were largely left to look after themselves. That this was indeed the dominant philosophy of the Labour leadership can be seen most clearly from the structure which it chose to establish for the management of the newly nationalized undertakings. They were each placed under the control of an independent board, which was loosely connected with a ministry. There was no compulsion, for example, on the Coal, Electricity, and Gas Boards to evolve a national fuel policy in unison with one another. They each went their separate ways, unless there was an exceptional assertion of authority by the Minister of Power.

Parliament, too, was given rather meagre powers of scrutiny over the affairs of publicly owned industries. It took many years before the Select Committee on the Nationalized Industries began to assert itself. Then in the early 1960s the Government at last made a determined effort to establish some kind of co-ordinated policy for the vast enterprises which it owned; the method which it adopted was to lay down a minimum figure for the financial return which each of the undertakings was required to achieve.[4] That forced the Government itself to examine its own aims as an entrepreneur, since it started off with a standard criterion of what should be considered a reasonable commercial rate of return on investment, and only accepted adjustments to it when these could be shown to be necessary to achieve specific objects of public policy. The financial yardstick adopted was different in each industry; but the difference had to be justified in argument. The new strictness was prompted partly by the revelation of the huge financial losses, largely unforeseen, suffered by British Railways. This provided the political impulse. In the event, it developed into a larger effort to look at the long-range investment activities of the public sector as a whole.

Labour Policies

In the field of social welfare there was, after the first impressive advance during the years immediately following the war, a similar failure to consolidate and to build further on foundations that had been established in Britain in advance of other European countries. This disappointing performance is also connected with the underlying view of the limited role of the state, which was shared in large measure by the Labour and Conservative leadership during this epoch. Most of the postwar welfare policies in the advanced countries of continental Europe were designed on an organic principle of growth. The complex of welfare services was envisaged as something which would of its nature expand, as the prosperity of the society as a whole increased. Moreover, the individual drawing on social welfare funds tended to be regarded increasingly as someone with rights

[4] See *The Financial and Economic Obligations of the Nationalized Industries*, Cmnd 1337 (1961).

beyond the assurance of a minimum subsistence standard. The difference between the British and the Continental approach to the problem is most readily apparent in the arrangements for old-age pensions and unemployment pay. In continental Europe it is generally accepted that a retirement pension should be related to the level of earnings of the individual person before his or her retirement; the aim is to avoid an abrupt drop in living standards when people stop working.[5] In the late 1950s this principle was further extended by some of the richest European countries. In Germany in particular the state pension schemes were remodelled to ensure that persons retiring on a pension of a given money value should have the right to an adjustment in line with the increase in the general prosperity of the country, which was confidently expected to result from the rising productivity of those at work. The state thus took it upon itself to ensure that the benefits of higher output were not retained exclusively by those who were fortunate enough to be working when better machines or new methods were introduced. Those who had worked under less favourable conditions and were now retired had a claim on the extra wealth generated in this way. Other countries, notably Sweden, had provided for automatic adjustment of pensions to rises in the cost-of-living index. The German scheme added the notion of automatic adjustment to the changing *volume* of national income.

The built-in principle of growth also applied to unemployment pay. Instead of the simple charitable idea of a fixed sum of money to provide a subsistence standard for anyone out of work, the advanced nations with sophisticated ideas of social welfare tried to ensure that the personal upheaval resulting from the temporary loss of a job was reduced to a minimum. To this end unemployment pay was graduated, so that the amount received was related to the earnings of the individual during the period when he was at work.[6] Again, the Germans have introduced a further refinement which graduates the actual proportion of previous earnings paid to the unemployed person in favour of the worker with relatively low wages; his unemployment pay may rise to as much as 95 per cent of his wage. A system of this kind naturally requires larger contributions from members of the social insurance scheme. It is indeed striking how small a proportion of British wages, compared with German, is taken by social security taxes.[7] A graduated pensions

[5] In the EEC, only Holland has a system of fixed old-age pensions which are not related to the individual worker's level of earnings before retirement.

[6] For example, in Germany, Holland, and Belgium the unemployed now receive between one-half and two-thirds of their previous earnings.

[7] Roughly 13 per cent of average wage earnings in Germany, compared with 4 per cent in Britain, during the late 1950s (see G. L. Reid and D. J. Robertson, eds., *Fringe Benefits, Labour Costs and Social Security* (London, Allen & Unwin, 1965), pp. 100–1). Some of the services financed by social security payments in Germany are met out of general taxation in Britain. Even so, the direct contribution made by the average British worker, in taxes and social security levies combined, falls well short of the German.

scheme was belatedly introduced in Britain in 1961,[8] but there was no system of automatic adjustment to compensate for changes in the cost of living, let alone to provide an equitable share for the old in any expansion of the real income of the country. On unemployment pay the principle of a fixed allowance, with variations only for the number of dependants of the person unemployed, continued in force—though by the middle of the 1960s there was strong political pressure for a graduated system related to individual rates of earnings.

It is interesting to observe that at least until very recently, the Right and the Left in postwar Britain were agreed on the basic doctrine governing the design of social welfare services—viz. that their sole purpose was to ensure that no man should fall below a certain minimum living standard. This is a conception of welfare which is directly related to the traditional act of charity; indeed, it may be regarded as a means of eliminating those individual acts of charity which are designed to mitigate poverty, by centralizing them in the hands of the state. The main difference between the approach of the two parties, once the postwar extension of the welfare services had been firmly established, was that Labour was inclined to be less demanding in its requirements of proof of need. The instinct of the Conservatives was to ask for clear evidence of an actual need for publicly provided assistance. But the Labour Party set the tone for the new welfare schemes immediately after the war by insisting on the rule that the same public services were to be automatically available to all, regardless of their financial circumstances. This attachment to the principle of equality allied itself easily, in practice, to the notion of social welfare as the provision of a basic minimum living standard. Plainly it could not be much more than a minimum if all were to have it equally. What seems to be missing in the British case is the impulse to extend the *depth* of public intervention—a feeling that welfare services, though collectively provided, ought to be tailored with increasing care to fit varying individual requirements. That is not the kind of thing the state is expected to do.

All this is an expression of the same mood which made the British Left, when it had power in 1945–51, so curiously reluctant to fashion the means of exerting the influence of the central government in the work of long-term economic planning. It was not, it hardly need be said, any hostility to state action as such. The assertion of public authority in new places was wholeheartedly approved; there was, and is, a constant demand from the British Left that the Government should intervene in more and more things. But the nature of this intervention is assumed to be of a strictly limited kind. It is in this sense that the traditional ideology continued to assert itself in the period immediately following the war. Old-fashioned *laissez-faire* had gone;

---

[8] Under the National Insurance Act, 1959.

but the old instinctive suspicion of positive government, which purports to identify the needs of the community before the community itself has recognized them, remained as vigorous as ever. It was reflected both in the behaviour of ministers who refused to plan, and in the administrative devices invented for them by civil servants, who were anxious above all to ensure that the exercise of the new powers of government did not saddle them with the responsibility for making choices, for which they might later be accountable. Administrative discretion, which is meat and drink to the French, is anathema to the British official. Of course, he has it in practice: without it a modern state could not function. But because it raises awkward problems about the division of responsibility between politicians and officials, the officials hold desperately to the pretence that they have no initiative of their own, that they are instruments only, wholly passive, in the hands of some masterminding minister. To give this pantomime verisimilitude, the powers attributed to civil servants must be seen to be kept to a minimum.

It is arguable that the Labour Government, had it continued in office, would sooner or later have been led on from the instruments of short-term economic control, which it had only recently developed and was trying to perfect, to the practice of long-term planning. Finding itself compelled to intervene intermittently at various points in the economy, in order to achieve the equilibrium which it sought—between its foreign exchange income and outgo, between the insistent demand for different forms of investment at home and the limited resources available to meet them—it would have jibbed before long at doing the job blindfold. To begin with, in the immediate postwar period, simply holding the economy in balance in conditions of full employment seemed to be a more than full-time job. The 1944 White Paper on full employment,[9] issued a year before Labour came to power, strikes the authentic note of innovation and adventure—'. . . in these matters we shall be pioneers. We must determine therefore to learn from experience; to invent and improve the instruments of our new policy as we move forward to its goal'.

In fact the instruments envisaged at the time were different from those which have since been employed. Most notably the designers of the full employment policy relied heavily on preparing in advance a 'shelf' of investment projects which the Government could take down and put into operation as soon as the economy showed signs of flagging.[10] This, rather than the fiscal adjustments in the Budget, was seen as the main lever for controlling the business cycle. As it turned out, the Labour Government was never faced with the need to find means of stimulating economic activity; it was always having to suppress it. There is, of course, no inherent reason why the negative selection of particular activities to suppress or restrain should not

[9] *Employment Policy*, Cmnd. 6527, p. 26.
[10] See Dow, *Management of British Economy*, p. 365.

have been carried out in the context of an overall picture of the country's long-range objectives. But perhaps psychologically there is more inclination to formulate such objectives in the course of a search for things which merit a special boost.

Later, when the problem of choosing the points at which to apply an economic stimulus in the recessions of the 1950s and early 1960s came to be tackled by Conservative Governments, the approach was deliberately neutral. The Government seemed to be positively determined to avoid an act of selection motivated by anything other than strictly short-term tactical convenience. The only question to be answered was which industries would most readily respond and provide some extra jobs to people out of work. It is only fair to say that the approach of the Labour Government to the opposite problem was equally tactical: in those of its crises caused by excessive demand it generally chose the points at which to cut back on grounds of convenience, measured by their degree of responsiveness to the treatment. Because a reduction in industrial investment could, it was thought, most easily relieve the pressure on the external balance of payments—either because industry would then need fewer imports or because it would be able to export more capital equipment—this was the sector which constantly had to make the sacrifice. One result of the dominance of the tactical motive in British economic policy for a decade and a half was that in the alternation of boom and slump the cuts in investment were usually followed by a boost to consumption. The long-term effect was bound to be debilitating.

However, if a government is to make choices of this kind on strategic rather than tactical grounds, it must do more than provide itself with a reserve of public investment projects on a 'shelf'. This is important, but it is only the beginning of the process. More significant is the relationship between the public authorities and the management of industrial enterprises, whether in private or public hands. We have already seen how the set-up of the nationalized undertakings made for a lack of co-ordination. There was at this stage a curious indifference or simply a lack of understanding of the fact that many, if not most, of the important decisions in the public utility industries were inevitably shaped by an implicit view of the state of the economy five to ten years ahead. It would therefore have been an elementary piece of prudence to exchange information about the views held on this subject in interdependent industries relying on the public purse. But in order to do this the underlying assumptions have to be made explicit; and when this is done, it soon becomes apparent that the operation cannot be sustained without a detailed survey of the economy as a whole.

It is, indeed, characteristic of modern capitalist planning that the impulse to embark on the seemingly speculative enterprise of long-range prediction comes from the industries which find that they are compelled, because of the nature of the technology that they employ, to commit large indivisible blocks of capital to projects that will only pay for themselves after the lapse of several years. Systematic economic analysis, preferably in collaboration with other industries similarly placed, whose decisions will also influence the outcome, is then the obvious way of reducing the size of the risk. In Britain, it was the steel industry which took the initiative in this field. The Iron and Steel Board, the public agency which had been set up in the early 1950s to supervise this industry, found that its attempts to guide the direction of steel investment and to check whether its volume was adequate, required a close examination of trends over the economy as a whole. The third five-year development programme issued in 1961[11] was in some ways a pilot project for the full-scale planning operation on which the British Government embarked with the establishment of the National Economic Development Council in 1962. It was not accidental that the first Director-General of NEDC, Sir Robert Shone, was an outstanding steel economist who as a member of the Iron and Steel Board had been responsible for working out the long-range investment programmes of the industry.

In steel there was a special relationship between the Government and private enterprise, which supplied a propitious soil for this type of experiment. It was unique in the Britain of the 1950s. The industry had been nationalized during the final year of the Labour Government in 1951, and when the Conservatives reversed this decision two years later, they went to some trouble in their attempt to demonstrate that a fully adequate means could be found to assert the public interest in steel while it remained in private ownership. To this end, the Iron and Steel Board was given the dual task of collaborating with the steel companies in the preparation of their investment plans and acting as their overseer when it came to setting maximum prices for their products.

It is instructive to compare the performance of the Iron and Steel Board, a key institution of the 1950s, with the attempt made earlier by the Labour Government to assert the public interest in a variety of other industries through the establishment of the Development Councils. These were an experiment of great potential significance. They followed on the systematic effort of self-examination conducted by government-appointed 'Working Parties' in a series of industries during 1945–7. Eleven of these Working Parties recommended the establishment of Development Councils in their industries, which were to provide common services like research and export promotion, designed to help the average firm to a higher level of efficiency. The Working Parties had uncovered a number of deficiencies in organization and performance. The idea behind this initiative was the same as that which prompted the establishment of the French *commissions de*

[11] *Development in Iron and Steel Industry, Special Report* (HMSO).

modernisation: a decade and a half occupied first by economic depression
and then by war had left many industries under-equipped and needing a
collective effort of renovation.

But when parliament passed the law providing for the establishment of
the Development Councils,[12] the response from industry was almost uniformly
negative. Only four councils were set up—in the cotton, furniture, clothing,
and jewellery industries. The last two were boycotted from the start by
several firms and they were wound up by the Tory Government in 1953.
The Cotton Board was not in fact a new body: it was a slightly modified
version of an organization set up by the cotton textile industry in 1940. The
sole lasting monument to the policy of industrial modernization hopefully
launched in 1947 is the Furniture Development Council, and even this
continued to be the object of hostility from the employers' association, which
demanded its abolition when the future of the Council was reconsidered in
1958,[13] This time however the President of the Board of Trade decided,
exceptionally, to overrule the critics and keep it going. The powers given to
the Government under the almost forgotten Industrial Organization and
Development Act of 1947 came in handy again some years later when a
Conservative minister wanted to impose a compulsory levy on the building
industry, to finance a new organization to provide it with collective research
and information services.[14] This was in 1964 when Mr Geoffrey Rippon,
Minister of Public Building and Works, launched a drive to induce the
British building industry to make itself more conversant with modern methods
of construction. But by then the wheel had come full circle, and the new
generation of young Tory ministers, of whom Mr Rippon was one, had
discarded many of the old inhibitions about intervening in the affairs of
private industry; indeed they had adopted economic planning as a Tory
party slogan.

What was the cause of the failure of the early British attempt in the
1940s to use the apparatus of government to foster the development of
particular industries? The blame cannot be simply laid on the Tories,
though it is true that when they took over in 1951, they were wholly
unenthusiastic both about the project and the philosophy behind it. There
is no reason to doubt P. D. Henderson's judgement who says in his summing
up of the story, 'it may be doubted whether the change of government made
any real difference' to the outcome.[15] The ultimate power to make or break
the Development Councils had been left with the firms belonging to the
industry. The whole tenor of the legislation of 1947 appears curiously

[12] Industrial Organization and Development Act, 1947.
[13] See P. D. Henderson, 'Government and Industry', in G. D. N. Worswick and P. H.
Ady, eds., *The British Economy in the Nineteen-Fifties* (London, OUP, 1962), p. 337.
[14] *The Times*, 11 Mar. 1964.
[15] Worswick and Ady, *British Economy*, p. 337.

confused in its intention. On the one hand the device had been heralded as a measure of radical reform designed to bring overwhelming pressure to bear on industrialists to put their house in order. They were also menaced by a compulsory levy to finance the work of the Councils. But on the other hand the Act laid down the condition that a Development Council was to be established in response to a demand by 'a substantial number of persons engaged in the industry'. Moreover, the Councils were designed in such a way, with a board of management composed of employers and trade union representatives flanked by a few 'independent' members, as to ensure that the conduct of their business would tend to be dominated by the views of the average firm in the industry. If there was no desire for research on the part of the member firms, then the mere fact that the Government had set up the Council would not ensure that any research got done. Thus when the Labour Government insisted on the establishment of a Clothing Development Council against the outspoken hostility of a majority of the firms in the industry, they simply boycotted it and nothing happened.

No doubt the political atmosphere of the time, in the midst of the postwar battle over the nationalization programme, which in the course of a couple of years absorbed a massive segment of British industry into public ownership, was not propitious to the venture. The employers, who were now asked to collaborate with the Government in an essentially voluntary task, which was going to cost them money, were ready to resent the ideological overtones which they detected in the exercise. The interesting question, however, is why the Labour Government, which might reasonably have been expected to foresee this, did not design a more effective instrument of public pressure on the representatives of private enterprise who would be called on to run the Development Councils. Perhaps it had been misled by the progressive outlook and sometimes radical proposals put forward by the Working Parties, which had themselves asked for the establishment of the Councils. What they appeared to overlook was that the industrialists in the Working Parties were among the most advanced in each industry, and by no means popular with the average run-of-the-mill manager; given a chance the latter was likely to reject the business eggheads anyway. In the event he found himself equipped with every opportunity for doing so. This was because the Government insisted absolutely on the representational formula; the Councils were not set up to lead an industry in the desired direction—which was likely to be a good deal farther than the average firm in it had thought of going. The French, it should be noted, never made this mistake. Their *commissions de modernisation* have a handpicked membership, and there is no secret made of the fact that they are generally dominated by the biggest and most dynamic firms in the industry concerned. Moreover, the administrative chores and all the work of the secretariat of these commissions remain firmly in the hands of government officials.

In sum, the Labour Government seemed unable to decide which of two objects it had in view. Did it wish to establish a regulatory body—rather like the Iron and Steel Board later became—which would also collaborate with the industry in the pursuit of certain defined long-range objectives? Or was it on the other hand to be an essentially corporatist body, an association of producers with some legal powers of compulsion over the individual members of the industry? There is little doubt that the result desired was the former; but the method chosen was designed to secure only the latter. In that case, the industrialists were bound to ask why they needed a Development Council, in addition to the industrial association to which they belonged. They were most of them already paying a voluntary levy to this; they were unwilling to add a compulsory one, inflicted on them by a Government of whom they were in any case deeply suspicious.

The story of the Development Councils also illustrates a more general difficulty about the traditional British view of the proper relationship between public and private power. The two sorts of power are thought of as utterly distinct from one another. They may enter into certain formal and well-defined relationships; but they do not mingle. Here, once again, there is the profound contrast with the traditional attitude of the French. In France the mixture of public and private endeavour is accepted as being of the essence of the economic process. It was therefore characteristic and predictable that the French would use their *commissions de modernisation* as an all-purpose vehicle which would carry them in any desired direction, while the British, presented with an analogous piece of machinery, were barely able to make it move at all. The outcome of the experiment has a moral with a wider application, as will appear later, to the problem of economic planning at large.

The Evolution of Conservative Government

For the greater part of the decade, following the advent of the Conservative Government in 1951, there was little significant development of the institutions of modern capitalism in Britain. The policy of full employment and the techniques of short-term economic management to secure it were continued by the Tories, as was the Labour Government's system of social welfare services. The outstanding feature of the period was a kind of vigorous spiritual back-pedalling, the expression of a nostalgia for some bygone age when market forces produced the important economic decisions, while governments merely registered them. The Tory ideologues, who exercised a profound influence on government thinking at the level of the permanent civil servants as well as the ministers, were during the period up to the mid-1950s passionate devotees of an aggressive cult of *anti-planning*. The ideological influence was reinforced by a widespread sentiment in Whitehall that Government had taken on too many tasks. There was an eagerness to shed many of them. It was not merely a matter of getting rid of certain physical controls which no longer fulfilled an important purpose; there was a systematic attempt to cut down the role of the public sector and to introduce in its place some natural or fabricated play of competing private interests. The fact that the competition so carefully nurtured was often of a kind which involved only a handful of contenders, ending with a gentleman's agreement between them rather than a fight to the finish, seemed to matter very little.

A certain exaggeration was perhaps to be expected from a rich nation in which the consumer's sovereignty had been denied for too long—first of all in a long war in which the distribution of most things was more effectively controlled than in any other belligerent country, and then in a highly disciplined and austere peaceful interlude which ended in another war, in Korea in 1950. Labour policy had tended to exaggerate the need for discipline as part of the price to be paid for its special gift of full employment. The Conservatives set out to demonstrate that full employment could be secured in modern conditions with a much smaller quota of government intervention in economic affairs. This was easily done. The British socialists had unnecessarily set up an Aunt Sally for their opponents to knock down. But this was all before full employment had come to be taken for granted throughout most of Western Europe and people had begun to measure success in comparative rates of economic growth. The confidence of the exponents of simple market doctrines, which developed during the first phase of Tory rule up to the mid-1950s, was no doubt due in part to the impression made on the Tories themselves by their success in handling what their opponents had warned them would be an exceptionally difficult problem.

The mood of the Government at the time is reflected very clearly in the scheme which figured prominently in the files of the Treasury during the early 1950s under the title of Operation Robot. This was a plan which was intended to abolish in one move all the restrictions and arrangements governing the permitted use of sterling abroad, and at the same time to make both the volume and direction of economic activity at home subject to the unimpeded play of world market forces. The public authorities were to be allowed to exercise their influence on economic events by means of two instruments only. These were changes in the bank rate, which would raise or lower the level of interest payments on all forms of credit, and adjustments in the rate of exchange of the pound sterling, which through its influence on the money value of foreign exchange earnings and expenditure would keep the external balance of payments automatically in equilibrium. The aim essentially was to simulate in Britain something close to the conditions of the pre-1914 world. It was hoped to subject the economy once again to maximum international exposure, while the removal of all controls would ensure that there was no possibility of any response to the external pressure other than total internal discipline. Market forces would be relied upon to impose the necessary adjustments in domestic living standards or in the level of employment. In the event, the Cabinet rejected the scheme,[16] in spite of the vigorous support of a number of powerful officials as well as of certain ministers. It continued, however, for a time to be treated as a serious practical possibility, promising, it seemed, a short cut to an altogether simpler style of economic policy, so greatly desired in the political climate of the time.

Although Robot failed to make the grade, the underlying notions which had gone into the making of the scheme retained much of their vigour. The essential idea was that the aims of economic policy could be achieved by means of a few simple operations—a shove forward or a pull back—applied at any point which happened to be conveniently at hand. The economy tended to be treated as an undifferentiated mass with a more or less uniform capacity for response, not as an articulated nervous system which would react very differently to particular stimuli occurring in different places. It was characteristic of this vision—a kind of sub-Robot view—that the attempt to counter the balance of payments crisis which occurred in the autumn of 1957 was based on a policy, recommended with brutal simplicity by Mr Peter Thorneycroft, the Chancellor of the Exchequer of the day, which saw the answer in a blank refusal by the monetary authorities to provide any extra cash or credit. If the flow of money was firmly blocked, it was argued, the inflationary problem would be licked. Of course it is possible to deflate by restricting the volume of credit and by putting up interest rates, as was in fact done in 1957. The significant point, however, was that this technique was envisaged as the basis of a long-term policy which would by itself supply the cure for Britain's economic ills. It would do so by restoring the discipline of the market. There was no hint at this stage that what was really required was a concentrated effort to increase the productive and selling power of British industry, so that the balance between what the country earned and spent in foreign exchange would be improved. Any proposal of that kind, carrying even a remote hint of the possible use of discriminating economic measures between different industries and trades, was wholly out of keeping with the official mood. The answers *had* to be simple and comprehensive. The stubborn insistence on a macro-economic approach to all problems meant a refusal to diagnose what was wrong in terms of the individual component parts of the economy.

In these circumstances there was naturally no need felt for any effort to co-ordinate the actions of the various government departments which impinged on the private sector. Indeed it was a matter of principle that their influence on private enterprise should be exercised, so to say, blindfold. It

[16] For an account of the circumstances see my *British Economic Policy since the War*, p. 217.

infringed the rules of the game if the different parts of government jointly made use of their commanding position to induce privately owned businesses to move in some chosen direction which was thought to be in the public interest, other than the path that business would have chosen spontaneously for itself. Describing the relations between government departments during the 1950s, P. D. Henderson notes 'a disposition to regard issues of policy as being normally if not necessarily decided by a somewhat stylized process of quasi-diplomatic bargaining between ministries'.[17] No doubt, some government departments treat each other with jealous suspicion in other countries too; but in Britain at this time the propensity to do so was unusually strong. That was partly because no one within the Government seemed to think it worth while to make any particular effort to restrain it.

The change in the mood of Government in the early 1960s bore all the signs of one of those sudden ideological waves which periodically seem to sweep through Whitehall. The excesses of market worship in the 1950s had been of a similar type. But now the doctrine of the 'invisible hand', which was supposed to look after the needs and desires of the community better than the community knew how to do the job for itself by any conscious effort, was entirely out of favour. The Tories declared themselves for 'planning'. But it was not a simple return to the techniques developed by the Labour Government of the 1940s, for whom planning was essentially the short-term management of the economy in conditions of scarcity. The new approach of the 1960s was based on the long view. It was a rebellion against the technique of administration by short-term expedient which had been given an extended run over the previous decade.

It is impossible to attach a precise date to the change. The establishment of the central planning organization, the NEDC, is perhaps the most striking manifestation of the new spirit. However, it should be noted that the minister officially responsible for the decision on NEDC, Mr Selwyn Lloyd, was himself very much an old-time Chancellor of the Exchequer. Indeed, he was at the time when he gave his approval to the planning organization, during the first half of 1962, in the middle of the traditional exercise of deflating the British economy in an effort to improve the balance of payments. As usual, industrial investment was the chief sufferer, so that the country's capacity for sustained growth was once again squeezed for the sake of strictly short-term ends. In fact the idea of a central economic planning body, analogous to the French system, had been under discussion for some time before this. There is little doubt that the impulse to embark on this experiment derived very largely from the Prime Minister himself. Mr Macmillan's part in the dramatic reversal of policies in the early 1960s was a decisive one. His personal contribution was only occasionally played out

[17] Worswick and Ady, *British Economy*, p. 374.

in full public view, as in the sudden upheaval in his Cabinet in the summer of 1962, when almost overnight one-third of the senior ministers in the Government lost their offices. This led to the dropping of some very old hands, including Mr Selwyn Lloyd himself, who were deeply imbued with the Tory spirit of the 1950s—essentially the spirit of economic non-intervention—and also gave enhanced power to a number of younger ministers with a technocratic bent and a radical spirit, brought in to run departments concerned with the problems of long-term national planning. The most important of these were in housing and other forms of construction and in education.

Equally important, though much less in the public eye, was the internal reorganization of the key government department concerned with economic policy, the Treasury. This, too, occurred in the second half of 1962. The date was a coincidence; the reform was largely the work of the civil service itself, and the process had been set in motion some time before. There had been criticisms of the efficacy of Treasury control over the spending of other government departments by the Select Committee on Estimates in 1957-8, and this was followed by the appointment of a special committee under Lord Plowden, consisting of five people from inside the civil service and three outsiders, to examine the whole question. Its report, published in 1961 as a White Paper,[18] set out the principles which guided the Treasury changes in the following year. There were two major deficiencies which it identified in the existing system. First, decisions about government expenditure were taken in an *ad hoc* spirit, and no serious attempt was made to place them in the framework of long-term trends, either of likely public needs or of the future resources available to meet them. Secondly, there was no adequate machinery for bringing the competing demands of the different departments of government together in a single coherent picture, so that decisions could be readily made by the Cabinet about the orders of priority in public spending.

The 1962 reorganization of the Treasury was designed to increase the range of administrative control by the government in these two dimensions. First, all decisions which involved the spending of public funds were to be subjected systematically to the techniques of forecasting several years ahead. Secondly, these decisions were to be looked at in relation to other immediately desirable forms of expenditure competing for public money. Since almost any government decision of any significance is bound to involve some

[18] *Control of Public Expenditure*, Cmnd 1432. The original Plowden Report was a confidential document submitted to the Chancellor of the Exchequer. But the version which was eventually published, according to R. W. B. Clarke, Second Secretary at the Treasury, 'covered most of the essentials' (lecture to Royal Inst. of Public Administration, 19 Nov. 1962).

spending of money, this pointed to a considerable reinforcement of centralized control throughout the public sector.

The new system involved some profound changes in the traditional organization of the Treasury. Because of the crucial position of this department in the whole apparatus of government, the rest of the civil service machine was caught up willy-nilly in the reorganization. The old Treasury system bore some resemblance to a royal court at the centre of a medieval kingdom, dealing with a lot of very independent barons. The convention was that each baron was allotted to a particular court official, who looked after all his needs and handed out orders or rebukes as they were required. What the baron finds after the reorganization is that the court chamberlains have disappeared and that he has to cope with a lot of specialists, each with his own limited function—as if, for all the world, the place had been turned into the headquarters of an army. This functional division of authority at the centre has other consequences for visitors from the outside. Some of those who were barely on speaking terms are now forced to rub shoulders with one another, and even to adapt themselves to each other's needs.

The effect of the new arrangement in Whitehall was, intentionally, to allow scope for more independent initiative in the government departments subject to ultimate Treasury control. There was no longer the single official overlord appointed to keep a supervisory eye on all the activities of any one ministry. But the new relationship was also intended to be more demanding; that was because the rearrangement of functions at the Treasury itself was designed to bring a wider range of different criteria to bear on the making of economic policy. Most important, a deliberate effort was made to escape from the old exclusive obsession with money; after the reform, one of the three main sections into which the Treasury was divided had the specific task of looking at government operations in terms of their effect on the real resources of the nation. This was the National Economy Group.[19] By contrast, the Finance Group is concerned exclusively with money. Its task is to look after the management of all money flows affected by government policy, both inside the country and as they impinge on the external balance of payments. Thirdly, there is the Public Sector Group, which looks after the expenditure of all public funds by government departments and agencies. Here again, those responsible for the reorganization made it clear that their intention was to go beyond the purely monetary aspect of securing efficiency in departmental spending activities. Getting 'value for money' was to be measured not only in terms of financial income and outgo at the Exchequer, but also by the effect which it had on the growth of the economy as a whole.[20]

[19] Subsequently transferred to the Department of Economic Affairs. This account of the Treasury deals only with its management of economic and financial policy. There is another portion of the Treasury, under a separate Permanent Secretary, which looks after the management and pay of the civil service.

[20] Clarke, lecture to Rl. Inst. Public Admin., 1962.

Clearly the significant novelty in the new set-up was the National Economy Group.[21] The ideas about long-term economic trends (now based on standard five-year forecasts), as well as about the long-range effects of public policy on particular issues, such as monopoly and restrictive practices, the supply of skilled manpower, impediments to productivity, industrial costs and prices, were supposed to be developed in this wing of the Treasury. It could be regarded as an embryo planning department.[22] But in practice everything depended on how effectively the influence of the new Group would be brought to bear on the other two—both more solidly grounded in the older conventional work of the Treasury, and commanded by officials (Second Secretaries) of greater seniority than the head of the National Economy Group. The interesting feature of the Treasury experiment was the establishment *within* the administration of a professional agency, packed with the best economists on the staff of the Treasury, whose specific task was to press the long-term viewpoint in the formulation of economic policy. It had the advantage, not possessed by NEDC, of operating on the inside of the administrative machine. The French, as will be seen in the next chapter, have always assumed that planners have to be insiders. So much of modern planning depends on making the multiple arms of governmental power move in unison. But of course over the rest of the field of planning, where private enterprise is ultimately responsible for the decisions, the Treasury is not equipped to do the work of either the Commissariat du Plan or the NEDC. It is still very far from being a Ministry of Planning.[23]

So far as can be judged, the establishment of the NEDC and the Treasury reorganization were the outcome of quite separate initiatives. Indeed, in

[21] When the Labour Government set up the Department of Economic Affairs in the autumn of 1964, with the task of supervising long-range economic policy, the National Economy Group became the central core of the new ministry.

[22] A senior Treasury official, who was closely concerned in the reorganization, described the function of the National Economy Group as follows: 'This group will in a sense co-ordinate and orientate the direction of the large-scale administrative operations of the Finance and Public Sector Groups' (Clarke, ibid.). It is not certain how far the original impulse which found its expression in the National Economy Group was effective in converting the Treasury to the practice of long-range economic planning. According to Mr. Robert Neild, there was no fundamental change of method. The Treasury, he stated, 'now looks at estimates of spending five years ahead and not just one year ahead. But this is a financial exercise which consists of adding up all the bits of departments and nationalized industries and scaling them down to fit some percentage of the national income. It is not an exercise in planning, in which long-run objectives are surveyed, alternatives are costed, and choices presented to ministers' (*Listener*, 27 Aug. 1964). All that can be said with assurance is that the administrative structure which *could* accommodate systematic planning of the type described in the last sentence was established in 1962.

[23] The Labour Government of 1964 again separated the function of liaison with private industry, which was left with NEDC, from the new Department of Economic Affairs. The Department meanwhile took over the 'pure' planning staff and functions of NEDC.

some ways they were competing initiatives. At any rate the Treasury seems to have been concerned to shift the main focus of its administrative energies from the traditional one of 'saving candle-ends' to the task of reshaping its policies, especially those which impinged on industry, in line with the requirements of long-term economic growth. Behind the new administrative thinking of the early 1960s there were two discoveries about the enhanced power of public authority which are central to modern economic planning in a capitalist context. Both are exceedingly obvious once they have been understood. But there was apparently a deep spiritual resistance to their recognition among postwar politicians and officials in the Anglo-American world. The resistance was stronger in the United States than in Britain, and continues. But in Britain it was strong enough to divert the attention of government from many of the crucial issues of contemporary economic and social policy during the 1950s.

The first discovery was that the volume of economic activity now controlled by the public authorities was exceedingly large, and exerted an overwhelming influence on particular sectors of the economy. Of course, the British Government had understood for a long time that it controlled the resources necessary to even out the short-term market forces which had been responsible for the violent alternation of boom and slump in the past. The advance in economic management during the 1960s was to begin to mobilize the mass of government power and influence in the pursuit of more ambitious objectives. Central and local government together employed 3 million people who earned 15 per cent of all wages and salaries. The public sector as a whole was responsible for over 40 per cent of all fixed investment and for as much as 50 per cent of the building work done in the country. In terms of strategic control this gave the Government outright possession of the 'commanding heights of the economy'—about which the socialists continued to talk wistfully as if they were a remote target for some ultimate assault. The lesson which the British Government learnt belatedly in the early 1960s, and which the French had absorbed much earlier, is that mere occupation of this terrain by public officials instead of private businessmen does not of itself make any difference to the result. A sustained and elaborate effort has to be made if this great mass of public power is to function in any kind of unison.

The second important discovery of the 1960s was that the character of this public economic power is of a kind which tends to produce its effects over long time periods. In the years immediately following the war, when the Keynesian techniques of short-term economic management were being given their first trial run, there was a tendency to exaggerate the day-to-day influence which the state could exert on the course of events through its control over public investment. But after a while it became clear that fiscal measures, in a society where the share of taxation in the national product had greatly increased,[24] provided a more powerful and quick-acting regulator of the economy, especially if they were combined with efficient management of the supply of credit. The central bank, working with the Chancellor of the Exchequer, especially after he was equipped with the power to vary certain consumer taxes by up to 10 per cent between his annual budgets,[25] made a formidable team. By contrast the big decisions about public investment cannot be easily shifted or changed in response to short-term fluctuations in the state of business or the balance of payments. This is partly because the objectives on which public capital is expended tend to be long-range ones. A decision to expand a social service like education or health requires first of all that teacher training colleges or medical schools are established; then the teaching capacity of these institutions has to be built up; and only after the lapse of some years can the extra schools and hospitals be manned and brought into full operation. Long range forecasting is of the essence of the social investment that is characteristic of our times.[26]

Uncertain Experiments of the 1960s

A number of forces contributed to the mood of self-examination and experiment in Britain in the early 1960s. But perhaps the most powerful one, which forced the pace of new thinking inside the Government and compelled it to bring the blurred and complicated and often tedious issues into sharp focus, was the negotiation in Brussels on the proposed British entry into the European Common Market. The future of agricultural policy, based on a system of guarantees to farmers quite different from that in use on the Continent, of the nationalized coal mines, of the regulation of the steel industry, of the method of taxing consumer goods, and of fixing freight charges on the railways—all these matters and several more besides had to be considered in the context of the probable need to create a common set of rules for their regulation with the six member states of the European Economic

---

[24] In 1962 total public expenditure, including interest paid on the national debt, was equivalent to 44 per cent of GNP. The ratio had varied but never fallen below 40 per cent at any time in the previous decade (see Cmnd 2235, 1963).

[25] This was the so-called 'regulator' which was introduced in 1961. Initially it was a crudely designed and rather rigid instrument, which required *all* consumer taxes to be raised or lowered by an equal amount, if the Chancellor of the Exchequer decided that he wanted a quick change between budgets. Subsequently he was given more room for manoeuvre and was allowed to discriminate in the tax increases or decreases to be applied to different classes of goods.

[26] That is not to say that there is no scope for short-term adjustments in social investment projects as part of business cycle policy. See the discussion of Swedish methods in Ch. IX. But to be successful this requires much more subtle and elaborate advance planning than the first generation of Keynesian policy-makers in Britain, the men responsible for framing the 1944 White Paper on Full Employment Policy, understood.

Community. The prospect of trying to bring the bewildering variety of principles embedded in different spheres of British economic policy into some sort of unison with Continental practice imparted a new urgency to the problem of co-ordination at the British end. The effect of being required to state as precisely as possible the doctrine behind some British administrative practice, in order to defend it against some alternative favoured by members of the European Common Market, was to prompt a wide-ranging review of the apparatus of British economic administration and law. Indeed, the intellectual questioning at one time—the moment when it looked as if Britain might be plunged straight into the European Community system at short notice—seemed to have some of the fervour and promise of the great debate which accompanied the dismantling of the British tariff and the policy of deliberate national exposure to the forces of free trade in the 1840s. In 1963 the process was halted before it had gone far enough to influence popular thinking; but it had the makings of a political upheaval of comparable dimensions, and one as fertile in new ideas about the proper way to run the country, as the controversy which culminated in the decision to abolish the Corn Laws in 1846.

It was a pity that the evolution of British ideas set in motion by the approach to the European Common Market in the early 1960s had to be telescoped into such a short period, in an effort to meet a political timetable. 1962 was, in this case too, the crucial year. However, the complaint of the dominant Continental partner in the negotiation, France, was that it had already lasted too long, and at the beginning of 1963, at General de Gaulle's behest, it was broken off. As *The Economist* pointed out afterwards,[27] one important loss which Britain suffered in consequence was the cessation of the work of the co-ordinating policy committee of the Cabinet under the chairmanship of Mr R. A. Butler, then First Secretary of State. This Cabinet committee had had the task of drawing together the different strands of British policy, on a great variety of topics, so that a coherent brief could be placed at the disposal of the men negotiating in Brussels with the European Economic Community. Much of the negotiation involved major matters of domestic economic policy. They were also frequently matters which depended on a long-term view of a combination of hypothetical circumstances. The issue was usually not just about the likely effect on a particular British interest of a certain arrangement with the EEC, but rather about the impact on a whole field of policy of a systematic shift, spread over several years, towards some emerging norm of common European behaviour.

When the negotiation in Brussels broke down, both sides retreated with some relief from this arduous exercise. But for Britain at least it had supplied an impulse towards administrative reform inside the Government, which

[27] 8 June 1963.

did not altogether lose its momentum. Summing up the process as it appeared by about the time of the General Election of 1964, it may be said that the intellectual and administrative preconditions for modern capitalist planning had been created or were in course of being established. This represented a remarkable change of attitude on the Right of British politics. There were, however, still some critical questions left unsettled. Chief of these was the proper relationship in a mixed capitalist society between government and private enterprise. How far should the considerably enhanced public power that exists in a modern European capitalist economy be employed deliberately to put pressure on the private sector to organize itself in certain ways and to pursue objectives which the Government deems to be in the national interest? This is not primarily a question to be settled by the adoption of the right legislative programme. It is rather a matter of how to employ the *incidental* power of the state from day to day, as a large purchaser of goods and services, as a big employer and producer, and as the guardian of long-term collective interests, over the use of scarce resources, e.g. land. The actual decisions are, and must be, largely made by officials.[28]

We have seen that in France there is an established intimacy between the representatives of public authority and the practitioners of private enterprise. This was the gift presented by French history to the planners of the mid-twentieth century. The tutelary role of the state in the economy is taken for granted; the only question is whether the different repositories of state power have taken the trouble to agree amongst themselves. But British history has deposited in government and in business an altogether different residue of assumptions and conventions governing their relationships with one another. These relations are often friendly and sometimes, in circumstances where the national interest can plainly be shown to be involved, notably in the sphere of foreign policy, there may be close collaboration over some specific issue.

---

[28] Some American Congressional committees have tried to insist that certain actions by Federal officials which impinge on private business, e.g. the buying of land, shall not be undertaken without the prior authorization of the committee concerned. In cases where this succeeds the Chairman of the committee then often becomes a kind of administrative overlord of some part of the Federal Government. This 'legislative veto', which makes for clumsy and inefficient administration, has been resisted with growing vigour by the US executive in recent years. In a tussle over property in the Panama Canal Zone at the end of 1963, President Johnson explicitly rejected Congress's claim to share in the administration, which had been written into the Public Works Appropriation Act 1964. Referring to the 'provision in the Act which precludes the Panama Canal Company from disposing of any real property or any rights to the use of real property without first obtaining the approval of the appropriate legislative committees of the House and Senate', he said: 'It is either an unconstitutional delegation to Congressional committees of powers which reside only in the Congress as a whole, or an attempt to confer executive powers on the committees in violation of the principle of separation of powers set forth in the Constitution'. He went on to say that he intended to treat the provision in the act merely 'as a request for information' (White House Press Release, 31 Dec. 1963, Statement by the President on H.R. 9140).

But the government side is normally very diffident about the use of the vast accretion of incidental power to influence private business decisions, which has come to it in the past quarter of a century. In part this diffidence is an expression of a simple liberal instinct: the state, now so mighty, must take extra special care to leave the citizen alone to get on with his own affairs. Life is only tolerable for the little fish if Leviathan deliberately adopts a lazy and sluggish posture. However, there is besides a particular strand in British Conservative philosophy which inclines strongly to the view that the state must, as a matter of principle, remain passive whenever any decision of an entrepreneurial character has to be taken. Outside the limited domain which belongs exclusively to the public services, the aim of policy should be to weaken the influence of the state to the point of total neutrality.

This is simply the doctrine of anti-planning. Curiously, it continued to be given expression inside the Conservative Cabinet, even after the planners had officially taken over in 1962, by a senior member of the government, Mr Enoch Powell, then Minister of Health.[29] It was not that Mr Powell's philosophical position on this matter, especially when stated in his characteristic style of academic intransigence, had any wide political support within the Conservative Party. But it did possess some of the moral force of a conscientious objection. It was the symbol of something profound and traditional and firmly rooted in the party, which at the very least acted as a restraint on other ministers, especially the new men who were trying to get things done in a hurry and whose instinct was to use the public power at their disposal in order to make private enterprise more efficient.

Thus the Minister of Works, Mr Geoffrey Rippon, appointed after the big Cabinet purge in 1962, consciously set out to use the vast mass of construction under his control—some £250 million worth a year—to induce builders to adopt new methods which would raise productivity and save labour. Chief of these was the introduction of 'systems building', construction based on standard factory-made components assembled on the site. The same objective was pursued by the Minister of Housing, Sir Keith Joseph, another appointment of 1962. All public building, including the considerable amount which each of the armed services had hitherto kept jealously under its own control, was centralized under Mr. Rippon's refurbished ministry (which was renamed the Ministry of Public Building and Works to mark the fact). Similarly, the Minister of Housing used his extensive powers of persuasion and pressure on public authorities to secure more joint planning and

---

[29] Later, in a speech deploring the encouragement of 'partnership' between public authority and private enterprise, as part of a general plea for 'less government', Mr Powell expressed the point as follows: 'Words should not obscure the fact that when one of the "partners" controls discretionary subsidies, public contracts, tax reliefs, honours, and other patronage, and can procure the power of enforcement, this too is a kind of government' (*Guardian*, 13 July 1964).

uniformity of standards in building.[30] However, it was plain from the start that the radical reform of industrial methods could only be achieved quickly if the structure of enterprise in the building industry was altered, so that the few large and dynamic firms—there were probably less than a dozen of them in Britain—captured a lot of new business at the expense of the large number of small and highly conservative builders. One way of doing this, and the most obvious, was to use the technique of the 'chosen instrument'—deliberately selecting a few promising firms who seem willing and able to move ahead fast, and then giving them every encouragement in the form of large contracts, financial help, and other favours. This would have been the French solution. In the long run the policy of the two ministries concerned with publicly financed building, responsible together for close to half of all the building in the country, pointed in this direction. New orders, with their encouragement, would in any case tend to be channelled to the building firms which were using standard dimensions and labour-saving methods. But it was another matter to single out particular firms in advance and then deliberately push them ahead of the others.

[30] The two ministries worked in close collaboration, using government building as the laboratory and pace-setter for the industry as a whole. When the Ministry of Public Building and Works laid down a series of new standard dimensions for various components to be employed in government building (DC 1, Dimensional Coordination for Industrialized Building, Feb. 1963), the Minister of Housing went on to issue a detailed list of 'recommendations' to Local Authorities, based on the same dimensional standards (*Design Bulletin* 8, 1963, Ministry of Housing and Local Government). 'I shall look to Local Authorities to use standard preferred increments and dimensions to the fullest possible extent', he told them. The Ministry's bulletin goes further in urging Local Authorities to get together and plan jointly for several years ahead. 'This standardization of types and sizes can be greatly helped by Local Authorities being prepared to agree on common standards . . . to pool their orders, preferably for a term of years, and so to ensure continuity of production' (ibid). It should be observed that the Local Authorities in Britain enjoy considerable formal independence in the conduct of their building programmes; however, they have every reason to seek the goodwill of the Minister of Housing, who is able in various ways to make life easy or difficult for them. In particular, they need his help periodically for a Compulsory Purchase Order, when they want to take over some land for a pet local scheme. Whatever the formal relationship, a Local Authority which is unco-operative with the ministry will not expect the minister to expose himself quite so readily on their behalf to the hostility which almost any compulsory order of this kind provokes.

The next step which the ministries were contemplating in 1964 was modelled on the French device of *agréments*—a centralized system of officially approved standards for building materials for all possible uses. The French have used this successfully to secure more rapid innovation in a notoriously conservative industry. The system was introduced in 1946, and it is startling to discover that the original inspiration for it—as with several other French institutional changes after the war—came from Britain, where the Building Research Station had done work which the French admired (see *Rl. Inst. of British Architects Journal*, Dec. 1963). What the French did was to introduce their own characteristic institutional stiffening—the generous subsidy from public funds, the active interest of the public authorities, and the powerful pressure to conform exercised from Paris.

In Britain at this stage the pressures for technical advance could only be applied lightly and obliquely; reforming ministers seemed to feel that they would have to work their essential purpose largely by stealth. Since their purpose required a major change in the essential structure of business enterprise in a privately owned industry, this approach was understandable. But it also implied the acceptance of a slower rate of technical progress than in those countries which were not trammelled by inhibitions on the use of public power in the private sector.[31]

Wage-Earners and the Unpaternal State

Perhaps the most striking illustration of the persistence of traditional British attitudes is to be found in the legal framework of the rights of labour in relation to their jobs. The line taken by the British courts is that the relationship between employer and employee is on exactly the same footing as that between a willing buyer and a willing seller of any other service. No one, for instance, can tell an employer that he has dismissed a worker without just cause and must reinstate him, or at least pay him damages. The most that a British worker can obtain if he is summarily dismissed is the amount of pay which he would have earned if he had been given the full period of notice agreed for the job on which he was engaged.[32] The principle of non-intervention by public authority in any matter involving a claim by workers on their employers is carried to extreme lengths. When in 1963 the ILO agreed by an overwhelming majority on a recommendation that all countries should move towards a maximum forty-hour working week, the British Government felt impelled to enter a solemn solitary dissent. It could not conscientiously accept this recommendation because such matters as this had to be left to the independent collective bargaining of employers and trade unions. It explained the point to the ILO: 'The Recommendation which requires governments to formulate and pursue a national policy designed to promote the progressive reduction of hours of work is not consistent with the methods by which conditions of employment are normally determined in the United Kingdom. The Government therefore does not accept the Recommendation.'[33]

[31] Officials of the Ministry of Housing were reported as saying at the beginning of 1964 that it might take five years before 'systems building starts to make a real impact on the whole industry', instead of the two years which it would have required if they had been equipped with wider administrative powers—described as 'powers of persuasion, influence and even coercion' (Michael Shanks, 'Revolution in Building', *Financial Times*, 31 Jan. 1964).

[32] The term 'wrongful dismissal' is somewhat misleading: the wrong for which the worker can claim damages is solely an employer's failure to carry out the proper procedure for dismissing him. The courts will not inquire into the reasons for dismissal.

[33] Cmnd 1993 (1963).

However, the British Government was, in fact, preparing at the time a major break with the principle of non-intervention, which was brandished like a battle banner at the ILO. The year 1963 saw the passage through parliament of the Contracts of Employment Act, which laid upon employers the legal obligation, new to Britain, to give certain fixed minimum periods of notice to any workers being dismissed. It started with a week's notice after six months. The Act also moved away from the hallowed principle of full reciprocity of rights between buyer and seller of labour: workers with two years or more of continuous employment in a particular job were henceforth to be entitled to longer periods of notice from their employer than the standard one week's notice which they were obliged to give him when leaving their jobs. Thus for the first time the British law recognized the existence of a special right generated by doing a job over a certain period—a right that could ultimately be translated into a money value, equal to the wages covering the legal term of notice."[34] It was something over and above the right to the fulfilment of an ordinary commercial agreement to buy or sell a number of hours of labour at a certain price. Both employer and employee were beneficiaries of the latter; only the employee could benefit from the former. However, the political implications of the change were evidently not grasped at once—at any rate, so it would appear from the philosophical aplomb with which the traditional view of the role of the state in labour relations was still put to the ILO.

It is to be observed that the Government was moved to intervene in this way partly because the trade unions had been slow to insist on even the minimum amounts of severance pay, when workers with long service to a firm behind them were summarily dismissed from their jobs on account of redundancy. The unions were caught in their own posture of militancy. They held rigidly to the principles of permanent employment, the traditional notion that the only form of protection for a wage-earner is to insist that he keeps on working in the particular job which he happens to occupy. The slogan of 'No redundancies!' and the formal posture of intransigence which the union leaders felt called upon to adopt towards the employers meant that it was extremely difficult for them even to raise the question of financial compensation for the loss of jobs. The result of clinging to an older ideology, derived from a time when jobs were scarce and cheap labour plentiful, was a failure to demand those workers' rights which had become especially valuable once full employment could be taken for granted—the right to a lump-sum payment to compensate for personal inconvenience when an old job closes

---

[34] The Labour Government carried the principle further with the Redundancy Payments Bill, 1965, which provided for the payment of a capital sum, varying with the length of service in a job, to workers dismissed through no fault of their own.

down and a new one has to be found, the right to retraining at public expense, and so on.[35]

The outcome is that in a country like France, where the trade union movement is much weaker than in Britain and there is generally far less tenderness about the rights of organized labour, the claims which are of particular importance to a wage-earner in modern conditions are covered by a more powerful system of legal protection. The French worker is entitled by law to a minimum of three weeks' holiday a year, whereas in Britain employers generally are not subject to a legal obligation to provide any holidays with pay.[36] The French worker has the right[37] to one month's notice or payment in lieu of notice, after six months' continuous employment in any one job, whereas in Britain, even after the 1963 legislation, the period of notice required in the same circumstances is only one week. Finally, the French system allows the worker to claim damages from his employer, if he has been dismissed from his job without good reason, the courts having a right to decide whether the employer's attitude showed 'legèreté coupable'. Indeed, nearly all advanced countries on the continent of Europe have arrangements for the legal control of dismissals. In some, notably Germany, the power of the courts over employers in this matter is very widely drawn indeed, and apparently used with vigour.[38] The whole trend of European law in recent years, except in Britain, has been to put employers increasingly under the necessity of providing evidence to show why the dismissal of a worker in any particular case was unavoidable. The burden of proof required differs from one country to another: in Germany the employer can be called upon by the courts, even when the general case for the dismissal

[35] When these matters began, belatedly, to be tackled in earnest by the Labour Government of 1964, the trade unions showed no enthusiasm for reform. The Government, rather, found itself in the position of having to persuade the unions to accept legislation guaranteeing certain rights for wage-earners, e.g. on severance pay. Typically, employers and trade unions were joined in their antipathy to the establishment of a statutory nation-wide industrial fund out of which people would automatically receive 'redundancy payments' to compensate for their hardships. The *Financial Times* reported (7 Jan. 1965) that the unions 'are opposed to the creation of a massive industrial fund because they feel that this would depersonalize their relations with the employers, narrow their scope for obtaining concessions from particular firms, and handicap them in obtaining other sorts of fringe benefits'.

[36] There are some Wages Council orders prescribing holidays in particular industries, but the majority of workers are outside their scope. Britain has refused to sign the ILO Convention of 1936 laying down a minimum of six days' paid holiday a year, on the ground that such matters ought to be settled by collective bargaining between unions and employers and 'that government intervention must be reduced to a minimum' (ILO, *Annual Holidays with Pay; a World Survey* (1964), para. 222). In practice two weeks is the normal minimum period of paid holiday; but unless he is protected by a trade union agreement or a Wages Council order, there is no redress for a wage-earner whose employer decides to give him less.

[37] Since the legislation of 1958.

[38] See ECSC, *La stabilité de l'emploi dans le droit des pays membres de la CECA* (Luxembourg, 1958), vol. ii: *Droit de travail*.

of some workers has been made out on business or technical grounds, to justify his *choice* of the individuals dismissed.[39]   In France it is up to the dismissed worker to make a case against the employer.   But in both countries the starting-point is that the employer is under legal compulsion to state the grounds for his action; the worker can then claim reinstatement or money damages, if the grounds given are proved to be baseless or false.   In Germany the maximum amount of damages awarded by the labour court is the equivalent of the worker's normal wage over a period of twelve months. Elsewhere the protection afforded by the law is not as great as this,[40] but generally in the industrial countries of continental Western Europe the worker is seen more and more as having certain rights as the 'owner' of a job—by contrast with the still dominant British view that employment is a commercial bargain, not to be especially distinguished from any other bargain merely because the commodity that is bought and sold happens to be labour.

In practice, of course, British employers are by no means free to dismiss whom they please at a moment's notice.   Here, and in the United States too, organized labour is quite powerful enough in many industries to protect workers' interests.   But it is to be observed that the protection does not extend—as it does on the continent of Europe—to those occupations in which workers' organizations happen to be weak.[41]   There are a lot of these,

---

[39] Ibid., p. 81.

[40] The case of the woman who was dismissed, in 1961, from her job in an undertaker's business, because she insisted on coming to work in a low-cut (pink) sweater, conveys something of the atmosphere of German labour law.   While it was conceded that the employer had some ground for complaint, the case (on appeal) went against him: his action, it was decided, had been too summary and he was ordered to pay damages. (See *Landesarbeitsgericht Berlin*, 9 Mar. 1962 (3 Sa2/62) for text of the judgment.)

[41] By 1964 there were signs that the British Government was beginning to respond to the pressure from ILO for the establishment of some formal machinery, whether by collective agreement between employers and trade unions or by law, which would guarantee *every* worker the right to a hearing and some form of redress in case he was dismissed for no good reason.   The White Paper (Cmnd. 2548, Dec. 1964) reporting on its response to the latest ILO proposals concedes that they could 'play a useful part in promoting a sense of security at work' and that this could make for more 'efficiency'.   The difficulty is that 'it is not the general practice in the United Kingdom for appeals against dismissal to be dealt with through collective machinery or through a neutral body'.   But the Government accept the need for reform and 'propose to discuss with representatives of employers and trade unions the provision of procedures to give effective safeguards against arbitrary dismissal'.   This could mark the start of a profound change on a major issue of principle—if it meant that in those occupations in which trade unions were not strong enough to protect workers by collective agreements, the Government would establish its own courts and enforce their judicial decisions.   Setting up a labour court (not just an instrument of arbitration) in Britain would be a large step towards continental European practice. Again, the hostility of the British trade unions to the principle of legal protection for their members was striking.   The TUC conducted an inquiry among its member unions in the early 1960s about a proposal for legislation against the wrongful dismissal of workers and found that the overwhelming majority of those replying— officials of unions with a combined membership of 4,600,000 out of a total of nearly

especially in the service trades. The other important issue is the precise definition of the obligations of employers to each individual wage-earner, both when he is at work and when he is unemployed. In the United States the strong trade unions go to great trouble, when bargaining over their labour contracts, to establish the different rights of workers in their jobs, on the basis of their length of service; this covers both the order of dismissals, in case the work force is reduced, and the order of reinstatement.[42] The courts will enforce these rights in case of dispute. In Britain, neither the law nor the trade unions provide any comparable form of protection. Matters are conducted much more informally. An American authority, Frederic Meyers, comparing British and American practice, argues that 'the pre-occupation of British trade union leaders with problems of full employment and their neglect of plant level problems of the employed worker have left a power vacuum into which shop stewards have stepped'. It is they who stand guard over the worker threatened with the sack—and they often do so in a trigger-happy fashion. Neither the employer nor the wage-earner, Meyers points out, has any clear idea of his rights; and the result of this lack of a formal procedure for judging a case makes it more difficult for British employers 'than for their American counterparts to establish and maintain standards of industrial discipline or to dismiss when good cause in fact can be shown'.[43] Evidently the successful British effort to keep lawyers as far as possible out of trade union affairs has its disadvantages too.

Continental practice, with its strong emphasis on legal rights, which have been impressively extended in the era of the welfare state, derives from a long-standing tradition of paternalism in labour relations. This has its dark side, notably in France. British labour relations right from the beginning of the industrial era were based on the principle of non-intervention by the state; workers were as free to walk out as employers were to sack them. This represented in the nineteenth century an advance on the practice of most of continental Europe. In France the notorious *livret*—the worker's pass-book containing the record of all his previous jobs and the reasons for leaving them, which had to be produced by the worker before he could take on fresh employment and surrendered to his current employer—remained in use until the late 1860s. It expressed the spirit of tutelage, a residue of the feudal tradition, from which the Continental countries have never purged themselves as completely as the British. In Britain the rule of the market, whether it applied to the buying of labour or to the import of foreign goods, was viewed as the necessary condition for personal freedom and equality before the law. In France, on the other hand, the traditional view of the

5 m. who took part in the inquiry—said that they preferred to do without the help of the law (see *The Times*, 15 Mar. 1965, 'Protecting Workers against Unjustified Dismissal').

[42] See Frederic Meyers, *Ownership of Jobs* (Los Angeles, Calif. Univ., 1964).

[43] Ibid., p. 103.

wage-earner was expressed by giving him something of the legal status of a minor—with a minor's rights as well as his disabilities. Indeed this particular legal fiction was advanced in the early twentieth century by lawyers who were trying to establish special rights for the workers: the worker, they held, could claim certain privileges from his employer, without being subject to equal obligations in return.[44] The interesting phenomenon of the mid-twentieth century is how the suspect and often reactionary paternalism of French and other Continental practice has been converted into an instrument for asserting the dignity and independence of the worker in conditions of full employment.

The same spirit which guides the British approach to industrial relations shows up in another guise in the treatment of industrial training since the war. In most West European countries the ground was well prepared for a major effort to train more people to a higher level of skill. There is no doubt that the success in doing so has contributed something to the high rates of economic growth which have been maintained, more especially in the period since the end of the 1950s when the earlier reserve of European surplus labour largely disappeared. At this stage, the pace of technological change demanded many more highly trained workers. As Gertrude Williams has pointed out in her survey, *Apprenticeship in Europe*,[45] making efficient use of available supplies of labour in conditions of full employment requires a systematic effort to down-grade certain jobs—what she terms ' de-skilling' them—as well as upgrading others. The effect of advancing technology is sometimes to simplify a process to the point where the technical know-how required by the worker engaged on it is much reduced.

But if the essential requirements of skill are to be kept up to date and the limited resources of able manpower deployed to best effect, then the jobs themselves and the standards of competence required for them must be constantly analysed and redefined. The authority to do this can come only from a public body. That, at any rate, is the conclusion that emerges from Gertrude Williams's survey of seven advanced West European countries.[46] Apprenticeship schemes may sometimes be operated by voluntary agreements between employers' and workers' organizations; but in all the countries in her survey the state has played an active role in the organization of industrial training.

In Britain for nearly two decades following the war this lesson was ignored; there was fierce resistance to any intrusion by the state into the sphere of industrial training. The most determined opposition, characteristically, came from inside the government itself. It was felt that it was somehow indecent for outsiders to presume to offer guidance to industry about what it ought to do to train the manpower that it so badly needed. Again and again during

---

[44] Ibid.
[45] London, Chapman & Hall, 1963.
[46] Germany, Holland, France, Italy, Switzerland, Sweden, and Belgium.

the 1940s, 1950s, and early 1960s, British industrial expansion came up against a series of bottlenecks caused by shortages of skilled manpower. At the same time, British workers were going through a longer period of apprenticeship than elsewhere in Europe. There was a fixed five-year period,[47] while in most other countries the time spent in training varied in relation to the job eventually to be done. Only in France was there a standard minimum time, but it was three years instead of the British five.

What is probably a more serious deficiency is that the British system of apprenticeship does not impose any test of competence before a man may call himself a 'skilled' worker in a particular trade. What counts is the number of years of his youth—the usual stipulation being that he has to be under twenty-one—that he has spent in doing apprentice tasks. The notion behind this form of tuition in a craft, which conceives of the master's knowledge as being somehow rubbed off on to the pupil by constant propinquity, is essentially pre-industrial in spirit. It belongs with Zen and other mysterious methods of conveying knowledge from one man to another.[48] The British, as pioneers of modern industrial craftsmanship, developed a species of artistic cult about it.[49] It has lasted into the era of mass production. So enduring was the attachment to the mute principle of learning—the cult of the implicit which goes with the refusal to set standards—that no serious effort was made, even in the 1950s, to define the missing 'skills' in modern terms. No doubt it was assumed, reasonably enough, that the ineffable was bound to elude definition. Meanwhile several of the newer industrial jobs requiring a high degree of special training fell outside the traditional list of apprentice skills. Other work which had been greatly simplified could not be 'de-skilled'.

Once more, it was the movement of national self-criticism, which we have located somewhere around 1961–2, that produced the demand for change. It was then that the Government issued a White Paper setting out a new and more vigorous approach to industrial training, which was embodied two years later in the Industrial Training Act of 1964. The novelty of the legislation lies in two highly untraditional principles. First, power was given to make a compulsory levy on all firms in an industry to finance training, regardless of whether they wanted trained men or not. Before this, the expenses of running an apprenticeship scheme had been borne by the individual firm. Henceforth those firms which conducted training of an officially

---

[47] Reduced to four years in certain building crafts in the 1960s.
[48] See E. Herrigel, *Zen in the Art of Archery* (London, Routledge, 1956).
[49] J. J. Habakkuk, *American and British Technology in the Nineteenth Century* (London, CUP, 1962) quotes a characteristic story of F. W. Lanchester, the pioneer motor manufacturer, about the attitudes that he encountered among British engineers, when he started to manufacture cars in England in the 1890s. Lanchester wrote: 'When a body-builder was asked to work to drawings, gauges, or templates, he gave a sullen look such as one might expect from a Royal Academician if asked to colour an engineering drawing' (p. 203). The underlying assumptions of the British skilled worker have not changed much during the twentieth century.

approved standard would not have to make any payment to the industry's scheme and might receive a financial contribution from the state. The second important departure was the introduction of official representatives of the government into the boards to be set up to supervise training in each industry.

It is impossible to say at this stage how these innovations will operate in practice. They may produce the drastic reform of British methods of industrial training which will bring them into line with the best practice of continental Europe. But certain features of the new organization at once raised doubts about its efficacy as an engine of rapid change. The status of the key representatives of the state's interest in vocational education—the officials of the Ministry of Labour and the Ministry of Education whose task is to set standards of performance and organization—is not as strong as it might have been. The most important decision to be made by these training boards, which is the amount of the compulsory levy to be imposed on the industry, will be decided by the representatives of the industry itself— there are to be equal numbers of employers and trade unionists—without the participation of the official experts. This may not prove in the end to be of decisive practical significance, yet it is symbolic of an abiding attitude towards any problem involving the relationship between public and private power, which has been the main theme of this chapter. It has to be remembered that Britain is peculiarly in the grip of petty craft restrictions on training as a preliminary to entry into certain occupations.[50] Yet the industrial training boards are so designed that the trade union side can block decisions on the training levy. The Government itself does make available an additional training grant; but it is noteworthy that no attempt has been made to use this as a means of asserting some measure of leadership on the part of the Government's own experts on the boards. Everywhere else in Europe the state has taken the lead in this way—and for a good reason, since its representatives are likely to take a wider view of the public interest than the people representing particular groups of employers and workers. But in Britain, in normal peacetime conditions (war is different), the state is not visualized as the carrier of an overriding national interest, but rather as one among several—admittedly *primus inter pares*—who compete with one another on behalf of their individual and differing interests.

There is no doubt that the British way makes for an unpompous state, a state which embarks on any venture with an intense consciousness of its

---

[50] See G. Williams (*Apprenticeship in Europe*, p. 204), who observes that Britain 'is the only European country in which the unions believe they are protecting their members by refusing to allow one worker to undertake the jobs normally done by another, for this policy depends directly upon British trade union structure. . . . In other countries . . . unions are anxious for their members to have as wide a training as possible so that they have greater security of employment by the ease with which they can move from one branch of the work to another'

own limitations.　Personal liberty is probably more secure under the shadow of such a state than elsewhere.　But its inhibitions also make it less active in pursuit of positive social goals.　And the more distant these goals are, or seem to be, the less inclination there is to believe that the sensible men who govern the state can do very much about them.

VII

THE DEVELOPMENT OF PLANNING
IN FRANCE

ECONOMIC planning is the most characteristic expression of the new capitalism. It reflects the determination to take charge rather than be driven by economic events. It also, however, has built into it something else which is alien to the traditional notions of economic planners, particularly of the communist school: the recognition of certain limits which the spontaneous choices of free people necessarily impose on the activity of planning, however benevolent and wise its intent. These limitations are of two kinds: they affect the range of economic behaviour that can be subjected to centralized economic decisions and they influence the manner in which these decisions are translated into fact. Sometimes, of course, the translation is a straightforward command—for example, when a government directs one of its ministries to reshape its policies in consonance with the central plan. But more usually there is a dialogue between planners and planned, with the latter answering back, and by their answers influencing the final shape of the plan. The state in other words finds itself, frequently and willingly, in the posture of a bargainer—a powerful bargainer, it is true, but one whose whole approach is influenced by the probability that at some stage it will have to enter into a compromise.

Planning, in the sense in which it is used in this book, is concerned with the attainment of specific objectives of a long-range character.[1] It has nothing in common with the activity of 'planning' as understood, for instance

---

[1] 'Long-range' is used very broadly in what follows to refer to a period of 4–5 years or more. This is sometimes called 'medium-term programming', to distinguish it from the very much longer periods which are required for town planning and the like. I prefer the terminology which emphasizes the difference between short-term (concerned essentially with adjustments towards some desired economic *equilibrium*) and all the rest, which I believe to be fundamental. To describe anything much longer than five years, 'perspective planning' seems the appropriate term: it aptly suggests the broad and unspecific character of the exercise. The 20-year projections, employed for the first time in the work on the French Fifth Plan (see *Réflexions pour 1985*, a report by the 'Groupe 1985'—a working party set up by the French Prime Minister in 1962—published by La Documentation Française, 1964) as an *extra means of orientation* for the planners, are a striking use of this device. Its value lies as much as anything in warning the planners about what they must *not* do. Commenting on the introduction of the 1985 projections into French four-year planning, the Draft of the Fifth Plan (Commissariat Gén. du Plan, *Projet de rapport sur les principales options du Vème Plan*, Sept. 1964, mimeo.) says: 'Il nous faudra . . . éviter d'hypothéquer l'avenir par des décisions irréversibles dont les conséquences risqueraient de peser trop lourdement sur la société de demain' (II–I–p. 6).

by the British Labour Government of the 1940s, where the aim was essentially short-term and of a very general character—like the maintenance of full employment or the achievement of equilibrium between the likely demand and supply of economic resources. There is, however, a political and historical connexion between the short-term and general, on the one hand, and the long-term and specific, on the other. For once the state has accepted the obligation to intervene intermittently in order to secure some desirable condition for society, it soon discovers that its actions exert a powerful influence, whether it likes it or not, on long-term trends. The usual grounds for interference in the postwar world—reversing a business recession, preventing a rise in prices, overcoming a crisis in the external balance of payments—involve decisions which tend to place some sector of the economy at a disadvantage compared with others. Repeated often, the result is likely to be a distortion of the underlying structure. It may be a healthy or desired distortion; but the main point is that a responsible government cannot opt out of the duty of assessing the long-term consequences of these intermittent interventions. Once it begins to make such an assessment, there is a strong inducement to examine the nature of the more fundamental objectives that it would in any case pursue, in default of these short-term pressures. The next stage is an attempt to organize these objectives into a coherent design, in which the various parts are consistent with one another, and then to put them inside the framework of a timetable. Introduce a periodic check on how far events are keeping pace with the timetable—and the main instruments of modern economic planning are in position.

Different National Styles

So far the following Western countries have embarked on a national economic plan: France, Britain, Italy, Sweden, Norway, the Netherlands, Belgium, and Austria. The degree of commitment to the exercise varies greatly, with France at the one extreme and Italy, judged at any rate by the performance to date, least committed to the practice of central economic planning. There are also large differences between individual countries in the role given to the planners inside the machinery of public administration. In some cases, notably France, the planning organization is simply one further arm of the government. It is different from other government departments in that it has no executive power, but the members of the Commissariat du Plan are officials in the same sense as the rest of the civil service. The British arrangement, which was established after careful study of the French system, so that the deviations from it may be assumed to be the outcome of deliberate decision, gave the planning body (NEDC) an official status, but placed it firmly outside the ordinary machinery of government.[2] Broadly, the methods adopted by other countries tend to approximate either to the French formula or to the British system.[3]

It often happens that the two countries appear at first sight to be quite close to one another. That is true in this instance. But they turn out, on closer inspection, to be exemplars of two profoundly different styles of managing the problems of contemporary capitalism. Because of certain important similarities between them—the existence of a large sector of nationalized industry, the emphasis on social welfare policies, the common aim of full employment, and latterly the effort to plan the rational use of the nation's resources—the contrasts in their behaviour, when they are actually faced with the same problems, emerge into especially sharp relief. They are like those differences of character that one only gradually observes among members of a family with a strong facial resemblance; the more subtle the difference, the more revealing it frequently is.

The first point, which relates directly to the historical account given in Chapters V and VI, is that the impulse to plan, although common to both countries in the 1960s, is wholly different in origin and spirit. In France the impulse did not have to be aroused by any special stimulus. The instinct to intervene in the management of the economy had never been curbed: the only problem, as the French have seen it, is how to make this interference more intelligent and coherent. Napoleonic government at the start of the nineteenth century may be regarded as one approach to the problem, modern economic planning as another; they both belong to the same single thread of history. In Britain, on the other hand, as the brief account of the two decades following the Second World War indicated,[4] the approach to planning involved a long and unwilling apprenticeship. It was the frustration caused by the series of *ad hoc* interventions, forced upon the Government by its desire to control the business cycle, maintain full employment and at the same time keep a weak balance of payments from running into deficit, which led to a new and sympathetic interest in economic planning. The development is all the more striking because it was the erstwhile ideological antagonists of a planned, as opposed to a market, economy who in the end created the machinery of planning.

In the early postwar years, the Conservatives had thought that although

---

[2] This describes the situation in the first phase of the British planning experiment, up to the advent of the Labour Government in the autumn of 1964. Subsequently NEDC's responsibility for formulating an overall national plan was transferred to the Department of Economic Affairs (see Ch. VIII).

[3] See Bernard Cazes for a discussion of the different forms of organization in contemporary economic planning, in a paper presented to a UN meeting of Experts on the Administrative Aspects of National Development Planning, Paris, June 1964. I have also drawn on Cazes' essay in OECD, International Trade Union Seminar on Economic and Social Programming, *Final Report* (1964) in the text which follows.

[4] See Ch. VI.

the Government would now have to interfere in the economic process to an extent that it had not done before, the interference could somehow be conducted in a neutral spirit. There would be no discrimination favouring one set of activities or hampering another. The state, when it imposed its short-term pressures on the economy, would endeavour to be as undiscriminating as the market. It made a virtue of its blindness, choosing the points at which to intervene by reference to administrative convenience. Hence the powerful attraction of a scheme like Operation Robot[5] which would allow the economy to be controlled by a species of automatic steering gear, thus relieving the Government of the need to think about the longer-term consequences of its actions. In fact, as we have seen, the British approach to the control of the business cycle, as practised after the Second World War, tended to result in a series of pressures discriminating against investment. For during a recession the Government's instinct, given the criterion of administrative convenience, was to apply a quick stimulus to personal consumption; while any restraints which had to be employed during a boom were directed chiefly against investment. It so happened that a great deal of investment was under direct government control, and also that it was easier to put a curb on the animal spirits of businessmen responsible for decisions about industrial investment than on the propensity of the ordinary consumer to buy more out of his increased income.

There is no inherent reason why governments should find it more difficult to moderate a rise in consumer spending than in business investment. Indeed, with the greater refinement introduced into the techniques of influencing demand, which have gradually been introduced during the 1950s and 1960s, governments can today exercise much closer control over short-term movements in the volume of consumption. However, it was an accident of history that most of the traditional instruments for the tactical control over economic activity operated through the machinery of credit, under the control of the central bank, and impinged chiefly on business investment. Changes in taxation, which would affect consumer spending, were normally made once a year on a fixed date, when the budget was presented. It was only after the lapse of some time that governments began to take the necessary measures to make their tax systems more flexible and responsive to changing conditions. Gradually they discovered that the machinery of credit too could be used at short notice—by altering the cost of hire purchase—to influence the behaviour of consumers, as well as businessmen. By contrast, while they were still struggling with uncertain effect to control short-term movements in personal consumption, they found that their influence over the volume and direction of the country's long-term investment was decisive. Whereas the sole concern of the Keynesian reformers had been to endow the public authorities with greatly enhanced control over the short-term management

[5] See above, p. 100.

of the economy, an equally significant but less understood change which occurred after the war was the vast increase in public power over long-term investment. In terms of its effect on the shape and content of life in any given society, the latter is the more profound influence.

Broadly, it is true to say that Britain arrived at long-term planning via the experience of the short-term management of the economy, while in France the process was reversed. The French did not seriously tackle the problems of efficient short-term management of the economy until the early 1960s, after a decade and a half of long-term economic planning. In this they were untypical of Western capitalist societies. The special historical circumstances which have influenced the use of public power in France go some way towards explaining why.[6] The more common approach to the practice of economic planning in the West approximates to British experience. Perhaps the most notable recent example is that of Germany, which has in the 1960s been moving gingerly towards new techniques for formulating central policy on the basis of a single overall view of the economy, related to long-term trends. In spite of ideological objections to the very notion of economic planning and the reverential official attitude towards the play of market forces, pure and unimpeded, the German Government has in practice been compelled to recognize that modern methods of short-term economic management necessarily involve long-term choices affecting the future of society. The real question is whether the choices are wittingly or unwittingly made.

After Monnet

French planning in its original form during the years immediately following the war was not very different from any other national reconstruction effort. It looked like the linear descendant of the familiar schemes of *Outillage National* in the late 1920s.[7] Wartime destruction and neglect had left France with a number of major gaps in the armoury of its productive equipment. Moreover, the depression of the 1930s had had disastrous effects on French industry—alone among the industries of the advanced Western countries, it had not managed to get back to the level of output reached in 1929, the high point of the prosperity of the 1920s. The first Plan of Modernization,[8] launched by M. Monnet in 1946, formulated its production targets in relation to the 1929 figures. This was the summit of French economic achievement, which now had to be recaptured.

The Monnet period of planning lasted into the early 1950s; it concentrated on a few basic branches of production, and used the power and influence

---

[6] See Ch. V. Japan, which is not included among the countries analysed in this book (see p. xiii) seems to conform more to the French pattern of experience—and for similar historical reasons.

[7] See above, p. 83. [8] *Plan de Modernisation et d'Équipement.*

of the state to back their claims on scarce economic resources. They were in the main the 'heavy industries', in the Russian meaning of the term— steel, cement, transport equipment, including tractors, fuel and power. Indeed, the similarity of approach, though not of course of method, with the earlier phase of Soviet planning in the Stalin period, is close. In both cases, the planners were aiming to increase the productive potential of the key sectors of the economy, on which the increase in all other forms of industrial output was believed to depend. The Russians tended to have a highly theoretical, indeed sometimes almost mystical, attitude towards the role of the 'heavy industries'; for the French the issue was more straightforward and pragmatic. That became very clear after the reconstruction phase was over and the French planners turned their attention, from about 1953 onwards, to the broader aspects of economic development, picking their way among competing demands for investment on the basis of a direct study of the country's changing needs, whereas in Russia the sacred doctrine of the priority of 'heavy industry' was still being fought over a decade later, in the 1960s. Khrushchev complained before his downfall that it had become an article of faith among the ideologues of Soviet planning that steel was of its nature more important for socialist progress than, for example, chemicals.

The French planners did, however, continue to make the distinction between key industries, the fulfilment of whose targets was essential to the success of the national economic effort, and others which could be allowed to lag without causing trouble. The division between the two is basic to the French approach to planning. But the composition of the group of 'hard core' industries changes from one Plan to another—and even in the course of an individual Plan. Thus, for example, the planners were arguing in 1963 that although the output target for French steel laid down in the Fourth Plan was likely to be missed by some 2 million tons, this failure of heavy industry would not affect the main structure of French economic development.[9] In identifying those activities which are regarded as crucial the planners think less about what socialists call 'the commanding heights of the economy' than about the mundane problem of actual or prospective bottle-necks. For example, the shortfall in steel in the Fourth Plan was not thought to matter much because supplies of additional steel at a reasonable price were likely to be readily available from the surplus of productive capacity abroad. There was the further point that part of this foreign surplus would in any case spill over into France from Belgium and Germany, with the elimination of tariff barriers inside the European Economic Community.

This case aptly illustrates the central feature of French planning as it has developed from the Second Plan (1954–7) onwards. It is concerned above all with the *interrelationships* between different economic activities—specifically to identify the bottlenecks (where supplies are likely to grow by an

[9] *Rapport sur l'exécution du Plan en 1962 et 1963* (Paris, 1963).

inadequate amount) and the multipliers (where a given change in demand at one point of the system will lead predictably to further changes, up or down, at other points; and everything depends on the size of the multiple effect between the first and subsequent movements). All this is implied by the increasing emphasis from 1954 onwards on what the French planners call *cohérence*. As Bernard Cazes points out, the earlier work of the Commissariat du Plan during the immediate postwar years was only 'partial planning'—partial in the sense that it did 'not attempt to define coherent macro-economic objectives'.[10] He goes on to say that 'the transition to global programming was made possible by improvements in national accounting. . . .'

The evolution of these statistical techniques in France is a particularly interesting aspect of the development of planning. It is, indeed, somewhat paradoxical that the nation that more or less invented the practice of modern capitalist planning, which rests on highly refined techniques of national income accounting and analysis,[11] should have had such a poor statistical apparatus at its disposal. Compared with either the United States or Britain, France was markedly backward in the new techniques of national income accounting. Compared with almost any of the advanced industrial countries, including Germany, Sweden, and Holland, the French started off with a smaller quantity and a poorer quality of statistical information. It is worth emphasizing this curious discrepancy, because it at once points to the distinctive aspect of the French contribution to the making of modern economic policy. It was not the French technical or intellectual effort—so often stressed by Frenchmen—which was significant. The British and Americans led in the development of modern national income accounting, and it was the Americans who were chiefly responsible for the further refinement of the investigation into the interrelationships among the key elements in the expansion or contraction of the national income—in the form of input-output analysis. The French were intellectual followers, not initiators. Their major contribution lay in the sphere of action rather than thought. They were the first people who systematically *used* the new techniques in an effort to control the future.

It is striking how, right from the start of French national income accounting —a start which occurred several years after the British and American pioneers had done their work—the new statistical instrument was actively employed in the making of national economic policy. The Commission des Comptes et des Budgets Économiques de la Nation, a parliamentary body set up in 1952 to review the information produced by national income analysis, became during the early and middle 1950s a platform for the magisterial examination of the economic policies of whichever government

[10] OECD, Internat. TU Seminar, *Final Report*, p. 80.
[11] Especially input-output analysis.

happened to be briefly in power. Typically, the national income statisticians were induced to employ their art right from the beginning, that is from 1952 onwards, when statistics of any reliability were first made available, to project forward the existing trends in the economy in the form of a series of estimates of the main elements of the national income a year ahead. The exercise was intended chiefly as a device for bringing current economic data into better focus—it attached figures to a trend—but it turned out to have considerable political significance. National income forecasts were ready-made raw material to be used by politicians and economists for a rigorous examination of current government policies. No doubt that is why the British Government so carefully avoided giving this hostage to its critics. It also made its calculations of the probable development of the national income, as part of the annual budget exercise; but the official forecast of the movement of the individual elements of the national product—the balance between investment and consumption, the probable rise in prices, the distribution of resources between the public and the private sectors—was treated as an internal administrative matter, not for the eye of the ordinary citizen or of his parliament. In France, on the contrary, national income statistics were employed immediately they became available as an instrument of pressure on the government, and by one part of the government on another.

A Conspiracy to Plan

But if the French statistical information available to planners was often not very reliable, the question is why did it not vitiate the national economic plan? Here the habit of the exercise of power by public officials over the private sector of the economy was crucial. The French economic plans in the 1950s were not a matter of making delicate adjustments to small economic changes from year to year. Rather, the officials understood it to be their business to secure a general bias in the important economic decisions, whether taken in the public or the private sector, in a given direction. The figures which appeared in the Plan were illustrative—they provided a general guide to the aims of official policy, not a precise set of instructions. The French official, being an interventionist by nature and by training, needed to be given a compass to steer by; and it was all to the good if the directions that he had been given were also known and accepted by the men responsible for major business decisions in the private sector of the economy.

In some ways, the development of French planning in the 1950s can be viewed as an act of voluntary collusion between senior civil servants and the senior managers of big business. The politicians and the representatives of organized labour were both largely passed by. The conspiracy in the public interest between big business and big officialdom worked, largely because both sides found it convenient. Since the Government had a substantial part of the nation's economic activity under its direct control and exerted an indirect, though powerful, influence on a great deal more, it was not too difficult to convince private business that its decisions would be more intelligently made, over a wider range of industry, if they were made in unison with the public authorities. Similarly, many of the objectives of the public sector depended for their fulfilment on the co-operation of privately owned business. Both sides had an interest in limiting the element of unpredictability and risk in their operations. Hence the conspiracy to plan. The word conspiracy is appropriate because the result depended on a recognition by private business that the government official personally disposed of considerable powers which could be used to influence the success or failure of individual businesses. It all depended, therefore, on a series of bargains between the main centres of public and private economic power. If the statistical information at their disposal was rather approximate and uncertain, the two sides were nevertheless able to make do by a succession of mutual adjustments in the face of the changing pressure of events. They were each extremely sensitive to the other's interests.

It is, however, pertinent to observe that the full and explicit commitment of the French government machine to the execution of the Plan was long delayed. It was not finally given until the early 1960s. Only then was the Budget formally involved—after the Minister of Finance issued an instruction in 1962 that all claims on Budgetary funds from government departments would in future be judged by the criteria laid down in the current Plan. That is not to say that the Plan had not been influential in shaping the French Budget before this date. On the interministerial committee, which meets each year to sort out the competing claims of different government departments on Budgetary funds, the Commissariat du Plan had for long been represented by a member of its staff. Its voice was frequently heard on these occasions; and because it was often listened to, several of the ministries had got into the habit of consulting the Commissariat in advance. They felt that this helped to give more intellectual substance to their claims on the Budget. There is no doubt that in this way the moral authority of the planners *within the Government* had been increasing steadily during the 1950s. Their most powerful ally right from the beginning was the Treasury (Direction du Trésor) inside the Ministry of Finance. This is an extremely influential government agency whose decisions impinge on the wide range of business activities which in France depend on the goodwill of the authorities.

The Treasury is responsible for the use of all government funds outside the nationalized industries; it also has the authority to underwrite certain favoured borrowing with a state guarantee. Its connexion with the Plan is firmly established through the Fund for Economic and Social Development (Fonds de Développement Économique et Social)—the body established after the war to provide public finance for investment projects deemed to be in the national interest—for which the Treasury provides the staff. Indeed, these two activities, the control exercised through the FDES over the investment of nationalized undertakings and the influence exerted over the flow of capital into the private sector of the economy, together provide much of the substance of French planning. Add to this that the Treasury is chiefly responsible for the statistical and economic analysis[12] which goes into the annual official forecast of the national income, mentioned above, and it is easy to see why it is the natural focus for the formulation of long-term economic policy. Indeed, it was largely the successful partnership between the Treasury and the Commissariat du Plan which provided the basis for the progress of French planning, under the succession of weak or collapsing governments in the final years of the Fourth Republic.

A typical device of this period was the *loi-programme*—a legislative arrangement, introduced by M. Mendès France when he was Prime Minister in 1954, which was intended to allow the planners to draw on public funds for certain purposes independently of the annual budget. The Second Plan referred to the *lois-programme* as a 'super budget',[13] which would go on regardless of whatever short-term decisions on the employment of public funds were made by the majority in parliament. It is worth pondering for a moment on the deeper political implications of this curious arrangement; they tell one a great deal about the tacit assumptions underlying the exercise of public power in France. Here was a parliament which voluntarily handed over to the permanent administration the authority to get on with certain things, and denied itself the right to interfere with them. The doctrine implied by this act of self-abnegation is that although the elected members of the Assembly may express the will of the majority at any given moment, there is a truer, deeper expression of the interests of the nation in the economic sphere, which resides inside the national Plan. There is of course a ready-made ideological framework for such an approach, deriving from Rousseau, which sees the Plan as a manifestation of the *volonté générale*— and that may quite easily be at variance with the *volonté de tous*, let alone with the *volonté du gouvernement*.

The Nineteen-Sixties

It is, therefore, not fanciful to describe French planning during this phase as a conspiracy in the public interest. It was a very élitist conspiracy,

---

[12] The SEEF (Service des Études Économiques et Financières) and the INSEE (Institut National des Études Économiques et Financières) are the departments of the Ministry of Finance concerned. They are responsible, jointly with the Commissariat, for the preliminary forecasts and final analysis and co-ordination of the reports of the individual planning commissions, which provide the basis of the Four-Year Plans (see P. Bauchet, *Economic Planning: the French Experience* (London, Heinemann, 1964), p. 43).

[13] The IIème Plan says that the *lois-programme* 'constitueraient un "super-document" budgétaire dont les pouvoirs publics s'interdiraient la remise en cause à propos des budgets annuels' (IIème Plan, *Journal officiel*, 1 Apr. 1956, p. 3226).

involving a fairly small number of people. One of the senior officials of the Commissariat du Plan once described the actual process of planning during the 1950s as 'a rather clandestine affair'. It relied essentially on the close contacts established between a number of like-minded men in the civil service and in big business. Organized labour, small business, and, most of the time, the ministers of the government of the day were largely passed by. Inside the civil service machine itself, there were departments where the objectives of the Plan were not taken very seriously. But fortunately the new postwar generation in the Ministry of Finance were committed to it.

It was not until the advent of the Fifth Republic in 1958 that economic planning became the full establishment doctrine in France—and then not at once. The testing time came halfway through the Third Plan, in 1960, when a couple of years of slow growth, caused by a deliberate policy of deflation designed to bring French costs down, had made production in a number of branches fall far short of the planned target levels. The question raised at this point was whether the Plan itself ought to be adjusted. But in the event the Commissariat put out a *Plan Intérimaire*, which was a sober analysis of how the available resources might, after all, be used to achieve the original targets of the Third Plan during the remaining two years of its life, by deliberately forcing the pace of economic growth. The outcome was that the substance of the Plan was reaffirmed and the full weight of the Government put behind it. The planners had won an earlier battle, during the period of deflation in 1958–9, in maintaining the planned programme of public investment substantially intact, in the face of pressure for budget economies from powerful elements inside the Ministry of Finance.[14]

It might, however, be argued that the 1960–1 episode, when France after a period of stagnation took off again at a rapid pace roughly in line with that projected in the Third Plan, really proves very little about the practical effect of planning. M. Jacques Rueff, the leading French opponent of the idea that a planned economy could in any way replace the virtues of an old-fashioned market system, said acidly that the planners of the Commissariat were like the cock who crowed at first light and believed that he had brought on the dawn. A hefty devaluation in 1958 gave French goods a decisive advantage in foreign markets during a period when tariff barriers were coming down

[14] See J. and A.-M. Hackett, *Economic Planning in France* (London, Allen & Unwin, 1963), pp. 32–33. Throughout the period of deflation, the authors assert, official policy remained 'fixed resolutely' on long-term growth objectives. It is not to be imagined, however, that there was unanimous support for the policy; the resolute officials happened to be more effective than their opponents. The expansionist group, notably represented at the time of the deflation in the Ministry of Industry, deliberately set out to encourage large manufacturing firms to increase their investment expenditure during this period of business uncertainty. The *ministère de tutelle*, which usually maintains close contacts with the big concerns of any industry under its supervision, was apparently able in several cases to do something practical to sustain business morale in advance of the general commercial recovery in 1960.

and international trade was expanding very rapidly. The big investment effort of the 1950s, which had itself contributed to the inflation that caused the devaluation of the franc, had endowed France with modern competitive industries. The deflation and the curb on wages during the first two years after General de Gaulle's return to power meant that French manufacturers had to look to foreign markets if they wanted an expanding outlet for their production; the home market did not provide it. Thus a quite special collection of circumstances—political as well as economic, for it was only the quite unusual political conditions of the early period of the Gaullist régime which made it possible to push down the level of real wages temporarily—allowed the French economy to be floated off, so to say, on the rising tide of international trade. The British, who tried something similar during the 'wages pause' of 1961–2, associated with Mr Selwyn Lloyd, failed entirely to attain their object; the element that was most obviously missing on the British side was the devaluation of the currency. So perhaps what the French experience chiefly illustrates is the great gain that results from devaluing when the circumstances are right. Everything else follows; the planners are otiose. Foreign trade can be relied upon, by itself, to provide the motive power for the revival of economic activity at home: business profits rise; there are more opportunities for employment; and in the end this leads to a new surge of industrial investment. The virtuous circle is complete.

On the other hand, the supporters of the Plan can reasonably point out that the damage to investment during the period of deflation in 1958–9 was limited through their endeavours. The long-term economic interests of the nation were successfully asserted against those who wanted to cut down public capital expenditure, in order tǒ secure a short-term budgetary advantage. In fact capital investment in the public sector increased during this period.[15] The contrast with the typical British postwar deflation is striking, for in Britain it is public investment which is invariably called upon to bear the main brunt of such adjustments. Thus at the very least it can be claimed that the existence of a lobby inside the French Government pressing the case for long-term economic growth did make a difference: it also stood ready in 1960 to seize the first favourable opportunity to reassert, with some success, the essential objectives of the Third Plan.

But perhaps the question whether the planners, in fact, deserve more or less credit for the rapid advance of the French economy from 1960 onwards is less important than the widespread belief in their power and influence, which was established at that time. The mythology played its part when the Commissariat set to work on the preparation of the Fourth Plan, covering the period from 1962 to 1965, more elaborate and in some ways more ambitious than any of its predecessors. France now had a government which prided itself on an indifference to short-term considerations and on its exclusive concern with the 'permanent' interests of the nation. The Plan was its chosen medium for expressing this fact in the field of economic and social affairs. The bargaining power of the planners in their dealings with private industry, already considerable after a decade of collaboration between French officialdom and big business in pursuit of economic growth, was further enhanced.

Yet the planners were, in some ways, in a more difficult position than they had been at any time since the war. While their official status had been enormously enhanced and their technical economic apparatus had been improved almost out of recognition, their ultimate control over at least one major sector of the economy had been decisively reduced. The advent of the European Common Market meant that France was now exposed to sudden and unpredictable pressures from the outside, and stripped of the traditional means of defence. It could no longer impose a set of import restrictions designed to help the balance of payments, and incidentally to support certain industries when they were in a difficult patch. The planners had lost their freedom to offer the bait of protection against trouble-some foreign competition, as part of their bargaining with big business. Their powers were trammelled in other, more subtle ways, which only began gradually to appear as the Treaty of Rome went into action. The tax arrangements of each individual member country of the Six were now watched carefully by its partners, who objected as soon as there was any sign that some national industry was receiving favours from the fiscal authorities which gave it an advantage by comparison with its competitors in the European Economic Community.

The EEC system was also found to put a very heavy premium on the maintenance of fixed exchange rates between the members of the group. That was because a dozen delicate and laboriously negotiated agreements, particularly in the field of agriculture, would be turned topsy turvy by any shift in the value of an individual currency. This could, of course, turn out to be a major inhibition on the pursuit of a national economic policy of high investment and rapid expansion. In the past the French policy makers had tended to pursue their long-range objectives with little regard to their short-term inflationary effects. They put first things first—and the first necessity in their view was to strengthen the productive power of the country; if prices rose, as a result of the investment boom, to the point where the currency had to be devalued, that was an inconvenience of an essentially secondary nature, which would just have to be borne.

There were other reasons—of national prestige—which in any case tended to give the French franc an increased weight in the scales of national policy under the Fifth Republic. All in all the effect of these various pressures was to increase the importance of short-term tactical considerations in economic policy. Politics counted for more. France, more powerful in Europe, was also much more exposed. From now on economic strategy, enshrined in the Plan, could be fulfilled only if the strategists mastered the art of responding flexibly to the changing current of events while maintaining the general direction set by their long-term objectives. If before this their habit was to set their sights on a fixed point and then move towards it, as nearly as possible in a straight line, henceforward their progress would of necessity be a zigzag course. For the first time the French found themselves up against the problem, so familiar to the British, of managing the short-term fluctuations of an economy exposed to international pressures without making it go groggy with constant changes of direction. The British meanwhile had invented a pejorative term for all this—it was called 'stop-go policy'—and planning in the French style, which the British believed themselves to be adopting in the early 1960s, was viewed as a means of escaping from the evil.

Targets and Pressures

The first and indispensable condition for successful economic planning in the context of modern capitalism is confidence on the part of the business community in the seriousness of the Government's intentions, as stated in the Plan. Once it is thought that the public authorities may, after all, not be in earnest, that their production targets are little more than maximized hopes, which will be readily foregone as soon as circumstances demonstrate that there is going to be some difficulty in achieving them, businessmen will hold back. They will refuse to risk their own capital on Plan projects, which they will come to regard more and more as unhedged bets.[16] Scepticism is corrosive to the whole exercise.

Yet there is a certain paradox here, for in practice individual French industries have frequently failed by quite large margins to reach the level of production laid down in the Plan. This has been particularly so in the large and miscellaneous group of manufacturing industries which are brought together in the Plan under the heading of 'Industries de Transformation'. It is an important group, which was responsible in the early 1960s for 34 per cent of all French industrial employment.[17] The planning reports on

[16] An interesting example of the effect of such a failure of confidence in the Government's ability to fulfil its part of the Plan is provided by the British chemical industry, which refused in 1963–4 to increase its investment by as much as the planners in the NEDC judged to be necessary. When pressed on this point the chemical industry answered breezily: 'This investment would be made if the industry was satisfied that the growth of gross domestic product would continue at a high rate after 1966'. And it went on to explain that it would be prepared to modify its plans 'if there were clear signs in 1964 that this rate was going to be maintained' (NEDC, *The Growth of the British Economy* (Mar. 1964), paras. 269 and 280).

[17] See *Rapport général de la Commission des Industries de Transformation, Quatrième Plan de Développement Économique et Social (1962–65)* (Paris, 1961). (The group excludes primary manufacture of metals—e.g. steel—and chemicals.)

these industries show some remarkable discrepancies between targets and outcome. The extreme case is agricultural machinery, where output was supposed to rise by 41 per cent above the 1956 level by the time the Plan reached its final year in 1961, and actually increased by 4 per cent. On the other hand, growth of output in the electronics industry and in 'metal construction' was twice as large as the increase which had been planned. But railway rolling stock, again, rose by only half as much as the target laid down in the Plan.

In some instances the causes of this failure of prediction could be identified. There were some glaring technical deficiencies in the preparation of the original Plan. The official report explains with engaging frankness that 'the very great discrepancy between forecast and realization' in the textile industry, where the increase in output fell short of the planned amount by more than one-third, was due to the fact that the planners had made a mess of the calculation of the probable elasticity of demand for textile goods in conditions of rising consumer incomes. They had first calculated a probable increase in the amount of *money* which consumers would spend on textiles and clothing, and had then applied the figure in a simple-minded fashion to their estimate of the increased *yardage* of textile factory output.[18] The resulting muddle would have been even worse if it had not been for the fact that French textile exports had been underestimated in the Plan. This error offset to some extent the gross overestimate of demand in the domestic market.[19] A similar compensating set of errors in opposite directions occurred in the calculations for the group of mechanical and electrical industries; the result was, as shown in the footnote below,[20] that the overall index for this group

---

[18] Ibid.   [19] Ibid. p. 22.

[20] The gap between prediction and fulfilment in the individual branches of the textile industry was even wider, as the following figures show:

France: Textile Industry
3rd Plan Targets & Actual Output
(1956 = 100)

	1957	1961	
	Actual output	Target	Actual output
Total output of textile industry	108	131	119·5
of which: Jute	94·5	102	79·5
Woollens & worsted	104·5	117	102
Synthetic fibres	117	231	168
Silk	102	128	147

In the mechanical and electrical group it looks at first sight as if the outcome was closer to the target; but examination of what happened in individual industry branches shows that this impression is the result of the accident that some very large errors happened to occur in opposite directions, and disappeared from view in the course of averaging. It is only in this sense that it is possible to accept the pleased comment of the Commission des Industries de Transformation on the results

appeared to be not very far off target, in spite of very big discrepancies in individual industrial branches of production.

Why do not these failures of prediction upset the Plan? Part of the answer lies in the distinction, which is made by M. Bernard Cazes, between what he calls *'objectifs'* ('where the public authorities dispose of effective instruments') and mere *'prévisions'*.[21] The latter are not serious targets in the sense that the state is prepared, or able, to put its resources fully behind the effort to achieve them. There is a further reason mentioned by Cazes for not taking the matter too seriously: the essential facts about some industries, including notably the *industries de transformation*, are 'more difficult to establish with precision'. Apparently it does not matter if production falls far short of the figures laid down in the Plan in these industries, because everyone concerned knows that they are not targets in any practical sense, but merely what Cazes calls *'prévisions cohérentes'*, that is hypothetical figures which fit in with the general pattern of the Plan.[22] Indeed, some of

as a whole (p. 20): 'Le résultat global de la prévision est satisfaisant puisque l'on constate la réalisation à 97% de l'objectif de production du IIIe Plan . . .'

France: Mechanical & Electrical Engineering Industry
3rd Plan Targets & Actual Output
(1956 = 100)

	1957	1961	
	Actual output	Target	Actual output
Total output of mechanical & electrical engineering industry	111	142	137
of which: Castings	116	142	127
Metal construction	120	124	149
Agricultural machinery	117·5	141	104
Railway rolling stock	105	129	113·5
Electronics	118	150	190

Source: Rapport Général de la Commission des Industries de Transformation, Annex 3, p. 134.

[21] *La planification en France et le Quatrième Plan* (Paris, L'Épargne, 1962, p. 84). M. Cazes is a senior official of the Commissariat du Plan.

[22] The mid-term report on the Fourth Plan (*Rapport sur l'exécution du plan en 1962 et 1963*) expresses the qualitative distinction between the different types of predictions and targets included in the Plan in a more formal way. Describing the difficulties encountered by certain industries, notably steel, during the previous two years, the report says that these had raised the question whether the stated objectives of the Plan would have to be modified. The decision to leave them intact was taken after an analysis of the effect of the shortfalls on the 28 broad sectors into which the economy is divided for making a systematic check on the performance of the Plan. This is the basic input-output table, smaller than the one used in the original planning operation. It was found that there were no consequential changes of significance in any of the 28 key magnitudes. It is to be observed that this manner of checking on the effect of deviations from the original production targets, adjusting the individual components of the Plan to shifting circumstances, reflects a considerable advance in sophistication on the techniques used in the earlier, heroic stages of

the planners in the Commissariat go further and refer, privately, to a third category of planned figures which have a 'purely moral significance'. Such figures may be put forward by the members of an over-enthusiastic planning commission for an industry and accepted by the Commissariat, even though they are known to be unrealistic, in order not to discourage them.

These explanations of how it all works, in spite of some wild figuring, still leave some questions unanswered. For the Plan only makes sense to the businessmen as a practical guide if they know precisely which production targets they are to take 'au sérieux', to use Cazes's phrase, and which not. It is as if the celebrated shooting of Admiral Byng, done as Voltaire explained 'pour encourager les autres',[23] had been conducted by taking the poor admiral out, blindfolding him, and then firing at him with dummy ammunition. Neither he nor other British admirals who were tempted not to fight hard enough would have been likely to derive much encouragement from that. It can only be supposed that a great many of the figures which go into these plans are of a quasi-ritualistic character. On the other hand, it must be emphasized that there is a good deal more to the actual process of French planning than the business of calculating appropriate production targets for each industry. The official in the Commissariat tends to see his relationship to 'his' industry in more intimate terms, as that of a day-to-day counsellor—part industrial consultant, part banker, part plain bully. His job is to maintain constant pressure on an industry, by any tactical means that happens to be available, to keep it moving in some desired direction. It may be that more modern equipment needs to be installed in it; or that the average size of the producing unit requires to be enlarged for the sake of greater efficiency; or that costs have to be brought down in order to sell more in export markets; or alternatively that certain types of product need to be produced in larger quantities in order to cut down some expensive import. Precise statistics, whether of actual production or of the planned level of future output, are only one of the tools of such a planner. He is mainly concerned to achieve momentum along some chosen route, and he will know whether this is occurring through his close daily contacts with the affairs of an industry, even if the figures that he has at his disposal are very approximate indeed.

One of the planners responsible for an industrial commission at the Commissariat estimated that in the course of a year the dossiers of as many as 500 firms pass across his desk; this, he explained, kept him up to date on the production and sales performance and investment plans of the relatively small number of businesses 'that matter'. It is indeed obvious, as soon as

French planning in the 1950s. Then the checks imposed on statistical forecasts, many of which were themselves based on extremely shaky figures, were very largely by guess and by God. The first modern industrial census in France was conducted only in 1963. The last one before that had taken place under Napoleon III.

[23] *Candide.*

one looks at the way in which French planning is actually conducted, that the planners can only cope if the number of firms with whom they have to deal in any particular industry is fairly small. Otherwise the task of keeping tabs on what is happening, of guiding or pressing individual managements to move in the desired directions becomes impossible. The Commissariat prides itself on its small staff: it employs about 100 people, of whom some fifty are professional planners.[24]

That has made it possible to preserve a certain collegiate atmosphere in the elegant, rather untidy old building, which houses the Commissariat in the rue Martignac. The officials of the Plan seem to live in each other's pockets: the celebrated 'cohérence', which is the mark of French planning, appears to be achieved at least in part by a system of communication among those ultimately responsible that most resembles a university common room. Informality and close personal contact are the hallmark of the planners' methods of dealing with their clients as well as their colleagues. They are strikingly unlike the popular image of the planner as a backroom boy with a slide-rule and a row of figures, and very little else. I remember one of them responding to a question of mine about how he checked up on some rather suspicious-looking production statistics for one industry. He picked up a piece of paper which was lying on the table in front of us and having brought it to his nose, sniffed at it energetically: 'One relies on one's sense of smell', he said. 'There is nothing else to do!'

These men talk among themselves in a kind of shorthand about the '80–20 ratio'. This expresses their view that to make effective planning possible the distribution of output in industry ought preferably to be such that something close to 80 per cent of production comes from about 20 per cent of the firms. Of course it is easier still to plan in this personal style, if the number of significant firms in an industry is an even smaller proportion of the total. The planners are able to cope, after a fashion, with industries in which ownership is less concentrated, but several of them seem to feel that a 60–40 relationship—i.e. 60 per cent of production in the hands of 40 per cent of the firms—would in the long run be unmanageable. The weakness of planning in such industries as textiles and capital goods is in large part due to their structure; nothing would help them more, it is felt, than the demise of a lot of small businesses and the emergence of a few dominant large ones. The planners make no secret of their belief in the iron law of oligarchy.

With this sort of approach it is natural that they should be eyed with suspicion by the typical small businessman; he tries to use his trade association to keep a watch on their activities. In 1962 some of the trade associations demanded that they should act as the 'intermediary

---

[24] This number excludes the staff of the Commissariat Général de la Productivité, which was attached to the Plan Organization in 1959.

between the planners and the individual firm'[25]—a method which would assuredly have destroyed the whole basis on which French planning has operated to date. For in any industry composed predominantly of small firms, the trade association is almost bound to become the spokesman for the views and the spirit of the average business—whereas the method of the Plan has been to select the above-average firms as active allies and to use them to force up the general level of performance of the rest. Needless to say, the planners have resisted the advances of these would-be intermediaries.

It would be a mistake, however, to suppose that the pressures in the process of planning always operate in one direction, from the official centre outwards upon the individual firm. The large corporations, who are interested in planning as a means of reducing the uncertainties of investment and of achieving the orderly development of their markets, exercise their pressures too. The Plan reflects, in large part, their ideas—or at least a compromise between their wishes and those of the officials responsible for government economic policy. The people in the Commissariat complain on occasion that the civil servants who come from the *ministère de tutelle* of a particular trade or industry too often act as if they were in some sense the representatives of these sectional interests, rather than the officials appointed to keep a watch on them in the public interest. On the other hand, it is also claimed that the Commissariat supplies a central forum where private business can argue out its case with the officials from the ministry, without being intimidated by them. Whichever way it is, there is no doubt that the activity of planning, as it is practised in France, has reinforced the systematic influence exerted by large-scale business on economic policy. Sometimes this influence is open and apparent, as when the Fourth Plan's investment policy for steel was modified in 1963 in deference to the wishes of the steel industry, despite the barely concealed objections of certain government officials. Subsequently, when the industry was offered a sufficient financial inducement by the Government—in the form of a reduction in the tariffs on imported US coking coal and a rebate on their social security payments—they agreed to an increase in the steel manufacturing capacity to be laid down in the Fifth Plan.[26]

More usually, the to-and-fro of bargaining over investment plans and about the size of the Government's contribution to the finances of individual firms takes place in private. There are occasions when the blandishments or pressures from the Government side simply fail to work—as, for instance, when the French motor industry in the early 1960s was investing more than the planners judged to be wise and a strong effort was made to induce them to cut back. Since they were very large and powerful firms, endowed with

[25] M. MacLennan, *French Planning: Some Lessons for Britain* (London, PEP, 1963, p. 345).

[26] See *The Economist*, 8 Feb. 1964. De Wendel and Sidelor agreed to build a new plant jointly on these terms.

very adequate funds—so that they did not have to rely on official help in raising money in the capital market—they could not be stopped. And it did not apparently signify at all that one of them, Renault, incidentally the largest single producer of cars in France, was a nationalized undertaking.[27] There are clearly certain rules of the game which apply to the relations between the French Government and successful big business, regardless of whether the latter is publicly or privately owned.

Flexibility

The demand for a high degree of flexibility in economic planning, which was a feature of the changed conditions of the early 1960s in France, was nothing new in the actual practice of the French planners. The rigidities of the Plan had always been more intellectual than practical.[28] Those who wielded the ultimate economic power, upon which the fulfilment of particular targets depended, had always acted with a wide measure of administrative discretion, using whatever tactical device came most readily to hand in pursuit of more important strategic objectives. This applied both to government officials and to the professional managers of big business. They belonged, in many cases, to a common élite, selected and cherished and trained in the same disciplines at the few traditional schools of higher education (the *Grandes Écoles*) where the country's top administrators were rigorously prepared for their task. These are men who take pride in assuming personal responsibility: their habit is to assume the initiative, and to think up formal justifications for their actions afterwards.

What was new in the 1960s was the feeling among politicians and others concerned with the making of economic policy that France was indeed much more vulnerable to outside forces and that therefore a significantly larger

---

[27] *Economist*, 13 July 1963. Renault was also in conflict with the Government at this time about the location of a new plant which it planned to establish at Le Havre. This was at variance with the Government's regional policy; but Renault resisted direction.

[28] The fate of the *lois-programme* (see above, p. 130) provides an apt illustration. They were introduced as a means of keeping governments on the straight and narrow path, forcing them to travel between the setting of the target and the point of realization by the shortest route. They were a parliamentary symbol of spiritual commitment. In practice, the money drawn for the finance of the *lois-programme* was sometimes used by the authorities for other, no doubt important, purposes; the system thus became a device for giving the administration *more* freedom of manoeuvre. Its employment was more closely supervised from the Fourth Plan onwards. The present intention is that a *lois-programme* should be used only where there is a clear promise of economic gain, as a result of lower costs and prices based on assured long-term orders (see MacLennan, *French Planning*, p. 376). The law of 1959 (Ordonnance 2 janvier 1959, Art. 2) was designed to limit the commitments undertaken by officials, without budgetary backing, towards private firms involved in the Plan. It says: 'Les lois de programme ne peuvent permettre d'engager l'État à l'égard des tiers que dans les limites des autorisations de programme contenues dans la loi de finances de l'année'.

portion of any future plan was going to be at risk—unless new measures of control could be invented. All this shows up clearly in the preparatory work on the Fifth Plan (1966–70).[29] The first reflex of the planners was to argue that since it was the European Common Market which had introduced all these inconvenient uncertainties into the conduct of French economic policy, the simplest remedy would be to subject the Common Market itself to economic planning. There were several snags of monumental proportions in this proposal—to which I shall have occasion to refer later—but before these could even be reached, there was the great barrier presented by the attitude of France's major partner in the Six, Germany, to the whole idea of economic planning *à la française*.

More realistically, the French authorities decided that in the formulation of future plans the emphasis would be shifted from production targets for particular industries to 'structural objectives'.[30] It may be argued that this is no more than admitting in public what had been implicit in the activities of the planners all along. They had always been concerned with the growth of the productive power and efficiency of French industry; output and investment figures included in the national plan had merely been used as means of attaining the more profound purpose. But to make these considerations explicit and central to the whole exercise is an important change. It can be treated as a further logical step in the increasing sophistication of French planning, which has been in progress since the early 1950s. The false precision of some of the earlier figuring is discarded because the statistics are improved and the economic data available to the planners have become more subtle. The distinction between targets, predictions, and mere guesses is more clearly drawn, and the extent of the hypothetical element in each is identified. In terms of method, it is a little like growing out of an exclusive preoccupation with arithmetic into the discovery of algebra.

The Democratic Urge

There is another aspect of the matter, which has more profound political implications. This kind of planning concerned with 'structural changes', once these are explicitly stated, brings out into the open the underlying

---

[29] The Draft says that 'the essential problem' of the Vth Plan is the adaptation of the system to the new conditions created by the Common Market (I–I–pp. 2–3).

[30] This is reflected in the *Programme de Travail* sent out to the *commissions* in 1964, instructing them on the procedures to be adopted in preparing the Fifth Plan The attempt by the planners to induce industry to think in terms of more fundamental structural changes is apparent even earlier in the following passage in the 'Instructions for the Presidents and Rapporteurs of Commissions' on the Fourth Plan (Oct. 1960) where businessmen are asked, in somewhat schoolmasterly terms, to put up ideas which show 'realism and imagination': 'Le Plan ne comporte pas seulement des prévisions chiffrées mais aussi des propositions de mesures à prendre par les pouvoirs publics . . . Leur propositions auront d'autant plus de chances d'être retenues qu'elles feront preuve à la fois de réalisme et d'imagination.'

motives of the planners where they have hitherto been barely recognized beneath the statistical targets. Planning as a 'clandestine affair'[31] had its convenience, often considerable, where an effective economic policy involved discrimination between individual firms; it will no longer be possible. M. Massé, the Commissaire Général of the Plan, and his senior staff clearly welcome the change, despite the inhibitions that it may place on their freedom of action; indeed, it is the Commissariat which has been most insistent in demanding more publicity, more democratic discussion, and finally more parliamentary control over the Plan.

It is an interesting and somewhat unexpected outcome of the advent of strong government in Gaullist France that the planners, who have for the first time obtained the full formal backing of the political executive, should nevertheless seek out the opportunities for imparting the uncertainties and discomfort of the parliamentary process into the heart of the Plan. The new procedures for the preparation of the Fifth Plan[32] are deliberately designed to associate the deputies of the National Assembly and the Senate with the business of planning in a way that has never been done before. Perhaps the most important change is not merely that parliament is brought into the centre of the discussion, but that it is asked to make decisions on policy at an earlier and more sensitive stage of the planning process. Instead of being presented by the planners with a few simple alternatives—a series of different possible rates of economic growth to choose from—after the broad pattern of future production and distribution has already been worked out, parliament is called upon at the start to fix the '*grandes options*', i.e. the desirable distribution of the increased wealth to be generated over the four-year period. Indeed, in the case of the Fifth Plan, it is being asked even more fundamentally whether economic policy should concentrate on the production of increased wealth, rather than on the provision of more leisure time.[33] Then, later on, when the Commissariat has made its calculations and argued them out with the *commissions* of the Plan (now increased to thirty), parliament is once again to be asked to consider the detailed implications of the broad choice it has already made.[34] These implications can never be fully foreseen, and it is of the essence of the democratic process that the elected representatives should not have to deliver themselves up, with no opportunity for second thoughts, to the technicians. The conclusions which the latter have reached on particular matters can frequently be modified, if there is sufficient will and ingenuity applied to meeting the wishes of parliament, without disrupting the essential framework of the Plan.

[31] See above, p. 131.   [32] *Programme de Travail.*
[33] The trade unions have been pressing for a cut in working hours.
[34] See Draft of Vth Plan, Preamble, where the claim is made that this double procedure for obtaining democratic assent, first of the '*grandes lignes*' of the Plan and then, a year later, of the detail 'has no equivalent in any other country'

However, there is no doubt that all this is going to make planning in France a more awkward and laborious process. After all, parliament was hardly allowed a say at all in three of the Plans: the First and Third were set in motion by government decree and the Second was submitted to parliamentary approval only in the course of its third year. The Fourth Plan did at least undergo scrutiny by parliament, but there was no serious attempt made to exercise control over it. The form of the eventual approval given to it conveys the atmosphere: the Plan is given parliamentary blessing as a 'framework' of the investment programme and as the 'instrument of orientation' for economic and social progress during the period.[35] The sense of commitment is lacking. On the other hand, parliament was prepared to let the planners have their head. Was it merely quixotry which led the latter to insist that they must have more parliamentary intervention—as if they were trying to assert that at a time when France was ruled by an authoritarian Government resting on the referendum, economic planning would provide a model of how to subject policy to the normal democratic process?

One does detect signs of such ambitions in the attitudes of the French planners, from M. Massé[36] downwards, in the early 1960s. But there is much more to all this than a political gesture. The essential fact is that those responsible have been learning during recent years about the practical value of a popular consensus for certain phases of economic policy. Specifically, the argument is that if France is no longer able to use the conventional economic weapons to combat a balance of payments crisis caused by an inflationary rise in domestic costs, then, in order to maintain a steady long-term economic policy, a direct means has to be found to curb domestic inflation through an agreement among the contenders for the annual increment in the national wealth. Prices will not be driven up so long as each of the main groups, the wage-earners and the owners of capital in various industries, agree in advance on how big a share of any increase they will expect to receive in wages and profits respectively. But of course such an 'incomes policy' could not possibly work without a basic identity of view about the main objectives of economic and social policy and the methods to be used

---

[35] See F. Perroux, *Le IVe Plan français* (Paris, Presses Universitaires, 1962), p. 108.

[36] He says explicitly in the preamble (p. 1) to the 1964 Draft of the Vth Plan, that his aim is to make the planning process 'more democratic'. Perhaps it is not entirely irrelevant that by this time Massé was struggling with a powerful current of opinion inside the French Administration, notably in the Ministry of Finance, which was unsympathetic to the whole notion of planning. Specifically, it objected to the burden imposed on the budget by the large-scale public financing of officially approved projects and saw in this a factor making for inflation. The new exponents of what was labelled 'Poincaréisme' insisted that the objective of balancing the budget must take precedence over programmes of public investment, and that in the last resort the Plan itself was an expendable item.

to attain them.[37]   Planning with the broadest possible democratic consent seems therefore to offer the way towards solving the problem.

What this implies is that the first French commitment henceforth has to be to the creation of the just society, not merely the efficient one which has engaged the planners since the end of the war.   The latter would undoubtedly claim that in the long run the society serviced by an efficient plan of production would tend to be more just in its distribution of wealth, if only because there would be that much more to distribute.   But the trouble is that the new popular consensus and the feeling that social justice is being done are needed for urgent practical reasons here and now.   There is no time to wait.   To run a successful 'incomes policy' a society must not only be just; it must immediately be seen to be so.   One way of putting the point, using Rousseauist language which remains the underlying stuff of so much French political thinking, is that planning must cease to be simply the expression of '*la volonté générale*', which may be in contradiction with the will of the majority at any single moment of time, and become in some sense '*la volonté de tous*'.

It is as if France has had to learn about the importance in economic policy of modern methods of persuasion, as opposed to the direct exercise of power by the state, through being subjected to pressures from the outside, centred on the balance of payments.   What the French are discovering in this way had long been familiar to other democratic societies, particularly in Northern Europe and in North America.   The characteristic procedure there is to start by looking for a consensus among the relevant interest groups and next to translate this into national policy and action, with the minimum intrusion of official authority.   In France, as Chapter V showed, the habit of positive interventionist government, exercised by officials enjoying a generous measure of administrative discretion, is old and ingrained.   It is this that is central to the new techniques of effective economic planning in a capitalist context. The arts of persuasion, as practised notably by the Anglo-Saxons, are at best a weak substitute.   That is not to say that persuasion, as well as government fiat, does not have an important role to play—the whole of the French postwar exercise in planning proclaims the fact—but it has to be persuasion backed by the knowledge that the power of the state is available for use and that there is a willingness to use it.   The recent emphasis on consensus and on a wider democratic participation in planning in France does not significantly affect this essential contrast.   The French can plan easily, because they

---

[37] The conflict between an 'incomes policy' and other objectives of planning is brought out vividly in the Draft Outline of the Vth Plan.   Commenting on the proposal to push up profits during the late 1960s faster than the rise in production (in order to support industrial investment) while wages are to rise more slowly than production, the Draft concludes sadly: 'C'est dire que le maintien de l'objectif d'équilibre exigerait que soit donné à la politique des revenus un contenu qui la rendrait difficilement acceptable' (I–IV–10).

have a system and an apparatus ready-made to take up the task of planning. Others who are not similarly endowed, notably the British, have had to fumble laboriously for a new way.

Power versus Persuasion

There has been a great quantity of double-talk about the role of public power in the process of modern capitalist planning, much of it promoted by the planners themselves. At times M. Massé has given the impression that the whole operation is essentially a species of intellectual confrontation, in the course of which the ordinary businessman, who is normally equipped to take no more than a short-term practical view of the forces of the market, is brought face to face with a longer perspective in time, as well as a wider one covering the whole economy. Out of this encounter there emerge spontaneously a number of wise decisions, and the planner's subsequent role is to stand ready to issue danger signals whenever there is any significant deviation between these decisions and the performance of business management. Once again, this is expected to lead, more or less spontaneously, to a number of concerted actions·among those responsible, which will put matters right. The intellectual and consultative factor in this account is given overwhelming importance. Planning is envisaged as a kind of spiritual illumination: because men understand more they behave better.

This emphasis on the voluntary character of the exercise was no doubt prompted in large part by the desire to mark off the civilized procedures of capitalist planning—with its central feature of the continuing 'dialogue' between the planners and the planned, speaking to one another on terms of equality, but coming so close together in the course of the debate that it is often impossible to say from which side the ultimate planning decision derives—from the Soviet method of planning by decree. It must not be forgotten that 'planning' initially during the postwar period, and in some countries throughout the 1950s, was a dirty word; it was associated with extreme forms of *dirigisme*. Naturally, the pioneers of the method in the West were eager to insist that what they were offering was nothing of the sort. Instead, they produced the image of something like a university seminar in continuous session or an orchestra successfully playing a score which they had composed together, without a conductor in sight. The typical form in which this was expressed during the 1950s was to say that the Plan was 'indicative' and never 'imperative'. But these simplified labels tended to blur an important issue of method: granted that the Plan was not imposed by direct compulsion, it was still open to the government to engage its greatly enlarged resources in an act of persuasion. If the government used all its considerable power, either to persuade the recalcitrant or to reward the obedient, the pressure behind the Plan could become well-nigh irresistible.

The intellectual exercise would then have a different and lesser role.

Whether they were conscious of it or not, the French certainly gave the appearance of trying to induce the rest of Western Europe to take up planning in the early 1960s by the technique of the 'soft sell'. Their main target was, naturally, the European Common Market. The practical motives behind this have been discussed earlier. What is curious and especially worthy of note is the manner in which the French exponents of 'European planning' seemed to go out of their way to cast a veil over the actual experience of the public authorities in France in persuading business to abide by the aims of the Plan in their day-to-day decisions. It was like describing a battle without ever taking account of the fact that anyone had been killed—or at least had been threatened with slaughter. With the corpses out of the way and weapons hidden, the mystery remained at the end of the valiant story why one side had moved forward while the other had retired from some strongly held position.

There is something faintly bizarre about the proposal, which was being freely debated at the time, that the European Commission in Brussels should double the role of the Commissariat du Plan and bring the national economic policies of the six members of the EEC into a single plan of the French type.[38] Planning of this kind only works, as has been indicated earlier, when it is backed by a highly centralized and powerful civil service strategically placed in the key economic ministries. The Commissariat is merely the spearhead of a pressure group inside the Government: its task is to persuade. The decisive role is that of the departmental officials acting in unison over a wide area of the economy. It was only by ignoring the factor of public power that the suggestion of European Common Market planning, at a time when the effective central authority exercised by the EEC over the day-to-day conduct of economic affairs was still tiny, acquired any slight degree of plausibility. It was in fact highly misleading to present the activity of the planners as if it were solely that of an intelligent broker, who is able to get his various clients to work in unison by pointing out to them the attractive long-term consequences of the chosen course of action. There is a great deal more to it than the species of administrative diplomacy cum political

[38] The work of the Medium-Term Economic Policy Committee of the EEC, which produced its first five-year programme in 1966, is something quite different. It is essentially a process of confrontation between governments, several of whom arrive on the scene with ready-made plans; its chief function is to pinpoint any inconsistencies between one set of national forecasts and another and to focus attention on the common purposes of the six members of the Community. In this sense it may be regarded as an advisory body, which like other such bodies, whether they are independent research institutes or representative of important interest groups, stand at the elbows of the national planners and point to apparent inconsistencies or urge upon them some modification in their scale of priorities. The Medium-Term Economic Policy Committee does not engage in any direct dialogue with the individual sectors of industry, so that the programme which emerges from its deliberations lacks the commitment or the involvement of the business community.

horse-trading which has been practised so successfully by the officials of the European Commission in Brussels.

It is easy to see why these officials should have sought to extend the range of their influence on the economic policies of member countries by offering them the bait of a 'European Plan', which was designed to reduce the element of uncertainty caused by their increasing exposure to pressures exerted wittingly or unwittingly by one another. No doubt, some method of more regular and systematic consultation between the Six on matters not covered by the Treaty of Rome will have to be developed, if the Community is to continue to grow without causing severe inconvenience to its member countries.[39] But that is a far cry from the scheme put forward by M. Robert Marjolin, Vice President of the European Commission, in a celebrated paper in 1962,[40] which would have had the EEC establish a European order of priorities for important investments—something which had hardly been managed at the national level in most European countries—and ensure that the necessary capital would be available to carry them out at the required speed. Apparently the only new instrument which M. Marjolin envisaged for this, and several other major developments of a concerted European economic policy, was a staff of economists who would produce long-term 'studies'; these latter, it was implied, would be of such compelling force that practical decisions would automatically fall into the slots prepared for them. 'In the beginning was the Word . . .'

The significant point in all this for the purposes of our present analysis is the assurance which Marjolin goes out of his way to emphasize in his conclusion—'en aucun cas, de telles études . . . ne devraient avoir pour effet de limiter en quoi que ce soit la liberté des entreprises, qui resteront entièrement maîtresses de leur décisions de production et d'investissement'. But, as we have seen, the direct threat to the ultimate freedom of management to do as it sees fit is not the issue at all. It is a question of how much the *environment* in which business management takes its decisions is to be altered by the deliberate intervention of the public authorities. What special inducements will be offered to the obedient and co-operative firm which will not be available to those who ignore the Plan? Is the reward for virtue to be solely the promise of higher profits to be earned by those who are wise enough to follow the advice of the experts? What do the planners do to influence the life and death of individual businesses when the manifest need is one of those familiar 'structural changes', designed to improve the general level of efficiency of a whole European industry? It is difficult enough, even

[39] The four EEC committees whose work acquired increasing significance in the mid-1960s, the Short-Term Economic Policy Committee, the Budget Policy Committee, the Monetary Committee, and the Medium-Term Economic Policy Committee, reflect in different ways the growing effort to cope with this type of problem.
[40] Read to a conference in Rome and reproduced in SEDEIS, *Bulletin*, no. 839, suppl. 1. See particularly paras. 21 & 25.

for a strong government inside a tightly knit national community, to make choices of this kind. What would it be like if the probable effects of the choice made by the planners of the European Community were seen to be that one member country would greatly improve its competitive position in a particular industry, while in another country a large number of firms would be forced out of business? That is not a fanciful supposition; it is what certain phases of planning are about. I remember the undisguised glee of a member of the staff of the Commissariat du Plan in Paris who was describing the success of a plan to change the structure of an industry in which there was a proliferation of small, backward firms: they were being killed off—'un vrai holocauste!' he said.[41]

The Example of Price Control

The formula which M. Massé eventually adopted for describing the method of his Plan—'less than imperative but more than indicative'[42]—is no doubt intended to express in polite language the realities of intervention in a society with a powerful officialdom and a responsive business community. Part of the problem is that even sophisticated French officials find it difficult to understand just how non-interventionist the officials of some other nations are—and want to be. What the French call non-imperative would seem extraordinarily imperious behaviour in Britain. In France it is the official style of the day which leaves its stamp on events far more firmly than the political views of the government which happens to be in power. The style often has remarkable stability.

Its staying power has been strikingly illustrated recently in the history of French price control. Back in 1958, in the early days of the Fifth Republic under the influence of the economic liberalism of M. Jacques Rueff,[43] it was proposed to reduce and finally to abolish the whole system of French price control. In the following years, during which French costs were successfully kept below the level of their competitors—largely as a result of the devaluation in 1958—the Office of Price Control in the Ministry of Finance did indeed have its activities reduced and its staff cut down. But at the first sign of a recurrence of the old inflationary trouble in 1963, the Government turned to

---

[41] It is worth recalling the reason given by the planners for trying to reduce the number of firms in this particular industry. The small firms, they said, were very weak sellers, and as soon as the balance of supply and demand was even slightly out of alignment, they proceeded to cut prices to ribbons. This caused excessive fluctuations and market uncertainties in an industry which, in fact, needed to invest heavily in order to make itself efficient. Once there were a small number of big dominant firms, conditions would become much more stable and predictable—because these large enterprises would tend to reduce their output temporarily, whenever the market was weak, rather than see prices broken. This defence of oligopoly as a way of planned life was delivered in an entirely matter of fact spirit—the planner speaking from direct experience—without any doctrinaire overtones.

[42] In the preface to François Perroux's *Le IVe Plan français*.

[43] See Rueff's *Rapport sur la situation financière* (Dec. 1958).

the familiar weapon of price control once again and in a matter of months it was functioning as vigorously as ever. This time practically every product and service was covered—generally at the point of production rather than retail sale. The interesting point is that after five years the administrative apparatus for this huge task was ready and available for use at short notice.[44] That it had lost none of its ability to cope during the interval became clear in the course of the Government's conflict with the butchers over the price of beef in 1963–4. According to the head of the Price Control Office, a total of some 500,000 inspections of butchers' shops had been carried out in the course of the nine months up to the middle of 1964, an average of 20 per shop.[45] The butchers were at this stage a decisive factor in the Government's battle to slow down the rise in the cost of living, and for tactical reasons the price controller was called upon to act with great vigour.

A closer insight into the underlying assumptions of the French official method can be gained by observing the behaviour of the reinvigorated Price Control Office in relation to the longer-term objectives of French policy. Maximum prices in a number of industries were deliberately fixed in such a way as to make it difficult for marginal, inefficient producers to survive. Advantage was taken of the opportunity to pursue desired structural changes with the help of yet another instrument of pressure. Meanwhile, the rewards offered to those who showed themselves willing to co-operate with the authorities provide an equally telling illustration of French official practice. Since retail prices were not, in general, directly controlled but ex-factory prices were, there was a problem of inducing shopkeepers to hold their margins down in the face of the temptations and pressures of a time of inflation. The reward offered to them required the collaboration of other government offices having no formal competence or concern with price control matters—notably the income tax authorities.

The French tax system allows businesses and people working on their own account to choose between two different methods of assessment: they can either be taxed on the basis of income actually earned, which may be difficult to establish precisely to the satisfaction of the authorities, or on a summary estimate of the figure of their turnover (*chiffre d'affaires*), made by the tax office itself. The latter is then adjusted by some standard figure reflecting the margin of profit deemed to be normal in that particular trade. Shopkeepers, for reasons which may be readily guessed, usually opt for the second method. The special concession offered to them in 1963 was that if they committed themselves to abide by the retail price 'recommendations' of the Price Control

[44] The essential regulation—which required a report to the Price Control Office of any proposed price increase two weeks in advance and allowed a stop to be imposed if objections were raised during this period—had been retained (see L. Franck, *Les Prix* (Paris, Presses Universitaires, 1964, p. 50)). But it had become the established practice to treat the report largely as a formality and not to raise objections.
[45] Information supplied orally.

Office—which meant joining the ranks of the organized virtuous, known officially as *commerçants pilotes*—they would be given a guarantee against any increase in the key figure of their assessed *chiffre d'affaires*, however much their turnover might expand.

The official explanation of this bargain was that retailers who held down their prices, in line with the Government's wishes, would probably have to accept a lower profit margin on sales, and so ought to receive a tax rebate of some sort. But if that had been all, the simplest method would surely have been to give the low-price shop the benefit of a realistic assessment of its reduced *profit margin*. In fact the scheme worked out by the officials was designed to hand out some tax prizes with a larger economic end in view. For the approved shops which did not raise their prices would, it was assumed, go out and make an exceptional sales effort to capture additional trade, knowing that the net profit on their extra turnover would be so much higher, because untaxed. And to further the plot to bring them additional customers, they were given free television advertising in a daily programme, put out at peak viewing time in the evening and paid for by the Price Control Office.

This story provides some useful pointers to the characteristic ingredients of the French official style. There is first of all the manner in which the officials seize on a negative instrument like price control, reshape it, and use it for their own positive purposes. They instinctively consolidate any extra bit of power which happens to come their way, even if it is as awkward and transient (in intention) as control over a price. Secondly, there is the move to mobilize allies in other, seemingly remote departments of government, whose essential functions are quite different, but which can be made to serve a particular tactical purpose.[46] There is a flexibility here which goes with the assumption of a large degree of administrative discretion: government offices make deals with one another over the heads, and no doubt sometimes at the expense, of the ordinary private citizens.[47] Thirdly, the officials automatically accept it as part of their task to discriminate between individual cases, to judge how far their performance comes up to some fairly flexible standard which they apply, to offer rewards to allies and to try to make life awkward for others.

---

[46] Franck, who was head of the Price Control Office during the 1950s, describes the active collaboration of different government agencies in the task of holding down prices. 'L'État acheteur, l'État client se préoccupait d'adopter une politique des prix des marchés publics, d'en coordonner les divers éléments, d'en régulariser le rythme, d'en spécialiser et d'en rationaliser les éléments en vue d'obtenir une baisse des coûts. L'administration des prix allait, pour une part essentielle, suivre de très près les prix de ce secteur vivant en symbiose avec les propres besoins de l'État' (*Les Prix*, p. 39).

[47] So far as I have been able to ascertain, the arrangements for retail price control described above have not been the subject of parliamentary questions or indeed of any form of official announcement or debate.

VIII

PLANNING: BRITAIN AND FRANCE COMPARED

HAVING identified the characteristic features of the French style of planning, we can now go on to a closer comparison of the organization and the practice of planning in Britain and France in the early 1960s. What follows is chiefly concerned with the period to the autumn of 1964—that is, up to the advent of the Labour Government in Britain, and the publication of the draft outline of the Fifth Plan in France. Both these events were important—the change of government in Britain especially so—and wherever possible their impact on methods of planning in the two countries is taken into account. (The significance of the draft Fifth Plan has already been mentioned in Chapter VII.) However, the implications of the altered British approach to planning under the Labour Government have not yet, at the time of writing, been fully documented. It *looks* as if the change of government may result in a definite advance on the methods of 1962–4 described in the following pages, though the amount of substantial evidence on this point is insufficient to build any confident projection of a trend. But the story of the first essay in planning, up to 1964, provides a reminder of some of the special obstacles which tend to impede any such exercise in a British context. The significance of this episode for any judgement on Britain's capacity to plan is more profound than the particular set of circumstances which happened to provide the setting for the experiment.

The British concentrated from the start on two aspects of planning—on the one hand, the propaganda aspect and, on the other, the plan as a forum for the establishment of a new consensus among the main economic interest groups. The latter objective was reflected in the organization of the National Economic Development Council: all effective power was concentrated in the Council—with the Office (NEDO), composed of the professional planning staff and corresponding broadly to the Commissariat du Plan in Paris, closely subject to its orders. The Council was established with an initial membership of twenty[1]—two independents and for the rest, three groups equally represented: employers, organized labour, and the state. The Government at this stage made it a point of principle not to claim any special status in this body: it behaved as if it were an interest group arguing its case with

[1] Subsequently raised to 22 by the Labour Government, with the addition of the Chief Industrial Adviser to the Department of Economic Affairs and the Chairman of the National Board for Prices and Incomes.

equal partners who were expected to have other interests; its only privilege was to provide the chairman of the Council, in the person of the Chancellor of the Exchequer.[2]   But no permanent officials of the Government were, under the Conservatives, allowed to take part in the Council's deliberations; it was only by an act of grace that a relatively junior Treasury civil servant was permitted to be present as an observer.

Of course, this procedure allowed the Government to keep the NEDC at arm's length too.   The planning officials were treated as persons working for an independent institution with which the Government happened to have intimate and friendly relations; they had no right of access to official documents or to the Government's discussions about its own plans.   Thus during the early stages of British planning in 1962–3 there was a slightly absurd game of hide-and-seek, with the NEDC trying to make shrewd guesses about the probable trend of public expenditure in different government departments for inclusion in its five-year plan for the economy, and the Treasury for its part refusing to disclose its own detailed calculations of future expenditure figures, but trying to ease the NEDC's problem by dropping helpful hints.   The nature of the Treasury's projections, covering precisely the five years ahead, was later revealed, with the publication of the White Paper on the future of public spending in the autumn of 1963.[3]   But before that the British planners had tended to understate the probable rise in government expenditure in the 1960s, and therefore its contribution as an expansive force to the higher rate of growth which the plan was intended to achieve.   Even after the publication of the White Paper the planners in the NEDC still encountered difficulties in their work as a result of the secrecy of government departments: they complained in their interim report on the progress of the plan (1964)[4] that 'only the broadest indication is available about the make-up of civil public consumption'.   This is of course the key element in French economic planning— the one piece of the jigsaw puzzle which can be foreseen with reasonable confidence.   It is not that the planners require precise guarantees about the level of government spending in different fields for several years ahead.   But what they must have, if they are to do their work efficiently, is a clear assurance that they will always be privy to the best and most up-to-date estimate of the future which the government itself can make at any moment of time.

There was another interesting wrangle about the structure of the NEDC involving the trade unions and the Government which has permanently marked the organization.   Its constitution, as originally proposed by the Government, would have contained a powerful contingent of independent members; but the Trades Union Congress vigorously resisted the suggestion

---

[2] Under the Labour Government, the Secretary of State for Economic Affairs.
[3] See above, p. 90.
[4] *The Growth of the Economy*, p. 102.

and made it clear, at a moment when their co-operation in the whole planning venture still hung in the balance,[5] that in their view the Council must either be a small, tightly knit body of powerful men representing the major interest groups in the country, or it was not worth having at all.[6] The TUC won their main point; the NEDC's role was designed, in effect, to be that of a second parliament with a corporatist character—and because of that character, expected to be able to conclude binding agreements between major interest groups of a type which a traditional British parliament could not compass.[7] However, the trade unions were not allowed to have their way completely. Some vestigial spirit of independence was preserved in the structure of the Council. First of all, two of the twenty members were to be appointed on the strength of their personal merits alone, without representing anyone. Secondly, and potentially more important, the industrialists appointed to the Council did not come in as representatives of collective business interests; they were chosen as persons of recognized ability responsible for the management of large business firms. Such men were plainly not going to regard it as their task to reflect the average businessman's point of view. Indeed, almost as soon as the NEDC held its first meeting in 1962, the trade union members were complaining (privately) that the employers sitting on the Council were altogether too experimental and bold in the ideas which they

[5] Mr Frank Cousins, the powerful General Secretary of the Transport and General Workers' Union, the largest union in Britain, was initially opposed to any form of collaboration.

[6] The TUC's letter replying to the invitation from Mr Selwyn Lloyd, the Chancellor of the Exchequer, said truculently, after putting the argument for a small representative body: 'This constitutes a convincing case against including in it persons appointed as individuals who would be responsible only to you or to themselves' (*Financial Times*, 20 Nov. 1961).

[7] There is a long established TUC doctrine of government by representative bargaining groups, negotiating behind closed doors and then presenting the result to be rubber-stamped by parliament, of which Ernest Bevin was a particularly forthright exponent. It was the subject of a celebrated parliamentary altercation in 1944 between him, as Minister of Labour, and Aneurin Bevan over a government order which had been issued (Order 1305) imposing heavy penalties on anyone organizing an unofficial strike. Mr Bevan argued that the content of the order should have been the subject of parliamentary debate, instead of being worked out in a series of private meetings between the TUC and employers' organizations and then presented as a *fait accompli*. One passage from Bevin's long, spirited, and somewhat puzzled reply to the criticism that what he had done was 'an affront to parliament', is worth quoting because of its overt allusion to the view of government as being essentially an extension of collective bargaining. 'What was Order 1305?' he said. 'Order 1305 was virtually a collective agreement, given the clothing of law in a Regulation.' He went on somewhat menacingly: 'This House can reject this Regulation today, and that is the answer to any understanding with the TUC' (HC Deb., 28 Apr. 1944, col. 1125). The status of the trade union as a closed 'corporation' was to be reinforced by the Order, for as Bevin explained, trade union members were to be free to urge people to come out on strike within the privileged context of a recognised trade union meeting. But anyone doing it outside—or anyone doing it at all, if he was not a member of a trade union—was made liable to five years' imprisonment.

put forward: these men, they said, were quite 'unrepresentative'—as the trade unionists knew better than anyone from their own contacts with the average British employer.

The TUC's view was accepted by the Labour Government when it undertook the reform of NEDC towards the end of 1964: it was decided that the industrialists on the Council would henceforth be the formal representatives of the major employers' organizations. But meanwhile NEDC's whole function had been curtailed, in a manner which was certainly not in line with TUC thinking. The planning staff of NEDC was lifted bodily out of it and put inside the government machine, in the new Department of Economic Affairs—in theory at least the senior department concerned with British economic policy, standing above the Treasury.[8] What was left of the central Council—as opposed to the series of Economic Development Committees, charged with the function of planning in individual industries—was viewed as being very largely an adjunct to the Labour Government's drive for an 'incomes policy', which was supposed to keep British costs down, while economic expansion went forward. It was central to Labour Party thinking that a government of the Left should assume full responsibility for the task of national planning. If the main residual purpose of NEDC was to help in the pursuit of an 'incomes policy', then the exercise clearly required the formal representation of the collective view of the employers, as a tactical device for exerting immediate moral pressure on the individual firm.

However, for a programme of strategic change in the industrial structure of Britain, something quite different was needed, something which must depend ultimately on the leadership of a selected minority of advanced firms, rather than on the representation of the average firm. The use of planning as a means of shifting the balance of national economic policy in favour of the firm or the managerial practice which is in advance of the average has already been discussed. There is a further issue of principle involved in this struggle between the 'representative' and the 'independent' in the British plan. In asking initially for many more independent members of the NEDC, the Government was no doubt moved by the hope that these people would achieve a quasi-judicial standing and that their recommendations on economic policy, even if unpopular, would have a compelling moral force, like those of judges handing down the law. This idea of bringing in a species of economic judiciary, to supplement the efforts of an executive in need of wider support for its policies, was a familiar one. It lay behind the establishment of the 'Council on Prices, Productivity and Incomes' in 1957—the so-called 'Cohen Council', after Lord Justice Cohen, its first chairman—which was supposed to provide the country with *ex cathedra* judgements on the permissible increase in wages, the likely trend of costs and prices and so on. This had

---

[8] This was reflected in the fact that the minister at the head of the Department of Economic Affairs, Mr. George Brown, was also the Deputy Prime Minister.

not been a success. People kept noticing the unstated political assumptions staring through the cracks in the façade of expert economic argument.

There followed the abortive experiment in 1962 with the National Incomes Commission, a body which was supposed to subject each wage agreement, as it was made, to impartial scrutiny, and to issue reasoned warning judgements on any which were likely to produce inflationary consequences. The TUC refused to have any truck with this body. With the advent of the Labour Government two years later, a further attempt was made, of a rather more sophisticated character than its predecessors, to impart a certain judicial element into the process of wage and price determination through a new body called the National Board for Prices and Incomes. This was intended to be the centrepiece of Labour's 'incomes policy'. It was an advance in sophistication on the earlier experiments in the sense that all incomes were explicitly to be taken into account by the Board, not wages in isolation. The level of profits would be subject to an automatic check when there was any out of the way movement of prices—in the same way as wages would be checked each time that there was a settlement of an unusually large trade union claim. Significantly, the first chairman of the Board, Mr. Aubrey Jones, insisted that its strictly judicial role was only one part of a much larger complex of activities, which included bargaining with interest groups.[9] To symbolize the fact that this was a judicial process organically related to interest group bargaining, the chairman of the National Board for Prices and Incomes was made a permanent member of the Council of NEDC.

The Role of the Expert

Going back over the story, one can see that the TUC's original insistence on the need for the explicit representation of differing interests in NEDC, when it was set up in 1962, was partly prompted by its experience of the earlier judicial fiasco of the Cohen Council.[10] But there was also, underlying the TUC's whole attitude, a certain easy contempt for the role of the expert in the field of economic planning. One of the leading trade unionists on the NEDC once described the activities of the professional staff in the Office— out of their hearing—as 'lad's work'. The phrase aptly describes this type of approach to planning. Its essence is seen as a bargain between interest groups; that is given a formal shape in terms of national economic policy and

---

[9] The task, he said, was 'partly judicial, partly diplomatic, partly administrative, very political and partly public relations' (*Financial Times*, 18 Mar. 1965). As if to mark the intention to take the subject of wages and prices outside the domain of party politics, the first chairman of the Board chosen by a Labour Government was a Conservative MP. Mr Jones resigned his seat in Parliament, but continued as a member of the Conservative Party.

[10] Consistently with this position, it rejected the purely judicial body, the National Incomes Commission, set up by the Conservative Government to pass judgement on the merits of wage agreements between employers and trade unions.

occasionally tidied up by the professional staff. Their work is necessary of course, but it is not anything which requires subtlety or maturity or qualities of judgement; it could be done by almost anyone with the right training and a certain amount of application. Plainly, you do not take much notice of the views of people like this, nor do you conceive of them as having any initiatives in the execution of policy.

There could hardly be a more complete antithesis to the role of the professional planner as practised under the French system. The chief reason why the presence of a strong contingent of independent members on the Council of NEDC would have been important is not that they would have added a judicial tone to the proceedings, but that since they might well have included a number of experts, they could have helped to reinforce the position of the professionals in the National Economic Development Office. In that case the tendency would have been for NEDO and NEDC to treat one another more nearly as equals, instead of as servant and master. What with the Conservative Government's willingness to be fobbed off with a couple of judicial types and the trade unions' insistence on pure representative types, the professional planners were turned into slightly depressed types. Symbolic mark of their status—they were not allowed to express any views of their own on any aspect of planning, independently of their masters. This was another point on which the trade unions insisted when they joined the NEDC and the Government was only too ready to agree. As a result the rule was laid down that no document would be published by the Office without the prior approval of the Council.[11] The further consequence was that the lobbying for policies of long-term growth by the British planners had to be done in secret. There was no public forum in which they could draw attention to their view of the long-term interests of the nation, in the course of the inevitable conflicts with the short-term imperatives which are all too readily accepted by governments in moments of economic or political stress.

Emphasis on the Short Term

Having designed the basic machinery of British planning in such a way as to concentrate all the power and most of the activity on the Council chamber of the NEDC, the whole exercise from 1962 to 1964 was given a characteristic bias. The impressive staff of professional economists, assembled under the Director-General, Sir Robert Shone, struggled manfully

---

[11] The degree of commitment of the Council to any particular document was indicated for the cognoscenti by the subtle variation of phrase in the introduction. Thus in the case of the report on *Export Trends* (1963), the Council 'considered that the survey should be made more widely available and asked the Director General to arrange for publication', while for *Growth of the United Kingdom Economy to 1966*, also published in 1963, the report was 'amended in the light of the Council's discussions . . .', after which the Council 'authorised' its publication.

with the analysis of the long-term problems of British economic development, which had been too long neglected; but the work which was given first priority was the rapid processing of material and the preparation of papers required for the monthly meetings of the Council. Naturally enough, the practical men who represented the major interest groups on the Council wanted to concentrate on what they judged to be urgent practical matters. That was true of no one more than of the ministers who were there to assert the interests of the Government. Their chief concern during the 1963-4 phase of the business cycle (moving out of the trough of a recession into a boom) and of the political cycle (approaching a general election) was with finding a method which would limit the rise in wage costs and prices, in the face of the usual upward pressure generated by a rapid expansion of the economy. Thus a large part of the intellectual resources of the NEDC, at a moment when they had only just been assembled and were still grappling with the novel and uncertain techniques of long-term planning, was flung wholesale into the task of securing a bargain on an 'incomes policy'.

This was a large problem with ramifications throughout the economy, involving such issues as the trend of retail prices, the probable rise in productivity, and the future costs of raw materials. Of course, what the Conservative Government was after was not a fundamental solution of the problem of keeping wages and productivity moving in unison, but a short-term arrangement which would prevent them from getting too far out of step during the year or two ahead. It is arguable that these discussions in NEDC did play a part in moderating the wage demands made by the trade unions during 1963-4. But what is certain is that the operation resulted in a diversion of the British long-term planning effort from important workaday tasks at a crucial moment when this delicate and complex exercise was undergoing its first trial.[12]

Weak Industrial Nexus

This concentration of NEDC on Council business also slowed down the development of part of the essential substructure of economic planning—the Economic Development Committees, the so-called 'little Neddies'. Much

---

[12] The comment of a leading article in the *Financial Times*, 7 Jan. 1964, 'Neddy in Difficulties', aptly expressed the point: 'The Chancellor has let it be known that he wants Neddy to produce, not just long-term plans, but a short-term agreement to be put into practice which would tide the economy over the next year or eighteen months without serious inflation . . . . Planning, in other words, is slipping away from being a matter of coordinating investment decisions into trying what has never before been achieved—synthesizing, in a capitalist economy, a 'fair' distribution of returns between capital and labour . . . . Neddy was to be the meeting ground for labour leaders and businessmen in an atmosphere devoid of the usual conflict, for the consideration of the needs of economic progress and for ways of removing blocks to this progress . . . . Putting on Neddy, as the Chancellor seems to be doing, a great deal of responsibility without any power could permanently damage its prospects.'

of the important work, especially in keeping the detailed operation of the plan flexible in the face of changing conditions, must depend on these committees which have responsibility for individual trades and industries. That at any rate has been the French experience. Effective planning in France, it is believed by its practitioners there, has been based on a continuing dialogue between the professional economists at the centre (with their emphasis on *cohérence* and the overall view) and the people in the *commissions de modernisation*; the latter know the practical detail of what is happening and can offer an expert judgement on the future performance which is feasible or probable. They provide a vital corrective to some of the broad simplifications used by the central planners to build up their model of the economy and to project a trend four or five years forward.

Forecasting the output available and the demands to be met industry by industry at some future moment of time, by the techniques of input-output analysis, relies heavily on the assumption of no change in many economic relationships. Thus, for example, the investment programme will be worked out on the basis of certain fixed ratios—fixed as a result of experience—of the amount of extra capital required to achieve a given increase in various kinds of production. But in practice, of course, these capital-output ratios are being modified all the time, as a result of changes in technology, changes in the quality of products, changes in the efficiency of management. The assumption of stability in the relationship between capital and output is a useful working hypothesis, which may not be too seriously out, taking the economy as a whole, over a period of four or five years. But, of course, it could be very wide of the mark in individual industries, and some of these might be crucial to whole sectors of production on which the fulfilment of the plan depends. It is frequently not possible to do more in such matters as this than make a judgement of *trend*—a qualitative judgement by men inside an industry with direct, up-to-date experience of what is happening there, which the planner then translates as best he can into a quantitative expression.

If the professional planners had had the initiative in Britain, as they had in France, they would no doubt have treated the creation of the Economic Development Committees as an urgent priority. These were, after all, to be their main partners in the operation. Their importance as an instrument of planning was likely, if anything, to be greater even than in France, since the British system deliberately kept the planners outside the ambit of the government machine.[13] Their influence on the government machine had to be exercised at arm's length, whereas inside the Committees the set-up allows for

[13] Neither the British nor the French planners have direct executive power. But the French were from the beginning part of the normal civil service machine, formally under the control of the Ministry of Finance, until 1962, and then the Prime Minister's Office. The statistical and economic department, INSEE, which performs a great deal of the economic analysis required for the Plan, is a section of the Ministry of Finance, like the Economic Section of the British Treasury.

a more intimate give-and-take relationship with those responsible for ultimate industrial decisions. With luck, NEDO's position on the Committees, if it had been effectively exploited, would eventually have induced government departments to establish closer working relations with it. However, in the event, this vital development in the planning process went forward very slowly; the first Committees were not appointed until the spring of 1964, two years after the establishment of NEDC.[14] The delay meant that when the Labour Government came to reconsider the whole basis of British planning towards the end of 1964, the organic nexus between the NEDO planners and private industry, which might have provided the special contribution of this type of planning, and might therefore have made it seem worth while to retain the NEDC system at the centre of the operation, had barely begun to develop. There was a pronounced tendency to create the Committees in the Council's own image—with perhaps a few more independent members, but with the emphasis firmly on the representation of interest groups in the industry concerned. Under this scheme the individual official brought in to represent a government department with an interest in the industry concerned was likely to feel that he had a junior status in a bargaining act where others made the running.

Here the contrast with French practice is striking. The civil servants and independent members generally occupy leading positions on the *commissions*. In sheer numbers they account for nearly 50 per cent of the total membership.[15] The effective influence of the civil servants over the actual conduct of business in the *commissions* is even greater. They provide either the chairman or the vice-chairman for all twenty-seven of them, and usually also the rapporteur. The latter has a key function in guiding the work of the group; he also is chiefly responsible for interpreting the sense of their conclusions in the central planning exercise.[16] Of the 22 'vertical commissions'— i.e. those which are responsible for individual branches of production—16 have rapporteurs who are civil servants; among the remaining 6, 5 have

---

[14] By the end of 1964 nine committees, covering some 6m. workers out of a total working population of nearly 25 m., had been set up.

[15] See B. Cazes, OECD Internat. TU Seminar, *Final Report*, p. 7, who gives the total membership of the 27 *commissions* and supplementary working parties in 1963 as 3,138, divided as follows:

Trade unionists	281
Farmers	107
Heads of firms (including nationalized undertakings, craft trades, commerce, banking)	715
Employers' organization	562
Civil servants	781
Independent persons (universities, liberal professions, experts)	692
	3,138

[16] See Cazes, UN paper cited p. 123 above.

civil servants as chairmen. The *commission* for the steel industry is the only one in which the jobs of chairman or rapporteur or both are not held by government officials; and in this case the vice-chairman is one.[17]

This story of the early stage of British planning suggests certain analogies with the case of Sir Stafford Cripps's Development Councils in the late 1940s, analysed in Chapter VI.[18] There, too, the original intention was to achieve a close and effective two-way dialogue between private industry and the Government, with the progressive elements in the industry taking the lead in a new form of collective effort to raise standards. This was foreshadowed most promisingly in the efforts of the industrial Working Parties, whose reports fired the interest of the French planners during the Monnet period. But as soon as the attempt moved on from the stage of ideas to the creation of permanent institutions, the British obsession with representation—the anti-leadership principle—began to take over and rapidly ruined the whole project. Remove the government official, suppress the independent person, ensure that there is equality between firms with no advantage for the dynamic enterprise, and the canker of the average firm will attack almost any scheme with a wider vision or a longer perspective than whatever happens to be the currently conventional norm.

The Control of Economic Power

Perhaps the fundamental point is a matter of ideology. The British find some difficulty in mingling government authority with private economic power and making ready use of the amalgam. A Conservative Government, designing the machinery for planning in collaboration with a highly traditionalist trade union movement, instinctively put the main emphasis on the role of the representatives of organized private power and played down the function of the public authorities.[19] The latter were thrown in as a kind of adjunct,

---

[17] 1962 data. See Hackett, *Economic Planning*, App. III.

[18] See pp. 96–97.

[19] The extent to which the NEDC at this stage was seen as replacing the normal process of government is shown by an unofficial proposal in 1964, which was backed at the highest level in the TUC, for dealing with the balance of payments crisis by a species of private treaty with the employers. As part of a general bargain on economic policy, it was suggested that they should agree to organize the deferment of a certain proportion of industrial imports until the balance of payments improved. Deep in the spirit of the British trade union movement is the belief that the country's economic affairs would be much better run if the method of collective bargaining between the two sides of industry were spread over the whole field, and the Government retired into a corner and kept quiet. Mr. George Woodcock, General Secretary of the TUC, went so far as to complain (Business Economists' Group Conference, Oxford, Apr. 1963) that the Government was going beyond its proper function, in the context of the incomes policy, if it attempted to set limits to the wage bargain by means of an official forecast of the increase in the national product that would be available for distribution during the year ahead. The matter should be left to the trade unions and the employers' organizations.

an interest group with perhaps a slightly wider range than the others. Characteristically, the alternative form of organization undertaken by Labour represents a drastic reversal of the relationship between public and private power. There is apparently no middle way. With the Economic Division of NEDO removed and put squarely inside the Government, the NEDC organization becomes essentially a federation of Development Committees. The national plan no longer supplies the common substructure; the job of planning is being carried out behind closed doors elsewhere. Once again there is the danger that the British penchant for the separation of powers in economic policy-making may be carried to extremes, for if planning of industrial development is in fact conducted without the active collaboration of those with effective power in individual industries it is likely to prove a fumbling operation. I say more about the actual prospects at the end of the chapter.

To sum up, the style of British planning in this first phase focused attention on a dilemma about the proper role of government in a system of guided capitalism. There are two questions to be answered: Who is to do the guiding? And how firmly is it to be done? The 1962–4 experiment adopted an essentially corporatist device, shifting the locus of decision in national economic policy from parliament to another body in which the representatives of the country's major economic organizations deliberate in secret and bargain with one another. The term 'corporatist' is not to be understood in a pejorative sense. All planning of the modern capitalist type implies the acceptance of some measure of corporatism in political organization: that follows from basing the conduct of economic affairs on the deliberate decisions of organized groups of producers, instead of leaving the outcome to the clash between individual competitors in the market. It is, however, a matter for concern when the new corporatist organizations bypass the ordinary democratic process—neither throwing their own deliberations open to the public nor subjecting the bargains struck between the main centres of economic power to regular parliamentary scrutiny. After all, many of these bargains, which are sought precisely because of their long-term implications, will affect the life of the average person more than a lot of the legislation which parliament subjects to close and protracted scrutiny. It is this which has led some of the radical reformers in France, notably M. Mendès France,[20] to propose that a second legislative chamber, openly devoted to the representation of economic interest groups, should be set up to supplement the first chamber elected by universal suffrage.

British complacency on this matter is indeed remarkable. At a time when the French planners are trying deliberately to inflict more parliamentary

---

[20] See *La République moderne* (Paris, Gallimard, 1962), ch. 5. He is supported in this by M. Bloch-Lainé in *Pour une réforme de l'entreprise* (Paris, Du Seuil, 1963), p. 133.

control on themselves and French political reformers are searching for means of bringing the operation of planning within the ambit of the democratic process, the problem of securing systematic public supervision of the work of NEDC has not even been seriously debated.[21] If it were, it is possible to predict with fair assurance what the reactions of the various members of the NEDC would be. The trade unionists would angrily point out that as private voluntary bodies they were not used to having outsiders prying into their doings; and that they were not going to begin now. The employers' organizations would withdraw, without rancour and with dignity, complaining that if they were to be subjected to the popular gaze and ear, they could hardly be expected to say anything serious or worth while. And the government representatives would no doubt argue that any extra control was wholly redundant, since, as ministers, all their decisions were already subjected to the close supervision of parliament.

It comes as something of a shock to the British when the strong and growing element of corporatism in the management of their society is pointed out to them. After all, Britain is the country in which the grant to corporate bodies of special legal rights or powers, that are not available to the other persons banded together as private citizens, has been most stubbornly resisted. In continental Europe the notion of the privileged corporation has, by contrast, been carried straight over into modern capitalism from the guild system. It is noteworthy that the power of the guilds was smashed more thoroughly in Britain than anywhere else. How, then, could it be that corporatist methods of government should find a congenial soil in which to flourish here?

The answer is to be found in the combined effect of two traditional British doctrines applied in a new set of conditions. One is the doctrine of the spontaneous association of individuals free from any form of surveillance from the outside. The fact that such an association is powerful gives no one the right to pry into its affairs, so long as what it does is not unlawful. The other doctrine is the one which underlies the instinctive British objection to 'positive government', discussed in Chapter VI. It is that since governmental decisions in a democracy of the British type are simply the resultant of a series of pressures and counter-pressures among free associations of individuals, agreed action by communal organizations themselves is to be preferred to the exercise of governmental power. The Government's role is essentially that of a long-stop: if the game of politics is being properly played, the other players will ensure that it has very little to do. There are two reasons why such an approach to politics leads to a reinforcement of the powers of professional corporate managers in the conditions of modern

---

[21] See my two articles, 'Who Controls the Planners?' and 'The Planners and Whitehall'. *Listener*, 13 & 20 Dec. 1962.

capitalism. First, the older forms of association among relatively small groups of people in clubs or their equivalent are in practice superseded, wherever important matters are at stake, by bigger organizations, which take over simply because they are more effective. The intimate relationship between members and club secretary, or whomever they chose to represent them, has little relevance to a world in which functionaries are chosen for their ability to out-general the bosses of other big battalions. Secondly, the economic system leaves much wider scope for the exercise of power by persons wielding the delegated authority of collective bodies. The traditional forms of economic decision emerging out of an uncontrolled competitive struggle are increasingly replaced by deliberate agreements among the spokesmen of big businesses and organized interest groups.

The upshot is that the British, for all their anti-corporatist tradition, allow effective power to slide into the hands of the corporations without subjecting them to public control—for the national doctrine insists that they are no more than free associations of individuals whose activities are essential to the emergence of a consensus. Continental practice, on the other hand, though much more tolerant of the privileged corporate body sometimes armed with para-statal authority,[22] is also more insistent on public surveillance. Indeed, inspection is the condition for toleration. In France, for example, the activities of the professional organizations are subject to official scrutiny and control by the Conseil d'État. These organizations are seen by the French as an important part of the apparatus of power in a modern society; and it is assumed to be the function of public authority to exercise a regular check on what they are doing, to ensure not merely that it is lawful—a policeman could do that—but that it conforms with the 'general interest'. Once again, the notion of the *volonté générale* is relevant; and it is to be observed that it is the Conseil d'État—that curious amalgam of judicial and administrative powers—rather than the elected representatives in parliament, which is chosen as its guardian.

Instruments of Pressure

It remains to consider the actual instruments of pressure used to secure the fulfilment of the national economic plan in Britain and in France. Of Britain in the NEDC phase of planning little more needs to be said. The Government approached the problem in a deliberately disarmed state; this was intended to be a persuasive posture. No one was trying to impose anything on anyone; what was being offered was a forum in which people were invited to do a deal. Such an operation rests on the ability of those concerned to commit their organizations to the performance of certain acts agreed to in principle, and that in turn depends on the extent to which each of these

[22] e.g. to collect compulsory dues from members of an industrial association.

organizations co-ordinates its own activities. In this the Government could provide an important lead: the effort to centralize control over major economic decisions in the public sector, begun in the early 1960s,[23] was a significant factor, since publicly financed investment accounts for between two-fifths and half of the national total. The other parties to the bargaining in the NEDC (and most notably the trade unions) find it more difficult to commit those whom they represent.

Power is, in fact, greatly diffused in the trade unions, with a shop steward movement frequently acting, at factory floor level, directly contrary to the wishes of the official leaders. Then the individual unions themselves, numbering a total of 175,[24] feel only very loosely connected to anything which the leaders of the TUC may in their wisdom decide is a reasonable bargain for organized labour as a whole. Similar limitations apply to the employers' organizations—with the important practical difference that effective planning is less dependent on the unanimous assent of management. Where industrial ownership is so concentrated—180 enterprises employ one-third of the labour force engaged in manufacturing in Britain and are responsible for one-half of all factory investment[25]—the decisive factor is the active collaboration of a relatively small number of leading firms. Once this has been secured, the probability is that the rest will follow—either through the psychological effect of fashion set by big business or as a result of more direct economic pressures exercised by the big on the small.

The NEDC system depends ultimately on moral pressures. Each party offers something which is conditional on certain actions by the others. The government must put something into the pot along with the rest. It may, for instance, offer financial concessions in the budget, which will help to make the cost of living or profits or savings move in some desired direction.[26] But the government's room for manoeuvre is generally very restricted; often the very basis for a conditional bargain is missing. For the truth is that there is no natural place in the British system, as it has developed to date, for the contractual relationships between the government and individual private firms covering the objectives of the plan, which have from the beginning been a feature of French planning. Mr Harold Wilson promised, before he became Prime Minister, that the Labour Government would discriminate in its treatment of firms on the basis of their contribution towards fulfilling

---

[23] See above, p. 103. [24] As at 1 Jan. 1965.

[25] *Net* capital expenditure. See *Board of Trade Journal*, 8 Mar. 1963, for a detailed breakdown based on a 1958 survey. Investment decisions are especially highly concentrated in the biggest firms; 74 businesses with 10,000 or more employees were together responsible for 38 per cent of net capital expenditure in manufacturing.

[26] For example, the income tax concessions made by Mr Maudling, the Conservative Chancellor of the Exchequer, in the Budget of 1963 were part of a deliberate policy which was designed to induce the trade unions to accept a degree of wage restraint in a period of economic expansion. There is evidence that the discussions with the trade unions which he had had in NEDC played some part in his decision.

the aims of a national economic policy.[27] All that can be said is that any such action, if it were systematically pursued in the French style as an instrument of economic planning, would have to overcome a powerful contrary tradition in the British civil service. Planning by this method could not just be conveniently left to ministers making occasional political decisions; government officials would also be called upon to exercise their personal judgement from day to day in meting out unequal treatment to people with theoretically equal rights; and the officials would not like it.

In France, as we have seen, planning began with the exercise of public power in the private sector of the economy, and only later came to concern itself with the problems of moral suasion. Moreover, public power frequently had a discriminating character; indeed, discrimination has from the start been of the essence of French planning. Particular firms have been singled out and induced to serve the purposes of public policy. There have been two main instruments of persuasion, one fiscal and the other dependent on direct financial inducements. These will be considered in turn.

The prizes which can be offered by the *Fisc* are so attractive partly because the burden of French company taxation is, by international standards, unusually heavy. That is so at any rate if the comparison is made in terms of tax *rates*; we have already had an example[28] of the way in which the actual amount of tax charged may be reduced by changing the basis of assessment. But leaving that particular instrument of discrimination aside, the official text of the Fourth Plan enumerates eight major categories of tax relief which the economic planners can employ to obtain the co-operation of individual private enterprises.[29] Some of these are described as 'véritables "contrats fiscaux"', i.e. contractual arrangements with the tax authorities under which 'a specific advantage is accorded to an enterprise as a counterpart of a programme of investment which is judged to be of interest'.[30] Among the most powerful incentives that can be offered to a French company is the relief from distributed profits tax for a period of seven years on dividends from new share capital. This is given when the new capital has been issued to finance an approved investment project.[31] Undistributed profits tax—which may incidentally also be moderated for favoured firms— amounts to 50 per cent; and the tax on distributions is 24 per cent of the remainder.[32] There are a number of further taxes to be met, which are calculated to reduce the actual sum that would be received by a middle-class shareholder, married, with two children, to only 25·3 per cent of the gross

---

[27] Speech on economic policy, Swansea, 25 Jan. 1964. [28] p. 149 above.

[29] Out of a total of 15 different varieties of discriminatory tax concessions applicable to business enterprises (see *Projet de Loi*, Nov. 1961, pp. 245–6).

[30] Ibid. p. 53.

[31] It applies to dividends of up to 5 per cent (Decree of 1957).

[32] Since 1960, when it was increased to this level.

profit distributed.[33] Not surprisingly, the interest of investors on the Paris Bourse is very firmly fixed—even more so than elsewhere—on new issues of shares with a bonus element (especially shares eligible for tax relief) and on capital gains generally. Dividend yields on French shares are very low. All this makes the other tax concessions on ploughed-back profits, employed in support of the Plan (e.g. higher than normal depreciation allowances based on the accelerated amortization of new capital investment) that much more valuable.

The Management of Credit

Tax relief should not, however, be viewed on its own: it is part of a larger complex of financial arrangements which help to ensure that French investment keeps moving in the direction and in the volume required by the Plan. The control over the flow of capital into industry is exercised in various ways. Historically, public authority has always played a much larger part in French banking than it has in the Anglo-Saxon world. This is no surprise in view of the traditional relationship between public and private enterprise in France, described in Chapter V. But there was a further factor in this particular instance: the technical backwardness of ordinary French commercial banking. It was slower to develop the services which were readily provided for industry and commerce elsewhere. The gap had to be filled by the Bank of France, which was called upon to supply

---

[33] The calculation is derived from an unpublished paper by Professor Cotta (of Caen University) and is based on the tax liability of a shareholder with an annual income of 60,000 NF (about £4,400). The following table compares the net income from investment of Professor Cotta's shareholder in France and the United Kingdom.

Taxation of Dividend Income [a]

		Per cent of gross profits	
		France	UK
Gross company profits before tax		100	100
Net profits after payment of:			
in France	in UK		
i. company profits tax	profits tax	50	85
ii. distributed profits tax	income tax (7/9d. in £ =38¼ per cent)	38	46.25
iii. surtax (less special tax allowances)[b]	surtax [c]	25.9	46.25
iv. 'Surtax surcharge'[d]	—	25.3	—
Net dividend income		25.3	46.25

[a] 1963 tax rates.
[b] Surtax payable amounts to 45 per cent of the amount distributed (after deduction of company tax, i.e. 38 per cent) less rebates equal to 9 per cent of this amount.
[c] Married and children's allowances in a British family of this size cancel liability for surtax. In the case of a single person earning £4,400, surtax rate is 2s. in £, resulting in a net dividend income of 43·5 per cent.
[d] Compulsory subscription to the Fonds National de Solidarité, equivalent to 5 per cent of net surtax (i.e. surtax minus tax allowances).

industry and commerce with the small credits required for everyday business. In the 1890s the Government went so far as to impose on the Bank the obligation to discount all commercial bills down to an amount of five francs (the equivalent of four shillings) so long as they met normal financial standards.[34]

No doubt the ready assumption of responsibility for the provision of commercial credit by the central bank tended to encourage the ordinary banks to be lazy and to lean on it. Indeed, it was a matter of complaint by the authorities that the commercial banks were inclined to work on too low a margin of reserves, threatening the security of the whole credit system—because they took it for granted that, in case of need, they would always be able to fall back on the Bank of France. Whoever was responsible, the effect of the underdeveloped state of French commercial banking was to reinforce the tendency towards the concentration of power, in a public institution, over the nation's credit business.[35] There were other public and semi-public enterprises which played an increasingly important role in French banking, as time went on. In modern times they have fulfilled two major functions in the finance of commerce and industry. First, they have mobilized supplies of loanable funds, which might otherwise have remained inactive in a country where ordinary deposit banking did not take hold. Secondly, they have provided a convenient mechanism for converting very liquid savings, which depositors wished to be able to draw at a moment's notice, into medium and long-term loans. The guarantee of the state gave depositors the necessary sense of security.

The agency which best expresses these characteristic features of French banking—indeed of French institutions generally—is the Caisse des Dépôts et des Consignations. It is much the biggest bank in France. It dominates the bond market in the Paris stock exchange; it commands all the money accumulated in small savings in the post office and savings banks; and it administers the pension funds of nationalized undertakings and local authorities. In addition, it handles the financial surpluses of the co-operative societies,

[34] Clapham, *Econ. Dev. of France & Germany*, p. 388. Clapham remarks that this burden laid on the Bank of France—to provide cash on demand for the whole of French business—may help to explain its rigid and sometimes unhelpful attitude towards France's neighbours. In its international relations the Bank of France has a long-standing reputation of being awkward and on occasion aggressively unco-operative, e.g. during the early stages of the world currency crisis in the 1930s—a reputation which it continues to sustain in the 1960s. It tends instinctively to see itself as charged with the overriding duty of hoarding gold in the national interest.

[35] The result, in the 20th century, was that French business had the benefit of an especially favourable credit service for activities like exporting, which were deemed to be in the national interest. As late as January 1965 the British, in the midst of an export crisis, were struggling with the problem of how to provide the exporter with credit on advantageous terms, such as those commonly employed in France, where, as *The Economist* pointed out, "export paper can be discounted at the Banque de France at a rate ½ per cent below the normal discount rate" (9 Jan. 1965, p. 141).

and it also receives on compulsory deposit any sums of money, notably inheritances, which are the subject of litigation. This enormous financial *masse de manoeuvre* has been built up and added to over a period of 150 years. But the essential structure of the institution and its basic idea, of mobilizing and concentrating all spare savings, however temporary, for profitable use in line with public policy, is a Napoleonic one—though the Caisse actually came into being in 1816, after Napoleon himself had departed to St Helena.

During the nineteenth and early twentieth centuries the role of the Caisse may be regarded as having been largely to offset some of the disadvantages caused by the relative backwardness of the French private banking system. Not until after the Second World War, when the French planners found this powerful instrument, so to say, lying around, was it systematically employed as part of a co-ordinated national economic policy. There is no legal compulsion on the Caisse to obey any political directives emanating from the Government; its 'independence' in the management of its funds is guaranteed and is as important to its clients as the Government's guarantee of their deposits. But as the Government's own banker, with its top manager and his deputy appointed by the state, it has a strong incentive to collaborate closely with those responsible for official economic policy.[36] It is also relevant that the president of the Caisse during the 1950s and early 1960s, M. Bloch-Lainé, was a senior official of the Ministry of Finance, who, as head of the Treasury, had played a major part in the early development of French planning.

It has become the regular practice at the start of each financial year for the three main sources of public funds—the Treasury, the FDES (Fonds de Développement Économique et Social),[37] and the Caisse—to divide up by agreement among themselves the financial responsibility for the large items of investment in the Plan. Choosing whether to put some project into the budget or to use the publicly financed Development Fund or whether it is wisest to bypass parliamentary scrutiny by employing the Caisse is often a delicate political decision. The Caisse is also an important factor in the private capital market; it may, for example, provide what amounts to underwriting support for a new issue of industrial bonds, by taking up any shares which are not immediately subscribed by the public. Although it is the Treasury which controls access to the stock market for approved investment

---

[36] The Caisse in its official history of the period 1950–60 described its two different functions as a long-term lender in the following terms: '. . . les placements sur le marché financier que la Caisse effectue avec la préoccupation exclusive de bien répartir ses risques et de faire fructifier le plus possible ses capitaux; les prêts et les participations, non négociables en Bourse, qui constituent la part la plus importante de ses interventions et pour lesquels le souci de favoriser l'expansion économique ou de satisfaire des besoins sociaux prime la recherche de rendement' (Caisse des Dépôts, *Dix années d'activité, 1950–60*, pp. 19–20).　　　　[37] See above, pp. 129–30.

schemes, the support of the Caisse means that a bond issue has a high chance of success. Finally, it helps to provide medium-term finance (i.e. up to five years) for industrial ventures approved by the Plan, through its regular purchase of bank bills from the Crédit National.

Most of the approved medium-term finance passes through the Crédit National, another important semi-public bank which has served as an instrument of French planning. Its original function, when it was founded after the First World War, was to finance postwar reconstruction in industry; it had the same task again after the Second World War, acting as the agent for the FDES. In addition it runs an ordinary commercial business in longer-term bank loans—now much the more important part of its activities. Gradually it has established itself as the key institution for the provision of medium-term finance for industry, again through one of those typically French devices for centralizing some economic activity—by licensing it. The Crédit National became in effect the authority responsible for issuing the licences. It did this by going into the business of rediscounting bank bills issued on a short-term basis to finance the requirements of industry. The Crédit National provided the instrument for converting very short-term finance, in the form of commercial bank bills, into loans which could be used for industrial investment. The French seem to be greatly impressed by the magic act of '*transformation*', by which short-term, excessively liquid savings are turned into solid industrial capital; the matter is discussed seriously and at length as if the postwar use of this device somehow constituted a significant technical break-through.[38] It is no more than a building society, for example, does everywhere else in the ordinary course of business. In France as we have already noticed the high liquidity preference of ordinary savers presented an extra problem. Its solution required the aid of some kind of public authority wielding the state's guarantee. The relevant guarantee in this case is the promise by the Banque de France that it will discount any bank bills coming to it from the Crédit National. It is willing to make this promise, however, only because the Crédit itself never takes over any medium-term financing from the other banks without prior consultation on each case with the Banque de France. And the Banque de France in turn depends on the advice of the Commissariat du Plan which examines the investment projects individually. In fact, French firms have learnt that it is not worth putting up a scheme for a loan of any size to their bank without clearing it first with the Commissariat.[39]

---

[38] See, for example, the report of the Comité Lorain, which enquired into the future of the French financial system (*Rapport présenté au Ministre des Finances et des Affaires Economiques par le Comité chargé d'étudier le financement des investissements*, May 1963).

[39] The minimum figure for a medium-term loan requiring approval by the Plan is 1 million francs, and for a long-term loan 2½ million francs. The Crédit National in its official leaflet explaining its procedures to industrial clients who are after loans,

The bank for its part goes to the Crédit National right at the start, as soon as its client asks for the loan, and puts the hypothetical question: Would the Crédit be prepared, in case of need, to take over the proposed credit to its client? It is then, at this early stage, that the project is placed before the Banque de France and the officials of the Plan. If it is approved, the word passes down the line back to the commercial bank, which proceeds to issue an ordinary three-month credit to its client—but with a clear understanding that the loan will be extended, in one way or another, for a period of up to five years. The bank itself may hold on to the credit for a while, in a series of three-monthly renewals, until it wants some more cash, when it turns it over to the Crédit National. It is ideally liquid financial paper. From the client's point of view it is indistinguishable from a straight five-year loan; for the bank it is a quick asset realisable at short notice, which counts as part of the minimum liquidity ratio that it is legally obliged to maintain.[40]

The Commissariat du Plan intervenes at three different points in the capital market where it influences the flow of funds into particular forms of investment. First of all, any new issue of industrial bonds requires the permission of the Treasury, which is given on the advice of the Commissariat; the latter also has to be consulted on any issue of ordinary shares if it is to qualify for dividend tax relief.[41] Secondly, medium-term bank credits (of 1 million francs or more) passing through the channel of the Crédit National will be looked at by the Commissariat before being approved for rediscount by the Banque de France. Thirdly, long-term bank loans which go through the Crédit National are passed directly to the Commissariat for vetting. Most of the large firms will be caught under the first heading, and the smaller ones under the second and third.[42] It is worth noting, incidentally, that the

---

tells them to go direct to the planners and get their support: '. . . à partir de 2,500,000 f. l'accord du Commissariat au Plan est nécessaire et les demandeurs ont intérêt à prendre contact, aussitôt après le Crédit National, avec cet organisme'.

[40] See J. S. G. Wilson in R. S. Sayers, ed., *Banking in Western Europe* (London, OUP, 1962); also official documents of Crédit National, in particular a paper by its Director, M. Maurice Lauré, entitled 'Le financement des investissements industriels et commerciaux par le crédit à long et moyen terme' (June 1962).

[41] See above, p. 165.

[42] There is another semi-public bank, the Caisse des Marchés de l'État, which looks after smaller loans to business and the important joint credits extended to groups of firms in certain industries. It also discounts its paper through the channel of the Crédit National, so that its activities too are ultimately subject to the inspection of the Commissariat. Lauré gives the following estimate of the way in which private industrial and commercial investment in France was financed in 1961 (in billions of old francs). The total amounted to some 2,000, of which 1,400 was supplied by the companies themselves. Of the 600 remaining, 400 was in the form of long-term capital supplied from three sources: new issues through the stock market (200), the Crédit National (100), miscellaneous, including Caisse des Dépôts, etc. (100). The last 200 was medium-term finance, which all passed through the channel of the Crédit National.

postwar nationalization of the major French banks,[43] which it is sometimes suggested was a key factor in the development of economic planning, has no relevance whatsoever to the tight control established by the Government over the French credit system. The fact is that the banks after nationalization were run by the same type of manager, and on exactly the same commercial principles as before. The authorities seemed to go out of their way to demonstrate that there had been no change. It was not public ownership but the traditional 'mixed enterprise', the fertile fusion of public and private power, which was used to take charge of the capital market. The instruments for guiding investment were there already, waiting to be used; all that the planners had to do was to pick them up and wield them in unison.

Why they succeeded in doing just this after the Second World War is a question which does not lend itself to an easy answer. Various explanations have been offered—the personalities of those involved;[44] the advent of a new generation of younger men to positions of power after the war at about the same time both in the public service and in large-scale private enterprise; the common background of education and ideas of these men, not only those drawn from the traditional *Grandes Écoles* but also the products of the new École Nationale d'Administration established after the war.[45] No doubt these things all contributed to the result. But it seems reasonable to put the question the other way about—to ask why it was that France, equipped as it was, did not achieve an effective centralized control over economic policy earlier. The odds have been in favour of it ever since Napoleon I. The coincidence of a few propitious circumstances, some of them technological (as suggested in Chapter V), made the favourable odds heavier.

Uncertain British Formula

One question which is prompted by this inventory of the powerful and varied armament at the disposal of the French planners is whether the British planning effort undertaken in the early 1960s, unarmed and with a

---

[43] The big four consisting of Crédit Lyonnais, Société Générale, Comptoir National d'Escompte, Banque Nationale pour le Commerce et l'Industrie. Their combined deposits amount to nearly 60 per cent of the total deposits in the French commercial banking system (see H. W. Auburn, ed., *Comparative Banking* (London, Waterlow, 1963), p. 54, 1961 figures).

[44] Besides men like M. Bloch-Lainé, first at the Treasury, then at the Caisse; there was also e.g. M. Baumgartner, who was head of the Crédit National during the period when it developed its new techniques for the finance of medium-term industrial investment, before he became governor of the Banque de France.

[45] It is interesting to recall that the ENA's idea of the professional administrator, who was not a specialist in anything but the art of administration, was inspired in part by the British model of the all-rounder in the administrative class of the civil service. The training applied to achieve the same result was remarkably gallicized in the process of transfer; the ENA is one of the important achievements of the French era of intense self-questioning and reform during the mid-1940s (see Brian Chapman. *The Profession of Government* (Allen & Unwin, 1959, ch. 2, esp. p. 82).

strong doctrinal devotion to disarmament, ever stood a chance of succeeding. Certainly some of the expectations which surrounded the birth of NEDC— for example that the mere psychological effect of setting national targets and obtaining a commitment from various industrial interest groups to their fulfilment would put an end once and for all to 'stop-go' economic policies— never had much more than mystical substance. On the other hand, the first British plan, viewed as a means of raising the average rate of economic growth and reducing the size of the fluctuations from year to year around this higher average, did represent a significant advance on what had gone before. Above all, there was the political effect of bringing into the centre of national life an agency whose job it was constantly to draw attention to the long-term aspects of economic policy.

It is something gained when a nation gets into the habit of thinking about its problems in a five or ten-year perspective, and doing so systematically. Already in the short time since the start of planning one can see the habit growing, in a variety of different fields—motor traffic, manpower and education, land use and regional development. It would be wrong, of course, to regard all these as the consequence of the NEDC; the truth is rather that the NEDC was itself one among several expressions of a new mood about the proper time perspective and range of deliberate decision in national policy.

The important contribution of NEDC was that it provided a single focus for efforts which might otherwise have remained only loosely, if at all, connected.[46] Above all, it served to establish a common intellectual base for the decisions made in the public and the private sectors. The effect of better communication on problems requiring joint action by independent centres of power, and of more systematic analysis of the problems themselves, is that the typical bottlenecks which are a recurrent feature of a full employment society are likely to be identified earlier. Again, the habit of looking for them, and then taking them seriously enough to do something about them, should make the process of economic growth smoother.

The benefits enumerated so far are essentially of an intellectual order. In a society in which the techniques of achieving a consensus are well developed—and Britain is outstandingly such a society—they are likely to have greater practical significance than they would possess elsewhere. But planning also involves a more extensive use of public power. Here the main advance in Britain to date is the effort undertaken during the early 1960s to co-ordinate the variegated activity of the public sector. This represents a large and little used economic armoury, especially in the field of investment,

[46] A number of important initiatives which were later absorbed into national politics originated or were developed in the NEDC, e.g. the schemes for improved industrial and management training, for a more radical approach to regional development in areas of high unemployment, and for a special redundancy fund to provide extra cash payments for workers thrown out of work as a result of technological change in their industry.

directed flexibly by strategists who have succeeded in bringing the main elements under a single effective command, its influence on the shape of the economy could be profound. That is why the remodelling of government administration with this end in view, reflected first in the reform of the Treasury in 1962, and subsequently in the creation of the Department of Economic Affairs by the Labour Government, is likely to prove of more lasting importance than the NEDC experiment.

However, the crucial issue in modern capitalist planning, which is the relationship between public power and private enterprise, remains open and undecided in the British case. The initial formula for NEDC was the product of an amalgam of motives, many of them having little to do with long-term planning. It is known that the Labour Government at one stage, just after it had taken office, contemplated abolishing NEDC altogether and making a fresh start. Once it had been decided to take the economic planning function fully inside the Government, the NEDC lost the greater part of its original *raison d'être*. It was retained very largely in order to provide a framework for the specialized industrial committees, the 'little Neddies', for which the traditional Whitehall structure could not provide a convenient niche.[47]

The danger which British planning faced at this stage was that the Government, which had in the early 1960s come a little way out of its shell, in the hope of securing a new form of collaboration with organized interest groups, would, now that the opportunity presented itself, retreat all the way back again. That was certainly the instinct of the civil servants who ran the government machine. The whole arrangement associated with an active interventionist relationship between officials in the public sector and private business is, as we have seen, profoundly alien to the spirit of the British civil service. The latter has a particular distaste for the job of discriminating between individual businessmen, handing out either rewards or penalties, with some long-range objective of economic policy in view. There are signs however that the Labour Government may have found more willing instruments for a discriminatory planning policy among the temporary officials, notably the businessmen, whom it has brought in to man some of the new positions in the Department of Economic Affairs. The key appointment is that of Chief Industrial Adviser to the Department of Economic Affairs, which has been filled by the managing director of one of the leading manufacturing firms in the country, lent to the government for a period of two

---

[47] A further consideration was that the NEDC was popular with the leaders of the big trade unions; the TUC wanted the institution to be retained. It is noticeable that employers wielding considerable power sit on the individual Economic Development Committees, and are able to make important collective decisions there. Persons of comparable stature in the trade union movement are to be found almost exclusively in the central Council of NEDC. A similar weakness of the French trade union representation on the *commissions de modernisation* can be observed (see p. 159).

years by his company.[48] His main task has been to organize the official side of the still embryonic industrial planning bodies, the Economic Development Committees ('little Neddies'), in which the higher management of the private sector, the trade unions and the public sector are supposed to coalesce in the conduct of a new and more far-sighted act of policy-making. In fact, as we have seen, the original structure of these committees emerging from the first phase of NEDC planning, tended to place the public official sitting on them in a distinctly junior role. Their main function was conceived as being to provide yet another forum for bargaining between employer and employee interest groups.

The characteristic feature of the Labour Government's approach, marking a sharp divergence from its predecessor, has been to shift the centre of gravity of the whole operation towards the public official, charged with the task of pressing the Government's point of view, and away from the bargaining between interest groups. Economic planning is recognized as something which depends on an act of leadership by the public sector. In consonance with this view—sharply at variance with the Selwyn Lloyd–Maudling doctrine of the role of the public sector in the planning operation as that of a 'third man'—the Department of Economic Affairs has, during the first phase of its experiment in long-range planning, set out deliberately to mobilize the available sources of public power, in order to exercise pressure on the 'little Neddies'. The official representation on these bodies has been strengthened; both the NEDC men and the officials from the appropriate department of government concerned with the industry in question have been organized into what is potentially an aggressive instrument of government long-range policies.

The approach moved Britain distinctly closer to the French conception of planning: its characteristic features were a new readiness to use something more than moral pressure against the recalcitrant industry which failed to act in accordance with the national plan, and to enter into private treaties with individual firms, foreign as well as British, whose investment policy could in this way be shaped to serve the plan.[49] The new thinking on long-range industrial policy was not simply a reflection of Labour ideology. It

---

[48] Mr Fred Catherwood, managing director of British Aluminium. His salary has continued to be paid by his company while he is in official employment.

[49] Typical of the changed mood was the proposal of the Machine Tool Industry Economic Development Committee, with the assent of the government representatives sitting on the Committee, that a government body should pick out machines of advanced design, place contracts for their manufacture, and then have them installed in suitable factories on trial production runs (NEDC Press Release, 10 June 1965). The whole scheme involved the use of public power in a novel fashion. The Minister of Technology, Mr Frank Cousins, told Parliament (14 June 1965) that the Government was prepared to order ' pre-production models ' of machine tools for 'approved new types'. He added that the Government was considering a further use of its incidental power as a customer; this was to stipulate particular methods of production for its industrial contracts, with the deliberate aim of encouraging advanced manufacturing techniques.

owed at least as much to the views of the new generation of radical industrialists—people who were in the main out of sympathy with traditional socialist ideas on nationalization, but who shared none of the traditional prejudice of the right wing in politics against the active use of public power to reshape the private sector of the economy.

It would be wrong, however, to conclude that the historic obstacles to the energetic deployment of the full range of public power in the service of planning in Britain have been finally overcome. The verdict must be left at least half open. The change in the style of economic policy in the mid-1960s is at least in part the expression of special circumstances—the appearance of a new Department of Economic Affairs manned by a lot of outsiders, many of them academic economists with no attachment to the tradition of the permanent civil service, some of them businessmen whose salaries are actually paid by their firms while they are on temporary leave of absence in the service of the state, with an exceptionally powerful politician in charge of the outfit, who also happens to be Deputy Prime Minister. This makes a formidable combination. But it is impossible to say at this stage how enduring the consequence of this fortuitous coalescence between political power and unconventional administrative method is likely to be. One essential element in the outcome is the issue of the struggle between an old and a new civil service style. The old remains very powerful and very entrenched; the exponents of the new are still comparatively few in number, and mostly temporary.

IX

VARIETIES OF EUROPEAN EXPERIENCE

1. The State as Entrepreneur: Italy and Austria

The French and the British approaches to economic planning illustrate two major themes in the development of modern managed capitalism. The present chapter will be concerned with some of the variations on them which have emerged elsewhere in Western Europe. These variations have been selected not on any systematic basis but as examples of different methods of tackling a problem, which serve to throw additional light on the underlying process. The social objectives of the countries concerned are broadly similar to those of Britain and France; and there is no overwhelming devotion to a market ideology which might get in the way of using the instruments of public authority to secure the two aims of postwar economic policy—accelerating long-term economic growth and controlling business fluctuations. (The 'market ideology countries' will be the subject of part III.) Two cases in particular are singled out for closer examination. They are Italy and Sweden, which in a sense stand at two opposite ends of the West European spectrum— Italy, the poorest in income per capita of the industrial nations of Western Europe, Sweden the richest. The chief problem for the Italians has been how to create enough new jobs to absorb their unemployed; for the Swedes how to manage their limited supply of labour so that each person capable of being employed will make the maximum feasible contribution towards increasing the national wealth.

Excepting the period of the 1963–4 balance of payments crisis, Italy has consistently had one of the highest rates of growth of any industrial country in the postwar period. Its GNP doubled during the twelve years 1950–62.[1] Outside Europe this rate of growth, averaging slightly over 6 per cent a year, has been surpassed by only one other capitalist country, Japan. Inside Europe, West Germany expanded faster over the period as a whole, but this was due to an exceptionally fast increase in production in the early 1950s, during the stage of repair and reconstruction of war-damaged industry; later on the Italian rate of growth was somewhat higher. There are some obvious special factors, peculiar to Italy, which have played a large part in this achievement. First, clearly, was the existence of a plentiful supply of labour to meet the rising needs of industry and the service trades. Secondly, the Italians derived some benefit from their relative technical backwardness

---

[1] OECD, *Statistics of National Accounts 1950–61* and *Monthly Statistical Bulletins*.

at the start:[2] a given amount of investment in the most up-to-date equipment would tend to induce a bigger improvement in the average level of productivity there than it would if it were applied to a more advanced economy. Thirdly, low wages after the war, improving during the 1950s but at a rate slower than the rise in productivity,[3] gave Italy a decisive advantage in international trade. This had two important effects on the growth of production: it gave a particular boost to export industries, whose output rose faster than the national average, and it allowed the country to go forward with a massive programme of domestic investment unimpeded by difficulties with its balance of payments.

Italian expansion proceeded smoothly, without the familiar stops and starts which occurred elsewhere as a result of official policies straining to keep foreign exchange income and outgo in balance. When the Italian balance of payments did eventually run into trouble in 1963—following a series of exceptionally large increases in wages, which in the early 1960s moved far ahead of the increase in productivity—the country's industries were able rapidly to make and sell the extra exports needed to meet the sudden shortage of foreign exchange. Admittedly, on this occasion the familiar measures of deflation were applied, with drastic effects on the import bill, and industrial investment suffered accordingly. But the striking thing about the financial crisis of 1963–4 was the extraordinary resilience of Italy's export industries which managed, in the face of what seemed to be a serious inflation of costs, to go out and increase their share of world trade in manufactured goods. Their competitive power reflected the high standard of equipment and technical performance which had been built up in the years of expansion.

Left-overs of Fascism

What is of especial interest in relation to the argument of this book is the role of the public sector in the Italian postwar system. The discussion which follows will be concerned very largely with this, not because it is believed that this was necessarily the decisive factor in Italy's success. It was one important contributory cause; but the main reason for picking it out for analysis is its relevance to a more general Western phenomenon noticeable among some of the most successful European economies since the war. In some ways, Italy is the most extreme example (with Austria) of public sector enterprise and intervention in the whole of Western Europe.[4] The state's

[2] See the discussion on pp. 58–59 above.
[3] See P. Baffi, 'Monetary Stability and Economic Development in Italy, 1946–60', Banca Nazionale del Lavoro *Quarterly Review*, Mar. 1961.
[4] See Chapman, *Profession of Government*, p. 58, who quotes La Malfa's assertion after his inquiry in 1951 that he had counted over 1,000 different state undertakings—excluding 'provincial or communal ramifications' which would have raised the figure to several thousands.

activities are more extensive even than in France—though, as we shall see, they are much less significant as adjuncts of a coherent national policy.

This proliferation of nationalized and semi-public enterprise is more the result of historical accident than of deliberate political decision. Much of it is the heritage of the Fascist regime between the wars—though not a deliberate gift by Mussolini to his successors: the business was wished on him by circumstances, rather than wished for. The circumstances were essentially the weakness of Italian industry and business organization in this early phase of development.[5] Unassisted, operating in the traditional style of Anglo-Saxon capitalism, it could not have coped with the heavy tasks into which it was plunged; indeed, Mussolini was making a valid point so far as Italy was concerned, when he insisted so vehemently on the need for policies opposed to economic liberalism.[6] Special measures were required, first of all, to give Italian industry the technical advantages of scale. This was gradually done over a period dating back well before Fascism by building up a few protected firms into monopolistic or quasi-monopolistic positions. Fiat, Snia Viscosa, Montecatini, Pirelli, Olivetti, Edison—they are the giants of postwar Italian industry, with an established habit of investment in sophisticated and advanced equipment, and a readiness to take long views which comes of being securely established as the dominant factor in a market. The ordinary run of Italian business meanwhile was hard put to it to lay hands on the risk capital that it needed for expansion. It became heavily dependent on the goodwill of the banks;[7] and the banks in turn, operating on too

---

[5] An underlying weakness which was brought to a state of crisis by the world depression of the 1930s, following on the earlier deflation of the Italian economy which accompanied Mussolini's prestige policy of raising the foreign exchange value of the lira in the late 1920s.

[6] That, of course, does not lend any colour to the inference, drawn by the Fascists, that *political* liberalism must necessarily be out too. The influence of Marxist doctrine, which automatically equated the two kinds of liberalism, must be held at least partly responsible for the tragic confusion. A typical example is the statement of Arnaldo Mussolini, official theorist of the early period of Fascism in Italy: 'Fascism clearly and resolutely denies the individualism of the 18th century' (quoted in S. B. Clough, 'The evolution of Fascist economic theory', *Harvard Business Review*, Apr. 1932). But if one looks at the context of this statement, one finds that what was chiefly being asserted was something about economic policy: a refusal to accept the decisions of the market place as a necessary guide to action. The essential point that is expressed with such vehemence is that the long-term economic interest of industry does not by any means always coincide with the sum of the individual short-term producer interests. That is commonplace enough today; but at the time (the 1920s) respectable economic thinking was still dominated by the model of the perfectly competitive market, with its corollary that there was an automatic correspondence between the undirected and unimpeded pursuit of personal ends by entrepreneurs and the achievement of the public good.

[7] Gerschenkron (*Economic Backwardness*, p. 88) describing the period of rapid growth of Italian industry under the umbrella of the banks during the period 1896–1908, says: 'As in Germany, the policy was to maintain an intimate connection with an industrial enterprise and to nurse it for a long time before introducing it to the capital market, which as often as not meant placing its stock among the banks' own

narrow a base of financial resources, looked for support to the public authorities.

This precarious pyramid of expectations finally came toppling down in the financial crisis of the early 1930s. The banks, more than ever responsive to the behests of the Government under the Fascist regime, had been encouraged to supply credit freely to businesses which were no longer solvent; they ended up by owning them. They had bought a lot of their shares in the course of support operations in stock markets. Then it was the turn of the banks themselves to come under serious pressure in the stock exchange. Again, under prompting from the Government, they supported their own shares by heavy purchases in the market until they found that they had become their own principal shareholders, using money which was not their own.[8] Ultimately the only escape from bankruptcy for this vast interlocked complex of industrial and financial interests was a take-over of the assets, as well as the liabilities, by the state. That is how IRI (Istituto per la Ricostruzione Industriale), Italy's biggest commercial enterprise, consisting today of some 120 companies employing a total of 280,000 people,[9] was born in 1933. It was an inauspicious beginning, and for several years the Government persistently tried to get rid of its unwanted child; the aim was to sell back to private enterprise as many of these derelict enterprises as soon as possible. It took until 1937 before the Fascist Government resigned itself to the idea that IRI was more than a temporary financial foray into alien territory; in that year it acquired the status of a permanent public agency[10]—perhaps the most absent-minded act of nationalization in history.

This was one of several economic left-overs of Fascism which was turned to positive purpose in postwar Italy. Another, which proved to be extremely important, was the tight control established over the operation of commercial and industrial credit by the central banking authorities. This was the end-product of a trend which went back to well before the advent of Mussolini; as in France, the public authorities have from the start of capitalism played an active part in banking. Banking was seen as the key to industrial

clients. As in Germany, the banks tried to influence and modernize the methods of inter-enterprise credit relations. As in Germany, they were ever eager to "discipline production" of industrial branches, which bland phrase meant reduction or abandonment of competition in favour of various monopolistic compacts.'

[8] See P. Einzig, *Economic Foundations of Fascism* (London, Macmillan, 1934), p. 89. Einzig reported that the banks at the time were finding their position exceedingly awkward, but added significantly: 'Their only comfort was the assurance that, should it become necessary, they could rely upon prompt and effective official support.'

[9] IRI, *Annual Report 1963*.

[10] Though still with the right to sell its constituent enterprises at its convenience back to private enterprise, a right which it has continued to exercise at various times. By 1937, with Italian industry tooling up for war, there was a current of thinking among the leaders of Fascism which was positively in favour of state intervention in private enterprise.

development, and therefore as the means by which Italy could regain her lost position as a leading nation of the Western world. There is, for instance, an organization corresponding to the Caisse des Dépôts in France[11]—the Cassa dei Depositi e Prestiti—which collects up all the money put into post office savings banks, acts as banker to all local authorities, and lends out funds for purposes approved by the state. It is not as powerful as the Caisse des Dépôts, for the instinct to centralize financial resources does not work quite so effectively in Italy; the Cassa is more of an adjunct than a major instrument of official policy. In addition, the biggest commercial bank, the Banca Nazionale del Lavoro, is largely nationalized, with 86 per cent of its capital owned by the state; and so are the other three major banks, through IRI, which holds over four-fifths of their capital.[12] There are also a number of special banking institutions, providing short and long-term credits to industry (e.g. Mediocredito) and regional development banks which are publicly owned in whole or in part. Indeed, traditional private banking plays a smaller part in Italy than in any other Western country.[13]

Bank of Italy

However, the fact of public ownership does not, as we have already seen in France,[14] by itself necessarily determine the way in which a bank's business is conducted. The heart of the Italian system of control over lending and investment is the central bank. To begin with, the governor of the bank plays a dominant part at the regular meetings of the Inter-Ministerial Committee on Credit—a powerful body composed of ministers in person,[15] which regularly examines all major public and private demands for credit, including share and bond issues through the stock market, and decides which, if any, should be rejected or reduced or postponed. The governor is often the only member of the committee with a grip on the technical aspects of the matters which come up for discussion, and if he is a man of character and ability— as the postwar governors have outstandingly been—he will usually get his way. (That at any rate is the impression that I have obtained from persons directly concerned. Normally the Bank and the Treasury are allies—a formidable combination against ministers of spending departments often competing against one another for public funds.)

A second instrument of control is provided by the system of *fidi eccedenti*— literally 'excess credits'—under which a bank must obtain special permission from the Banca d'Italia, whenever it wants to make a loan which is equivalent

---

[11] See above, pp. 167 ff.
[12] See V. Lutz and L. Ceriani in Sayers, *Banking in W. Europe*, ch. 3.
[13] Ibid.   [14] p. 171 above.
[15] The only other permanent official, besides the Governor of the Banca d'Italia, present at these meetings is the Director-General of the Treasury (Ministero del Tesoro), who attends, however, merely in the capacity of adviser to his minister.

to more than one-fifth of the value of its paid-up capital and reserves. The result of the postwar inflation, which has not been reflected in the official valuation of the share capital of the banks, has been to bring many more individual loans under central bank surveillance. Dr Lutz comments in her survey of postwar Italian banking: 'The control over *fidi eccedenti* obviously offers scope for qualitative control. The Bank of Italy . . . takes into account the branch of economic activity in which, and the purpose for which, funds are to be used.'[16] There is no evidence, however, that the power has been used by the Bank to further any *systematic* policy of selective investment, either of its own or of the Government.

On the contrary, the clear impression that I formed directly from those concerned was that the instincts of the senior officials of the Bank are deeply antagonistic to the notion of any form of long-term planning dependent on their control of bank lending policies. Here the contrast is most striking with French readiness to throw the central bank's powers in as a weapon, indeed the main weapon in the armoury of the Plan. That is not to say that the Banca d'Italia has not in practice exercised a deliberate and sometimes decisive influence on the direction of industrial investment during the postwar period. For example, it took a strong line during the 1950s, under the governorship of Signor Menichella, against investment which was merely intended to create more opportunities for employment, regardless of the effect on the productive efficiency of Italian industry. Indeed, the successful resistance to the popular clamour for the use of whatever capital resources were available to produce as many new jobs as possible, and the stubborn pursuit of the objective of higher productivity during a period of high unemployment, is one of the major achievements of public enterprise in Italy. It appears both in the conduct of banking and also, in spite of occasional compromises, in the management policy of the industrial concerns controlled by IRI.

The central bank's ultimate control over the flow of investment and credit derives chiefly from the sheer concentration of financial resources in the Italian system; a very few large commercial banks face a governor endowed with immense authority to supervise the conduct of their affairs. He rarely has to apply the formal powers at his disposal. Everyone knows that he can, if he is displeased with the way in which an individual bank is running its business, cut down the immensely valuable facilities for rediscounting its paper at the central bank. In that way he can largely determine how much cash any bank has at its disposal.[17] Rediscount is a privilege, not a right.

---

[16] In Sayers, *Banking in W. Europe*, p. 159. At the end of 1963 there were over 3,000 permissions or renewals of permissions previously granted and still outstanding—a permit runs only for one year at a time—with a total value of around £1,600 m.

[17] Not entirely, however. During the 1963 financial crisis the banks were able for a time to overcome the effects of the central bank's squeeze on their supply of credit, by borrowing abroad.

There are no fixed margins of central bank credit upon which the individual banks know that they can draw, as under the French system. By these means the central bank has in fact been able to achieve a greater measure of control over business spending in the private sector than has so far been attained over spending in the public sector by the formal machinery of government. It is partly because of this ability to make its will effective in the few centres of financial power that matter, that the Banca d'Italia is called upon periodically to carry some of the burdens of workaday government, which in other countries are regarded as the natural responsibility of ministers and their departments. This was most noticeable during the balance of payments crisis of 1963–4 when the task of formulating a drastic deflationary policy and imposing it on the country—all of which involved a series of highly political decisions—was carried out, in the initial phase at any rate, almost single-handed by the bank.

It is here perhaps that the incidental consequences of running a largely nationalized banking system make themselves felt. The advantage is not any formal power to command the management of those banks that are subject to the overriding authority of the state as principal shareholder. In practice, the managers of the state-owned banks are almost invariably officials who have come up the conventional ladder of promotion inside their own 'firm'; the big four banks, in particular, regard themselves as autonomous enterprises, largely responsible for appointing their own management, and the state for its part is just as eager to insist on their character as independent, and occasionally competing, businesses.[18] But when it comes to the point over any issue of policy, the men in charge readily act and think, like the central bank, in the style of public officials. As one of them put it in conversation: 'Today we are all of us bank *functionaries*—not bankers venturing money.'

This atmosphere has almost certainly contributed something to Italian economic growth. It has done so in a subtle fashion, by reinforcing the confidence of the authorities. Because the central bank has known itself to be so firmly in charge of the country's credit system and the system itself has been constructed in such a way as to respond sensitively to pressures from the centre, financial policy has been boldly geared to expansion. The analogy which comes to mind is with the Bank of England in the second half of the nineteenth century, when, sustained by confidence in its technical mastery and its power to dominate the City of London, it was providing a model for other central banks of how to take calculated risks of a novel type, in support of the expansion of trade. The remarkable thing was how small a gold reserve the Bank of England thought it necessary to keep in its vaults

---

[18] However, in some of the other publicly owned banks decisions about whom to appoint as general manager are sometimes the subject of protracted negotiations of a political character between powerful ministers and party representatives.

to sustain a world-wide network of financial transactions, each carrying some degree of hazard. In both cases, of course—in nineteenth-century Britain, as well as in mid-twentieth-century Italy—the underlying economic circumstances were highly favourable to the experiment. But economic circumstances do not of themselves produce boldness; the accident of particular institutions, and the habits of using them engendered by history, are necessary too.

More specifically, the tight Italian system of centralized credit control has made it possible to channel a vast flow of investment funds into the public sector.[19] Since a significant portion of productive enterprise is publicly financed, this in itself has been a factor in the country's rapid economic advance. The connexion can be seen most clearly in the employment of public funds to back investment, in private as well as in public projects, in the regional development schemes for Central and Southern Italy.[20] Not all of this investment has paid off; but in a number of places new 'growth points' have been firmly established, with the result that local economic resources that would otherwise have been wasted have found productive use. The chief benefit of a well conceived regional policy is to secure in the long run a more efficient employment of all forms of national capital taken together—including of course social capital—than would result from an entrepreneur's conventional profit-and-loss approach to the problem of investment.[21] It is not to be imagined that Italian public initiative in this field has been applied only to the derelict villages and barren lands of the South. There has, for instance, been the successful effort in the Veneto to establish a lot of small industrial plants in a predominantly agricultural area suffering from underemployment; this has been financed in part by Mediocredito, which is subsidized out of government funds. A wide range of other economic activities scattered over the country have been supported, in one way or another, by public money.

---

[19] Baffi ('Monetary Stability', p. 21) estimates that 'approximately one quarter of the overall increase in financial assets, other than shares, during the thirteen years 1948–60 (4,600 billion lire in a total of 18,100 billions) was made up of borrowing by the central government'. His comment on the official treatment of minimum bank reserve ratios imposed by the authorities is also of interest, since he is Director-General of the Banca d'Italia. These reserves—equal to $22\frac{1}{2}$ per cent of deposits since 1962, either in Treasury bills or deposited at the central bank—have not been used 'to regulate liquidity in order to meet the needs of the business cycle; the use made so far in Italy of obligatory reserves has been rather to channel to the public sector a considerable proportion of the expansion of bank credit (p. 8).

[20] It is estimated that three-quarters of all industrial investment in the South in the mid-1950s was 'assisted' in this way. Often it was the large and dynamic firms which were attracted. The two main industries which benefited at this time were chemicals and electricity (see PEP, *Regional Development in the EEC* (London, 1962), ch. 2).

[21] For a further discussion of this point, see below, p. 279.

The 'Condottiere Principle' : ENI

The special role of public sector enterprise in postwar Italian industry is seen at its most spectacular in the performance of the two great corporations ENI[22] (oil and natural gas) and IRI (the diversified group based on the bankrupt companies which were taken over in the 1930s). Together they were responsible in the early 1960s for over one-fifth of all capital investment in manufacturing industry, transport, and communications.[23] They include several of the most rapidly growing and technically advanced enterprises in Italy. The origins of IRI have already been described.[24] ENI was a postwar creation, founded in 1953, though it took under its wing nationalized undertakings in the field of oil and gas which had been set up under the Fascist régime.[25] Its great achievement in the 1950s was the exceedingly rapid development of the newly found reserves of natural gas in North Italy.

It is highly improbable that any of the international oil companies who were so eager to get into the business, and whom Signor Mattei, the head of ENI until his death in 1962, regarded as his personal enemies, would have done the job with equal speed. The other alternative, an indigenous private enterprise organization, could hardly have matched ENI's high-speed performance in bringing to Italian industry all the supplies of the newly discovered natural gas that it could use, in so short a time. The speed with which any normal private business would have set about the venture would have been determined by commercial criteria, such as the desire to husband reserves or the wish not to disrupt other established supplies of fuel, which would have slowed down the process. Indeed, it is sometimes argued that ENI's pace was excessive: the consequence is that known Italian reserves of natural gas are in danger of being exhausted in a matter of a few years. However, those who took charge of Italian gas development were guided by other considerations than this. They were, of course, anxious to make a profit; but their main objective was to apply to the national economy the stimulus of plentiful domestic fuel for industry at a cheap price. It was the first time in Italian history that this had happened.

It is perhaps no wonder, in view of the national interests which were felt to be at stake, that the management of ENI treated the organization as a fighting company. It always seemed to be carrying some flag, and its normal posture was one of defiance. Leaving aside the emotional overtones which occasionally dominated the argument, there were shrewd economic reasons

[22] *Ente Nazionale Idrocarburi.*
[23] *The Economist*, 25 May 1963, p. 309, estimates their combined fixed investment in Italy in 1963 at some 700 billion lire. Total investment in manufacturing, transport and communications in that year amounted to 3,150 billion lire (see OECD, *Econ. Surveys, Italy*, June 1964).
[24] p. 179.
[25] See Vera Lutz, *Italy: a Study in Economic Development* (London, RIIA/OUP, 1962), ch. 12, for a good account of the development of Italian nationalized undertakings.

why the Italians should have regarded it as a venture which ought to be buttressed by public power.   The French, trying to make an entry into the international oil industry in the 1920s, after the major companies had already established themselves, had also felt the need for a special form of organization which would protect the national interest.   Their answer to it was the characteristic mixed enterprise, part public and part privately owned, the Compagnie Française des Petrôles.[26]   The truth is that in the oil industry any new entrant facing the competition of the international majors can only hope to capture any significant share of the market if it is backed by an unusually large concentration of economic power.   In Italy this concentration was naturally sought in the public sector.

There are, of course, risks in using public money in this way.   A fighting company like ENI, commanded by a dominant personality like Signor Mattei, does not readily accept any form of outside supervision.   Indeed it seems nowadays that the bosses of great public enterprises often operate with greater personal freedom of decision than the typical head of the big corporation in private industry.   Few of them, however, have carried the method of personal rule to such lengths as Signor Mattei did in ENI.   He worked on the *condottiere* principle: he had been handed a fief to look after and he saw it as his task to enlarge its power and extent wherever possible—if at the expense of rivals, so much the better.   ENI was paid a remunerative price for the gas which it sold, and it used the money to invest in petrol stations, pipelines covering half of Europe, chemicals, motels, as well as in large oil concessions overseas.   By the time Signor Mattei died in 1962, the finances of the organization were seriously over-stretched.   In particular, some of his foreign ventures in oil exploration do not seem to have been well judged. However, these were incidental episodes to the main business, which was to provide Italian industry with cheap and assured supplies of fuel.   ENI's venture into Russian oil was part of this pattern, for the prices which it paid were considerably below those charged by the international oil companies. Certainly, if Italian industry suffered from a disadvantage during its early development by comparison with other industrial countries because of its lack of cheap domestic fuel, then the balance of advantage was decisively reversed from the early 1950s onwards.

State Capitalism : IRI

IRI is a more complicated and in some ways more interesting case. Because of the great variety of enterprises brought haphazardly under its

---

[26] The state holds 30 per cent of its shares, but exercises a powerful influence on the management.   It is interesting to note the contrast with British Petroleum, where the British Government owns 51 per cent of the equity capital but makes a point of keeping the two directors, whom it nominates to the board of the company, out of the active running of the business. See p. 82 above.

umbrella, it offers a richer field for study of the possible functions of public enterprise in a dynamic capitalist economy. It was not asked to meet a clear and straightforward national objective, as ENI was. Nor did it come under the direction of a determined managerial dictator able to give this rambling organization a simple sense of direction—his own. To many observers after the war, IRI seemed like a great incubus on the state, a complex of decrepit looking enterprises pressing constantly on the Treasury for more money; and itself exposed, in turn, to every form of political pressure. Perhaps it was the sense of its unpromising appearance which made the managers of IRI insist so powerfully on their independent managerial status. Without this, the group could never have made its major contribution to the growth of modern Italian, industry in the postwar period.

From the beginning it was riven by a conflict between two different objectives. It was the biggest single employer of industrial labour in a country suffering from heavy unemployment. Its primary task, as the average politician and the average voter saw it at that time, was to keep as many people as possible in their jobs. On the other hand the management of IRI viewed itself as the guardian of a number of the key sectors of modern industry, on whose efficiency the performance of the rest of the Italian economy would depend. This was outstandingly true of steel, with more than half of the industry in IRI's hands. If the price of Italian steel was too high, or the quality below the best international standard, there would be little chance for Italy's engineering exports in world markets. Cement was another key industry whose prices affected many other products at home, in which the IRI management set out to impose high standards of technical efficiency. In this case its factories produced a relatively small part of total output, around 10 per cent; but, it is claimed, their strong competitive power, based on large investments in modern plant and high technical efficiency, has been deliberately used to hold down prices.[27]

The conflict between a policy of job creation and the pursuit of higher productivity was firmly resolved in favour of the latter. Not that the decision received much publicity at the time. It was another one of the characteristic Latin conspiracies in the public interest, of which France, in particular, has provided some outstanding examples. In Italy such things have to be done

[27] See Aldo Fascetti (former President of IRI), *Scritti e discorsi* (Milan, 1960), p. 97, and Annual Reports of IRI. A paper by Dr Carlo Obber, financial manager of IRI, on 'The Role of IRI in the Italian Economy' read at Europe House (London) in 1962 gave the following summary of IRI's share in the various sectors of the Italian economy: 62 per cent of passenger shipping; 85 per cent of pig-iron output; 55 per cent of steel output; 80 per cent of shipbuilding capacity; 65 per cent of mercury output; 10 per cent of cement output; 8 per cent of passenger car output. In addition, it owns several large blocks of shares in individual engineering concerns, and runs the nationalized airline, the broadcasting and television company, and the urban telephone service, as well as a number of banks and the bulk of the toll motorways.

with greater stealth, because there is neither the instinctive French respect for the high public official, nor any of the confidence in his moral purpose. It was necessary to make political compromises from time to time which involved using capital to keep people in jobs for which there was no economic justification. This was especially true of the shipyards. But even here the management was able to introduce a long-term programme of reconversion of plant and retraining of shipbuilding workers, which has had some notable successes, especially in the big Ansaldo yard in Genoa. Of course, all this was more expensive than simply turning the unwanted workers on to the streets—for the company, if not for the nation. It is worth remarking that IRI, with ENI, are the only businesses in Italy which have engaged in any serious work of retraining workers. They are also the pioneers in management training.

The success of the effort to avoid the dilution of labour and to use investment as a means of raising the efficiency of the individual worker is reflected in the high ratio of fixed capital at the disposal of the average employee in the manufacturing companies of the group. By 1963 the average had reached the equivalent of over £3,000 per head.[28] The finance for the impressive investment effort of the postwar years came from three sources. First, there was the very generous plough-back of profits, secondly, the issue of bonds to the public by IRI and the various companies in the group, and thirdly, direct contributions from the state. The sheer size of the group, which allowed profits in one part to be set off against losses in another, added to the backing of the state, which meant that it would be able, in an emergency, to fall back on public funds to meet its obligations, made it a safe vehicle for investment. The state also contributes more directly to IRI's investment programme—recently at a rate of some 50 billion lire a year—but does not demand any share of the income it earns. It could do so in theory, though there is very little to spare. The net profits of this vast enterprise, after the payment of interest and dividends to private investors, and meeting its other expenses, amounts to the equivalent of under half a million pounds sterling annually.[29]

The Government's profitless investment in IRI and what prompted it are

---

[28] IRI, *Annual Report 1963*. Net fixed assets in manufacturing (after deduction of allowances for depreciation) divided by numbers employed. Capital per employee in the group as a whole is much higher than this, because of the expensive nature of the plant employed in the particular service industries—telephones, airways, radio and television transmission—in which IRI is engaged. This tends to reinforce the management of the group in its view of itself as the natural leader in the capital-intensive, and technologically advanced, sectors of the economy.

[29] The Annual Report for 1963 showed a total income of 45 billion lire. Payments to bond holders were 37 billion; other interest payments 1·4 billion; administrative expenses 2·7 billion; tax payments 1·88 billion; other expenditure (including training and education and contribution to staff funds) 1·27 billion. The net profit remaining was 0·75 billion lire, compared with 0·6 billion in the previous year—giving an average for the two years equivalent to something less than £400,000.

worth examining more closely. The money from the Government may be regarded as being, in large part, a subsidy to support an accelerated pace of investment in certain vital areas of the Italian economy. Here there is a close analogy with ENI; if the industries which have been helped in this way had been left to fend for themselves, their investment would have proceeded more slowly, and so presumably the rate of growth of the whole Italian economy would have been less. The subvention to IRI is, formally at any rate, temporary and repayable; it appears on the books of the corporation as an investment which, like any other, will rank for dividend payments ultimately—when sufficient profits are available. That is not likely to be for a long time yet. The group seems to have considerable freedom to decide how to treat its expenditures for accounting purposes; and the more rapidly new investment can be written off against current income, the less is left over to figure in the profit-and-loss account. Moreover, the scope for offsetting profits in one section against accumulated losses elsewhere provides ample room for manoeuvre: the final 'profit' is very largely what the management wants it to be.

Alternatively, the state's financial contribution may be regarded as a means of increasing the return on capital available for distribution to IRI's private investors. At any rate it is evident that if the group were not in the fortunate position of having one shareholder, responsible for contributing a third of the equity capital,[30] who was ready to go without any dividend, there would be less left over to distribute to the other investors. In practice the shareholders and bondholders in IRI companies, although they have done quite well, generally receive little more than the going rate of return in Italy on investments of this type. So perhaps the proposition ought to be put the other way about—that if the state had not been prepared to play the part of the rentier who never squeals, it would not have been possible for IRI to obtain the large amounts of money that it needs for investment from the ordinary capital market. The terms that it would have been able to offer, without this public support, would not have been sufficiently attractive to tempt the private investor. The final outcome would then have been that the group would have invested less in those of its enterprises which the stock

---

[30] At the end of 1963 the total value of the equity owned by shareholders in IRI companies was 740 billion lire, while the Government's contributions to the share capital of the company (shown in the balance sheet as the 'Endowment Fund') amounted to 370 billion lire. Of course if all the sources of IRI's finance—not merely the equity shareholding—are included, the Government's proportion is very much smaller. IRI itself, which seems to be at great pains to point out in its official annual statements how small a part the Government really plays in financing its business, puts the matter as follows: 'For every lira therefore which the government has supplied to IRI, the capital market has supplied the group with 11 lire' (*Ann. Rep. 1963*, p. 89 of English text). This formulation might cause one to overlook the fact that this is a business into which the Government has put some $600 m. of public funds and from which it has never taken any profit.

market would have regarded as hazardous, either because they were old and in need of expensive reconversion or because they were too new to be trusted.[31]   The state's annual investment in IRI is really to be seen as a disguised subsidy to a number of industrial enterprises which require to be nursed along for a while—some of the older ones no doubt for a very long while—until they have become sufficiently profitable to be able to go directly to the capital market for finance on favourable terms.

A Philosophy of Public Entrepreneurship

It would be surprising if a business enterprise of this unusual kind had not built up over the years some kind of 'company philosophy'; and IRI has. Like other doctrines of this kind, it tends to spill over occasionally into the mythological.   But it is interesting because it at least tells one something about what the management are *trying* to do.   The president of the group, Signor Petrilli, in his Annual Report for 1961, summed up what he conceived to be the special advantages of the IRI method as follows.   First, and 'most important', it creates a large and varied complex of technical cadres, which are able quickly to exploit new opportunities for industrial investment. Secondly, there is the commercial stability of such a group containing 'complementary sectors', e.g. shipbuilding and shipping, which are able to support each other by means of orders during slack periods.   The shipping companies will be ready to accelerate their programme of renewals in order to provide work for the shipyards.   Thirdly, the financial strength of a group with such a wide spread is such that there are likely always to be sufficient profits to support enterprises 'in temporary crisis'.   These are, of course, the familiar claims that are made by any big business—greater stability of employment, more security for investment, and more rapid technical innovation.   There is the further point that out of the confidence born of such strong positions come the big adventurous projects, which may take many years to mature to the point where they show a profit.   No doubt General Motors would be able to substantiate most of IRI's claims.   But the truth is that the local equivalent of a General Motors in private hands would be impossible to accommodate in Italy without severe political strain.[32]   Through a series of

---

[31] The management of IRI takes the view (see *Ann. Rep. 1963*) that the state's contribution to its capital is the offset for its management of a number of unprofitable enterprises put into its keeping.   The 370 billion lire of government money provided 'is *grossomodo* equivalent to the Institute's non-earning assets, the bulk of which consists of investment in shipbuilding and certain heavy engineering firms (in the course of rationalization, but with restraint on dismissals of redundant labour) and in *Autostrade* (whose investment in motorways is still in the construction stage)' (Eng. ed. p. 89).

[32] Unilever is the only European private enterprise concern which is larger than IRI in terms of numbers employed: in 1963 Unilever employed 290,000, IRI 278,500 (*Fortune*, Aug. 1964 and IRI, *Ann. Rep. 1963*).

accidents starting with a desperate piece of salvage by the Fascist Government, the Italians arrived at an alternative formula.

But bigness is not all. There is also the part played by the motivation of management. Professor Pasquale Saraceno, who is chief economist at IRI and has also been an outstandingly subtle analyst of Italy's postwar economic problems, has offered some illuminating comment on the mixture of motives required in a dynamic national business corporation dependent on public funds.[33] He is certainly in a position to know. Apart from his work in IRI, he has played an active part in the formulation of regional development policy in Southern Italy, and more recently has been the effective head of the Economic Planning Commission set up by the Government in 1962. Saraceno argues that although the manager of a public enterprise has an important advantage, because his actions are not exclusively determined by the pursuit of profit, it is very dangerous for him to be liberated from the need to show *some* profit. The danger is to his own position. For the imperative of profit is the means that he can use to assert his independence, in the face of pressures coming from the Government to adopt policies which will serve political purposes.

The obvious example is the pressure that was exerted on IRI at the height of Italian unemployment after the war to direct its capital investment to the supply of extra jobs rather than the improvement of efficiency. That is why Saraceno argues that a 'semi-public corporation' is a better device than a wholly nationalized undertaking. It has the advantage of being constantly subject to the tension between the objectives of public policy on the one hand, and the need to satisfy shareholders that their capital is being used on projects which will show a good return on the other.[34] Although the parent company of IRI is wholly 'owned' by the state,[35] while the private bondholders merely lend money to it at a fixed rate of interest, it does in practice meet this prescription. That is mainly because there is an unending need for extra cash for investment, and the greater part of it comes from the capital market. Management therefore has to defer constantly to the intending investor's desire for evidence of profitability.

---

[33] See *Lo stato e l'economia* (Cinque Lune, 1963) and also Saraceno's course of lectures at the University of Venice published under the title *La produzione industriale* (Venice, Libreria Universitaria, 1962).

[34] The recent action of the Dutch State Mines—a conspicuously successful and dynamic public enterprise, which has spread from coal into chemicals and other fields— is worth noting. It has adopted the IRI formula and turned itself into a 'mixed company', with two-fifths of its share capital owned by private investors (see *The Economist*, 25 Mar. 1963).

[35] The parent company invests money (which it derives partly from the state and partly from the issue of bonds) in the equity of companies belonging to the group. In many of the individual companies part of the equity belongs to private shareholders (see p. 188, n. 30), but no part of the equity of the parent. IRI bonds issued to the public amounted to 608 billion lire, compared with the Government's holding 370 billion lire of shares (*Ann. Rep. 1963*).

It is also essential, Saraceno argues, that such an undertaking should have a wide spread of industrial activities. If it is governed by a restrictive statute which puts close legal limitations on the functions that it may perform, this is bound to constrict the entrepreneurial drive of the publicly owned concern. It must be in a position to pop up, like any other lively entrepreneur, in unexpected places. On these grounds, Saraceno criticizes the British brand of nationalization, which has its counterpart in the Italian State Railways.[36] Clearly, if public enterprise is seen as the means of creating fighting companies, which aim to influence the tempo and direction of whole industries in which private business is active, the argument for allowing management the maximum freedom to choose its targets is strong. On this view, the public or semi-public enterprise is a gadfly, fulfilling a function rather like that which has been assumed by the Swedish co-operative movement in the field of consumer goods and services—looking for places where private enterprise is soft or where its prices are too high or its profits too large.

It is a curious role to ask a public undertaking to fulfil in a democratic society where its management is exposed to regular parliamentary scrutiny and irregular pressures from the representatives of all the interest groups in the land. The answer is, of course, that such an arrangement is only possible where the officials in charge are given the maximum administrative discretion.[37] Saraceno makes it quite clear that the device of building into an organization like IRI the countervailing power of private investors is to provide the management with even more freedom of action than it would have if it were ruled by private enterprise alone. It is characteristic of the mood of his time and place that he is entirely unconcerned about the problem of exercising some form of democratic control over enterprises set up with public money and backed by the authority of the state in their operations.

---

[36] And in France too: see e.g. the severe restrictions placed on the Charbonnages de France, which must confine itself to production only, and cannot engage in marketing or in technical work on the use of coal.

[37] It is interesting to find one of the British nationalized undertakings, the Transport Holding Company established in 1962, demanding some of the freedom of the IRI formula. Because of its variegated activities in the field of transport—which include shipping, tourism, and road haulage—it insists in its first annual report (for the year 1963) that it 'should not therefore be thought of as a "nationalized industry"—a point of some consequence'. It goes on to assert that it does not intend to be bound by its present activities and that it 'is specially ready to take up new investment, subject to the consent of the Minister, in the constantly widening field of transport'. The ministerial proviso reflects the distance that separates British public enterprise, even after this 'new experiment' (the report's phrase), from the managerial freedom of an IRI. The point emerges very clearly in the financial section of its report, where it complained that it had been compelled to hand over to the Exchequer profits which ought to have been devoted to investment. There is a note of indignation in its conclusion: 'The Board of the Holding Company therefore feel bound to record their view that it would have been more in accord with the practice of successful commercial enterprises for the Company to have been permitted to retain profits in the business to a greater extent' (para. 24).

Indeed he says outright that the absence of any 'substantial control' over management, whether by parliament or by government departments, is 'the obvious consequence' of the choice of the type of industrial organization which he describes and recommends.[38] It is interesting to find the old corporatist ideal which was deeply embedded in Italian pre-war thinking—the ideal of a balanced and responsible economic group with quasi-sovereign powers administering itself—cropping up in this new guise.

Underlying all this is a view that while the rapid advance of technology offers unusually high returns nowadays on innovation in the right places, it also makes capital investment itself that much more risky. Saraceno points to all the familiar factors which add to uncertainty—the increasing proportion of uncontrollable overhead costs in modern industry, the premature obsolescence of capital equipment, the long lead time before the typical large unit of investment in modern manufacturing industry comes into full operation and pays for itself, and finally the increasing exposure of industry to international competition.[39] What is therefore required is a system which builds into industrial investment some additional elements of security. These can be provided either by large private enterprise with ample reserves—large-scale business has become so institutionalized, he says, that it can now be regarded as a form of 'permanent' organization, no longer seriously vulnerable to the threat of bankruptcy—or by the organization of producers into industrial groups which carry out certain activities in common, or by a concern with public funds at its disposal.

This approach to the problems of modern capitalism has some obvious affinities with the views of the French planners. Their central problem, too, is how to reduce the factor of uncertainty which inhibits the act of expansion. The Italian answer so far has been very different, and it has little connexion with planning.[40] The form of economic organization chosen to cope with the new problems emerges as the incidental product of national history and ideology, stretching many years back, rather than as the outcome of systematic ratiocination. The same was true, as we saw, in France. The whole process is a little reminiscent of the way in which a wilful and confident artist like Picasso constructed some of his sculptures, picking up the objects which happened to be to hand, including his children's toys, and incorporating them in some design of his own.

Managerial Democracy: The Austrian Experience

The other West European country with a body of nationalized undertakings as extensive and varied, and as haphazardly put together as the Italian, is Austria. It has also been outstandingly successful in the postwar world. Here

---

[38] *Lo stato e l'economia*, p. 63.   [39] *La produzione industriale.*
[40] See below, pp. 196 ff.

too, much of the nationalization was the result of historical accident rather than ideological purpose—first, the expropriation of German concerns after the war, and later the transfer to the Austrian state of enterprises taken over by the Russians during the postwar occupation. All told, the nationalized industries account for 24 per cent of industrial output and 27 per cent of total exports.[41] Because the solution adopted by the Austrians to the problem of political control is so sharply in contrast to the Italian method—or lack of method—it serves to throw some additional light on one of the key institutional questions of modern capitalism.

The basic political doctrine of postwar Austria, a kind of maid-of-all-work employed to make life easier for the politicians, is *Proporz*. This is an agreed formula for the proportional representation of the two main parties, the Socialists and the Österreichische Volkspartei (OVP), in all public bodies, based on the voting in the general election. Since the votes cast by the two main parties[42] have been fairly evenly matched at the polls, *Proporz* rather than the principle of straight majority rule has been seen as the means of securing domestic peace in a small nation with a bad record for violent quarrelling. The need for some formula which would allow the parties to collaborate actively in the national interest became urgent when the country faced severe economic strains immediately after the war; the establishment within the economy of a very extensive terrain where the state was either in direct control or in a position to exercise a decisive influence brought the problem to a head.

The first point to observe is that the insistence on unmitigated party democracy throughout the public sector has had the result of downgrading parliament.[43] No doubt any prolonged government coalition between a couple of parties representing the overwhelming majority of the electorate is likely, in any case, to take some of the edge off parliamentary debate. But in Austria the process has gone much further than that. Again, the subsoil of national institutions produced its own characteristic growth. The corporatist form of organization seems to be almost second nature to the Austrians. It is not that they are undemocratic; they nearly all belong to their business and professional associations, their trades unions, their religious and other groups—indeed membership of some of them is compulsory. And the Government is in turn under legal compulsion to consult these organizations

---

[41] *The Economist*, 9 Feb. 1963. In addition to a variety of electrical and engineering firms, the steel industry, the oil industry, and all mining are nationalized.

[42] There are some minor parties, including the Communists, but their combined share of the vote is only about 10 per cent.

[43] See K. W. Rothschild, *Österreichs Wirtschaftsstruktur* (Berlin, Duncker & Humblot, 1962), who describes the postwar reaction against 'ideologizing', which he says has led to a distaste for public debate as such. Everything is fixed up inside the various interest group organizations—the *Kammern*—and then adjusted in the course of bargaining between the groups. See also an interesting account in Uwe Kitzinger, 'The Austrian Election of 1959', *Political Studies* (Oxford), June 1961.

before it takes legislative or administrative action of certain specified kinds.[44] Since the organized interest groups are also represented in an especially powerful way inside one or the other of the two main political parties, politicians are more or less invited to discuss the real work of government almost anywhere other than in parliament.

It might be argued that this Austrian system merely provides a model, in an extreme form, of the destination towards which several of the democracies of Western Europe are now heading. There is, however, a further feature of these arrangements for which it is hard to find any analogy elsewhere. The delicate balance of representation between the two parties has been carried right down into the boards of management of the numerous undertakings which are publicly owned. As Kitzinger says, 'Positions which involve major acts of economic decision-making are thought to entail ideological opportunities and power—and therefore to be a vital matter for the parties and the people.'[45] The Coalition Pact between the parties, which is a kind of Social Contract more fundamental than the constitution, lays down that 'leading positions' in nationalized industry and in the nationalized banks shall be carved up between the parties in a ratio corresponding to the *Proporz*.

What is remarkable is that this device has not seriously reduced the efficiency of the large sector of Austrian industry owned by the state.[46] Part of the explanation lies in the deliberate effort made by the Socialist Party after the war to train up a body of able and qualified party men to take over their share of these managerial jobs.[47] It is clear that the system could only have absorbed these newcomers so readily in a country where the ordinary standards of management and of management training were high. However, the Austrians, for all the skill that they have displayed over rather more than a decade and a half in working a machine which seemed initially to have been designed to be productive of little more than the sustained excitement of unstable equilibrium, have recently been agitating for its reform. They have come to the conclusion that if their nationalized industries are to function effectively in a period of increasing international competition, their boards of management will have to be more homogeneous and less subject to political pressures from parties.

No one would deliberately wish on themselves a repetition of the Austrian

---

[44] Kitzinger, *Political Studies*, June 1961.   [45] Ibid.

[46] The right-wing OVP claims that it has, and it is now common ground between the parties that the system could, and ought to, function more efficiently. But by any objective criterion of output or export performance Austrian nationalized industry does not come off badly.

[47] See F. Parkinson, 'Austrian Socialism Today', *The World Today*, Mar. 1964, who points out that the Bund Sozialistischer Akademiker, created after the war, was designed to supply the managerial talent which would ordinarily have come from the right wing Catholic students' organizations, CV (*Cartell-Verband*).

experiment. But it ought to be noted as a serious attempt to keep the conduct of undertakings which form part of the public patrimony under some
kind of political surveillance. The obvious people to do the job are the
elected representatives of the people; but since the Austrians had so organized
their affairs that the main stream of political life by-passed parliament, this
option was not open to them. It is doubtful whether it is, in fact, open to
the parliaments of other West European countries, as they are at present
constituted.

These parliaments do not normally contain a sufficient body of professional
expertise to set themselves up as effective supervisory boards representing the
public shareholder in nationalized undertakings. The result is that the
managers of the undertakings run things pretty much their own way, so long
as they make sure to respond demonstratively every now and then to the
distant bark of the parliamentary watchdog tethered to his post. It is worth
noting an alternative device, characteristically developed by the French. This
is a quasi-judicial body working from inside the public service: it is called
the Commission de Vérification des Comptes des Entreprises Publiques and
is attached to the Cour des Comptes, the agency traditionally responsible for
the regular audit and check on all government expenditure. The Commission
was set up in 1948, because it was felt that something other than the formal
and somewhat inflexible approach to the inspection of public spending was
required for the job of supervising the mass of undertakings newly nationalized
after the war.[48] The intention was that the Commission should provide
parliament with an expert technical comment on the operation and finances
of the nationalized enterprises, pointing to matters which raise important
issues requiring the attention of parliament. The investigators are usually
magistrates of the Cour des Comptes and they are assisted by specialists,
officials who may be either drawn from the Cour or seconded from other
government departments. Their method is to argue through each detailed
report, before its publication, with the public enterprise concerned. Any
undertaking in which the state owns 51 per cent or more of the capital is
subjected to this treatment; there are around 110 of them.[49] Professor Chapman, who judges this to be 'the most successful attempt so far' to put public
enterprise under effective surveillance, believes that it exercises a positive
function in guiding management, analogous to that of the Conseil d'État in
the sphere of administrative actions. This is because there is a built-in
tendency under the French system for such judicial controls to become a
positive assertion of the public interest. He concludes: 'Just as legal control
of administrative acts tends gradually to extend to a control of their reason-
ableness and impartiality, so financial control tends to shade imperceptibly
into an examination of efficiency and the rational . . . use of public resources'.[50]

[48] Chapman, *Profession of Government*, ch. 13.   [49] Ibid., p 265.
[50] Ibid. ch. 13.

Here is another illustration of the manner in which all roads in the French administrative system seem to point the way towards some form of planning.

Italian Approach to Planning

The Italians do not have the built-in administrative bias of the French to push them towards a national economic plan. Rather the contrary. Yet the need for a system of planning is, if anything, more acute in a country like Italy where the structure of large-scale industry weakens the play of market forces and the economic life of the country is largely determined by disparate decisions made in a series of unconnected centres of power, both in the public and the private sector. In Austria the Socialists, devotees of public ownership, have come to see that the way to effective public control over state-owned, as well as private, industry lies in the process of central planning.[51] Nationalization solves nothing. The problem of inducing the managers of industry to act in unison and in the public interest remains, whether the shareholders who formally own the business are private persons or public authorities. In Italy, as we have seen, the problem of democratic control is not an important public issue. The motives which led the Italians to the effort to set up a system of economic planning in the early 1960s were chiefly the desire to deal with public investment in a more rational and businesslike fashion.[52]

The truth is that behind an administrative façade which bears many of the French labels and whose design has been deliberately modelled on French ideas, the Italian system of government is in practice among the least co-ordinated in Western Europe.[53] There is none of the French esprit de

[51] See a series of articles in *Die Zukunft*, the Socialist Party journal (nos. 7 & 8, Apr. 1964), discussing the proposed reform of management structure in nationalized industry.

[52] The so-called Vanoni Plan, presented in 1955, was a sketch for a long-term policy, rather than an exercise in comprehensive national planning in the contemporary style. For the motives behind the latest effort in planning, see La Malfa Report to parliament, 22 May 1962, published by Min. of the Budget under the title, *Problems and Prospects of Italian Economic Development*, p. 46. '. . . Planning has first and foremost to do with public investment as the latter is only justified in so far as the purposes to which it is put are well-defined and the net social benefits are plainly evident.' It goes on to describe the impact of the plan on the private sector as follows: 'Development planning can, furthermore, reduce private enterprise's insistence on underestimating investment opportunities for reasons long known in economics—the necessarily limited economic outlook of private enterprise which has neither the means nor the opportunity of working with broader aims in view as the State may do; the existence in certain fields of risks for the private investor but not for the community; and the impossibility for private firms to enter on the balance sheet investment benefits which are not in the form of immediate returns but are for the good of the community at large'.

[53] The La Malfa Report remarks: 'It is a well-known fact that serious and sometimes insuperable co-ordination difficulties arise between one part of the administration and another (and even in different sections of one department)' (p. 48). It goes on to record

corps uniting the great officials of the state, none of the feeling that they *ought* to have a purpose in common. Instead the *'condottiere* principle', which has been noted before,[54] takes charge. Inside government Italian individualism seems to have scope to run riot. There is a tendency, which many foreigners must have observed even in the streets of Italy, to use public office and, where these are available, its outer trappings of uniform and weapons, as a means of adding a further dimension to the personality of the office-holder. This self-indulgence is not, it seems, entirely absent in the highest offices of the state. There is moreover, partly no doubt on this very account, little public trust in the integrity of high officials. Relations between people in private enterprise and the public service are usually distant and often strained; they are treated as belonging to two entirely different worlds, and there is none of the easy movement from important official positions into business management which is a feature of modern France. There is instead widespread resentment felt in private business about the favours and special advantages, real and imaginary, enjoyed by anyone working in the public sector—a feeling which occasionally finds expression in the view that the whole of the public service is a grand conspiracy against the captains of industry.

The effect of these conflicting pressures and sentiments is illustrated in the story of the Ministry of State Holdings set up in 1957. It was established with the worthy aim of securing some co-ordination in the behaviour of the variegated array of Italian public and semi-public enterprises. However, it was from the start the object of hostility from both the freebooting managers inside the public system and the industrialists outside it. In order to counter any attempt to turn it into a new instrument of government intervention in the economy, its total staff was restricted by law to a maximum of 100. In view of the size and variety of the public sector, this limitation should have been quite enough to stultify any serious effort to establish an effective central control over nationalized undertakings. But in the end even this provision of the law was by-passed—by means of a device which tended to weaken the exercise of central authority still further. Some of the public enterprises obligingly took extra members of the staff of the ministry, which was supposed to supervise them, on to their own payrolls. The practice has, of

that when the Government embarked on the large-scale regional development pro-gramme for Southern Italy, it was decided to set up a new organization, the Cassa per il Mezzogiorno, which would by-pass the normal channels of departmental authority. This was the only way in which the co-ordination required for regional planning was capable of being secured. It was buttressed by one of the many 'inter-ministerial committees' through which officials achieve the form, if not the content, of co-ordinated administrative policy. However, La Malfa goes on to record sadly that through being outside the traditional channels of authority, the Cassa 'encountered such obstacles that the ensuing difficulties could not be solved'.

[54] p. 185.

course, never received any publicity. It is no doubt regarded as no more than a continuation of the tradition whereby firms make a small financial contribution to officials who might some day be in a position to cause them some inconvenience.

It remains to observe the manner in which Italy's planning effort has evolved in the period since its initiation with the La Malfa Report in 1962. In the public sector, there has been no progress towards the integration of the investment activities of the different departments of government. Instead, the tendency has been to look to the various interest groups, whose representatives sit on the Planning Commission, to do the job of co-ordinating national investment as a whole, somehow taking the Government along with them. This whole approach has come in for some sharp criticism from Pasquale Saraceno in his latest guise as Vice-President of the Planning Commission—deputy to the Minister of the Budget, who is the titular President. Running through his interim report[55] on the work of the Commission is the persistent demand for 'political decision' by the Government. It comes up on one subject after another; the important issues of national policy, he points out relentlessly, cannot be left to be settled by a series of bargains between interest groups. There is no way of turning planning into a non-political exercise.

Once again, one observes historical attitudes reasserting themselves. Presented with an opportunity such as this, the old corporatist instincts of Italian business and other interest groups—the instinct to clothe the representatives of the 'corporations' with semi-sovereign powers of legal regulation and then leave them to fix things up among themselves—came immediately to expression. The Communist-led trade union movement, Confederazione Generale Italiana del Lavoro (CGIL), was just as ready to engage in this kind of bargain as the Confindustria, the central employers' organization, by-passing the ordinary machinery of democratic government entirely. Although it derives from quite another tradition, the analogy with the behaviour of the British trade unions in NEDC suggests itself.[56] It is highly doubtful whether the 'corporations' in either country have it in their capacity to plan in any meaningful sense, without the political decision, the explicit commitment by the Government of the resources of public power, which Saraceno so urgently demands.

---

[55] *Rapporto del Vice Presidente della Commissione Nazionale per la Programmazione Economica* (Mar. 1964). This report is a personal document issued by the Vice-President, effectively the man in charge, without committing the other members of the Commission. It was indeed evident that these carefully balanced interest groups, whatever bargains they might make among themselves, would never be able to produce a common view on a long-term plan for Italy. The report is in the nature of a sketch for an exercise in Italian economic planning, setting out a list of problems to be tackled and the possible methods of doing so, rather than a plan of action.

[56] See above, pp. 152 ff.

2. Manpower Planning: Sweden

The Active Consensus

In Sweden there is a society in which interest groups are so strongly organized, their democratic basis is so firm, and their habit of bargaining with one another independently of the government so well established, that here, if anywhere, 'indicative planning' in the full sense—that is planning without any dependence on the power of the state—looks as if it ought to be feasible. Indeed, it is a matter of pride for those involved in what is probably the most important single act of Swedish economic policy, the annual bargain on the national wage level, that the Government is made to keep its distance. It is not merely that it is excluded from the colloquy between the two sides; it does not even, any longer, attempt to exercise guidance from the side-lines by providing an official view of the likely trend of the national product for the year ahead and therefore of the scope for increases in wages and other incomes. It used to do this at one time, but the principal bargainers evidently made it clear that they would regard it as more tactful if they were left alone to do their own sums.

I recall a British trade union leader after an organized visit to Sweden—there were several such visits undertaken by the British trade union movement in the early 1960s in an attempt to discover the secret of Swedish labour's success—expressing his frustration over the whole business. The secret was either too banal or too opaque to yield to intelligent investigation. 'All they can tell you when you ask them how they do it', he said, describing some particularly difficult decision which involved the concerted action of competing interest groups, 'is: "We has a meeting." *We has a meeting!* I'd like to see how they'd make out with our blokes over here.' The Swedish trade unions and employers have not always shown this propensity to reach agreement by means of protracted and no doubt tediously polite dialogue, rather than by direct action and strife. Sweden before the war had a bad record for working days lost through strikes.[57] Indeed, the Basic Agreement of 1938 between the employers and the trade union organization, the foundation of the whole system from which all else including the central wages pact has followed, was only signed under strong pressure from the authorities. As one Swedish commentator on the labour side has said: 'To prevent legislation was the principal motive.'[58]

This is not by any means the sole occasion on which the overhanging presence of governmental authority has been the decisive factor in the outcome. The fact that the Government does not intervene—indeed is publicly seen *not* to intervene—does not mean that it fails to let its views be known to those concerned. That incidentally is also true of the annual wage

[57] See Jack Cooper, *Industrial Relations: Sweden Shows the Way* (London, Fabian Research Ser., 1963, p. 20). [58] Ibid.

negotiation. It just happens that it is the Swedish way to treat the process of government as being in large part an extended dialogue between experts drawn from a variety of bodies, official and unofficial, whose views are expected to be merely tinged rather than finally shaped by those who pay their salaries. This active search for consensus, which is a preliminary to any important action, is in fact one of the means of governing. It influences the effectiveness of government just as certainly as more formal methods of law enforcement.

The interesting thing is that in spite of the variety of built-in mechanisms for compromise, working through a system of wide-ranging consultation and organized argument, the Swedish Government still manages to act in a decisive fashion when circumstances require it.[59] Even more striking, the leading organizations, which are so bound up with the process of government, have provided the impulse for innovations in the field of policy which boldly lead, rather than follow public opinion. The achievement is especially worthy of note because Sweden offers the solitary instance in the postwar capitalist world of a trade union movement which has made a significant intellectual contribution to the development of the system. Elsewhere the trade unions have, in the main, been followers, reacting with old ideas to a changed economic environment; sometimes they have been active resisters. There have been neither the political ideas nor the initiatives in social organization which were a feature of the vigorous trade unionism of the interwar years and of the period immediately preceding the First World War. The leaders of Swedish organized labour, almost alone, seem actively to have welcomed the opportunity to adapt their doctrines to the social needs of a mixed economy of the modern capitalist type. No doubt the circumstance of having its allies in the Socialist Party running the Government at the same time favoured the effort.

Typically, the Swedish Left, which has about the longest experience of office of any socialist party in the West, is very little concerned with the extension of public ownership. There is probably less nationalization than in other advanced West European countries; even public utilities like electricity are not entirely publicly owned. The Swedish Socialists were among the first to realize that there was no necessary connexion between the exercise of effective

---

[59] The Swedish system seems to be a refutation of the view that either the pressure of public argument in advance of action or public accountability afterwards has the effect of paralysing the initiative of government officials. Swedish officials are especially exposed to the latter, both through the Ombudsman (who is essentially the agent of parliament inside the administrative machine, checking that the administrators are carrying out their duties in accordance with the intentions of the legislature) and the Supreme Administrative Tribunal. In fact it is arguable that this elaborate system for talking out the rights and wrongs of any given administrative action tends to make officials more, rather than less, confident in taking decisions. See Ch. XVI for a more detailed account of the Swedish administrative system.

control over the pace and direction of a modern economy and the proliferation of public enterprise. The special feature of postwar Sweden is that the focus of national economic policy is on the use of the labour force—how to increase its size, how to improve its quality, how to achieve its more rapid deployment in response to changing needs. There is also the problem of controlling its remuneration in circumstances of full employment, when it is assumed that wages will almost inevitably rise faster than productivity.[60]

The Swedish Government has taken the policy of full employment more seriously than other Western countries. Having rejected the notion that the rise in wages should be restrained by securing a sufficient margin of unemployment to enhance the bargaining power of employers, it actively cast around for new ways of restraining costs and prices. The central wage bargain, related to a carefully calculated forecast of the probable rise in the real national product, is one of the expedients. The other, and the more important part of the effort, is the collection of measures grouped under the heading of 'Active Manpower Policy'. This is a strategy for mobilizing labour of the kind and in the amounts that are going to be needed to make the most of the economic opportunities offered by new technology, and to do so at the maximum feasible speed. This is the heart of Swedish economic planning. Since the supply of labour is seen as the limiting factor on economic advance, long-term policy is concerned with identifying the probable shifts in the demand for different skills and organizing training and incentives accordingly.

Labour and Investment

The centrepiece of the system is the Labour Market Board. It is an immensely powerful body whose brief includes the tactical control of economic policy, as well as its strategy. For a full employment policy also requires that any fluctuations in the demand for labour caused by the business cycle should be evened out. Fewer fluctuations in employment also mean a higher average rate of growth of national production. By the same token, an increase in demand at a time and a place where it cannot be met by an increased supply of labour is wasteful and a source of disruption: it is, so far as is possible, to be prevented. There are two main instruments used by the authorities to secure these ends, one a direct physical control over building, and the other a financial control over investment.

The financial control is particularly interesting as an instrument of policy, because it offers scope for discrimination between different industries in guiding national investment policy. The system is essentially a simple one. Firms which make good profits in times of boom are given the opportunity of avoiding tax on them if the money is frozen in a special reserve fund, to be

---

[60] See T. L. Johnston, ed., *Economic Expansion and Structural Change* (London, Allen & Unwin, 1963), the Swedish trade union manifesto of 1961, for a discussion of these ideas; also OECD, *Labour Market Policy in Sweden* (1963).

used later for investments whose content and timing have been approved by the authorities.[61] The amount of money accumulated by firms in this way in the early 1960s was large enough to have a significant effect on the level of investment. For example, the 1,200 million kronor which was channelled into additional building during the winter of 1962–3, when there was a threat of unemployment in the building trades, amounted to the equivalent of rather more than one-quarter of all fixed investment in the manufacturing and construction industries.[62] The authorities also appear to have grown more skilful in the handling of this powerful tool since it was introduced in the mid-1950s; the timing of releases was better planned in the small incipient recession of 1961–2 than it had been in the business downturn of 1958–9. With practice, the management of the country's investment programme has become more subtle and selective. Some of the conditions imposed on firms which benefit from these releases of funds are precise and detailed: for instance, they stipulate the type of person and age-groups to be employed on certain approved projects.[63] Alternatively, the condition applied may be that the releases are to be used for particular kinds of capital goods: in this way a special boost was given to the shipbuilding industry and also to machinery manufacturing industries in 1962–3, when they were held back by thin order books.[64]

This type of investment planning, which is closely attuned to the ups and downs of the business cycle, is supplemented by the careful management of a timetable of capital projects in the public sector. Local authorities are encouraged to accumulate a 'shelf' of investment schemes which can be brought into action at short notice, and to ensure that this physical investment reserve is kept replenished. The numerous regional offices of the Labour Market Board follow the work done on the individual blueprints for projects in some detail. The incentive which they can offer is the payment of a government subsidy to cover up to 50 per cent of the costs incurred at the planning stage. A scheme is judged to be ready to go into the 'investment

---

[61] In addition, when the money is released for an approved project, the firm can claim an income tax rebate amounting to 10 per cent of the sum withdrawn (see B. Olsson, 'Employment Policy in Sweden', *Internat. Labour Review*, May 1963).

[62] Olsson and OECD, *Labour Market Policy*. In practice, only a portion of the profits set aside for the investment reserve is actually deposited in the special account of the central bank (46 per cent) and it is this sum which is formally released, on the understanding that the firms concerned will make up the remainder of the 100 per cent required for the finance of the approved projects. Thus, the actual amount released for these building works in 1962–3 was some 600 m. kr., which went towards the finance of an additional 1,200 m. kr. investment in building. The tax report for 1962 shows 2,400 m. kr. of deposits accumulated in reserve investment funds under the control of the Labour Market Board—the equivalent of some 15 per cent of total Swedish fixed investment in that year.

[63] This was done in the pulp and paper industry in 1961–2 (see National Labour Market Board's *Annual Report 1962*).

[64] Ibid.

reserve' when the plans allow for a maximum interval of two months between the date of its authorization and the actual engagement of man-power. Similar arrangements cover the capital programmes of the central government departments. Finally, all these projects are brought together into a comprehensive national plan—not a plan of firm commitments, but rather of desirable objectives ready to be pursued at the first favourable moment—and submitted to parliament for approval. In the early 1960s the amount of building work in the 'investment reserve' was equivalent to 10 per cent of the annual value of all forms of construction—which was quite enough to offset any business fluctuation of normal postwar dimensions. It also contained orders for large amounts of manufactured goods and equipment.[65]

What is especially interesting to observe is the way in which the Swedish concern with short-term economic fluctuations and their control has pushed the Government inexorably towards systematic long-term planning. It is exactly the opposite of the French experience, where the long term was the initial and overriding consideration, while the problems of the short term were only gradually identified as a significant factor in economic policy, having been treated at first merely as a troublesome element making for untidiness in a set of beautifully balanced calculations. Both stories illustrate the pressures in contemporary capitalist society which push governments to formulate their economic objectives with increasing precision in the framework of a comprehensive national plan.

Centralized Power

For several years after the war the Swedes tended to treat the preparation of long-term economic plans as a peripheral aspect of national policy—an intellectual exercise setting out alternative possibilities of growth, prepared by an *ad hoc* group of independent experts. It was only in 1962 that the Government set up the Economic Planning Council, still composed pre-dominantly of experts drawn from outside the Government, but now for the first time brought inside the governmental machine: the Minister of Finance is the chairman and the permanent secretariat of the Council is provided by the Economic Department of the Ministry.[66] The motive for the reform, it was explained, was 'a need for greater continuity in the long-term planning process'.[67] This is another way of saying that planning, if it is to be effective,

---

[65] Olsson, *Internat. Lab. R.*, May 1963.
[66] The Economic Dept., in its new role, has been given the task of 'working out the next long-term planning report', i.e. for 1965–70 (see OECD, *Growth and Economic Policy* (1964, mimeo.), pt. 2, ch. 3: 'Sweden'). Thus the guiding professional arm is firmly attached to the body of the Government. The Council itself, which has 14 members, is partly composed of independent experts and partly of representatives of trade unions and of industrial associations.
[67] OECD, *Econ. Surveys, Sweden*, 1963.

must be steadily related to the day-to-day work of government. This is the truth which the French have grasped most clearly, right from the start. It does not follow, however, that the reform presages the complete conversion of Sweden to the French system. Although it is clear that the two countries are moving broadly in the same direction, along with several other West European nations, each continues to do so in its own very distinctive vehicle.[68]

It is interesting to observe how much of the French way is vigorously repudiated by the dominant school of thought in the Swedish establishment, centred on the trade union movement, despite its demands for more active government planning. The trade unions say that they are against the centralization of economic authority; that they do not like selective subsidies which are supposed to encourage the growth of particular sectors of industry; that their preference is for the use of competitive market pressures on firms; and that they want the maximum possible free trade, because this will compel both capital and labour to move from less productive to more productive industries.[69] One is tempted to ask, after this formidable list of demands for non-intervention, whether the 'planning' which the Swedish trade unions are after would not also satisfy the most zealous devotee of old-fashioned market forces. The answer is that in a country which is so exposed to the pressures of international trade, it is believed that the starting point for planning must be adaptation to extraneous market forces. The job of the planner is chiefly to help the nation to adapt itself to the market more rapidly than it otherwise would do. Broadly the view is that firms must fend entirely for themselves— whether they survive or not is a matter of indifference—and that the whole of the public effort is to be concentrated on the welfare of the wage-earners.

It is only fair to point out that this robust attitude towards the fate of private enterprise and the beneficent working of market forces has emerged in a country endowed with special economic advantages. It is not merely that the productivity of the average worker in Sweden is considerably higher than it is anywhere else in Western Europe. There are in addition some

---

[68] The Swedes, for instance, have been very reluctant to make use of the discriminatory techniques of economic intervention, which are an essential element of French planning. Here the spirit of Swedish administration and laws is much closer to the British than to the French tradition. Commenting on the use made of the investment control exercised through the individual licensing of every building project (covering dates of starting and finishing the work; the numbers to be employed month by month; and the age-groups of workers employed) the OECD reports: 'This individual licensing of each project gives a possibility of discrimination between firms, trades or geographical regions. Such discrimination has, however, been avoided, although in some cases where local variations in labour supply existed it would have been desirable. This non-discrimination has been considered necessary to maintain confidence in the system' (*Labour Market Policy*, p. 43).

[69] Johnston, *Economic Expansion*.

unusual social forces which are well designed to keep Swedish private enterprise on its toes. One of them is a powerful and aggressive co-operative organization, equipped with plenty of funds and actively trying to smoke out any firms with a monopolistic element in their profits resulting from a protected position in the market. There may be a hankering after more decentralization of power; but in the meanwhile the characteristic feature of the country is the highly centralized structure of its major organizations. The Swedish co-operatives present in this matter the extreme contrast to the British co-operative movement. So do the trade unions. Even the employers, who have been united for many years in Sweden in a single tightly-knit body, are divided into three independent organizations in Britain.[70]

A further significant factor in Sweden is the existence of a wide-ranging apparatus to educate public opinion for use as a force in the economic process, notably in the field of consumer standards. The state plays a major part in this. Indeed it is worth remarking that when it comes to the subject of consumer research and information—which is normally regarded in Western countries as a function of voluntary bodies—the Swedes plump for a very etatist solution. Not for them the embattled body of private citizens clubbed together in Consumers' Associations, on the original American model later copied in Britain and in other European countries. That is thought to be far too uncertain a challenge to issue to the manufacturers of shoddy goods. It is assumed that this is a function which belongs naturally in the sphere of government responsibility.[71]

It would thus be wrong to accept too readily the conventional Swedish view of the relatively minor part played by governmental authority in their society. The power of the state is considerable. This is no corporatist system in which interest groups are endowed with legal privileges and act as independent semi-sovereign entities. Rather they are the instruments of public policy used by the state, wherever this is feasible, in the place of its own paid servants. There was an interesting exchange in the course of an OECD investigation of Swedish manpower policy in 1962 which neatly expresses the underlying attitude. The visiting OECD examiners commented after they had looked at the organization of Labour Market Board and its various affiliates on which organized interest groups outside the Government are heavily represented: 'It would seem as if, through the central labour market agency, the employers' and employees' organisations have to some extent been put in a position to pursue their own policy.' The Swedes plainly did not like this suggestion. Their formal reply to the OECD, though polite enough in tone,

---

[70] Arrangements are now being made (1965) to unite the British employers, though the negotiations for doing so have proved laborious.
[71] The trade union policy statement (Johnston, *Economic Expansion*, p. 118) refers disdainfully to the proposal to form a voluntary consumers' association in Sweden as 'a second best alternative' to the existing state-run system for the protection of consumers.

carries the tiniest hint of suppressed indignation: 'It should be added', they say, 'that the organizations, thanks to this close co-operation, not only influence but also take responsibility for the efficient pursuance of the policies and measures decided upon; they have not only rights but duties as well.'[72]

The Central Wage Bargain

How important in practice is the central wage bargain between the trade union and employers' organizations in the Swedish system of planning? It might appear at first sight that once the question of the level of wages—and incidentally profits, and therefore the prices of all goods produced at home— has been settled, the rest is fairly easy. Perhaps, in that case, what Sweden ought to offer to the rest of us is a lesson in the uses of an 'incomes policy' rather than anything else. The problem of how to control cost inflation, which seems to be a built-in feature of postwar Western society, has become in the 1960s a growing preoccupation of governments. As full employment has come to be taken for granted among the advanced industrial countries of Western Europe, leaving only a residual and diminishing exception in Southern Italy, the uninterrupted rise in costs and prices tends to occupy the centre of the stage in popular political discussion of economic policy. The issue has been invested in some countries with more urgency by the systematic lowering of the barriers to international trade, inside the European Common Market and the European Free Trade Association. As domestic markets are more and more exposed to foreign competition, there is immediate danger to the balance of payments from any rise in costs which goes beyond the level of competing countries. Since it is usually impossible to forecast precisely what the other guy will do, this is a subject of constant anxiety. Especially for a nation which feels that its gold reserve is insufficient to meet a temporary deficit caused by miscalculation, there is a strong incentive to avoid the risks of an all-out policy of expansion.

However, judged by the results to date, the Swedish experience does not appear to supply a very promising guide on how to keep wages moving in line with the rise in productivity.[73] Indeed, it could be argued that the annual rise in wages for the country as a whole is greater than it would be if each individual group of workers were left to fend for itself, without the support of a central body of bargainers determined to ensure that no one gets left behind. The leaders of the trade union movement are, not surprisingly, a great deal better at the latter task than at preventing workers, who are favourably placed in a profitable industry, from pushing their wages ahead faster than was planned. What happens is that the two organizations, the trade unions (Landsorganisationen, LO) and the employers (Svenska Arbetsgivare-

---

[72] *Labour Market Policy*, p. 52 n.
[73] See, *inter alia*, B. C. Roberts, *National Wages Policy in War and Peace* (London, Allen & Unwin, 1958).

föreningen, SAF), work out separately their own estimates of the probable increase in the national product, of the trend of profits, the external balance of payments, industrial costs, and so on over the year ahead. The LO then presents its overall wage claim for the year, supported by its calculations of what extra real resources are going to be produced. It used to take two to three weeks for the SAF to work out all the implications of the trade unions' case and to prepare an answer to it; nowadays with the aid of computers, the employers can react 'in a matter of minutes'.[74] The next stage is some highly expert bargaining about percentage points of wages and profits, based on the forecast figures of production and prices put forward by the two sides.

The national figure for the basic wage increase which is ultimately agreed is, however, not the end of the story. LO now proceeds to recommend larger than average increases for particular industries in which earnings have lagged behind, because of the weak bargaining position of organized labour in them. This corresponds to the element of so-called 'wage drift', i.e. the additional earnings received by some workers over and above the standard rates negotiated by the trades unions. In recent years 'wage drift' has averaged around 4 per cent in Swedish manufacturing industry. What LO does is to insist that workers in less prosperous industries—an example is textiles—should be enabled to capture some of the benefits of the extra earnings that have been obtained elsewhere, in the course of the regular trade union negotiation. It is in this way that wage increases which in other countries might be confined to particular groups of workers or areas where labour is especially short are, in Sweden, generalized over the whole system.

The deeper implications of this policy adopted by the trade union leadership—which it calls the policy of 'wage solidarity'—are worth considering. If enterprises in an industry where productivity is low are compelled to pay the same wages as more productive workers earn elsewhere, three possible results may follow. Either the prices charged by this industry will have to be raised or it will have to accept a lower average level of profit than is obtainable elsewhere or a number of firms in the industry will have to go out of business, leaving only those with an above average level of efficiency who are able to produce a satisfactory return on their capital even after their wages have gone up. The trade unions reject the first alternative, and the deliberate policy of keeping tariffs low and exposing Swedish industry to international competition means that domestic prices are, in any case, under constant pressure from abroad. The second alternative is unlikely to be sustained in the long run, since firms requiring outside finance must be able to offer investors a normal rate of return on their money. So it is the third solution which is the most probable outcome. The trade unions are well

[74] This and following information on the procedure and content of the central wage bargain is derived from a description of it given verbally by the heads of LO and SAF in London in 1964.

aware of this; indeed, they welcome the process of killing off enterprises in which productivity is below the national average.

All this is part of the robust view taken by the Swedish Left of the role of market competition: competitive pressures are regarded as something to be accepted and used, rather than resisted. The unions are determined to ride the market, but not to be driven by it. They see their purpose as being like that of a skilful pilot in a sea of fast currents and high winds, who sets out to employ the energy of the elements to bring his boatload of passengers to their destination. It may be a bit uncomfortable at times, but at least they know where they are going and get there with the minimum of diversions. Specifically, in their wage policy the union leadership aims to reinforce the normal pressures of the market moving investment capital towards the places where it shows the highest rate of return—which, in a competitive situation undisturbed by monopolistic factors, are also the places where labour tends to be employed most efficiently. Labour's reward is a higher level of real wages than it would otherwise have been able to earn. Beyond that, it is the stated ambition of the trade unions to reduce, in the long run, the share of the final product taken by the owners of capital and to increase the share of labour. Again the means by which it hopes that this shift will be secured is through the more active use of the market—the capital market this time, where it is believed that the standard rate of return demanded by investors could be lowered if the national supply of capital were made more mobile. An efficient capital market which succeeded in mobilizing the funds of a lot of marginal investors for use in productive enterprise would, it is argued, provide investment finance for new ventures more cheaply than it is secured at present, especially as the savings represented by the ploughed back profits of companies are also withdrawn from the market. Reduced dependence on the plough-back, as a result of lowering the rate of profit, would therefore make for a better distribution of capital.[75]

In the meantime the way in which a carefully calculated wage bargain builds up into a powerful inflationary force is best demonstrated by an actual example. The 1962 agreement is fairly typical.[76] It started with a national wage increase of 2·75 per cent agreed between LO and SAF after their bout of bargaining and national income calculations. To this a sum equivalent to 1·5 per cent of the national wage bill was added to finance special wage increases for lagging industries (including a 7 per cent rise in the standard

---

[75] The state pension fund, greatly enlarged since the introduction of the supplementary pension scheme in 1960, is expected to provide a lot of the extra money going into the capital market in the future—it is already a major source of investment finance— thus incidentally withdrawing some unearned income and realised capital gains which would otherwise accrue to private rentiers, as a result of raising a higher proportion of the funds required for investment through the market.

[76] The figures which follow were given by Mr Per Holmberg, economist of LO at the Business Economists' Group Conference, Oxford, Apr. 1963.

rates for textiles and 10 per cent for transport). Then there were the increases for workers organized outside LO, in the white-collar unions and in agriculture.[77] These included a big rise (11 per cent) for all civil servants and an even bigger one (18 per cent) for shopworkers. The combined effect of all these special arrangements was to add a further 2 per cent to the nation's total wages. Finally, the normal process of wage drift was expected to put on another 2 per cent. In all, therefore, the Swedish wage bill was estimated to go up by something of the order of 8 per cent. The actual outcome for 1963 was a rise of 7·5 per cent in the national wage bill, against an increase of 3·3 per cent in the national product.[78]

What, then, it may be asked, is the purpose of the whole elaborate exercise—if in the end Swedish wages go up by more than they do even in a hopelessly unco-ordinated bargaining system such as Britain's?[79] The Swedish answer is that there are other benefits, in the form of improved economic efficiency, which result from a technique of wage determination that is generally accepted as a way of doing justice between different groups of workers. A central wage bargain which fixes the amount of the basic increase that all wage-earners can expect reduces the pressure on the individual union leader, who is at least assured that his members are not going to be left out in a general free-for-all. He does not feel that he has to use whatever industrial power he has at his command to protect the short-term sectional interests of his particular group. Once the principle is established that the level of wages is not to be determined by the bargaining strength of the individual union, the nature of the bargain between employers and workers changes too. An atmosphere is created in the course of the long and detailed negotiation, covering a wide area of industrial and economic policy, which leads easily to a discussion of methods for achieving a more productive use of labour in various fields. After all, the wage increase eventually agreed depends on the size of the prospective increase in output. The effect of this type of industrial negotiation, at any rate when it takes place in the context of Sweden's unusually sophisticated institutions for managing the labour market,[80] is to

---

[77] TCO (Tjänstemännens Centralorganisation), which is the trade union organization of the white-collar workers, is growing fast; it is expected to overtake the LO in membership by the late 1970s. Although LO does the actual negotiation, TCO arrangements for wage increases to be granted to their affiliated unions are fixed up in an inter-union agreement with LO, before the latter embarks on the central wage bargain.

[78] OECD, *Econ. Surveys, Sweden*, 1964.

[79] The annual increase in the wage bill in Britain averaged around 5 per cent in 1960–3—admittedly a period when the Government's deflationary policy had put some slack into the economy. The gap between the increase in earnings and the increase in productivity was also somewhat smaller in Britain than in Sweden during that period.

[80] The whole network of supporting institutions connected with the Labour Market Board contributes largely to the result. The summing-up of the OECD report on Sweden's *Labour Market Policy* (p. 69) is worth quoting on this point: 'The clear

create the conditions in which advantages of technological change can be exploited more rapidly than in other countries in which labour is equally scarce.

Perhaps the most important brake on the pace of technological progress in a full employment society is the immobility of labour. The Swedish way is designed to speed up the movement between jobs. The trade unions, having achieved a large measure of security for their members—not only through the assured annual increments of wages, but also through the various welfare services provided by the state for workers on the move between jobs, including generous cash payments during retraining, priority for housing and adequate removal allowances—have the confidence to pursue the objective of high labour mobility. Their view is that once the worker has been equipped with this protective shell, the labour market ought to be encouraged to operate with the maximum vigour. For it is assumed that it will, like any other market when it is properly harnessed, serve the purpose of the community.

Other European countries have begun in the 1960s to show an interest in 'active manpower policies',[81] in the Swedish style, as an aid to economic growth. Gradually it has come to be realized that since the limiting factor on expansion is no longer likely to be inadequacy or uncertainty of demand or lack of capital, but rather a shortage of labour of the right type in the right place, the sensible thing to do is to plan the use of this scarce resource to better effect. One part of the answer is to increase its mobility; the other is to improve its training. Both involve forecasting the demands of particular industries for some time ahead. The second answer, better manpower training, must, where skills of increasing sophistication are concerned, involve planning of an especially long-term character.

In a sense, active manpower policies are the natural corollary of the policy of full employment. To begin with, the remedy for the growing pressure on labour supplies was sought in the traditional fashion, by importing more of it from abroad. But after a few years of this several countries began to express anxiety about the social problems of running a country or even individual towns and districts with a high proportion of foreigners in the working population. In fact the postwar immigration policies had never been

definition of their employment policy tasks has converted the labour market agencies from passive agents able to serve only limited sectors of the labour market; they now form an organization which seeks to anticipate the changes in supply and demand for labour on a broad scale and to facilitate the adjustments of individuals and enterprises to oncoming changes. This policy has inspired confidence among workers in the probability of their placement in new jobs after loss of employment, and in financial maintenance during the adjustment period. The result has been a greater willingness on the part of trades unions and the people as a whole to support technological and economic changes which will benefit the national economy'.

[81] The phrase used by the OECD, which has taken the lead in organizing the exchange of ideas on this theme (see OECD, Social Affairs Division, Seminar on Active Manpower Policy, *Reports* (Brussels), 14–17 Apr. 1964).

regarded as more than an interim solution: while the plethora of jobs lasted, they would be filled by foreigners; but as soon as there was any threat of unemployment the foreigners would be sent home. France between the wars had supplied the tragic model for this kind of arrangement.[82] But when the threat of unemployment failed to materialize—rather the demand for labour became ever more insistent—governments faced worries of another sort.

The way out of the social and the economic problem, it became evident, was to speed up the movement from old and declining jobs to new and expanding ones inside the domestic labour market. This implied a policy of inducing weak industries to decline faster, and shed their labour in the process—the opposite of the traditional effort to make such changes as slow and as long drawn out as possible. Agriculture was the most obvious example of large reserves of manpower which could be transferred to new occupations. There was also an increasing number of industrial jobs of a traditional kind which were becoming redundant, notably in coalmining and in certain kinds of transport. Yet meanwhile the difficulty of shifting people under the pressure of harsh economic circumstances had increased, as a result of the spread of social welfare and the attitudes of an affluent community, in which politicians could be fairly readily blackmailed into providing a subsidy to keep an insistent and obviously unfortunate pressure group quiet.

The Swedish experience has pointed the way to an alternative approach. It is, of course, quite expensive—though not nearly so expensive as either the permanent subsidy to the sectional interest that cannot support itself or the deflationary method of raising the level of unemployment, in order to induce workers to become more mobile. Sweden, which was probably more firmly committed than other nations to the triple objective of full employment, rapid growth, and a very high level of social welfare, was the natural source of innovation in this field.[83]

3. The Control of Wages and Incomes

Dutch Experience

The other outstanding example of postwar economic policy based on the central control of wages is the Netherlands. It is pertinent to describe the differences between it and the Swedish system, with which it is sometimes

---

[82] See p. 85.

[83] It is worth noting that the Swedes have not made use of the device of large-scale immigration, even as a stop-gap measure—something for which the Government has been criticized by the trade unions (see Johnston, *Economic Expansion*). This no doubt added to the incentive to find an alternative solution to the problem of labour shortage. They have also been relatively unconcerned about the effect on the geographical balance of Swedish industry and population of a large-scale movement of labour to a few centres of high employment. The latter is no doubt one of the effects of having a great deal of space and few problems of human or industrial congestion.

associated in the discussion of incomes policies. It should not be. The chief similarity with the Swedish experiment is a common inability to cope with the problem of 'wage drift'—in spite of the fact that the Dutch have armed their wage controllers with statutory powers, contrasting with the purely advisory function of those responsible for the Swedish central wage agreement. The instrument used in Sweden is the pressure arising out of highly centralized organizations, both moral and straight financial pressure.[84] In Holland it has been the law, powerfully buttressed by direct government control over prices.

The direct intrusion of governmental authority in a process which is generally regarded in the Western world as standing outside the ambit of state power is the distinctive feature of the Dutch political experience since the war. It is because some governments of Western countries in the 1960s have begun nibbling at the problem, however gingerly, and others show every sign of being tempted to do so, that the uncompromising method of direct wage control adopted in Holland invites attention. After all, if a nation with a democratic tradition as firmly grounded as the Dutch is willing to stand for the full treatment, then perhaps there may be more scope than is generally imagined for direct intervention by the state in support of an 'incomes policy'

In fact, the circumstances of postwar Holland are too special to permit any significant generalization to be founded on the experiment. The Dutch saw themselves immediately after the war facing a serious problem of surplus population, in a country whose industries were much less developed than those of her neighbours in Western Europe. The only hope of providing large-scale opportunities for additional employment through the expansion of home industry seemed to be by keeping Dutch wages deliberately below the West European standard. This, it was thought, would permit the Netherlands to compete on level terms for an outlet for its industrial products in world export markets. The argument was in fact a variation on the traditional case for protecting infant industries. Only in this instance, instead of providing shelter for these industries at home by means of a high tariff wall, it was to be supplied by putting an artificially low ceiling on wages and holding it there by decree. The remarkable willingness of the trade unions to collaborate actively in this policy of wage restraint is to be explained by their anxiety about the future supply of jobs for Dutchmen.

It was precisely the kind of policy which Italy—for similar though more pressing reasons—might have been expected to adopt. In fact, the Italians during the 1950s managed to achieve the same essential purpose as the Dutch, by keeping the rise in wages below the rise in productivity, but they

---

[84] e.g. the Swedish trade union organization LO has large funds on which individual unions rely to supplement their own strike funds in case of need. It could be awkward for them if they moved into a dispute against the wishes of the central trade union body.

did it with the help of covert pressures rather than overt dictation on the part of the government. In both countries the arrangements broke down in the early 1960s. But it should be noted that by then the Dutch had had several years of very full employment. They were induced to go on exercising some restraint in spite of it. In Italy the mere approach of full employment, still some way from being realized, was sufficient to bring on a spectacular rise in wage rates in the early 1960s, far greater than any possible increase in productivity. This was the chief cause of the Italian balance of payments crisis in 1963–4, which then led to a bout of deflation and a slowing down of economic growth.

The breakdown of the Dutch system was not formally registered until the autumn of 1963. It had been visibly shaky for some time, as increasing numbers of Dutchmen found work on the German side of the frontier and brought back a considerably larger wage packet than they could earn at home. Dutch employers who wanted their services had to compete. In 1962 and 1963 average wages rose by 8 per cent a year, which was several times more than the rather modest increase in the productivity of Dutch workers during that period. The wage controllers appeared to be helpless. Evidently trying to counter the danger that the whole system would be brought into disrepute by the exercise of a control which when it worked did so uncertainly and in spots, they decided at last to ride out the forces of the market—in Swedish style—rather than go on resisting them. Under a series of agreements, ratified by the Government, it was estimated that average hourly wages would be jacked up by an estimated 16 per cent in the course of one year, 1964.[85] However, the mechanism of control was still retained intact. Indeed, the powers of the Government to control prices, an essential instrument for imposing discipline on employers, were reinforced. The Government found itself, against its earlier intentions, relying more heavily than ever on the indirect pressure of price control to stiffen the resistance of employers to wage claims. Businesses were in fact served notice that if they conceded more than the permitted wage increases in the future, the price control would be used to force them to finance the extra amount by a cut in their profits.

The extreme readiness to use the weapon of price control—the Government had already assumed additional powers early in 1963 to fix retail ceiling prices for individual firms—is the striking feature of Dutch postwar economic policy. They seem to have fewer inhibitions about this kind of detailed intervention even than the French.[86] In Holland any firm which proposes to raise its prices is under an obligation to discuss its intention with the government department concerned before it makes any move. It is partly because business is so highly concentrated in several Dutch industries and the country

---

[85] OECD, *Econ. Surveys, Netherlands*, 1964.   [86] See above, pp. 148 ff.

itself is small that such close consultation can be conducted between government departments and individual firms with so little apparent fuss. The Government for its part takes great trouble to equip itself for these encounters with a large amount of relevant economic information and with the advice of a high-powered Central Planning Bureau, which itself maintains close contacts with the business world. Price control on so broad a front clearly involves an overall view of economic strategy. Without the guidance of a national plan, such intervention could easily deform and impede the process of economic growth.[87] It is not clear how far the experience of the Netherlands is relevant to the problems of other countries. On the face of it, the Dutch seem to have discovered in price control a powerful tool of economic pressure, especially in relation to 'incomes policies', which is generally neglected in other Western countries[88]—except as part of an occasional emergency operation of a strictly temporary character.

Dutch economic planning, like Swedish, was initially focused very largely on the short term. The Central Planning Bureau's task was to look one year ahead. But the Government has found itself gradually compelled, in order to deal sensibly with a series of short-term decisions, to extend the time horizon of its plan. In 1963 it decided to embark on a system of 'medium-term forecasts', looking ahead for five years.[89] It is also to be remarked that the words used to describe the method of planning employed, both in Holland and in Sweden, may mislead if they are taken at their face value as a guide to the true role of public power in the management of the economy in these countries. There is the constant insistence that their kind of planning is purely 'indicative', which might suggest to the unwary that the plan depended for its fulfilment on intellectual persuasion alone.[90] In fact, there

---

[87] There appears to be a large measure of administrative discretion in interpreting the rules governing the control of prices. The main point is that industry is made to operate in a gold-fish bowl: the officials demand to know the full detail of costs and earnings item by item. They can even prescribe the form in which company books are to be kept, so that they are enabled more easily to follow the movement of real costs. But there is no rigidity when it comes to the practical application of the criteria of price control. The economic circumstances of individual enterprises are taken into account. The OECD remarks in its report on Dutch practice that 'the departures from these criteria (of price control) may be permitted if necessitated by considerations related to the earning-power of the industry or enterprise concerned' (*Policies for Prices, Profits and Other Non-Wage Incomes* (1964), p. 63).

[88] Ibid.

[89] OECD, *Econ. Surveys, Netherlands*, 1964, reports that 'both employers and wage-earners seem more and more convinced of the usefulness of medium-term forecasting of the overall economic trend, especially to guide investment decisions or wage negotiations' (para. 33).

[90] There is a certain terminological confusion, because the use of the word 'indicative' by the planners is sometimes intended merely to convey that their task is not an executive one. But the real point is not whether the people in the planning office have the formal right to issue orders to anyone, but rather how much notice those

are very powerful instruments of pressure available for use by public authority on private enterprise. Broadly, price control is to Holland what the system of investment reserves is to Sweden.[91]

On the other hand the technique of statutory wage control does not make a very impressive showing as a tool of economic policy. It did admittedly serve its purpose during the period of reconstruction immediately after the war and then in the crash programme of investment and modernization which followed. But once the sense of national emergency was removed, the difficulties multiplied. In particular, the Dutch authorities could not design any satisfactory method of keeping the movements of wages in different industries and trades in some reasonable relationship to one another. For several years they seemed to be intent on treating the labour market as if it was a national parade ground. on which everyone was supposed to march for ever steadily in step. The first break came in 1959 when some concession was made to claims by the workers to a share of the prosperity and extra profits of their particular industry. But the attempt to limit the effect on wage differentials by applying a standard national formula, allotting so many marks for the rise in productivity in the particular industry and so many for the anticipated rise over the economy as a whole, did not work out.[92]

The Dutch have refused to contemplate anything like the Swedish system of compensating workers in less favoured trades who were found to be lagging behind. This, as we have seen, provides an efficient built-in device for spreading the effects of 'wage drift' throughout the economy. Its immediate impact is highly inflationary. However, in the long run it has the attraction that it gives wage-earners a sense of security and order, so that they are ready to consent to a degree of centralization of trade union power which they would

who do possess full executive power take of their advice. Note that the Commissariat du Plan has no executive powers either. It is characteristic that the Dutch Central Planning Bureau in the official document setting out its functions first of all goes out of its way to explain the limitations imposed on its activities by its purely advisory role, but then goes on to point out that because of the loose administrative structure of Dutch government, with public authority widely dispersed and individual government departments very independent, the influence of an advisory body which spans the activities of a variety of government departments can be considerable. It then turns out that the same limitation which is placed on the executive powers of the planners also applies to the Cabinet and to the Ministerial Council of Economic Affairs! Both 'serve more for joint consultation than as authoritative bodies above the departments' (*Scope and Methods of the Central Planning Bureau*, The Hague, 1956, p. 215).

[91] See above, pp. 201–2.

[92] The formula for permissible wage increases introduced in 1961 was as follows: $\dfrac{3a + b}{4}$ with a equal to the average annual increase in productivity achieved in the particular industry over the previous nine years or so, and b representing the expected increase in national productivity calculated for the year ahead (see OECD, *Econ. Surveys, Netherlands*, 1963).

otherwise be unwilling to accept. Ordinarily each group would want to keep a tight hold on its own separate organisation to fight for its interests. The Swedish arrangement thus creates the conditions for more rational behaviour over the whole field of industrial relations. What the Dutch have tried to do is to have it both ways. When they finally embarked on a radical reform of their system in 1962, they copied the Swedes to the extent of giving the trade union and employers' organizations more responsibility for wage agreements; but on the other hand, the Government continued to insist on its ultimate power to inspect and to declare illegal any wage bargain which did not meet with its approval.

The reform was intended to meet the criticisms made by the Economic and Social Council of the whole approach to wage control on the basis of a single national formula. 'There is increasing unanimity in thinking', it had said in its report to the Government, 'that wage trends really depend on a large number of factors which are so diverse that they cannot be reduced to a single formula. . . . In determining wages, these factors can best be appreciated in the first instance by private enterprise. But this means that private enterprise must have adequate freedom of action in this field.'[93] In practice, private enterprise certainly seemed to feel much freer after the reform. Its new initiative, which was first exercised in 1963, began to show its effect in the following year when a series of agreements approved by the Foundation of Labour—the central body of employers and trade union organizations responsible for wage bargains—resulted, during the first quarter of 1964 alone, in a wage rise of $11\frac{1}{2}$–12 per cent.[94]

The débâcle of Dutch wage restraint, which had been regarded for so long as a kind of beacon light for less disciplined countries, induced the OECD to comment on its general significance in the contemporary struggle to achieve a rational 'incomes policy'. What scope was there for 'a policy designed to co-ordinate the growth of wages with national priority and not simply, even in the short run, to reflect the state of the market'? The lesson which it drew from the events in Holland was 'that too much cannot be expected from a wage policy which is not combined with other economic policy measures to match supply satisfactorily to demand'.[95] Certainly it is a fair point that wages cannot be handled in isolation from a general economic plan. But the more difficult question is whether in conditions where supply and demand *are* in balance, the growth of money wages can be limited to the prospective increase in real resources. The Swedish view, accepted by both trade union and employers' organizations, is that even after demand inflation is eliminated,

[93] Quoted ibid.
[94] Ibid., 1964. The increase in Dutch wages over 1964 as a whole was estimated by Dr J. E. Andriessen, Netherlands Minister of Economic Affairs, as 15–17 per cent (*Financial Times Survey of Europe*, 7 Dec. 1964).
[95] OECD, *Econ. Surveys, Netherlands*, 1964.

an underlying cost inflation will tend to push up prices. There is room for argument about how large and how inevitable, in the long run, this element of cost inflation is. But for all practical purposes it is treated by the Swedes as an autonomous factor, whose influence on prices can be mitigated, though not eliminated, by a combination of economic measures (designed to speed up the increase in productivity) and political ones (asserting some social principle in the division of the spoils). This view seems to correspond pretty well with the realities of economic life in Western Europe during the 1950s and 1960s.

Chasing an 'Incomes Policy'

There was a curious unrealism about the fervent expectations which suddenly came to be attached to the pursuit of an 'incomes policy' in a variety of Western countries during the 1960s. It was talked of by practical hardheaded men as if it offered an immediate short cut to an ideal economic world of steady prices and uninterrupted growth. It was alleged by some to be the precondition for effective economic planning. A great deal of time and energy was expended in efforts to induce trade union leaders to commit themselves to various abstract propositions about policies on wages which were designed to deal with the problem of inflation once and for all.[96] Whence came this sudden euphoria about the prospect of solving to the satisfaction of all concerned the most stubborn of all questions of social justice? What the fashionable exponents of 'incomes policy' seemed constantly to ignore was that they were asking wage-earners to accept that the existing division of wealth and the income derived from it was basically fair. Their concern, they insisted, was only to agree about the way in which the annual *increment* of national production—after all, a very small percentage of what was already possessed—was to be distributed. Perhaps the optimism arose out of the conviction, which had become widespread by the early 1960s, that economic growth could now be taken for granted: with the secure prospect

---

[96] Notably in Britain during 1963–5. A 'Joint Statement of Intent' by representatives of employers, trade unions, and the Government was signed (16 Dec. 1964) under the aegis of Mr George Brown, Minister for Economic Affairs. This was the culmination of an extended period of bargaining and pressure involving the previous (Conservative) Chancellor of the Exchequer (see Ch. VIII) as well as Mr Brown. The statement covered all incomes, not only wage-earnings. It also included a wide range of proposals about raising the level of industrial performance—rather more than about controlling the amounts of remuneration—which made it read like a general statement on production policy and planning. Indeed at this stage the British Government appeared to be undecided between the Swedish type of approach to a policy on incomes, which is to use it primarily as an aid to higher industrial efficiency and production, and the Dutch type, which is exclusively concerned with it as a means of controlling the level of money wages. The two approaches may easily conflict, for example, when wage incentives have to be used to secure greater mobility of labour.

of an annual bonanza to be shared out, it was argued, why should people quarrel about it? Especially, the argument went on, when it is clear that if some people do nevertheless insist on trying to take more than their fair share—which in this context means taking an increase in money wages greater than the increase in productivity—their action is bound to be self-defeating. That is because costs and prices are supposed to be driven up by precisely the amount corresponding to the excess taken by the greedy ones; and so the real value of the money which they earn will, in the end, be no more than they would have got on the basis of an agreed share-out.[97]

The conclusion although presented as a simple piece of economics is, in fact, a highly political argument. It implies that no group has it in its power to increase its share of the nation's income by more than it contributes to national production. Such intellectual plausibility as the argument has derives from the curiously vivid imagery invented by the classical economists—that of a perfectly competitive economy in which the various factors of production, the owners of capital, the managers and the labourers, are each rewarded to the extent necessary to bring out the marginal contribution required to secure the maximum possible output of saleable goods and services. Disturb this delicate balance of market forces, we are warned, and the well-being of the whole of society is imperilled. Reduce the reward to the marginal owner of capital and he will withdraw his contribution; there will then be less than full employment of labour. No doubt it would be a great convenience if an 'incomes policy' could start from these assumptions of perfect competition; all that would then be needed would be some minor adjustments in relative shares of different branches of production every now and then, to allow for changing economic opportunities. Such assumptions are, however, too blatantly in contradiction with the facts of our highly managed economy.

Moreover, even if this were not so, labour might still decide that it was worth while to pursue certain social ends by changes in the *relative* rewards of different factors of production, even at the cost of a slower increase in output. Full employment in the plain man's sense—not the classical economist's—can be achieved by reducing the number of hours which each person works. This rather theoretical point is worth mentioning, because it serves to emphasize that what is implied by arguments derived from theoretical economics about the proper remuneration of factors is the acceptance of a large block of the *status quo*. Labour is really being asked to give its consent to a particular type of social order. There is no reason why it

---

[97] In the particular case of the British Labour Government after 1964, there was a further political factor. This was the belief of the new Government that there was sufficiently widespread confidence among wage-earners in its determination and ability to use the power of the state to secure social justice for them that they would be willing to accept a new system of sharing out the prospective increase in the national income among themselves, the employers, the owners of capital and the Government.

should willingly do so—or for that matter why the owners of capital should positively assent to any alternative proposed.

They may, of course, be compelled to do so. But what a fully fledged 'incomes policy' really implies is the equivalent of a new Social Contract: it presupposes a society in which the different interest groups have marked out a sufficient area of agreement about the present distribution of wealth to deny themselves the right to try, in the future, to obtain certain advantages at each other's expense. Without this, one or another will surely find sooner or later a tactical opportunity for redistributing some of the existing wealth, and exploit it—even if that results in inflation. The common interest in avoiding the erosion of money values will not, by itself, be an overriding argument against making such an attempt. All this is another way of saying that a practical approach to a more rational wages policy must be deliberately and extensively political. It must stand ready to include in the bargain a wide range of issues concerned with the ordinary man's notions of social justice. Specifically, as the OECD notes in its description of the more sophisticated approach of some countries to the problem of an 'incomes policy' during the 1960s, 'the taxation of capital and capital gains, treatment of business expense allowances and measures to promote a wider distribution of wealth' are the type of issues that are brought within the compass of the argument.[98] There is also the need to ensure that justice is *seen* to be done. In the matter of opening up the economic process to effective public inspection, most of the Western capitalist countries are still at a very primitive stage. It seems unlikely that people in a democratic society will accept a policy of wage restraint unless the composition of all other domestic incomes which affect costs, however remotely, is brought under close and expert scrutiny.

That is why the Dutch insistence on the right of official inspection of costs and of the pricing policies of individual companies is especially noteworthy. It is a device which expresses the principle that decisions hitherto regarded as private matters belong increasingly in the domain of public responsibility. The British Labour Government, judging by its emphasis on the need for a new authority with the power to examine increases in prices as part of an 'incomes policy',[99] has also recognized that this a crucial element in the operation. The demand for transparent prices may, in the second half of the twentieth century, replace the more familiar demand for competitive prices. It will not be enough for a company to be able to show that it is selling its goods in competition with others at prices which it judges that the market will bear; it will also have to show why, in cases where its own profits are

[98] *Policies for Prices*, para. 91. Germany is cited as a country in which these aspects of an 'incomes policy' have received particular attention.

[99] This is the task of the National Board for Prices and Incomes, established in 1965 (see p. 155). Significantly, it chose price increases rather than wage claims as the first targets for its critical attention.

unusually high, it does not reduce its prices. The Dutch price control authorities in the Ministry of Economic Affairs make a practice of asking this question already. It is very doubtful whether the question can be asked in the right tone of voice, unless the ultimate power to fix the price at the level required by the public interest exists too.

X

PLANNING IN GENERAL

It may be useful at this point to draw some of the threads together in this story of planning. As the reader will have observed, there are a lot of loose ends. That is only to be expected in an activity which has so many different starting-points and whose direction is so powerfully influenced by individual national styles. It is also in most countries an activity of very recent origin,[1] belonging to the 1960s rather than to the 1950s. Nevertheless, it is basically—to use a different metaphor—the same tune which is being played in so many places, though you have to listen carefully sometimes in order to be sure, because each orchestra is performing with a different set of instruments and is determined to make the most of its own very special variations. Still, the tune is the thing.

It should be observed first of all how planning connects up with the improvement in the control over the business cycle, which was the theme of earlier chapters.[2] Indeed, in several countries it was the search for better methods of short-term control over the economic system which led to long-term planning. (The short term in this context is thought of as a period of about one year and the long term as four to five.) The Swedish case clearly illustrates the interaction between the short and the long-term motifs. The emphasis initially is all on the short, and the central aim is focused on maintaining full employment at the highest level of national output capable of achievement with the technology available at any given moment. Out of this came planned training related to an estimate of future national needs for various types of labour. In addition, the direct control of the business cycle itself required the preparation of a 'shelf' of investment projects, ready to be started at brief notice. And that, allied to the public control exercised since the middle 1950s over the investment reserve fund of private industry, provided a strong inducement to the Government to apply itself more systematically to the problem of long-term priorities.

In Britain too it was the desire to escape from the cycle of 'stop-go' policies which finally moved a Tory Government, elected to office in the early 1950s with an almost fanatical market ideology, to adopt economic planning as a central theme of its domestic policy a decade later. In the British case, unlike

[1] The point is illustrated in the international comparisons of planning procedure in J. Tinbergen, *Central Planning* (New Haven, Conn., Yale UP, 1964), pp. 32 ff. and Appendix, which show the preliminary and uncertain methodology of many of the planners at this stage and their reliance on what they called 'trial and error' techniques.   [2] See Part I.

the Swedish one, the final decision had very little to do with the control of the ordinary business cycle. The British authorities were not at all worried by this time about their ability to manage any downturn in the economy. It was the upturn which was their sole concern. How to prevent this from straining the balance of payments to the point where expansion had to be halted in order to protect the gold and foreign exchange reserves? The answer which was eagerly accepted was that an economy in which major decisions in both the public and private sectors were guided by precise long-term objectives, rather than the fluctuating circumstances of the market, would have a steadier rate of growth from year to year; being steadier, it was likely that the average rate for the period as a whole would also be higher.

Broadly, it is true to say that whereas in the earlier postwar period the main preoccupation of economic strategy was with the downswing of the business cycle—how to control and reverse it—later on the centre of concern came to focus increasingly on how to contain the upswing without actually reversing it. There is no symmetry between the two contrasting phases of trade-cycle policy. Indeed, it may be argued that the stubborn tendency of economists to believe that trade-cycle policy was all one, and that what was required to deal with the problem of controlling the movement in either direction would always be identical and opposite to the treatment required if the trend were reversed, was a serious intellectual impediment to the conduct of an effective economic policy. Only gradually were governments induced to recognize the fact that the forces making for inflation during periods of prosperity were different in kind from those responsible for deflation during a downturn of the business cycle. The British Government, for instance, persisted during the late 1950s and early 1960s in believing that the sole cause of its economic ills, including the slow growth of the national product, was an excessive demand on resources—just as the troubles of the 1930s had been caused by an excessively small demand. There was supposed to be a simple calculable figure for the optimum level of aggregate demand which would at one and the same time keep prices steady and maximize production.[3] Guided by this doctrine, the Government pursued a policy which from 1961 to 1964 maintained British unemployment at two to three times the level of the German.[4] The experiment did not, in the event, justify itself either by giving

---

[3] The most influential exponent of these views, which guided the thinking of the Treasury for several years, was Professor F. W. Paish (see e.g., *Policy for Incomes?* (London, Inst. of Econ. Affairs, 1964)). Paish calculated that the 'equilibrium rate' of unemployment, corresponding to full utilization of British productive capacity without inflationary pressure, was 2¼ per cent. A level of unemployment somewhat above his figure was in fact sustained for a whole year, from the fourth quarter of 1962 until the third quarter of 1963.

[4] OECD, *General Statistics*. The ratio is between the *absolute* number of unemployed in the two countries. Since the total labour force (including self-employed persons) was somewhat larger in Germany than in Britain, the proportion of unemployed there was even lower by comparison with the British.

Britain a price advantage over Germany or by raising the British rate of growth to the German level.

The essential truth about cost inflation is that any policy designed to mitigate its effects must concentrate on the management of production rather than of demand. That means that the whole *style* of intervention has to be different. Whereas the management of demand can deal with large aggregates using well-tried instruments, like the control of credit, a plot to raise the volume of production beyond the level which it would reach through the unaided operation of market forces requires a highly selective strategy of intervention. The problem here is the identification of individual bottlenecks —whether in capital equipment, in the supply of certain goods and services, or in particular types of labour—which threaten to hold up the advance on a much wider front. To eliminate these requires the active concentration of effort and resources at particular points in the productive system. All this is more like the function of government in a contemporary underdeveloped country than the traditional behaviour of government in Western capitalist society of the liberal Anglo-American type. It is of course closer to the way in which governments have behaved in Western societies on the continent of Europe, particularly those which were late starters in the industrial revolution and were deliberately trying to catch up fast. There, too, it was accepted as the natural task of the state to intervene in favour of particular branches of production, selected on the ground that their progress would exercise a more pervasive influence over the tempo of development of the economy as a whole.

It is worth emphasizing this contrast between the two kinds of prophylactic treatment required at the opposite ends of the business cycle. Its recognition is an especially characteristic feature of the more sophisticated capitalism of the later postwar years. Many other things in the conduct of economic policy flow from it. And an essential element in the change was the advance in techniques of economic analysis. As J. Tinbergen has pointed out, so long as there was no proper understanding of the nature of business recessions, 'governments resorted to regulation of single markets strongly affected by the decrease in demand. Such regulation was highly esteemed, and ironically some business groups willingly gave up more freedom of action than was actually necessary'.[5] With greatly improved methods of short-term economic forecasting, the necessary measures to stimulate demand can be taken at an early stage of a business cycle. At that stage, the job can be done with very little government interference in specific markets or types of employment. The authorities may, of course, wish to use the opportunity, as in Sweden, to further specific investment schemes. But there is no *need* to do so merely in order to overcome the recession. With greater sureness of touch, the governments are able to intervene more delicately, causing less disturbance to

[5] *Shaping the World Economy* (New York, 20th Century Fund, 1962), p. 68.

private business, and this in turn helps to create the atmosphere in which private enterprise collaborates readily and easily in the pursuit of long-term objectives of public policy.

The big discovery of the postwar period was that, contrary to the view widely held in the 1930s, the bludgeon was not the sole or the most effective instrument of economic policy. Events would respond to subtler pressures, if these were applied in time. Governments of the Left found that it was not necessary always to take enterprises into public ownership merely in order to be able to exercise control over some of their actions. And private enterprise came to see the greatly reinforced public sector less as a dangerous rival than as a useful ally, indeed almost as a hostage—for it was now so vast and heavy that it could not move in the wrong direction for even a moment without rocking the whole boat. Keynes with extraordinary prescience pointed in the 1920s to the chief elements in economic policy which have been responsible for the recent great change. Writing in *The End of Laissez-Faire* about the miseries of business depressions, he said:

I believe that the cure for these things is partly to be sought in the deliberate control of currency and of credit by a central institution, and partly in the collection and dissemination on a great scale of data relating to the business situation. . . . These measures would involve society in exercising directive intelligence through some appropriate organ of action over many of the inner intricacies of private business, yet it would leave private initiative and enterprise unhindered.[6]

It bears saying again how much more profound was this Keynesian vision of control through a combination of financial pressure and improved economic information, than the socialist formula, which guided the dominant movement of reform for close on half a century, of capturing the 'commanding heights' of the economy. What Keynes did not envisage, however, was the problem of almost continuous boom-control, once the menace of a serious slump had been removed. As suggested earlier,[7] his vision in this matter was impeded by the curious belief that Western nations were on the brink of material satiety, which would make them largely indifferent about whether the volume of production increased slowly or fast. The typical problem of modern economic planning—related chiefly to the need for greater mobility of resources in order to take advantage of more rapid technological change— did not figure in his thinking. The law of diminishing returns provided his natural intellectual framework; there was no hint of an offsetting principle of increasing technological opportunity.

Limitations of Planning Techniques

The shift in emphasis from slump-control to boom-control, which was analysed in the last section in terms of its effect on the broad thrust of

---

[6] London, Hogarth Press (1926), p. 47. The original lecture on which the text is based was given by Keynes in 1924.   [7] See above, p. 64.

economic policy, is, of course, a simple reflection of changing expectation. Either it is expected that there will be normally too little demand, and then the problem is how to fabricate some more of it—or it is expected that there will usually be too much demand and the main effort turns to increasing supply beyond the amount that market forces would spontaneously provide. What emerges from an examination of the story is that long-term planning came to be generally envisaged as a proper answer to the second situation only after the lapse of many years—rather more than a decade and a half—following the war. It took as long as that to get prosperity and full employment, and therefore cost inflation, accepted as the norm.

The contribution of France in the field of planning was not that the French saw earlier than the others what was coming. They were simply determined for their own reasons, having a worse record of stagnation since the late 1920s than any other advanced industrial country, to grow considerably faster than before. Their intellectual contribution was that they did not rely exclusively on increasing the *overall* level of investment to achieve their ends, but developed a strategy on a national scale for deploying this investment at those points in the system where it produced an especially high return. This is the technique which the second wave of would-be planners, outside France, in the early 1960s were anxious to copy. Their objective was to make a given amount of investment go further; specifically, by a more careful timing of interconnected capital requirements, to improve the average capital-output ratio of investment as a whole. When economic growth is fast, the precise timing of individual bits of investment becomes more important. And the complementary character of large indivisible units of investment in the crowded urban industrial society of today means that the timetable must be laid out several years ahead and must also aim to be as comprehensive as possible. Otherwise some crucial element in the mosaic of capital projects is likely to be missed.

Of course, it is highly probable that the planners, at any given stage in the timetable, will have failed to put in something which proves to be important—as well as setting up some ill-considered piece of investment which turns out to be wasteful, either because of unforeseen changes in technology or spontaneous shifts in demand. This likelihood has been held by some critics of planning to invalidate the whole procedure. Their argument is that if the forecasts of what is going to be required some years hence are inaccurate, action based on them is likely to be foolish. Better not plan at all. What this ignores is that if responsible people were not prepared to predict future needs some years ahead, certain kinds of investment would always be late—with the result that the rate of growth of the economy *as a whole* would be significantly slowed down. The port capacity needed to take the extra exports and imports in a period of rapid economic growth would never be ready on time; the road connecting with the port would always be congested; factory order books would be over-full and deliveries would be delayed. In the end it would be the customer who would find himself compelled to plan ahead, anticipating his own needs in order to get them met on time. All that has to be shown in order to justify the effort of central planning is that it makes it more probable than it would be under a pure market system that complementary investments involving a long lead time will be carried out when they are required. There are more and more such investments in our rich and crowded societies. If foresight has any value at all, a planned system will tend to work with a lower margin of underemployed capacity in any given productive sector. That is another way of saying that it will suffer from fewer bottlenecks. And it also implies that the capital-output ratio will be more favourable. This last is certainly one of the outstanding features of postwar France; and the French planners have, plausibly enough, claimed some of the credit for it.[8]

It would be wrong, however, to suggest that economic planning as it has developed in Europe to date is overwhelmingly concerned with making the total volume of national output increase faster than it otherwise would, regardless of how it is composed. It is true that this kind of approach is dominant in one or two countries, notably in Britain, but it is quite alien to the French view of the problem. In France the planners explicitly regard it as one of their tasks to ensure that the distribution of the anticipated increase in the nation's wealth over a period of years ahead is biased towards the attainment of certain social objectives. Again, one is struck by the Anglo-French contrast—the willingness of the French authorities to assume a tutelary role in the division of the prizes which result from a more efficient management of the economy, while British planning in the early 1960s was concerned exclusively with enlarging the aggregate volume of supplies; so far at any rate it has recoiled from any attempt to plan demand.[9] The French

---

[8] See the essay by Pierre Massé, *Revue du Marché Commun*, no. 55 (Feb. 1963), where he asserts that 'the Plan's . . . merit has been to reduce, thanks to better coordination of policies, overlapping and spare capacities, and thus to achieve the same growth target with a lower rate of investment' (p. 50). A report by the OECD in March 1962 puts this saving on investment at 2 per cent of gross domestic production. *Statistics of National Accounts 1950–61* (1964) shows that the rate of growth of French GNP from the mid-1950s onwards was slightly higher than the average of European OECD countries (4·7 per cent per annum against an average of 4·5 per cent), while the proportion of the French national product devoted to fixed capital investment was between 1 and 2 per cent below the OECD European average.

[9] The whole approach of NEDC was to discover from the various industries and other branches of the economy what each one of them would require in the way of resources, on the hypothesis that national output in the aggregate rose by 4 per cent a year. No attempt was made to argue systematically about the best way of distributing the national effort, so that the various increments of output—adding up to the national average of 4 per cent—would occur in the places where they would produce the greatest return, measured by some explicit criterion of social benefit. This is, of course, a political question and one that cannot be burked; but so far the

Fourth Plan insisted vigorously on its objective of achieving 'a more complete view of man'[10]—by which it meant that the additional resources becoming available between 1961 and 1965 must not be used merely to satisfy consumer demands which would find their normal expression through the market, but must be devoted to more profound purposes, for which the ordinary citizen might not opt spontaneously today but for which he will be grateful in the future—because by then he will be a different man. Specifically the French planners set their faces against a 'civilization of gadgets'.[11] The point of planning is thus in part an ethical one: it imposes choices about the use of resources other than those which the market would produce.[12]

This frank emphasis not on what people want now but on what they will want (or ought to be wanting) in the future is characteristically French in style. But leaving aside the transcendental overtones, it is in practice closely in line with the thinking of the growing body of planners elsewhere in the Western world. Increasingly the realization is forced upon us that the market, which purports to be the reflection of the way in which people spontaneously value their individual wants and efforts, is a poor guide to the best means of satisfying the real wishes of consumers. That is because market prices generally fail to measure either social costs or social benefits. In our civilization these grow constantly more important. Simply because some amenity— let it be a pleasant view or an uncongested road or a reasonably quiet environment—is not paid for directly by those who enjoy it, there is no measure of the cost of the disinvestment which occurs when a profitable economic activity destroys what already exists. Unless the state actively intervenes, and on an increasing scale, to compel private enterprise to adapt its investment decisions to considerations such as these, the process of economic growth may positively impede the attainment of things that people most deeply want.[13]

British idea has been to keep planning out of politics. A national plan is thought of as the reflection of a tacit consensus, something that all right-thinking persons agree about implicitly. It is therefore only the practical detail which is worth discussing; the criteria are not.

[10] See e.g. Massé, *Revue du Marché Commun*, Feb. 1963, p. 51.

[11] See Cazes, *Planification en France*, and Massé's article, 'La France, le Plan et les gadgets', *Entreprise*, Mar. 1962. Cazes admits (and laments) that the argument for social investment is not accepted by more than a small fraction of public opinion— which is why care is taken not to present the issue of social versus consumer goods as a straightforward matter of choice (p. 118).

[12] This is a fairly recent development. Pierre Massé has explained: 'We have, in the Fourth Plan, for the first time, emphasized social policy, which previously had been left completely out of the Plans . . .' (see *Planning*—papers read at the Business Economists' Conference, Oxford, Apr. 1962). The new emphasis was reflected in the projected use of resources: personal consumption was planned to rise by 23 per cent between 1961 and 1965, while social investment was to rise by 50 per cent.

[13] The Swedish trade union organization LO urged its case for more planning on the government in 1961 on the ground that the 'price mechanism is becoming an increasingly unreliable indicator of real alternative costs because of . . . distortions of prices and through the divergence between social and private costs' (see Johnston,

Social benefits tend to be left out of account, or at best played down, in any hard-headed calculation of the return on any proposed piece of investment. It is the pride of hard-headed men, especially when they are accountants, to include in the arithmetic of prospective profit and loss only those items which are sufficiently precise to be measured in monetary terms. The rest, the things that you do not pay for, may be thrown in—where they are too obviously significant to be entirely ignored—as 'incidentals'; they may marginally add to the force of a conclusion emerging from the monetary calculation, but rarely affect its substance.

It is instructive to observe how the slow advance in intellectual techniques, in this case the technique of measuring costs, may result in denying to millions of people for several years the benefit of some desirable piece of investment. A recent example is the building of the new underground railway, the so-called Victoria Line, across the most congested area of central London. The project was argued over, examined, and re-examined for well over a decade from the time when it was first proposed, and always it was turned down on the ground that it could not be made to pay its way. Then in the early 1960s someone had the bright idea of bringing into the calculation the secondary benefits of having this extra channel of rail transport across London—notably the saving in travel time and motor-vehicle operating costs which would result for people *not* using the new line, from the reduction in traffic congestion in the central streets. When monetary values were calculated for these and other savings, it was found that the true return on the investment in the Victoria Line was over 10 per cent of the capital cost of the project.[14] This answer, on the basis of which construction of the railway has gone ahead, was arrived at by cost-benefit analysis—a method which has come into vogue since the war, as public authorities have tried to struggle out of the windowless intellectual box prepared for them by upright business accountants. There is nothing complicated or subtle about the method: it is merely a way of bringing into a profit-and-loss account relevant but not

Economic Expansion, p. 165). The other side of the medal is that the classical capitalist system, which allowed the entrepreneur to pocket all the gains while meeting none of the social costs of any innovation, established, as Hirschman has pointed out, an exceptionally powerful incentive for business investment. Once these external costs become 'internalized', i.e. have to be taken into the calculus of profit and loss of those responsible for innovation, business may become less dynamic (see A. O. Hirschman, *The Strategy of Economic Development* (Yale UP, 1959), pp. 57 ff.

[14] See C. D. Foster and M. E. Beesley, 'Estimating the social benefit of constructing an underground railway in London', *Rl. Statist. Soc. Journal*, vol. cxxvi, pt. 1, 1963. The answer, which is calculated on the basis of the discounted 'present value' of capital and operating costs set against the future benefits of the project over the assumed 50 years' life of the line, obviously varies with different assumptions about the level of interest rates. If the rate of interest to be charged is 6 per cent, the estimated return on the investment is 11·3 per cent; even with interest rates at 8 per cent, the return is 10·9 per cent—quite respectable by commercial standards.

immediately obvious products of an investment which occur beyond the immediate confines of the investment project itself. As such, it provides a handy weapon in an argument with practical men who trust arithmetic above all else.

It is, however, a blunt weapon for any other purpose. The problem is that the values imputed to the products of social investment usually include a large element of the arbitrary. The gains are real enough—benefits like time saved, less wear and tear on the nerves of people travelling in cities, a smaller intake of motor exhaust fumes—but they do not lend themselves to precise assessment in terms of shillings per man-year. The best that can be done in most cases is to relate the item to be measured (e.g. wasted time) to some activity which does actually produce or cost money; in this way the cost-benefit accountant is able to establish an upper and a lower limit for the value of the service (or disservice) which he is trying to measure. The exercise sometimes calls for a great deal of ingenuity. If it seems at times to have a certain unreality, one has to remind oneself that the practical purpose of these intricate calculations of tenuous social returns is to supply an indication of a broad order of magnitude, which can be set against some conventional standard rate of return on capital as a means of judging whether a project is going to be wildly wasteful or not. But any attempt to determine an order of priorities by this species of arithmetical juggling is more difficult. In particular it provides little help in making a choice between competing social investment projects, each with a claim on public funds. The imputed magnitudes carry too large a margin of error to make any exact comparisons possible.

What this means is that public investment policy is less amenable to unambiguous answers derived from a scale of profit and loss than private investment is in its own sphere. Even an apparently straightforward issue like the return to be expected from public investment in education is subject to very hazardous and various answers.[15] Some economists have dreamed of a world in which price tags of social as well as private costs and benefits are attached to all things, so that a large high-speed computer simulating the behaviour of a market would make its rational choices on behalf of society. But in the present and foreseeable state of the art of costing there seems little chance that the automaton will be able to replace the judgement of the planner. Computers will surely have a growing part to play in this too; but as auxiliaries not principals.

[15] See Robbins Report, *Higher Education*, Cmnd 2154 (1963) for a summary of the various attempts that have been made by economists to measure the product of educational investment. None of them is satisfactory, largely because it has proved impossible to isolate from among the various interconnected factors, which are together responsible for any given increase in productivity, the particular element that is due to the increased knowledge of the worker derived from additional tuition.

Corporatism and Public Power

It is as if the European nations needed time to arrive at their own deeper motives for embarking on a permanent system of economic planning. To begin with, planning was seized upon as a device for dealing with some specific problem—overcoming past neglect of certain industries or catching up with other countries or helping to smooth out fluctuations in business and employment. Only later did they come to see the relevance of what they were doing to the whole range of economic policy issues. Some of the original motives are still very pertinent. Thus, for all the contemporary feeling of greater security in the economic environment, there are also new forces making for increased instability in the postwar world. Outstanding among them are the two factors discussed at length in Part I: the acceleration of technological change and the removal of barriers to international trade. Both of these make for sudden jolts. Planning is seen as a means of making them less sudden.[16]

There has also been a certain ambiguity about the practical methods employed to make a plan work—assisted in this instance by a good deal of double talk on the part of some of the planners. Perhaps this obfuscation of what is really going on, whether conscious or unconscious, derives from a deeper reluctance to recognize that some of it does not fit at all well with the existing structure of Western democratic institutions. Who controls the planners? It is not just a matter of getting parliamentary approval for the broad outline of a scheme for raising the standard of living of a nation by a certain amount over a stated period of years. A plan is a living body of economic policy, adapting itself constantly to changing circumstances, sometimes undergoing drastic alteration in its component parts in order to secure particular objectives which come in time to acquire a new order of priority. The traditional Western parliament, a non-expert body, by instinct non-interventionalist unless there is some manifest abuse or need for legislation, is hardly equipped for the job of supervising the systematic intervention which planning implies. That is perhaps the justification for the tacit consensus among the planners that it is, on the whole, best to bypass the parliamentary process.[17]

---

[16] There are, of course, other types of machinery, international in character, which have been developed since the war specifically as an insurance against the additional risks of international trade. Outstanding among these is the enlargement of the resources of the IMF and their more flexible use to assist countries whose currency reserves are under temporary pressure. This book is, however, concerned with an analysis of the national institutions of modern capitalism; the role of the new international institutions (EEC, GATT, IMF, and others) in the economic performance of the West since the war is a large topic which deserves treatment on its own.

[17] With the exception, as noted above, p. 142, of the French planners in the early 1960s. It is no reflection on the sincerity of M. Massé and his colleagues to point out that the Fifth Republic under the presidency of General de Gaulle was not a

Among the variety of methods and expedients employed in postwar planning in Western Europe, there are three broad strands which can be identified. There is first of all the intellectual approach. It is 'indicative' planning in its purest form. The plan is made to work because the quality of the analysis done by the planners convinces the men wielding economic power, in the private and the public sectors alike, that the conclusions offered to them provide good advice. On this showing, the plan does the same sort of thing as watching the market normally does for managers of enterprises, only better: it presents them with additional signals to guide their decisions. Secondly, there is the approach which relies on reinforced governmental powers. The state controls so large a part of the economy that a planner can, by intelligent manipulation of the new levers of public power, guide the remainder of the economy firmly towards any objective that the government chooses. The third approach, by contrast, eschews whenever possible the use of direct governmental intervention, and places its reliance instead on the corporatist formula for managing the economy. The major interest groups are brought together and encouraged to conclude a series of bargains about their future behaviour, which will have the effect of moving economic events along the desired path. The plan indicates the general direction in which the interest groups, including the state in its various economic guises, have agreed that they want to go.

The French method of planning, it is clear, is predominantly a combination of the first and second approach; the British—in the NEDC phase of planning—a combination of the first and third. But the mixture is not exclusive: most of the planning efforts to date contain elements of all three. Thus, an important aspect of the British planning effort is the attempt to unite previously disparate branches of state activity in the pursuit of a single policy. Once having been co-ordinated, this aggregation of public power inevitably has a quite different weight in the economy—and presents a fresh element in the planning equation—even though it continues to be used with restraint in dealings with the private sector. The weight does not have to be chucked about to be felt.

By the same token, the *commissions de modernisation* fit into the third, corporatist, approach to planning. The 3,000 individuals who are brought in by the Commissariat du Plan to take part in the formulation of the Plan are selected in such a way as to include representatives of the most powerful interest groups in the country. The intention is that in the course of their discussions of what ought to be done and what is likely to be done, they should also agree among themselves to do certain things in unison. How far the individual commitment goes in matters involving commercial agreements is never revealed to outsiders. On one point those involved in the

place in which the French parliamentarians were showing the kind of vigour that would make them either awkward or effective

business are unanimous when they are questioned about it: the meetings of the *commissions* are not used to discuss cartel arrangements for the division of future markets among the firms planning an expansion of output or the prices to be charged. There is no reason to disbelieve this assertion. Indeed it would be surprising if industrialists argued about such matters as these in the presence of trade union officials. The trade union representatives on the *commissions* have in fact complained that some of the key information and figures in the possession of the employers are never revealed in their presence, let alone discussed.[18] One of the planning officials put the point to me as follows: 'We invite the industrialists to meet us in Paris, and we know that at this meeting no cartel business is discussed. But of course at the meeting which they hold among themselves the day before, we are not present, and we do not know what happens.'[19] It would in fact be strange if the atmosphere created among groups of businessmen who have collaborated over several years in a planning exercise of increasing range and complexity, demanding a close interchange of ideas in sessions lasting for hours at a time, did not lead to some useful commercial arrangements among the big firms concerned. Sometimes the industry as a whole is asked to expand its output by a certain amount (e.g. in steel) or to reduce it by cutting down existing investment projects (e.g. in motor cars)—then the incentive to allot approximate output quotas, as part of a patriotic endeavour, must be overwhelming.

However, in the formulation of policy at the national level the representatives of French commercial interests come up against some pretty formidable countervailing power, in the shape of government officials and independent experts who sit in large numbers on the planning *commissions*. The actual conduct of the work of the *commissions*, the preparation of the agenda for meetings, the circulation of papers, and the writing of minutes and reports, is very largely in their hands. The permanent officials of the government—and these of course include the officials working in the Commissariat du Plan—are expected both to provide the leadership and to have the last word. In Britain during the NEDC phase of planning the professional planners were not officials of the Government but servants of the Council, on which the interest groups—the employers and trade unionists—were in a majority. The set-up of NEDC and of the subordinate Economic Development Committees was such that if the leadership did not come from the

---

[18] See G. Mathieu, three articles on French planning, *Le Monde*, 2, 3, 6 Mar. 1962, written from a moderate trade unionist standpoint. Mathieu points out that the trade union representatives are without authority in the *commissions*—not one of them has ever become chairman of any *commission*—and that the businessmen are inclined to cut them out of discussions when these are alleged to involve 'business secrets'.

[19] D. Granick, *The European Executive* (London, Weidenfeld, 1962), p. 154, reports that the chairman of one of the planning *commissions* said that 'it was really the big firms themselves who have decided by negotiation which one was to undertake which investment—and when they were to take joint shares in some new company'.

interest groups, it could hardly be provided by anyone else. The Labour Government's distinctive contribution in the course of the reform of planning during its first six months of power in 1964–5 has been (*a*) to bring the whole process inside the government machine, and (*b*) to make a start in mobilizing the hitherto unused instruments of pressure on the private sector. The open question, as we have seen, is whether having concentrated the power and added to the instruments for its exercise, it will be able to persuade the official bureaucracy, in the face of a contrary tradition, to employ them with the dash and skill necessary to make a success of modern planning. The techniques that have to be employed for the purpose offend against a number of cherished conventions. It has still to be shown whether the British civil service, at any rate in its present guise, will reverse the usual relationship between the private and the public domains in Britain, and proceed to pressurize the pressure groups.

It was Keynes, once again, forty years before NEDC was established, who unwittingly wrote the blueprint for this very English type of organization. Discussing the kind of body that would assume responsibility, as the traditional market economy ceased to function, he said:

I suggest therefore that progress lies in the growth and the recognition of semi-autonomous bodies within the state—bodies whose criterion of action within their own field is solely the public good as they understand it, and from whose deliberations motives of private advantage are excluded, though some place it may still be necessary to leave, until the ambit of men's altruism grows wider, to the separate advantage of particular groups, classes, or faculties—bodies which in the ordinary course of affairs are mainly autonomous within their prescribed limitations, but are subject in the last resort to the sovereignty of the democracy expressed through Parliament.[20]

It is curious to observe how close this kind of thinking was to the corporatist theories of the earlier writers of Italian fascism, who flourished in the 1920s. Corporatism got its bad name, which has stuck to it, essentially because of its association with the one-party state: this was the opposite of what Keynes was after. Indeed, his preference for semi-autonomous 'corporations', rather than a state with greatly reinforced powers, which would fill the vacuum as the old *laissez-faire* system disappeared, was precisely because they were likely to provide a better context for a pluralistic society, and therefore scope for dissent. The instinct which led to the curious and uncertain formula of British planning in the early 1960s, enshrined in NEDC, was the same. There was so much power here that it was felt it must not be left to the government.

The Planner as Politician

The common element in all the varieties of postwar capitalist planning is the large role given to the independent intellectual. The continental European

[20] *End of Laissez-Faire*, p. 41.

tradition has found it easier to accommodate him than the British. In France, the independent expert is elevated to the position of master of the whole operation; in Britain he is a respected servant of others. The British system does not contain any established place high up in the hierarchy of power for a person who is not a judge, who is paid, and whose claim to status is personal independence combined with expertise.[21] That is perhaps because the obligation of loyalty and batting for one's own side is assumed to attach automatically to any employed person not engaged in a judicial occupation.

The difficulty is aggravated because the head of a national planning organization has the obligation to engage in a certain type of politics. His job as a public servant is to lead a lobby for long-term economic growth inside the government; this may conflict with the party politician's short-range imperatives. Like the governor of the central bank, he is ultimately subject to the orders of the government of the day, but it is expected of both governor and head planner that they will urge the policies which they judge to be right, in their fields of expertise, on the country at large as well as on the government, and do so with clarity. Plainly this does not give either of them a licence for unrestrained feuding. But it does make them politicians of a discreet variety.

The combination of a politician with the pretensions of an independent expert is something which the British especially find hard to stomach. The Continental tradition much more readily accepts the paid public official who slips into the occasional political role. After all, the device, which originates with the French, of a ministerial *cabinet* including permanent civil servants, who are chosen on the basis of their personal attachment to the minister, implies that government officials are not expected to remain altogether aloof from politics. Indeed the ambitious civil servant can sometimes push several moves ahead in his career by coping successfully with the mixture of delicate tasks, personal, political and administrative, in the *cabinet* of some powerful politician. It is generally assumed that these tasks cannot be carried out by a self-respecting man, unless he is in some degree attached by sentiment to the person and the politics of his minister.[22]

---

[21] The post of Chairman of the National Board for Prices and Incomes (at a salary of £15,000 a year), created by the Labour Government in early 1965 (see above, p. 155), represents a departure—and possibly a precedent.

[22] It is instructive to observe the alternative British practice, as it applies to the Prime Minister's Office. Although in theory the Prime Minister's Private Secretary behaves like any other member of the civil service in contact with a politician—i.e. carefully separates the administrative and political functions of the minister, and assists him only in the latter—it is pretty evident that the work cannot be effectively done unless the private secretary is devoted wholeheartedly to the Prime Minister's person, anticipating the moves of his enemies, advising him on tactics which are designed to strengthen his political position in the country, and generally thinking for him in any matter where he can save the Prime Minister time and trouble. None of this, however, is officially recognized, although it must be apparent to anyone with a

It is especially important that the technician in charge of the national plan should be someone who is able to talk to the politicians directly and on equal terms. For if parliament is to play an effective part in the business of national planning—and if it does not, the outlook for the future of democracy is bleak—then members of parliament will also have to learn to recognize some theoretical, as well as practical, limitations on the exercise of their collective sovereignty. These theoretical limitations apply to the whole procedure of introducing a parliamentary amendment to a set of planning proposals, whose merit is their intellectual coherence and self-consistency. If any significant element in them is changed, the whole structure must be adapted to accommodate the alteration. It follows that the essential relationship between planners and parliament is one of sympathetic negotiation: the parliamentarians cannot work out the answers—that is the job of a technician who is a specialist at making coherent economic models—the elected representatives of the people can do no more than demand that a new set of choices be presented to them by the planners. Plainly, the back-and-forth dialogue will work successfully only if the two sides know how to parley with one another—the parliamentarians being sufficiently trained in the material to know how the economic system functions, and the planners sufficiently versed in politics to offer the solution which parliament is after, but is unable to express in the language at its disposal.

It is this difficulty of reducing the arguments about the options open to society to manageable parliamentary terms which has led Bernard Cazes to suggest that the mastery of mathematical means of expression is necessary for the exercise of any effective democratic control over planning. This, he contends, is the only way of conducting a dialogue about complicated and interdependent choices between experts and non-experts in a meaningful fashion.[23] The suggestion serves to emphasize the point that if parliament is

nodding acquaintance with the problem that the strict division between political and administrative duties will not work in the Prime Minister's Office. It is somehow believed that the requirements of the job do not damage the self-respect of the civil servant concerned, even if his personal views on politics are opposed to those of the Prime Minister whom he serves. It is hard to see how the problem can be resolved except by the choice of a very special type of man for the task, someone with the temperament of a janissary who is willing to apply complete devotion to the person of the office-holder whom he is paid to serve. Anything in fact to avoid the realism of the *cabinet* system, which the British civil service especially abhors.

[23] OECD, Internat. TU Seminar, *Final Report*, p. 126. Cazes makes the following points about the difficulties of discussing the 'variants' on the sets of choices presented in a fully fashioned national plan. First, the number of possible variants is very great—'they must not be so numerous as to prevent all discussion, and must relate to the most significant development problems'. Second, the way in which they are combined affects the answer—'isolated analysis of each variant is technically justified, but in fact an alternative economic policy will require a combination of several variants'. Thirdly, the manner of formulation of an alternative choice is laborious—'it is important that as far as possible all conditions which must be fulfilled to achieve a particular variant be specified, together with its positive aspects, lest the choice

to establish effective control over the national economic plan, it must equip itself with a corpus of specialist ability. This is by no means as difficult as it sounds. What should be envisaged is a high-powered parliamentary committee of the American Congressional type backed by an able full-time staff of a technical calibre equal to that of the national planning staff itself. Indeed it is to be hoped that, as under the American system, there would be a movement of staff from the parliamentary to the administrative side and vice versa.

As it is at present conducted, economic planning greatly reinforces the already powerful trend of 'the flow of power towards the executive'.[24] It is perhaps unreasonable to expect that at this early stage, when the techniques of planning are themselves still experimental and highly tentative, an answer should already have been found to the major political problems which they bring in their train. But the problems themselves urgently need to be identified. The worst danger to democratic institutions would be if it were pretended that there was nothing whatsoever to worry about—because a standing committee of the nation's major interest groups working in collaboration with a team of high-powered economic experts had succeeded in taking the issue right out of politics.[25]

---

be distorted'. He concludes: 'Hence the importance of expressing a programme's variants in mathematical terms, so that a democratic discussion of the options is possible'.

[24] The phrase is Professor Arthur Miller's (see 'Evidence before the House of Representatives Committee on Banking and Currency', 14 Apr. 1964) who was describing to the committee the resistance of the US to the trend—'in many respects the last country in the world that has not almost completely gone over to more of an executive type of government'.

[25] See Part 4 for further discussion of the political problem.

Part 3
MARKET IDEOLOGIES

XI

ORGANIZED PRIVATE ENTERPRISE: GERMANY

Two counties, Germany and the United States, appear to be out of the mainstream of modern capitalism as it has been described in the preceding chapters. They show no enthusiasm for the increasingly organized pattern of economic behaviour, replacing the older methods of arriving at decisions through the autonomous, if haphazard, movement of the market; indeed, they evince an ostentatious antipathy for the whole process and loudly advocate resistance to it. Their official doctrines continue to carry a high content of simple traditional capitalist folklore. Since one of these countries is the most dynamic industrial state in Western Europe, and the other constitutes by far the largest concentration of economic power and wealth in the history of mankind, they make two very important exceptions. It is necessary, therefore, to face the possibility that the postwar development in other countries, which has been the subject of Part II, is not after all the mainstream but a lesser tributary, perhaps momentarily excited by a quirk current.

In the chapters which follow the two cases will be examined in turn. This will involve a closer scrutiny of postwar developments in the private sector of the economy than we have conducted so far. Up to this point the main focus of attention in the analysis of the apparatus of modern capitalism has been on the active role of the public authorities, with private enterprise responding—or not, as the case may be. Now the latter comes into the centre of the stage—an active agent in shaping the postwar capitalist system, as well as reacting to the pressures and designs of others. After the particular circumstances of Germany and the United States have been considered, Chapter XV goes on to a more general discussion of the changing structure of private enterprise in the 1950s and 1960s.

In Germany after the war official policy deliberately set about the task of reducing the power of the state in the management of the economy. The effort was crystallized in the person of Dr Erhard, Minister of Economics during the period which took the Germans through the reconstruction phase into the era of prosperity and full employment, and Chancellor since 1963. It is sometimes suggested that Erhard's fervent defence of private enterprise against the pretensions of governmental power is in large part a public relations job—that his role is that of a kind of paper lion of German capitalism. In fact his whole approach symbolizes part of the conscious effort made by a new generation of Germans to break right away from the past, in which the state had appeared either as a kind of universal busybody or as a selectively brutal bully. Economic liberalism was seen by Erhard as a way of cutting down overweening public power to size. The approach has the authentic Victorian English liberal touch: freer trade as the answer to arbitrary authority.[1] But of course he was operating in an economic and social context as different as it is possible to imagine from that of nineteenth-century England. The defeat, division, and chaos which Germany suffered in the 1940s did not wipe out the legacy of the past; it only lifted temporarily the pressure of history. When the Germans began to reconstruct their economy, they built upon the familiar structural foundation and plan, much of it invisible to the naked eye, as if guided by an archaeologist who could pick his way blindfold about some favourite ruin.

Centralized Power

Most striking was the overwhelming instinct to centralize economic decisions. The obstacles which it had to surmount were considerable. The country was divided into eleven states,[2] each with its own separate budget and considerable taxing powers. The Federal Government's authority over the national economy was deliberately weakened; each state was encouraged to go its own way. Large industrial enterprises were broken up, and the old nation-wide commercial banks were replaced by dozens of smaller ones, which were not allowed to do business outside the *Land* in which they were registered. The economic arrangements of the occupying powers reflected chiefly the thinking of the Americans. The system which they fastened on the country was intended to establish firmly and for all time the economic base to sustain Erhard's doctrine of economic liberalism—whether Erhard was there to sustain it himself or not. Whatever the views of the German central government, business would in future be kept small, divided, and competitive.

German industry thought otherwise. It was highly organized in a hierarchical system of industrial associations—dating back to imperial Germany and enormously reinforced under the Nazi régime—which survived largely intact in the Federal Republic. The last thing that German industrialists contemplated was to establish a free market economy of small producers, in the Anglo-Saxon spirit. Their problem was in any case how to

---

[1] In the preface to the English edition of his book, *Germany's Comeback in the World Market* (London, Allen & Unwin, 1954), Erhard put the point as follows: 'More perhaps than any other economy the German one has had to experience the economic and supra-economic consequences of an economic and trading policy subjected to the extremes of nationalism, autarky and government control. We have learnt the lesson; and if the basic principles of a liberal economic policy are championed in the following pages with a vigour possibly startling to foreign readers, the reason must be sought in the special circumstances of our recent history.'

[2] This was reduced to nine in 1951 when Baden, Würtemburg-Baden, and Würtemburg-Hohenzollern were amalgamated. In addition, West Berlin was given the status of a *Land* by the Federal Government; and a further *Land* was added in 1957 when the Saar was returned to Germany, bringing the number back to eleven.

mobilize economic resources and power on the scale required to do the job of reconstruction as rapidly as possible. They needed big enterprises, which would undertake ambitious investment projects, and large concentrations of venture capital in the hands of powerful financial institutions, ready and able to take risks. In fact the concentration of economic power among the large firms in German industry steadily increased. By 1960 the hundred biggest firms were responsible for nearly 40 per cent of total industrial turnover, and they employed one out of every three workers in industry.[3] Admittedly the two largest combines of the prewar era, I. G. Farben and the Vereinigte Stahlwerke, were never reconstituted; but that is largely because the companies into which these giants were broken up are in any case very big indeed by European standards.[4]

The argument is not that German industry is today exceptionally highly concentrated: merely that there has been a powerful undertow throughout these postwar years which has irresistibly brought together pieces of economic power that were supposed to have stayed apart.[5] This is nowhere more clearly illustrated than in the story of the three big banks—the Deutsche Bank, Dresdner Bank, and Commerz Bank—which were broken up into small pieces after the war. Although the ex-directors of the big three were forbidden to establish any formal relationship with the new banks constituted out of their old branches, they nevertheless continued to exercise a pretty effective

---

[3] See *Bericht über das Ergebnis einer Untersuchung der Konzentration in der Wirtschaft*, Bundestags-Drucksache IV/2320, June 1964 (report of a German Government inquiry into economic concentration).

[4] The merger between Thyssen and Phoenix Rheinröhr in 1964, both members of the prewar Vereinigte Stahlwerke group, has established the largest single unit in the European steel industry.

[5] It is extraordinarily difficult to compare the degree of industrial concentration in different countries. The EEC's survey in 1958 (*Rapport sur la situation économique dans les pays de la Communauté*) produced data which suggested that the structure of German industrial enterprise was, at that time, not out of line with that of other members of the Community. On the other hand, a survey of the 50 largest West European (including British) firms in the 'energy, steel, chemical, vehicle, engineering and allied industries' by the ECSC in 1962 showed that 19 of them were German— three times as many as the French firms in the group. In Britain, it appears, the degree of concentration among the very largest firms in manufacturing industry is not as high as in Germany; the top 180 British firms accounted for only one-third of employment in manufacturing and for 38 per cent of net output (*Board of Trade Journal*, 8 Mar. 1963). The British figures are not strictly comparable with the German ones quoted above, because the coverage is different: the German figures refer to industry as a whole, including e.g. mining and power production, whereas the British apply to manufacturing industry only. There is, however, no *prima facie* reason to suppose that the predominance of large firms was markedly less in German manufacturing than in the rest of industry. Another interesting and more up-to-date pointer is that 50 per cent of German industrial exports in the early 1960s were supplied by the 100 largest firms (see report on concentration in the economy, Bundestags-Drucksache IV/2320), whereas in Britain it took twice as many companies to produce the same proportion of export sales (see article by Sir Norman Kipping, *The Times*, 16 Nov. 1964).

influence from afar. How explain otherwise that the new directors of independent banks never seriously asserted their independence?[6] It took until 1952 before the occupying powers were willing to give up any of the rigours of the American principle of 'state banking', i.e. each bank with all its branches to be confined to a single *Land*. The 1952 reform divided the country, for banking purposes, into three regions (instead of the nine *Länder*[7]) in any one of which, but not in more than one, a bank had freedom to operate. The greatest care was still taken to prevent any 'reconcentration' of nation-wide banking power; the new law laid down that no bank could own more than 5 per cent of the share capital of another. None of this, however, had much relevance to the exercise of effective influence by the unfrocked representatives of the old and officially defunct banks. By 1950 two of the big three—the Deutsche and the Dresdner—were more or less in full control of all their branch banks again; the Commerzbank followed in 1958. The law was changed to suit the facts in 1957.

The Industrial Associations

The postwar reassertion of power by the German commercial banks is important, because, as we shall see later, they occupy a special position in the organization of German industry. Another force making for organized economic effort, which should be noticed, is the pervasive German industrial association and more especially the central body, the Bundersverband der Deutschen Industrie (the Federation of German Industry). The latter was established in 1949 with an organizational structure, based on thirty-nine national industrial federations, taken over largely intact from the Nazi era. The system is very hierarchical: the smaller industrial associations have to rely on the support of the so-called *Spitzenverbände* (the 'top associations') to make their views heard at the centre. The German constitution, which gives the *Verbände* an unusual consultative status in the process of government, lays

---

[6] One attempt was made by three of the successor banks in one city to merge and form a new company out of their joint resources. According to Mr Abs, managing director of the Deutsche Bank, they desisted when he told them firmly, though informally—since he had no official standing in any of the banks and had indeed been forbidden by Allied Military Government to set foot on their premises—that legal proceedings would at some stage be taken against them. The incident is an interesting illustration of the moral authority wielded by the leaders of German commerce and industry at that time. Abs recounts that at the end of the war in 1945 the Deutsche Bank directors met in Berlin and appointed a group of twelve overseers, of whom he was one, to take charge of the interests of the Bank while the Allies were in occupation of the country. Thus, although he could in theory do no more than 'advise' the managers of the newly independent banks set up under the occupation, the managers were no doubt made aware of the fact that they were dealing with someone who would quite probably, some day, be able to assert some legal as well as moral authority.

[7] Excluding Berlin.

down the general practice in ministries—'not to bring in for consultation *Verbände* which do not have a nation-wide authority'.[8] This carries an echo of older arrangements established under the Weimar Republic for collaboration between the state and the powerful industrial associations; the law of 1926 charged the big *Verbände* 'to give a hearing to the *"Unterverbände"* and to take note of their views'.[9] The hierarchical principle was more than an administrative convenience; it was the basis of the system.

In the 1930s under the Nazis the hierachy of power was greatly reinforced. The whole structure was strengthened so that the lines of authority were unequivocal, and responsibility was concentrated in a small group right at the top. The system was modelled—originally by Krupp, shortly after Hitler had taken power—on an industrial army. The associations were renamed *Reichsgruppen* and placed under the command of captains of industry; and further down the scale were the managing directors of companies who became 'enterprise leaders'—junior officers subordinate to the generals at the centre of German industry.[10] The story is worth recalling not merely for its eccentric interest. It expresses, in an admittedly extreme and bizarre form, something of the underlying mood pervading the structure of German business for a long time before the 1930s, and which was not without its residue when German businessmen regained their freedom in the late 1940s. The favourite Nazi word for their method of organizing industry was *Wirtschaftslenkung*, which might be freely translated as 'guided private enterprise'. It was not by any means all sterile or vicious. There were aspects of Nazi industrial planning in peacetime which foreshadowed some of the methods that have come to be commonly adopted in postwar Europe. One feature of the Nazi system,

---

[8] See article by W. Hennis, 'Verfassungsordnung und Verbandseinfluss' in *Politische Vierteljahresschrift*, 1961, ii, 23. Hennis says in his analysis of the place given to the *Verbände* in the official 'Rules for the conduct of business in ministries' that 'It opens the way into the ministerial bureaucracy . . . in a way which so far as I know is unique' (p. 27). He points out that government officials are given specific permission to discuss certain matters, e.g. preparatory work on new legislation, with the *Verbände*, which they are not allowed to reveal to members of parliament. There have indeed been complaints from MPs that they are not able to get at official information which is readily available to members of certain powerful *Spitzenverbände*.

[9] Ibid. It is a point of interest that Gustav Stresemann, the outstanding figure in the government of these middle years of the Weimar Republic, was a former top bureaucrat of a big industrial association.

[10] The account of industrial associations under the Nazis is based on an unpublished thesis by W. Sorgel of Frankfurt University, 'Zur Soziologie Industrieller Interessen-Organisationen' He points out that before Hitler came to power there had been a long-standing rivalry between two groups of industrial associations, those representing the large firms on the one side and the associations of smaller enterprises on the other. The Nazis originally came to power as the declared protectors of the small businessman; but when it came to the point, they put the tycoons like Krupp and Siemens in charge, with a new legal authority to discipline the small businesses and the trade associations more firmly than ever.

where it worked effectively, was a planned investment programme covering a whole industry and an effort to achieve more collaboration in research deliberately aimed at accelerating technical development.[11]

The BDI and the individual industrial associations in postwar Germany have reacted strongly against the methods employed in the Nazi era. Not that the continuity of management has been widely interrupted; people like Herr Zangen, the head of Reichsgruppe Industrie, the summit organization of the Nazi industrial hierarchy, continued to play a leading part in German industry after the war. So did several other important figures. But there is no reason to doubt the genuineness of the recoil from the arbitrary procedures, the cartel-mongering, the compulsory price agreements, and the general atmosphere of bullying by the big of the small. In my personal encounters with the postwar German industrial associations, I have been struck by the contrast with the attitude displayed for example by comparable persons in France and in other European countries. The Germans are almost neurotically anxious to explain that they are not trying to organize relations between firms in their industry, and that they have nothing whatever to do with price agreements or commercial arrangements of any kind. Part of the industry's antipathy towards French-type planning is an uneasy feeling that it would be dangerous for Germany, with her particular experiences, to expose herself to temptation of this sort.

However, a change of doctrine does not suddenly destroy a well-established habit of collaboration. The residue left over from the Nazi era includes, for example, a notable improvement in the standard of German industrial statistics. The industrial associations had compulsory powers to collect these statistics under the Nazis. That made the statistics more comprehensive and precise—and they have remained so since the collection became voluntary. Indeed one occasionally finds the German industrial association spontaneously providing the kind of forecasting service which in France is officially supplied by the *commissions de modernisation*. It may not be such a complete service of prediction, but on the other hand it probably competes quite well with the French in accuracy.[12] It may even be of more practical use on occasion, because it does not purport to have such a high degree of precision.[13] The

---

[11] A typical example was the Wirtschaftsgruppe Fahrzeugindustrie (the motor industry) whose aims included 'the furtherance of economic production through understandings about [motor car] types and development programmes', as well as 'organizing scientific research and collective efforts to achieve rational industrial methods' (ibid).

[12] See p. 135 n. 20.

[13] See the interesting comment by Dr Hans Wolter, the chief economist of the German Iron and Steel Association and the man responsible for its investment forecasts, in an article on the limitations of planning as practised by the ECSC in *Stahl und Eisen*, 82/62, 6 June 1962. He called on the investment planners of the ECSC for more realism in forecasting and 'the deliberate renunciation of an excessive degree of precision and perfection' (p. 780).

steel industry, for example, has since 1953 been making 3–5-year forecasts of productive capacity, on the basis of current investment plans. This is matched by an estimate of future demand for various steel products. The whole exercise is conducted very cautiously, almost clandestinely, with the results presented to the industry tagged with warnings—'Speculation! Handle with care! For internal consumption only'. Nevertheless all the evidence is that when the individual steel firms come to plan their own investment programmes, these forecasts are treated very seriously. They have certainly played a part in encouraging some of the major steel companies to embark on joint long-term supply arrangements for particular products, in a conscious effort to avoid the creation of surplus capacity in the industry *as a whole* some years hence. These arrangements will be discussed later.[14]

The general point is that German *Verbände* have traditionally seen themselves as performing an important public role, as guardians of the long-term interests of the nation's industries, and they continue to do so.[15] The development that one observes since the war is that the approach to problems of policy has become more consultative, with the emphasis on technical advice. Power and influence are still exercised; but the manner is different. Individual associations vary widely in quality and in importance. Where they are a significant force in an industry, as for example in steel, in chemicals, and in machine tools, the technical performance, in terms of information given and leadership supplied to members, is of a high order. The means used to guide the consensus of industrial decisions in any given direction are distinctly of an intellectual order in postwar Germany. The technical directors who are employed by the associations tend to see it increasingly as their task to take a systematic long-term view of the interests of their industry, both in the sphere of legislation, where they are regularly consulted by the Government well before any law becomes a matter for parliamentary discussion, and in matters of investment and technological development.

Their well-advertised distrust of French planning does not prevent them from taking a keen interest in the development of techniques of analysis which help to extend the time horizon of business decisions. Contrary to the somewhat complacent view commonly expressed in Paris, German antipathy towards the French method of planning is not simply the result of a lack of

---

[14] See pp. 255–6.

[15] A Rand Corporation study, *West German Leadership and Foreign Policy*, by H. Speier and W. P. Davison (New York, 1957) which discusses the postwar role of these interest groups, puts the point as follows: 'In Germany, there is a sharp break between the public and the private spheres. Political and social responsibility is an attribute of office whether in the parliaments, the ministries, the churches, the trade unions, or the interest groups. What is more, within these various political structures a strong hierarchical spirit . . . dominates. . . . In England and the United States, on the other hand, there is a gradation from public to private' (p. 238).

economic sophistication. The results of the inquiry conducted by a working group of the BDI in 1963 into the subject of economic planning, circulated as an internal memorandum for members,[16] indicated that German business had been following the technical side of the operation with close interest. German business suspicions of the whole process were, rather, based on a political view—that planning, like Bismarck's alliances, implied a horse and a rider; they were determined not to be the horse.

The average German industrialist who recoiled from what the French offered him was not objecting primarily to the principle of central guidance for industrial decisions. It would be a mistake to imagine that Dr Erhard and the ideologues of economic liberalism had suddenly converted him from a disciplined member of his particular industrial community into a passionate devotee of the free-for-all of the market place. This is not to deny that German businessmen are in practice extremely responsive to the market and sometimes compete powerfully with one another. Competition is an accepted fact of life; but so are collective business decisions—if they are imposed by the right people.

The discipline of the German businessman when faced by the massed power of the *Verbände*, acting deliberately in their role of semi-public institutions, was illustrated in dramatic fashion in 1960 when industry and commerce were subjected to what amounted to a forced loan. The sum was considerable, DM 1,200 million; the money was needed by the Government to finance a new German aid programme for the underdeveloped countries, in the face of growing complaints around the world that Germany, with her vast balance of payments surplus, was not carrying a fair share of the load. But to convert part of this surplus into usable funds, it had first to be extracted from its individual German owners. For fear that the alternative might be more uncomfortable, the BDI and the other central business organizations (covering banks and commerce) agreed to get the money subscribed voluntarily. They did so by dividing up the responsibility among the various trade and industrial associations, who in turn assessed their members on their individual capacity to pay. There was no legal sanction whatever behind this operation. To appreciate its significance, one might ask how the ordinary British businessman would react if he were notified by the Federation of British Industries that he had been assessed for a certain contribution to a public loan for £100 million, at an unattractive rate of interest—and would he please pay up promptly.

Banks as Prefects

German institutions and habits thus produce a climate which favours industrial collaboration. The climate does not change much, whatever the

[16] BDI Circular VwA 29/63, 7 Oct. 1963.

currently fashionable economic doctrine. Moreover, the nation's history tends to reinforce the natural bias: no businessman is an island. After all the Germans started on their industrial revolution rather late and with a number of handicaps: their great success in the second half of the nineteenth century was based on 'national economics',[17] not on the Anglo-Saxon legend of the 'invisible hand' wisely guiding the destiny of a lot of little men who struggle blindly with one another in the market. The Germans never shared the strong, almost religious, taste of the British for the image of these massed gladiatorial struggles in a merciless commercial arena. Not that the Germans rejected the brutal exercise of power in business enterprise. But their penchant was for the organized and deliberate, not the blind hand-to-hand encounter.

In this articulated industrial system, the banks played from the beginning a major tutelary role. They were perhaps the most powerful force making for the centralization of economic decisions. It is broadly true to say that what the great public and semi-public institutions are to the French economy, the big banks are to Germany. This is an old story. Alfred Marshall described its origins in his wide-ranging survey, *Industry and Trade*, published in 1919 and reflecting the experience of some fifty years of European economic development, as follows:[18] 'The German great banks are, as a rule, remarkably well managed. But they are also inclined . . . to venture beyond their strength; especially by carrying to excess the locking up of their capital in loans, which cannot be called in under grave emergency.' This, he said, was the result of their intimate relationship with German business firms, to whom the banks were over-generous in their grants of long-term credits, and whom they supported to the limit of their strength in the issue of shares and bonds. They felt, in consequence, that they had a permanent stake in the businesses which they had nursed to maturity.[19] Marshall concludes: 'Each of the great banks has representatives on several other banks and on a vast number of industrial enterprises. . . . Representatives of banks have exercised, for two generations at least, a strong control on industrial businesses which they support.'[20]

An important channel for the exercise of bank influence is the *Aufsichtsrat*, the Supervisory Board of a company. This is a peculiarly German corporate institution, not known in the company law of Anglo-Saxon or Latin countries. It was originally set up as a device to provide more effective representation

---

[17] See above, p. 80.   [18] Macmillan, p. 342.

[19] Marshall (p. 342) quotes a German authority, Dr Riesser, who wrote: 'By such an issue [of shares and bonds] the connexion between the banks . . . and industrial production is drawn so tight that they are thereafter joined "for better or worse". Sooner or later this connexion finds further expression in the appointment of members of the bank directorate to the supervisory council of industrial enterprises' (trans. in Report of American Monetary Commission, 1911).

[20] Ibid., p. 567.

for the interests of the shareholders in decisions taken by the management of public companies. Without the *Aufsichtsrat*, the only occasion on which the ordinary shareholder had a chance to press the management in any way was at the annual general meeting. The *Aufsichtsrat*, on the other hand, generally meets at least four times a year and is usually small and compact enough to make a mark on the managers, who are subject to its ultimate sanction on any major investment decision and on matters like the employment of senior staff. Since the *Aufsichtsrat* also decides how much the managers themselves are to be paid, there is an added motive for the latter to show that they are responsive to the views of the supervisors, as well as merely obedient to their formal decisions.

The theory behind this arrangement is analogous to the doctrine of the 'separation of powers': the management (*Vorstand*) stands in the place of the executive and the *Aufsichtsrat*, which is completely separated from it, is composed of the parliamentary spokesmen for the shareholders. In the British system the whole board of directors of a company is treated indiscriminately as representatives of shareholders, with no distinction made between those who are executive directors (corresponding to the *Vorstand*), and those who are not.[21] However the original German bid for shareholder democracy has led in practice to effects which are very close to the opposite of those intended. The power of the managers is, if anything, enhanced, and that of the ordinary interested shareholder diminished. That is because the shareholder's representative, usually a professional man himself, is the natural ally of the management; meanwhile the establishment of a system of representation weakens the position of any individual shareholder who tries to press his views directly—unless he has a very big shareholding indeed. Appearances might suggest that shareholder democracy in Germany is unusually vigorous; there are many more votes cast at annual shareholders' meetings of companies than in other countries.[22] That, however, merely reflects the greater efficiency of interested organizations in collecting shareholders' proxies. And the most interested organizations of all are the banks.

German investors have every incentive to use their bank as an agent. They

[21] Granick (*European Executive*, p. 284) argues that the uniqueness of the German system with its sharp distinction between 'an inside board of directors and an outside supervisory board' is largely a matter of form, which is matched by the American and British convention of having inside and outside members of a single company board. It is true, as will be shown later, that the German supervisory board is not in any profound sense more representative of the shareholders than any of the other directors of a company. But the sharp distinction between the two boards in the German system is important, because of the way in which it reposes an ultimate veto on certain decisions in the hands of the *outsiders*—and in particular in those of the Chairman and Vice-Chairman of the *Aufsichtsrat*.

[22] The average for public companies in the year 1961 was 70–80 per cent (see report on concentration in the economy, Bundestags-Drucksache IV/2320, 1964).

must, in any case, generally go to a bank in order to buy or sell their shares, since bank officials are the only people, other than specialized brokers,[23] who are allowed to trade on the floor of German stock exchanges. The banks run substantial investment departments for their clients; and the small investor knows that the way to get his business done efficiently is to allow the bank official a wide measure of discretion on prices for buying and selling. The whole operation of the stock market is in fact highly centralized. First of all the stocks of only fifteen large companies account for 43 per cent of the nominal value of all quoted shares.[24] Secondly, the bulk of all share dealings are concentrated in the investment departments of the Big Three banks, the Deutsche, the Dresdner, and the Commerz. Finally, any company other than the very largest is usually dependent on a bank's goodwill for making a market in its shares. Indeed, the power of the banks in relation to the company on the make is reinforced by a law, dating from 1896, which prohibits dealings on the stock exchange in the shares or bonds of any company until one year has elapsed from its registration. In other words, it is impossible to solicit investors' funds for a new enterprise unless it has at least a year's trading as a public company behind it; and during this probationary period it is entirely dependent on bank finance.[25] Here one catches a clear glimpse of the underlying vision of the lawmakers who shaped the institutional structure of the German economy—the banks as prefects who will keep a watchful eye on a new company for a test period (one year), who will restrain the speculative excesses of undisciplined investors, and who have the authority ultimately, through their control of shareholders' proxy votes, to tell the managers of German industry where they get off.[26]

An elaborate German government inquiry of 1960 into the degree of business concentration in the postwar economy[27] found, in a sample of companies whose aggregate share capital amounted to three-quarters of the nominal value of all quoted shares, that 70 per cent of the capital was controlled by the banks. This depended only to a minor extent on the direct ownership of shares—though the banks have acquired some major shareholdings, notably in retail and wholesale trade, where they own over one-quarter of all quoted shares. But in most industrial and commercial enterprises in which they had an interest, their control was overwhelmingly dependent on the voting power which they wielded as shareholders' proxies. Again, the German system of proxy voting by the banks has certain peculiarities: the proxy vote is not exercised solely on specific questions, about which shareholders have been

---

[23] The so-called *freie Makler*, who sometimes acts as the agent of a bank when the latter does not want to reveal its identity in particular share dealings (see K. Richebächer, *Börse und Kapitalmarkt* (Berlin, Knapp, 1963), p. 18).

[24] Ibid., pp. 47–48. [25] Ibid., p. 14.

[26] The banks are also responsible for appointing 50 per cent of the boards of control of the stock exchanges.

[27] Bundestags-Drucksache IV/2320.

informed in advance and have given instructions, but also as a general voting
right transferred by a depositor to his bank, the so-called *Depotstimmrecht*,
for a limited period of time.[28]   Incidentally, it is extremely difficult, as the
German official inquiry pointed out,[29] to identify a bank as the wielder of a
shareholder's proxy, since all that is reported is the name and address of an
individual who has been appointed to cast the votes on behalf of the bank
concerned.

It is, moreover, a common practice for proxies to be exchanged between
banks under the system of *Stimmenleihe* ('loaned votes'). This can be done
without referring back to the shareholder on each occasion when his vote is
passed on for casting to another trustee. The advantage of the exchange
system to the bank is that it is enabled to increase the weight of its voting
power in any enterprise in which it has a particular interest. It is also a
convenience for some of the smaller banks, where they are not interested in
the affairs of a company, to avoid the trouble and expense of representing their
depositors at its annual general meeting. The official inquiry noted, not
surprisingly, that the Big Three banks collect more 'loaned votes' than they
hand out to others. All told, some 70 per cent of all shareholders' proxy
votes cast by the banks at company meetings were controlled by the Big
Three.[30]

Company Supervisory Boards

It is plain that any bank which has managed to amass a large block of
shareholders' votes can make its influence felt with the management of a
company, whether or not it has a representative actually sitting on the
Aufsichtsrat. It seems that it is a common ambition among banks to gain
control of a minimum of some 25 per cent of the shareholding of any company in which it is particularly interested; this gives it the status of the
'leading bank' for that company, and certain business advantages usually
follow. All this is a matter of convention, and there is no guarantee that
any individual company will abide by the rules. In the very biggest German
enterprises especially, the management takes pride in its independence. So
long as a company is successful and making good profits, its *Vorstand*
usually has an ultimate say in deciding the membership of the *Aufsichtsrat*.
It normally does so on the basis of a careful mixture of the main outside
interests on whose co-operation the company is dependent—either as customers for its products or as suppliers of materials or providers of finance.
The result is that one company will be represented on the *Aufsichtsrat* of
another as a supplier, and receive a representative of the second company on

[28] Under the present law it has to be renewed every fifteen months.
[29] See report on concentration in the economy, Bundestags-Drucksache IV/2320.
[30] Ibid.

its *Aufsichtsrat*, as a valued customer.[31]   Friendly relations between firms in allied, but not competitive, industries are thus cemented by associating each with the investment decisions of the other.[32]

The function of the *Aufsichtsrat* as a device for systematic consultation between businesses whose interests are intertwined is most clear in relation to the banks. The official inquiry covering a large sample[33] of companies whose shares are quoted on the stock exchange showed that only one-fifth had no bank representative on its *Aufsichtsrat*. The others, numbering 318 companies, had a total of 573 bank representatives distributed among their boards. This gives the banks roughly one in every three *Aufsichtsrat* places in this group of companies, other than those reserved for the trade union representatives. Moreover, in nearly all of these companies, a bank representative was either the Chairman or the Vice-Chairman of the *Aufsichtsrat*. These two posts are endowed with special responsibilities for certain management decisions. Their status is of a different order from those of the ordinary members of the Supervisory Board; the management must consult the Chairman or Vice-Chairman and obtain their approval before they can take action on certain matters. Most important of these is the timing of investment expenditure: the final decision about when to go ahead with an extension of the works or some other capital project, and on what scale, depends on these two members of the Board. Plainly, they are questions in which a firm's banker is especially concerned, since it may be called upon to find at least part of the cash to finance the proposed investment scheme. There are no doubt some moments for doing so which are less convenient than others.

'The banks', says one critic of the system, 'collect *Aufsichtsrat* places the

---

[31] The company law reform of 1965 makes it illegal for two companies to exchange *Vorstand* and *Aufsichtsrat* places directly. There is, however, nothing to stop each of the two companies from having a trusted executive (who is not a member of the *Vorstand*) sitting on its own *Aufsichtsrat* and on that of the other company. Interlocking is legal so long as it is all done at *Aufsichtsrat* level; this is in fact the method now being adopted.

[32] One-third of the members of the *Aufsichtsrat* are trade union representatives; the proportion is raised to half in the steel and coal industries. There seems to be a widespread convention that these trade union members do not intervene in the ordinary conduct of the business in the sphere of investment and other 'technical matters'. They tend to concentrate on questions affecting employment and conditions of work. The system has in practice turned out to be a valuable way of associating the trade unions at an early stage with management discussions which may ultimately involve changes on the factory floor.

[33] This is the same sample—425 companies—as that used on p. 249 above, less the 34 banks included in it. Of the remainder, 73 companies had no bank representative on their *Aufsichtsräte*, leaving a total of 318 companies (i.e. about half of all the German quoted companies) with one or more bank representatives on the *Aufsichtsrat*.

way other people collect postage stamps.'[34] It is indeed the way in which
the hobby is pursued with such intensity by a few large banks which makes
it noteworthy. Three-quarters of all the *Aufsichtsrat* places controlled by the
banking system are held by eleven banks; and the Big Three alone hold over
half.[35] In the smaller sample of 318 companies examined in the official
inquiry, a total of 297 places were filled by representatives of the Big Three;
and the majority of these were either chairman or deputy chairman of their
boards. It would be wrong to conclude, however, that the position of a
bank on an *Aufsichtsrat* is simply a reflection of its power as a controller of
shareholders' proxies. The official inquiry found no apparent correlation
between weight of voting power and position on the supervisory board.
Rather, the membership of the board is to be regarded as an additional
source of information and influence in a company in which a bank is
interested.

It is not clear how far the distribution of influence is covered by tacit
understandings among the banks themselves. The system of *Stimmenleihe*,
whereby the proxy votes of bank depositors are exchanged, allows plenty of
scope for collaboration in pursuit of particular business objectives. This does
not, however, prevent competition among the Big Three for places on the
Aufsichtsräte of the largest industrial concerns. These are much sought after;
there have been occasions when even a big banker has not been above trying
to manoeuvre himself into one of them at the expense of a sitting member
from a rival bank. But when it comes to really serious business, like dealing
with shareholders' votes at the annual general meetings of the banks themselves, the rule of collaboration among the Big Three is apparently absolute.
Each dutifully delivers up to the bank concerned the proxy votes collected
from its shareholders—with the result that an estimated 65–80 per cent of all
the shareholders' votes at the annual general meeting of any one of the Big
Three banks are controlled by the management of the bank itself.[36] Here,
then, at the peak of the German system we arrive at the apotheosis of
managerial self-government. The official report on concentration in the
economy, commenting on the widespread ownership of the shares of the Big
Three, remarks how easy it might have been for some outsider to buy up a
large shareholding in one of these banks during the stock-exchange slump of
the postwar years. That this never happened is a tribute to the efficiency of
the banks in managing the market for their own shares.

However, the big banks are careful not to behave like a closed shop. The
directors of large industrial firms are brought in on the banks' *Aufsichtsräte*—

[34] D. Schneider in an article in the trade union paper, *Die Welt der Arbeit*, 24 July
1959.
[35] See report on concentration in the economy, Bundestags-Drucksache IV/2320.
[36] Ibid.

often from the same firms on which the banks have their own *Aufsichtsrat* representative. This form of mutual supervision applies to most of the 47 public companies whose representatives sit on the supervisory boards of the Big Three banks. All but 10 of these 47 firms have one or more Big Three representatives sitting on their boards.[37] This interchange covers a number of the largest concerns in Germany. A detailed survey of the boards of the largest industrial public companies, those with more than 40,000 employees — 17 companies in all—showed that the Deutsche Bank had a representative on the *Aufsichtsrat* of ten of them. Six of these companies were in turn represented on the *Aufsichtsrat* of the Deutsche Bank.[38] The Deutsche Bank is in an outstandingly strong position in large-scale industry, partly by tradition and partly as a result of the personal status of the managing director of the Bank, Herman Abs. The Deutsche Bank's close industrial links go all the way back to its foundation at the time of the Franco-Prussian War in 1870 by Georg von Siemens.[39] As to Abs, he is probably the largest single collector of *Aufsichtsrat* places in postwar Germany: he sits on a score or more boards and is chairman of eight of them.[40] It is not known with certainty how many other seats on supervisory boards are held by officials of the Deutsche Bank; the Bank itself does not publish the information. One newspaper estimate, which independent evidence suggests is not far out, put the figure at around 400.[41]

Co-ordination by Banker

How does this network of influence radiating from the Big Three banks affect the day-to-day management of German industry? Certainly it would be wrong to see it as a modern substitute for the old-fashioned industrial cartel, in the formation of which the German banks played a leading part during the late nineteenth and early twentieth centuries. There are in fact some well-established conventions against one man sitting on the *Aufsichtsräte*

---

[37] Ibid.

[38] The data on business positions held was derived from *Leitende Manner der Wirtschaft* (Darmstadt, Hoppenstedt, 1961) and from company prospectuses, 1961–3. The companies examined were the following: AEG, Badische Anilin, Bayer, Bosch, Daimler, Gelsenkirchner Bergwerke, Gutehoffnungshütte, Hoechst, Hoesch, Klöckner, Mannesmann, Rheinstahl, Salzgitter-Konzern, Siemens, August Thyssen, Veba, Volkswagen. Four places on the *Aufsichtsräte* of these companies were held by the Commerz Bank, and three by the Dresdner Bank.

[39] See Marshall, *Industry and Trade*, p. 567. The traditional relationship with Siemens has, incidentally, continued for more than 90 years, and today the directors of the two companies continue to sit on each other's supervisory boards and to do business together. These long-standing links between a particular bank and a big business are not uncommon.

[40] In 1964. Under the 1965 reform the maximum number of *Aufsichtsrat* places that may be held by any one person has been reduced to 15.

[41] *Die Welt der Arbeit*, 22 May 1959. This total included companies whose shares were not quoted on the stock exchanges.

of two firms in the same industry. Indeed, one banker told me that when he had been invited to join the supervisory board of a certain motor company, he went to the trouble of asking a competing motor firm, which did a lot of business with his bank, whether they would object. They didn't. The incident serves to illustrate the delicacy of the relationship between a German bank and its big industrial clients. It has to be remembered that there is a tradition, dating back to the early years of German industrial development, that a businessman expects his banker to have an intimate knowledge of all phases of his business. That was also the least that the banker on his side expected, if he was to lend on the lavish and sometimes hazardous scale that German industry demanded for its rapidly expanding operations. Unlike the British banks, for example, the German banks were equipped from early on in their history with technical departments whose job it was to make a judgement on clients' requests for loans on the basis of their scientific and industrial merit.[42] This ability to make a technical judgement, or at any rate to deploy enough technical knowledge to understand such a judgement, is still the pride of German bankers.

Certainly one of the purposes served by plural membership of the *Aufsichtsräte* of various companies is to provide a channel for the diffusion of advanced business practice. The bank's representative, especially if he is chairman or deputy chairman of the board, will regard it as part of his duty to bring to the attention of the management new ideas and techniques which have been developed by other companies in which he is concerned. Sometimes he will go further and organize formal exchanges on specific technical or managerial matters between two firms which employ him independently on their supervisory boards.

But the banker on the *Aufsichtsrat* is not merely a carrier of useful ideas between different industries; he will also make it his business to inform himself about what is happening to other firms competing in the industry with which he is concerned. From his vantage point inside a bank he is well placed to do so. Moreover, although the convention is that he may sit on the *Aufsichtsrat* of only one firm in any given industry, there is nothing to stop his colleagues in the same bank from accepting jobs on the boards of other firms in the same industry. Great care is taken to assure competing concerns using a bank in common that their business secrets will not leak from one to the other through the bank officials sitting on their respective *Aufsichtsräte*. These men, however closely they may work together inside the bank, are charged to keep any company files, which they handle as members of an *Aufsichtsrat*, meticulously concealed from one another. They are supposed to behave rather like father confessors, who happen to be lodged in a seminary with a lot of other confessors; indeed the bank official is under

---

[42] See Marshall, *Industry and Trade*, p. 347.

even greater restraint, because he must make a secret of the successes of his clients, as well as of their failures.

However, in practice a bank is not a monastery, and the priesthood of mammon working there are not exclusively concerned with the individual material progress of those committed to their care. Their interest is ultimately in the bank itself; they, as its executives, are responsible for its lending policy. The more skilfully they choose their borrowers, the bigger the profits they can show at the end of the year. This is their primary objective. It would therefore be surprising if the directors and senior staff of a big German bank who are actively engaged in industrial affairs, either as members of the supervisory boards of companies or in the ordinary course of banking business, did not constantly try to reach a consensus about the prospects and problems of the industries in which they are concerned. That need not involve a breach of the confidence of any individual firm. Still, communication on certain crucial matters is bound to involve some delicate problems. For example, should firm A be encouraged to hurry ahead with an investment in some new plant, using a loan from the bank, when firm B (another client) is planning increased production of a competing product? Will the output of either one be on a large enough scale to force down the market price if both firms go ahead? And what about firms C and D in the same line of business—are they not angling for an agreement to rationalize production by specializing on different products, in order to cut costs and increase their share of the market?

The Steel Industry

The above is not a fanciful case. The German steel industry in 1962–3 faced just such a situation. After many years of heavy investment, continuous expansion of output, and handsome returns on capital, the industry faced a surplus of several million tons of steel. Yet the leading firms were clear that more investment was required, to meet the rising demand for particular steel products and to modernize various production processes. The question was: would each of them go forward independently with its own investment plan, and aggravate the glut and the gloom in the industry as a whole? It is hard to say who contributed most to shaping the answer that was given to the problem—a new form of inter-company agreement— but there is every indication that the big German banks, in their role as supervisors and carriers of ideas from one firm to another, played a significant part in it. The indications are clear, but they are not explicit. They could hardly be so, in the nature of the case. One such pointer is the fact that the Deutsche Bank has one of its directors or a member of its senior staff on the *Aufsichtsräte* of nearly every one of the dozen important steel companies. There is no doubt that the bank was deeply concerned during the period of steel surplus about the danger of involving these firms in heavy spending on new plant which might not be fully employed. The consensus pointed to the need for some rationalization and division of functions between companies; indeed there was some self-criticism inside the bank that the consensus had not operated more effectively to curb investment in steel earlier on.

The new arrangement designed to meet the problem was described in the *Deutsche Zeitung* of 8 November 1962 under the engaging title, 'Gemeinsam leben ist besser' (roughly 'Togetherness is better'). Two of the largest steel companies, Thyssen and Mannesmann, were dissuaded from going ahead with separate and expensive hot strip mills for the production of wide steel sheets. Instead, it was agreed that one of them, Thyssen, would set up a single large plant with an annual capacity of nearly $1\frac{3}{4}$ million tons, and be given an eight-year contract for 'hire-rolling' by the other. Under the contract, Mannesmann supplies its own steel slabs to be rolled by Thyssen and to be returned to it in the required form, paying merely for the use of the capacity 'hired' from Thyssen. Mannesmann for its part committed itself not to put up a plant of its own. Finally, in order to make the Thyssen operation larger and more economic, a third company was brought in, Hüttenwerk Oberhausen AG. (HOAG), to share in the long-term contract for hire-rolling. The agreement was to run from 1964 until 1972. Independently, a further agreement was made at about this time between HOAG and another company, Nieder-rheinische Hütte, covering wire rod. Niederrhein was persuaded to postpone the construction of a new steel rod mill of its own, which threatened to create surplus capacity, in return for a promise by HOAG to take the billets supplied from Niederrhein's works and roll them into wire rod at an agreed price.

There is nothing especially novel about these agreements except their formal long-term character. They involve a measure of joint long-range planning by companies, based on calculations of the future capacity of the industry as a whole; the operation bears some analogy, in its practical effects, to the control exercised over investment plans in the British steel industry through the statutory powers of the Iron and Steel Board. The first German arrangement of this kind dates back to 1959, between the iron and steel firms of Hoesch and Dortmund-Hörder. It had the enthusiastic support of the Deutsche Bank, and provided the model for the more formal trade treaties between companies, running a specific number of years, which followed during the period of widespread and sustained surplus in the early 1960s.

Now it is not suggested that all this was the result of the efforts of bank officials sitting on the *Aufsichtsräte* of steel companies and plotting the long-term future of the industry. There were other forces working in the same direction. One of these has already been mentioned—the systematic long-term forecasts of supply and demand for steel products, developed by the Iron and Steel Industry Association in the 1950s.[43] By the early 1960s the forecasts

[43] See above, p. 245.

were pointing clearly to a future surplus of steel strip capacity, if current investment plans were carried out. It may be asked why the Germans had to wait until as late as the 1960s in order to engage in the rationalization of their steel production. In other European countries it had been accepted readily and earlier as a way of securing a better return on the large blocks of capital, which had to be assembled for investment in modern plants, by avoiding duplication. The answer is simply that the German steelmasters had been able, for more than a decade, to invest in ever-increasing capacity with the assurance of finding a ready market for their products. Only when the threat of a cut in the rate of return on their capital became apparent did they feel the need to plan. They responded to the feeling promptly enough.

Once started on this type of venture, its momentum carried the steel companies forward into new experiments in collaboration, and these continued even when their production and order books had staged a strong recovery in 1964. In that year four of the steel firms who had figured in the earlier arrangements came together in a new kind of agreement, called the 'Carousel' (i.e. merry-go-round), under which they pooled all their orders for certain products and took it in turn to produce them. It works on a production plan which is fixed in advance for a calendar quarter and is designed to give each steelworks the opportunity for longer runs in certain specialized products. The plan is switched round from quarter to quarter in such a way that each of the four steelworks covers the whole range of products included in the agreement—which come under the heading of bar and section steel[44]—in the course of a single year. The four firms are a significant, though not dominant factor in the market, accounting between them for a quarter of total German output of these products.[45]

Again, the interesting feature of this arrangement is the effort to increase the return on capital—by lowering production costs—through the joint planning of production, while preserving the separate identity and commercial independence of the individual firms.[46] They specifically stated that they were not contemplating a joint sales organization for these products; each firm would deal with its own customers, regardless of which of them actually produced the goods supplied. Nevertheless, although nothing was said about it, it will be surprising if, when the moment comes to think about adding to production capacity in order to meet the needs of the group, they do not reach an understanding on an investment plan and on a long-term programme for marketing the extra output. It is worth remarking that this is not to be mistaken for an old-fashioned cartel agreement, designed to keep prices artificially above the market level by controlling the sales of the individual

---

[44] Stab und Formstahl.   [45] See *Frankfurter Allgemeine Zeitung*, 26 Oct. 1964.
[46] It was estimated that the specialization of each works on a smaller range of products with longer runs would increase the effective productive capacity of each of the four steelworks by 15 per cent (see *Handelsblatt*, 22 Oct. 1964).

producer. That is not the best way to capture extra profits in an industry which has a growing market for its products, but faces the constant danger that its big and expensive capital investments may be timed so that they give rise to surplus capacity. The method chosen is to try to obtain a better return on the capital invested, first by joint planning of current production schedules, and secondly by agreeing on a long-term sales programme designed to secure the full employment of any new plant.

It would be wrong, however, to suppose that joint company planning of the kind which has developed in the steel industry in recent years is either widespread or systematically performed in Germany. The existence of a German institutional substructure which, it is plain, could readily support a nation-wide industrial plan has misled some observers into believing that the rest of the building really exists, only has somehow been rendered invisible. Thus M. Pierre Uri in his survey of economic policies in the countries of the Atlantic area says:[47] 'Coordination has proved possible in other countries [i.e. other than France] which do not use central planning. In some cases, the basic sectors were, as in Germany, in the hands of a small number of very big concerns whose plans, in effect, added up to an overall one for the whole economy.' This is too facile a conclusion. In any case it is not, as we have seen, the bigness of German firms which leads to the co-ordination of economic policy in any given industry. It arises out of a combination of more subtle and less readily identifiable factors, dependent on habits and assumptions inherited from the past.

Once the period of urgent postwar reconstruction was over in the early 1950s, and the main landmarks on the German industrial landscape were back in position, there was no overwhelming force pushing the managers of German businesses into a systematic planning endeavour with one another. Uri's comment suggests that a national plan can somehow be achieved merely by the aggregation of the separate plans of individual enterprises. The truth is that if they are to make an integrated whole, somebody has to do the adding up—and the subtractions. How far Germany is still removed from this process was indicated by a direct survey of the business planning practices of a number of the largest German manufacturing concerns in 1964.[48] This showed that the method, the organization, and also the underlying aims of the whole exercise differed widely from one firm to another. There was no evidence even of the acceptance of a rough standard time-period for use in forecasting; each company had its own ideas and did not seem to be much interested in any device for securing comparability with others. Altogether,

---

[47] *Partnership for Progress*, published for the Atlantic Institute (New York, Harper and Rowe, 1963), p. 75.
[48] Including the following: Klöckner-Werke, Siemens & Halske, Opel, Bayer, Badische Anilin, Daimler-Benz, Telefunken, Ford-Werke, AEG.

there appeared to be markedly less standardization of company planning techniques than exists, for example, in the United States.

Business Planning

There is no doubt, however, that the practice of long-term forecasting by the individual firm of profits, production, investment, etc. at some point in the period ahead, has taken hold in large German businesses in recent years. Some of them have ventured into more detailed calculations, including such matters as the size of stocks, their share of the market for certain products, order books and so on. The one feature common to all of them is that they use the official national income figures as the basis for their calculations. Another noticeable tendency in recent years has been to extend the *time horizon* of the business plan. Evidently management in German large-scale enterprise has found—as it has in large-scale enterprise elsewhere—that important business decisions, notably in the field of capital investment, require a lengthened perspective. The data in such an exercise are bound to be speculative; yet it is believed by a number of very large concerns to be worthwhile to make the effort and accept the expense of organizing these forecasts in an increasingly elaborate and systematic fashion. Usually there are alternative assumptions, and therefore several possible answers. It is well understood that no single one of them may prove to be correct; the purpose is to achieve clarity in future management decisions, rather than firm prophecies now.

An extreme devotee of systematic planning is Siemens, the largest company in German industry.[49] It runs a varied group of factories, each of which is required at the start of every year to make a five-year forecast of the main elements in its operations. This is followed by a joint exercise six months later, in which all works managers are involved, together with headquarters senior staff, lasting for two weeks. It is a full-scale conference with analytical papers, reviewing first of all the actual performance of the half-year to date against the forecasts made earlier, and secondly analysing the content of the longer-term plan. The management of the company seems to be convinced— and so are its bankers, the Deutsche Bank—that this systematic study of the actual, and probable, deviations of results from forecasts throws up important ideas which are closely relevant to practical business decisions. Siemens is admittedly an extreme case. In its business of selling heavy electrical machinery it has traditionally found itself involved in taking a long view. But the elaborate intellectual drill of a six-monthly exercise, with a new plan arising out of the analysis of the errors of the old, was adopted only in the 1950s.

There are many German companies which remain sceptical about the practical uses of such detailed planning exercises. But a considerable number

---

[49] Measured by the size of its labour force.

of firms evidently take long-term forecasting seriously enough to pay for the job. IFO, the Munich institute of business forecasting, set up a special department in 1957 to develop a service of longer-term economic predictions. Initially it was given a subsidy of 300,000 Marks; but it was soon found that there was sufficient demand for its work to make the department self-supporting. In 1958 the BDI established a parallel office of its own to examine the long-term forecasts being supplied to its members.[50]

It is easy to see that if the urge towards inter-company arrangements of the type employed by the steel industry recently were to be more generally adopted, the individual firm would be driven to put its own company plan on to an industry-wide basis. It would need to be able to use common assumptions and a common intellectual framework for its forecasts. These are the minimum equipment required for the formulation of a collective strategy for long-term investment programmes. The German steel industry was supplied with some of these necessary instruments ready-made by a high-powered industrial association. The association's investment surveys and forecasts had in fact been going for some years, having been started in the early 1950s, before they were picked up and actively used by the industry. It happened when it found itself, at the beginning of the 1960s, facing the unfamiliar problem of surplus capacity and weak markets. Up to that point, capital invested in German industry as a whole, and in the steel industry in particular, had produced an extremely high return.[51] So long as there appeared to be no significant investment risks, the main motive for industry-wide planning, which is to reduce the area of uncertainty about prospective supplies and markets, was missing. It seems unlikely that it will continue to be quite so markedly absent in the second half of the 1960s.

'Politico-Economic Agency'

To sum up, the Germans are equipped with both the business habits and institutions which would allow them to make an easy transition to a planned economy of the modern capitalist type. The contrast with Britain, for instance, where commercial customs and national history both argue against

---

[50] The predominant view in the BDI in the early 1960s was a sceptical one. But there was no lack of interest in the techniques of long-term planning.

[51] See ECE, *Econ. Survey Europe 1961*, pt. 2, 'Some factors in economic growth in Europe during the 1950s', ch. 6, for a discussion of the causes of the exceptionally favourable incremental capital-output ratio (ICOR) achieved by Germany. During the 1950s the annual average for the German economy as a whole was twice as good as the British. Industrial planning based on a series of long-term inter-firm agreements, designed to economize capital during a period of slower growth of demand, as in the steel industry in the early 1960s, is one way of maintaining a favourable ICOR when market forces begin to be less favourable. More formal national planning in France helped to produce a similar effect on the ICOR there during the 1950s; the ECE Survey (ch. 6, p. 7) makes the point that through 'the efficient use of scarce productive resources', the French achieved a high rate of economic growth 'with a relatively modest investment ratio'.

the process of central planning, is very marked. German businessmen, right from the start of the country's industrial development, have been influenced in some measure by considerations of collective economic policy, whether applying to groups of firms thrusting for some special advantage or to the whole of an industry. The banks have usually been either the leaders or active partners in this process; typically, they were the organizers of the original cartels.[52]

The big banks have always seen it as their business to take an overall view of the long-term trend in any industry in which they were concerned, and then to press individual firms to conform to certain broad lines of development.[53] They saw themselves essentially as the grand strategists of the nation's industry, whereas the British banks, by contrast, were content to act as its quartermaster general. There is no doubt that the British banks were, and are, extremely responsive to changing business needs, once these needs have been recognized by the businessmen themselves and clearly stated. The Germans are probably less responsive; but they anticipate, and sometimes no doubt cause the business needs to appear. The contrast is connected with the banking history of the two countries: the British system of specialized banking made the business of industrial investment the exclusive concern of the merchant bankers, and left the much larger joint-stock banks out of it; while in Germany the all-purpose bank, covering the whole range of activities requiring credit, proved to be a remarkably powerful instrument for financing the rapid growth of a country which was a comparative latecomer to the industrial revolution.[54]

It would be wrong, however, to cast the German banks in the role of the ringmaster, with the big horses of industry galloping round them and responding to the crack of the whip. The lines of influence between the large bank and the large industrial enterprise are reciprocal. What tends to emerge out of this process is a consensus of big business about the affairs of an industry. Of course it does not by any means always work. The very large firms or the new and exceptionally dynamic firms, proud of their own separate personalities, will sometimes go their own way. The common feeling in postwar Germany is that Krupp—still a private company and therefore without the supervision of outsiders on an *Aufsichtsrat*—is such a business.[55] It should be observed that in France too there are great family concerns, for example

---

[52] See Clapham, *Economic Development of France and Germany*, p. 394.
[53] C. H. Wilson, *New Cambridge Modern History*, xi. 74, describes the function of German banking in the late 19th century as follows: 'The joint stock bank was not merely a credit organization but a politico-economic agency for converting Germany into an industrial state.'
[54] Clapham, pp. 393 ff.
[55] Private companies are not compelled to have an *Aufsichtsrat*, though they must meet the legal requirement (applying to the *Aufsichtsrat* of public companies) of workers' representation on whatever organ of control is established by the company.

Michelin, which notoriously resist any attempt to involve them in the process of national planning. The French planners have experienced difficulties with very large firms even when they are nationalized, like Renault. As the analysis in Part II suggested, it is size and the sense of economic power, not whether an enterprise is in public or private ownership, which tends to determine its amenability to a national plan or any other form of collective pressure.

The most clearly visible manifestation of banking influence in German industry is the presence of the representatives of the big banks on the supervisory boards of important businesses. But there are many other means of pressure available to the banks which are less immediately obvious—notably the control over large blocks of shareholders' proxy votes in companies and the power of the big banks over almost every phase of the operations of the German capital market. The sheer technical competence of the banks, especially in matters concerned with industrial innovation, is another factor.[56]

Finally, the banks have a recognized special status—an almost para-statal position, as the natural and trusted ally of public authority in managing any intervention that is to be made in the private sector of the economy. Thus, for example, the subsidies which the central Government hands out for a wide variety of capital projects undertaken in development areas—notably

---

[56] See Marshall, *Industry and Trade* (p. 347), who quotes a writer in *The Economist* (5 Feb. 1916) on the contrast between the treatment of inventions and new ideas in the City of London and in Germany. In Germany, he said, 'the pioneer would take his proposal to one of the great banks with an industrial department; and the proposal would immediately be put before experts, scientific and technical, well known to the bank and thoroughly trusted who (on the assumption that the proposed business was really good) would report well on it, and *would be believed*.' Marshall's conclusion is that 'the German banks have surpassed even those of America in the promptitude and energy with which they faced the risks of turning a large flow of capital into an enterprise . . . to which the future belongs' (p. 558). All the evidence suggests that the lending departments of the modern German banks make a conscious effort to maintain this tradition, of which they are proud. A notable postwar example is the establishment of the new Zeiss optical concern in Western Germany, when all the assets of the company, centred on Jena, had been lost in the Soviet zone of occupation. The Deutsche Bank, on the say-so of Mr Abs, made available to a group of refugee Zeiss technicians, who had been conveniently rounded up in a British internment camp, an investment loan of several tens of millions of D.Marks to set up a new works. There was no collateral for the loan, the lenders say proudly in retrospect, other than the technical competence of a body of penniless men in a prison camp ! Indeed, one can hardly fail to observe the satisfaction felt in pointing out that loans such as this were not 'bankable' by any conventional standard. The destruction of most forms of conventional credit-worthiness in Germany during the late 1940s, at the time of the currency reform, gave the German bankers a generous opportunity to exercise their talent as industrial venturers—in a spirit which recalled the early years of the German industrial revolution. The postwar experience seems to have created a momentum of investment in new industrial ventures, which continued after the immediate cause of the emergency had disappeared.

the areas bordering the Soviet Zone[57]—are all distributed by banks. They play an active part in helping to choose the recipient. Each project that is put forward to the Ministry of Economics for a subsidy—which takes the form of a cheap loan—must be approved by the applicant's bank. Only if the latter is sufficiently satisfied with the details of the project and the solvency of its client to guarantee the loan are public funds made available. What this means in effect is that if an entrepreneur with a business confined to a single locality had earned the ill-will or suspicion of the bank concerned with his affairs, he would be hard put to it to qualify for the normal government subsidy in support of a regional investment scheme. His only hope would be to obtain the support of another banker—not always an easy thing to do for a small businessman dependent on his personal reputation for credit. The subsidy comes in the form of a rate of interest well below what the business-man would be charged for an ordinary commercial loan. In 1963–4 the going rate for subsidized loans for regional development was $3\frac{1}{2}$ per cent, against a normal rate for bank advances of around 7 per cent. The bank, which is expected to do all the work of sorting out the affairs of claimants, received the money from the Government at a rate of 2 per cent and pocketed the extra $1\frac{1}{2}$ per cent charged to the recipient, as a fee for its management service and credit guarantee.[58]

It would be wrong, however, to imply that it is the banks alone which are responsible for the characteristic flavour of collective purpose in German industry. They are the most notable expression of a much more general phenomenon. Industrial collaboration in pursuit of long-range objectives is fostered by powerful trade associations in certain industries. And these spokesmen for the collective view of organized industry have a direct and privileged entrée to the government machine, via the ministry concerned with their affairs. They normally sit on the Standing Advisory Council (*Beirat*), representing the major interest groups, established by the ministries for each of their main activities. The officials in Bonn seem often to regard the *Beirat* not as an instrument for outside intervention in departmental business, but rather as providing them with an umbrella under which they are able to shelter in their dealings with parliament. It is another kind of democratic sanction for official acts. On the other hand, it can sometimes be more trouble than it is worth. One official explained to me that he had deliberately avoided establishing a *Beirat* in his sphere of activity, because he was dealing

[57] This is an important and fairly successful programme which has been in operation since 1950. It was extended in 1959 to other economic problem areas away from the Soviet border regions. The technique used is to choose a 'growth point', usually in a small town with under-used amenities, and then actively to seek out individual firms to go there and take advantage of the cheap loans provided out of public funds.
[58] Information from the Regional Development Section of the Ministry of Economics. These loans were usually for 15 years at the time. Some of them, notably for agricultural investment, were at even lower rates of interest and for longer periods.

with problems which required the exercise of administrative initiative in the public interest. This might not be universally popular. His fear was that once a *Beirat* was established, he would be faced with collective recommendations, the product of careful compromises between competing interest groups, which it would be difficult for him to ignore. He could not, in any case, avoid consulting the interest groups; but, he said, he preferred to do so singly and in private.[59]

A close relationship between an organization representing the views of the major firms in an industry and its *ministère de tutelle* is another one of the conditions of French-type planning which the Germans would be able to satisfy with little trouble. Indeed, all that seems to be missing in order to bring these disparate pieces of an embryonic planning exercise together into a working system is a plan. But that is not an insignificant gap in a society where the government seizes every opportunity to express its hostility to the very idea of planning. The evolution of official economic policy in Germany since the war and its probable future direction is the subject of the next chapter.

---

[59] Although the law governing the *Beiräte* (GGO 23) says that the members of these committees are to act in their personal capacity as experts, and not as the representatives of organizations, these advisory committees are in practice a recognized form of official representation for major interest groups—'as much a part of the machinery of government as the Bundestag' (Hennis, *Pol. Vierteljahresschrift 1961*).

XII

GERMAN ECONOMIC POLICY: THEORY AND PRACTICE

THERE is a popular image of the postwar German economy as the nearest European approximation to the American way of life. Private initiative is always preferred to public, and the state is kept vigorously in its place. Public enterprise and central planning under the aegis of the government are both firmly rejected. That at any rate is the political legend. It is not wholly false; such ideas as these genuinely express the intentions of those who have, since the end of the war, been responsible for the government of Germany. However, they do not entirely fit with the way in which the governors have in practice behaved.

For instance, the conventional image of the German Government would hardly lead one to anticipate the fact that it regularly takes in taxation a higher proportion of the nation's output than the government of any other advanced Western country.[1] The United States, in spite of a much larger burden of defence expenditure (relatively as well as absolutely) belongs at the other end of the scale, among the least taxed Western nations. It is especially interesting to compare the German with the British case, because of the remarkable persistence of a legend that Germany's much more rapid economic growth is correlated with the greater freedom of her citizens from the attentions of the tax collector. It was true right at the beginning of the 1950s, when the Labour Government was still in power in Britain, that the level of British taxation was higher than the German. But by 1960 the position had been dramatically reversed. That was the outcome of a progressive movement by the two countries in opposite directions, as the following figures show:

Taxation as Per Cent of Gross National Product*

				1950	1955	1960
Britain	...	...	...	32.5	29.0	27.6
Germany	...	...	...	30.3	32.2	33.9

*At market prices

Source : OECD, Statistics of National Accounts 1950–61 (1964).

[1] 35 per cent in 1961 (OECD, *Statistics of National Accounts 1950–61*). A large part of the burden falls on the working class; but rates of taxation on middle-class incomes are also heavy. NIESR, *Econ. R.*, no. 15 (May 1961), p. 8, compares direct taxes paid at various levels of income for a standard family consisting of two adults and two children between the ages of five and ten years in different countries, and shows that a German family with an earned income of between £3,000 and £5,000 paid a larger part of it in tax (including social security contributions) than an Englishman in the same economic circumstances (see also ibid., no. 14, Mar. 1961).

It should be observed that the increase in the absolute amount taken by the Germans in taxation over these years was even bigger than the figures suggest, because the rate of increase in the German national product between 1950 and 1960 was three times as great as the British. Indeed, the striking thing about the German case is that rising prosperity, which produced windfalls for the exchequer in the form of extra revenue both from income taxes and from the sales tax, was not seized upon as a reason for cutting down the share of income claimed by the state from the nation. That is precisely what happened in Britain. In part, the difference between the two countries reflects a contrast in attitudes towards the social services during a period of increasing affluence. In the second half of the 1950s the Germans embarked on a major extension of their social security system; and by the end of the decade the tax revenue required to support it absorbed one-tenth of the gross national product. In Britain the objective of tax reduction took priority over schemes for the extension of social welfare.[2]

But the high level of German taxation was not solely for the support of ambitious social welfare schemes. The money was needed for a variety of subsidies to support one or another of the activities favoured by the state, and also to help in the finance of the nation's capital investment at large. Without the massive contribution from public saving, it is very doubtful whether Germany would have been able to maintain her exceptionally high level of investment—around 25 per cent of the national product in the early 1960s. Public saving financed nearly a third of this; in Britain it provided about one-tenth of a much smaller total of national investment. The only advanced European nation which makes any comparable contribution out of public saving to the national investment effort is Sweden.[3] Indeed, anyone judging the relative importance devoted to the role of the state in national economic policy by the obvious fiscal criteria—level of taxation, public savings, collective social expenditure—would be bound to conclude that the German policy-makers belonged naturally with the Scandinavian group, while the British were allied with the Americans, the Belgians, and the other traditional antagonists of public initiative.[4]

German public investment in education, transport and communications, social services, etc., has grown especially fast in recent years. During the five years from 1958 to 1963 annual expenditure on all forms of public investment nearly doubled. It was already significantly larger than the equivalent British figure at the start of the period. The table in Appendix III (p. 432) compares the changes in the main items of public investment with those which occurred in Britain, where the period 1958–63 was also one in which investment on

[2] See above, pp. 91 ff.   [3] OECD, *Statistics of National Accounts.*
[4] For note see p. 267.

public account[5] made a notable spurt. It rose by some two-thirds in the five years. The main fields of investment activity were also very similar—roads and other forms of transport, education and housing. But only in public housing is the British advance comparable in magnitude with the German—and the reason here is partly that the starting point in Britain was comparatively low. At the end of the period the absolute value of public investment in housing in Britain was still well below the German figure.[6]

Whence came this extraordinary burgeoning of German public investment, on top of an earlier effort which many other countries would have regarded as quite impressive? It seems clear that it flowed, in large part, from the success of the German authorities in collecting tax revenue and their stubbornness in maintaining high tax rates—that it was the effect of decisions on fiscal policy rather than their cause.[7] There was no attempt, for example, to make the timing of public investment fit the broader needs of economic policy for controlling the business cycle. The Bundesbank, reviewing the five years in question, says wrily: 'It would be wrong to conclude . . . that the capital

---

[4] The point becomes most readily apparent from a comparison of public saving as a proportion of GNP in a scatter of industrialized countries:

	Gross public saving as % of GNP at market prices
High saving	*1961*
Sweden	8·8
West Germany	8·7
Austria	8·6
Norway	8·0
Netherlands	6·7
Low saving	
France	3·7
Italy	3·2
USA*	2·2
United Kingdom	2·0
Belgium	0·8

* Includes saving of public corporations

Source: OECD, *Statistics of National Accounts*.

[5] The comparison covers central and local government expenditure, excluding the nationalized industries.

[6] Converted at current rates of exchange.

[7] The Bundesbank, commenting on the rise in public investment during the period, in its Report of Aug. 1964 (vol. 16, no. 8, p. 4), says: 'The disproportionately great increase of capital expenditure was rendered possible . . . by the fact that owing to the progressive rates for important taxes, not only did tax revenues grow faster than the national product, but the additional receipts from taxes materially exceeded the increase in the public authorities' current expenditure.' The central bank also published some interesting figures showing the time-lag between the appearance of an increase in the tax revenue surplus and the consequential rise in public investment: tax revenue increased faster than public investment in 1959–60; public investment caught up in 1961; then went ahead very much faster in 1962–3 than tax revenue. In the latter two years, when the public authorities were evidently given their head, their investment expenditure rose at twice the rate of increase in fixed investment over the German economy as a whole.

expenditure of public authorities in the period . . . operated to even out private investment activity.'⁸ The British, on the other hand, deliberately tried to moderate the rise in public sector investment when the private sector was booming and vice versa. Perhaps it is characteristic that as a result of their greater concern with short-term business cycle policy—and it must be admitted, greater skill in handling it—the British reduced their taxes more than the Germans, and got a lot less public investment done.

Divided Authority

What adds a certain piquancy to the story is that the orginal reason why the German authorities insisted on their high taxes, from which so many of these generous public initiatives flow, was their anxiety over the lack of unified fiscal control at the centre. Because the power to levy taxes was so diffused, with the *Länder* governments claiming the lion's share of direct taxes before the central Government even got a look in, the tax authorities in Bonn were inclined to over-insure in order to make certain that their minimum needs were met. The original constitution of postwar Western Germany, framed under the influence of American federal doctrines with a strong decentralizing bias, put the centre in the position of a suppliant *vis-à-vis* the rulers of the *Länder*. The latter were given legal control over the revenue from both income taxes and corporation taxes.⁹

It was only with the tax reform in 1955 that the central Government was able to assert its claim on a regular and substantial share of this revenue.¹⁰ The Federal Government's proportion was initially fixed at 35 per cent; it has risen subsequently in a series of concessions on percentage points, made after protracted arguments, to 39 per cent in 1964. Even so, the Federal Government continues to occupy a very exposed position as the manager of the nation's economic policy. It is the only one of the taxing authorities which takes an overall view of national income trends, the balance of payments and so on. The other ten governments are interested in taxes solely as a means of getting certain specific jobs done on their bit of territory. If they have the money in hand, they will not be easily deterred from spending

---

⁸ Ibid., p. 5.
⁹ The Federal Government's own source of revenue is chiefly the turnover tax, levied on all sales.
¹⁰ See H. H. Götz, *Weil alle besser leben wollen: Porträt der deutschen Wirtschaftspolitik* (Dusseldorf, Econ-Verlag, 1963), p. 180. The central Government was able to persuade the *Länder* to give way, partly because the law left it with the ultimate power to impose a 'supplementary income tax and corporate tax levy', if it required this money in order to be able to function. The right has in fact never been used, but the existence of the threat was a strong inducement to the *Länder* to give up some of their gains. Even after 1955, however, as Götz points out, the *Länder* continued to get the better part of the bargain: during the period 1955–61 their total tax receipts increased by 130 per cent, while the Federal Government's receipts rose by only 68 per cent (p. 183).

it on their favourite projects by arguments about national economic policy, and even less by talk about the dangers of inflation resulting from their actions. Say there is a danger, why pick on us to cut back our spending?— each of them asks in turn. In the early 1960s, when they were putting this sort of question, the *Länder* showed how easy it was to embarrass the central Government by drawing on the considerable reserve funds which they had by then accumulated at the Bundesbank. No wonder, then, that the Ministry of Finance feels it has a strong incentive to err on the side of taxing too much, rather than too little.

Moreover, the limitations on its financial control over the nation's affairs are not confined to the sphere of taxation. Most modern governments expect to be able to use their central banks to regulate the volume of money flowing into the economic system. The latter normally have the power to decide the terms of any new credit to be granted by banks and other lending institutions throughout the country, and to fix the price that borrowers will have to pay. They can also influence the volume of money in the system by their 'open market operations'—buying securities (and therefore increasing the amount of money flowing in) or selling them (thus decreasing the flow, by withdrawing money from the buyers) in the gilt-edged market. In Germany, however, the central bank is very much a law to itself. The most that the Minister of Economics or the Minister of Finance can do, if they object to a Bundesbank decision, is to demand a delay of up to two weeks in its execution. The Chancellor, Dr Adenauer, on one occasion in 1956 in a speech to the Federation of German Industry, publicly rebuked the central bank for raising the bank rate, which he said would harm business activity. He went on to develop the point that the bank's action was directed especially at 'the small man'.[11] But the most that he could do in the end was to turn on his Ministers of Economics and Finance and promise his audience that he would demand a full account from them of their dealings with the bank. The bank itself was beyond his reach.

The government is, indeed, more dependent in some ways on the goodwill of the directors of the Bundesbank than the latter are on the government. The law limits the amount of money which the government may borrow on short term, either direct from the Bundesbank, or by the issue of treasury bills with the bank's permission, to cover temporary gaps in its finances caused by the seasonal ups and downs of tax payments, to a total of DM 3,000 million (about £270 million). This is keeping a government whose annual budget runs to around DM 50,000 million[12] on a very short rein indeed. But the bank has not generally been willing to provide even this amount of help, if the loans are required to tide the government over for anything more than a few weeks; in that case the government is invited to borrow the sum that it

---

[11] Ibid., p. 72. [12] In the early 1960s.

needs by an issue of bonds in the market. It still does not escape from control, however, if it adopts that expedient, for there is a legal restriction on the
size of any borrowing, up to a maximum of DM 4,500 million in any one
year.[13]   And as a final inhibition on any possible remaining impulse towards
financial ebullience, the German constitution formally charges the government with the duty of balancing its budget *each year*; in theory it can be
hauled before the Federal Supreme Court for running a deficit.[14]

Even when taxes are collected centrally and escape the grasp of the *Länder*,
the Federal exchequer may be denied the use of them altogether.   Certain
important revenues are hived off into separate funds, which are effectively
placed beyond the reach of the government, even for temporary use in the
course of its short-term financial operations.   This applies to the vast sums
which are collected annually in social security payments.   They account for
more than one-quarter of all the taxes levied by public authorities in Germany.   The two funds with the largest reserves are Unemployment Insurance
and Old Age Pensions; they make up the greater part of the accumulated
reserve of some DM 27,000 million of the social security services.[15]   They
have in recent years been in very substantial surplus.   Over the period 1960–3,
covered in an analysis of their operations conducted by the Bundesbank, their
savings amounted to DM 8,600 million (nearly £800 million).[16]

These surpluses have become a significant factor in German capital
markets; they financed, among other things, nearly 9 per cent of all purchases
of new issues of fixed interest securities during the years 1960–3.   But the
favourite form of investment is in deposits and loans to banks; three-fifths
of the accumulated public insurance funds are deployed in this way.   The
managers of the German social security funds have a quite unusual freedom
in the conduct of their investment policy.   In France and Italy there is a

---

[13] If the government does not redeem these bonds by the end of the year, its issuing
rights for the subsequent year are reduced by the amount outstanding.   The government is also allowed to obtain short-term credits direct from the commercial banks
by the issue of commercial paper, again on condition that the Bundesbank gives its
approval.   It has never in fact used this expedient.

[14] Fortunately the German system of budget accounting is so complicated and confused
that it would be hard to prove, in anything but an extreme case, that a 'deficit' had
actually occurred.   It would always be open to the government to amend its
accounting definitions in order to accommodate its financial needs.   Indeed, it can at
a pinch treat certain of its borrowings not as debit items, but as revenue received!

[15] End 1963 figures.   See Deutsche Bundesbank *Monthly Report*, July 1964.   The Sickness Insurance Fund has a larger annual income and outgo than the other two, but
does not accumulate any significant reserves.

[16] The published figure of the reserve of the Public Insurance Funds increased
by DM 10·6 billion during this period (to a total of over DM 27 billion) but of this
about DM 2 billion were derived from a special payment by the government (ibid.).
Since 1963 there has been a change of trend and the social insurance funds have just
about managed to balance their books with an increased outgo for pensions.   It
looks as if they had now ceased to be a significant source of net savings in the
German economy.

deliberate policy of concentrating control over the employment of all such funds in the hands of a public or semi-public agency, which is responsive to the government's wishes. Even in the United States and in Britain, where the funds are cut loose from direct government control, their investments are confined to loans and stocks issued by public authorities. But in Germany there are no such restraints; and the men responsible for the disposal of these large sums of public money are it seems drawn irresistibly, like so many other investors in Germany, towards the banks.

Commenting on the financial impact of the social insurance funds over the period 1960–3, the Bundesbank remarks: 'These amounts greatly strengthen the ability of the banks to grant credit to their customers'. The funds are not guided in their choice of outlet by considerations of public policy, though the central bank concedes that they 'readily complied' during 1960–1 when asked to give 'support for its restrictive measures'.[17] However, since all that this required was a willingness to subscribe to some short-term public bonds with a very handsome yield, little sacrifice of advantage, and none of autonomy, was involved. There is indeed no secret about the fact that the central bank regards the absence of effective control over the rapidly growing surpluses in the hands of the public insurance funds as a source of serious weakness in the conduct of German financial policy. The German Federal authorities have no legal means of deploying this vast mass of public saving in the public interest. Again, the publicly owned savings banks have been especially successful in postwar Germany and now hold around 50 per cent of all bank deposits in the country,[18] and employ their funds pretty much as they please. This is the opposite of the principle of centralization pursued by the French and which is given its characteristic expression in institutions like the Caisse des Dépôts.[19]

The remarkable thing is that in spite of the proliferation of these competing centres of power, German economic policy has achieved a high degree of apparent coherence. In part this seems to be due to the irrepressible administrative instinct to centralize authority, even in the face of serious legal obstacles. The method of the highly successful Prussian bureaucracy was inherited by Imperial Germany and automatically passed on to successor governments. It leads to an obsessive concern with the observance of standard practices, as though the smallest deviation from established drill threatens disruption to the whole apparatus of governing.[20] The vision of

[17] Ibid.
[18] See Auburn, *Comparative Banking*, p. 59 (1961 figures).
[19] See above pp. 167 ff. The Caisse holds all the funds of the French savings banks, as well as the various public pension funds.
[20] In postwar Germany this spirit was expressed most typically in the behaviour of the *Oberfinanzpräsident*, the old-style senior financial official, devoted to a rigid accounting procedure, which was uniform in all its detail for the whole of the Reich, and to high standards of honesty. The officials who manned the independent Finance

parade-ground chaos, as a single man gets out of step, is the underlying nightmare. The hierarchical principle asserts itself, partly no doubt because it is more efficient to know precisely where authority is located. It should not be forgotten either that the division of German sovereign authority into a lot of semi-independent entities, each charged with the duty of maintaining a high degree of autonomy and separateness from all the rest, was an idea wished on the Germans by their Allied conquerors. The Americans seem to have been particularly keen on trying out another experiment with their favourite political device, the separation of powers. There was no reason why the Germans should show any special interest in sustaining it—nor why they should not seize any opportunity that offered to move in the direction of the older and more familiar unitary system.

Orderly Housekeeping

Another point to observe is that the German economic policy-makers did not set themselves any very ambitious aims in the early postwar years. If the policy looked effective, it was at least partly because the targets were traditional and modest. They were to get back to some point which the country had reached before. Most notably, the new objective of full employment on a permanent basis, which occupied a leading place in the thinking of the postwar governments of the Anglo-Saxon world,[21] hardly figured at all in Germany. Full employment, even in the modest sense in which Lord Beveridge had defined it in Britain, i.e. an average of 3 per cent of the labour force out of work,[22] was not at this stage a serious objective of official policy, either in the Bundesbank in Frankfurt or in the government departments in Bonn. A typical example of their approach to the problem was the decision

Ministries of the *Länder*, with their greatly enhanced tax and spending powers, were drawn from this class. Their rigid notions of financial and procedural orthodoxy certainly helped to save the postwar German state from the administrative fission, which the new constitution might so easily have produced. Intent above all upon standardized practice and the assertion of clearcut administrative authority, these men were instinctively driven to collaborate with one another closely, even at the expense of the sectional *Länder* interests which most of them were paid to serve. A characteristic example of the way in which they behaved occurred in the late 1940s, when the Allied Military Government charged each *Land* to work out its own tax code and financial arrangements. Beginning in the American Military Zone, the financial authorities of the various *Länder* came together to formulate a standard fiscal practice, from which none of the individual states would deviate. Later on each of the *Länder* in the British and French zones voluntarily adopted the same standard book of rules. It is interesting to speculate what would have happened to the German financial system after the war, if it had not been equipped with this stiff administrative backbone, but had instead, as the Americans and others evidently expected, been run by people who were intent on exploiting the wide range of opportunities offered to them for the assertion of separate regional interests.

[21] The US Employment Act (1946) and the British white paper, *Employment Policy* (1944), give clear expression to the new mood of official thinking in these two countries.

[22] W. H. Beveridge, *Full Employment in a Free Society* (London, Allen & Unwin, 1944), pp. 126–8.

in 1951 to increase taxes by a substantial amount at a time when unemployment stood at over 6 per cent.[23] 1951 was admittedly a year of strain on the German balance of payments caused by the Korean War boom, and this might have lent some colour to the argument for deflationary measures; but there is no doubt that what, in fact, prompted the Finance Minister's demand that the turnover tax should be raised by one-third[24] was the simple imperative of 'orderly housekeeping'—a conviction that any self-respecting government must, in all circumstances, collect at least enough revenue to cover its spending. This conviction was shared by the rest of the Cabinet and especially by the Chancellor, Dr Adenauer. The effect of the state's housekeeping on the level of employment in the other parts of the economy outside the state's immediate financial orbit was the last thing to be considered. It was the business of the state to look after its own affairs, and above all to set an example of transparently honest behaviour.

The German authorities behaved as if the revolution in economic thinking which derived from the work of Keynes in the 1930s had never occurred at all. It is indeed remarkable how few people in Germany, even among the professional economists, had taken in this great intellectual change, before the second half of the 1950s.[25] It took even longer to penetrate the embattled outworks of the Ministry of Finance. The Ministry of Economics, Dr Erhard's department, was not quite so tightly in the grip of conventional financial orthodoxy; and this ministry was gradually able to establish its ascendancy, in alliance with a group of professional economists more in touch with modern ideas, some of whom had by this time found their way into positions of influence in the Bundesbank.[26] It is indeed a notable, and

[23] OECD, *Manpower Statistics 1950–62*. It is fair to say that the tax increase was originally prompted by complaints from the OEEC countries about Germany's balance of payments deficit which, they thought, required the remedy of a dose of deflation.

[24] From 3 per cent to a standard rate of 4 per cent on most transactions, where it has stuck ever since. There are, however, important exceptions, e.g. the rate in wholesale trade is 1 per cent.

[25] It is the more remarkable in view of the strong tradition of *Konjunkturforschung* in Germany which continued after the war; indeed the Germans were the leaders in Western Europe in applying modern techniques to business cycle forecasting. The systematic monthly questionnaire on business conditions and intentions initiated by the Munich Institut für Wirtschaftsforschung (IFO) in 1950 provided the model followed later by several other European countries (see 'Short-term Business Indicators in Western Europe', in ECE, *Econ. Bulletin for Europe*, Nov. 1955). However the German *Konjunkturforschung* institutions were not much interested in economic analysis of underlying trends; they were concerned at this stage almost exclusively with the identification of short-term changes in business intentions and expectations.

[26] Notably, Dr Eduard Wolf, a key figure on the professional staff of the bank in the postwar period, editor of its publications and a member of the board of managers from 1951 until 1964. He explained to me that he had had the unusual opportunity, for a German economist, of following the development of Keynesian ideas in the 1930s, when he ran the American desk at the Berlin Institute of Economics.

unusual, circumstances that the new thinking along Keynesian lines in Germany found expression in the central bank first, rather than in the departments of government concerned with economic policy. In the end the exceptionally powerful and independent position which the postwar constitution gave to the central bank was a factor in hastening the long delayed Keynesian revolution in German economic thinking. It was assisted by the accident of personalities—Dr Erhard's special position in the Ministry of Economics—which in the long run allowed the department concerned with the broad questions of economic policy to take precedence over the traditionally all-powerful Ministry of Finance.

But that was only in the long run. Until the second half of the 1950s 'orderly housekeeping' by the Minister of Finance, Fritz Schaeffer, closely supported by Adenauer as Chancellor, took precedence over everything else. It was not merely that no attempt was made to use tax policy to smooth out the ups and downs of the business cycle; the tax changes introduced to satisfy the needs of financial respectability sometimes served to sharpen the economic fluctuations. There was a striking example during the boom and recession of 1950–2. As Henry Wallich pointed out, 'the tax cut of 1950 aggravated the Korea boom, the increase of 1951 contributed to the subsequent lull'.[27]

Germany was saved from the economic damage and human misery which might otherwise have resulted from this anachronistic approach to the use of public finance by a number of providential circumstances. First and most important was the continuing boom in world trade[28] which always kept the order books of German industry filled, however consumer demand might fluctuate at home. German manufacturing capacity at the start of the period was grossly under-employed, so that when the concentrated investment effort began to ease the industrial bottlenecks at critical points in the economy— notably in steel, coal, and electric power, but also in a number of other key goods and services—a vast additional productive potential was brought into play.[29] While the Ministry of Finance was busy keeping house, and conscientiously disregarding the effect that this frugal exercise might have on the

[27] *Mainsprings of the German Revival* (New Haven, Conn., Yale UP, 1955). Wallich remarked at this stage on the curious 'philosophy of the Finance Ministry', which he, as an American, found was sharply in contrast with postwar views of fiscal policy in the United States. 'According to the Finance Ministry's view the important effect of a deficit-creating tax cut is not the increase in purchasing power of consumers. . . . The deficit is viewed more as an unfortunate byproduct, a temporary violation of the principle of a balanced budget, soon to be made good through rising revenues from a higher national income' (p. 110).

[28] See Part I, Ch. II.

[29] See ECE, *Econ. Survey Europe 1961*, pt. 2, ch. 6, p. 5, which estimates that the increase in 'capacity utilisation between 1949 and 1955 corresponded to 4½ years gross fixed investment at a 10 per cent annual rate of addition to the gross fixed capital stock'.

rest of the economy, the Ministry of Economics was most actively intervening wherever opportunities for more production, aided by strategically placed subsidies or tax concessions, presented themselves. Rarely can a ministry so vociferously devoted to the virtues of economic liberalism and market forces have taken so vigorous a part in setting the direction and selecting the targets of economic development.

It is, indeed, not at all apparent that there was any great difference in practice between the special effort made by the German authorities to refurbish their basic industries at the beginning of the 1950s and the early phases of the Monnet Plan in France. If the Germans did not use the apparatus of a plan, as the French did—though it should be observed that the French apparatus of planning had at this stage a very primitive, ad hoc character—the difference could be accounted for, in large part, by the much greater self-reliance of large-scale German industry. The industrialists did not have to be told where to go. Once given their opportunity, in the form of high profits, a plentiful, skilled and low-cost labour supply, and the backing of a series of generous tax concessions on certain kinds of investment, they went ahead very fast in the required direction. In a sense, it was unnecessary for the German authorities to plan the growth of the country's productive capacity as a formal exercise in prediction, in the French manner, because what had to be done was essentially to reconstruct something which had existed before. The guide-lines were provided by the past; there was no need for a German Monnet to invent them.

Another factor was that when the German Government intervened to accelerate the growth of certain sectors of the economy, it went to great lengths to present the matter, wherever it was possible to do so, as if it derived from or supplemented some primary private initiative, whereas in France the natural tendency was, and is, to insist on the public character of any such initiative. Indeed, the German Government seemed at times almost to be trying to disguise what it was doing even from itself. Thus, when it embarked on the great investment effort in the bottleneck industries—steel, coal, and selected public utilities—in 1952, and collected a forced loan from the whole of industry to cover the cost, it did not issue ordinary government bonds to those who had paid the levy. No—arrangements had to be made to give them securities in the individual concerns which benefited from the loan and which the lenders had had no part in choosing.[30] The fiction of private investment was maintained, even though the DM 1,000 million collected by the levy was allocated by the Government to enterprises selected by it in amounts which it decided. The iron and steel industry obtained the largest share (DM 278 million); electric power got only a little less (DM 252 million); and the coal industry came next (DM 234 million). The rest of the money was shared between gas, water undertakings and the Federal Railways.

[30] See Wallich, *Mainsprings*, p. 177.

Private Enterprise and Public Guidance

The 1952 investment programme was not an isolated one-shot operation. The heroic legend of German reconstruction as a spontaneous upsurge of aggressive private enterprise has been so sedulously fostered that the crucial part played by the public authorities in the process tends to be overlooked. In fact, they not only supplied money, but also exercised a significant influence in selecting the projects on which it was to be spent. This was especially true during the critical early years from the currency reform of 1948 through the Marshall Plan period until 1952. What made the operation possible in the first place was the inflow of large amounts of American aid. The aid itself consisted, of course, of physical goods shipped from the United States and elsewhere. But there was a further financial consequence of the transaction, in the shape of 'Counterpart Funds'. These funds represented the value in local currency, i.e. Deutschemarks, of the goods that had been provided; in theory the money stood in the place of the dollars which the recipient country was too poor to pay. It could only be used with the permission of the American authorities, and was intended for such purposes as providing loans to local businessmen to buy the aid goods which had already been shipped over.

Now it does not take much analysis to see that there was an element of formalized nonsense in this whole procedure. Once the aid goods had arrived in the country, there was nothing to stop a government from making its own arrangements to create the extra money to provide businessmen with additional credits in order to be able to buy the stuff. The Counterpart Fund could then be ignored. That is more or less what the British Government did with its Marshall Aid receipts. The pound sterling Counterpart which had accumulated was 'used' to cancel public debt. What this meant in fact was that certain British government loans were redeemed, in the ordinary course of business, and the Americans agreed that a book entry showing assets of equivalent value to these loans in the Counterpart account should be cancelled. Had they not agreed, it would not have made any practical difference —except to the people keeping the books, who would have continued to show the government in possession of a large fund (in pounds sterling) derived from the original gift of Marshall Aid.

The Germans, however, decided to play the Counterpart game very straight indeed. It is even conceivable, in view of the attachment of officials and ministers to somewhat eccentric doctrines on how a modern system of public finance works, that they actually believed in it. In any case, since the central bank had the power to impede any government attempt to create credit, it was a matter of practical political significance that additional money could be pumped into the German economy, legitimately, out of the Counterpart Fund. A special institution was set up for the purpose, the Kreditanstalt für Wiederaufbau (Reconstruction Loan Corporation). This was conceived of as a banker's bank—a source of additional funds to supplement the exiguous resources of the ordinary commercial banks, which had been sharply reduced by the currency reform. Its first general manager was Herman Abs, the leading figure in postwar German banking, temporarily out of commission because the Allies had insisted on going through the motions of abolishing Abs's bank.[31]

It was a characteristic German arrangement: the public authorities and the banks collaborating in the execution of a national recovery programme. The strategy was agreed between the American authorities and the government departments concerned, above all the Ministry of Economics. The latter was, and remain today, the tutelary ministry of the KW[32] and gave it instructions about the priorities to be accorded to various types of investment. The managers of the KW were in charge of the tactics of the investment operation and wielded the ultimate power to decide which firm should carry out any particular investment project. However, in practice the choice was often determined by the commanders actually in the field—the individual commercial banks. They were given the task of sifting their clients' requests for investment loans and then passing on those which they thought were suitable—backed by each bank's own guarantee—to the KW.

This proved to be an efficient way of getting industrial capital quickly to the places where it was most needed. Whether it would have been quite so efficient in another national context than that of Germany, where bankers were not traditionally endowed with the same technical competence or institutional dominance, is open to question. Where the German instinct proved to be especially sound in this instance was in the way that it converted these public funds into a wide-ranging investment effort which was directly complementary to the capital sums that the banks were spreading, all too thinly, over German industry. The German banks were especially well equipped to know where the worst gaps were, and where the addition of a relatively small amount of capital, which would ease some especially troublesome bottleneck, would produce a disproportionately large return. It was not that the total amount of money involved was very large: it averaged $3\frac{1}{2}$ per cent of gross investment during 1949–53, reaching a peak of 9 per cent in 1950. As Wallich points out, the main value of these funds was 'qualitative: they represented the chief *masse de manoeuvre* of investment planning'.[33]

---

[31] The Deutsche Bank, see pp. 241–2. [32] Kreditanstalt für Wiederaufbau.

[33] *Mainsprings*, p. 366. During the period when the normal German capital market was barely functioning, KW supplied a significant proportion of the 'free funds' used for industrial investment. From 1948 to 1953 KW issued loans amounting to some DM $5\frac{1}{4}$ billion, while the issues of 'financial paper' (i.e. bonds and shares) through the capital market produced a total of some DM 7 billion. By the mid 1950s, when the capital market had revived, KW was still making a significant marginal contribution: its loans in 1955 amounted to nearly DM 1 billion, against market issues of DM $5\frac{1}{4}$ billion of financial paper (Annual Reports of Kreditanstalt, 1953

That German business was well satisfied with the results is shown by the decision in the late '50s to make the KW permanent, after the specific purpose that it was set up to fulfil in the process of reconstruction had been completed. No one seems to have doubted that a public banking institution of this type would find useful work to do in directing the flow of money into particular types of investment. Indeed, it is interesting to observe how readily this novel and alien bit of public enterprise has been absorbed into the German financial system. Unlike the British or the Americans who would, no doubt, in similar circumstances have engaged in furious ideological argument about the principle of using public funds to make profits, and losses, in commercial banking business, the Germans accepted the institution without fuss as something which would probably make a useful adjunct to the country's credit machinery. At any rate, there was no harm in trying the experiment.

It is true that everything had been done to make the bankers comfortable about the new venture. Their unfussed pragmatism was well grounded in a number of cosy facts. To begin with the KW was prohibited by law from engaging in any competition for business with the existing banks;[34] moreover, it was charged to bring in other credit institutions 'as intermediaries' in granting loans. It was only 'in exceptional cases, and only with the assent of the [Supervisory] Board of Directors' (*Verwaltungsrat*)[35] that loans could be granted direct to clients.[36] Finally the law made it clear that the head of the Supervisory Board of the KW and his deputy would always be commercial bankers.[37] And who do we find has in fact been chosen to head the Board? The reader will by now not be wholly surprised to learn that it is Herman Abs.[38] After he ceased to be general manager of the Kreditanstalt, in order to take charge of the reconstituted Deutsche Bank,[39] he moved onto the KW Supervisory Board. He has stayed there ever since—a kind of permanent surety against any attempt by the managers of the KW to compete in the private banking field. Abs is clearly proud of the achievement of the institution which he helped to establish—among other things it

and 1955). Thereafter its share of investment business diminished very rapidly, though it still remains an important source of funds for certain classes of investment—notably 5–15 year loans to medium and small businesses. KW has in fact deliberately set itself the task of filling this gap in the ordinary German capital market machinery.

[34] See Art. 2 of 'Law concerning the Kreditanstalt für Wiederaufbau' dated 5 Nov. 1948 (with amendments to Oct. 1961) which allows the KW to grant loans 'in so far as other credit institutions are unable to raise the necessary funds'.

[35] This body corresponds to the *Aufsichtsrat* or Supervisory Board in other German companies and performs the same functions. Since the Board is unusually large—some thirty people have a right to sit on it—the usual leading role of the chairman tends to be especially pronounced. [36] Art. 3 (1), ibid.

[37] Art. 7 (1), which says that they must be 'persons with special experience in the field of credit' is interpreted to mean that.

[38] From 1959 onwards. Previously he had been deputy chairman of the Board.

[39] See above, p. 242.

makes a profit on banking of over £2 million a year[40]—and he is also better equipped than anyone else in Germany to decide whether some piece of attractive business offered to the KW *might* after all be done by a private enterprise bank instead, if the proposition were brought to its notice.

A New Type of Nationalized Bank?

Broadly the function of the KW in the German system might be described in terms which are the opposite of those in which socialists have traditionally seen the role of public enterprise: the 'commanding heights' are all to be closely occupied by the private banks, and the public banks[41] are to be confined to the lowlands. Yet it would be a mistake to minimize the significance of this type of public enterprise as an adjunct of national economic policy. Just as the KW in its initial phase, during the reconstruction of the German economy, directed its attention especially to bottleneck investments, trying to identify those projects which yielded an especially high national return because they helped to activate additional productive capacity in allied though separate industrial enterprises, so later it continued to concern itself with other and less obvious kinds of bottleneck which commercial banking tended to overlook. Thus from the middle 1950s onwards it devoted a considerable part of its funds to financing business investment in areas marked out as requiring special assistance under the government's regional development schemes. The bank is, in fact, an extremely active agent of official regional policies.

The rationale of this effort from a public banker's point of view was well described by the chief economist of the KW, Dr W. Hankel, in terms of its effect on the efficiency of the nation's capital as a whole.[42] In addition to the normal effect of a productive investment in giving rise to additional income, there is, he pointed out, also a 'capacity effect'—i.e. the effect which an extra bit of investment has on the degree to which the *existing* productive capacity of the country is used. It is evident that the yield on a capital project in a development area might seem unattractively low, when measured solely in terms of the money income derived from it by the investor, and yet turn out to be an efficient use of capital once the calculation takes in the additional return accruing from the venture to other investments indirectly affected, both private and public. If roads or sewage or housing, which already exist and have been paid for by the public, are used fully, instead of being underemployed because an area is decaying, all this capital is more efficiently employed. The alternative, if the new business were to

---

[40] The 1962 figure was DM 26 m. (KW Annual Report).
[41] There are in addition to the KW three other specialized public banks: Lastenausgleichbank, the Berliner Industriekreditbank, and the Landwirtschaftliche Rentenbank.
[42] See *Volkswirt*, 15 May 1964, pp. 917 ff.

decide to set up in an already crowded region where the public services are working to full capacity, would be to impose on the community the cost of additional public investment. An investment bank like the KW, which has public funds at its disposal, can look at both aspects of any investment project. If its calculations suggest that the total return on a project will be worthwhile, it may offer to finance a private investor at a lower rate of interest than he would have to pay if he obtained his money from the ordinary capital market.

The theoretical argument about what constitutes the true return on an investment is interesting because it illustrates the way in which, for all the cult of private enterprise, postwar German thinking on economic policy has not allowed itself to be mesmerized by the vision of the market as the 'invisible hand', effortlessly guiding all productive factors to their optimum uses. No one is surprised that the market needs to be supplemented by active public enterprise, which sees further than the market is able to do. The British and the Americans tend to assume that devotion to private enterprise necessarily implies an equal devotion to the market as an overwhelming force for good. But German devotees of capitalism have never found any difficulty in keeping the two things separate. This undoubtedly makes it easier for them to adapt their methods of business and government to accommodate the typical institutions of modern capitalism, of which the KW is one.

Dr Hankel in his analysis of the performance of the KW,[43] argues that this is an institution that responds to a particular mid-twentieth century problem which is common to the experience of many Western countries. The earliest model for this kind of enterprise was, he points out, the Crédit National in France, founded after the First World War. We have already had occasion to observe how that institution has been especially adept in developing the services to meet the needs of a modern economy, where public and private initiative freely intermingle.[44] There is no analogy between the function of the Crédit National, today at the centre of the French system, and the KW, which most conscientiously sticks to the periphery. But they have an underlying principle in common. This is that certain types of private investment are to be supported by a combination of public and private business initiatives, making their junction through a bank. The operational device used in such ventures is the cheap loan at something below the market rate of interest. The cost to the state of guiding investment in any given direction tends to be relatively small: it is the difference between what the state pays in interest on loans and the rate charged to the favoured investor. This may be as little as one per cent a year, as it is for KW loans. The

---

[43] *Die Zweite Kapitalverteilung* (Berlin, Knapp, 1961), ch. 15.
[44] See above, pp. 169–70.

benefit to the recipient is often much greater, for the state or one of its agencies can usually borrow on far better terms than the individual small businessman.

The evolution of the KW in the 1950s and early 1960s is characteristic. It starts off after the war as a bank entirely dependent on public funds concentrating on a massive and essentially temporary investment operation in a number of key industries. Gradually it becomes involved in long-term problems of development, notably regional investment and the finance of small and medium-sized business. Additional public funds are made available for these purposes and the bank becomes in part the agent of the government (just like the Crédit National in some of its operations) in distributing money for certain specific investments which the state wishes to finance.[45] The bank, while co-operating closely with its equivalent of a *ministère de tutelle* (the Ministry of Economics), acquires a certain independence in the conduct of its financial affairs as its own funds are built up. This process goes forward more rapidly after 1958, when the bank begins to issue its own bonds and notes through the market. By 1959–60 the bank's own resources or borrowings are large enough to finance half of all its new domestic lending business.[46]

At this stage the bank tries to find a clearer sense of purpose. How independent ought it to be? What are the principles which should guide its choice of investment projects? We saw earlier[47] how the great Italian public enterprises actively sought to increase their dependence on private capital, because this gave them an additional handle in any dispute over policy with the government. In Germany the publicly owned banks are ridden on a very loose rein by the Federal authorities. In some cases, indeed, there seems to be nothing there for the rider to pull on. But the KW does not need to be driven; it is anxious to conduct its affairs in the closest unison with the Bundesbank. Its objective, in Hankel's phrase, is to be the nation's 'second central bank', looking after the public interest in the conduct of long-term investment policy.[48]

---

[45] The analogous case is the Crédit National's function in distributing funds on behalf of the government drawn from the Fonds de Développement Économique et Social (see above, p. 169). The KW's role as agent for the direct disbursement of government funds was enlarged in the 1960s when it was given the task of handling official loans to underdeveloped countries.

[46] An interesting sidelight on the keenness of the KW as a competitor for funds in the capital market is the way in which it has from the start managed the market in its own securities, buying whenever they tended to fall below par, and selling whenever they rose above. In this way its financial paper carries an effective guarantee that it will be turned into cash at a moment's notice at its original face value. It thus became an ideal form of liquid investment for any banker's funds which might have to be realized in a hurry. Again, it is worth noting the analogy with the French technique of *transformation* (see above, p. 169), by which public or semi-public institutions manage to convert short-term funds into medium and long-term credits to industry.

[47] See pp. 191–2.   [48] *Zweite Kapitalverteilung*, p. 153.

As to the principles guiding the choice of investment by this type of bank, the recent annual reports indicate that the chief purpose envisaged for the institution is to take a *longer* view of the probable fruits of an investment than an ordinary commercial lender would. Regional development is one example. More generally the aim is to speed up the process of 'structural change' in industries which are, or should be, adapting themselves to new conditions. This applies not only to 'weak industries', but also to those with strong and rapidly expanding markets which could be helped, by additional capital supplied on the right terms, to increase their output faster. The public interest would, it is argued, be served in such a case, because the rapid increase in supplies coming onto the market will help to check the rise in price that would otherwise have occurred in response to unsatisfied demand. The long view connects up with the attempt to take a wider view of the return on an investment, beyond the simple measurement of the effect on the money income of the investor. All this is done in a cautious spirit; the radicalism lies more in the deeper implications of the rules of the bank than in any actual practice so far. The rules amount to a form of public entrepreneurship whose function it is to seek out opportunities for making the nation's capital yield a larger return in the long run, even at the cost of some sacrifice of investment income in the short run.

A Policy of Discrimination

The German Government's use of tax concessions to speed the postwar economic recovery is a familiar story. What is not always so clearly recognized is that the device was employed not merely to accelerate but to discriminate actively between one industry, and one purpose, and another. Special tax benefits went to the favoured basic industries—steel, coal and iron ore mines, and electric power plants—during the early 1950s; firms in these industries were given exceptionally large depreciation allowances for any new investment, which they were able to set against their profits for tax purposes. The result was that the declared profit on which tax had to be paid was sharply reduced. The only condition was that the money corresponding to the reduction in taxable profit was not to be distributed to shareholders, but reinvested in the business.

To make the trick work, tax rates had to be high. They were. The large company and the businessman with a big income were the most eager beneficiaries of the concessions. They were also given the chance to cut their tax liability further, as exporters. This was done through a tax remission which applied to all industries and was proportional to the amount exported. The rebate on income tax and corporation tax was only a fraction of the value of export turnover, but evidently the marginal benefit to highly taxed incomes was an effective incentive to switch more goods abroad, when there was a choice between the home and foreign markets.[49] The export tax rebate, which was introduced in 1951 when the German balance of payments was still weak, was retained until 1955, by which time it had become stronger than that of almost any other country in the world.

There were other discriminatory tax reliefs given on incomes which were invested in the building of dwellings and in the shipbuilding industry. The latter played a big part in the rapid comeback of the German shipyards, which had been largely destroyed during the war. This tax incentive was removed in 1954—in response to fears, aroused by its extreme effectiveness, that it would soon give rise to surplus shipbuilding capacity. The tax relief on income and profits devoted to housebuilding lasted much longer. It led to a vast output of new housing, which may in turn fairly be given part of the credit for the remarkable mobility of German labour during the 1950s. The availability of housing in the great industrial centres may also have contributed something to the sustained low average of unemployment in the early 1960s. At any rate there does not seem to have been the same obstacle as existed in Britain, for example, at that time to movement from areas of higher unemployment to those of labour scarcity, because of a shortage of houseroom in the latter.[50]

Thus the German Government set up a series of targets for economic recovery—basic industries, exports, housing— and concentrated the resources of the nation on them, one after another. Public saving, combined with the great ploughback of profits by firms fed on tax concessions, provided the finance for these extensive investments. It would be wrong to suppose, however, that this was the outcome of a wise and deliberate calculation of the best way to employ the national resources. The capital surplus from the public sector, which proved so fertile, was largely coincidental. Those who were chiefly responsible for its appearance and persistence, the honest officials and their master, Schaeffer, in the Finance Ministry, were intent solely on their own 'housekeeping' purposes; they pursued them regardless. In other circumstances, for example in the economic crisis of the early 1930s before Hitler took over, the stubborn pursuit of transparent financial solvency produced disastrous results. The failure to stimulate internal demand, which had resulted in millions of active people being kept idle, was the first thing that Hitler put right. It was perhaps his greatest success; the horrors which followed would not have been possible without it. But in the 1950s the same

[49] The export rebate scheme took two alternative forms: one was a once-for-all cut in tax, the other was the right to transfer a sum of money corresponding to a fixed fraction of exports sold to a temporary tax-free reserve. Under the latter arrangement the tax was merely deferred; it had ultimately to be paid over ten yearly instalments. Its attraction was in part that of an interest-free loan, provided in effect by the tax authorities, and also that it could result in lowering the marginal income bracket, on which the highest rate of the progressive income tax had to be paid.

[50] Germany was building 60–80 per cent more dwellings per year than Britain in the early 1960s (see OECD, *Industrial Statistics*). Its unemployment ratio from 1961 onwards was consistently below the British figure (see pp. 36–7).

simple-minded fiscal probity worked magnificently: world demand for the goods that German industry could supply was extremely buoyant; more and more labour was drawn into satisfying it. Meanwhile the task of remaking the foundations of the German economy provided a ready-made investment programme, on which all the spare resources of the nation were deployed. The high taxes which held down consumption supplied the extra room for manoeuvre. In particular, they supplied the opportunity for the Government to intervene, by means of direct subsidies, cheap loans, and special tax allowances, in support of a variety of favoured economic activities.

Breaking Through the Fiscal Barrier

What was missing was any serious effort to take an overall view of the economy—on the one side the claims likely to be made on it from all sources, private as well as public, and on the other its capacity to produce, using public finance as a means of keeping the two in balance at the highest possible level of output. The antipathy of the postwar German government towards a Keynesian mode of thinking about economic policy showed up most strikingly in the mid-1950s, after the German economic recovery had been largely achieved, in the bizarre affair of the so-called *Juliusturm* ('Tower of Julius'),[51] built up by Fritz Schaeffer, the Finance Minister. The Tower was a great accumulation of tax revenues, which was watched intently by the most heavily taxed people in Western Europe as it grew year by year. What started off the venture was the decision that Germany was, after all, to have an army. The Chancellor, Dr Adenauer, was anxious that rearmament should not impose any extra burden on the German taxpayer, and in agreement with his Finance Minister set about the business of accumulating as much as possible of the money that would be required, in advance. It was the apotheosis of good housekeeping, and Schaeffer applied himself to it with a will. It was estimated that the rearmament programme would cost some DM 45 billion over five years. Although the bulk of this money would only be spent much later, the Finance Ministry's scheme, starting from 1954, was to tuck away DM 9 billion a year. It did not quite achieve this figure, but for two or three years, at a time when Germany was still not within striking distance of full employment, the Finance Minister steadily put a damper on home demand by extracting more money from the taxpayer than the state needed to cover its current budget expenditure.

It seems that Schaeffer was unaware of the economic consequences of what he was doing; it was deflation by accident. Some of the funds that he collected were used to pay off public debt. His intention, he made it clear, was to re-borrow the money that he had paid back to government bondholders

---

[51] The original Tower was built by the Prussian Prince Julius in the 16th century in Spandau, and was used both as a fortress and as a treasury for the nation's war reserves (Kriegsschatz). The nickname applied to Schaeffer's hoard became part of the popular shorthand of the great debate on German tax policy in the mid-1950s.

when he needed it later on, so that over the period as a whole the Government's accounts would be balanced. The notion that the economic cost of rearmament—the claims that it would make on productive resources—would have to be met *at the time* by withdrawing a corresponding volume of resources from other uses, that taxes imposed in advance of the need to transfer these resources served not to accumulate treasure but to put a damper on demand, was not even seriously considered by him. It was an excuse for procrastination. St Anthony could not have resisted the temptations offered to him with more fervour. Their very plausibility made them especially obnoxious.

In the end Schaeffer was defeated not so much by the Keynesians as by other simple housekeeping types, who decided that since the money was there, it ought to be used for some good purpose. The Finance Minister was unable to prevent his Tower from being pillaged. The first raids occurred in 1956. At this point, the metaphor of the popular debate changed: the body of MPs appointed to consider alternative uses for these large funds was known as the 'Cake Commission' (*Kuchenausschuss*). When Schaeffer heard how it had decided to divide up the cake, he is reported to have wept.

He was in fact right to see the decision as the beginning of the end of orthodox German fiscal policy—although that was by no means clear at the time. The big spending operations followed, notably the new and greatly improved old-age pension scheme in 1957 and the massive extension of agricultural subsidies known as the 'Green Plan'. But it was not merely that the public purse-strings were loosened. As we have seen, the burden on the German taxpayer was not diminished. A series of unconnected circumstances made the period 1957–8 a turning point in the making of postwar economic and financial policy. First of all Schaeffer himself retired in 1957. He was replaced as Finance Minister by Franz Etzel, a man who was not irretrievably separated from the ideas of modern economics by a barrier of traditional financial probity. He was no Keynesian; but he was prepared, for the first time, to look at his budget calculations in terms of modern national income accounting. Their effect on real resources was formally noticed in a statement annexed to the Budget.

At least as important as the events in Bonn, perhaps even more so, the management of the Bundesbank in Frankfurt also changed in 1957. Dr Vocke, another staunch representative of the traditional school of German finance, who had shaped the postwar central bank and contributed a distinctive and very independent note to all its operations, retired and was replaced as President of the Bank by Karl Blessing.[52] Vocke believed that a central

---

[52] A special instrument forged by Vocke in his fight for central bank independence was the monthly bulletin of the Bundesbank (previously Bank Deutscher Länder)—an unusually frank and forthright commentary on economic events. He would always insist on seeing the proofs and would re-write bits of the text.

bank should concentrate exclusively on two objects: first make certain that prices did not rise, and second ensure a sufficiently large volume of savings to finance essential investment. The balance of payments, which by the time he retired was in chronic and embarrassing surplus for Germany, concerned him very little; the objective of full employment even less. The bank's constitution was revised, in the year that Vocke retired, and the powers of the executive directors on the Bundesbank Council were increased: they were given independent voting rights, which meant that the President no longer had quite the unchallenged authority which he had possessed previously. His status came to approximate more that of *primus inter pares*. This also helped to provide more scope for the newer generation to assert itself.

Something similar was happening at about this time in the senior bureaucracy of the Finance Ministry in Bonn. The older men in key positions were beginning to move out and to make way for men who were less firmly devoted to traditional ways of doing things. 1958 happened to be a recession year in Western Europe and North America; German economic growth continued, but at a markedly slower pace. At this point the remnants of Schaeffer's 'Tower' came in very useful: the billions of DM which had been accumulated in his tax reserve provided an excuse for deficit financing on a large scale, which might otherwise have been difficult to justify. The 1958 budget also contained some useful tax reliefs for people with modest incomes; notably it separated a husband's and a wife's earnings for tax assessment purposes, with the result that the marginal rate of tax was generally lower than it had been when they were assessed jointly as one income. Many families found themselves with more money left over to spend. None of this seems to have been consciously designed as part of a policy to offset the downswing of the business cycle. The increase in spending power during 1958 was providential rather than designed; moreover its effect was enhanced by delays in the actual collection of taxes, caused by the extensive budget changes in the basis of assessment and in individual allowances. The Bundesbank acted with rather more deliberation. It took measures to keep up the volume of money and credit in the system, instead of allowing itself to be governed, as it would almost certainly have been earlier in the 1950s, by the market forces making for contraction. And it followed this up a year later, in the 1959 boom, by a move to tighten credit, which it justified in explicitly Keynesian terms, as an attempt to moderate a rise in demand that was threatening to outpace the economic resources available to meet it.[53]

Controlling the Business Cycle

All in all the experience of coping, more by luck than by judgement, with the 1958 recession seems to have left a certain political residue—a willingness to give more serious attention to the problem of tackling a future business

[53] See Deutsche Bundesbank, *Monthly Report*, Nov. 1959.

downturn, when the accidents might not be so uniformly favourable. The mood was fostered by changing economic circumstances: in 1959 Germany for the first time achieved and held full employment. For the whole of that year the total of unemployed averaged just under 2 per cent of the labour force. Thereafter the proportion continued to fall, in spite of heavy immigration of workers from all over Europe, and from 1960 onwards remained steadily below 1 per cent.

The authorities became far more responsive to the need for an effective business cycle policy which would prevent the recurrence of even temporary unemployment. It was no longer assumed that the pursuit of absolute price stability ought necessarily to take precedence over every other objective. The first practical result was a law passed in 1961—a modest measure but establishing a novel precedent—which gave the Government the right to decree an increase in tax allowances for new investment, without recourse to parliament, on the basis of its own judgement of business cycle trends.[54] In the same year a start was made on a major official inquiry undertaken by the Ministries of Economics and of Finance jointly, with the advice of the central bank, to determine how far the instruments at the disposal of the authorities were adequate to cope with the menace of business fluctuations. It was a new sort of question for the German authorities to be asking.

Once it had been asked the investigation was thorough, with a series of inter-ministerial study groups reporting on specific practical problems. The work went on for over two years and was finally published in 1964.[55] By that time Adenauer had gone out of office—in his eighties, still an over-lifesize representative of the prejudices as well as the virtues of the old order. His departure and the consequent reshuffle of official posts brought more of the younger generation into the seats of power at Bonn. The report reflected the change in the political climate which had taken place. It was a plea for a radical reform of the financial machinery of government, designed to enable

[54] The law gave the Government the power to institute a *Sonderabschreibung* (special depreciation allowance) by executive order, of 5 per cent for investment in land and buildings and 10 per cent for investment in capital equipment. This device was intended to serve the same function as the short-term 'regulator' in Britain—the right to vary indirect taxes by up to 10 per cent which was introduced in the same year. The German instrument was however a feeble one compared with the British, which affected a bigger segment of the national income and operated directly upon the spending of consumers (see above, p. 107). The German report on 'Instruments of business cycle control' (see n. 55) proposed that the *Sonderabschreibung* percentage should be increased, in order to make the system more effective as an instrument of business cycle control.

[55] 'Proposals for the development of the instruments of business cycle control', presented jointly by the Ministries of Finance and of Economics, Mar. 1964, published as App. I of the Supplement of the *Annual Report on Economic Development in 1963* (Bundestags-Drucksache IV/1752, June 1964). It was completed by the summer of 1963, but publication was delayed until the promised resignation of Chancellor Adenauer had taken place in the autumn and Dr Erhard was firmly established in his new office.

the state to intervene with greater speed and enhanced power in the nation's business.

The authentic Keynesian note is struck, almost provocatively, right from the start by the use of the English phrase 'deficit spending' in the German text. It is a foreign idea—and a good one. There must be no nonsense about balancing the budget during a downturn of the business cycle: the authorities must be prepared in advance to spend their way into a deficit, and to do so fast. The danger, which provides the underlying theme of the report, is that the lack of sufficient central power may slow down the reaction to an emergency. In addition to a specific proposal to establish a 'shelf' of prepared investment projects which can be started at short notice—on the Swedish model[56]—the report argues for a more general need to mobilize the large resources at the disposal of the public authorities within the framework of a co-ordinated national programme governing all forms of investment.[57] It points out that 32 per cent of all fixed investment in Germany is done directly by the public authorities, and that when private investments financed by public funds are included, the proportion of the total dependent on government money in one form or another rises to over 50 per cent.

Perhaps most significant of all, in terms of postwar German history, is the political tone of this document, which was issued on the authority of the Federal Cabinet. A solemn preamble to the dry and technical analysis begins as follows: 'Germany's fate after 1933 was connected by a causal sequence to the inability of the Weimar Republic to master unemployment. . . '. It goes on to state the imperative that now 'in the light of the East-West conflict' public policy must ensure that there is no risk of any similar failure. This is the Beveridge note,[58] struck on a German keyboard twenty years after. It took as long as that for German economic policy to get set finally in a modern mould. The delay was in part the result of too many diversions and too many successes—the diversions of the massive, yet essentially simple, task of economic reconstruction and the successes of an immensely competitive and productive export industry, selling to a world market with an insatiable appetite for its goods. Admittedly German export salesmen played an active part in stimulating the appetite; tax discrimination and cheap export credit[59] provided by the authorities helped them; underemployed industrial capacity and practically unlimited supplies of well-trained labour, combined with a tight control over the volume of demand at home, drove business into

---

[56] See above, p. 202.
[57] The independent powers of the *Länder*, it says, make it important that 'all investment expenditure be coordinated in the light of business cycle policy needs'.
[58] See *Full Employment* (1944).
[59] The Bundesbank led the way; other institutions followed—including the Kreditanstalt, which fulfilled in this matter a function analogous to that of the US Export-Import Bank.

markets abroad. Exports came to represent a much larger proportion of the German national product than ever before. Because of the country's commanding position in export markets, the problems of economic policy in the two recession years of 1952 and 1958[60] were greatly simplified for the German Government. A drop in home demand simply meant that more goods were sold abroad. This was a formula which Britain, through successive credit squeezes, sought in vain to copy. For Germany international trade, even in years when it was relatively slack by postwar standards, automatically provided a large part of the answer to the ups and downs of the business cycle at home.

Even by the time that the new 'Proposals on Business Cycle Control'[61] were issued in 1964, the reforming spirit was by no means triumphant. The Government is still bound by the restrictive clause which allows it to borrow funds 'for productive investment' only, and by other official inhibitions on its freedom to manage the finances of the country in a sensible way.[62] There is no doubt that if there were a recession, a strong government faced with an emergency would today be able to take all the measures necessary to force up the level of economic activity. It would no longer have to overcome the serious administrative and doctrinal barrier that Germany would have faced if such an emergency had occurred as little as five years ago.[63] It is only a weak or uncertain cabinet which might be seriously trammelled by the restrictive financial rules imposed on the Federal Government after the war. The intention then was to put the Government into a financial straitjacket—one whose design happened to suit the predilections of an older generation of officials, who were guided by views formed well before the experience of the 1930s. The straitjacket has by now largely been stripped away; but what remains of it makes the German Government look rather like a runner whose chosen costume for the race track is an especially tight waistcoat with a lot of little buttons on it. There is no reason why he should not finish the course; but it is likely to be a bit of a struggle.

[60] See p. 9. [61] Bundestags-Drucksache IV/1752.

[62] Notably the directives which place it under a legal compulsion to 'balance the budget'.

[63] The ECE *Econ. Survey Europe 1959* (ch. 6, p. 17), in a review of German postwar financial policy up to the date, concluded: 'In Western Germany, government-sector operations have not so far been used deliberately to counteract what were considered short-term inflationary pressures or to reverse deflationary tendencies. The main objectives of budget making have been to finance by traditional means the traditional tasks of government . . .' Modern business cycle policies were, by the late 1950s, adopted by the central bank. But as late as November 1959 it was having to plead with the fiscal authorities for a more rational approach to the problem thus: 'A counter-cyclical behaviour of budgetary policy would be highly desirable. . . . The Central Bank Council therefore appeals urgently to all the authorities responsible for the conduct of budgetary policy to behave as far as possible in a counter-cyclical way when they establish the next budget and thus to support the credit policy of the Bundesbank and even, as far as possible, to reduce the burden placed on it' (*Bundesbank Monthly Report*, Nov. 1959).

Approach to Planning

In several other countries the postwar effort to control the ups and downs of the business cycle has pointed the way towards more systematic economic planning on a national scale.[64] Germany is no exception. But because it is Germany, there has been rather more semantic trouble than elsewhere about recognizing the fact. The evidence of changing official attitudes, beneath the disguise of unchanging official slogans, came late—in the Government's first annual survey and forecast for the year ahead, published in early 1963. Its official title *Report on Economic Trends in 1962 and Prospects for 1963*[65] appearing on the light blue cover gave no indication that this was in fact a bold and highly speculative document containing a series of detailed predictions of the individual components of the national income over the year ahead. These included forecasts of production in each of the main sectors— agriculture, trade and transport, industrial and other goods, services—of the amount of profits, of average wages, of how much would be saved, and how much invested in building on the one hand, and industrial equipment on the other. Now there was no doubt that these figures were intended solely to provide illustrative orders of magnitude: they were not predictions in the sense of being fixed points on the horizon of expectations, with the rest of public policy built up rigidly around them. It is, however, a delusion, to which the Germans seem incidentally to be especially prone, that any Western planning of a serious type, including in particular French planning, is based on any such rigid predictions. A large part of a modern French plan consists, as we have seen, of figures which are intended as a rough shorthand expression of a putative trend, rather than anything resembling a target or, more remotely still, a prophecy.

Still, that is not to say that the German annual economic report is in any sense the equivalent of a French economic plan. The French plan is, first of all, far more detailed, taking a view of the economy industry by industry and calculating the inter-relationships between them. Secondly, the French exercise is a long-term plan, covering four years in detail, and up to twenty years in some of its broad projections.[66] The Germans have however discovered that trying to make systematic sense of economic trends and .policies for a year ahead involves them almost at once in taking a long-term view. The short term, says the first economic report, cannot be isolated.[67] How could

---

[64] See p. 221.   [65] Bundestags-Drucksache IV/1010.
[66] See Pt. II of the draft of the Fifth Plan, *Projet de rapport sur les principales options du Vème Plan*, Sept. 1964, notably ch. 1 on the new series of projections to 1985.
[67] See para. 36, Bundestags-Drucksache IV/1010, 1963. The report goes on at once in the same paragraph to insist virtuously that it is not going to have any truck with 'hypothetical advance calculations and long-term detailed forecasts which are of no use for guiding economic policy, and which hinder free development of entrepreneurial initiative unafraid of future risks.' It is going to confine itself to 'data and trends which can be more or less realistically assessed'.

it be, when the essential purpose of the Ministry of Economics, which produced the report and invited parliament to discuss it, was precisely to issue an advance warning about the consequences that would emerge over a period of years from certain deep changes which it had just detected in the structure of the German economy?

The whole argument of the first report on 1962–3 is, in fact, about how Germany should adapt itself to the weakening of the two main forces which had provided the motive power for the great economic advance of the 1950s. 'On the side of demand', it says, 'the expansive factors which were strongest in past years, namely capital investment and exports, are tending to lose weight.' On the other hand, the relative weight of demand 'for both private and government consumption' is increasing. The country must in the long run depend more on the last two than it has in the past to maintain full employment and economic growth. However, if the switch were allowed to occur too abruptly, it might be ruinous. It was reasonable to expect that both the export surplus and the proportion of the nation's resources devoted to new investment would decline from the high levels of the late 1950s and early 1960s; but if the ordinary wage-earner took this as a signal to go on a spending spree and the Government insisted on a rapid build-up of the social services and other forms of expenditure, the German balance of payments would be put severely out of joint.

Behind this simple presentation of the problem, there were a number of new factors, which were hinted at rather than spelled out in the report. First, there was the fear that if existing trends continued, the country would become over-dependent on non-German immigrants—already some 4 per cent of its labour force[68]—and an unwillingness to let the proportion of foreigners in the population increase at anything like the rate of recent years. The decision to curb the pace of immigration was central to the thinking of officials at the Ministry of Economics on long-term economic policy.[69] Secondly, there was the effect of the freer movement of international capital into and out of Germany. The stringent control over German domestic finance exercised during the 1950s had rested very largely on the insulation of the domestic capital market. But investment funds sucked in from abroad could, and did, nullify the effects of a credit squeeze at home. This pointed to the need for something more than conventional monetary policy, on which postwar Germany had heavily relied, as an instrument for managing the economy.

Similar considerations applied to the problems raised by the removal of barriers to the movement of goods between member states of the Common

---

[68] Some 800,000 people at this stage; well over 1 million by the mid-1960s. The report also pointed to the small contribution to the labour force that would be forthcoming from any increase in the indigenous population up to the early 1970s.

[69] A decision, it should be noted, that was made by several other European countries, including Britain and Switzerland, independently at about this time.

Market. If Italy or France had a bout of inflation, they could no longer use import restrictions to prevent the inflow of a flood of goods from a country with a relatively stable price structure, like Germany. And that in turn might well impose a strain on the resources available to meet Germany's home demand at moderate prices; the monetary balance of the economy would then be upset, unless counter-measures were taken. But what kind of counter-measures? Again, the old-fashioned market remedy, which would mean inflicting a credit squeeze on the Germans in order to offset the inflation caused by the indiscipline of other countries in the Common Market, did not seem to be a wholly satisfactory solution. Finally, underlying all this was the come-back of the German consumer; with the rapid rise in wages of the early 1960s and the cut in working hours, there was a smaller proportionate surplus available both for government spending on social purposes and for all forms of investment.[70] The response to this was to organize a more discriminating use of resources in the public sector, by more efficient planning of programmes, and to try to achieve a more economical use of capital in the private sector as well by selecting investments that produce more. The latter depended on more skilful commercial strategy, which in turn required improved information about, and analysis of, economic trends.[71]

The father of the new venture into annual forecasting and systematic analysis of economic policy trends was Ludwig Erhard. He had first proposed something of the sort as early as 1957 and had been overruled by Chancellor Adenauer. At first sight, it may seem an odd venture for so vociferous an opponent of 'planning' in any guise, but Erhard himself was evidently unaware of any difficulty in reconciling it with the rest of his policies. In fact, it conforms with the tenor of a great many of the measures for which he was responsible during Germany's recovery, and after it. The mistake that observers have tended to make with Erhard is to listen too attentively to his words, of which he produces very many, and to pay too little attention to his actions—or for that matter, inactions. He is a strangely successful politician, who seems markedly under-equipped for his chosen task. German intellectuals have on the whole regarded him with scant respect, as a person too given to an over-simplified, rhetorical approach to economic and political problems. Outside Germany, his achievement while he was at the

---

[70] In the long run a smaller proportion of the national product was expected to be required for investment in enlarging the country's stock of equipment; but in the meantime the danger was that the supply of capital might be insufficient to meet national needs.

[71] The preamble to the Report, para. 3, put the point as follows: '. . . narrower limits are now set to the further extension of prosperity. Increased importance accordingly attaches to the inter-play of the forces supporting the economy, as well as to better coordination of all the agencies responsible for economic policy'. It is the systematic analysis of this 'interplay' between economic forces, with the aim of securing a more efficient use of capital than the market on its own would achieve, which is the novel feature of the German thinking behind the 1963 annual economic report.

Ministry of Economics was to attract the approbation of a reactionary fringe—sometimes more lunatic than reactionary—which saw him as the exponent of an extreme form of economic liberalism, worshipping the market-place and abhorring all forms of public power. In fact he has never been averse to using the authority of the state, or his own official position, to mould the decisions of industrial entrepreneurs in the way that he or the Government wanted.

On occasion he has openly attempted to force their hand, presenting him-self as the representative of the public interest against narrow views of selfish business concerns. He did this in a notable dispute with Volkswagen in May 1962, when he tried to prevent the company from raising the domestic prices of its cars. The company was subjected to a variety of pressure tactics by the Government, including an officially organized line-up of the *Aufsichtsrat* of Volkswagen against the management.[72] When this failed to move Dr Nordhoff, the Volkswagen general manager, the Government hastily brought in a bill to halve the duties on imported cars from other Common Market countries; this brought the price of the Renault Dauphine down below the German home cost of the Volkswagen.

Erhard's actions in this case, and in several others, suggest that he is ready, indeed anxious, to intervene in the private sector—so long as he can convince himself that what he is doing is only to bring about, somewhat faster, results which an ideal market would in any case have achieved in the long run. This ideal market often bears as little relationship to the real market as Rousseau's General Will, which was supposed to express the true wishes of the people, bore to the apparent will of the majority of voters. Erhard's interest is not in the market as an institution, but as a process. If the real-life market does not behave as markets should, then non-market forces must be brought in to do the job for it. This whole approach fits easily with the philosophy of the first *Report on Economic Trends* of 1963. Erhard's inter-ventionism does not make him a planner in the French sense; rather he is a jogger and nudger, closer in spirit (though not in his ultimate social aims) to the Swedish view of the role of public authority in economic change.

---

[72] See *Frankfurter Allgemeine Zeitung*, 3 May 1962. The Government at this stage held 20 per cent of the shares of Volkswagen and had its own representative on the *Aufsichtsrat*. It is interesting to observe that in this case, once again, a semi-public enterprise, run by a person with something of the status of a public servant—Dr Nordhoff, the general manager, was originally put in to manage the company as a public official at the time when it was fully nationalized—was especially eager, and able, to assert its independence of the wishes of the Government of the day. We have seen other examples in the behaviour of the management of Renault (see above, p. 140) and the performance of Mattei in Italy as manager of ENI (see above, p. 184). These cases are in striking contrast to the manner in which the US Steel Corporation—a much larger business than any of them, and fully privately owned—caved in promptly, under protest, when President Kennedy objected to its decision to raise steel prices in April 1962.

Indeed, Erhard's design for the 'Council of Economic Experts', who have since 1964 been given the responsibility for producing the annual report, has a certain family resemblance to the old Swedish Planning Commission, which functioned until the early years of the 1960s.[73] The Swedes, too, were anxious that the periodic surveys of economic plans (differing from the German annual reports in being long-term, but otherwise very similar in their intended function of providing analysis rather than formulation of policy) should be conducted by independent persons standing right outside the Government, and not committing the Government in any way to their views. It was precisely this notion of an independent body of outsiders with the right to an insider's view of the Government's economic performance which made the scheme unacceptable to Adenauer, when it was originally proposed to him in 1957. It seemed to be an unnecessary slight on the majesty of the state. When the idea was revived in 1961, as a result of pressure from a parliamentary committee,[74] it was proposed that the body of economic assessors should be fully controlled by the Ministry. The first two annual reports, for 1962-3 and 1963-4,[75] were the work of government officials, with some assistance from economic consultants in institutes concerned with the study of economic trends.

Only after Erhard became Chancellor was he able to return to his original idea of a solid body of outsiders. The Council of Economic Experts was set up as an independent agency in March 1964. It consists of five members who, in addition to their annual report, are free to conduct special studies on any subjects of their choice and publish them.[76] The only restriction placed on them is that actual publication may be delayed for up to eight weeks, in order to allow the Government time to present any comments of its own in answer to the Council's conclusions. Thus it has more independence than was given for instance to the economic planners of NEDC in Britain, who are outside the Government but who are not allowed to publish anything without the explicit permission of their Council, which includes representatives of the Government.[77]

The Use of Public Power

The interesting question is whether the Germans, having established their Council of Economic Experts at arm's length distance from the government, will find, as the Swedes have, that if it is to do its work properly this body must somehow be brought back into an integral relationship with the

[73] The Swedish Commission was replaced in 1962 by the Economic Planning Council (see above, p. 203).
[74] Unofficially prompted by the Ministry of Economics.
[75] Bundestags-Drucksache IV/1752.
[76] See OECD, *Growth and Economic Policy*, report of Working Party no. 2 to the Economic Policy Committee (1964, mimeo).
[77] See above, p. 156.

apparatus of public power.[78] The same need has been felt in other countries, the most recent example being in Britain since the advent of the Labour Government in 1964. A great deal more than party politics is involved in the change. The regular and systematic analysis of economic policy, whether in the framework of a long-term plan or an annual forecast, must, if it is to have practical relevance to what is actually decided by the government, be something more than a detached academic exercise. The economic advisers must engage; they must have an intimate awareness of which policy decisions are, or may be, in the making inside the government, and what the motives, implicit as well as explicit, behind them really are. Otherwise there is little prospect that the Rational and the Real will mesh with one another. After all, the economic advisers, if they are doing their stuff, will on occasion be saying some drastic and uncomfortable things to the nation's legislators and ministers: they will be telling them about the limitations on their own power to achieve some highly desirable, perhaps politically imperative, set of objectives. The message will quite frequently be that in order to make the particular combination proposed *coherent*—so that the various lines of endeavour contained in it do not contradict or impede one another, and therefore waste the nation's resources—certain items will have to be cut or changed. The ultimate choice remains with the legislator, but he must first of all accept the discipline imposed by those who tell him what the true range of choice really is. And the disciplinarians must in turn be sufficiently close and sympathetic to the current purposes of the government to offer the best combinations of politically relevant alternatives that ingenuity can devise.[79]

The French, as we have seen,[80] have recognized the ultimate power of initiative possessed by these intellectuals in the business of modern government; they have been given an important status inside the official machine. In Germany, the law establishing the Council of Economic Experts says specifically that it is to avoid making any political recommendations; these are to be left entirely to parliament or to the authorities appointed by it to execute its decisions. On the other hand, the Council is charged with the duty of offering alternative choices to the government, on the basis of different assumptions about the priorities to be given to various political aims.[81] The truth is of course that it is impossible for anyone to give useful advice of this

---

[78] See above, pp. 203 ff.

[79] The type of relationship between legislator and technocrat outlined here can be observed at work most clearly in a quite different context—that of the EEC. Under the Treaty of Rome the *proposing* function is largely reserved for the European Commission, with its nine appointed officials; the Council of Ministers rejects proposals on a majority vote or sometimes on a single objection, but can only amend them by unanimous vote. In practice, the division of function that results is that the Council chooses, but the Commission sets the limits of possible choice.

[80] Ch. VII.   [81] See OECD, *Growth and Economic Policy*.

kind, especially if it involves the normal complicated combinations of political and economic variables, without limiting his range to the realistic political choices. A planner, even an independent one who offers an analysis rather than a prescription, must also be in some measure a politician.

The Germans would certainly deny that what they have created is a board of planners in any proper sense. My argument is not intended to imply that they have in fact started to plan clandestinely, but that the institutions they have now established belong to the same family as the planning organs that have been set up elsewhere in Western Europe since the war. The conclusion of the OECD Working Party which conducted a series of studies in depth into the conduct of economic policy in six different European countries, Germany, France, Britain, Sweden, Norway, and Holland, is apposite:

There is of course a wide variety of practices to be found in the various countries studied. These however proved to have much more in common than would be thought from the countries' own theoretical definitions and statements of principle. If one tries to avoid disputes over words, it can be observed that countries do not neatly separate into those that do and those that do not have an explicit growth policy, between those that do and do not use long-term planning techniques. . . . In fact, the six countries examined could be arranged along a continuous spectrum according to the greater or lesser emphasis they put on measures for the promotion of growth.[82]

What can be said about Germany is that the basic bits of apparatus which are required for systematic economic planning are more readily available there than in many other countries. So are the requisite forms of collaboration in the private sector and the appropriate habits of mind. These things do not have to be laboriously invented, as in Britain or the United States. There are also a lot of German assumptions about the thrust and the spread of public power in the sphere of private enterprise, which have no place in traditional Anglo-Saxon thinking.

In its fiscal practice Germany is much closer to France than to Britain. Subsidies, cheap loans provided by the state, and above all, discriminating tax allowances which support favoured activities, are used with an abandon that could only be acceptable in a society where the average citizen expects the state to choose its favourites and to intervene on their behalf. The extent of this intervention was revealed in a series of elaborate calculations made by the Ministry of Finance in 1959 and 1961. It was answering a parliamentary question about the total sum of money, either paid out by the Government or lost by it in taxes forgone, for such purposes. At Appendix IV (p. 435) an attempt is made to compare the German figures with the corresponding British items. The German total, converted at current rates of exchange, amounted to around £960 million in 1961, against a British figure of some £620 million—about one-third less.

[82] *Growth and Economic Policy*, pt. I, para. 20.

What emerges most clearly from the comparison is the enormously greater German propensity to use public finance to discriminate in industry and trade. Both countries are saddled with a vast bill to cover the cost of special favours given to their farming communities. That is now common form among all the advanced Western countries. The absolute amounts of money devoted to the support of agriculture by the British and German Governments are broadly comparable—though it should be noted in passing that the German farmer is given the benefit of artificially high prices as well.[83] Agricultural subsidies add up to over half of the total cost of financial discrimination by the state in Britain. But the Germans put a further sum of money, only a little smaller than the contribution to their farmers, into industry and commerce as well. The aggregate cost to the exchequer of the latter group of concessions is over three times as great in Germany as it is in Britain.

Measured in terms of the impact on the budget, the total German bill for fiscal discrimination is larger than the comparison of the absolute figures suggests. It amounts to nearly one-quarter of all budgetary expenditure of the central Government, compared with less than one-tenth in Britain. Moreover the German total shows no signs of decreasing.[84] Rather it is Britain that has been moving during the 1960s towards more discrimination in its tax system, as part of the policy changes associated with economic planning.[85] It has been a cautious and thus far reluctant movement away from the traditional Anglo-Saxon ideal of a fiscally neutral state. Officially this is the German ideal too;[86] but as we have had occasion to observe before, economic doctrine is on the whole a less useful guide to economic practice among the Germans than it is among the British or Americans.

Thus here, once again, Germany is seen to be better endowed than others with the essential discriminatory equipment required for modern planning, especially planning of a long-term character. It seems unlikely that in the long run it will not be used. To adopt a principle of economic non-intervention by the state is at least intelligible; what does not make sense is to intervene constantly and yet not to plan.

---

[83] In Britain the subsidy to farmers is chiefly in the form of 'deficiency payments', making up the difference between the cost of home-produced produce and world prices. The latter set the price in the home market.

[84] The two detailed investigations of the Ministry of Finance covering the years 1959–61 showed that in spite of the run-down of the special tax favours associated with the era of postwar reconstruction, the total bill for discriminatory tax reliefs and subsidies went up.

[85] Notably regional planning.

[86] See e.g. parliamentary answer by the Minister of Finance, published in *Bulletin*, 31 July 1959, no. 137/S, para. 9, where he speaks of the 'fundamental principle of neutrality in a competitive market (*Wettbewerbsneutralität*)' as the aim which guides his department.

XIII

THE UNITED STATES: THE UNCERTAIN ROLE OF PUBLIC POWER

THE stout American defence of old-style capitalism has been discussed in earlier chapters.[1] The United States is indeed one of the few places left in the world where 'capitalism' is generally thought to be an OK word. Elsewhere even a politician of the far Right, abusing socialism and the welfare state, will normally hesitate to base his appeal to popular sentiment on a call for the reassertion of good old capitalist principles. And if he did have the impulse to do so, his election manager would almost certainly suggest the use of some more discreet euphemism. The label attracts an opprobrium, not only in Europe but also in most of the underdeveloped countries, which Americans sometimes find puzzling. Newspaper articles have been written suggesting that perhaps the name of the thing ought to be changed, in order to give others a fair chance to appreciate it without prejudice.

But there is something more than a semantic eccentricity dividing the common ideology of the United States from that of the rest of the world. Among the Americans there is a general commitment to the view, shared by both political parties, of the natural predominance of private enterprise in the economic sphere and of the subordinate role of public initiative in any situation other than a manifest national emergency. The West Europeans, who have no such assumptions—for even the Right in Europe tends to believe in the abiding place of active paternalistic government—have in consequence been spared the awful doctrinal wrestling, in which Americans tend to engage whenever any bit of the economic field has to be divided afresh between the public and private sectors. The commandments which issue forth after the struggle is over carry a portentous and urgent note. It is plain that something more serious than mere political decision is being exercised.

Thus the current policy directive of the US Bureau of the Budget[2] to all Federal Offices and Agencies on the use of government-owned production facilities introduces the rules with the resounding preamble: 'Because the private enterprise system is basic to the American economy. . . .' It goes on to warn any civil servant who proposes to use public enterprise for the 'provision of a product or service' that 'the burden of proof lies on the agency

---

[1] See Ch. I.
[2] 'Criteria of Commercial-Industrial Activities of Government', *Bureau of the Budget Bulletin*, 60–62, quoted in Joint Economic Committee of Congress Hearings Sub-Committee on Defense Procurement, Mar.–Apr. 1963.

which determines that an exception to the general policy is required'. Nor must the civil servant imagine, if he comes across a piece of public enterprise which is already in operation, that he has no duty to put matters right. 'The existence of the government-owned capital assets is not in itself an adequate justification for the government to provide its own goods or services. The need for continued government ownership or operation must be fully sub-stantiated.' Finally, he may be tempted to believe that his obligations have been met, once private enterprise has been brought in to take charge of and operate the publicly owned undertaking. Nothing of the kind. 'Even the operation of a government-owned facility by a private organization through contractual arrangement does not automatically assure that the government is not competing with private enterprise. This type of arrangement could act as a barrier to the development and growth of competitive commercial sources and procurement through ordinary business channels.'

All the evidence suggests that these regulations are very strictly obeyed. The hostility to public initiative has deep roots in American traditional mythology. Yet that does not mean that in practice private enterprise has it entirely its own way. Indeed, coming from Europe and observing the behaviour of people in industry and commerce, one may well be struck by the way in which it seems to be accepted that it is part of the lot of businessmen to be pushed around intermittently by one Federal agency or another. The Securities and Exchange Commission in Washington has established standards for comprehensive and frequent reporting of the affairs of companies whose shares are publicly quoted which are far more stringent than anything in Europe. Even Britain, which is probably more advanced than any Con-tinental country in the requirements of company reporting, is not nearly so demanding as the US Federal authorities. This type of government super-vision is sometimes defended on traditional grounds, as belonging to the same order of ideas as those which have made the American anti-trust laws tougher than anywhere else. Making the market function properly means, if it is a stock market, that investors must be given a lot of relevant information of guaranteed accuracy. How else can firms compete on level terms for the public's money? The foreign businessman in the United States may remark wryly that the belief in the beneficent power of the market place leads the American Government to impose a number of obligations on companies, which they manage to escape in other countries where competitive capitalism is less well-regarded. These obligations apply particularly to statements of fact which a firm puts out—not merely in its company accounts, but also in the form of advertising and the labelling of its products. Except perhaps in Sweden, labels are nowhere so closely regulated as in the United States.

There are besides some controls which interfere directly with the decisions of private enterprise about how much it is to produce. The most notorious example is the restrictions, which have operated since the early 1950s, on the acreage which American farmers are allowed to employ in the production of cereals, of cotton, of tobacco and a variety of other crops. Areas to be cultivated for particular purposes are fixed farm by farm, and are subject to inspection by officials who have grown increasingly anxious, as surpluses have mounted, to check on anyone who is inclined to cheat. On occasion the inspection has taken on features of a military exercise, with the government men engaging in surprise aerial reconnaissance over suspicious fields of corn. Even so, the great flood of pròduce coming off American farms has not been checked.

By the early 1960s it had become evident that the real trouble was not the farmer's traditional capacity for deceiving inspectors from outside the parish, but rather his new-found ability to draw more and more output from less land. The Government did not shrink from drawing the inference: the controls would have to be made tougher and more direct. It proclaimed the need for 'supply management': farmers who had previously been told merely how much land they could devote to what, were now to have the actual quantities of each commodity to be produced laid down for them. The first attempt to introduce this system failed. In 1963 the Government's proposals were defeated in the annual wheat referendum, a procedure which up to that point had regularly produced a majority of the farmers' votes for the controls that the Government required over their productive efforts, in return for a guaranteed price for their products. There is little doubt, however, that in the long run some form of still closer control over the amounts which the American farmer is allowed to produce will be established. Even now, it is hard to argue that the $2\frac{1}{2}$ million independent farmers working on their own account in the United States enjoy much entrepreneurial freedom, compared for example with most of the people who work the land in Western Europe. That is not to say that the West Europeans will be able to avoid facing the same problem for long. But the Americans must have the credit for pioneering the *dirigiste* solutions.

That the authorities should have had the confidence to go to the farmer in 1963 in the expectation that he would voluntarily accept their scheme for a still more advanced kind of dragooning indicates a set of assumptions derived from a well-established relationship of close government tutelage. The relationship is not peculiar to farming. Indeed an even more niggling control is exercised over the output of producers in the oil industry. It has been in operation since the early 1930s. The glut of oil at that time and the collapse of prices caused by the competitive struggle for markets led first of all to direct regulation of output in the early days of the New Deal, and later to the Inter-State Oil Compact, under which the individual states agreed to impose strict limits on the amounts which they would allow to be sold. Under the present system the power to regulate domestic supplies in the United States is in effect delegated to a single state-run public authority operating out of Texas, whose writ is obeyed by the governments of other states.

The Texas Railroad Commission, which controls the area with the largest volume of production, announces its figure of 'allowable production' each month and the output of other oil-producing states is then fixed in relation to this. (The detailed working of the system is described in Appendix v, p. 439.) Within the production quota of any state there is not much room for competition among individual firms; enforcement of the rationing rule is ensured by the big refineries which reject crude oil that has not been officially authorized. Evasion is made still more difficult by a Federal law which prohibits the transport across state boundaries of 'hot oil' produced outside the allotted quotas. Evidently rugged individualism, even of the Texas variety, finds it possible to operate inside very tight limits indeed without feeling tamed in the process. No one seems to want to fight the Railroad Commission, let alone abolish it. The explanation presumably lies in the power of the myth; it is hard to think of any other. And the myth is buttressed by what seems to be a native histrionic ability; a lot of people positively want to act out the part of their national stereotypes, once the public relations men, the schoolmasters, and the journalists have established it clearly by iteration. Thus, by contrast, British business, which nowhere has to suffer the kind of detailed control over what is to be produced, and when, that is exemplified in the United States oil industry,[3] is widely convinced that it is subject to extremes of government regulation that no American would tolerate. The ordinary British businessman, too, seems to be ready to act out a part— the national stereotype of *un*enterprise, resting on the belief that circumstances make it barely worth while trying.

Tradition of Public Enterprise

I do not intend to imply that the sole difference between American and British entrepreneurial behaviour is the influence of two different and arbitrarily chosen mythical structures. There is a great deal of historical fact behind the myth. But the point that has to be established first, before analysing the real nature of the relationship between the private and public sectors in the United States, is that the conventional view of a business community with a zero margin of tolerance for public intervention is false. Historically, American capitalism in its formative period was much readier to accept intervention by public authority than British capitalism. The doctrines of *laissez-faire* bit very deep into the social and political life of England for a

---

[3] Adolf Berle, in *The American Economic Republic* (London, Sidgwick, 1963), pp. 157–8, cites the American sugar industry as another example of a well-established system of detailed government control over individual producers. The sugar factories are allotted production quotas on the basis of an annual estimate, made in Washington, of the volume of US consumption during the forthcoming year.

century and more. The constant effort to push back governmental authority of any kind from entrenched positions which it occupied in the economic process became the preoccupation of several generations of reformers. In nineteenth-century America the attitudes towards public authority did not—at any rate until the last quarter of the century—acquire the ferocious doctrinal consistency which they assumed early on among the English. The reasons are not far to seek. After all, public authority, in a territory with a vast amount of rich land being steadily opened up and a frontier constantly threatening to get out of control, had a much more obvious part to play than in a settled island where people were used to operating within well-defined social as well as physical limits.

But it was not simply that American conditions imposed the need for more active use of governmental power in order to keep the peace. The characteristic role of government in the United States during the first half of the nineteenth century, in sharp contrast to what was happening in Britain, was its emergence as an entrepreneur on a large scale, either on its own independent account or, more commonly, in partnership with private interests. Railways, canals, and banks were all treated as proper spheres for public enterprise. In the first two, several state governments were exceedingly active, at a time when in Britain private enterprise owned and ran virtually all public transport. The argument for the use of public funds was forthrightly stated in the legislative address of the Whig Party of New York State in 1838. 'We hold it to be wisest . . .', it said, 'to apply the means of the state boldly and liberally to aid those great public works of railroads and canals which are beyond the means of unassisted private enterprise.'[4] It is somewhat ironical that today the United States is the only advanced country of the Western world in which the railways are stubbornly preserved, against considerable odds, almost as a kind of museum piece of private enterprise. Everywhere else the state has taken over the service—for the very reasons which were recognized in New York in the dawn of American capitalism.

In his profound study of the development of economic policy in Pennsylvania during this period,[5] Louis Hartz mentions a total of over 150 'mixed corporations', in which the state government and private enterprise were partners, shown in the official records of the year 1844. He observes that the political pressure behind this remarkable movement to involve the state in business enterprise came from 'the mercantile group' centred on Philadelphia; these early American businessmen regarded government as a natural partner in their efforts to compete with the trading and transport services

---

[4] Quoted in Lee Benson, *The Concept of Jacksonian Democracy* (N.J., Princeton UP, 1961), p. 103. The author remarks that the Jeffersonian doctrine of non-interventionist liberal government was at this time 'for the most part ignored in practice by all state governments'.

[5] *Economic Policy and Democratic Thought: Pennsylvania 1776–1860* (Cambridge, Mass., Harvard UP, 1948). See pp. 290–1.

provided by their rivals, the merchants of Baltimore and New York. The relationship between public and private enterprise at this stage of American history seems indeed to be guided by many of the underlying assumptions of the traditional French approach.[6]

It is a widely believed legend in the United States that Andrew Jackson's Presidency (1829–37) marked the decisive rejection of the older forms of tutelary government and the assertion of the typically American principle of free enterprise at any cost. All this is somehow symbolized in Jackson's struggle against the privileges of the United States Bank, culminating in his veto on the renewal of its charter in 1832. 'Free banking' was one of the popular slogans of the time. So was the demand for payments in specie, instead of banknotes. It is hard to make any serious economic sense of either; both belong in the category of primitive money magic, which has somehow to be exorcized before modern capitalism can develop efficient institutions. One of the consequences of the confused Jacksonian ideas on currency and banking was to delay the establishment of a central banking system in the United States until 1914,[7] long after the leading European nations had fully equipped themselves with this essential piece of machinery.

Jackson was the first of the great populist leaders who seem to be so readily spawned by the American political system. His political notions had neither the consistency nor the narrowness which his subsequent admirers have sometimes attributed to them. In some ways, Jacksonian democracy served to reinforce the movement for active government, in the form of public welfare services, which already existed.[8] Its opposition was not to the use of public power in the economic system, but only to any reinforcement of central power wielded through the Federal authority. State and municipal government were at liberty to expand. The fear was only of the potential Leviathan in Washington; the American principle of preserving individual freedom by dividing up public authority into separate pieces was not threatened by the vigorous growth of rival governmental power away from the centre. On the contrary, the theorists of pluralistic government were often inclined, and still are sometimes, to talk of the state in relation to the Federal authority as if it were a precise analogue of the heroic private individual standing against the overweening pretensions of arbitrary government power. It is the image of David being armed with more powerful weapons for his future struggle against Goliath.

At times the degree of tutelage which state governments arrogated to themselves in Jacksonian America appears so extreme that it suggests the direct inspiration of Colbert, rather than anything that belongs to the Anglo-Saxon tradition. Colbert would surely have approved of the systematic regulation

---

[6] See Ch. V.   [7] The year of the founding of the Federal Reserve system.
[8] See Arthur Schlesinger, Jr, *The Age of Jackson* (London, Eyre & Spottiswoode, 1946).

of the standards of quality of all exported goods, instituted by the government of Pennsylvania in the 1830s.[9] The Pennsylvanians were in fierce competition with the state of New York and afraid that they might lose business to their aggressive neighbour unless they made a special effort to maintain the reputation of their goods. Their views were reflected in the report of a committee of the state's House of Representatives in 1833 which says: 'If the article . . . forms an important item of export a well-regulated inspection is productive of benefit by preventing the exportation of inferior descriptions of the same article and thus giving it a character in foreign markets.' Two years after this a law was passed which went a stage farther. After bringing all the existing inspection measures into a systematic code, it proceeded to fix detailed regulations for each individual commodity, covering the dimensions of containers, the methods of packing, and the brand marks to be put on goods.[10] The mood which prompted this active use of public power to improve the performance of private enterprise lasted into the middle years of the century. As late as 1853 the Chief Justice of the state, in delivering judgment in a case brought by a citizen, who argued that the investment of public funds by the Pennsylvanian government was unconstitutional, declared with a feeling of confidence which reverberates through the words a century afterwards:

It is a grave error to suppose that the duty of the state stops with the establishment of those institutions which are necessary to the existence of government: such as those for the administration of justice, preservation of the peace, and the protection of the country from foreign enemies. . . . To aid, encourage, and stimulate commerce, domestic and foreign, is a duty of the sovereign as plain and as universally recognised as any other.[11]

The Reversal of the Late Nineteenth Century

Yet a couple of decades later the Pennsylvania Supreme Court judgment would have been thought to reflect a highly eccentric view of the role of government. By then business, and above all big business, seemed to have made a successful take-over bid for all the economic power that was worth having. In the last quarter of the nineteenth century, at just about the time that Britain was beginning to turn slowly away from some of the excesses of the old doctrine, the exponents of an extreme version of *laissez-faire* came to dominate the public life of the United States. The philosophy stamped itself on the country through the agency of the courts even more than through the conventional political process. Judges have at various crucial periods of American history—including most recently during the Civil Rights movement of the early 1960s—acted as conscious agents of a political trend. The task

[9] See Hartz, *Economic Policy.*
[10] Ibid., pp. 204 ff. The regulations covered a wide variety of goods ranging from flour and fish to tobacco, potash and gunpowder.
[11] Judgment in the Sharpless case (ibid., p. 122).

of interpreting the constitution in a system where the Federal Government's room for manoeuvre is in normal times constricted by the 'separation of powers' sometimes gives the Supreme Court the initiative in the nation's politics.

What happened to change the balance between public and private initiatives so violently during the third quarter of the nineteenth century? Part of the explanation is possibly the shift in the alignment of the political parties during and after the Civil War, with the earlier exponents of active interventionist government, in the northern states, absorbed into a Republican Party which was now dominated by the big business interests.[12] But there were in addition two economic factors which helped to sharpen the reaction against all forms of public enterprise at this stage. The first was simply that there was no longer any lack of private risk capital on a sufficient scale to finance large enterprises, particularly in the field of public transport. Private investors were now eager to engage in this lucrative business. Secondly, and probably more important in terms of national politics, the management of too many public enterprises had been thoroughly inefficient. It was widely felt that some means had to be found to curb the multifarious initiatives of state governments like that of Pennsylvania, which had ended with the waste of the taxpayer's money. They also, incidentally, destroyed the credit standing of states which too often failed, through mismanagement, to meet their obligations to those who had lent them money.

The essential trouble was that state legislatures tended to regard the management of a public enterprise as merely an extension of the conventional political process. It was not so much that the managers were corrupt as that they were committed to an amateur's view of the needs of management. As was the established practice with elected political representatives in an egalitarian democracy of the American type, managers were also appointed for short periods and subject to political rotation. Only in this way, it was felt, could their exercise of power be checked. They were treated as if they were no more than passive agents of the committees of the state legislature who had to make the real decisions. Thus, while the state governments embarked on public enterprise and public regulation of industry with a vigour that is reminiscent of the traditional French approach to economic policy, they entirely failed to equip themselves with a core of professional administrators of French quality. Indeed, the whole notion of a professional public officer, acting on behalf of the state rather than of the politicians who happened to make up the government of the day, was alien to the spirit of nineteenth-century American democracy. It is hardly surprising in these circumstances that public enterprise came to be regarded as inherently inferior, in its level of efficiency, to private enterprise.

[12] See Schlesinger, *Jackson*, pp. 505 ff.

J. W. Hurst points out[13] that the public authorities continued to exercise an important influence on economic development even after the popular reaction in the third quarter of the nineteenth century which forced the state governments to divest themselves of their business interests. But now government lent its power to private corporations which were developing public utilities. It did this in a variety of ways, but most blatantly by giving them the right of 'eminent domain', which meant that they could compulsorily acquire any land needed for their operations.[14] These 'delegated powers of legal compulsion' assisted the rapid growth of certain fortunate businesses which were able to claim that they were fulfilling a public purpose; they were one of the factors in the build-up of the massive concentration of power in corporate hands during the 1880s and 1890s.

Direct public enterprise was not immediately extinguished in all its forms. For a while municipal authorities were able to find a hole through the net which had closed on the economic ventures previously run by state governments. But the courts gradually introduced a restrictive set of criteria which made it unconstitutional to use tax money for anything other than an essential 'public purpose'. The decision on what constituted a proper 'public purpose' depended in the last resort on the judge's view of the relationship between public and private responsibilities. And in the late nineteenth century fashionable judicial doctrine in the United States squeezed the former almost to vanishing point.

Debate on American History

It is possible to regard the extremist version of the private enterprise doctrine in the late nineteenth century, from which so many of the simple and certain formulae of the popular political debate in mid-twentieth century America seem to derive, as no more than a temporary distortion of the straight limb of the continuing American liberal tradition. Some eminent historians have argued this way. Affirmative government, which intervenes in the economic affairs of a nation on the basis of a long view of its collective interest, is, it is claimed, of the essence of this tradition. It was only a shabby manoeuvre of the big businessmen who captured the Republican Party after the Civil War which made it appear otherwise. As Arthur Schlesinger, Jr, puts it,[15] they were able to use the 'Jeffersonian myth' that any strong government was of its nature bad, 'to defeat Jefferson's essential purposes'.

Whatever President Jefferson's true intentions, the myth continues to have a powerful influence in the politics of contemporary America. At any rate the words used in the political debate seem to refer to concepts implying a suspicion of public power as such, which strike a bizarre note on the average

---

[13] See *Law and the Conditions of Freedom* (Madison, Wisconsin UP, 1956).
[14] Ibid., pp. 63 ff.
[15] *Jackson*, p. 518

European ear today. Are the American historians right who say that all this verbiage conceals, rather than expresses, the underlying reality of American political history? The point has some practical importance, because as we have seen (in Part I), the United States has so far appeared as the outstanding laggard in the general movement of the Western world towards the eager acceptance of a vastly enlarged role for the central government in economic affairs. The question is whether the apparent lag is due to special circumstances—notably that the United States is so much richer than the rest of us and has been under less urgent political compulsion to reform itself than Western Europe in the past couple of decades—or whether there is some more deep-seated impediment in the American system to the adoption of the new order.

One version of the evolution of public economic power in the United States sees it as a dialectical process in three distinct phases. J. W. Hurst, the legal historian, describes them as follows: 'Over the first three-quarters of the [nineteenth] century we used law to help determine priorities among competing uses of our scarce working capital';[16] next there was an interlude lasting into the early years of this century during which private business power was unnaturally inflated at the expense of public authority; then came a 'familiar pendulum movement of policy during the twentieth century', which reversed the movement. 'The depression of the 1930s', he concludes, 'enormously strengthened but did not initiate this swing back towards promotional use of public finance.' Arthur Schlesinger, Jr, marks out the various stages on the voyage from precedent to precedent during the twentieth century in these terms: 'Slowly the liberal tradition was overhauled. . . . The Hamiltonian progressivism of Theodore Roosevelt ushered in a period of energetic government. Woodrow Wilson understood even more plainly the need for executive vigor and government action. Franklin D. Roosevelt carried out these tendencies more decisively than Wilson, and the New Deal achieved the emancipation of liberalism from this aspect of the Jeffersonian myth.'[17]

On this view the New Deal was not a sharp break with American tradition but simply a continuation, at a somewhat accelerated pace, of a process which went back to the start of the twentieth century and affected Republican and Democratic governments alike. Schlesinger's comment was written in 1941. Many American liberals at that stage thought that the antipathy to positive government had finally been overcome as a result of the experience of the New Deal. Adolf Berle, who is perhaps the most abiding spokesman of New

---

[16] Hurst (*Law and the Conditions of Freedom*, p. 53) distinguishes four types of investment decisions in which government actively intervened. 'Listed in descending order' according to degree of priority attached to them by public opinion, they were: 'the allocation of capital to transport, to the development of commercial agriculture, to the fostering of credit facilities, and the encouragement of industry'.

[17] *Jackson*, p. 520.

Deal radicalism, untiring in his series of attempts to adapt its principles to changing conditions during the subsequent two and a half decades, wrote in 1940 about the future of public enterprise in the American system: 'I am pretty clear . . . that, within ten years, we shall be forced into a vast expansion of direct production of one sort or another. . . . The Tennessee Valley Authority may well prove to be the great example. . . .'[18] Berle envisaged a further development of New Deal policies in the private sector too. Private ownership could not simply be left to the unpredictable and often perverse guidance of market forces; there had to be central control—'some sort of cartel formation or other organisation of industry'. He singled out three categories which especially required public supervision. They were first of all industries where, for technical reasons, the average size of the single unit of production was large, for example steel; secondly, those where market forces tended to result in damaging fluctuations in output (e.g. the automobile industry) or in long-term depletion of a natural resource (e.g. oil); and thirdly, those whose products ought, for reasons of social welfare, to be supplied in a 'reasonably continuous . . . even flow' to consumers.[19]

All this reads rather like a blueprint for modern capitalist planning, with a slightly more radical twist, on the French model. Indeed, there were many elements in the early New Deal which pointed, at a time when few of the European politicians of either the Right or the Left were ready for it, in the direction which much of Western Europe has taken since the war. The special virtue of the American reformers was their refusal to accept the simple dichotomy between socialism and capitalism which then dominated European political thinking. The New Dealers—or at any rate the leading group which stayed the course and occupied a political position a very little left of centre, close to that of Franklin Roosevelt himself—perceived the future as a new mixture of public and private initiatives, with the public side very much reinforced but still operating in the framework of a predominantly capitalist system.

Considering the opportunities for radical experiment offered by twenty years of uninterrupted Democratic administration from 1933 to 1952, it is surprising how little follow-through there was from this original impulse into the postwar world. By the 1950s the typical view of the liberal establishment in the United States had probably moved closer to that of Professor Eugene Rostow, former Dean of the Yale University Law School and another highly sophisticated lawyer-economist, in an American tradition of which Berle him-

[18] *New Directions in the New World* (New York, Harper, 1940), p. 95.
[19] See also *Power Without Property* (London, Sidgwick, 1960), where Berle has shifted the emphasis away from public ownership—in the light of twenty years of further experience—but the basic techniques of the regulation of private enterprise to secure a public purpose, developed by the New Deal, are vigorously recommended for the treatment of postwar American economic problems.

self was a notable product. In *Planning for Freedom*[20] Rostow felt able to assert, after surveying the experience of American business fluctuation and economic growth during the 1940s and 1950s, that the United States system was of its nature opposed to 'collectivism' in any form. Whatever measures the government might have to take in order to keep the flow of money and the flow of goods moving in step inside a market economy did 'not require any change in the prevailing pattern of power distribution'. Private enterprise in something very close to its traditional form was in his view a necessary condition for the survival of the American democratic system—'. . . competitive capitalism is a characteristic expression of the American culture . . . [U.S.] policy is always to avoid concentrations of authority . . . Capitalism stands with federalism, the separation of powers, the disestablishment of religion, the antitrust tradition, the autonomy of educational bodies . . . in expressing a deep suspicion of authority. Americans are committed pluralists'. Here then is the antithesis, intransigently put, to the concentration of economic authority and the centralized planning of the use of resources, which have become the characteristic instruments of dynamic postwar capitalism elsewhere in the Western world.

Two Doctrines of the New Deal

The paradox is that the Americans who, in the 1930s, acted as the precursors of the new capitalism, seemed to stall in their course just when the system was coming to fruition in the Western world—showing its full powers to provide the great gifts of economic growth, full employment, and social welfare. Why was the original momentum of the New Deal halted? In order to answer the question it is necessary, briefly, to take a closer look at the New Deal itself.

Among the great variety of political impulses which went to make the heroic period of New Deal reforms (roughly the years 1933 and 1934) there are two major themes which constantly recur. They both appear, at first, to be accommodated in a natural ideological coalition; but once Washington has managed to cope with the immediate economic crisis, they come to be seen increasingly by their supporters as alternative and essentially conflicting policies. Arthur Schlesinger, in his history of *The Age of Roosevelt*,[21] has subtly delineated the gradual emergence of these distinct lines of thought, out of what started off by being little more than a couple of ragbags of ideas. One may be broadly described as the corporatist view. This envisaged an entirely new relationship between government and business, collaborating actively with one another in the pursuit of agreed economic objectives. The principle of competitive enterprise in pursuit of maximum profits was regarded as superseded; in its place there was a vision of organized industries in which the producers shared out their task on a rational basis. The other

[20] New Haven, Conn., Yale UP, 1959, p. 43.   [21] New York, Houghton, 1959.

view emphasized supervision rather than collaboration: public supervision, of an essentially judicial character, of the activities of private enterprise. Its purpose was to ensure that certain clearly stated business rules were obeyed, rather than to exact any active help from private enterprise in the objectives of public policy. It was expected that public aid in various forms would be required from time to time, in order to make some businesses function properly; but this was regarded as an underpinning for market forces, not as a means of replacing them by some alternative device.

During the emergency phase of the rescue operation in 1933, the supporters of the second view found themselves compelled to accept government intervention on the grand scale; private enterprise was so much flotsam which had to be salvaged in any way possible. But after a short while the battle between the two groups was joined around the issue of the National Recovery Administration. The NRA was given powers to compel industry to reorganize itself, fix prices, allot quotas of production, and so on. General Hugh Johnson, its head, saw it as the instrument for bringing together under one co-ordinated control the work of all the economic departments and agencies of government. Public authority would speak with a single voice and be spoken to in turn by the single corporate voice of each industry.

The inspiration of European corporatist ideas, which were fashionable at the time, is apparent. Indeed, Johnson explicitly recognized the fact when in his farewell speech he invoked 'the shining name of Mussolini'.[22] He was not referring to the doctrine of the one-party state or approving of the characteristic forms of Fascist violence. His concern was with the 'corporations', the autonomous organizations governing the various sectors of the national economic life, which figured so prominently in the theory—though less in the practice—of Italian Fascism of the 1920s. Not by any means all of the enthusiastic supporters of the NRA were prepared to go as far as this. Johnson was an ebullient character who enjoyed pushing matters to extremes. But he expressed a view widely held at the time, when he insisted that the traditional form of American competitive enterprise was outmoded and must be deliberately replaced by something else. He eventually demanded of President Roosevelt 'a clean-cut decision' between the established theory of American capitalism, based on anti-trust and the encouragement of small business enterprise, on the one side, and the NRA on the other. 'You can't escape the issue', he said. 'Cooperation or competition.'[23]

Somehow or other, and not for the last time, the President did manage to escape from some seemingly ineluctable choice. He selected the pieces of policy which suited his immediate purposes, and never worried if they appeared to make a grossly inconsistent pattern. Thus, in the other major arena of the economic depression where the Government's policies were being

---

[22] Schlesinger, *Roosevelt*, ii. p. 153. [23] Ibid., p. 171.

deployed, in agriculture, they involved thorough-going controls over the output of each individual producer and over the prices of commodities. The state stepped in as an active partner here, and itself bought up the amounts necessary to maintain prices at the desired levels. The managed agricultural system of contemporary America is a permanent monument to the interventionist school of the New Deal, which believed that the era of the competitive market had gone. It is tempting to speculate about what might have happened if the methods used by the Agricultural Adjustment Administration, with the backing of Henry Wallace, the radical Secretary for Agriculture,[24] had been effectively applied to American industry.

But the industrialists recovered their nerve far more quickly than the farmers. Industry had been badly shaken by the collapse of the markets for its goods and the failure of the financial system in the early 1930s. But unlike the farmers, it did not have to face a long crisis of over-production. As soon as the Government had done what was necessary to make the banks function again and had put some money back into people's pockets, business morale perked up. Businessmen were soon ready to launch an attack on a Government which simply assumed its right to interfere, and when they resisted, bullied them. The counter-offensive against the New Deal reached a climax with the campaign against the NRA. In 1935 it was finally abolished, after the Supreme Court had declared it unconstitutional. It was potentially an instrument for centralized economic planning of the modern type. It was also the symbol of the rejection of old-style capitalism, which was the central theme of the first phase of the New Deal. Schlesinger lists 'the tenets of the First New Deal' as follows—'that the technological revolution had rendered bigness inevitable; that competition could no longer be relied on to protect social interests; that large units were an opportunity to be seized rather than a danger to be fought; and that the formula for stability in the new society must be combination and co-operation under enlarged federal authority'.[25]

It is remarkable how soon this wave of new ideas, seemingly so powerful, was reversed. All the evidence suggests that the decisive change came round about 1935. There was no particular event that can be blamed for it, though the revulsion against some of the excesses and inefficiencies of the NRA,[26] culminating in the Supreme Court's ruling against it, certainly played an important part. It was, of course, unreasonable to expect that a new and highly experimental enterprise of this kind, which had been plunged suddenly into the task of writing codes of detailed commercial regulations and good

---

[24] Vice-President of the US, 1941–5.   [25] *Roosevelt*, p. 179.

[26] It is to be observed that some of the most radical supporters of the original New Deal, those who favoured the most active government intervention in the private sector, had also meanwhile turned against the NRA, which they saw increasingly as a device for giving business the effective power to administer itself.

conduct for 546 industries,[27] would function smoothly. It was bound to make a lot of mistakes. The enormously ambitious venture of devising a substitute, in the form of a new system of collaboration between public and private power, to replace the classical rules of competition could not possibly have succeeded without being given, first of all, time to correct errors and secondly, the support of an unequivocal political decision. Neither was forthcoming.

The New Deal's Permanent Legacy

In the second half of the 1930s the United States seems to have reverted contentedly to the familiar course—seeking out the remedies for the deficiencies of capitalism by regulating the behaviour of individual capitalists. The emphasis is once again all on trust-busting, on sustaining the little man in his struggle against the power of big business, on making competition work. Policy was still bent on reinforcing the exercise of public authority in the economic system; but the authority was judicial rather than administrative. It aimed at an arm's length relationship with private enterprise, not at the kind of active huddle which General Johnson had envisaged in the NRA.

Not that there was any lack of radical spirit in the design of these reforms. One example, the Securities and Exchange Commission, set up to regulate the behaviour of companies which issue shares or bonds, will serve to illustrate the use of the judicial approach to bring about significant institutional change of a kind which has not yet been compassed elsewhere. Established in the first phase of the New Deal, when the tide seemed to be running strongly in favour of the corporatist doctrines, it was regarded as a contemptibly cautious effort by the advanced reformers. Yet thirty years after the SEC was set up, Western Europe is still groping for some means of matching the public supervision of the activities of private enterprise management which it secured in the United States. All directors and officers of companies whose shares are publicly traded are forced, as one member of the official committee inquiring into British company law in 1961 (the Jenkins Committee) put it, 'to operate as if in a goldfish bowl'.[28] They have to report to the Commission every one of their share transactions, within ten days of the end of the month in which it took place, and these are then set out in a regular monthly publication issued by the Government printing office. Also included in this compilation are the dealings and holdings of any person who owns 10 per cent or more of the shares of a public company. According to M. F. Cohen, a senior official of the SEC who gave evidence to the Jenkins Committee, there were in 1961 approximately 40,000 people who were subject to the

---

[27] See E. F. Goldman, *Rendezvous with Destiny; a History of Modern American Reform* (New York, Vintage, 1956), p. 272.

[28] Memo. by Professor L. C. D. Gower, *Minutes of Evidence, Company Law Committee*, 10 Feb. 1961.

reporting rule.[29]   Professor Gower, a lawyer on the Committee, remarked wistfully: 'If rules similar to these were adopted in Britain it would undoubtedly be a potent sanction against abuse of inside information'.   There was no sign however that any British Government of the early 1960s, whether of the Right or the Left, was prepared to contemplate any reform of company law as radical as this.

Yet at the time when the SEC legislation was being introduced in the United States in the early 1930s, it was dismissed by Professor W. O. Douglas (later Justice Douglas of the Supreme Court) as 'a nineteenth century piece of legislation'.   Moreover it was, he said, 'wholly antithetical to the programme of control envisaged in the New Deal and to the whole economy under which we are living'.[30]   He was, of course, expressing the views of the interventionist school of reformers, and on this view of what the New Deal was about he was justified in his strictures.   It only became clear later on, particularly after 1935, that the New Deal—or the bits of it which lasted—was really about something else.   Even when there was active intervention by the Government in the running of the economy, it never amounted to Douglas's 'programme of control'.   Above all, there was no serious attempt to co-ordinate the various activities of the Government in the economic sphere into a coherent policy endowed with purpose and direction.   Each section of the Government concentrated more or less independently on its own sphere of influence.

It is worth insisting that if there had been the urge towards positive government and economic planning on the part of the Roosevelt Administration, the opportunities for securing co-ordinated action were not lacking. The NRA was not a unique chance, which had to be passed up because of the Supreme Court's action against it.   We have already seen how the Government's intervention in the agricultural field opened the way to a permanent and profound change in the organization of American farming. This happened in spite of the fact that the official crop controls operated by the agricultural agency were also declared to be unconstitutional by the Supreme Court at the time of the NRA case in 1935.   Some of the New Deal radicals had seen equally rich opportunities in another of the great administrative agencies whose task was to salvage the economy—the Reconstruction Finance Corporation.   In the face of the collapse of American

---

[29] *Minutes of Evidence*, 23 Mar. 1961.   The reporting requirement is especially important, because if the persons concerned are shown to have taken a short-term profit on dealings in the shares of their company ('short-term' is defined as being a six-months' period) they can be forced by law to surrender the whole of the sum to the company.   As Professor Loss, another American witness, told the Jenkins Committee, section 16(b) of the 1934 Act, which deals with the recovery of profits, 'is probably the most cordially disliked single section in the entire SEC armoury by those it affects'.

[30] Quoted in Schlesinger, *Roosevelt*, ii, 445.

banking and the desperate shortage of capital of any kind, the RFC had almost unlimited power to control the direction of national investment. Adolf Berle, who was a leading official of the Corporation at the time, urged that the power should be used. The RFC could determine not only investment policies, but also the dividends distributed by the banks to their shareholders, their employment of staff and even the salaries paid to their employees. 'As long as additional capital is needed through the Reconstruction Finance Corporation', he pointed out, 'just so long there must be acquiescence in the views which it happens to express'.[31]

It is to be observed that it was precisely through its control over the key institutions for the provision of credit that the French state forged its most potent instrument of economic planning in the postwar period. There was no inherent reason why the RFC should not have been used in the same way. Berle in fact wanted to use the Federal Government's control over the sources of credit to establish a chain of banks whose task it would be to seek out opportunities for new investment promising a social return, as well as a profit to the borrower. In such a scheme the state would of course have been doing more than providing the wherewithal to sustain a prosperous level of business and employment; it would also have been seeking out agents for its own economic policies. Characteristically the chief aim—as with the postwar European planners—would have been to speed up industrial innovation. 'Outside of the large corporations', Berle said, 'men who have ideas for new enterprise cannot expect to find much assistance in the commercial banking system'.[32]

In the event, the spirit of experiment in the RFC was held under close restraint. Although the New Deal introduced major reforms into the American financial system, they were of quite a different character. Thus laws were passed to regulate the proportion of bank credit that might be used for a purchase of shares in the stock exchange. It is worth noting that there is still no such official control over stock market 'margin requirements' in Britain and several other European countries. In the United States changes in the minimum cash margin have come to be used nowadays as a regulator of the flow of speculative credit, and form part of the general apparatus of business cycle policy. The central bank also tightened its control over the minimum reserves to be held by commercial banks. Under the Banking Act of 1935 the Federal Reserve Board was given the authority to change bank reserve requirements as an instrument of credit policy. But the most novel feature of the reforms was the device providing government insurance for all bank deposits. This was a peculiarly American arrangement, using public authority to underwrite the finances of the banks—the end effect being to assist them in obtaining deposits from the public more easily and on better terms

---

[31] Ibid., p. 432.   [32] Ibid.

than would otherwise have been possible. Like the Government's parallel scheme for the insurance of house mortgage loans, it provides, at small public cost, the means of making money flow into enterprises for which bankers, acting unaided, would not have been able to provide the funds.[33] The Government guarantee against default mobilizes extra money for commercial transactions of which the state approves, but without any active state participation in commerce. Thus it stands ready both to regulate and to buttress the system, although always from the outside.

All this contrasts sharply with the failure to achieve even the minimum rationalization of the grossly inefficient structure of American banking either during the New Deal or after. Sir Denis Brogan has suggested[34] that the reason why nothing was done about this was the irrational prejudice of the old-line Democrats on all matters connected with currency and credit. No doubt that played a part; but if the only difficulty had been the traditional ideological stance of the party, means would surely have been sought, and quite probably found, to overcome it—as happened over other equally explosive issues. The remarkable fact is that no serious attempt was made to change the power structure of American banking, to regroup the banks so as to increase their combined lending capacity or to convert them into a more flexible instrument of public policy. This was done in Western Europe by far less radical governments than Roosevelt's during the 1930s. The independent, under-capitalized, small town bank was, and still is, a hallowed institution—with an honoured and ancient place in the folklore of American free enterprise—and it has to be kept in active business, even if that means stopping the large banks from setting up branches in places where they might be dangerously efficient competitors.

Roosevelt and the Fragmentation of Government

Eric Goldman[35] tells the story of a conversation in 1933 between Raymond Moley, senior member of the New Deal Brains Trust, and Roosevelt on the evening when the President was about to deliver a 'fireside chat' on the radio about the establishment of the NRA. Moley, who had drafted the text of the speech, had put in a passage explaining that this institution, together with the AAA[36] to look after agriculture, were to be the instruments of a new era of national planning. He was anxious to impress on the President the 'enormous step' that he was taking when he turned his back on the old ideals of free market capitalism. Did he really approve of planning? Roosevelt replied: 'I never felt surer of anything in my life.'

---

[33] There is a certain analogy with the French technique of *transformation*—turning short-term savings into usable investment credits with the aid of the state (see p. 169).

[34] *New Cambridge Modern History*, xii. 169.   [35] *Rendezvous with Destiny*, p. 265.

[36] Agricultural Adjustment Administration—an innocuous-sounding name for a revolutionary device of a highly *dirigiste* character (see above, p. 311).

Yet when it came to the point, Roosevelt's instinct was profoundly hostile to the change in the method of government which was necessary to convert 'national planning' from an attractive abstract idea into a reality. To a large extent planning in a capitalist context, as we have come to know it since the war, is a matter of tightening the hierarchical structure of government, compelling all departments to put all the decisions which have significant long-term consequences into a single intellectual framework, determined at the highest level of administration. New lines of authority are established, and at each level of power there is a more precise definition of the area in which choice and local initiative are allowed. Planning thus requires a high degree of explicitness in the relations between the different departments of government and a clear division of responsibilities.

But Roosevelt always preferred to conduct his operations in a kind of extended twilight zone where responsibilities were blurred. Schlesinger describes the results: 'His favourite technique was to keep grants of authority incomplete, jurisdiction uncertain, charters overlapping. The result of this competitive theory of administration was often confusion and exasperation on the operating level. . . .'[37] All this was designed to keep the initiative firmly in the President's hands; the constant likelihood of jurisdictional disputes required his presence as final arbiter. Richard Neustadt in his analysis of the different methods of governing of modern Presidents[38] contrasts with Roosevelt's technique the hierarchical system of administration employed by President Eisenhower—to the disadvantage of the latter. The task of the head of the executive in the United States, in Neustadt's view, is an unremitting process of bargaining among competing centres of power. The President must constantly manoeuvre for advantage; he is lost if he imagines, like Eisenhower, that his job is to establish a series of chains of command and then to ensure that a consistent set of orders is sent down them.

No doubt Eisenhower overdid the analogy between the White House and a military staff headquarters. However, other soldier Presidents, notably in contemporary France, seem to be more efficient both in thinking out orders and in getting them obeyed than he was. It may be that Eisenhower's real deficiency lay in his lack of understanding, and even more in his absence of any liking for politics, rather than in his failure to keep everyone guessing about the nature of their true responsibility, in the Roosevelt manner.

Indeed, it is arguable that Roosevelt's penchant for the role of bargainer-in-chief, his evident delight in the exercise of a kind of administrative athleticism, caused him to miss an opportunity which another President, endowed with less political virtuosity, might have seized. The opportunity was the sudden expansion of the small and not very professional American civil service into an enormous administrative apparatus of the modern type. Before 1933 the

Federal administrative service was small and tended to be treated as a very subordinate element in the national life. It was a recognized patriotic purpose to keep it puny and somewhat depressed. With the coming of the New Deal it was hurried into a drastic change of role, pushed into the centre of the stage, and told to take charge of the plot. The number of Federal officials multiplied several times over during the New Deal. A spate of legislation endowed these men and women with extended new powers; as the Federal Government found itself compelled to engage in a mass of fresh activities, the area of administrative discretion left to officials was greatly enlarged. It is hard to avoid the reflection that if the head of such a government had been seriously concerned with the formulation of a coherent social and economic policy, he would have insisted on a clear pattern of relationships between the disparate organs of authority on which the reform depended. If the commitment to national planning meant anything, it implied at least this.

That Roosevelt preferred the blurred and uncertain lines of demarcation to a more conventional administrative system may have been partly temperamental. There is a story in *The White House Papers* about the President's astonishment and admiration when he was told by Robert Sherwood (the author of the book) that he had had to leave Washington for a few days in order to sack one of his subordinate officials in the Office of War Information, of which Sherwood was the head. 'And did you fire him?' asked Roosevelt. When Sherwood said yes, he wanted to know more. 'How did you do it?' he asked. It became apparent from Roosevelt's unaffected curiosity about the detail of the incident that he himself found it almost impossible to sack anyone.[39] His preferred method was not to remove a man who had failed from his job, but to deflate the job, leave the same man in it, and invent a new post alongside it with more authority to be filled by someone else.

This was of course marvellously designed to exacerbate the process which Theodore Roosevelt had described back in 1910 as 'the over-division of governmental powers'[40] The elder Roosevelt had become convinced by that time—when he was launching his break-away reform movement outside the established two-party structure of US politics[41]—that this was one of the peculiar deficiencies of the American system: it was responsible, he argued, for the 'impotence' of the Government in the pursuit of positive and coherent policies designed to serve the public interest. The evidence suggests that he really did possess some of the impulses of a planner to which his nephew, a quarter of a century later, laid not very convincing claim. However, it would not be fair to blame Franklin Roosevelt's temperament solely for this enlarged obstacle to coherent government in the United States in the second half of the

[39] *The White House Papers of Harry L. Hopkins* (London, Eyre & Spottiswoode, 1949), i. 72.
[40] Quoted by Goldman, *Rendezvous with Destiny*, p. 162.
[41] The Bull Moose Party, hived off from the Republicans.

twentieth century. He was in fact only allowing himself to be moved along by a powerful and abiding undercurrent of American political life, and acting out the process with an American politician's characteristic zest. He was responding to a national instinct to break up government into many small parts, an instinct which seems at times to be guided by some eccentric model of a system of administration in which a lot of independent bodies engage in furious competition with one another—the nearest thing in fact to a market place. It is fashionable to praise Franklin Roosevelt for his lightness and skill in manoeuvring over the muddy terrain of American government. It is less usual to recall that he left it a lot muddier than he found it.

American political analysts of the Neustadt school seem at times to imply that the fragmentation of government, the presidential manoeuvring and generally the huge impediment to the execution of coherent public policy, are essentially the consequence of the separation of powers.[42] But this is only true because Americans have been inclined to interpret the doctrine of separation in an extreme sense. This has something to do with the national culture, not with the constitutional doctrine. In France, where constitutions express at least an equal devotion to the separation of powers—which is after all by way of being a French idea[43]—the opposite trend operates. Independent public agencies may be created and their independence protected by laws; yet somehow they all seem to end up centralizing the important decisions in a small circle of offices in Paris.

The Federal Agencies

Thus the advance of public regulation and public welfare activity since the early 1930s, which is the common experience of the Western world, has had a noticeably different outcome in the United States from anywhere else. The difference is not simply a matter of the relative importance of governmental activities in the US economy. Public consumption of goods and services, by all forms of government, although not as large as in many West European countries, still amounts to over one-fifth of the GNP[44]—a respectable *masse de manoeuvre* in conducting the nation's economic policy. Of course, the division of powers between the individual states and the Federal authority creates special problems for the conduct of a coherent domestic policy. But federalism by itself hardly accounts for the extraordinary propensity to fragment authority at the very centre of the life of the nation.

In order to see just how far the United States deviates from the techniques of government in other Western societies, where the general trend is to use

---

[42] Neustadt (*Presidential Power*, p. 191) does at the same time make some interesting practical suggestions for mitigating the divisions in American government, e.g. by reforming the electoral process, so that President and Congress are both elected at the same time and serve for the same period.

[43] Partly derived from a not very accurate interpretation by Montesquieu of English 18th-century practice.

the aggregation of public power in order to create a coherent force whose significance will be greater than the sum of its individual parts, it is necessary to examine the detail of the curious disorder which seems to have been deliberately organized at the heart of the American administrative process.[45] There are altogether over eighty different government departments and agencies which report direct to the President of the United States. They are not grouped in any hierarchy which would permit the President to restrict his dealings to a smaller number of intermediaries who would make reports and carry back the Government's decisions to the agency chiefs. Each of them has the right of access to the man at the top and is determined to use it. It is almost inconceivable that a coherent policy could emerge out of an administrative welter of this kind. Its effect under any but the strongest President is to turn the offices of the Government into a loose confederation of more or less hostile bodies competing with one another for more money and more power.

The competition for money is perhaps the one salutary aspect of the situation. It means that the agencies are constantly forced to refer to the Bureau of the Budget for permission to spend more. The Budget Bureau has, indeed, over recent years come to be the chief instrument for the co-ordination of government available to the President. It is not only the sole authority for the spending of money; it has also been given the job of formulating the whole of the Government's legislative programme for each session of Congress. In theory this task is merely one of bringing together the bits and pieces of legislation proposed by all the various government departments and then presenting the result in a tidy form to the President for his approval. This is in line with the fiction that the Director of the Budget Bureau is a rather subordinate member of the government apparatus, without even a place in the Cabinet. (Franklin Roosevelt himself was sufficiently caught up in this illusion of the 'non-political' character of the Budget Bureau to offer at one stage to make the post of Director a career civil servant appointment.) In fact, the job of 'legislative reference' performed by the Director, when he decides which bills shall take precedence in the queue of government business and which shall go to the bottom or be left out altogether, is the closest that any member of an American Government gets to the power exercised by the Leader of the House of Commons in Britain. The difference is that in America he still has to wait on the pleasure of the Chairman of the Rules Committee before a government bill is allowed to go before Congress and be voted on. The US Budget Director also has some of the power that normally goes with the UK head of the civil service; he is supposed to ensure that official business gets done and to sort out jurisdictional disputes about the boundaries of authority between competing government agencies. It is freely

[45] The argument which follows incorporates part of the text of my article, 'Transatlantic Differences', which appeared in *Encounter*, Sept. 1963.

admitted inside the Bureau of the Budget that it is much easier in practice to work out the most complex legislative programme than to compel a couple of government departments with overlapping spheres of influence to agree on which of them shall do what.

The most striking example of free-wheeling government is provided by the Federal Agencies, which regulate a host of basic economic activities including railroads, oil and electric power, air travel and shipping, radio and television. An examination of these agencies provides an insight into the mood and atmosphere in which the American Administration conducts its affairs, and points to the obstacles that would have to be overcome before this style of doing business could accommodate a set of coherent policies. The system originated with the belated effort to assert the public interest in the management and the fixing of rates on the American railroads in the 1880s. Congress was loth to hand this power over to the Department of the Interior, which had up till then been responsible for railway matters, because this would have strengthened the power of the executive and ultimately of the President.[46] On the other hand, Congress realized that it could not itself directly hand down the stream of decisions which would be necessary to ensure the effective supervision of the railways. It therefore set up in 1887 an independent executive agency, the Inter-State Commerce Commission, which was not subject to any government department or indeed to the President's own orders. This was regarded as a triumph for the legislature in its constant struggle to curb the power of the central government, which was firmly established by then as the chief menace to the freedom of the individual citizen. Since the area of government regulation could not be prevented from growing, in view of the way that private enterprise, not in railways only but also in other spheres, impinged increasingly on the public interest, the best solution was to break it up. It was a new variety of the traditional pluralist formula: if you can't lick it, atomize it.

Moreover the legislators came to see the independent Federal Agency as a special instrument for the assertion of its own power—an 'arm of Congress', it was called, inside the executive. The formula was used increasingly during the twentieth century as the range of activities which had to be regulated or promoted by the Federal Government widened—banking and credit through the Federal Reserve Board, business practices through the Federal Trade Commission, the stock exchange through the Securities and Exchange Commission, right through to the establishment of the Atomic Energy Commission, after the last war. In fact the decision whether to place some new governmental activity inside an existing department under the control of the

---

[46] The President of the day, Grover Cleveland, happened to be a former railroad lawyer (see Mark S. Massel, in *Administrative Regulation, Law and Contemporary Problems* (Duke Univ.), Spring 1961, to which I am indebted for much of what follows on the subject of the regulatory agencies).

President or whether to float it off in a separate agency was pretty haphazard. However it was necessary to create some doctrine which would provide the theoretical framework for this curiously separate piece of government. One of the things which all the agencies appeared to have in common was that they interfered, more or less, with private business. They could be treated as a set of regrettable exceptions to the principle of *laissez-faire* capitalism— itself, in the national myth, the guarantor of the freedom of the individual from oppression by the Government. Here was the justification for picking out this one sphere of activity for Congress's special attention.

Nor was this all. Because the typical work of the Federal Agency involved it in relations which could either help or hinder private enterprise—sometimes make or break it—its primary role was thought to be a judicial one.[47] Characteristically, its function as an instrument of positive government, which ought at its best to secure the public good with the minimum of friction, was underplayed; all the emphasis was on its appearance in the guise of a judge between competing private interests. Professor M. H. Bernstein sums up the historical process which led to this curious device as follows: 'The inability to come to terms with the political character of regulation has been glorified as an honourable escape from politics, and it has sanctified the drive towards further judicialisation of administrative regulation.'[48]

The judicial rot, once it set in, went deep. In the effort to establish a consistent doctrine for the regulatory agencies, the lawyers have tried to isolate and heighten the judicial element in the process. More and more the trend

[47] e.g. Massel (ibid., p. 193) estimates that 'a television licence in a town of moderate size can be worth between $3 and $4 million'. No payment is made for this franchise. The trouble, and the public expense and finally the enormous delays incurred through the insistence on the full judicial treatment, designed to ensure 'equal opportunity' for all contenders, have been described by Newton N. Minow, Chairman of the Federal Communications Commission, 1961–3:

'When an applicant seeks a television license, he fills out the prescribed application forms and the regulatory processing begins. If it is a desirable channel, then, wholly apart from the massive influence the broadcaster will have upon his viewers, the license is also worth millions of dollars. Willing contenders compete vigorously for the prize. The contest will cost the applicant many hundreds of thousands of dollars and the government invests a staggering sum of man-hours and dollars to determine the winners.

'To make the choice, the FCC follows a course prescribed by law. There will be a hearing on the public record before a trained Examiner, followed by appeals and arguments to the Commission, followed by appeals and arguments to the courts. The transcript will run into thousands of pages with hundreds of charts and exhibits. While I served at the Commission, we sometimes heard cases that had begun as long as five, ten, and even fifteen years earlier. Once, while testifying in Congress, I was asked about the status of a specific case, and upon checking I discovered that it had begun when I was in the army in India during World War II. It is still pending' (*The Mazes of Modern Government* (Santa Barbara, Calif., Center for the Study of Democratic Institutions, 1964)).

[48] See *Administrative Regulation* (Duke University, Spring 1961), p. 330.

has been to hive off the 'judges' (who are usually the most senior people) from the rest of the staff, whose business is to promulgate administrative laws governing the activities which fall within the agency's responsibility. For example, the five Commissioners who are in charge of the Federal Trade Commission are not allowed to consult their own staff of economists and accountants when they are reviewing a case. This is because their impartiality as judges might be reduced through receiving advice from someone engaged in the formulation of long-term policy for the Government.

The result of this kind of attitude is that the people with ultimate authority in the field of policy tend to abdicate it to the junior officials, in order to keep their own minds clear and their hearts pure for the vital judicial process. Like some tireless primitive organism exclusively concerned with reproduction, these agencies divide themselves again into yet more parts, each with an independent body and soul. It has to be understood that, in the American context, it is the judicial role which attracts high public esteem. Lesser people merely make policy—and, if they value a quiet life, they make as little of it as possible, at any rate overtly. For once a Federal Agency lays down a general rule governing some activity which it is supposed to supervise, Congress is tempted to question it. It is, after all, a piece of rival legislation. But so long as the agencies stick to the business of case-by-case judgement, the legislators will be less inclined to feel that they ought to argue about the outcome of a judicial ritual. Thus a large slice of American government is farmed out in pieces to a number of individuals who neither know nor are expected to care about the long-range purposes of the President and his administration. It is the principle of *anti-planning* deliberately elevated into a way of life.

The central government can from time to time make its influence felt through the Bureau of the Budget. All Federal Agencies need some legislation at some stage, in order to cope with their tasks; their place in the queue depends on the goodwill of the Director of the Budget Bureau. But if a majority on some Federal Commission decides to oppose the Government's policies, the President cannot get rid of them. Commissioners cannot be prevented from serving out their full term of office, which is usually about five years. It is only when that is over that the President can bring in his own men to conduct the policies that he desires. It may take more than one presidential term to alter the composition of a Federal Agency sufficiently to provide a majority for some new policy. That may sometimes be too long to wait, not only for the President, but also for some of his appointees.[49]

---

[49] For example, Newton Minow, the radical Chairman of the FCC, appointed by Kennedy in 1961, was able to make little impression on his fellow Commissioners, largely hard-line Republican nominees left over from the Eisenhower régime, and retired after two years.

Government by Bargaining—with Exceptions

It may be thought that the independent Federal Agencies are an offbeat and eccentric manifestation of a certain riotous pluralism in US public life. On the contrary, their aims and ideals pervade the whole system of American government. Each Bureau within a government department aims to secure the maximum freedom of manoeuvre, and generally thinks of itself as being connected with the Cabinet minister who is officially in charge of the department only by the loosest rein. Some of the subordinate offices of government, like the Bureau of Land Reclamation (Department of the Interior) or the Corps of Engineers (Army), are notorious for the way in which they have built up their autonomous power by peddling their influence both outside and inside Congress. A mere Cabinet minister would think twice before ordering them to perform some action which conflicted with the ideas of the Bureau chiefs. Each Bureau takes pains to organize its own 'constituency' of people who are dependent on its goodwill and interested in maintaining its independent power. The civil contractors behind the Bureau of Land Reclamation, for example, are known to be a formidable lot with an extensive influence in Congress. They could, if they were crossed, make life very awkward for a minister when he came on the unavoidable trip to Capitol Hill to ask a Congressional Committee for support on some task for which he needed legislative authority. There is no secret made about the process of mutual backscratching; it is accepted in Washington as the natural way of life of a society in which power is dispersed. Chairmen of powerful Congressional Committees will make it quite clear to a high officer of state appointed by the President that he will not get his way on A unless he makes a deal on B, even though it has no apparent connexion with the case.

Bargaining is the essence of government. So everyone tries to have something to bargain with. Autonomy inside and influence outside the executive are recognized as the two main instruments. It is regarded as normal for a subordinate organ of government to seek to strengthen both. Congress for its part encourages the process openly: it is its special contribution in the fight against 'big government'. Thus the budget of a department is broken down and allocated in advance to the subordinate Bureaus; the heads of these Bureaus are then asked to come before the Congressional Committees and justify their claims for funds or explain how the money already spent has been used.

This constant stimulus to rivalry is applied to the armed forces too, and shows up in competition for funds between different branches of the same service—e.g. in the Navy Department between the sailors in the Bureau of Ships (BuShips) and the airmen in the Bureau of Aeronautics (BuAer) over a project like the Polaris missile. The planners of Polaris, when they started the project in 1956, wisely decided to bypass these jurisdictional disputes by setting up an entirely new office, the Special Projects Office, inside the Navy Department with the right to draw people in from any arm of the service. Only in this way was it possible to overcome the natural inertia of service departments, which have been graphically described as 'holding companies' for a number of government Bureaus, each with its own separate and diverse interest. As Samuel Huntington puts it: 'The Services become holding companies serving a variety of purposes rather than integrated companies devoted to a unifying goal.'[50]

Congress is constantly seeking new levers of power to insert in the hidden interstices of government. One such device which proved especially efficient was the ruling, which Congress imposed on President Truman in 1949, that the individual members of the Joint Chiefs of Staff were to be empowered to speak to any Congressional Committee freely in their own personal capacity, without any commitment to the official line of policy adopted by the government. Since the members of the JCS are put there with the expectation that they will represent the interests, as well as express the expertise, of each of the armed services, it is a well established forum for bargaining. Congress was able to ensure that the bargaining would not be confined within the walls of the Defense Department, but would be extended into a richer and more dramatic argument on Capitol Hill. This changed after Robert McNamara appeared in Washington in 1961 as Secretary of Defense in the new Democratic Administration, and seriously set about the task of converting the US military effort into a coherent enterprise. But until then the arrangements with Congress had provided much aid and comfort to each of the services in their struggle to counter the threat of a co-ordinated US defence policy.

When public power is systematically fragmented, its ability to control the over-mighty subject tends to be weakened. In the American context there is also the effect of a species of officially sponsored inferiority complex in regard to any form of public enterprise; it is clearly expressed in the directive of the Bureau of the Budget quoted at the beginning of this chapter. The underlying doctrine of that directive is: anything the public sector can do, the private can do better. Its explicit reference is admittedly confined to the production of goods and services—this is where the private alternative must invariably be preferred—but it would be reasonable to expect that some of the distrust for public initiative would spill over into other activities of the state. That perhaps explains why it is a commonly heard complaint that the officials of some Federal Agency are acting as the representatives and spokesmen for the people whom they are supposed to supervise. In a competitive system of government, where effective administrative power often is drawn from sources outside the official machine, an official may easily come to

---

[50] *The Common Defense: Strategic Programs in National Politics* (New York, Columbia UP, 1961).

regard it as part of his normal function to seek the goodwill of his 'constituency'.

But this is by no means the consistent pattern of official behaviour when it is called upon to regulate the affairs of private industry. We have already observed[51] that some government controls over the activities of private enterprise in the United States are unusually fierce, by the standards of other countries. The Food and Drug Administration since the reforms of 1962 has introduced rules requiring positive proof of the efficacy claimed for any medicinal preparation, which are extremely stringent. And actions like the seizure of three different 'anti-wrinkle' preparations by officials of the FDA in the summer of 1964[52] suggest that the officials who have been armed with these extra powers are not inhibited about using them promptly. They demanded scientific evidence, which was very hard to come by, that wrinkles were actually removed as a result of the treatment proposed. In the same spirit the Federal Trade Commission in 1964 ordered tobacco manufacturers 'to disclose clearly and prominently' on all packets of cigarettes that 'cigarette smoking is dangerous to health and may cause death from cancer and other diseases'.[53] This was regarded by the tobacco companies as far harsher treatment than anything that had been meted out to them in other countries which prided themselves oh their systems of social welfare and protection.

It might be argued that hazards to health and use of drugs have an emotional significance which put them in a class apart. But officials from other departments have at times been equally aggressive in their behaviour towards private enterprise, when they conceived that it was not abiding by the rules of the game. One outstanding case, which occurred during the militant pro-business crusade at the beginning of the Eisenhower régime in the early 1950s, concerned the use of a chemical called AD-X2, which when added to a battery was supposed to make it last longer. The Bureau of Standards tried some tests and decided that the chemical did not in fact add anything to the life of batteries. The Post Office then refused permission for the use of the US mail service for the transmission of advertisements for this product. This is a powerful sanction which has been used in other cases to prevent the propagation of falsehood by advertisers. The Secretary of Commerce, Sinclair Weeks, was furious and tried to sack the head of the Bureau of Standards. His testimony to a Congressional Committee which was investigating the affair in 1953 reads like the apotheosis of the spirit of private enterprise. 'I am not a man of science . . .', he said, 'but as a practical man, I think that the National Bureau of Standards has not been sufficiently objective because they discount entirely the play of the market place.' But

[51] See above, pp. 299 ff.
[52] See *The Economist*, 6 June 1964.
[53] Quoted in *Financial Times*, 25 June 1964. The regulation was due to come into force in 1965.

Congress upheld the Bureau of Standards, and in the end both the Secretary of Commerce and the makers of AD-X2 had to admit defeat.[54]

It is not claimed that this case is typical. But what it shows is that when a government office possesses an established status, like the Bureau of Standards, and is also supported by Congress, it can exercise effective power. It is, after all, unusual even in the most advanced welfare states for the Post Office to take responsibility for the scientific veracity of advertising claims made on behalf of some not very important consumer product. The significant point, however, is that all these examples are concerned with matters where government intervention can be justified ultimately by reference to some simple true-or-false criterion. Public authority is seen, once again, to be active and confident once it appears in a judge's robe.

Judicial Instruments for Political Ends

Yet in practice the line between the judicial and the policy decision is often a blurred one. Perhaps the outstanding example of the deliberate employment of the judicial process to develop the content and extend the range of official policy is the behaviour of the Anti-Trust Division of the Department of Justice. There can be no doubt about the aggressive ideological spirit in which the 300 lawyers on the payroll of the Division set about their task. They do not conceive it to be their duty merely to uncover the individual wrong-doer and bring him to justice. As a senior member of the Division, G. B. Spivack, put it, these officials have other functions 'as well as imposing punishment or obtaining relief in a particular situation'—notably they must help to create 'a social environment in which businessmen are induced to conduct their businesses in accordance with not only the letter but also the spirit of the Anti-Trust laws'.[55] Again, when the Anti-Trust Division lawyers are engaged in litigation, they should not be exclusively concerned with the merits of the particular case; they 'should consider how valuable a conviction based on particular evidence and particular issues might be on subsequent damage suits in determining their trial strategy and tactics'.[56]

When the methods actually employed by these lawyers are examined at closer hand, it becomes clear that their power over American industry extends

---

[54] F. C. Newman and S. S. Surrey, eds., *U.S. Legislation: Cases and Materials* (Englewood Cliffs, N.J., Prentice Hall, 1955). The chairman of the FTC giving evidence before the Commerce Committee in 1964 in the cigarette labelling case explained the wide-ranging principles guiding his intervention in the market place as follows: 'The Commission has the authority to proceed against any actual or potential deception in the sale . . . of any product in commerce. . . . Such deception may result either from a direct statement concerning a product or a failure to disclose any material facts relating to such product' (see *Financial Times*, 25 June 1964).

[55] British Inst. of Internat. & Comparative Law, Conference on Comparative Aspects of Anti-Trust Law in the US, the UK and the EEC, *Report*, Suppl. 6, 1963.

[56] Ibid.

much further than the identification and suppression of monopolistic practices. Through the Justice Department's 'consent orders'—that is an arrangement whereby the authorities consent to certain business practices which have been questioned, but on condition that the business concerned obeys a number of specific instructions in the conduct of its future policy—the government engages increasingly in detailed interventions which influence the structure of whole industries. These consent orders are in fact the result of what Mark S. Massel has called 'shirt sleeve negotiations' between the Anti-Trust Division and the individual management concerned, a bargain on business conduct in return for a promise to be left alone.[57]   Moreover, the legal action and the court case are often used merely as a device to put an official stamp on a decision whose essentials have already been agreed in private. 'The Anti-Trust Division', Massel says, 'frequently formulates the complaint after it has negotiated the consent decree.'[58]   Matters which have been subjected to official supervision in this way include the disposal of patents (an order that certain firms must be given the opportunity of acquiring them), the future behaviour of a business under examination towards firms which are dependent on it, either as suppliers or customers, and even the manner in which a concern is to conduct the affairs of its sales department.   A notable instance of the latter was the case of International Business Machines[59] which was directed to dispose of fewer of its data-processing machines under rental agreements and to increase its proportion of outright sales.   This was specifically intended to loosen the company's established hold on the goodwill of its rental customers.   By the early 1960s there had in fact been a noticeable shift in the composition of IBM's sales, with a diminished, though still large, proportion of rented machines.[60]

The special character of the American anti-trust operations becomes very clear when one tries to transpose them into some other national context.   It is hard to imagine a British judge being called upon to decide not the question of ascertainable fact about the existence or not of monopolistic conditions in a given market, but whether a particular merger between two firms *was likely at some future date* to create conditions in an industry which would weaken the competitive process in it.   The conclusion reached must depend on such factors as the judge's interpretation of an underlying historical trend. Is this an industry, he must ask himself, where technological developments or the possible management success of particular firms or the financial backing at their disposal will probably lead to certain changes in ownership over the next ten or twenty years?   Thus in the crucial Brown Shoe case in 1962

[57] *Administrative Regulation*.   Massel estimates that 'between 85 and 90 per cent of the consent decrees of recent years have been negotiated in this manner' (p. 192).
[58] *Ibid*.   [59] The decision was issued in a consent order of 25 Jan. 1956.
[60] This was assisted by the independent decision of the Department of Defense in the early 1960s, to buy its computers, on grounds of economy, instead of renting them as it had done in the past.

the Supreme Court refused to allow a large but by no means dominant shoe manufacturing firm, Brown—the third largest in the industry—to buy out a firm of footwear retailers, Kinney, who were responsible for less than 2 per cent of retail sales, on the ground that by tying up this retail outlet the scope for Brown's competitors would be diminished. The essential point was that the Court came to the conclusion that, on the evidence available, there was in this industry a trend towards vertical integration by the larger manufacturers which threatened in the long run to create a situation in which a few big firms dominated the market.[61]

Now, it was not suggested that this particular firm, Brown, producing less than 10 per cent of the output of the footwear industry, would be able, by itself, to have a significant effect on competition. It could not therefore be held to have transgressed any regulation laid down by public authority. Yet the firm was penalized by having this important commercial transaction declared illegal, because of a judgement about the probable future behaviour of other persons whom it could not in any case control. As one American lawyer has remarked, this kind of doctrine 'requires the Federal courts to make economic judgements of a kind that would seem entirely non-judicial to most civilian [i.e. exponents of Roman civil law] and British observers'.[62] Such judgements would also be regarded in Britain as intolerably unfair to the individual firm which found that a normal commercial transaction had become illegal because it affected some long-range objective of public policy concerning the future structure of an industry. This is an essential point of principle. In the traditional British system there is no place for the use of the courts to further some evolving purpose of public administration. In America there is.[63]

Moreover, the purpose itself is frequently subject to considerable intellectual confusion. It is not clear on what principle vertical mergers, like Brown Shoe, should be treated more strictly than horizontal mergers (i.e. those within the same branch of industry or trade). A recent judgement suggests that the barrier to acquisition applies in the latter case only when the new business resulting from the combination accounts for 30 per cent or more of the sales in its market.[64] Then there is the problem of what are termed 'conglomerate mergers'—unions between firms of significant size in industries which are not related at all to one another. These have become a matter of particular concern to the Anti-Trust Division in recent years. It does not like them. It feels that these powerful and diversified industrial groups, which have 'deep pockets' out of which to finance the operations of their individual member

---

[61] H. M. Blake, 'Mergers and US Anti-Trust Law', *Internat. and Comparative Law Q.*, Suppl. 6 (1963), p. 88.   [62] Ibid.

[63] G. B. Spivack (ibid., p. 49) says that it is a principle 'clearly established that the court may not only prohibit otherwise lawful activity and direct action not otherwise required by law, but may also reorganise corporate structures'.

[64] Ibid. See *US* v. *Philadelphia National Bank*, 1963.

companies, place any new entrant to an 'industry affected by a conglomerate merger' at an unfair disadvantage.[65]   But there is no clear doctrine in sight which will allow businesses contemplating a deal to predict how their case will be treated.   The only safe thing to do is to get permission in advance, by persuading the authorities that the arrangement will, in some sense, positively serve the public interest.   To succeed a firm must, in fact, be able to offer its collaboration in the pursuit of some objective of policy which transcends the mere making of extra profits.

Observing the aggressive interventionist spirit of public power in this instance and the readiness with which private enterprise is guided by official directives, based on a good deal of administrative discretion, one is led to ask whether the obstacles to positive centralized government in the United States are, after all, as great as the earlier argument seemed to suggest.   If the trust-busters can do it, why not those in charge of social welfare or bodies concerned with economic planning?   The answer seems to be that anti-trust in the United States is a unique case; it is best understood when it is treated as a form of national religion.   Moreover, unlike the other, merely theological religions in the United States, the propagation of this one doctrine by public means is entirely constitutional.   Indeed the whole American way of life is believed to depend on it: it is the only firm guarantee of pluralism, the only defence against overwhelming private power.   Public authority having been deliberately weakened by division, private power must be kept divided too.

[65] Ibid

XIV

UNITED STATES POLICY IN THE 1960s

THE last chapter surveyed some of the ideological and institutional impedimenta which American policy-makers have to carry around with them. The conclusion that emerged was that what the Americans have to carry is pretty solid and weighty stuff—in contrast with the Germans, where a similarly impressive baggage train turned out, on inspection, to include a large number of half-empty suitcases. The outcome shows up very clearly in the contrasting German and American attitudes towards the business of government. Whereas the Germans instinctively concentrate public power, the Americans divide and diffuse it. The American instinct is, besides, non-interventionist: if public authority has a choice, it generally opts for the role of referee rather than that of manager.[1] There is no evidence of any comparable political inhibition on the German side. In this matter American political assumptions about the relationship between public and private power are closer to British traditional practice, whose remarkable staying power was described in Chapter VI, than to anything in Germany. The explicit ideology seems to be of less account than the implicit content of established institutions. However, the British are equipped, unlike the Americans, with a unitary and hierarchical form of executive government, which is fully capable of projecting a single set of centrally determined policies to cover the whole national economy. The basic prerequisites for planning therefore exist in Britain—even though the administrative habits required to make a success of the planner's task have not yet been much cultivated. In America, there is no reason why the competing centres of power concerned with different aspects of economic policy should ever agree.[2]

[1] Though not invariably. We saw at the end of the last chapter how in the sphere of anti-trust the judicial approach spills over into political interventionism of an active and detailed kind.

[2] The following interchange between Mr William M. Martin, Chairman of the Federal Reserve Board, and Senator Russell Long, in the Senate Finance Committee (Aug. 1957), illustrates the nature and extent of the problem:

'*Mr Martin*: . . . In the field of money and credit, . . . regardless of what the decisions of the Administration may be—we consult with them but we feel that we have the authority if we think that in our field, money and credit policies, that we should act differently than they, we feel perfectly at liberty to do so.

'*Senator Long*: In other words you feel that you have freedom . . . to adopt policies that may not be the policy of the Administration itself?

'*Mr Martin*: That is right. . . .

'*Senator Long*: And you believe that the Federal Reserve Board, if it does disagree, has the right to pursue a policy that is completely contrary to the policy that the

330

It is true that the same forces which we have observed at work in other countries have also been pressing on the United States government. Above all there is a growing demand for better control over fluctuations in business activity and employment. Yet as late as 1957, Mr George Humphrey, the Secretary of the Treasury and one of the most powerful influences on the domestic policies of the Eisenhower Cabinet, made it clear that he would resign rather than accept the use of a budget deficit as a legitimate means of avoiding an economic depression.[3] This was typical of the sentiment which continued, even after Humphrey's departure from the Cabinet, to inform the later years of the Eisenhower Administration. The chronicle of the fiascos of that period has already been recounted; so has the deliberate change of course after President Kennedy took office at the head of the Democratic Administration in 1961.[4] From 1961 onwards each successive year brought some fresh stimulus by the Government to economic growth, culminating in the series of massive cuts in taxation in 1964–5. It required a great spiritual heave, and a major propaganda effort, before the American legislature could convince itself that it was decent to aim deliberately at a budget deficit in a period when business was good. Deficits which happened because of a down-turn in business and employment could just about be borne, as acts of God. But to cut taxes below what were known to be the needs of government expenditure, merely in order to impart an extra boost to economic activity, to take effect some time in the future when it was thought that it might be flagging, was a moral decision of some gravity.

Having achieved this break-through, the makers of American economic policy have embarked on the systematic exploitation of their new opportunity. Henceforth the technique of tax-cutting, abetted by increases in government expenditure, will continue to be applied—at any rate while a Democratic Administration remains in power—until unemployment has been brought down to the target figure of 4 per cent.[5] In early 1965, after four years of continuous economic expansion, unemployment still stood at 5 per cent.

A simple, though ingenious, accounting device has been used to make the

Administration proceeds to follow, not meaning that you are doing this or that you have done it, but that you feel that under the law you do have that right?

'*Mr Martin*: Under the law we feel it is our prerogative; yes sir.'

To appreciate the practical significance of this 'prerogative' it should be remembered that the Chairman of the FRB has a 14-year tenure of office and during the period is as irremovable as a judge, whereas the President of the US is elected to his office for four years only and may at best stay for eight. One of the controversial reforms proposed in the early 1960s was that the terms of office of the Chairman and the President should coincide with one another (see 'The Federal Reserve System after fifty years', Hearings before the Subcommittee on Domestic Finance, vol. 3, 1964).

[3] *New York Times*, 17 Jan. 1957.   [4] See above, pp. 29–30 and 56–58.

[5] As indicated above (p. 15), there is a difference of nearly 1 per cent in the official US and British figures of unemployment caused by the use of different techniques of measurement. The American figure of 4 per cent would on the British basis be close to 3 per cent.

whole operation morally acceptable to the American public. Budget receipts are calculated not only on the basis of the actual prospect for the year ahead, but also in a separate account on the expectation of the revenue that *would* accrue if the economy were operating at the target rate of 4 per cent unemployment. On the second basis the Federal Budget for the fiscal year 1964–5 was shown to be in approximate balance—though of course in actual deficit. Moreover, there was the promise of further tax cuts in the years after that, because at the rate of economic expansion that was anticipated once the economy had reached this 'full employment' level, an additional $6 billion of revenue was estimated to accrue to the exchequer each year.[6]

The Government has at the same time sought to extend its specific powers to deal with short-term fluctuations in the economy. President Johnson asked Congress in his 'State of the Union' message at the beginning of 1965 to embark on two reforms which are familiar from the practices developed by West European countries since the war. One was the creation of a special fund available for use by the Government at short notice for 'job-creating public programmes' if a business recession threatened; and the other was a new procedure to produce a quick cut in taxes if this was judged to be necessary in order to give an extra boost to a flagging economy. Both ideas were tactfully presented, so as not to appear to be whittling away either the spending or the taxing powers of Congress; these are very tender subjects indeed.[7] But the intention behind the Administration's policy is nevertheless clear: it is to concentrate a greatly enhanced tactical control over economic policy under the thumb of the Government. Admittedly, the public works fund proposed is not thought of as anything so elaborate as a 'shelf' of planned investment projects ready for use at short notice, on the Swedish model[8]; but it is reasonable to expect that, once established, it would readily evolve into something of this sort fairly quickly. Having got the principle accepted, the demands of technical efficiency, especially in an American context, could be relied upon to do the rest. Similarly, the scheme for accelerated tax-cutting does not quite amount to a 'regulator', of the kind with which the British Government equipped itself in the early 1960s for short-term control of the economy.[9] But the essential purpose is the same.

All told, these American policies of the mid-1960s bear a close resemblance to the moves which were taking place in Germany at about the same time.[10] Cautiously and belatedly, both countries were trying to provide themselves with a modern armoury of economic weapons of a Keynesian type. The striking thing is how long it took before the intellectual message delivered

[6] OECD, *Econ. Surveys, United States*, 1964, p. 12.
[7] President Kennedy had asked Congress to grant him similar powers, without success.
[8] See above, p. 202.
[9] See above, p. 107. The main difference is that the British Government can act first and then argue with Parliament afterwards.
[10] See above, pp. 288–9.

more than a quarter of a century earlier was translated into practical politics. In Germany the delay could be at least partially explained by a certain intellectual backwardness in the field of economics, dating from the Hitler era. No such excuse is available to the Americans. They were the intellectual leaders in this business. They were, however, also the outstanding institutional laggards.

Government and Business

The open question is whether the Americans will go on from the point that they have reached in the mid-1960s to the practice of regular economic planning in the West European style. We have seen how in other countries the choices which are imposed on government by the business of active short-term economic management, together with the problems incident to a full employment economy, always on the edge of inflationary trouble,[11] have tended to make for a new and much more intimate relationship between public and private power. This is the political meaning of planning in a mixed economy of the modern capitalist type. Its expression is the establishment of a single framework of long-range policy in unison between private enterprise and public authority.

In 1962 Professor Edward S. Mason devoted his presidential address to the American Economic Association[12] to an examination of European planning experience and its possible application to the United States. He found compelling reasons why the European, and more particularly the French, method was likely to be rejected. Chief of them was the general attitude of Americans, and of American business especially, towards government. The important fact, he said, was 'that the really revolutionary changes in the role of government and in the relations of various groups to government produced by the great depression and the war have not yet been fully accepted in this country'. On the government side there was an established tradition of 'contracting out' to private enterprise the activities which it wished to support.[13] 'Government has gone very far in turning over to, or permitting business participation in, decisions which elsewhere are made only by government. . . . This is one reason why Federal employment has not increased as rapidly as

[11] An outstanding feature of the American experience of continuous economic growth, without full employment, from 1961 until 1965 was the comparative stability of the price level. Wage costs per unit of output, which were almost continuously and sometimes steeply on the increase throughout Western Europe during that period, rose hardly at all in the US. It seems reasonable to attach some of the responsibility for the outcome to the comparatively weak bargaining position of American labour in conditions where the number of unemployed greatly exceeded the total of job vacancies.

[12] Reprinted in *AER*, Mar. 1963.

[13] Mason cites as examples the employment of private enterprise in publicly financed research and development and 'the loan insurance and loan guarantee schemes of the Federal Housing Authority'.

Federal expenditures.' Yet this favourable treatment of business interests by public authorities had not, Mason averred, led to any intimacy or sympathy between the two.

It is clear to the most obtuse observer that there is a much more distant relationship between business and government leadership in the United States than, say, in Britain, France or the Netherlands. The Federation of British Industries has an entrée to government, whether Conservative or Labour, that neither the National Association of Manufacturers nor the Chamber of Commerce has or, for that matter, would desire. A British businessman can say, "Some of my best friends are civil servants," and really mean it. This would be rare in the United States.

Mason saw the lack of rapport between these two groups as part of a general phenomenon of American life, which militates against easy communication between people working in different professions. After discussing the social effects of the 'geographical dispersion' of the population of the United States, he went on: 'The dispersion however does not adequately explain what seems to me a much sharper separation of élite groups, government, business, professional, artistic, academic, etc. than one encounters in most Western European countries. Despite the continuing rapid vertical social mobility in the United States, horizontal penetration appears to encounter greater difficulties.' There were, therefore, he concluded, major obstacles to the kind of collaboration between different centres of decision, outside and inside the government, which had made the French plans, with their targets for economic expansion, 'credible to the people who make investment decisions'. American conditions[14] 'tend to deprive such targets of the credibility they would need to possess in order significantly to affect business decision making'.

These views, coming from a respected academic figure with a close practical knowledge of American economic processes, must carry weight. Yet the assertion that American business is somehow divorced from the day-to-day activities of government seems odd, in the light of the picture of the Federal Agencies and Bureaus which emerged in Chapter XIII. Indeed, to an outside observer it seems rather that private enterprise has had some striking successes in actually capturing a number of enclaves inside the structure of the Federal government. And even where its marauding parties have not been able to establish full rights of conquest, they do seem in several instances to have taken up permanent residence inside and to be living on terms of equality with those officially in charge. The combination of Congressional pressures and the spontaneous desire of Bureau and Agency chiefs to live on

[14] Mason includes 'balance of payments considerations' as one of the factors that would tend to make American business especially sceptical about target rates of growth set by a national plan—which seems odd when one remembers that external payments represent a much smaller proportion of the American national product than of the French.

terms of amity with their 'constituents' has secured for a number of important interest groups a powerful influence over the decisions taken by the authorities charged with the supervision of their affairs. Some of these groups are so well entrenched—e.g. the organizations of civil contractors dealing with the Army Corps of Engineers, or those involved in the business of the Rural Electrification Administration, or those concerned with the distribution of favours by the Small Business Administration—that it is legitimate to describe what happens as joint government by public and private bodies.

The chairmen of certain Congressional Committees insist on being consulted about any decision of even moderate importance made by the Agencies or Bureaus subject to their surveillance. This is the channel through which the 'constituency' can make its voice formally heard. But the senior officials do not normally wait to learn about the views of outside interests from the members of their Congressional Committee or Subcommittee; it makes for less friction to consult them in advance. The Committee has a professional 'staff director', a man who usually makes it his business to be as well versed in the affairs of any government agency within his purview as the government officials themselves; and often the details of policy are worked out by a system of informal collaboration among the professionals, inside and outside the administration. It saves time and trouble.

The Real Impediment to Planning

Professor Mason's observations can, therefore, hardly have been intended to cover all aspects of government, including its varied 'regulatory' activities, but solely to the formulation of policy at the centre. We have seen that in practice the distinction between regulation and policy-making, a traditional favourite among American lawyers, frequently does not work. There is, however, an identifiable group of major government departments explicitly concerned with Policy (as opposed to policy)—broadly those departments whose chiefs are members of the President's Cabinet—and it may well be that in this sphere American business organizations do not readily penetrate. But probably the more significant element in the relationship between the government and business is contained in Professor Mason's second observation, about the difficulties of 'horizontal penetration'. Individual interest groups and other organized bodies inside and outside government tend instinctively to separate themselves off from the rest and to function as autonomous entities. Thus, even without the stimulus derived from the forays made by business interests, the structure of American government was already riddled with enclaves of its own making. The significant point is not, it seems, that organized business lacks ready access to the topmost level of the administrative apparatus; it is rather the doubt whether it would be able to settle the major practical issues which are of interest to the business community by penetrating there. Perhaps this is the real reason why the American business organizations do not 'desire', as Professor Mason says, 'the entrée' to the senior officials of the civil service which comparable organizations have in Britain.

We are therefore back with the old problem of the fragmentation of public authority, discussed in Chapter XIII. Can a society, which is devoted to this riot of pluralism in public as well as business affairs, plan itself? It is, in fact, the feebleness of the magnetic pull at the centre of the public sector which sets the pattern for the rest of society. And the weak magnet belongs to the constitution; its weakness is jealously guarded by Congress. The separation of powers, on the one hand, excludes the members of Congress from any direct part in the work of administration, but on the other hand gives them enormous powers of oversight of individual administrative acts. The Congressional system is indeed one of the very few examples of vital democratic control in the Western world today. The professionalism[15] of the best committees and their whole apparatus for conducting a dialogue with the Administration on equal terms are the admiration of other countries, where the parliamentary process seems to penetrate less and less into the important activities of government. Bertrand de Jouvenel has pointed out that the vitality of the American system of democratic control is reflected in the unique expansion of the physical appurtenances of Congress, above all their office space and staff, compared with those of the legislative bodies of other nations; the American legislature visibly reflects something of the growing range of modern government.[16]

It is not the powers of outside surveillance which by themselves necessarily inhibit either active or co-ordinated government. Swedish officials, for example, have to conduct their work in a goldfish bowl which is if anything

---

[15] Their expertise derives partly from the fact that the people concerned tend to stay with the jobs of surveillance assigned to them for a long time. A survey of the House of Representatives Appropriations Committee, which consists of 50 members manning more than a dozen subcommittees concerned with various aspects of government expenditure, showed that in 1961 the average member had spent 9·3 years on the Committee. The 15 professional staff employees included in the survey also showed remarkable constancy in their employment; they had an average of 10·7 years of service with the Committee (see R. F. Fenno, 'The House Appropriations Committee', *American Political Science Review*, June 1962). The average senior official appointed by the President normally stays in Washington a much shorter time than this. It is no wonder, therefore, that there is a natural nexus between the long-service professional civil servant, typically the head of a Bureau or some organization in the lower reaches of government, and the men running the Congressional Committees. Both are specialists in their subject. By contrast, the men holding the highest offices in government departments are, as one survey puts it, 'the transient amateurs who are often incapable of exerting firm control over the professional bureaucracy' (Bernstein, *The Job of the Federal Executive*, p. 86 (Brookings, 1958).

[16] 'On the evolution of forms of government', *Futuribles Studies in Conjecture* (Geneva, Droz, 1963). De Jouvenel remarks that even so, the physical growth of the Congressional establishment is 'insignificant' by comparison with that of the executive branch.

more transparent than the American.[17]   That has still left plenty of scope
for the development of Swedish central planning.   It is rather the special
conditions and the mood of Congressmen in their dealings with the executive—especially that part of the executive which they identify as 'big
government', as opposed to the individual Bureaus and Agencies dealing with
specialized matters.   Anywhere else one would expect that party discipline
would put a sufficient curb on the personal politics of members of Congressional Committees to provide, in normal circumstances, a steady majority in
support of the government's decisions.   The President of the United States
is, after all, the official leader of his party as well as the head of the executive;
so that if he has a majority in Congress, he should in theory be able to get
his way. But that is not how American parties work. Each of them is more
like a broad collection of disparate local interests, making a temporary
alliance at election times.   On any given piece of national legislation the
coalition may be deeply divided.   Indeed it is arguable that the absence of
party discipline, in the sense that it is understood in European politics, is, in
the long run, the biggest single factor impeding the exercise of systematic
initiative by the executive of the kind that is required for modern planning.
The emphasis on *cohérence*[18] in the making of policy, which is the characteristic feature of modern planning, the treatment of all aspects of the
economic activities of government, present and future, as interdependent parts
of a single system of aims and expectations, imposes fresh demands on the
relationship between legislature and executive.   The strain becomes impossible if the executive is not sufficiently sustained by a majority of the
legislature to embark on the comprehensive formulation of national policies.

There were signs after the landslide victory of the Democrats in the 1964
election that the way might be opened for closer liaison between the President
and his party's representatives in Congress than there had been for many years
past.   At any rate, the road-block in several Congressional Committees, which
had impeded the domestic policies of successive Democratic Administrations, as
a result of the tacit alliance between conservative Southern Democrats and
Northern Republicans, was being broken down.[19]   The essential issue is a

---

[17] See Nils Herlitz, 'Publicity of Official Documents in Sweden', *Public Law* (London,
Stevens, 1958) and below, p. 399.   [18] See above, p. 127.

[19] An important reform in the structure of Committees was the change from the
established 3:2 ratio (between majority and minority party representatives) in two
crucial Committees of the House of Representatives, the Ways and Means Committee and the Appropriations Committee.   On the new 2:1 basis, the liberal
Democrats were expected to be able to rely on a majority.   An interesting feature
of this and other reforms—including a new arrangement to limit the power of the
Chairman of the Rules Committee to keep legislation from being taken to the floor
of the House, which had been a serious impediment to the rapid execution of
government policy—is that they emerged out of a programme agreed among an
organized group of Democratic Congressmen, the so-called Democratic Study Group
consisting of 115 Representatives (see *The Economist*, 9 Jan. 1965, p. 116).   Such
a body as this, functioning between elections and working in close accord with the

change in the balance of initiatives between executive and legislature. A change in the balance of *power* between the two is not what is required. What the American system would have to provide, if it were to accommodate economic planning, is more room for administrative discretion. The exercise of such discretion in any particular case would remain subject to democratic control—but after the event, not before it. Perhaps the most pernicious device invented by Congressional Committees to stultify initiative in the use of public power is the technique of 'legislative veto'. This requires officials to give advance notice to Congress, or specifically to named Congressional Committees, *before* they undertake certain administrative acts which are a normal part of the work of their department. Sometimes there is specific provision in the law for a Committee veto on these actions; but even the requirement of 'advance notice' is a sizeable impediment to efficient administration.[20] In recent years there has been increasing resistance by the President to these Congressional invasions of administrative authority; and President Johnson in particular has rejected them outright.[21]

The Limits of Ideology

If in this argument about the impediments to planning in the United States I have put the main emphasis squarely on the structure of government, it is not out of disregard for other important objections that would almost certainly be made to any such proposal, notably the ideological objections. These constitute the most obvious immediate barrier to movement in the direction which Western Europe has taken. Indeed, the one experiment in a tentative approach to indicative planning so far undertaken was defeated in the sphere of ideas, before it had even had a chance to come to grips with the problem of institutions. The experiment was an interesting one, partly because of its use of what may be termed the technique of intellectual infiltration. No one admitted officially that what they were trying to do was to persuade the various departments of government and the leaders of private enterprise to make decisions in unison about the future, by the use of a common framework of aims and expectations.

Administration, *could* provide the nucleus of a system out of which the regular exercise of party discipline might grow. But it is hard to envisage the emergence of someone resembling the conventional party whip, unless there are some sanctions that he can apply against recalcitrant party members. There is no sign at the time of writing of any device which would serve this purpose. The most obvious means of pressure would be provided by a large centrally administered party election fund, on which loyal members of the party, but not others, would be able to draw for the finance of their election campaigns. The growing expense of American elections may thus turn out to be, in the long run, a force making for more party discipline.

[20] See Joseph P. Harris, *Congressional Control of Administration* (Washington, Brookings Institution, 1964).
[21] See above, p. 109 n. 28.

What happened was that shortly after the Kennedy Administration took office in 1961 the President's Council of Economic Advisers produced a document called 'Full Employment Perspective' which tried to look ahead, on certain closely defined assumptions, to what might happen to the economy in 1963. Great pains were taken to insist that it was 'not a forecast'.[22] However the form of the exercise immediately aroused suspicion. This was because the businesses to which it was circulated found, at the end of the Government's own forward estimates, a blank table which they were asked to fill in, giving their own calculations of what their output, their investment, their employment, dividends etc. would be in the year 1963, on the basis of the same assumptions as those made by the Government. The businessmen did not like it. They felt that the hypothetical exercise was in danger of getting out of hand and impinging on reality.

They were, of course, right in their assessment of the intention behind the document. The man responsible for the venture was Professor James Tobin, one of the three members of the Council of Economic Advisers, and there is no doubt that he intended the results to be used as the basis for a more elaborate guide to long-range economic policy. Once the answers from the important firms or industrial groups came in, the next stage would have been to try to weld the various calculations made by the public and the private sectors into a single consistent model of the economy. The answer would no doubt have provided scope for the construction of several alternative models. Businessmen—and government bodies—would have to start choosing, and arguing about their choice. But even before that, each of the alternative models would probably have involved some modification of the forecasts and plans of individual enterprises and industries. Once these alternatives began to be passed back and forth among the people concerned, followed by discussions aiming at a consensus on the model which was most acceptable for the year in question, something rather like the planning effort of the French *commissions de modernisation* would have been achieved.

Beyond that stage it was possible to envisage that government economic policy would have been equipped to develop a more powerful directional thrust; having secured this insight into the private sector's plans, the Government might have been tempted to push and prod business management, whenever it considered that some part of the economy was not working according to the model. Was it the fear of this reinforcement of public authority *vis-à-vis* private enterprise which caused the angry rebellion against

---

[22] See OECD, International Trade Union Seminar, Paris, 22–25 Oct. 1963, *Economic and Social Programming (1964)*, p. 108, for an account of this document. The assumptions which it used for its own estimates included: 4 per cent unemployment; economic growth at 3·5 per cent per annum; an average price rise of 1·5 per cent per annum; government consumption 20 per cent of GNP; and an export surplus of $9 billion.

the operation? Those who were involved in the experiment on the government side believed that the reaction was not based on practical considerations of this type. It was more emotional than that. One of the officials concerned dismissed the incident of the meeting with the representatives of industry, which had brought the project to a premature end, with the comment that the government side had asked for a meeting with business economists and found itself instead facing a lot of 'business ideologists'. It was they who killed the scheme.

Yet it hardly seems plausible to interpret this incident as the simple expression of an overwhelming American hostility to any form of joint government and business forecasting for industrial purposes. At any rate the Department of Labour, using a somewhat different approach, was able in the early 1960s to develop a series of systematic forecasts of precisely this type. No doubt that was due in part to the established semantic prejudice which made 'manpower planning' a humane and honourable thing to do, whereas 'economic planning' was known to be plain wicked. There is a long history of public effort in the United States to make the most of immigrant manpower and to provide certain kinds of minimum training to enable people to earn their living. But in an age where a plan for the training and deployment of labour depends on anticipating the industrial skills which will be needed five or ten years ahead, what is required is indistinguishable from a long-range and fairly detailed economic forecast. The Department took up this task after the advent of the Kennedy Administration, when the main focus of American economic policy shifted to the problem of unemployment.[23] Five-year forecasts were made of the likely demand for labour of different types in a variety of industries, on the basis of certain assumptions about the state of the economy over the period. Three separate models were worked out using alternative assumptions.[24] Curiously, the Department of Labour found itself in dispute at this stage with the Council of Economic Advisers about the function of long-range economic planning as a primary technique of government. The Council, whose earlier experimental venture had aroused the hostility of the business world, attached little practical importance to planning, and contended that there was not much wrong with the American economy which the systematic application of Keynesian techniques for the

[23] Professor W. Leontief, the man responsible for the development of input/output analysis, together with Professor J. K. Galbraith of Harvard, were influential in persuading the Administration to revive the exercise in manpower planning by the Department of Labour, which had been in vogue immediately after the war, stimulated by the problem of absorbing great numbers of people into civilian employment, but had been stopped in 1953 under the Eisenhower Administration.

[24] They were (a) 4 per cent unemployment, (b) 5 per cent unemployment, (c) a special set of assumptions about the level of investment. The first product of this venture into long-term forecasting was a preliminary sketch of the state of certain important sectors of industry in 1970, *Technological Trends in 36 Major Industries* (Washington, 1964).

management of demand would not cure. Tax cuts and other simple unselective measures, designed to stimulate demand and raise the general level of economic activity, were seen as the long term answer to American unemployment.[25] By contrast, the thinking in the Department of Labour was dominated by the evidence of widespread structural unemployment, caused by the lack of certain industrial skills of increasing complexity, which an expansion in the sheer volume of demand, however large, would not cure. Long-range planning was therefore necessary in order to ensure the supply of the required type of labour at the right time.[26] It followed that equally long-range forecasts of the detailed development of individual sectors of the economy were necessary to supplement the short-term, macro-economic approach of those who sought the key to economic policy in the management of demand.

Economic Disciplines from the Department of Defense

The Department of Defense provides another example of the development of government planning in the 1960s, narrower in range than manpower planning though more spectacular in its effects. The aim here was the familiar one of using a common intellectual framework, in which trends were projected and future needs established by all the service departments and their subordinate offices, in order to compel them to co-ordinate their decisions here and now on what to buy and how much. The combined buying power of the three services is enormous. Particularly in the development of new products and techniques their impact is decisive; they finance over half of all the research and development done in the United States.[27]

The chief objective of the Secretary of Defense, Robert McNamara, who was personally responsible for the thorough-going reforms in the Department from 1961 onwards, was to eliminate the element of duplication in this immensely costly business of the development of new weapons. In order to do this, each of the services had to collaborate in an exercise in systematic prediction covering its armoury of weapons as they would be several years ahead. All the weapons in the pipeline, i.e. those covered by the huge research and development programme—absorbing as much as 15 per cent of the whole defence budget—were thus subjected to review. It was in fact

---

[25] Supplemented by special programmes of regional aid and other measures to overcome specific social and economic problems.

[26] Active short-term training programmes for workers whose occupations were disappearing as a result of technological change were also undertaken by the Department of Labour under the Manpower Development and Training Act. Over 60,000 workers received such training in 1963 and the aim was to raise the total number of people undergoing training at any one time to 100,000.

[27] See R. R. Nelson, 'The Impact of Arms Reduction on Research and Development', *AER*, May 1963. Nelson, a member of the staff of the Council of Economic Advisers, estimated that defence expenditure on research and development represented 50–60 per cent of the cost of all research and development done in the US.

closely analogous to the first step in the preparation of a French Plan, when firms which have been competing with one another come together in order to establish an investment programme with a timetable over a stated period of years for their industry as a whole. The different services and their subordinate branches engaged in the $50 billion defence programme of the United States tended to behave, as we have seen,[28] precisely on the model of rival firms in a keenly competitive market. The technique of confrontation and joint planning imposed on them by the Secretary of Defense, in the face of a powerful resistance movement, has resulted in some remarkable savings. Those which have attracted the greatest attention are the cancellations of some expensive and beloved project of a single service, found on closer examination to add an insufficient amount to the military output of the United States to justify the additional cost.[29] But there have been many other substantial though less dramatic economies achieved through the techniques of long-range planning, for example the reduction in the unwieldy volume of military stocks held.[30]

In this instance, it is clear, the techniques developed in large-scale private enterprise were being deliberately imported into the public sector. Robert McNamara had been President of the Ford Motor Corporation, one of the five biggest industrial firms in the United States, before coming to Washington. But there has also been a movement of ideas and standard practices from the government departments back into the private sector of industry. To begin with, the Department of Defense, the Atomic Energy Commission, and some other Federal Agencies imposed an elaborate standard reporting procedure on

[28] See above, pp. 323–4.
[29] McNamara's most controversial project in his programme for cutting costs by better co-ordinated planning to meet the needs of the different armed services was the fighter-bomber called TFX, developed in the early 1960s. The special feature of the machine, which was estimated to cost around $1,000m. to develop, was that its basic design was intended to meet both navy and army air force needs. Previously the two services had kept their design work jealously under their own separate control. In the end the contract was awarded, in the face of strong opposition from the army side and noisy protests from Congress, to the General Dynamics Corporation. The special advantage of the winning design over its nearest rival, presented by Boeing, was that 91 per cent of its components consisted of interchangeable parts (common to the machines required to meet the needs of the two services) compared with Boeing's proportion of 44 per cent. It was, it seems, the principle of the thing, the idea that a firm should win a contract on the grounds that it had found the highest common factor of two different service customers, instead of concentrating exclusively on meeting the design specifications of each one of them, which prompted an especially violent attack on McNamara, including an attack on his personal character, on this occasion (see *Sunday Times*, 17 Jan. 1965).
[30] This has already been mentioned in another connexion—see pp. 51–52. For other examples of economies see McNamara's report to the Subcommittee on Defense Procurement of the Joint Economic Committee of Congress, *The Impact of Military Supply and Service Activities on the Economy* (1963). Some indication of the scope for economies in stock-holding is provided by McNamara's estimate (p. 45) that at the end of 1962 there were 3·9m. military items, 'individually identified with a unique number', held in stock.

all their contractors. The next stage has been to require of these contractors that they employ certain management techniques, notably the so-called PERT system, in the government work on which they are employed.[31] PERT is a method of setting out a very precise time and cost schedule—particularly relevant to the development of a new industrial product or one containing novel elements—and then checking rapidly on the probable effect on time and cost of any proposed changes in the original plan, which come up as the actual work proceeds. Such changes are almost inevitable. The initials stand for Program Evaluation Review Technique—a forbidding huddle of abstractions, which turn out to be a description of an extremely practical set of management rules. Their function is to break down a complicated task containing elements of uncertainty—typically the task of developing something which has not been produced in the same form before—into a number of precisely defined component parts, showing how far any single bit of the operation is dependent on the performance of others. The nature and degree of this interdependence will often determine the speed at which the total job can be completed, in the face of unforeseen delays at particular points in the process. As the government pamphlet recommending the method to business management points out, one of the points in its favour is that 'it provides visible proof that a planning job has been done'.[32]

The Changing Mood of Government

It would be wrong to suggest that the introduction of these standard management devices by the government dates only from the arrival of McNamara in Washington in 1961. In fact PERT was used by the contractors on the development programme for the Polaris submarine as early as

---

[31] See *PERT Guide for Management Use*, June 1963, issued jointly by the Department of Defense, the Bureau of the Budget, and certain Federal Agencies for the use of contractors and government officials. Page 9 says: 'Full PERT implementation will be required on many major programs. In addition, the use of PERT will be encouraged, whenever it is applicable, as an effective management technique'. PERT is, of course, only one of several methods of 'critical path' analysis now in use.

[32] Ibid. The other advantages listed in the government document are: 'It imposes a more rigid discipline for considering the various elements of effort required to achieve the desired objectives. . . . It is a quick and effective method of communicating plans. . . . It provides a structured plan which lends itself to a systematic determination of the total estimated required time, which can then be compared to a directed or desired completion date. It provides a means for appraising progress against approved plans and for forecasting problems in meeting a schedule.' The Government Agencies clearly intend that the diffusion of this standard management device should go beyond those firms of contractors which have direct relations with Washington. The official pamphlet asks the question on behalf of the smaller sub-contractor: 'Are the Government Agencies going to help . . . in the initiation of PERT?'—and answers that for any advanced training, 'normally this responsibility will rest with the prime contractor'. It adds in the style of candid friend: 'Cost of PERT training, as with any managerial training in industry, is simply part of the cost of doing business'.

1957. The Special Projects Office of the Department of the Navy, which was responsible for Polaris, was indeed one of the chief sources of innovation in this field of management control.[33] But what happened after 1961 was that a systematic effort was made to ensure that all government offices working on the defence programme and all private firms connected with it marched in step. The experimental novelties of the second half of the 1950s were thus turned into the clichés of management in the 1960s.[34] The need for standard forms of reporting, which could be absorbed directly into the computer systems run by the government offices concerned, accelerated the process.

But what chiefly prompted the introduction of these standard techniques was the recognition that the old style of government supervision by means of some modified version of the competitive criterion was no longer workable over a wide range of production. Even the pretence of open tendering for orders could not be seriously kept up in some of the most valuable and important government contracts.[35] The strict planning of projects, stage by stage, in collaboration between government department and private contractor, the frequent reporting and the devices for automatic checks on any deviation from the original plan, were intended to provide a substitute for the absent pressures of the market. The outcome has been that some of the most advanced and dynamic firms in American industry—among them the contractors for armaments, aviation, and atomic energy—have had part of their management processes redesigned for them on certain standard patterns.

---

[33] See US Dept of the Navy, *Polaris Management* (1962).

[34] Certain forms of American defence planning have been criticized for an excessive and illusory precision which has been dubbed 'inventing on schedule' (C. J. Hitch and R. N. McKean, *The Economics of Defense in the Nuclear Age*, Cambridge, Mass., Harvard UP, 1960). PERT is in fact only one of several different methods of management control applied to problems of production and development carrying varying degrees of uncertainty. The aim of the planner in each case is to establish a technique which will (a) identify the area of uncertainty and define its range, (b) allow a rapid estimate to be made of the effect on time and cost of any new proposals which come up for decision as the work proceeds. No doubt some of the less sophisticated planning techniques applied to projects in very new fields of scientific research underestimated the degree of uncertainty which *had* to be accepted. It was partly in order to meet this problem that McNamara introduced the standard procedure of the 'program definition phase' of planning, 'in the early stages of which no attempt is made to establish rigorous specifications; preference is given to initiative and innovation on the part of the contractors' (evidence by McNamara to the Subcommittee on Defense Procurement, 1963).

[35] The Assistant Secretary of Defense, Thomas D. Morris, in his evidence to the Joint Economic Committee of Congress in 1963 was very frank on this point. He said: 'The production of new aircraft and missile systems cannot be economically procured on the basis of price competition, due to the high start-up costs and the lead time required to introduce a new production source after a long period of development. It is estimated that to establish a new production source on the Polaris missile, for example, would require up to three years and an investment of over $100 million in facilities and special tooling' (Hearings of Evidence before the Subcommittee on Defense Procurement of the Joint Econ. Ctee of Congress, Mar.–Apr. 1963, p. 41).

Defence planning is admittedly a rather special case; and the American agencies concerned with defence were especially in need of co-ordination. The conclusions to be drawn from the McNamara experience in the early 1960s are therefore of a limited character. There are however two observations which are suggested by it. The first is the remarkable responsiveness of American industry to pressures making for the standardization of techniques. This is an abiding feature of American business; it was noted in the middle of the nineteenth century.[36] The second point is that other departments of government in Washington were encouraged by the Defense Department's example to make an effort to secure better co-ordination between separate and sometimes competing centres of public power, and to use long-range planning as a means to this end. It was not that any single department tried to copy the McNamara formula; rather it was the general influence exercised by his success on the climate of opinion in Washington. In this climate the Bureau of the Budget, which we have already noted as a motor centre in the nervous system of government,[37] acted with increasing vigour. Once again its favourite device for securing better co-ordination among the departments and agencies of government was the long-range economic plan. The five-year budget forecast was introduced as standard procedure for all Agencies in 1962, and the first results incorporated into the 1963 Federal Budget.[38]

---

[36] e.g. in the development of interchangeable parts, the so-called 'American system' (see T. K. Derry and T. I. Williams, *A Short History of Technology* (London, OUP, 1960)). Simplicity of manufacture in a country in which skilled labour was scarce was one consideration. Moreover, because of the great distances between the centres of industrial production and the users of such things as agricultural machinery, it has always been important to arrange matters in such a way as to spare the buyer of the machine the need to employ the services of a skilled mechanic. Agricultural machine parts were designed very early on to meet this kind of problem. Much later in the 1920s Herbert Hoover, as Secretary of Commerce, acting with the full support of the business community, deliberately used the authority of his office to further the standardization of products. The standards promulgated by the Department of Commerce during his period of office covered a total of some 3,000 articles. Hoover believed that standardization of this kind was of the essence of efficient capitalism, and that it was a proper use of public power to further it (see *The Memoirs of Herbert Hoover, 1920–33* (London, Hollis & Carter, 1952), p. 67).

[37] See above, p. 319.

[38] See George Steiner, ed., *Managerial Long-Range Planning* (New York, McGraw Hill, 1963), article by Samuel M. Cohn of the Bureau of the Budget. He says that the Budget Bureau itself developed some long-range forecasts for the Kennedy budget of January 1962, and that as a result of this 'the Director of the Bureau got the President's approval to encourage major Agencies of the Government to begin making plans at least five years ahead. Dollar estimates were then required for these plans as part of the regular Budget submissions' (p. 50). A report by the Bureau of the Budget entitled *Goals Setting and Comprehensive Planning* (Washington, Feb. 1963), points out how rudimentary the planning efforts of the Federal Agencies still were at this stage: 'The Director's letter to the Agencies, last spring [1962], requested a brief statement of the major goals and objectives proposed, the major changes and developments which can be foreseen in the next five years

Again, the beginnings of this venture antedated the Kennedy Administration. The last Director of the Budget Bureau under President Eisenhower, Mr Maurice Stans, initiated some preliminary work on long-range forecasting of government expenditure, the results of which were issued in mimeographed form as a special study, *Ten Year Projections of Federal Budget Expenditures*, in January 1961. (The whole process is reminiscent of the efforts that were being made by the British Treasury—which occupies a central position in the process of government, comparable to that of the Bureau of the Budget— to grapple with the problems of long-range forecasting of public spending at about the same time.)[39] With the change of Government in the United States, the new Director of the Bureau took up the task with vigour. The most important change was that the independent Federal Agencies were, for the first time, brought in as active participants in the formulation of government plans. A senior official of the Bureau, Samuel M. Cohn, summed up the results of this and the subsequent reform as follows: 'I think one of the basic distinctions between the pre-Kennedy and post-Kennedy plans is that budgeting in the first was used principally as a control. It was used too much as a control tool. Now budgeting is used in important measure also as a positive planning and coordinating instrument.'[40]

Corporations as Planners

According to a report on American planning issued by the Bureau of the Budget in 1963,[41] it is a 'development pioneered by private corporations which is only recently being generally applied in peacetime government activities'. Business planning was well established by the time that the government began to take a serious interest in it during the late 1950s.[42] But to begin with, only a select few of the Federal Agencies were seriously concerned. In the large government departments headed by members of the Cabinet, the independent behaviour of the Bureaus (only nominally controlled by their department chiefs), was, and has remained, an obstacle to effective planning. The outstanding exception is the Department of Defense. The report sees this exception as the manifestation of a more fundamental trend, common to both private industry and government: the urge to plan, it says, is strongest

and the quantitative indicators of work load. . . . Unfortunately, many Agencies were unable to submit meaningful programs directed to multi-year goals or objectives since they have not yet been adequately formulated.' The report concludes that 'the emphasis on the longer-range implications of budget year decisions is . . . forcing consideration within Agencies of the possible future consequences of current program decisions' (pp. 30–31).

[39] See above, pp. 104–5.
[40] Steiner, *Long-Range Planning*, p. 53. Cohn was replying to the discussion on his paper at a conference on planning, whose proceedings are recorded in this volume.
[41] *Goals Setting and Comprehensive Planning*.
[42] The Government's effort, the report says, dates from 'the beginning of the "Sputnik" era', i.e. 1957 (p. ii).

in organizations concerned with new technology and in 'non-routine situations'.

How did it all begin? The report dates the original impulse in the business world from 'shortly after World War II', when, it says, 'many business corporations began formalizing a systematic means whereby a company seeks to become what it wants to be by the formulation of corporate-wide objectives and systematic performance controls . . . for at least five years ahead'. However, other evidence suggests that this may present a rather too favourable picture of the intellectual dynamism and foresight of even the big American corporations. The McGraw Hill Company, which has been running a Survey of Business Plans for New Plant and Equipment since 1947, has recorded that at the start, 'only a handful' of companies could provide a forecast of their investment going beyond the current year.[43] The questionnaire for the survey is sent out in the spring of each year and businesses are asked to make a statement on their investment plans for the three years after the end of the current year. This means that they must in effect make a four-year estimate[44] of production, sales, and capacity in order to give intelligent answers to the questions. By the early 1960s the proportion of companies in the McGraw Hill sample who were able to provide the data had risen to over 90 per cent, compared with some 20 per cent (the 'handful') in the late 1940s.[45] The size of the sample has meanwhile increased, and it now represents a substantial proportion of the total manufacturing capacity of the United States.[46]

What is noteworthy is not only how rapidly the practice of business planning appears to have spread, but also how ready American business is to engage in a species of communal activity in this field. The collective element in a venture such as that of McGraw Hill should not be overstated; there is certainly no active collusion. Indeed, part of the purpose of the exercise would be lost if managers answered the questions influenced by the knowledge of what the other guy was saying that he was doing. The interest for the individual firm lies in the discovery of how far its own expectations—on which its investment plans are based—deviate from any consensus about the future that may emerge in its industry. McGraw Hill in fact offers two different services to clients, based on the data derived from its inquiries into business investment plans. One is a 'forecast', which is an expert attempt

---

[43] D. M. Keezer, ed., *New Forces in American Business* (New York, McGraw Hill, 1959), p. 36.

[44] i.e. including about three-quarters of the current year; even the data on the first calendar quarter will often not be available at the time when they answer the questionnaire.

[45] Information from McGraw Hill, Dept. of Economics. According to Keezer (p. 36), the proportion had already reached 'some 90 per cent' by 1959.

[46] Because of the high concentration of American manufacturing in comparatively few firms, the sample is able to take in the businesses responsible for some 50 per cent of all factory investment in the US. The coverage in the service and other trades is much smaller—12 per cent of total investment.

to use the data, after statistical corrections for various kinds of bias in the answers, to make a realistic prediction of what an industry will actually do.[47] The other service, the 'Survey', is simply a tabulation of what people *say* they are going to do. Of the two, businessmen overwhelmingly plump for the latter. They are evidently more interested in the opinion poll of their industry than in the expert prediction.

There is a further development of the active search for consensus. Individual firms in the sample which find that their own plans are out of line with the collective view of their industry, as established by the Survey, will nowadays phone the McGraw Hill economists in order to check more closely on the reasons for the discrepancy—and no doubt to consider whether they ought not to adjust their own forecasts and investment plans in the light of the discussion. Here is something which, in an embryonic form, provides a service for business management analogous to that of a *commission de modernisation* under the French Plan. The French industrialist too is interested in the consensus about the future of his industry, rigorously expressed in a series of detailed forecasts over a period of years, against which he will check his own investment programme. The difference is that the Frenchmen can do so directly by questioning one another in a smoke-filled room under official auspices, with the Government's plans thrown in too, while the Americans have to get it all second-hand. Yet it is not certain which of the two methods would, if perfected, produce the more accurate guidance for the small or medium-sized firm trying to find a rational basis for its own investment plans. The French method is undoubtedly superior for the large enterprises, and it is, after all, they who do most of the investment in most of manufacturing industry. But the smaller firm in France probably does not receive much more information that is of use to it than it would under the American system—and gets rather more tutelage.

It is too early yet to judge the aggregate effect of the growth of business planning in the 1950s on the American economy. The McGraw Hill economists assert 'that the widespread prevalence of long-range business investment planning during the 1957–8 business recession accounted very considerably for what, in historical perspective, was the remarkable brevity (about a year) of the decline of this type of investment'.[48] If this claim is justified— and there is no statistical evidence for it—then American private planning is beginning to perform at least one of the functions aimed at by the government plans of Western Europe, which is to smooth out cyclical fluctuations in business activity and employment,[49] or, in British parlance, to avoid 'stop-go'. No one, however, would pretend that the American method does the job very efficiently. All that can be said with confidence about it so far is that since the classical cause of the downturn of the business cycle was a sharp and

[47] This service is provided only to individual clients. [48] Keezer, *New Forces*. p. 37.
[49] See in particular the Swedish case, above, pp. 199 ff.

cumulative cut-back of investment, any widely diffused optimistic view about the longer-range prospects for profitable investment is a good help.[50]

One striking feature of American business planning is its high degree of standardization. George A. Steiner, summing up the findings of a research seminar on the planning methods of a group of large business and government organizations in 1963, remarked on the 'surprising uniformity in practice among widely different types of organization'.[51] The detailed plans usually covered a period of five years ahead, though most of the organizations represented at this seminar also engaged in special studies with a longer time perspective of ten to twenty or more years. The usual procedure is to revise the five-year plan in an annual exercise, and then extend it forward by one year. There was insistence on the point that the company planners were not merely making forecasts; this had been common practice in a lot of businesses for many years. As the representative of American Airlines put it: 'Our planning process aims to develop a course of action which American Airlines will attempt to *make* happen, not to ask what *will* happen. . . . Financial planning normally simply prices out the most conservative assumptions. Our plan is not a table of financial results; it is an approved detailed plan of action, supported by specific plans for each major functional activity.' It is the shift from the conventional financial framework for analysing a company's policy and operations to their analysis in terms of the flow of physical resources—raw materials, equipment, buildings, manpower—which the large organizations tend to see as the most significant aspect of the new techniques. It is analogous to what happened after the war in the public sector when the traditional budget accounts, expressed in terms of revenue and expenditure, were translated into national income calculations, showing the impact of the government on the output and distribution of the nation's goods and services.

One can only guess at what prompted the surge of interest in company planning in the United States during the 1950s. A contributory factor seems to have been the growing awareness of the effects of speeded up technological change. Many more new products and processes were being marketed, and

[50] Although undoubtedly influential by the early 1960s, it would be wrong to conclude that long-range business planning had become anything like a general practice among the ordinary run of American firms. According to one survey in 1962, less than 20 per cent of the manufacturing firms with annual sales of over $10 million had 'organized long-range planning on a corporate wide basis'. Only about one-quarter of these firms had been engaged in systematic planning for longer than four years (see R. H. Mason, 'Organizing for Corporate Planning', *Proc. of the Long-Range Planning Service Client Conference* (Stanford Research Inst., 1962), quoted by Steiner, *Long-Range Planning*). There is some apparent discrepancy between these estimates and the McGraw Hill experience. However, the high proportion of American investment in manufacturing done by companies which engage in business planning that is shown by the McGraw Hill sample is largely explained by the heavy concentration of the largest manufacturing concerns in it. This sample does not purport to reflect the planning behaviour of the typical medium or small-sized firm.

[51] *Long-Range Planning*, p. 318.

they entered increasingly into the business calculations of the ordinary firm. Businesses got used to another time scale. They also recognized that although there is more innovation, it still takes quite a long time before any individual piece of innovation begins to pay off. There is scope for planning on the basis of identifiable changes, if you begin early. The McGraw Hill economists, using their experience of American business plans and performance since the war, suggest as a rough guide that it is 'at least seven years before research programs begin to affect product sales or capital investment for new plant facilities'.[52] How important this element in business decisions had become by the late 1950s is indicated by the results of the 1958 McGraw Hill Survey in which 'companies reported that, on the average, they expected some 12 per cent of their 1961 sales to be in products that were not on the market in 1957'.[53] The precise degree of novelty of such 'new products' may often be open to argument. The Survey is more indicative of *attitudes* towards the prospect of technological innovation than of anything else.

The Approach to Consensus

Is it plausible to envisage that in the long run a national economic plan for the United States will gradually emerge as a kind of natural outcrop of private enterprise planning? There are in fact several other ventures, besides the McGraw Hill Survey, actively engaged in the propagation of ideas about planning and the improvement of its methods. Some of these, like the National Planning Association in Washington, deliberately set out to span both government and business efforts in this field. More modest, yet somehow very characteristic of the practical American approach to this kind of problem is the workaday 'Federal Statistics Users Conference', which was set up in 1956. It is an experts' body devoted to the task of keeping the public and the private sectors in touch, and where possible in step, in the development of statistical information and techniques. The new generation of business planners is particularly interested in getting the government to present the data about what it is doing, and even more about what it is going to do, in a form which will allow the implications to be drawn out and absorbed into long-range company forecasts. The Federal Government on its side has the declared purpose of securing the widest possible spread of common standards and concepts in the work of planning. Inside industry the same sort of function is performed, whether consciously or not, by such bodies as the National Association of Business Economists. I noticed during a short visit to the United States in 1964 that separate expert conferences on forecasting and planning by the National Planning Association, the National Association of Business Economics, and the National Industrial Conference Board (New York) were starting or finishing or in progress during the ten days that I was there.

[52] Keezer, *New Forces*, p. 62. [53] Ibid., pp. 61–62.

There is indeed a kind of intellectual underworld of American business which seems to have escaped from some of the conventional inhibitions of the Anti-Trust laws that bind the rest of the community; it has assumed a licence to exchange ideas both on how firms see the future of the market and on some of the things that they are going to do about it. All this, in spite of the fact that making economic forecasts in common is a form of communication that seems most likely to lead to other forms of common action. Business communication is, of course, an established form of virtue in the United States, pursued, as anyone who has made a round of visits to American firms will be able to testify, with intense vigour. But it is well known that this cherished activity can, in the twinkling of an eye, be converted into deepest sin—if the exchange of ideas is allowed to extend at any point to a discussion of even the possibility of collaboration between competitors in any conceivable market for their goods. The great advantage of the business economists who meet to discuss their market forecasts and their techniques of planning is that everyone, including the Anti-Trust Division of the Department of Justice, recognizes that they are engaged in communication and not collusion. It is as if the faculty for winking or nodding were unknown to the law. I should add that there is no evidence that these people do, in fact, wink or nod when they get together on such occasions. But perhaps in any case, whether the explicit gestures are made or not is less important in the long run than the achievement of an implicit consensus among those involved—an understanding about the views and intentions which they hold in common, reached by a process which may be only half recognized by those taking part in it.

The next question is whether a comprehensive national plan could be accommodated within the institutional limitations of the United States. Surveying the impressive growth of American planning activities up to 1964, Gerhard Colm, Chief Economist of the National Planning Association, concludes that 'these various efforts have more mutual consistency than appears on the surface'. He argues that the type of planning which has developed in the United States 'has some similarity with the planning in other Western countries', and that 'it is beginning to have a significant impact on the performance of the American economy'.[54] Nevertheless his final judgement is that, on balance, an overall national plan on the French model is not for the United

---

[54] *Economic Planning in the United States* (Hamburg, Weltwirtschaftliches Archiv, 1964, Heft 1), p. 54. He also comments that there is 'considerable interdependence' between the planning activities, in spite of their apparently disparate character. In fact, this process of knitting together the assumptions underlying the plans of numerous independent bodies into a coherent whole is one of the features of the work of the NPA. The organization makes five- and ten-year projections, annually revised, for the major metropolitan areas, for each of the fifty states, and for the United States as a whole. These are used by a variety of public agencies—local authorities, as well as Federal and state government departments—and by around three hundred big corporations. Together, these bodies are responsible for a sizeable portion of the annual investment done in the public and private sectors.

States. The reason is that 'the more individualistic attitude of entrepreneurs' is likely to get in the way—for Colm sees the essential element in the success of French planning as being the 'self-enforcement' of discipline among businessmen in the execution of a national plan, which they have helped to formulate. It is that, he avers, which cannot be reproduced in the United States.

On the face of it, this hardly appears a decisive obstacle. Americans often seem, to an outsider, to be inclined to over-stress both the extent and the dire consequences of their unbridled individualism; it feels at times suspiciously like the description of a lovable defect, which is the opposite of self-criticism. Perhaps it belongs with the cult of the frontier, the lone ranger, and the awkward American. Observing American behaviour, rather than the myths about it, one is struck, when something has to be done which involves the conflicting interests of individuals or groups, not so much by the spirit of intransigent personal initiative, as by the urge to achieve a palpable consensus. The patience and energy with which this latter objective is pursued, both in politics and in business, often comes as a surprise to a European. Americans believe in competition, but they like to agree. In the greater part of Western Europe —excluding Britain and Scandinavia—there has traditionally been neither the belief in the one nor the desire for the other.[55]

More serious as an obstacle to American economic planning than the jungle urges of the American entrepreneur is the behaviour of his government. We have seen in the discussion of the mechanics of planning in Part II that there is a great deal more involved in making a national plan work than the spirit of 'self-enforcement' in private industry. Colm comes nearer to the truth when he discusses the other difficulty, which is to make an American plan *credible* to business, for, as he points out, the exercise will only work if 'business is convinced . . . that the government will play its role in implementing policies for the promotion of economic growth'.[56] Where the central power of government is weak and a large number of competing agencies of public authority are able to assert their independence of decisions made at the centre,

---

[55] The pervasive itch for consensus is a long-standing feature of American society. Its immense political implications are sometimes missed even by the most perceptive commentator like de Tocqueville. His analysis of the politics of an egalitarian society in *Democracy in America* led him to the conclusion that its outstanding characteristic is conservatism. The observation was—in the 1830s when he wrote in the midst of the upheaval of Andrew Jackson's Presidency—and remains, profound. But this American trait is consistent with a principle of constant movement in American political life, the result of the endless bargaining process between political groups searching conservatively for a consensus, which was, it seems to me, insufficiently stressed by de Tocqueville. The capacity of American society for profound political change in pursuit of a shifting consensus, e.g. on the Negro question in the 1960s or on the amount of poverty that is tolerable, continues to be underrated.

[56] *Economic Planning*, p. 43. This therefore comes back to the same point as that raised (but also only as a subsidiary objection to American planning) by Professor E. S. Mason (see above, pp. 333–4).

the proper posture for private business, when it is asked to go ahead on the assumption that the government's planned targets will be achieved, is one of scepticism. It is in fact the competitive theory of administration inside the government, rather than any ungovernable competitiveness outside it, which makes the American case special.

A Disappearing Surplus of Resources

It is characteristic of the relationship between the public and the private sectors in America that government, having been formed in the image of private enterprise, now justifies planning on the ground that it is essentially a private enterprise technique. It is also noticeable that the most vigorous planning efforts by the government—outside the field of defence, which is a special case—appear in those areas where the pressures of private consumption and of private industry supplying consumer needs actively call for collective action by the public authorities. Roads and urban development, as offshoots of consumer demand for more cars and nicer houses, are outstanding examples. These are of course essential elements of an economic plan. However, the more profound collective choices, those which ought to find their expression in a comprehensive national plan for the distribution of the national product among its main uses, and which are logically prior to decisions about the level to be reached by particular kinds of consumer demand, go by default. It is of the essence of planning by business that it is *partial* planning. This has been reproduced in the public sector. A national plan is something quite else; it deliberately engages the transcendent power of the state in a design which is more than the sum of all the individual pressures in a society.

Apart from the fragmentation of the Federal Government which has figured very largely in the argument so far, there is the equally serious problem of the independent and competing public power of state and local authorities. If I have not stressed this obstacle to economic planning on a nation-wide scale in the United States, it is not because it is unimportant, but only that it is more familiar. It is especially relevant to the Federal Government's recent attempt to bring the multifarious activities impinging on urban development into a rational programme of town planning. This provides a clear illustration of both the successes and the limitations of the current phase of American planning, which have been conveniently recorded in an analytical report by the Advisory Commission on Inter-Governmental Relations.[57]

[57] *Impact of Federal Urban Development Programs on Local Government Organization and Planning* (Washington, 30 May 1964). The report was 'the first attempt to provide a systematic survey of requirements for local government organization and planning in all Federal aid programs affecting physical development in urban areas and to assess the extent and nature of inter-agency coordination of these programs within the Federal Government'.

The Advisory Commission was established in 1959 with the task of recommending ways in which the various parts of the American government, state and local government as well as Federal, could co-operate more effectively in the execution of a common policy. Its appointment was prompted by the recognition that, as the official pamphlet on its operations explains, the 'expansion of governmental activity at all levels has correspondingly increased the number of actual and potential friction points in our federal system'. Since it was inaugurated it has dealt with a variety of subjects and has winkled out some remarkable absurdities. It has made a particular contribution in the field of town planning where Federal, state, and local activities impinge on one another, sometimes violently, and where jurisdictional disputes are reinforced by the normal jealousies associated with local government. The need for a new approach had been pointed out by President Kennedy in his 1961 Housing Message to Congress. The old jurisdictional boundaries were no longer appropriate. 'The city and its suburbs', the President said, 'are both interdependent parts of a single community bound together by the web of transportation and other public facilities and by common economic interests. . . . This requires the establishment of an effective and comprehensive planning process in each metropolitan area embracing all activities, both public and private, which shape the community.'[58]

Some progress has been made along the lines laid down by President Kennedy during the early 1960s. The technique employed by the Federal Government has been a combination of cajolery and financial pressure. Direct Federal subsidies to state and local authorities to pay for the work of 'comprehensive planning'[59] have been used as a means of imposing uniform minimum standards for urban development projects. A more powerful compulsion has been applied by the Bureau of Roads, which insists on a regional planning exercise involving separate and competing local governments, as a condition for making a grant for highway construction. The rules have gradually been tightened, and from 1965 onwards urban areas with a population of more than 50,000 will not be eligible for Federal funds to construct highways unless they have a 'comprehensive transportation planning process for the urban area as a whole, actively being carried on through co-operative efforts between the States and local communities'.[60] Since the Federal grant covers up to 90 per cent of the cost of such road construction and runs to an expenditure of over $3 billion annually, the Advisory Commission's report is probably not over-stating the case when it says: 'This condition provides the strongest possible encouragement for the establishment of cooperative arrangements between the governmental units concerned with each major

---

[58] Ibid., p. 1.
[59] These grants had risen to an annual total of $18 m. in 1963; they cover between two-thirds and three-quarters of planning costs.
[60] Ibid., p. 106.

urban area.'[61] The planning of transportation may appear to cover only a narrow segment of community life, but it is one which impinges on almost everything else in a modern city; that is why 'economic, land use, and population projections' must all be included in any plan that is to qualify for a road grant.[62]

The procedure is typical of the way in which a single energetic agency can use its incidental power to enlarge the area of co-ordinated government. The effort of the Bureau of Roads has been reinforced by the pressures coming from the Urban Renewal Administration, another Federal body with a big budget.[63] In order to qualify for its grants, state and local authorities have to produce comprehensive plans subject to similar conditions to those demanded for a road-building subsidy. Local governments are thus being told both to plan more systematically by looking further ahead and to extend the geographical ambit of any individual piece of planning to include other bodies whose jurisdiction they have hitherto been able to ignore. All this is part of a deliberate policy, as the report of the Advisory Commission on Inter-Governmental Relations indicates, of making the excessively separate bits of public power in the United States enter into a series of coalitions. Planning is the means to overcome their unwillingness to coalesce.

But meanwhile what happens in Washington itself? In spite of the pressures for togetherness in the new style of urban development planning, it is clear that some of the best-known practitioners of the competitive theory of government have succeeded in keeping out of the huddle.[64] There are altogether 40 programmes and 13 different Federal agencies involved in the business of urban development. The Advisory Commission comments that there are 'programs of long standing found in so many major departments and agencies of the Federal Government that a reorganization to combine them into one operating unit would be impossible'. It should be noted that a proposal by President Kennedy to meet the problem by establishing a single Department of Urban Affairs was turned down by Congress in 1962.[65] This was supposed to start off with only roads and housing under its direct control; but it would have provided the nucleus for a spreading organ of supervision over the great range of social and economic activities connected in one way

---

[61] Ibid. It is also, in the long run, likely to be a powerful influence making for uniform national planning standards, as well as uniform assumptions about long-range objectives, for the Federal agencies concerned with the preparation of such plans increasingly claim the right to make 'qualitative judgments' on them (p. 63).

[62] Ibid., p. 106.　　　　　　　　　　　　[63] Nearly $600 m. in 1963 (ibid., p. 68).

[64] The Corps of Engineers (responsible for projects involving water and drainage) and the Rural Electrification Administration (which is also concerned with telephones) have both managed to stay outside the new comprehensive planning arrangements in the field of urban development (ibid., pp. 134 and 170).

[65] The bill was prevented from reaching the floor of Congress by a majority vote in the Rules Committee in January 1962. The scheme was revived by President Johnson, and the Department of Housing and Urban Affairs was established in 1965.

or another with the development of cities in the United States. That was plainly the intention. Congressmen smelt co-ordination and bucked. A big department under the control of a member of the President's Cabinet was likely to be less amenable to the pressures of local and other special interest groups than a lot of little government agencies, each jealously guarding its own independent fief from interference by the centre.[66]

But the Congressmen who, as members of the Advisory Committee on Inter-Governmental Relations,[67] examined the working of the urban development programmes in 1964, joined in the general indignation about the failure of the Federal Government to exercise effective control. The Commission summed up its findings as follows:

The President himself has been given legislative authority for allocating and coordinating public works acceleration funds. The Bureau of the Budget maintains a consolidated six-year program of the public works being proposed by Federal Agencies. No evidence was found, however, of a unified Federal Urban Development policy, nor of general coordination procedures between Agencies in this field. Inter-Agency contacts are largely informal. . . . If conflicts between programs are not resolved by State or local officials they may not be resolved at all. No one in the Federal Government is specifically charged with the job of promoting consistency between all the programs affecting urban development.[68]

I have described the urban development programme of the early 1960s in some detail, because this is in fact a particularly promising field for public planning in the United States. Whereas in Europe, long-range planning was originally prompted by straightforward economic objectives—the desire for faster growth of the national product, interrupted by fewer business fluctuations—and only later came upon the task of settling major social options,[69] in America the active political interest in government planning has derived chiefly from social rather than economic problems. Washington in the mid-1960s—after the crucial tax cut of 1964, and with it the acceptance of

[66] Congressman Widnall explained in the House of Representatives Subcommittee on Domestic Finance what the issue really was: 'Part of the great fight over the Urban Affairs Cabinet post position was the fact that there would be set up an administrative head who actually would just be responsible to the President. This Urban Affairs Secretary would not be an elected official but would have almost unlimited powers as far as the national economy is concerned, because his department would take in mass transportation; it would take in housing; it would take in many things in many other fields' (*The Federal Reserve System after 50 Years*, vol. iii (Apr. 1964), p. 1691).

[67] The Commission contains members of both houses of Congress, as well as State Governors, members of State Legislatures, and people engaged in local government. Three members of the Administration, including the Secretary of the Treasury, are also members.

[68] *Impact of Federal Urban Development Programs*, p. 38.

[69] The French planners, for example, only began to tackle the problems of social policy in the Fourth Plan, beginning 1962 (see above, p. 227 n. 12). Regional policies, in which these social options (involving the future of whole communities, their livelihood and land) appear in a sharp form, were not absorbed into the French planning process until the early 1960s (see Bauchet, *Economic Planning*, p. 46).

deficit financing as a respectable instrument of policy—was fairly confident that American unemployment could be largely overcome by the efficient short-term management of the volume of demand, supplemented by subsidiary measures to deal with special problems of a long-term character, like regional poverty and decay and the racial barrier to the development of modern industrial skills throughout the nation. While these structural problems were recognized as serious and the effort being concentrated on them in President Johnson's second term was considerable, the prevailing view in the Administration at this stage was that economic planning on a national scale was not required in order to provide American people with the extra jobs that were needed.

Long-range planning is concerned, above all, with the detailed management of supply. Why do it, if you have a surplus of resources—not only of labour but of most other things, including, until recently, space for all the buildings that anyone seemed likely to want to put up and the roads to drive on? Congestion is a relatively new phenomenon in the United States. The problem of improving the long-term management of supply in conditions of full employment has not been reached yet. When the achievement of full employment[70] gives it the status of a problem, the other pressures making for new policies analogous to European planning will have gained a powerful ally. But even then, there is no reason to suppose that the transformation of policy in a country that is deeply devoted to institutions which express an opposite principle of government will happen either easily or fast.

[70] Even when the US reaches the 'short-term objective' of 4 per cent unemployment, the limit of ambition of the Democratic Administrations of the early 1960s, it will still be a long way from the kind of full employment which most of Western Europe has lived with for most of a decade.

XV

THE CHANGING STYLE OF PRIVATE ENTERPRISE

IT would be misleading to leave this account of the mechanics of modern capitalism without some more general discussion of the changes that have occurred in the conduct of private enterprise. The subject has come up intermittently in earlier chapters;[1] certain common trends were noted in Chapter III.[2] It is now possible to examine the problem further against the background of the major institutional developments described in the intervening argument.

The significant facts about the behaviour of private enterprise are less readily established than about governments. This is partly because of the sheer volume of disparate elements, each pursuing its own separate interest, which make up the private sector; at best, one is dealing with statistical aggregates. The other factor which makes the study of the public sector easier is that even at its most secretive its actions in the conduct of economic policy are, in a democracy, subject to scrutiny, whereas private enterprise has often managed to escape it. That is not due merely to its talent for evasion; the observers themselves have been remarkably undemanding. Knowledge about such matters as how the typical business sets about pricing its goods or deciding how much to invest has only recently begun to be established by systematic empirical tests.[3] Economic analysis, during most of the time that it has been practised as an academic discipline, has been much less concerned with what businessmen actually do than with what they *would* do on certain assumptions, including the major assumption that they are strictly rational men.[4] My purpose at this stage is not to attempt a survey of the whole field of entrepreneurial behaviour, but only to comment briefly on some trends which are directly relevant to the theme of this book.

---

[1] Notably in Part I and in Chs. XI & XIV.   [2] See pp. 54 ff.

[3] The US is in advance of other countries. For interesting examples of recent British work see R. R. Neild, *Pricing and Employment in the Trade Cycle*, NIESR, Occ. Paper XXI, Cambridge 1963, and NIESR, *Econ. R.*, Nov. 1964, 'Replacement Policy'.

[4] The favoured technique of analysis has been to concentrate attention on the 'limiting case'. In this way certain problems involving economic choice are clarified. But the next stage in the development of the subject, when empirical data are collected on how businessmen actually do choose in different circumstances, has been a long time coming. The further stage of analysing their motives, both conscious and unconscious, with the aim of uncovering relationships which could be useful for predictive purposes, has hardly got going yet—beyond the occasional do-it-yourself efforts of an economist with a taste for psychoanalysis.

First of all, there is the changed attitude of management to labour costs. Partly this is the effect of full employment: the difficulty and expense of recruiting workers have made employers less willing to sack them as soon as business turns bad.   More fundamentally, there has been a marked rise in the permanent salaried staff of industrial firms.   In the ten years from 1950 to 1960 the total number of workers in this category increased in Britain from 17 to 22 per cent of the labour force, and in the United States from 18 to 25 per cent.[5]   Since staff salaried workers get paid more, the impact of this change on the overhead costs of the individual firm was even greater than these figures suggest.   Moreover, the upward trend seems to be continuing. By 1962 the total amount paid to salaried workers in Britain had reached two-thirds of the sum paid out in wages.   This was an abrupt change from the mid-1950s, when the proportion of salaries to wages was one-half—very close to the prewar ratio.[6]

The rapid increase in 'white collar workers' compared to 'blue collar' has been observed in many other Western countries.   It reflects the growing sophistication of methods of industrial production.   The penalty which business pays for carrying this increasing load of sophistication is that its production costs are more rigid.   When trade is bad and production has to be cut back, wage costs per unit of output tend to rise sharply.   One might have expected that this would make firms more vulnerable to cut-throat price competition for the reduced amount of business.   But market pressures no longer seem to work in this way.   Rather the contrary.   An American study of the effect of labour costs on business behaviour since the war concludes that 'in most industries prices are raised in the face of declining demands if costs increase, even when those cost increases are largely attributable to the decline in output itself'.[7]   Profits do, of course, decline during a recession and businessmen may have to accept a smaller mark-up on their goods.   But the broad conclusion of the American evidence is that in manufacturing industry 'pricing policies are strongly cost-oriented' during periods when demand is falling.[8]

---

[5] Neild, *Pricing and Employment*, p. 47.   The coverage is slightly different in the US, where those included are all workers other than 'production workers'.   The figures are judged by Neild to be 'broadly comparable' with those for the category of 'salaried workers' in the UK.

[6] *Treasury Bulletin for Industry*, Nov. 1963, which says that from 1938 to 1955 there was 'near stability' in the relationship between aggregate wage and salary earnings.

[7] See Charles L. Schultze and J. L. Tryon, *Prices and Costs in Manufacturing Industries*, Study Paper No. 17 for the Study of Employment, Growth and Price Levels, Joint Economic Committee of Congress, 25 Jan. 1960, p. 50.   Neild (*Pricing and Employment*, p. 49), however, suggests—on the basis of indications drawn from the behaviour of American profits, rather than direct comparison of prices—that prices set by manufacturers in the US are more responsive to short run fluctuations in demand than in Britain.

[8] Ibid.   There is a great deal of detailed evidence about the way in which prices of certain important American products, e.g. steel and automobiles, are determined by cost and 'target profit' calculations, rather than by movements in market demand.

In a careful study of the behaviour of prices in British manufacturing industry from 1950 to 1961, Robert Neild found that there was no response to short-term changes either in market demand or in workers' productivity. A rise in wages or in the cost of materials was reflected fairly promptly in the price of the finished product; but the equally important effects on the costs of firms caused by changes, either up or down, in the volume of output per worker were, during the short period, ignored. The evidence indicated that there was some normal long-run trend of costs which was used by firms in setting their prices, regardless of what was happening to their actual costs, for example as a result of a slump in demand. When that occurred, costs went up, because labour was retained in employment, and even working hours were not seriously cut. In the event the usual response was to let profits bear the burden of the discrepancy between short-term reality and the assumed long-term trend. By and large the fluctuations in demand during this period, which were quite sharp in some industries, neither induced British manufacturers to cut their prices, in order to increase the volume of sales, nor to raise their prices in an effort to compensate for the increase in production costs caused by the drop in business. They kept their eyes firmly fixed on the long term.

No doubt a generalization of this kind can be faulted in individual cases; it is not intended to do more than explain the behaviour of certain aggregates, derived from the statistical analysis of the observed movement of costs and prices in a variety of industries over a number of years. No alternative explanation so far offered fits the facts. The interesting point is that the behaviour of business management during this period was in marked contrast to the prewar pricing policy of British business, analysed in an earlier study.[9] This study had shown that the tendency then was for prices to respond to sharp movements of the market up or down, rather than to the calculation of costs and 'target profits' over a long period.

Big Business and the Long-Term View

It is impossible to say how far the behaviour of British manufacturing industry is typical of what has been happening in other countries. What is to be observed, however, is that the motives for 'full cost pricing'—i.e. prices which cover all of the overheads, as well as current production costs—are much stronger when the overhead element is a greatly enlarged proportion

See, for instance, the study by O. Eckstein & G. Fromm, *Steel and the Post-War Inflation* (Joint Economic Committee of Congress, Study of Employment, Growth and Price Levels. Study Paper No. 2, Nov. 1959), who conclude that the rapid rise in steel prices during the 1950s depended to a large extent on 'the exercise of market power by the steel industry', notably its endeavour to increase the amount of profit that could be used to finance its investment program without drawing on outside funds.
[9] See Neild, *Pricing and Employment*, who refers to the article, by R. L. Hall and C. J. Hitch, 'Price Theory and Business Behaviour', *Oxford Economic Papers*, May 1939.

of a company's expenditure. It is not only staff overheads but also the proportion of fixed capital costs in the total which has increased. That reflects the more rapid obsolescence of machines and equipment, as technology advances; costs are saddled with a larger proportion of the value of the plant which has to be written off each year. Moreover, in Europe investment in fixed assets as a proportion of total business expenditure has been running at an unusually high level for many years.[10]

A striking example of the way in which these trends influence the structure of costs is provided by the textile industry. An OECD survey of the state of this traditionally labour-intensive industry in the early 1960s shows that investment in new and more productive machinery has raised annual charges for the amortization of fixed capital 'in the most modern firms' to the point where it is as large as the wage bill.[11] Employment has steadily fallen while investment has risen; so that an industry which in the past has been exceptionally volatile, more given to alternations of boom and slump than others, tends to find its room for manoeuvre has become restricted. Almost inevitably, it has to adopt a much steadier policy both in regard to its labour and to its prices, in order to adapt itself to the combined effects of full employment and technological change. The trend towards larger units was especially marked in the British textile industry after 1960; and with it went the elimination of small, typically 'weak' sellers. An interesting feature of this development was that the pressure to enlarge and amalgamate textile firms came from the two giant producers of synthetics, Imperial Chemical Industries and Courtaulds, who deliberately set out to improve the efficiency of their customers, in order to secure a more predictable, as well as a larger, outlet for their products. Thus bigness tends to spread in modern industry through sheer propinquity. In the traditional market situation the big firm positively prefers to sell to a lot of little ones; that enables it to obtain the maximum short-term advantage from its greater market power. But the predominance of long-term considerations in the thinking of big enterprises nowadays leads them to a desire to have customers who are rather closer to their own size.[12] There is in any case a common language of the big and a common employment of sophisticated techniques which the average small firm does not easily master.

---

[10] Of course, the more rapid rate of replacement is itself a cause of the higher level of investment in new equipment.

[11] *Textile Industry in OECD Countries 1962–1963* (1963), para. 16.

[12] So eager was ICI to bring about the change in the structure of the textile industry that it lent money to favoured companies, very much like a banker, in order to help them to finance *their* take-over bids for other firms, without itself acquiring any part of the ownership of the business. ICI's £13 m. loan to Viyella was on these terms, yielding only 6¼ per cent, against ICI's normal requirement of a prospective profit of 15 per cent on its own ventures into the manufacture of any new chemical product (see *The Economist*, 23 Nov. 1963).

There is no means of telling how far such factors as these have influenced management behaviour over the whole range of private enterprise. As was pointed out earlier, there is a lack of systematic data on which to base precise and comprehensive generalizations in this field. Many of the changes which have occurred are in any case so recent that it would be surprising if much more were available at this stage than suggestive indications of underlying trends. The development of business planning is an obvious case in point. There is no way of measuring its significance.

Its considerable potential as a force making for stability in markets was discussed in the United States context.[13] Outside North America the information about business planning practices is much harder to come by. That is no doubt partly due to the fact that the practices themselves have been slower to take on in European business. Government planning, in those countries in which it is practised, does not appear to have been the decisive factor in business behaviour. At any rate such data as are available do not suggest that large French enterprises have been more energetic or systematic in the formulation of medium and long-range business plans than the corresponding German concerns, for example.[14] That is not to say that the government plans in France have had no effect on the methods of French firms; a study by Mussard and Taboulet showed, for instance, that some concerns fixed their regular planning period at four years, in order to conform with the *Commissariat du Plan*.[15] But the extent of business planning in any individual country seems to be little influenced by whether it has a national plan or not.

Indeed, the impression that one gains is that American business planning experience has exercised a more powerful influence on European business— whether directly through contact with American subsidiaries, which are involved in the planning exercise of their parent company, or indirectly by employing the services of industrial consultant firms, many of whom are either American or have adopted American methods—than the planning activities of their own governments. Not surprisingly, large firms, particularly international ones, have been most receptive to planning ideas.[16] The practice of

---

[13] See above, pp. 348 ff.

[14] B. R. Williams, *International Report on Factors in Investment Behaviour* (OECD, 1962), says that the evidence of his survey, covering the mechanical engineering industry, suggested that 'investment planning is less firm in France than in Germany, the Netherlands, and Sweden'. He found that the larger German firms in the industry, responsible for 80 per cent of the turnover in the national sample, had developed the practice of planning for more than one year ahead. The result, he noted, was that there was a solid proportion of the investment planned for each year which 'was not blown about by short-term changes' (ch. X, p. 13).

[15] A. Mussard and H. Taboulet, *Les Plans à Cinq Ans dans les entreprises françaises* (*SEDEIS Bulletin*, Suppl. no. 815, 1962) state that the practice of 'medium-term planning' (i.e. of several years' duration) started in earnest in France around 1957; it was largely confined to big business.

planning has spread during the early 1960s; it tends to be treated by a growing number of firms as an integral part of the techniques of scientific management. Moreover, the methods used, even by firms with a long established practice of forward budgeting several years ahead, show a marked increase in sophistication. At the same time, the whole exercise comes to be regarded less as a backroom operation—to be taken out and dusted on special occasions—and more as an active tool of management. There is, however, still some way to go before business planning in Europe achieves the fashionable status that it had acquired in American big business by the early 1960s. In the United States it has an established place among the techniques of large-scale enterprise, where it often commands the services of highly paid economists and the attention of senior members of boards of management.

Trying to rig an international commodity price *below* what the market is proclaiming is the most obvious and dramatic way of asserting the primacy of the long-term, hypothetical view of an industry's interests over the realities of immediate advantage. This has been done by the international copper companies in recent years, though because of the American anti-trust laws— four of the major companies are American—the arrangements have never been formalized; they rest on tacit understandings. The understandings nevertheless seem pretty reliable. They derive from the conclusion reached in the late 1950s by the seven major producing companies, which effectively control world supplies of new copper, that the chief threat to their future was the sharp fluctuations in the price of the commodity in international markets. Users of copper, above all the large-scale enterprises in the electrical industry,

---

[16] See e.g. T. Barna, *Investment and Growth Policies in British Industrial Firms* (London, CUP, 1962). In his sample of firms in the food processing and electrical engineering industries, eight of the largest concerns (employing over 20,000 persons) used plans of 2–5 years' duration, and of these half were foreign-controlled companies. Two of the British firms in this group had introduced planning either at the time that the study was undertaken (1959) or a little while before (p. 26). There is independent evidence that business planning of a systematic character did not begin to take hold in British industry—even among very large concerns—until the late 1950s and early 1960s. Among the evidence, admittedly impressionistic, are the answers to a questionnaire (which I devised) given by business executives attending the course at the Administrative Staff College, Henley, in December 1963. Mr J. P. Martin-Bates, the Director of the College, organized the exercise. It showed that even among this biased sample of firms—biased in the sense of being progressive enough to be willing to send a senior executive away on a course lasting several months—business planning of a systematic and rigorous kind was by no means general. It was also clear that for most of those who did engage in planning, it was a comparatively recent tool of business management. Further personal inquiries among large British concerns confirmed this conclusion. One famous international company selling consumer products, which is well known for its progressive management practices, only moved on to five-year planning in 1963—having previously taken the view that anything longer than two years was of little value for purposes of prediction, because of the probable amplitude of short-term fluctuations. Evidently by the early 1960s their view of the short term had changed.

wanted something whose cost they could predict for the purposes of their own long-term calculations. In this respect copper compared very unfavourably with its most dangerous competitor, aluminium.

The operation of fixing a price for copper and then sticking to it, regardless of what happened on the London Metal Exchange, was started as an independent venture by Rhodesian Selection Trust. It seemed a quixotic gesture. Yet it evidently corresponded to a common conviction among the major world producers that the metal market ought to be organized to respond less sensitively to short-term movements in supply and demand. Once the initiative had been taken, they proved to be eager to engage in a collective effort to this end. The actual level at which this ideally stable price was to be set was determined by a careful calculation of the counter-attractions of aluminium as a long-term proposition. A curious feature of the present world copper arrangement is that it does not depend on any form of overt bargaining about commitments to produce—or not to produce—certain tonnages by the individual companies. What the producers do is to engage in an innocent form of analytical exercise: they organize an annual exchange of data and ideas about the probable trend of demand and the potential supply of copper for a year ahead. Once agreement has been reached on the facts, the appropriate action to hold the market at the fixed price usually follows. If there are any failures of control, they can, it seems, usually be traced back to an unresolved difference in the estimate of future prospects.

The whole operation has certain features which are reminiscent of the American style of non-collusive business planning.[17] The copper companies are, however, occasionally forced into the open. This happened dramatically in 1964 when shortages of immediate supplies started a scramble for copper on the London Metal Exchange. Instead of managing the market by skilful purchases and sales, as they had done previously, so that its fluctuations were contained within the narrow range of prices fixed by them, they found it necessary to fight the market from the outside. They announced early in the year that they would continue to sell copper to their customers at a fixed price of £244 a ton, however high the London market price went. In fact it went as high as £500 a ton for a brief period in the autumn of 1964. The companies, which were by that time rationing their customers, could not entirely resist the pressure; they raised their selling price—to £260 a ton.[18] Summing up the

[17] See above, p. 347.
[18] See *The Economist*, 22 Aug. 1964, and various *Financial Times* market reports in 1964. The original price set by the Rhodesian producers, Rhodesian Selection Trust and Anglo-American, at the start of 1964 was £236 a ton. This was raised to £244. It was finally the pressure from the Chilean Government, which felt that it was being denied the benefit of the high profits available by selling on the London Metal Exchange, that compelled Anaconda, the US company which owned the Chilean mines to give way and lift the price ceiling to £260 a ton. The long-term view of

curious quarrel between the copper producers and the brokers on the London Metal Exchange who were trying to get them a higher price than they wanted, H. Heymann, the Swiss authority on commodity markets, argued that the decisive factor in it was the change which had taken place in the scale and structure of the industry: 'What has changed in copper over the last few decades is not the operations of the London market . . . but the emergence of . . . bigger units in both production and consumption of copper and, with it, a growing inclination towards "administrative" pricing.'[19]

Moreover, copper's example has proved catching. The aluminium price was already safely administered—by an even smaller number of major producers endowed with greater market power, because of their more extensive control over the manufacturing process down to the finished products. Zinc is the latest recruit to the doctrine of market stability above all else, including the making of a quick big profit. It looked at first as if it might be a more difficult metal to administer than the other two, because of the far greater number of independent mining companies. But it turned out that the concentrated control over the zinc smelters by a few large concerns effectively established their market power. Again, the aim was to keep the price down—against the strong upward pressures being exerted through the London Metal Exchange in 1964. In July of that year the major zinc companies formally announced a uniform range of selling prices, much lower than those which marginal supplies were fetching in the Exchange. During the first few months of the operation of the scheme the zinc producers appear to have been outstandingly successful—more so than the copper producers—in managing to keep supply and demand in the world market in nice balance.

Prices and the Public Interest

While business management was intent on the pursuit of policies which rode over market fluctuations, fixing prices by reference to other factors of more enduring interest to large productive enterprises, prices in general were coming to be regarded as belonging in the domain of public policy—a subject in which governments had a natural right to intervene. The doctrines which were used to justify the active interference of the state in the pricing policies of private enterprise, over and above the outlawing of price conspiracies

producer interests evidently does not recommend itself so readily to governments, especially governments of poor primary producing countries, as it does to large corporate enterprises endowed with plentiful financial reserves.

[19] *The Times*, 14 Aug. 1964. Heymann pointed out that the US had been a decade or two ahead of Europe in this process. There the 'changeover was fought out in the '20s and early '30s; in the rest of the world the fight has been on ever since the re-opening of the London copper market in August 1953'.

among sellers,[20] were often confused. But there was no doubt about the direction in which policies were pointed.

President Kennedy's dispute with the American steel companies in 1962 provides an especially striking illustration of the changing role of public policy in determining prices—partly because the incident occurred in a country where arguments about the exact line of demarcation between public and private authority tend to be passionate and explosive. Led by the United States Steel Corporation, several firms had raised the prices of their products against the President's wishes. The action was regarded as especially pro-vocative, because it followed on a wage agreement with the steelworkers in which the unions had agreed to a moderate wage settlement. Kennedy had no legal power to control the movement of steel prices. However, that did not prevent him from engaging the steel companies in an open battle. He explained his tactics to a press conference in April after United States Steel prices had been raised: 'I was hopeful that the others would not follow the examples and therefore the pressures of the competitive market place would bring United States Steel back to their original prices.' But the market did not work. He discovered that 'nearly the entire industry was about to come in'. He added, to explain his own intervention—'therefore the amount of choice we have is somewhat limited'.[21] His view was that it required the intervention of the President of the United States in order to invigorate the cowed com-petitors of US Steel. Nevertheless he insisted that price decisions 'are and ought to be freely and privately made'. He did not address himself to the possibility that US Steel's competitors might after all not be cowed but merely complaisant—pleased to see prices go up in an inelastic market containing a relatively small number of sellers, none of whom was anxious to undercut the others' prices and thus invite retaliation.[22] Kennedy was determined on the theory of conspiracy. 'The American people', he said, 'will find it hard, as I do, to accept a situation in which a tiny handful of steel executives whose pursuit of private power and profit exceeds their sense of public responsibility can show such utter contempt for the interests of 185 million Americans.'

The reaction of business leaders and of their Republican allies to Kennedy's action was remarkably fierce. In a series of counter-accusations the Repub-licans alleged that Kennedy's actions 'imperilled basic American rights, went far beyond the law, and were more characteristic of a police state than a free

[20] There was a spate of anti-trust legislation in a variety of West European countries during the 1950s and early 1960s—not an attack on bigness as such in the American style, rather an effort to outlaw overt price agreements, often among small firms (see Louis Franck, *La libre concurrence* (Paris, Presses Universitaires, 1963) for a summary of the legislation of the 1950s and 1960s). In the US too (see above, pp. 326 ff) the anti-trust laws were being interpreted with increasing severity.

[21] All quotations from USIS transcript, 12 Apr. 1962.

[22] The normal condition of several leading American manufacturing industries, as J. K. Galbraith indicated in *American Capitalism: The Concept of Countervailing Power* (London, Hamilton, 1957), competition by all means short of price-cutting.

government'.[23]   In fact his intervention did have precisely the effect intended: it employed the apparatus of the state to stimulate other companies, also large but much smaller than the US Steel Corporation,[24] to challenge the latter's position of 'price leadership' in the industry.   US Steel then found it had to cut back its price.   Moreover, the American business community as a whole, for all the protests against Kennedy's 'interference', was in no doubt that what had been done was not just an odd deviation by a President who was thought to be anti-business, but the expression of a new and abiding relationship between private and public authority in decisions about the price of anything which was deemed to be a key product—whatever that meant.[25]   Two years later, in the benign atmosphere of President Johnson's Administration, which businessmen felt to be much more sympathetic to their cause, the Secretary of Commerce, Luther Hodges, was boasting that prices would not rise, in spite of the gathering boom in demand, because of what he called the Administration's 'psychological control' over business and labour.[26]

The doctrinal confusion over the proper relationship between public and private power in determining prices is common to other Western countries. At times it seems that governments are simply demanding that businessmen behave like decent old-fashioned capitalists and take more heed of market forces.   (This is invariably when demand is slack.)   But on other occasions, they are exhorted to disregard such short-term considerations and to focus on the long-term perspective.[27]   But even though there is little consistency in the principles guiding government intervention on prices, it is clear at least that the practical effect is to add yet another brake on any sudden large movement.   It reinforces the placid behaviour of modern markets.

We have already discussed the more formal effort that has been made in some countries to control prices as part of an 'incomes policy'.[28]   Its relevance to the present theme is that it is yet another force tending to relate prices to an assumed long-term trend (in productivity) rather than to the fluctuating

[23] *The Economist*, 28 Apr. 1962.

[24] The output of the latter was about as large as that of Britain and France combined. The revolt against the price rise, by a minority of the industry, was led by Inland Steel and Kaiser.   Once it had these allies in the private sector, the Government could make US Steel do what it wanted without the appearance of taking charge of price decisions in the domain of private business.

[25] Steel was regarded as a key product largely because there was a convention that it set the trend of prices for a lot of other products.

[26] *The Times*, 16 Mar. 1964.

[27] An interesting example was the rebuke delivered by the British Chancellor of the Exchequer, Mr James Callaghan, to building societies for increasing their lending rates in early 1965 after the Government itself had sharply raised the bank rate from 5 to 7 per cent.   The building societies, he indicated, ought to base their lending rates on a long-term view and not on 'a temporary increase in bank rate' (HC Deb., 19 Jan. 1965).

[28] See above, ch. IX, 3.

balance of supply and demand. Perhaps the most ambitious piece of machinery of this kind set up by any of the major industrial nations so far is Britain's National Board for Prices and Incomes, created in 1965. It is not yet possible to say how this will work. But its essential purpose may be expressed as being to provide an alternative mechanism, in a situation where market forces have been blunted, which will produce the same answer as a competitive market would have done in the long run—only do so more quickly and without the violent ups and downs on the way.

It should be observed that the objective of price stability is not normally pursued at the expense of business profits. On the contrary, governments of Western countries in the 1960s tend to see it as part of their duty to safeguard the level of profits—on the theory that these in turn determine the level of investment. Modern price policy is not to be seen as merely an extension of the traditional warfare between the grasping merchants and the prince who tries to force them to disgorge their gains. The practical aim is price restraint rather than a bar on price movement: the message that governments are chiefly concerned to convey to business is that if prices have to go up, in order to maintain profits, the movement should be gradual.[29]

There are a number of other forces making their contribution towards taming the traditional violence of markets. I shall not attempt to list them all. But it is worth making special mention of two of them—one is the greatly increased importance of institutional investment (notably by insurance companies and pension funds) in the market for capital and the other is the changing character of commercial banks. The latter are in many European countries to be regarded by now as, in effect, semi-public institutions, licensed to make a profit, whose day-to-day operations are under the close supervision, and sometimes direction, of the public authorities. The supervision is just as complete in countries where the big banks are privately owned as in those, like France and Italy, where they are nationalized.[30] That is not to say that the greatly reinforced machinery for the control of financial affairs is always

---

[29] On public policy towards profits, see for example the proposal in the Draft Outline of the Fifth French Plan (*Projet de rapport* (1964), I–IV–10) that profit margins should be deliberately increased during the second half of the 1960s by arranging matters so that profits as a whole would rise by 2 per cent more than production each year. This was seen as a necessary measure to give a fillip to investment. The same argument was used in Italy in 1964–5 to justify a measure introduced by the Centre-Left Government to reduce employers' statutory payments for social security by the equivalent of nearly £40 m. a year (see *The Economist*, 20 Mar. 1965).

[30] In a country as devoted to private enterprise as Belgium, one finds the institution of the *reviseur*. He is the agent of the central bank—or more strictly the Commission Bancaire, which it controls—with a permanent office in the bank building and the right to inspect all its books. His task is to exercise a measure of direct tutelage over the policy of the individual banks on behalf of the governor of the central bank. This arrangement, like several of the other banking reforms elsewhere in Europe, grew out of the financial crisis of the early 1930s and dates from before the war; its full significance did not however emerge until after the war.

effectively used; Western governments in the 1950s and early 1960s were still in process of learning how to handle the power at their disposal.

In return the big banks have been endowed with a certain privileged status, which makes it extremely difficult for any newcomer to challenge their command over a large and lucrative business. They are, indeed, the most advanced model of the category of the 'permanent corporations',[31] which are characteristic of our epoch; public policy is committed to keeping them alive, just as surely as if they were nationalized undertakings.[32] What has been created out of this complex of forces is a credit system which can rely on a *steadier* flow of funds for investment (from institutions like insurance companies and pension funds) and one which is immeasurably more responsive than in the past to the requirements of public policy, when the latter is directed towards offsetting the shifts and turns of the business cycle. As the previous chapters have shown, by the mid-1960s public policy in all the major countries of the Western world had been deliberately geared to this end.

Science-based Industries

It may be objected that the forces making for the increasing emphasis on the long-term view and the element of systematic calculation in business decisions are likely to be offset by another factor which was given much prominence in the earlier chapters of this book. This is the exploding technology of our epoch.[33] By its nature it must surely add to the uncertainty of business plans, and make almost any investment more hazardous.

Yet it is a striking fact that the very concerns whose business depends on taking a view a long way ahead in industries peculiarly subject to the most rapidly changing technology, notably the great chemical firms of Western Europe and the United States, have also been among the most successful and profitable businesses of the postwar era. Their success might, of course, prove nothing more than that each of them had been lucky enough in its research and development to hit on one or more very lucrative line of production. That is clearly part of the truth. But there is more to it. A big business organization working in a field of rapid technological change nowadays plans its research strategy with 'defensive' as well as 'offensive' objectives in view. The methods that have been evolved by American concerns have been described by J. B. Quinn and R. M. Cavanaugh,[34] who show clearly that a large research and development programme, especially one involving basic

---

[31] Saraceno, *La produzione industriale*, see above, p. 192.

[32] On the assumption that they do not defy public policies—and also that they have reached the size that would make it indecent for them to be subject to a take-over bid (i.e. are among the 'big three', 'big four', or 'big five'—whichever happens to be appropriate to the size of the country concerned; in Holland there are now only the 'big two').

[33] See in particular Part I, Ch. III.

[34] 'Fundamental Research Can be Planned', *Harvard Business Review*, Jan.–Feb. 1964.

research, introduces a more than usually strong inducement to subject all phases of a business to a careful long-range plan.

As research has become a major item in the costs of a number of dynamic industries, companies in them are compelled to calculate as meticulously as they can the timetable for the development of possible new products—not only their own but also, so far as they can, the probable innovations of others. They have to take a wide view, as well as a long one, of the trends of technology in order to identify likely areas of innovation which may either compete with or duplicate their own efforts—or put some existing selling line out of business. This is where 'defensive' research is relevant—that is research which is not aiming at a break-through ahead of anyone else, but merely to maintain sufficient contact with new work in a field other than the company's own speciality, to be able to respond quickly in case some new advance there impinges on the company's existing market.[35] It is alleged that in America possible sources of competition resulting from fundamental research 'can be fairly easily estimated because liberal publication policies often allow a careful analyst to name each person that a competitor has working in the field'.[36] But not everything is published. What is actually done by the 'defensive' research worker—or the 'offensive' one for that matter—is not readily distinguishable from scientific espionage. All sources of information have to be used in this anxious business of defending your organization against the surprises of another firm's innovation. The aim may simply be to be ready in case of need to launch a 'crash programme' so as 'to force competitors to cross-licence otherwise damaging technology'.[37]

The upshot is that nowadays a major company operating in a field of rapid technological advance must spend a great deal of money not merely on the development of its own new products, but also in maintaining a wide network of other research activities related to work going on in the rest of its industry —and to some work outside it. Evidently, once the system has been set up, the business of keeping in touch with a world of speculative possibilities is not quite so nerve-racking as it sounds. What saves the situation is that although innovation is frequent, there is, as was pointed out in an earlier chapter,[38] an interval of years before any individual piece of research matures

[35] A typical example of such activity which I came across in the early 1960s was a research project, conducted by a large manufacturer of detergents, on the properties of sonic waves. It was basic research, and it was being done by a small unit. The intention was not to discover anything new, but rather to be sufficiently abreast of the discoveries of others to be able to report periodically to the company, well ahead of developments, on the prospects for the use of sonic waves as a means of cleaning textile materials. The detergent company was hoping by its defensive research to buy time in which to sort out a new commercial policy—if one were needed.

[36] See Quinn and Cavanaugh, *HBR*, Jan.-Feb. 1964, p. 119. This statement has some practical authority, since one of the authors of the article, R. M. Cavanaugh, was director of research in a department of Du Pont—a firm which spends more on research each year than any other chemical company in the world.

[37] Ibid.   [38] See above, p. 350.

into a saleable new product. McGraw Hill used seven years as a rough guide; for a piece of fundamental research the 'lead time' before anything saleable is produced may be much longer—estimated on the basis of recent American industrial experience to be from a minimum of five years up to as much as fifteen years.[39] For a firm which has set itself up to receive the proper signals, the odds are that some early warning of any major technological advance will be registered.

The Factor of Size

Bigness is especially important in science-based industry; it makes possible the wide spread of resources and the employment of expensive expertise required for success.[40] The consequence is not that there are no small or medium sized firms in these advanced sectors of industry—many of such firms run some speciality which allows them to survive, often with handsome profits—but that the substantial concern, which aims to offer its customers a wide range of an industry's products, has to be very big indeed. Some notion of the order of magnitude involved is given by the results of a survey of the distribution of the research and development expenditures in the United States by the National Science Foundation in the mid-1950s. This found that seven companies alone accounted for 26 per cent of the total expenditure on research of the 15,500 American firms which had research and development laboratories at that time.[41] The results are even more striking when broken down into individual industries. In each of the half dozen manufacturing industries which are together responsible for nine-tenths of all industrial research—chemicals, machinery, electrical equipment (including electronics), scientific instruments, motor vehicles, aircraft—there were, according to a later analysis by the US National Science Foundation in 1959, four big firms which accounted for at least 45 per cent, and often more, of the total amount spent on research in that industry. The proportion was commonly 60 per cent and over.[42]

[39] Quinn and Cavanaugh, *HBR*, Jan.–Feb. 1964.

[40] In fact each firm tries to achieve a quasi-monopolistic position in some particular branch of technology, where it aims to be the most advanced innovator. It is during the short period when it can stay ahead of the rest of the field that the very big profits are made. By the time its competitors catch up—or have been granted a licence to produce—the innovating firm aims to have achieved a lead with another new product. The fifteen years during which Du Pont enjoyed, practically unchallenged, the fruits of its invention of nylon are regarded as quite exceptional (see *Financial Times*, 27 May 1963, 'Du Pont digs deeper for its profits' by Geoffrey Owen).

[41] US National Science Foundation, *Science and Engineering in American Industry* (Washington, 1956), quoted by Carl Kaysen in E. S. Mason, ed., *The Corporation in Modern Society* (Cambridge, Mass., Harvard UP, 1959), p. 86.

[42] See OECD, *Science, Economic Growth and Government Policy* (1963), table 12, based on National Science Foundation figures.

In Britain the Advisory Council on Scientific Policy, in its 1964 annual report summing up seventeen years of work since its foundation, concluded that there was a special problem in dealing with research which offered the 'possibilities of substantial technological advance' but which was costly and would require an extended effort over a period of years. 'In such cases the expenditure and the risks involved may be so large that the enterprise is beyond the resources in men and money of any one firm acting in competitive conditions'.[43] The report went on to comment that it might be difficult to bring about 'a merger of firms' or other forms of industrial collaboration, which would create the required concentration of resources, and that in consequence the process of innovation might be delayed. In order to cope with just such a situation, the British Government in the 1950s had prompted a series of company mergers in the aircraft industry, so that by the early 1960s there were only two major manufacturers left in the field. Even this number began to seem as if it might be excessive by the middle of the decade, when a review of Britain's strategic commitments was undertaken with the aim of adapting them to the economic resources of a country of 50 million people.

Looking beyond the defence and aviation industries, the Advisory Council on Scientific Policy stated: 'Our own discussion of these problems points to the conclusion that there is an increasing number of fields in which very advanced research and development of long-term national importance needs to be undertaken, but is beyond the capacity of industry as now organized in this country.' And it went on to suggest that the state, 'taking a longer view' than industry, would have to provide more of the finance for the purpose.[44] In fact the British Government is already supplying nearly two-thirds of all the money spent on industrial research and development—about the same proportion as in the United States. In France the proportion is even higher.[45]

Governments thus possess an extremely powerful means of influencing the long-term direction of growth in the most dynamic sectors of the economy. It is remarkable in fact how little use has so far been made of it. The advantages implicit in a large research contract won by a firm in a science-based industry are considerable. Moreover, many of the beneficiaries are likely to be precisely the big well-established firms, with a proved reputation for the execution of research or development programmes and the quality of staff required to do the job well. It is largely their research capacity which

---

[43] Annual Report of the Advisory Council on Scientific Policy, 1963–4 (Cmnd 2538), para. 34.

[44] Ibid., para. 36.

[45] See OECD, *Science, Economic Growth, &c.*, table 1. The report showed that industrial research, outside the defence field (where Britain and the US spent very heavily) reached a figure of $1\frac{1}{4}$–$1\frac{1}{2}$ per cent of the national product in most of the advanced countries. The proportion of the national product devoted to research and development rose very sharply in the 1950s.

has been responsible for giving these firms their position of overwhelming dominance in the postwar defence industries.[46]

In the early 1930s Adolf Berle and Gardiner Means in their influential book, *The Modern Corporation and Private Property*,[47] advanced the thesis that the trend of business organization in the twentieth century was to make the centres of corporate power progressively larger and fewer. Despite the series of pressures enumerated above, the thesis does not fit the facts of postwar America.[48] On the other hand the official German inquiry into concentration in the economy[49] concluded that there had been a marked increase in the importance of the largest industrial corporations during the 1950s. The top fifty in size, who had been responsible for 17·7 per cent of industrial sales in 1954, accounted for 29 per cent by 1960. The report pointed specifically to the influence of technological change as one of the factors making for the concentration of industry; it increased the basic burden

[46] In the US, for instance, ten large concerns, including the three largest companies in each of their respective industries—General Motors, American Telephone and Telegraph, and General Electric—captured nearly one-third of all the military contracts placed in the period covered by the Korean War and immediately after, 1950–6 (see Kaysen in Mason, *The Corporation*, p. 86). The advantage that goes with a government research contract and also the dependence of the Government on the goodwill of the large efficient concern is well illustrated in the following exchange between Senator Paul Douglas and a representative of the US Defense Department (see Hearing of Evidence before the Subcommittee on Defense Procurement of the Joint Econ. Ctee of Congress, Mar.–Apr. 1963):

'*Douglas*: . . . When a firm gets a research contract it has a stranglehold on development. Of necessity, the research contract carries with it the production of the prototype. . . . When research and development is carried on with the private ownership of patents, as I understand it . . . then others are foreclosed from coming into the field to bid on the production items' (p. 53).

'*Bannerman* [Deputy Assistant Secretary of Defense]: . . . No invention is ever the product of one contract. It is the product of an on-going technology, usually in some company. These companies, for the most part, are in business for commercial reasons, for making profits in the commercial markets. We want to tap their technology for governmental use.' In reply to the suggestion that patents derived from government-sponsored research should be made freely available, Mr Bannerman said: 'If we were to demand that they [i.e. the companies] give away their commercial rights, we feel quite confident that they would be very reluctant to devote their best research talents to our work' (p. 55).

[47] New York, Macmillan, 1932.

[48] Berle recognized as much in his later book, *The Twentieth Century Capitalist Revolution* (New York, Harcourt, Brace, 1954). See J. Lintner, 'The Financing of Corporations' in Mason, *The Corporation*, for a careful analysis of the Berle and Means thesis on the basis of the company data for the 25 years following its publication. His conclusion is that the main movement towards concentration in American industry occurred during the first part of the twentieth century and was further reinforced in the 1920s. It underwent a reversal in one field of industry as a result of the enforced break-up of the public utility holding companies in the 1930s. In manufacturing the concentration of industrial power has remained unchanged at a very high level.

[49] See above, p. 241.

of capital costs, which could be more readily carried by larger industrial enterprises.[50] Elsewhere in Western Europe, there are indications—though no comprehensive statistical information—that the series of company mergers and take-overs of business in Britain and several other countries during the late 1950s and early 1960s resulted in a movement of concentration parallel to the German one, though it is impossible to say whether it was on a comparable scale.

The evidence available points to the conclusion that there is no simple uniform trend towards fewer and bigger firms, but rather that there is an increasingly important range of industrial activity, dependent on research and development of the wide-ranging type characteristic of industries in the most dynamic sectors of modern technology, which requires the support of firms that have grown beyond a very substantial size.[51] The same factor also tends to impose new limitations on the industrial capabilities of otherwise advanced nations. The International Economic Association, in a symposium on the *Economic Consequences of the Size of Nations* published in 1960,[52] pointed to the tentative conclusion that the minimum size required to secure the typical economies of scale of modern industry was a nation with a population of at least 10–15 million, but that most of the advantages of scale were available to a country whose population reached 50 million.[53] What has been happening in some of the most advanced European industries during the early 1960s suggests that the threshold of size over a widening range may by now be well above a national population of 50 million.

A Trial Run in Computers

The European electronic computer industry in the early 1960s has provided a dramatic insight into the problem of scale as it affects the structure of enterprises working on the frontiers of new technology. During the 1950s the

---

[50] The comment of the OECD report, *Science, Economic Growth &c.*, is pertinent: 'It is much more difficult to borrow money for investment in research and development than for investment in fixed capital, and firms which, for one reason or another, cannot finance R. and D. from their own resources will find it much more difficult to engage in research than firms which have better possibilities of self-financing' (para. 46).

[51] The OECD report, *Science, Economic Growth &c.*, says that there is no 'strong positive linear correlation' between the size of firms and the performance of research and development. That may mean no more than that some large firms do not engage in R. and D., and that many medium-sized firms do. In fact the OECD's own figures (table 11) show that the large firms are responsible for 85 per cent of total research expenditure in the US and 93 per cent in the UK. The 'medium' firms accounted for 8 per cent in the US and 6 per cent in the UK.

[52] E. A. G. Robinson, ed. (London, Macmillan).

[53] Robinson pointed out that there were certain benefits of extra specialization, e.g. in sub-contracting, which the US had over the West European nations in the 50 m. population class. Simply because the market was that much bigger the economy could support more specialist firms of small or medium size, with a very narrow range of products, enjoying the benefit of long runs.

French and Italian firms which were in the business of computers were among the brightest hopes of European industry—go-ahead, proud of their big research laboratories and their skill in bringing new products to the market, and above all immensely profitable. The two biggest companies, Machines Bull in France and Olivetti in Italy, were treated as great national assets. And so they were: they endowed these countries with centres for the development of the advanced instruments which were rightly seen as the key to the new production techniques of the second half of the twentieth century. But by 1963 both companies were in serious financial trouble. The details in each case were different, but what was common to both was that they possessed neither the technical resources nor sufficient funds to stand up to the competition of the leading American firm in the computer industry, International Business Machines. When the pace of innovation in an industry becomes very hot, the distance between the front runner and those who are equipped to move forward only at normal speeds of technical advance is glaringly apparent. The typical customer for the products of such an industry is likely to be more than usually aware of what is the very latest thing—and determined to have it. The technical lifetime of data processing machines has in fact shortened progressively. To begin with, a seven-year life was regarded as reasonable, and machines were hired out to customers on rental agreements which reflected the expectation that it would take that long before any major technological advance would make the machine uncompetitive. The period was then cut to five years; and by the early 1960s it had come down to something closer to three years.[54]

It was not inevitable that Bull and Olivetti should fail to hold their own in these circumstances. The British firm, International Computers and Tabulators, which was itself the product of the merger of several quite substantial concerns, did manage to survive as an independent company in the face of similar pressures. But it was clear that an ordinary European company, working on a scale corresponding to European nation-state size, was under a severe disadvantage in competing with IBM, whose base was in a vastly bigger and also more sophisticated market. If it was to overcome the handicap, a European company might well need some form of special support from an interested government; and there was in fact one government at least, that of General de Gaulle, standing ready and eager to do its stuff. The French authorities worked out a scheme to put Machines Bull on a new and stronger financial basis. Various organizations, all in some way dependent on the favour of the Government, including the Caisse des Dépôts, the semi-public

---

[54] For the last figure, see *The Economist*, 26 Sept. 1964, p. 1252. The earlier estimates of the market life of computers are based on the notional periods used by European companies to calculate charges under their rental agreements. Plainly, the longer the expected life of the machine, the smaller the annual rental that has to be charged.

bank which looks after the bulk of official funds, were pressed into a financial consortium. Their task was to go out and save Bull from the American take-over bidders who were known to be lurking near at hand.

But in the event, neither the saviours nor the victim marked out for saving had much stomach for the scheme, which had been patriotically labelled '*la solution française*'. The management of the company made no secret of the fact that it wanted to be able to command the technological resources of an American-size business, in order to be able to meet IBM on level terms. In the end it got what it wanted by entering into a partnership with General Electric, the biggest electrical firm in the United States, which paid cash in return for half of the company's shares in 1964.[55] Olivetti too found it expedient to turn to General Electric in 1964, when the latter took over 60 per cent of the shares in its computer business.[56] Meanwhile in Germany the Radio Corporation of America had already developed an arrangement with Siemens for the production of computers there.

There is room for argument about the influence of special factors peculiar to the individual firms concerned in deciding the outcome. But in this instance what may prove to be as important as the facts themselves is the lesson that business management in Europe derived from the story. It confirmed the widespread view that there was a need for greatly enlarged scale in a number of industries subject to rapid technological change and making expensive products.[57] Rightly or wrongly, there is a suspicion that economists, particularly economists under the influence of Anglo-Saxon ideas, tend to underestimate the advantages of size, which are so apparent to management. By managers, the scale of the enterprise is treated as an offset to the additional risk and uncertainty attendant on doing business on the frontiers of technology. It seems likely that the common view of management is what will influence the actual shape and size of the firm of the future.

The Politics of Private Economic Power

The changing style and structure of modern private enterprise, described in the preceding sections, raise some important political issues. The typical business organization in Western society in the second half of the twentieth century is a much steadier employer of labour; it is much more amenable to pressures from public authority; it is more sensitive to the public view of its

---

[55] See *The Economist*, 1 Aug. 1964. General Electric obtained a 49 per cent interest in two of the companies into which the Bull organization was divided and a 51 per cent interest in the third, judged to be the most important of the three.

[56] Ibid., 5 Sept. 1964.

[57] The lesson was taken to heart by the EEC, which was by the mid-1960s actively seeking means of promoting mergers between *large* European companies in these industries, whose scale was still judged to be insufficient to match the technical and financial advantages of the giant American concerns operating on the frontiers of known technology.

behaviour; it tends, especially if it is big, to be powerfully influenced by the long-term view; above all, it is inclined, if it is a substantial enterprise, to view itself as a *permanent* institution, with functions distinct from making the maximum profit, and sometimes not even compatible with it. The taming of the market—in the sense that sudden movements of market forces are no longer permitted to disrupt the life of civilized society—is the condition for a style of private enterprise which tends to grow more like the behaviour of certain public institutions.[58]

Of course, there is still a lot of competitive enterprise about. Small building firms still go bankrupt in considerable numbers in any off-boom year. And bustling parvenu businessmen, selling a new product or service, still regularly demonstrate their ability to push their way into an industry or trade and to establish a powerful position in it, against the desires of the sitting tenants. Nevertheless, it remains true that the large corporations occupy a position of impressive authority and influence. Their power cannot be precisely measured; but it is illustrated by such facts as that about half of American manufacturing output is produced by the 130 biggest corporations, and that in German industry one out of every three workers is employed by the 100 largest concerns.[59] Moreover, the great more than ever tend to set the tone for the rest of the business community. Fashionable business journalism, whose volume has grown enormously since the war, concentrates on their doings. This is partly because they are more open and easy to get at, and have set themselves to explain to outsiders what they are about.

In counting the blessings that go with a more urbane form of commercial life, we should not overlook the fact that the violence of the old-fashioned market place did, after all, produce certain benefits which we can no longer take for granted. For example, the relentless pursuit of profit by a lot of tough owner-entrepreneurs hustling one another and their workers did tend, so long as none of them was in a position to exercise monopolistic power, to bring prices down to the lowest level compatible with economic production. The entrepreneur's behaviour had a certain automaticity. Nowadays the manager, who is not the owner, is neither driven into automatic responses by the forces of the market place nor guided by the exclusive desire to make the maximum profit on behalf of his shareholders. This is where the political problem arises. So long as the management of a large public company is

[58] Professor Edward Mason observes shrewdly: 'While large private corporations have been forced by their sheer size, power and "visibility" to behave with a circumspection unknown to the untrammelled nineteenth century, government on the other hand has attempted to give its "businesslike" activities a sphere of independence approaching that of the private corporation'. He concludes that 'managerial practices and attitudes in the public and private sectors of most Western economies tend to become more similar' (*The Corporation*, p. 17).

[59] See Mason (ibid., p. 5) for the US and Bundestags-Drucksache IV/2320 for Germany.

reasonably successful at making a profit, it is normally left alone to conduct the business as it sees fit and to appoint its own successors. The position of the shareholders, which is sometimes presented by the ideologues of business in the image of a parliament telling ministers what to do, is in fact much closer to that of a highly disciplined army, which is permitted by law to riot against its generals if, but only if, rations should happen to run out.

The ordinary shareholder who disagrees with the policy of a company in which he has invested does not usually stay to argue; he prefers to sell out. The case is different when there happens to be a single big shareholder with a long-standing interest in the business. But in the large public companies whose shares are widely held by investors, it is only *after* a disaster has happened that the shareholder's voice is normally heard. Such disasters are not very frequent. Moreover, the right to participate in disaster salvage seems a meagre formula for democratic control. It is not, for instance, the sort of formula which would readily be accepted by the voters of a modern colonial dependency as the sum total of their constitutional rights.

Shareholders, of course, are different. There is no reason why they should have the same interest in self-government as colonial peoples. But that still leaves unsolved the problem of defining the political status of management power. What, for instance, are the limits of the authority of management in a German bank, where shareholders' proxy votes have been faithfully collected and handed over to be cast as management sees fit?[60] This is not an isolated or eccentric case. The biggest Belgian holding company, the Société Générale, has as its two chief shareholders a couple of insurance companies, the Royale and the Assurance Générale. But these two companies are in turn controlled by the Société Générale whose management appoints directors to their boards. A mere owner of part of the equity in any one of these business organizations would be unable to come within shouting distance of the closely interlocked circle of non-proprietary managers, where all the real power resides. One of the consequences of the phenomenon of managerial autonomy, of which the Belgian holding companies and the German big banks are only the extreme manifestations, was stated as follows by Paul Harbrecht in his study of *Pension Funds and Economic Power*:[61] 'A man's relationship to things—material wealth—no longer determines his place in society (as it did in a strong proprietary system) but his place in society now determines his relationship to things.'

It is worth making the general point that socialist reformers, as well as right-wing ideologues of business, have tended to exaggerate the lasting importance of the property relationship. They took it for granted that it was, and would remain, in its crude form, the fundamental feature of capitalist

---

[60] See above, pp. 249–50.
[61] New York, Twentieth Century Fund, 1959, quoted in Harbrecht & Berle, *Toward the Paraproprietal Society* (Twentieth Century Fund, 1960), p. 39.

society. Ownership, it was assumed, was the pure form of power, and all other types of power were sub-categories of it. It therefore followed that the only way to change the manner in which economic power was used was to take away the property rights of the existing owners and transfer them to the collective ownership of society, embodied in the state. The important discovery of the postwar period is that ownership is of itself much less important than either revolutionary proletarian or conservative bourgeois philosophy alleged. It has become clear that these two agreed about altogether too much.

Nevertheless, ownership does convey legitimacy—the legal right to exercise certain kinds of power. Although big business management is in fact largely a self-perpetuating oligarchy, it claims its right to issue commands as the democratically appointed representative of the owners of the enterprise.[62] Professor Edward Mason has remarked on the special advantages which this confers on managers of enterprises working in the private sector compared with those working in the public sector: 'As we have seen, management has pretty much escaped from ownership control, but though private ownership may no longer carry with it control, it does guarantee corporate management against most of the political, ministerial and legislative interference that commonly besets public management. Perhaps in a corporate society this is becoming one of the primary contributions of private property.'[63] We have had occasion to observe how, for example in the Italian nationalized undertakings run by IRI, the management is in practice very adept at resisting interference—and the Government, it is fair to say, rather diffident about trying it on. There are signs of a certain convergence between the behaviour of the public and the private sectors in this matter too. Nevertheless, Mason is surely right to stress the importance of the legitimacy conferred on management initiatives in the private sector by the myth of private ownership control. In the public sector the powerful manager is sometimes able to assert his independence, even in overt defiance of the government's wishes; but it usually requires a special kind of personality to do it—preferably one

---

[62] Adolf Berle's comment on this point is telling. 'Interesting parallels suggest themselves. The administrator of a Soviet state operation, if asked where he acquired his right to run it, would answer that the competent authorities of the Communist government put him there. If asked how they got that right, he would probably answer that they derived it from an oligarchic group known as the Central Party Committee in Moscow. To the inquiry why this oligarchy had authority to make decisions, he would take refuge in mythology. . . . If the same questions were asked of the president of the American Telephone & Telegraph Company, he would probably say he was elected to his job by the board of directors of his company. If inquiry were made where they got the right to give him the job, he would probably repeat the myth that the directors were "elected by the stockholders"—though the undeniable fact is that they have been chosen by their predecessor directors as vacancies occurred for the last thirty or forty years' (P. P. Harbrecht and A. A. Berle, *Toward the Paraproprietal Society*, p. 11.

[63] *The Corporation*, p. 11.

that is rather over life-size.[64]   In private enterprise it can be done with far less personal effort and panache.   The humdrum manager can get away with more.

Who Manages the Managers?

Governments have their own problems in dealing with big corporate enterprises which possess some special technical and managerial know-how.   The US Assistant Secretary of Defense, Thomas D. Morris, giving evidence to the Joint Economic Committee of Congress in 1963, estimated that if he wanted to turn to an alternative source of production for the Polaris, it would cost 'over \$100 million in facilities and special tooling' and an extra three years of waiting.[65]   The Department of Defense has tried to avoid total dependence on any one company by the system of 'back up' contractors—firms which are paid to keep in touch with the technical development of a given project and follow it through from stage to stage, in order to be able in case of need to take over the production contract.   But this form of simulated competition is expensive, and with only two firms in the field, is bound to have a limited effect.[66]   The truth is that in most Western societies, although the Government possesses plenty of means which it can use—if it has the will—to bully or to cajole big private firms, it also has to be ready on occasion to bargain and to compromise with their independent wishes.

The political and social power of corporate management is far more marked in other fields, outside its relations with government.   It frequently nowadays bears a benevolent look.   But even its benevolence has aroused opposition in the passionate debate on the true function of the modern corporation which has been engaged in the United States.[67]   By what right do the managers of an enterprise which they do not own presume to distribute largesse from its

[64] Mattei in Italy was the outstanding example (see above, p. 185), but there have been several others less well known, including some in British nationalized industries.

[65] See above, p. 344, n. 35.

[66] In 1965 the US Department of Defense decided, when it was about to embark on the project of a new giant transport aircraft, the C5A, that it was too expensive to maintain the trappings of competition between firms for the production work on the aeroplane after the research and development contract had been placed.   The Defense Department spokesman was reported as saying that 'production work had to be awarded to the development contractor on a non-competitive basis unless the government was willing to duplicate, at great cost in money and time, much of the work already performed' (*Financial Times*, 15 March 1965).

[67] See the discussion on this question in *The Corporation in Modern Society* (Mason, ed.), which is of an unusually high quality.   It is noteworthy that no comparable interest in the subject of the rights and duties of the corporate enterprise and its place in society has apparently been aroused either in Britain or in Germany.   It is as if in these countries there were only two possible positions: either the corporation is taken completely for granted or it is the object of total distrust and hostility.   Only in France does there appear to have been any comparable *philosophical* interest in the subject of the role of the corporation (see in particular, François Bloch-Lainé, *Pour une réforme de l'entreprise*).

profits? There are great dangers, it is argued, in encouraging business management to be dominated by considerations of public policy, at the expense of normal commercial motives. Eugene Rostow is perhaps the most powerful advocate of this school of thought.[68] Recognizing the large degree of autonomy in modern business management, he claims that the only way in which a proper check can be kept on its behaviour in the public interest is by imposing the rule of 'profit maximization as a legal principle'.

The proffered solution illustrates, more than anything else, the profound nature of the dilemma which is posed by modern corporate management. The Rostow formula is really an attempt to extend the principles of American anti-trust, which are supposed to compel people to compete, one stage further—by forcing the individual firm to demonstrate that it has concentrated on making the maximum profit for itself regardless of the effect on anyone else. Indifference to the public interest, in the sense that governments understand it, is, he believes, of the essence of efficient private enterprise. This is a consistent, if extreme, view. It is the authentic expression of the nostalgia for the automatic checks and balances which used to keep management in its place. That management itself would reject the idea out of hand, because it represented a serious diminution of its social functions, would no doubt be regarded by its author as a positive recommendation for the proposal.

Alternative suggestions for dealing with the excessive autonomy of management envisage the creation of a 'second chamber' inside corporations, consisting of a group of experts to whom shareholders would delegate their votes and their rights of supervision.[69] This is close to the German idea of the *Aufsichtsrat*; it at once raises the problem of whether these representatives of the shareholders will themselves be managerial types. If they are, the chances are that they will gang up with the existing managements. If not, it is hard to see how they will acquire the expertise necessary to control them. Partly in order to meet the latter problem, Justice W. O. Douglas of the US Supreme Court has made the suggestion that a new post of 'paid director' should be created, with the exclusive function of acting as watchdog for the shareholders, their permanent full-time representative on the board.

It is characteristic that the American thinkers who tackle this problem instinctively turn towards devices which are supposed to ensure better forms of representation for the interests concerned. By contrast, the formula offered by one French reformer of the 1960s with a considerable following, is an extension of the judicial process. M. Bloch-Lainé, in his *Pour une réforme de l'entreprise*,[70] argues that a modern enterprise, having ceased to be a piece of simple property, has become a complex institution controlled jointly by three different parties with claims on it. They are the equity shareholders, the

---

[68] *The Corporation*, pp. 46 ff.
[69] Ibid., pp. 57–58. Professor B. Manning, Jr. (1958), quoted by E. Rostow.
[70] See in particular chs. 3 and 7.

public authorities, and the employees. He suggests that businesses should be subjected to the surveillance of an independent *magistrature*. This would be separate from the government and would maintain its professional standards, like any good judiciary, by collective self-discipline. The emissaries of the *magistrature* would look into the affairs of any individual business, in the same objective spirit as an accountant, and 'verify' whether the obligations of the management to the three parties with rights in the enterprise were being fulfilled or not. The government's interest, as Bloch-Lainé sees it, is in ensuring that the firm makes its proper contribution to the national Plan; this has to be accommodated with the interest of the workers in high wages and the interest of the shareholders in large dividends.

Once again, the idea may seem somewhat far-fetched and even eccentric; its significance is that, like Eugene Rostow's proposal, it comes from an eminently sensible man who finds that the problem of modern management demands radical and offbeat solutions. Bloch-Lainé's book putting forward these proposals was the outcome of extensive discussions among groups of reformers many of them working inside the French civil service.[71] It also had a considerable popular success, when it was published in 1963, among the French reading public.

The purpose of this summary account of questions raised in the current debate on the proper role of corporate power is not to point to any particular solution, but rather to indicate something of the flavour of the argument that has begun to emerge, as a concomitant of the changing style of private enterprise. It is an argument which is likely to grow in intensity. Whatever the outcome, one prediction about its practical consequences seems secure. The unresolved problem of the legitimacy of management separated from the ownership function will reinforce the trend towards an expansion of the supervisory role of public power over the private sector. It may be judicial, legislative, or merely administrative supervision. However, public power raises its own problems of legitimacy and effectiveness. These problems are discussed in the essay on the future of democratic institutions under modern capitalism in Part 4.

---

[71] The Club Jean Moulin (see Bloch-Lainé's introduction to *Pour une réforme de l'entreprise*, p. 7).

Part 4

AN ESSAY ON SOME POLITICAL IMPLICATIONS OF ACTIVE GOVERNMENT

AN ESSAY ON
SOME POLITICAL IMPLICATIONS OF
ACTIVE GOVERNMENT

THE political institutions in current use in Western society were designed, for the most part, to cope with a set of circumstances that are remote from those which have been described in the preceding chapters. This concluding section is concerned with the problems raised by the process of adapting these institutions to new functions. It tries to analyse the questions and to suggest directions in which remedies may be sought, rather than to propose a complete answer. I cannot in fact see a satisfactory answer, and suspect that one will only begin to emerge after there is much more widespread worry about the problem itself and active discussion of its nature. The central question is how far an active government wielding great and varied economic power, intervening in the detailed conduct of private business affairs, discriminating between one citizen and another on the basis of subtle and complex judgements of the community's needs ten or twenty years ahead, driving bargains with particular interest groups as administrative convenience dictates, can be subjected to effective democratic control. My concern is primarily with the relationship between the individual and the state. There are other important aspects of the democratic process which demand attention, notably the organization of collective entities like trade unions, parties and pressure groups, and the ways in which they exercise political power. It is noteworthy that the line between government and non-government activity tends increasingly to lose its sharpness in the course of an exercise such as economic planning; the future structure of these influential organizations outside government is therefore of great significance. But it is the individual in his private capacity who is most vulnerable to the erosion of old style capitalism—which allowed him considerable freedom so long as he had a bit of money and a steady job—and to the crowding in of more and more public power. That this power often has a beneficent purpose does not make it any less awkward to deal with.

It is noticeable that some of the nations which made the most complete and successful adaptation to the political problems of the earlier era of capitalism seem to be stuck with especially inefficient and stumbling political machinery when they apply themselves to the new problems. This is outstandingly true of the Anglo-Saxon countries. Britain and the United States, both holding to the Common Law tradition, were brilliantly inventive in using their legal systems to create an environment in which a great reserve of previously suppressed business initiative was liberated. They concentrated the main weight of their effort on the protection and enlargement of the rights of private property: the arrangements governing society were turned into a series of contracts between owners of various things, including the owners of their own labour, about the terms on which such property was to be used. The system was harsh, but its by-product was a degree of personal liberty rarely, if ever, realized before.

The political techniques adopted by the two countries to secure their ends were different. In Britain the method, pursued with evangelical vigour during most of the nineteenth century, was to limit the sphere of government—while recognizing the need to maintain the strength of an irreducible hard core of governmental power. The enlargement of private freedom, by the assertion of property rights, was held to be dependent on reducing the *range* of public power. The Americans were more radical: they deliberately weakened the public power itself by dividing it into separate parts. We have seen how the separation of powers in the US system and its concomitant, the competitive theory of government, make it extraordinarily difficult for the United States today to achieve a coherent long-term economic policy. In Britain, on the other hand, the trouble is that although there is an established principle of strong unitary central power, there are other potent traditions ingrained in the political system which impede the development of active, interventionist government. There is an abiding prejudice which sees it as the natural business of government to react—not to act.

France, by contrast, never adjusted itself fully to the needs of the capitalist entrepreneur of the nineteenth century: there governmental power was neither limited nor divided. The national image of the successful modern state, based on that of Napoleon I, was Louis XIV's state writ even larger. There was never any conscious break with the traditional modes of exercising public power. The French Revolution, unlike the English or the American ones, did not secure the rights of the ordinary citizen by forcing the executive power of the state to retreat and then setting up an independent judiciary to consolidate the result. The French purpose, as it unfolded after 1789, was above all to secure the active participation of the individual citizen in the doings of the state; in the process the power of the state, and of the whole apparatus of government, was enhanced rather than diminished. Typically, the spirit of judicial independence which is in the keeping of the ordinary courts in the Anglo-Saxon system, emerged in France out of the centre of the administration itself. The ordinary judiciary was comparatively weak. But the great official, with his high professional standards and his personal confidence deriving from the majesty of the state, was much stronger than elsewhere. He came to see himself as the independent spokesman for the public interest, often against the popular and political interests represented by the politician. It is characteristic that the most renowned court in France, renowned above all for its spirit of independence, is the Conseil d'État—a body of professional administrators who are appointed as independent judges of the actions of the administration.

Broadly, it is true to say that whereas in Britain the separation of powers meant that the judiciary was divided off from the administration,[1] and in the United States that the legislature was hived off too, in France the great and enduring separation was between the professional politicians and the *permanent* administration. The historical point is worth making, because these two contrasting traditions, the Anglo-American and the French, continue to exercise a profound influence on the political structures and styles of government throughout the Western world. One of the themes of the earlier chapters of this book has been that we are much more firmly the prisoners of our national histories than we imagine; we can knock off a shackle or break a hole in the wall, but it requires a conscious and sustained effort to get the job of demolition done. There is no need to repeat the argument in detail here. The conclusion suggested by the discussion of French economic history[2] was that a set of institutions which were largely pre-capitalist in design could be adapted more readily than others to serve the purposes of the new capitalism, with its large built-in segment of public power, in the second half of the twentieth century.

Three Safeguards

The point is not that they order politics better in France. Indeed, it is clear from even a cursory examination of modern history that the British are far more successful at managing great changes with little violent upheaval. British institutional equipment seems to have been especially well designed for the purpose, and it has been supported by civilized and subtle political habits. Britain, in fact, demands special attention in any discussion of the future of Western political institutions. It provides a model of what was probably the most admired piece of political machinery of the age just past, at once most sensitive and most stable, and now stands out as particularly ill adapted to cope with the problems of the present age.

A nation which is unable to establish effective democratic control over the processes of modern government faces one of two alternatives. Either it

---

[1] The Act of Settlement of 1701 did envisage, in addition to the establishment of an independent judiciary, the complete separation of the legislature from office-holders under the Crown, i.e. the executive. This was the formula which the Americans later adopted; but in Britain it never established itself. In fact the formula used by the 17th-century reformers who were trying to limit the power of the executive in England was not 'separation' but, characteristically, 'mixed monarchy'. It was a system of active collaboration—laws to be made by the King *in* Parliament—which was the objective; this was gradually realized in the early 18th century (see Maurice Ashley, 'Constitutionalism and the Sovereign States in the Seventeenth Century', in *Chapters in Western Civilization*, vol. i (New York, Columbia UP, 1961).

must accept that the liberties of its citizens will be diminished or it must forego the great material benefits which can be made to flow from the opera·tions of the active interventionist state of today. In practice, what this means for those countries which have a firmly established system of representative institutions is that the full potentialities of the new economic system will not be exploited unless fresh political techniques to secure the effective control of enlarged governmental power are brought into being. Political invention is therefore in this sense part of the equipment required for economic growth.

It may be useful at this stage to list some of the major political safeguards which need to be reinforced in order to meet the changes in the economic system. First of all, the greatly enlarged scope for the exercise of administrative discretion must be made more visible—and audible. On the one hand, we want officials to take more initiative, to exercise judgement on a wider range of subject matter than they have in the past; but on the other hand, we must be able to call on the person who makes these decisions to give an account of the reasons which moved him in deciding one way and not another. The fiction that all the acts of a government department are the personal responsibility of the minister placed in charge of it, who has to explain them on demand to parliament, fits the facts less and less. Indeed, ministerial responsibility, in its extreme British version, is a device for preventing the public from learning about the actual reasons which determine the behaviour of the great body of administrators who intervene increasingly in their daily lives.[3] It should also be recognized that certain administrative acts involving the exercise of discretion can be more suitably examined by the courts than by parliament.

Secondly, if parliament is to exercise an effective supervision over the great range of work which is, or ought to be, done by a modern administration, it must re-equip itself for this highly technical and exacting task. The plenary session culminating in a vote taken along party lines has limited relevance to the problem. The obvious alternative is the small specialist committee, developing over a period of time a considerable degree of expertise, and supported by professional staff of its own sufficiently knowledgeable to talk to the professional civil servants on equal terms.[4]

[3] The only exception to the rule that parliament's powers of direct investigation do not extend beyond the ministers to those who actually do the work of their departments is in the Public Accounts Committee and the Committee on Estimates. They question civil servants, in theory only about how money voted by parliament was spent, but by implication. on some occasions at least, about how they exercised their judgement.

[4] The US Congressional committees, see p. 336 n. 15 above, provide an example of how this can be done. The defect of the American committees, as was argued in Chs. XIII and XIV, is that they have individually accumulated great and separate powers, which they use to keep the Federal Government fragmented and less effectual than it should be. However, this is in large part due to special constitutional arrangements peculiar to the US, and it is not to be assumed that expert parliamentary committees in other countries would prove to be either as indifferent to the needs of the executive or as impervious to party discipline as the American ones are.

Thirdly, the necessary intimate relationship between the public authorities and private interest groups has to be made more explicit and open. The great enlargement of the sphere of public power does not make that power less sensitive to the pressures of private interests and individuals. On the contrary, the increased range and subtlety of the relationship between the public and the private sectors have made it less feasible to govern effectively by decree. The system will not function unless private organizations give their willing collaboration to the pursuit of public purposes. What is therefore required is the opposite of a bully state—rather a wheeling and dealing type of public authority constantly seeking out allies, probing and manoeuvring for the active consensus.[5] On the one hand this creates an additional force making for a new kind of political equilibrium: enhanced governmental power generates its own offset. But on the other hand the important private interest groups, on whom the government depends for active collaboration over a widening range of its activities, often play little part in the overt democratic process conducted by the officially elected representatives of the people. The essential dialogue in a country like Britain tends to take place out of earshot, between the faceless government official and the discreet emissary of some 'recognized' association with an interest in the business in hand. By the time a legislative proposal reaches the floor of parliament, many of the substantial matters for parliament will have been settled at another level.

Making Power Visible

There is nothing wrong with this dialogue at the level of interest groups—so long as its existence is fully recognized. One of the advantages of the American system of 'public hearings' before Congressional committees, it has been pointed out by French admirers of the device, is that it forces all the lobbyists and other interested parties out into the open. By this method, 'which marries ingeniously the inquest and the petition'[6] everyone, including the Congress, is made aware, before it is too late, of what the issues really are in any projected piece of legislation. Elsewhere the spokesmen of interest groups are sometimes given an official status inside the apparatus of government—the Planning Commissions in France and the National Economic Development Council in Britain are familiar examples—but the public's information about what they are up to is usually confined to a newspaper photograph of a backview of a man disappearing into a pompous building. At best there may be a few muttered syllables to a television camera on the way out again.

[5] An outstanding example of the mid-1960s is the devious and complicated bargaining conducted in pursuit of an 'incomes policy'. See above, pp. 217 ff.
[6] Club Jean Moulin, *L'Etat et le citoyen*, p. 389. Another interesting device, which the Americans use as part of their effort to make the interest groups involved in the process of government more visible is to insist on the official registration of 'lobbyists'.

The development of this type of body has led some commentators to suggest that the future lies with expert 'hybrid committees' containing some members of parliament alongside the representatives of the interest groups.[7] That may indeed turn out to be the way in which these increasingly important corporatist organizations will try to accommodate themselves to the outward conventions of popular democratic government. The presence of MPs will help to give the exercise an air of legitimacy. But it will also serve to emphasize more sharply than ever the unsorted jumble of notions on which our current doctrines of legitimate government are founded. For the interest group's spokesman owes his place on such a committee to a quite different set of circumstances from those which bring the member of parliament there; the former is usually an operator, a professional appointee with a particular job, and the man who corresponds to him inside the apparatus of government is the permanent official, not the MP. That is not an argument for excluding the MP, but for bringing in the civil servant as well.[8] The important issue of principle is that if it ever comes to a vote, the views of such persons ought to count differently in the scales of the ultimate decision from those of people who owe their position to an open choice by a democratic majority of the electorate. The men who represent public or private interests in an official capacity on these committees are 'notables' in the old-fashioned sense of the term; in pre-democratic times they would have found their natural place in an Assembly of Notables with recognizable titles. They have the right to speak because of their status; they do not stand on terms of equality with an ordinary citizen: they have special rights because of the tasks that they are called upon to perform.

All this may be seen as part of what Professor John Mitchell has described as 'the movement from contract to status'.[9] In a society in which the violence of market forces has been tamed, in which people have established rights to a rising standard of welfare, and in which change involving discomfort is negotiated rather than just allowed to happen, the professional administrators appointed to guard the interests of one group or another are a force of great and growing significance. Because most of them have never fought an election, they have little taste or sympathy for the processes of representative

[7] See Bernard Crick, *The Reform of Parliament* (London, Weidenfeld, 1964), p. 199.
[8] Civil servants are, of course, heavily represented in the French planning commissions, and in Britain they also sit alongside the interest group spokesmen in certain planning bodies, e.g. in the National Economic Development Committees for individual industries, the so-called 'little Neddies' (see Ch. VIII).
[9] Reversing Sir Henry Maine's dictum that the progress in the evolution of modern society since the Middle Ages is the movement from status to contract (see J. D. B. Mitchell, *The Contracts of Public Authorities* (London, Bell, 1954)). Mitchell makes the observation specifically in connexion with the rights of French public servants, including officials of nationalized undertakings, in relation to the state. The French state, he argues, is not prepared to be trammelled by a formal contractual obligation towards those whom it employs, but instead is eager to reinforce their special status.

government. They instinctively resist the suggestion that they should be made accountable for their actions to the general public. Reporting to their own executive committees behind closed doors is as far as they will willingly go. The conclusion, therefore, is that means will have to be found to compel the 'notables' to be articulate. An interesting suggestion for constitutional reform designed to serve this purpose has been made by Pierre Mendès France. He proposes that there should be a second chamber of parliament, corresponding to the senate, composed of people appointed by major interest groups, professional, commercial, territorial and so on.[10] Plainly the collective power of any such chamber would have to be strictly limited. There is, indeed, no apparent reason why it should operate as a chamber at all; on the contrary, once it acquired the form of a parliament, it would tend to be manned by professional parliamentarians instead of by the *managers* of the interest groups. The objective is, after all, not to arrive at a comprehensive sum of the views of all interest groups, but to provide a visible forum for the work of the specialized bodies of senior bureaucrats (drawn from both public and private organizations) who nowadays exercise such a powerful influence on the shaping of a nation's laws and on the execution of its policies.

Clearly, the pursuit of visibility should not be pushed to the point of insisting that all such discussions are held in public. The same point would indeed apply to certain sessions of the specialist parliamentary committees too, when they were checking on the work of the administration. If there were no routine for making discussions confidential, some important questions would never be asked—or if asked, never satisfactorily answered. But while it is necessary to have a set of rules which will permit an argument over public policy to be conducted in private, the purpose of democratic control will fail to be met unless the privilege is used with conscientious reluctance. One possible device for ensuring this would be that an independent judgement, by an outsider with no interest in the outcome of the discussion, should always be applied to the decision whether it is to be taken into secret session or not. The bias ought to be strongly in favour of publicity—privacy being something which always has to be justified. It is, indeed, a common discovery of even very great powers with especially terrifying secrets, like the United States, that many more facts can be usefully subjected to public discussion than the specialized and somewhat narrow sense of responsibility of the expert official normally suggests.

British Theory of Executive Authority

There are two separate problems of democratic control which need to be distinguished. One is how to ensure that the elected representatives play a meaningful role in the business of government. The other is how to secure

[10] See *La République moderne*, ch. 5.

the protection of the individual citizen against the arbitrary exercise of an ever more extensive public power.

The British case, as suggested earlier, serves especially well to illustrate the nature of the difficulties that have to be overcome in order to achieve these two objectives in the context of the new conditions that have emerged in Western society since the Second World War. The essential issue is how to expose the active and ubiquitous government which we face today to more effective pressure from public opinion and from the courts. The growth of public power demands the reinforcement of both. In Britain the parliamentarians treat it as an axiom that the country ought to have a strong executive. The rules of the game allow the government to be endlessly teased but not to be seriously incommoded in the conduct of its ordinary work. The British tend to see it as one of the chief defects of the French parliamentary system that the lack of restraint of the contending parties under the Third and Fourth Republics weakened the executive to the point of exhaustion. The criticism that can be levelled at the performance of the British parliament today is that it continues to be excessively preoccupied with the problem of allowing the executive to be strong, at a time when the latter's strength has in fact become overwhelming.

The point can best be made by way of examples. We have already mentioned the need to induce parliament to organize itself into a system of specialist committees. The members of the existing Standing Committees do not stay for long enough with any particular segment of government to become expert in it. Moreover, even if their work were differently organized, they would hardly have the opportunity to educate themselves since the committees have no research staff. Why do not the MPs insist on being properly serviced? The answer which is suggested by the experience of another committee, an unusually successful one by British standards, the Select Committee on Nationalized Industries,[11] is that the MPs themselves have no desire for the kind of help which experts can give them. They are generalists—and proud of it. When this Select Committee took a look at its own varied work of supervision in 1958–9 and considered proposals that have been made for improving it, or simply for easing the burden, by calling in some outside specialist assistance, it unerringly found strong reasons why it could better do without. The most illuminating commentary on its underlying attitude is provided by the reasons which it gave against employing a high-powered investigating officer with the status of a senior civil servant:[12] this, it objected, might seem to point towards a 'grand inquisition' of the nationalized industries.

[11] It was established in 1955 and has issued a number of influential reports on the conduct of individual nationalized undertakings (see Crick, *Reform of Parliament*, App. D).

[12] Someone corresponding to the Comptroller and Auditor General employed by the Public Accounts Committee.

Why not? one might ask. To someone fed on the British parliamentary tradition the answer is clear. Such a relationship between parliament and any operating agency would involve an obnoxious degree of tutelage by the legislature over the executive power.[13] The only case in which parliament feels it right to intervene in this way, with expert facilities for investigation at its disposal, is in its control over the spending of public money exercised by the Public Accounts Committee. But this is because parliament is supposed to be expert in only one thing, and that is in securing the proper expenditure of the money which it votes for public purposes.

For the rest, the executive must be permitted to get on with its own work as it sees fit, subject only to the need to answer queries from MPs put at Question Time every afternoon in the House of Commons. That this system of questioning does not begin to meet the problem posed by the huge extension of the apparatus and range of modern government is sufficiently shown by the fact that the duration of Question Time—something under an hour—is no longer than it was in the early years of this century.[14] The same attitude is apparent in the permissive approach towards delegated legislation—the purest expression of modern executive power. The theory is that parliament is given the opportunity to consider all executive orders, made in the form of Statutory Instruments, before they become law. They are published and circulated to members of parliament forty days in advance, and during that period are examined by the Scrutiny Committee of the House of Commons, whose task it is to draw attention to any anomalies. But in practice parliamentary control over the content of such delegated legislation is far less complete than it sounds. First of all, a large number of Statutory Instruments escape the procedure of being laid before parliament altogether; the proportion was estimated in the mid-1950s to be as high as 50 per cent.[15] This is the result of legislative laziness, the failure of the legislature in drafting the

[13] Thus, for example, Michael Ryle, a Senior Clerk of the House of Commons, after making a series of radical proposals to reform and strengthen the committee system of parliament, produced the following argument against experts: 'The members' own standing would be significantly weakened if they came to rely on their own expert advisers on the American model. And it would probably destroy the necessary good relations with the departments if responsible civil service experts were, in effect, to be examined by non-responsible, unofficial experts. The committees should therefore obtain their expert advice from those giving evidence' ('Greater Committee Scope for MPs', *The Times*, 17 Apr. 1963).

[14] D. N. Chester and N. Bowring, *Questions in Parliament* (London, OUP, 1962), quoted by Crick, *Reform of Parliament*, p. 48. At the same time parliament is getting through fewer oral questions during the period (see *Second Report from the Select Committee on Procedure*, HMSO 1965). This is because more supplementary questions are being asked. The result was that in early 1965 there were questions which were waiting up to three months for an answer. *The Economist* (13 Mar. 1965) remarked that 'many of the subjects . . . are out of date by the time they are reached'.

[15] J. E. Kersell, *Parliamentary Supervision of Delegated Legislation* (London, Stevens, 1960), p. 19, who quotes the estimate of Sir Cecil Carr, Counsel to the Speaker of the House of Commons, 1943–55.

original enabling Acts. The interesting point, however, is that no one seems to object when the executive exploits the opportunity thus presented to it to extend its law-making powers independently of parliament.

Secondly, the scope of the Scrutiny Committee is subject to strict limitations. It may not comment on the merits of any piece of delegated legislation put before it, even to the extent of giving its view on whether it is in fact a proper use of the power delegated to the executive. Its task is solely to draw the attention of the House of Commons to any Statutory Instruments which raise doubts on certain stated grounds. Among these grounds, it is true, is that the proposed law makes 'unusual or unexpected use of powers'[16] that have been delegated. But the Committee cannot explain its doubts; it can only point dumbly. When Sir Gilbert Campion, as Clerk of the House of Commons, suggested in the mid-1940s that the Scrutiny Committee's functions might be stretched to allow it to report 'on the merits of a Statutory Instrument, as an exercise in the powers delegated', the Government rejected the idea out of hand. The whole operation would, it alleged, become an intolerable burden on busy ministers. It 'would mean that ministers would have to attend before the Select Committee to defend the policy embodied in subordinate legislation'. But in fact Campion's proposal had nothing to do with policy; its purpose, as A. H. Hanson has pointed out, was to allow parliament to make an assessment of the actual use of 'that discretion which parliament . . . intended the Minister to exercise'.[17] No doubt it was this which made the Government of the day shy away from the proposal like a frightened horse. For, as Campion went on to argue, the people who would naturally be called upon to explain the intended use of the discretionary powers embodied in any particular Statutory Instrument would not be ministers, but the officials responsible for the actual drafting of the order. If the officials were competent to make the orders, he argued, they 'would be competent to explain their purpose and the reasons for making them'.[18]

Thus the real threat in this proposal for reform was to the myth of total ministerial responsibility. There seemed to be a danger that parliament was about to extend its finger and touch, ever so lightly, some part of the actual business of public administration. However, all that was necessary was for the Government to draw attention to the peril and parliament desisted. Why this extraordinary self-restraint? No doubt, the answer is that parliament, having evolved over a long period a technique for securing government which is strong enough to be efficient and yet malleable enough to be changed without disturbance, is very wary of anything which might upset the system. The anonymous civil servant, separated from parliamentary contact by an

---

[16] Ibid., p. 50 ff.
[17] 'The Select Committee on Statutory Instruments: Further Note', *Public Administration*, Autumn 1951, quoted by Kersell, p. 50.
[18] Kersell, *Parliamentary Supervision*, p. 51.

opaque screen, has come to be regarded as an essential element in this arrangement; he must be politically 'sterilized', to use the somewhat contemptuous term applied to him by one French commentator,[19] in order to make possible those marvellous frictionless changes in the political composition of British government. This element in the machinery is, in fact, of comparatively recent origin. Britain was later than other European nations in developing a professional civil service; it dates only from the second half of the nineteenth century. But having decided, somewhat belatedly, on the need for a non-political body of officials, the British proceeded to make their divorce from the world of politics more complete than it is anywhere else.

To this end the old notion of the separation of powers contained in the Act of Settlement of 1701 was revived.[20] We have seen that the practical significance of the doctrine of separation from the early eighteenth century onwards was, in Britain, the independence of the judiciary. Walter Bagehot in *The English Constitution* makes amusing play over the misunderstanding of the Founding Fathers of the American Constitution, who thought they were copying the English model, but in fact 'were contriving a contrast to it'.[21] The Americans most carefully separated the legislature from the executive, whereas the characteristic feature of the English system is 'the fusion of the executive power with the legislative power'.[22] Writing as he was in the 1860s, Bagehot did not foresee the growth of an administrative branch of government, endowed with an initiative of its own over a wide area of activity and effectively removed from parliamentary scrutiny. This is not quite the separation of powers, as the eighteenth-century theorists envisaged it. The civil servant is in the last resort subject to the orders of his minister who in turn depends on the support of parliament. But in practice, the fiction that all the actions of a department are the personal responsibility of its minister and that therefore parliament cannot carry its enquiries beyond the confines of a dialogue with the minister, means that there is a considerable, and constantly growing, range of administrative activity which escapes effective legislative oversight.

The people with the strongest interest in preserving this system are the civil servants themselves. They may be 'sterilized' in terms of overt party politics; but this is regarded as a small price to pay for being almost entirely

[19] Charles Fourrier, *Liberté d'opinion du fonctionnaire* (Paris, Pichon & Durand-Auzias, 1957). Titre II, in particular pp. 100 ff.

[20] The official handbook for the civil servant refers to the Act explicitly in connexion with its prohibition on members of the House of Commons from holding an 'office of profit' under the Crown. It says: 'This prohibition was later modified, and Ministers and holders of certain other "offices of profit" under the Crown are now allowed to sit in the House; but as a general rule civil servants are still excluded, and if a Member of Parliament should become a civil servant his seat in Parliament will automatically become vacant' (*A Handbook for the New Civil Servant*, 11th ed., 1964, p. 34).

[21] Fontana Library Ed., 1963, p. 219.   [22] Ibid., p. 81.

protected from the rude gaze of outsiders, and even more from their questions about what they are doing in the exercise of immense power. Any attempt by the press to identify the particular civil servant responsible for certain actions is especially resented.[23] Meanwhile the minister often enjoys the over-lifesize role which the civil servants are anxious to help him to perform—being not merely the head but the personification of a portion of the apparatus of state.

It hardly needs to be said that the minister himself, working under the personal pressure which the conditions of modern government impose on such a person, cannot be expected to do the job of oversight on parliament's behalf. In any case, as Bagehot shrewdly remarks, an especially important task of parliament when it questions the doings of the executive—more important than its legislative activity—is its 'informing function'.[24] It enables the public to learn what the issues are and what considerations have been, or ought to have been, taken into account in shaping the actions of the government. The minister in private conversation with his civil servants cannot do that.

The 'Informing Function' of the Bureaucracy

Indeed, the senior civil servants, who are in fact taking an active hand in the making of the nation's policy, whatever the theory may say to the contrary, might reasonably be expected to regard it as part of their duty to contribute personally to this 'informing function', even if parliament happened to be more efficient than it is as an intermediary between them and the public. In order to do so usefully they would, of course, have to be given some freedom to express opinions of their own, without committing the minister in charge of their department to their conclusions. This is readily done in other countries, notably in France, where officials of any intellectual distinction tend to see it as part of their business—unmistakably a pleasurable part— to bring the underlying issues in their administrative work to the attention of the public. Some of them are prolific writers of books and articles. Their subjects, moreover, are often right on top of some issue of popular controversy. It is recognised, of course, that they cannot engage in such an argument at the level of unrestrained popular polemic, without damaging their professional reputations for impartiality. As Fourrier puts it, a civil servant must always

---

[23] In the early 1960s there were the beginnings of an attempt, in such books as *The Treasury under the Tories* by Samuel Brittan (Penguin, 1964) and *Anatomy of Britain* by Anthony Sampson (Hodder & Stoughton, 1962), to break down the myth of ministerial responsibility in its extreme form which treated civil servants as a species of *un*person. The pained reaction to the naming of officials held to have influenced certain decisions suggested that they would fight hard to retain their cocoon of anonymity.

[24] *English Constitution*, p. 153. Bagehot lists as the most important function of parliament that of maintaining an effective executive in being. The 'informing function' comes next.

appear *'serein'* and therefore in his public utterances must show *'réserve'*.[25] But this is a matter of individual self-discipline; there is no system of internal censorship for members of the civil service. They are not required either to obtain permission before they write something for publication or to submit the text to official scrutiny by someone else in the service before publication. British civil servants in all but the very lowest grades must do both.

Thus in recent years there have been books on French price control policy by the civil servant who was for many years in charge of the Price Control Office, and on the government's economic planning by a senior official of the Commissariat du Plan—to mention two examples of works which have been quoted in the earlier chapters of this book.[26] They are typical products of a certain highbrow journalism, what the French call, with a touch of self-deprecating affectation, *haute vulgarisation*, in which high French officials engage on a wide range of topics and with undisguised gusto. No one doubts that they benefit by exposing their ideas to public comment and criticism by book reviewers and others. It is also assumed to be a help to the administrator in the conduct of his work, if the public has been given an insight into what the problems of administration really are. Admittedly the French approach to the whole question of freedom of expression has a certain doctrinaire quality. The right of the civil servant to publish, it is argued, is guaranteed to him by the Declaration of the Rights of Man; it is built into the constitution.[27] Indeed, it is regarded as the duty of the authorities positively to help an official who wishes to take part in a political election—for example by granting him paid leave during the election campaign.[28]

[25] *Liberté d'opinion*, III–II–chs. II & III. There is only one exception to the rule of political freedom of expression, within the limits of 'réserve', and that applies to the Prefects and Sub-Prefects (p. 311). They are held to be in an especially close political relationship with the government of the day, through the Minister of the Interior who is their chief. Roger Grégoire, in the standard work on the subject, *La fonction publique* (Paris, Colin, 1954), mentions two specific regulations governing the publications of French civil servants on political matters. They are not supposed to make damaging statements about their superiors in the service and 'in certain cases' must avoid making 'a direct attack against the authority of the state' (p. 298). These limitations both clearly come under the general rule of 'réserve'. All the evidence is that they are liberally interpreted by the Conseil d'État, which is the ultimate arbiter of civil servants' behaviour. That is not to say that a French official who expresses views which are unpopular with the politician in charge of his department suffers no disadvantages whatever. He will very likely not be the first person to be considered when there is an opportunity for promotion, in which the minister has a say. But he cannot be demoted or dismissed for the views which he expresses; the Conseil d'État, with its highly developed sense of professional solidarity, has quite sufficient power to protect him in case of need.

[26] Louis Franck and Bernard Cazes (see p. 148 n. 43 and p. 136 n. 21).

[27] See Fourrier, *Liberté d'opinion*, p. 304.

[28] See Grégoire, *Fonction publique*, p. 339, who remarks that the provisions of a 'recent circular' on the subject seem to be generously interpreted, so that not only the officials who are actual candidates, but also those who merely wish to take an active part in the campaign in support of someone else are able to claim election leave. If

No doubt the instinctive British reaction to all this would be to say: 'Well, just look at the result. The French may enjoy throwing off all these irksome restraints; but once they have done so, the only way in which they seem to be able to give themselves an effective government is by setting up an authoritarian régime under a strong man, preferably a general.' Without attempting to judge the merit of the accusation, it is at least possible to reply that even within the limitations of the Fifth Republic there is a more frank and informed debate on certain matters of public policy, for example the choices implicit in the national economic plan, and a more effective scrutiny of the actions of the bureaucracy, including most notably its delegated legislation, by the Conseil d'État than by the parliament in Britain.

The French way is only one of various possible methods of putting the essential work of a modern administration on public view. The Americans have another technique. A much larger segment at the top of their bureaucracy is filled by political appointments. It is to be observed that most of the men who occupy these posts, which in other countries would be occupied by civil servants, are not politicians in the ordinary sense, but men of administrative experience or ability who are politically committed.[29] Once in office, it is their business to be articulate. Further down the scale of the American bureaucracy, among the 'career officers', there is still considerable scope for the public expression of opinion. The rule is that all civil servants may speak without submitting their speeches in advance, even though it is known that the speech will be published, but that anything written specifically for publication is subject to certain restrictions. Officials working in the two most sensitive areas of public policy, in the State Department and the Department of Defense, must submit everything that they write for preliminary vetting; indeed, there is a well understood though informal rule—informal because Congress might object to the restriction if it were made explicit— that even the spoken words of officers of these departments are, wherever this is feasible, subject to advance censorship. But over the wide range of economic and social affairs, the rule is that only articles or books which set out to discuss some aspect of government policy, rather than do so incidentally in connexion with a more general argument, have to be submitted for official approval before being published. Plainly with several hundreds of

elected to parliament, a French official is treated as being on secondment and has full rights of reinstatement at the end of the parliamentary term. He can even get some extra pay out of the government while seconded; if his parliamentary salary is less than the official salary he was receiving beforehand, the difference is made up (ibid., p. 341).

[29] The French achieve something not altogether dissimilar by the device of the *cabinet* of the minister. This is composed of civil servants and others chosen by the minister because of their political affiliations with him. Admittedly the *cabinet* does not have the same formal position of commanding authority in the French system as political appointees have in the American system; but it can at times exercise an influence which is as powerful as theirs.

articulate political appointees in the field, the scope for journalism by the 'career' men is, in any case, limited.

Sweden : The Principle of the Goldfish Bowl

More radical than either the French or the American is the Swedish rule that all government documents must be made available for inspection by any member of the public who wants to see them. Such a person need not give any reason why he wants to do so or show that he has any personal stake in the case.[30] There are exceptions to the rule—plainly efficient administration in certain fields would be impossible without some measure of secrecy—but it is not left to the discretion of the official bureaucracy to decide what is to be withheld: specific legislative authority has to be given in the Secrecy Act. Moreover, the officials who are being bothered by the inquisitive outsider are not allowed to get away with excuses about administrative inconvenience. It is up to them to arrange matters inside their offices in such a way as to make the prompt production of documents possible. There is also an obligation on the authorities to keep a complete and up to date index of documents received, to help the inquirer. The only part of their files which government offices are allowed to keep private, apart from matters covered specifically by the Secrecy Act, is internal correspondence or memoranda about a case which is under discussion, in advance of an official decision.

The effect of this remarkable arrangement is most apparent in the level and quality of information available in the newspapers. Professor Herlitz has described what happens: 'Every day, in the great offices in Stockholm for instance, documents which have been received will be brought to a room where representatives of the newspapers are welcome to see them. A representative of the leading news agencies will never fail to appear, and through him a flood of news will go to the newspapers and to the general public'.[31] He goes on: 'Just as publicity in the courts all over the world makes it possible for everybody to know how justice is administered, the publicity of documents has the same effect insofar as documents reflect the activity of the authorities.' This applies not only to the official decisions themselves but also to the 'background of decisions: the complex of facts, interests, arguments, motives, on the basis of which an authority has decided or is going to decide. I underline the words "is going to"; the authorities are under observation not only after a decision is taken but also at the preparatory stage.'[32] The result is to change the whole atmosphere of the debate on any important issue of public policy. 'It is not unusual', Herlitz remarks, 'for the opinions of central offices or of province governors to become powerful elements in public opinion.'[33]

[30] See Nils Herlitz, 'Publicity of Documents in Sweden', *Public Law*, 1958, from which the account that follows is derived.
[31] Ibid., p. 54.   [32] Ibid., p. 55.   [33] Ibid., p. 56.

The principle of ubiquitous publicity is also bound to have an effect on the behaviour of interest groups in their relations with government. We remarked in an earlier chapter on the extraordinary faculty of the Swedish authorities for achieving a consensus in matters of national policy, in such a way as to blur the line of demarcation between the public and the private sectors.[34] No doubt, the knowledge that any pressure applied on the Government by some interested group or any argument put to the Government is likely before long to become public property contributes to a habit of frank argument and compromise among the conflicting parties concerned in any issue. In most other countries government is, or is believed to be, the most clandestine of all the organizations which affect the life of the citizen. Any other organization approaching it therefore tends instinctively to adopt a clandestine manner. The pompous password 'affairs of state' is automatically taken to mean that voices are to be hushed. The Swedes have shown what happens when there is a deliberate attempt to make it mean the opposite. The most important consequence, as Herlitz has put it, is 'that the publicity of documents has created a peculiar spirit of openness. It is natural for the authorities to answer without severe restrictions when they are asked. And also spontaneously they will be rather generous in giving information on public affairs, particularly to newspapers—so that it is unnecessary to ask for documents.'[35]

Of course, the whole business is immensely inconvenient. Some things never get said for fear of being reported; arguments which are relevant are not put in writing, but are whispered in somebody's ear; public action may sometimes be delayed, because a person needing aid is shy of publicity. The catalogue of possible inefficiencies is large. Plainly the extent of the actual damage likely to be caused depends on the habits and manners of the people working the system. The British, for example, would regard it as impossibly indiscreet; the Americans, on the other hand, with their fondness for explicit personal statements, might well discover that it caused them little trouble. The Swedes themselves are not such rollicking, jovial extroverts as to feel that life in a goldfish bowl causes them no difficulties. But as Herlitz explains: 'That, in spite of them [the difficulties], we maintain publicity shows how highly we value it: the advantages are regarded as counterpoising very considerable disadvantages.'[36]

Parliaments and Juries in Britain

Sweden thus lies at the extreme opposite end of the spectrum from Britain. The British on the whole tend to see first of all the negative aspects of any proposed piece of publicity. Will the uttering of certain words prejudice someone who may be called upon to judge the case in question? Might the words of an official embarrass the minister charged with the sole responsibility

[34] See above, p. 205.   [35] *Public Law*, 1958, p. 58.

for a decision? If there is the slightest risk of either result, then suppress the chatterer. The notion of matters being *sub judice*, and therefore not to be publicly discussed, is readily extended into other fields in which it has no natural place. A striking instance of this propensity to tell people to shut up, in order to leave the field absolutely clear for those officially authorized to pass judgement on a matter, was the notorious 'fourteen day rule' imposed on the radio and television services of the country in 1955. The Postmaster General ordered the British Broadcasting Corporation and the Independent Television Authority not to discuss any issue 'during a period of a fortnight before the issue is debated in either House [of Parliament] or while it is being so debated'.[37] The actual practice of reducing the country's radio and TV services to silence on a topical subject, while parliament girded itself to dispute it, was not new. The BBC had voluntarily observed the rule for some years before this, and it was only because it was beginning to feel irked at last by its role of dumb friend of parliament that the formal order was thought to be necessary.

The public argument on the subject forced the Government, after an initial display of truculence, to retreat. The 1955 order has not in fact been enforced since the late 1950s, when the Postmaster General agreed to suspend the rule, though not to rescind it, for an indefinite period. But there was one condition. The broadcasters had to give an undertaking that they would not deal with topical affairs in such a way as to 'derogate from the primacy of Parliament'.[38] No doubt a very good debate on television, involving a selection of the most able MPs talking at the top of their form, might do just that.

Presumably the theory underlying the objection to a great public debate before parliament has had its say is that the electorate—the jury of the nation—might in a simple-minded way be unduly influenced by the earlier performance, so that its response to the speeches of its elected representatives could be, in some sense, prejudiced. This, at any rate, was the kind of analogy that was drawn at the time with the conventional notion of a matter being *sub judice*. The interesting point is the notion of extreme simple-mindedness which tends to be attributed to juries of all kinds in the British system. Immense trouble is taken to protect an ordinary trial jury from the knowledge of any information from which it might just conceivably draw a false inference. Advance publicity is the greatest enemy of the *tabula rasa* of the juror. But it is not merely that the juror is allowed no knowledge of an accused person's past crimes, which may after all be pertinent to an assessment of probabilities about the behaviour of the accused, or that the judge will deny the juror the right to hear evidence in court, which although relevant might, he thinks, be

[37] H. Street, *Freedom, the Individual and the Law* (London, Penguin, 1963), p. 85.
[38] Ibid., p. 85.

misread by an untrained mind.[39]   He is also refused the normal intellectual equipment that is used by anyone trying to take a systematic view of contradictory evidence—viz. a written record of what has been said.   At any rate, when the jury in the Hanratty case in 1962, after the longest murder trial in English legal history, asked to have the record of the proceedings put at its disposal in the room where it was considering its verdict, the judge said no.[40] The incident, which was barely commented upon at the time, is worth attention because it provides one of those brief and profound glimpses of the unstated assumptions underlying a respected institution.   These include an active distrust of the understanding of the written word by the plain man; at the same time, an almost mystical belief in the plain man's natural sense of justice, undisturbed by systematic ratiocination; and over all a kind of protective anti-intellectualism on the part of the judge towards the ordinary citizen, from whose untutored instincts he expects illumination to arrive.   The amateurs—and an English jury is, as Louis Blom-Cooper says, 'the apotheosis of amateurism'—must at any cost be defended from the taint of professional judicial expertise.

It is here that the spirit of the English jury exhibits an analogy with the spirit of parliament.   Both are devoted to the cult of the non-expert.   In both, issues are deliberately cast in a crude mould requiring rough straight answers. The task of elaborating the answer, so that it makes administrative sense, indeed of framing the original question and finding the responses to it, all come from the judge in court or the executive in parliament.   The jury and the MPs occupy the stage; but in their present guise they have a limited utility.

At the heart of the system there is the notion of the 'adversary procedure'. A court case is made to conform to the image of a fight between two sides, with judge and jury in the role of referee.   Parliament too is cast in the image of a battlefield, with the two front benches divided by a couple of sword lengths and complicated legislative proposals treated like declarations of war. It is noteworthy that whenever suggestions are made for reforming parliament— as they have been with increasing frequency in recent years—by setting up a series of specialist committees which would be able to take a grip on what the executive is actually doing, the standard objection made is that this would tend 'to blur party lines'.[41]   It could convincingly be argued instead that this is in fact one of the most useful purposes that such a reform could be made to serve—by adapting the formal posture of parliament to the realities of public

---

[39] See the argument put forward in the Hanratty murder case in 1962 by the defence counsel that a certain piece of evidence ought to be excluded because, although 'a trained tribunal' would probably be able to put it into perspective, a jury could not be expected to do so.   The judge accepted the defence counsel's contention (Louis Blom-Cooper, *The A6 Murder*, London (Penguin, 1963), p. 108).   [40] Ibid., p. 15.
[41] See *The Times*, 16 Mar. 1963, reporting on the House of Commons debate on parliamentary reform.

power today. The set battle is no longer an efficient means of fulfilling the 'informing function' of parliament, nor is it a sensible way of dealing with most of the work of legislation.

That is not to say that the party system is outmoded; the point is only that the manner in which the competition for power is conducted between the parties has too little relevance to the process of contemporary government. The simplification of issues and dividing lines—allegedly required in order to help the simple-minded voter to take sides—has been carried to excess. In practice, a considerable body of the electorate in a Western society today is more sophisticated than the impresarios of the party battle seem willing to allow. It is common for voters to declare at election time that they will support a given party because they are in favour of it 'on balance', and they will often go on to explain that this is 'in spite of its attitude on X or Y'. There are also signs of a wider appreciation among the electorate that the act of governing is a genuinely complex and difficult task; nowadays governments which have been in office for a while and have shown themselves capable of taking charge, tend to have an advantage, even if they have done some unpopular things, over opponents who have not proved themselves. On the evidence of the longevity of governments in many Western countries during the postwar period, there is a much less ready response to the old election-time cry: 'Throw the rascals out!'

It would help to restore meaning to party politics if the exercise were less exclusively occupied with the clash of wooden swords and cardboard shields in furious battle. At the cost of making the conflict appear less deadly, it might acquire more administrative reality. At present the way in which nations tend to deal with a problem which is both serious and complicated is to agree to 'take it out of politics'. What this means in fact is that the great coalitions of factions and interest groups, which make up the mass political parties, are not committed to a simple fixed position on the issue in question. It does not mean that the bulk of the membership of any given party are unable to agree on a distinctive doctrine on this matter. After all, to become a member of such a party expresses a view about the statistical probability of a coincidence of opinion on major questions. The point about the big issues which are 'taken out of politics' is not that party positions are irrelevant to them, but that there is no deep rift between the common positions arrived at by one party and another.

In fact, a large part of contemporary politics is of this kind. Parties can still provide the vehicle for expressing a series of political preferences, which in the aggregate do serve to mark off the position of one voter from another. To be a member of the Labour or Conservative Party in Britain, of the Democrat or Republican Party in the United States, is for many people a means of expressing a definite bias towards public measures of an identifiable general shape or colour. There is no reason to suppose that parties will fail to fulfil a similar function in the future. Of course, by the time party proposals are converted into administrative acts, many compromises will have been made by the politicians in power, to meet the wishes or fears of influential groups and individuals in their own party, in the opposition party, and inside the government apparatus. The last category is particularly important: the views of officials naturally carry weight, because they are the people who will eventually have to try to make the measure work.

But there is no ground for thinking that officials, whose views may exercise a profound influence on political decisions, are moved solely by considerations of the technical feasibility of what is proposed. They have preferences too, views about what is wise or proper or merely convenient for a government to do. We have seen how publicity for official documents in Sweden not only provides some extra safeguards for the individual against arbitrary acts of government, but also influences the political debate by making known the opinions of high officials on matters which fall within their competence. One of the probable consequences of making officials more articulate about policy would be that the party argument, grown more sophisticated, would spill over from parliament into the bureaucracy. I do not ignore the problems which such an arrangement would present, especially for an administration of the British type. But on balance the disadvantages of keeping the great official inarticulate and divorced from any politics which are conducted in public view seem to be far greater.

The Independent Official

One question which is raised by the argument in the preceding sections is the degree of personal independence which is appropriate to officials of states of the Western capitalist type. The British adopt an extreme theoretical position which is symbolized in the legal doctrine that a civil servant holds his post 'at pleasure' of the Crown and can be summarily dismissed without redress. The reality is quite different, and the civil servant is thought of in Britain as being a more than usually permanent fixture in his job.[42] Nevertheless the notion that he is in an essentially military relationship with his employer, the Crown—a good servant who obeys orders to the best of his ability but has suppressed any independent will of his own—has bitten deep into British institutions.

This whole approach is, as we have observed on several occasions, sharply at variance with French ideas on the role of the public servant. In France the characteristic quality ascribed to the great official is his 'independence'.

---

[42] See L. Blair, 'The Civil Servant—Political Reality and Legal Myth', *Public Law*, 1958. However, as Professor W. Friedmann says, 'the problem of dismissability at will remains . . . of practical importance in times of public nervousness and preoccupation with security and loyalty considerations' (*Law in a Changing Society*, abridged ed. (London, Penguin, 1964), p. 299).

This is not intended to describe a quality of mind which is indifferent to political considerations: to be 'independent' does not mean to be exclusively devoted to the autonomy of individual conscience, regardless of how its behests impinge on others. On the contrary, it goes with an active readiness to compromise, if this will serve to achieve the expression of some real consensus among colleagues engaged in the joint exercise of power. That is the spirit which animates the members of the Conseil d'État. It is the opposite of that displayed by French parliamentarians, who have tended to treat the floor of the chamber as a forum for professional displays of political intransigence—and have in consequence divorced parliament from an effective role in the business of government.

The 'independent' official is, above all, a person who is loyal to certain professional standards. Being in a position of trust, he must actively resist the pressures of mere convenience, whether private or public; there is no excuse for failure to press an honest personal judgement. Loyalty to the professional service of the state is not supposed to swamp the individual personality; rather, the service is seen as providing the opportunity for an especially noble expression of the private *persona* in a public context.[43] The notion is complex and sometimes confused;[44] it certainly lacks the logic of the English doctrine of the civil servant. It has, however, proved its usefulness in practice—and not in France only. To obtain a clearer view of its significance, it is worth looking at its further elaboration in another context, where it has produced some striking results.

The apotheosis of independent officialdom in the postwar world is the European Commission set up in Brussels by the European Economic Community. In the course of grappling, rather effectively, with some of the most complicated administrative problems of economic policy, it has evolved methods which have a relevance to the national, as well as international, institutions of contemporary Western society. What follows is not intended as a systematic exposition of the functions of the European Commission; my purpose is solely to point to certain of its activities which seem to be germane to the theme of this chapter—viz. active government by consent.

The first point to observe is that the elected parliament of the European

---

[43] It is interesting to observe that the notion of the independent public official in France goes back to the *ancien régime*, before the Revolution. W. R. Brock remarks that in the eighteenth century, by contrast with the absolute obedience exacted from the civil servants of the Prussian and Austrian imperial régimes, 'an *intendant* could and did resist and criticise the central Government' (*New Cambridge Modern History*, vol. vii, *1713–63*, p. 159).

[44] The French, for instance, seem to have difficulty in running a genuinely independent public corporation, like the BBC. Here the sharp British distinction between those who are 'servants' of the minister in a department, with no independent initiative of their own, and those public officials (e.g. in the BBC) who are not covered by the doctrine of total ministerial responsibility helps to secure more genuine independence for the latter than the French have been able to achieve.

Community is a body without effective authority. The nearest thing to a body of men who have a direct relationship with the electorate is the Council of Ministers, made up of the ministerial representatives of the governments of the six member countries. These are the men who have the ultimate power to determine what the Community does. But it was clear that from the start the intention was to use the European Commission—the executive body of the Community consisting of nine officials appointed by governments for a term of four years at a time—to get various things done which the governments, acting solely through their ministerial representatives, believed themselves incapable of doing. There is a certain abdication of initiative by the politicians implied by the Treaty of Rome. The procedure laid down by the Treaty is that most of the important proposals for joint action by the Community—broadly those which are legislative in character—are to be formulated by the Commission and put to the Council for decision, and can only be modified by a unanimous vote of the Council.[45] If there is disagreement within the Council on such a proposal so that it fails to command the necessary number of votes, it goes back to the Commission which amends it as it thinks necessary and then presents it again.

The result in practice is to keep the law-making initiative always in the hands of the Commission. It makes the running. Its task is to produce the ideas required for the further development of the Community, and then to bombard the Council of Ministers with a series of proposals for action, until one that is acceptable to the Six has been found. Moreover, once a measure has been agreed by the Council of Ministers, the decision cannot be reversed by any one of the national parliaments; at most a parliament may force the minister who agreed to the measure to resign. Thus, in addition to the loss of initiative by the politicians at the centre, there is a surrender of certain powers by the national legislatures.

The task of the Commission is firstly, as Dr. Hallstein, its President, has put it, to act as an 'arbitrator between member countries'.[46] It is supposed to bargain actively for the kind of compromise between the separate national interests of the member states, which will serve to forward 'the European interest'—i.e. will achieve the most rapid integration of the six nations.[47] Secondly, it is the 'guardian of the Treaty'; in this capacity it issues orders to

---

[45] Treaty of Rome, Art. 149.

[46] Speech at Strasbourg to the European Parliament, 18 June 1964 (see *Community Topics No. 13*, European Community Information Service).

[47] Hallstein (ibid.), referring to the 113 regulations, directives and decisions issued by the Council of Ministers in 1963–4, said: 'A great number would doubtless never have seen the light of day if the Commission had not striven constantly for compromise'. He added, however, that in certain matters, 'the Commission has continued to press for the acceptance of its proposals even after the Council of Ministers, or part of it, has arrived at other opinions'.

desist to governments, if it considers that they have infringed the Treaty.[48] Thirdly, it is 'the prime mover' of the Community, pushing, prodding and guiding the representatives of governments in the Council of Ministers towards the surrender of powers to the collective organs of the EEC.

Who are the men who exercise these unusual political powers? The Treaty of Rome lays down that they must be persons 'whose independence can be fully guaranteed'.[49] That emphatically does not mean, however, that each of the nine members of the Commission is supposed to be indifferent to the interests of the particular government which was responsible for appointing him. It is difficult to define precisely the nature of the special relationship between the European official and the rulers of his own country; but it is clear that if he ignores it altogether, he does so at his peril. The case of M. Étienne Hirsch, the first President of Euratom, shows what may happen. When his term expired in 1962 he was widely supported for a further spell of office, but the French Government refused to renew his appointment. It was well known that M. Hirsch was given to expressing a spirit of excessive independence—at any rate by French official standards—in relation to General de Gaulle's nuclear policies. The incident provided a brutal reminder of the fact that although the members of the European executive organs have the status of appointed officials, they are expected to behave with the tactical adroitness of politicians. While the European Community has, in practice, achieved a remarkable spirit of collective responsibility in the Commission,[50] it is clearly understood that the individual Commissioners are not intended to forget their relationship with their 'constituencies', the particular governments which appointed them.

It is of the essence of the task that the members of the Commission are people who could just as easily be politicians as public officials. Indeed two of the Vice Presidents of the Commission are intermittently active in the politics of their countries, M. Marjolin in France and M. Mansholt in Holland.[51] The European Commissioner is in fact the most prominent

---

[48] In the form of an *'avis motivé'*. The state to which this is directed must either comply within a time limit set by the Commission or take the matter to the European Court of Justice (see É. Noel, 'How the European Economic Community's Institutions Work', *Community Topics No. 11*).

[49] Art. 157—'offrant toutes guaranties d'indépendance'.

[50] The Commission will, for instance, never reveal how individual members voted on any issue nor indeed whether it was a unanimous or a majority decision. Once a vote has been taken, the nine will give unanimous public support to the decision taken.

[51] Marjolin stood for parliament in the French general election of 1962 as a socialist in opposition to the Gaullist régime. He returned after his electoral leave of absence (defeated at the polls) to his job on the Commission, and was reappointed as one of the two French Commissioners by de Gaulle in the following year. Mansholt, another socialist, was all set to take high ministerial office in the Dutch Cabinet, if his party was victorious in the 1964 election. It was not, and Mansholt stayed put.

manifestation of an increasingly common hybrid type in Western society, the professional administrator cum political operator. He often has a particular field of expertise in which he has achieved some eminence, but he is not content merely to tender expert advice. He is a lobbyist, an intriguer—in short, a fixer who is also a technician. Indeed, precisely because he does possess the technical mastery over his subject, he knows better than any ordinary politician just how far he can go in making a compromise with the interest groups involved in any question, without losing the substance of his cause. Again and again the European Commission has demonstrated to outsiders, who have expressed anxiety about some compromise which seemed to put a part of the highly technical process of European integration in jeopardy, that its mastery of technical detail gives it a special facility for taking nicely calculated political risks.

A Reversal of the Separation of Powers

The currently fashionable word used to tag this kind of person is 'technocrat'. His relevance to the general problem of the political institutions of modern capitalism is that he is normally called in to deal with the type of problem whose solution cannot be precisely defined in advance, and where the area of administrative discretion is therefore recognized as being very large.[52] In practice such a person combines a large part of the law-making function with the executive function. He is the embodiment of a principle which is the opposite of the classical separation of powers. Indeed in the European Commission the *mixture of powers* is carried a stage further, for the Commission is also endowed with limited judicial functions in relation to certain matters.[53] Here again there are intimations of a wider administrative phenomenon. It is essential that in neither its judicial nor its legislative functions should the power of the executive arm be final. The issue is to establish an enlarged area of initiative for the executive in both these functions, not to give it any absolute authority in either of them. What should be recognized, as

---

[52] See Alfred Frisch, 'L'Avenir des Technocrates', *Bulletin SEDEIS, Futuribles*, no. 84, 1964, who argues that the growth of technocratic power is a natural consequence, as well as an offset, to the inevitable process of increasing centralization in government. While policy covering various aspects of national life is coordinated more and more at the centre, the degree of discretion accorded to those who actually execute the policy is inevitably extended; otherwise the system would become excessively rigid in action. 'Plus un système est centralisé, plus sa marge technocratique devient grande' (p. 8).

[53] In regard to restrictive practices, under Art. 85–90 of the Treaty of Rome. The Commission issues general regulations on this subject and also judges individual cases according to an established legal procedure—the latter in order to decide claims that particular restrictive agreements have beneficial economic side effects which would justify their retention under Article 85(3) of the Rome Treaty. It has wide judicial discretion on this point, subject to the ultimate authority of the European Court (see EEC *Annual Report 1963–4*, pp. 62 ff).

Friedmann says, is that 'cooperation rather than separation . . . between legislature, executive and judiciary, reflects the reality of the legal process'.[54] He adds that 'by far the most important aspect' of the doctrine of the separation of powers is the ability of judges to resist administrative direction, though even judicial independence is not absolute. We have seen that in a more modest way a similar spirit of independence is required of the modern official, in the face of pressures from politicians located in the legislature. At any rate the administrator must be prepared to engage them and to argue back, even though he recognizes, like the judge, that the legislators must have the final say.

The high official can only do his task efficiently in this style if he is fortified by direct contact with public opinion. He must not only speak but also allow himself to be questioned. Although the official is not personally elected, he fulfils in a democracy a representative function. He ought never to be permitted to forget it. Again, the European Commission, partly through the accident that it faced the problem of operating as an executive without effective parliamentary institutions, while being even more dependent than the ordinary national executive on active democratic consent, has some lessons to offer. With a large part of the European élite mobilized in support of the general enterprise of integration, it has found it possible to bring the universities, the press, and the other organs of publicity into a series of debates on controversial issues of European Community policy *before* executive decisions are made. The debates are consciously employed to provide a substitute, often at a more expert level, for a full parliamentary forum. Immense trouble has also gone into the effort to keep the Commission exposed to the currents of opinion in the governments and the important interest groups of the member states.[55] The Commission takes pride in its capacity for frank and extensive argument; notoriously its favourite word in describing almost any of its activities is 'dialogue'. Journalism in its widest sense, oral as well as written, including especially highbrow or technical journalism at the level of *haute vulgarisation*, is treated as a professional duty by the officials of the Community. Anyone who has had experience of their behaviour during the formative years of the European Common Market from 1958 onwards must

---

[54] *Law in a Changing Society*, p. 66.

[55] Émile Noel, Executive Secretary of the European Commission, reports that in one year, 1961, more than 1,000 meetings of 'experts' from the national governments of the member states were organized by the Commission. 'These experts' he comments, 'do not formally commit their governments, but, as they are informed of the interests and opinions of the latter, they perform a useful function in guiding the Commission in its search for solutions that are technically accurate and generally acceptable to the six governments'. And these contacts 'are supplemented by many consultative meetings organized by members of the Commission or its various departments, with, for example, leaders of the Community-wide groupings of trade unions, employers' associations, farmers' unions, and traders' associations' (*Community Topics No. 11*).

have been struck by the extraordinary readiness of people burdened with the heaviest administrative tasks, from the President of the Commission downwards, to take off from Brussels to give a speech, or preferably to engage in an active debate, if there is a serious audience on hand.

The contention is not that parliament can be dispensed with; only that given a willingness to articulate on the part of officials, the public debate can be richly supplemented in other ways. The techniques used by the European Community to secure the active participation of interest groups are, indeed, reminiscent of the traditional practice of ubiquitous consultation used by a country like Sweden to secure active democratic consent.[56] It is noteworthy that not only in Sweden, but also in other European countries, like Austria and Holland, which have been ruled rather effectively by coalition governments since the war, the set parliamentary battle has been downgraded. The common assembly of parliament has come to be seen as only one of several places where elected and appointed persons argue about policy.

What is striking is that probably the most radical and complicated set of reforms of our time, those undertaken by the European Economic Community, have been achieved substantially by a group of appointed officials at one remove from the conventional democratic process. The moral of this achievement is not that the representative process is dead, but that it may well assume additional and more subtle forms than the conventional parliamentary encounter. Effective democracy has always depended on a limited suspension of judgement by the electors, on a willingness to clothe people with power and then give them a period of time for action, before reporting back to those from whom they derived their mandate. The principle has been further extended in postwar national planning; the plans formally recognize that decisions once made cannot be quickly unravelled. In the short or medium term they are irrevocable. The work of the European Commission offers another kind of example of the contemporary political method at work.

The underlying notion is that the rulers of a democracy, whether elected or appointed, must have the consent of the ruled to do more than the latter would willingly do for themselves if left to take charge of the whole process. Representative democracy is not a substitute for direct democracy; it is a quite different form of government. The general point which Edmund Burke made in his *Address to the Electors of Bristol* in 1774 has a wider application today, beyond parliament, to the body of ruling officials appointed for a term in the public service. 'Parliament is not a congress of ambassadors from different and hostile interests; . . . You choose a member indeed; but when you have chosen him, he is not a member of Bristol, but he is a member of *parliament.'*[57]

---

[56] See above, pp. 199 ff.
[57] *Speeches and Letters on American Affairs* (Everyman Library), p. 73.

Discretionary Power versus Judicial Authority

The second of the two major questions which we distinguished earlier—the first being the problem of democratic participation in modern government—is how to protect the individual against the growing range and penetrating power of public authority. The collective provision of so much more welfare and the progressive effort to relate it more subtly to varied individual needs, coupled with the central control over many more decisions which in one way or another affect private initiatives, whether in business or in personal life, argue the need for new techniques of judicial supervision. In this section of the argument I shall again use the British case as a reference point, because here too its institutions have in the past, especially during the formative period of Western capitalism in the eighteenth and nineteenth centuries, proved especially effective in defence of the individual against the exercise of arbitrary public power. Of late, however, their success in this regard has been less in evidence.

In a sense the trouble with the British courts is the same as that which we observed earlier in parliament: there is too much concern with the problem of providing the executive with the conditions that it deems to be necessary for the efficient conduct of its work. This may seem a surprising conclusion about the courts in Britain, in view of the tough way in which they insist on the letter of the law regardless of administrative convenience. But it may be precisely because they are so tough about the letter that they feel themselves to be obliged to be pretty lax on occasion about the spirit. The criticism applies particularly to cases where justice would seem to require analysis of the *intentions* of the legislators, in addition to the actual words used by the drafters of the law, and those where the exercise of administrative *discretion* is involved.

It is in the treatment of the latter that the executive in Britain can rely on the courts to give it vast benefit of the doubt. The point is best illustrated by the statement of the Lord Chief Justice in a recent case involving some campaigners for nuclear disarmament, who tried to organize a demonstration on an airfield in 1962. Some of the demonstrators were sentenced to imprisonment and appealed. Lord Parker, in dismissing the appeal, said that there were certain matters into which the courts could not inquire because they concerned the exercise of powers left to 'the unfettered control of the Crown'. The defending counsel had previously argued that evidence of harm to the national interest should be produced and that it surely could not be right that 'all the Crown had to do was to call a government official of some kind to say "that act is in fact prejudicial because I am the only person who knows" '.[58] But Lord Parker pointed to 'the general power of Ministers whether in war or peace to claim Crown privilege'. He added: 'A similar

[58] *The Times*, Law Report, 3 Apr. 1962.

principle underlies the power of the executive . . . to requisition or to do other acts where in its discretion that is considered necessary in the national interest.'[59]

The principle that the courts do not inquire into the reasons which lead officials to exercise administrative discretion granted to them by law is well established. As C. J. Hamson put it in his comment on the judgment in the case of *Liversidge* v. *Anderson* (1942), concerning a man who claimed that he had been wrongly imprisoned under a wartime detention order: 'The detention order accordingly was valid by reason of the mere statement of the Home Secretary that the Home Secretary believed himself to have reasonable cause to believe that the appellant ought to be locked up.'[60] Some judges have been increasingly irked by the petty way in which the executive's right to refuse to give reasons is exercised. In a case in 1964 involving a dispute between the British Railways Board and a group of hotels (the *Grosvenor Hotel* case), in the course of which the Minister of Transport, responsible for the Board, refused to produce a document that was held to be relevant, claiming Crown privilege, one of the judges commented that he 'detected a desire in the official mind to push ever forward the frontiers of secrecy'—a process which he regarded 'with distaste'.[61] Another judge in the same case went further. He said that when Crown privilege was unreasonably claimed in matters like this, 'the Court ought to have the power to override the Executive'. In his view,

it was incredible that the public service should not function properly unless commonplace communications between one civil servant and another were privileged from production. . . . Industry seemed to have got along very well without privilege for communications even at the highest level. The law had already given the Executive complete protection in respect of high level communications and communications made under a statutory duty.[62]

The rebellion of these High Court judges is not an isolated incident. The three judges, led by Lord Denning, Master of the Rolls, who had presided over the *Grosvenor Hotel* case, repeated their strictures on the arbitrary exercise of administrative discretion by government officials in another department, the Ministry of Housing and Local Government, in December 1964. Again, it was a question of producing official documents, which were relevant to a dispute with some borough councils, for examination by the court; this was refused without other explanation than that it was 'necessary for the proper functioning of the public service to withhold from production' documents in

---

[59] *All England Law Reports*, 15 May 1962, p. 320.
[60] *Executive Discretion and Judicial Control* (London, Stevens, 1954), p. 13 n. 7.
[61] Lord Justice Harman, *The Times*, *Law Report*, 30 July 1964. The case was about the refusal by the Railways Board to renew the lease of the Grosvenor Hotel (at Victoria Station) on a site which the Board owned.
[62] Lord Justice Salmon (ibid.)

this class.[63]   This statement was covered in the usual way by the signature of the minister, and, it was claimed, his say-so was sufficient to settle the matter.   Lord Denning asserted, on the contrary, that when a minister put a blanket of secrecy over a whole class of documents 'he *must* justify his objection with reasons.   He should describe the nature of the class and the reason why the document should not be disclosed, so that the Court itself could see whether the claim was well taken or not.'[64]

He admitted that the blanket statement of refusal by a minister had been accepted as 'common form' before the *Grosvenor Hotel* case, and indicated that the court would in future try to control the unrestrained—and unexplained—use of ministerial discretion.   However, so far the challenge to the executive is no more than a promise, for in both cases—the Grosvenor Hotel and the borough councils—Lord Denning and his fellow judges ruled that the official documents which had been demanded by the litigants against the Government were not, in fact, necessary for the court's decision.   The match between judicial authority and discretionary power has, therefore, for the present, been postponed.[65]

How did it happen that the frontiers of British justice had been allowed to retreat as far as this?   The chief cause lies in what Mitchell has called the conception of 'the Minister-judge' in parliament, who must answer for all administrative acts done on his responsibility and 'against whom the Common Law can do nothing'.   He describes the further process as follows:

> From that fact, coupled with the dependent fact of the anonymity of the civil service, flowed the judicial answers that the individual was not entitled to know or see the individual official who decided (this being, it was considered, immaterial, since the Minister was responsible) and that decisions need not be reasoned.   The last was an acceptance of administrative practice which was itself dependent upon the doctrine of ministerial responsibility.   The decision, it was thought, should, if need be, be justified in Parliament but not elsewhere.[66]

The story is a telling example of the way in which a useful piece of mythology—the absolute sovereignty of parliament and the total subordination of servants of the Crown—may actively impede progress if people insist on remaining loyal to it when circumstances, and the problems to be solved, have changed.   There is no mystery about what is lacking: it is a system of administrative law which will allow acts of official discretion to be judged by an independent tribunal.   But there is no means of accommodating such a

---

[63] The case involved the reorganization of local government and the objections of Wednesbury Borough Council and four other local authorities in the Midlands to the decision of the Ministry.   They claimed that the inquiry held by the Ministry had not been properly conducted and was therefore invalid.

[64] Ibid.

[65] Lord Denning's view of the proper role of the courts in this matter is not by any means uniformly accepted by the rest of the British judiciary.

[66] 'The Causes and Effects of the Absence of a System of Public Law in the United Kingdom', *Public Law*, Summer 1965, p. 102.

reform without pulling the doctrine of ministerial responsibility up by the roots. The result of not making the wrench is a profound distortion at the centre of the administrative system. 'The civil servant in England', C. J. Hamson says,[67] 'necessarily suffers a gross professional deformation, not by reason of any naturally inherent vice but mainly by reason of the condition in which he operates—namely, as the bearer collectively within the community of a power which is as great as it is arbitrary'. It is a comfort that civilized administrative habits and a strong tradition of fair play limit the actual employment of this arbitrary power. But it might also be argued that the cultivated reticence of the British civil servant, the restraint on his initiative, and the damper on verbal expression, which he accepts as the price for being left undisturbed in the twilight zone between parliament and the people whom he administers, endow Britain with a less effective form of public power than the natural talent of the nation is capable of providing.

Conseil d'État

For purposes of comparison it is useful to begin with another case, in France, involving a refusal by the Government to produce documents for a court. This is the case of the five students, now celebrated in French administrative law (*'Barel and others'*), who in 1953 tried to enter the École Nationale d'Administration, the school which has to be attended in order to gain entry to the senior grades of the civil service, and were refused permission to sit for the competitive examination. The person responsible for the order turning down their applications was the State Secretary acting on behalf of the Prime Minister, at that time M. Laniel; and there is no doubt that he did so because he believed that these men were communists. The students applied to the Conseil d'État for relief, and the Conseil, after considering the case, asked the minister for an explanation. This he refused to provide, alleging that he had full discretionary power to ·decide who should sit for the examination; the Conseil's request to inspect the official documents in the case was turned down. The Conseil thereupon annulled the minister's order, and the students were given the right to take the examination.[68]

The case, as M. Letourneur, the noted French jurist and member of the Conseil d'État, has since argued, consolidated some important principles of administrative law.[69] First, it used the fundamental notion of *détournement de pouvoir*—i.e. of an administrative act which distorts the *intention* of the law—to pass judgment on an administrative action, even though there was no specific legal limitation on the exercise of ministerial discretion in the case. The manner in which this was done was to assert that the Conseil d'État was

---

[67] *Executive Discretion*, p. 19.   [68] See ibid., pp. 24–25.
[69] See *Études et Documents, Conseil d'État, 1962* (Paris), 'L'étendue du contrôle du juge de l'excès de pouvoir', p. 56. He insists that the case 'did not innovate'; but it served to give greater precision and clarity to certain powers which the Conseil had been exercising.

the guardian of the 'public interest', in relation to the actions of the administration, and that this particular action, which denied equal rights of access to the French government service to certain citizens of the country, appeared to be in conflict with the Declaration of the Rights of Man guaranteeing such equality for all.[70] Secondly, the judgment asserted that the minister was under an obligation to produce evidence to show whether his assessment of the case was correct. Letourneur makes the point that this case was part of the systematic effort undertaken by the Conseil to squeeze 'the margin of administrative discretion' and subject it to legal rules.

An interesting legal device which it has employed since the case of *Barel* to reduce this margin still further is the notion of 'manifest error' (*erreur manifeste*) in certain administrative decisions. It has served to introduce a form of judicial surveillance in matters where the administrative services had previously felt themselves to be free to decide for themselves, without anyone questioning their judgement. The case of the mayor of Montfermeil who, in 1962, sacked one of the workers employed by the commune, because his job had lapsed, shows the way in which this kind of control may be extended. The law laid down that workers in such circumstances were to be retained, if there was a vacancy in an 'equivalent job' elsewhere, in the employ of the local authority. The mayor alleged that such a job did not exist. But according to the Conseil d'État's judgment, there was a vacancy which filled the bill—it was 'manifestly equivalent to the job which had lapsed'—and so the dismissed worker was taken back on to the books of the local authority, in spite of the mayor.[71] Thus judicial inspection of the circumstances revealed that the latter's view of the degree of equivalence between certain kinds of employment was mistaken; this was the 'manifest error'.

The detail of such cases as this is less interesting than the principle which moves the lawyers of the Conseil d'État to seek out the arbitrary element in acts of administrative discretion and devise ingenious ways of subjecting it to some degree of explicit discipline. It is its constant pressure on the administration to explain itself which is the Conseil's most valuable contribution. Not that this is done in a hostile or niggling spirit. On the contrary, the authority of the members of the Conseil depends in part on the fact that they are members of the administrative service and know at first hand what the problems of administration are really like. When they hand down a judgment, they do not, as English judges would deliberately try to do, exclude such considerations from their thoughts. Professor Georges Langrod remarks that the Conseil 'preserves a remarkable moderation, seeing to it that the Administration is not hindered by a minutely detailed and burdensome judicial control'. There is above all a permissive attitude towards actions

[70] See Hamson, *Executive Discretion*, pp. 28–29.
[71] *Études et Documents, Conseil d'État, 1962*, p. 57.

which officials take in extraordinary circumstances; in an emergency the administrative court will even countenance 'certain extra-legal powers of the Administration which permit it to exceed the authority conferred by legislative statute, thus allowing the administrative judge to modify the content of the law *extra* and even *contra legem* (the so-called "war powers" theory)'. Langrod comments that this arrangement is 'by no means limited to wartime events', but extends to all '*périodes critiques*'. He concludes that 'administrative decisions which would be illegal in normal times thus become legal by virtue of certain circumstances'.[72]

It is thus apparent that the whole operation relies on a spirit of self-criticism. How effective it is in practice depends ultimately on the professional pride of the bosses of this great bureaucracy who sit in the Conseil d'État. All accounts agree that their *esprit de corps* is immense. A recent striking example of this spirit was the unanimous verdict of the Conseil, in October 1962, declaring that General de Gaulle's proposed use of a referendum to change the procedure for electing the President of the Republic[73] was unconstitutional. Among those who took part in the voting of the Conseil sitting in '*assemblée générale*' was its Vice-President, M. Parodi, himself a fervent Gaullist.[74] The Conseil has an intimate and complex relationship with the government of the day. On the one hand it acts as its close counsellor, especially in the delicate work of preparing delegated legislation. It has to be consulted on and to approve all laws and regulations made by executive order. Yet in its other, judicial, incarnation (acting through the Section du Contentieux) it can subsequently, and does, annul these orders if they are judged to be legally unsatisfactory in some respect. This may cause considerable inconvenience, since the annulment is retroactive; it is as if the order in question never had any legal force, so that any person who suffered loss through obeying it has a claim for damages against the government department concerned. In the year 1962, for example, the list of ministerial orders, decisions, and circulars declared illegal added up to a total of 57.[75]

Hamson's comment on this dual and apparently contradictory role of the Conseil is apt:

There is here an extraordinary paradox—the Conseil d'État consists of a body of men who are in one of their functions the confidential advisers of the executive, sharing their inmost secrets and who yet, at the instance of the subject and in another function, set themselves up as the uncommitted judges of the executive act. . . . It is precisely this paradox which is the essence of the matter. . . . The Conseil d'État will retain its efficacy—which today is extreme—only if and so long as it is able to retain, in their most uncompromised state, both of these apparently opposite and contradictory functions.[76]

---

[72] 'The French Council of State', *American Political Science Review*, Sept. 1955.
[73] To direct popular voting.   [74] See *Le Monde*, 3 Oct. 1962.
[75] See *Études et Documents, Conseil d'État, 1962*, list on pp. 177–80.
[76] *Executive Discretion*, p. 46.

The arrangement, however, depends in the last resort on the acceptance of the primacy of the judicial function by the administrative sections of the Conseil. Of course, it is inconvenient to have an order to which they have given their approval subsequently annulled; but they readily submit to the referee, and even take some pride in the fact that the referee is so indifferent to questions of mere convenience.

Development of French Administrative Law

It is a curious fact that this remarkable curb on administrative discretion, which has been copied, though in a milder form, by various other European countries, originally arose out of the French government's determination after the Revolution of 1789 to secure for itself total administrative discretion, unchecked by any court of law. The fear of the régime was that the lawyers in the traditional *parlements* would try to obstruct, as they had done in the past, the effective work of the central administration; so all official acts were declared to be outside the jurisdiction of the courts.[77] Gradually what Bernard Schwartz calls the 'dual system'—a case of separation of powers with a vengeance—was subjected to a measure of judicial control; but always with the authority to judge the administrative act kept firmly inside the administration. The Conseil d'État itself was established by Napoleon, and initially its independent judicial activity was slight. There were no regular proceedings in open court until 1831. Even then, the decisions that it reached about administrative acts were still only advisory in character; the government was not compelled to accept them.

The great authority to annul official decisions directly was given to the Conseil in the early years of the Third Republic, in 1872. Thereafter its position of independent authority was steadily reinforced. During the twentieth century it managed to establish a species of tutelary relationship towards the government of the day; especially if it was a weak government without a dependable parliamentary majority, it needed the goodwill of the Conseil for the day-to-day business of governing. The failure of successive French parliaments to provide the necessary steady support for the executive meant that the Conseil's role was greatly enhanced. In so far as a government succeeded in bypassing the legislature and governing by executive order, it became more dependent on the approval of the Conseil. To some extent it stood in as a substitute for the supervision of government that parliament was unable to provide.[78]

[77] See B. Schwartz, *French Administrative Law and the Common-Law World* (New York UP, 1954), p. 6.
[78] See *Études et Documents, Conseil d'État, 1947*, Introduction, p. 13, which points out that the Conseil itself was responsible for a great deal of what it calls 'secondary legislation', based on acts of parliament which were deliberately very widely drawn. From passing judgement on the legality of government decrees and helping in their original drafting the Conseil thus moved over into an active law-making role.

As might have been expected, the Conseil has not had quite such an easy passage under a strong Government, such as that of the Fifth Republic, as under the Third and Fourth Republics. Nevertheless it has continued to assert itself quite effectively in the face of a greatly reinforced executive, at a time when parliament was particularly enfeebled.[79] There was some anxiety aroused in the early 1960s by a much heralded project for the reform of the Conseil, after it had been involved in some friction with General de Gaulle. But the changes introduced in the summer of 1963 did not reduce the independent judicial authority of the Conseil. Their aim, more subtly, was to enlarge the active administrative role of the men who sit in judgement on administrative acts. The idea, it was explained, was that this would make the members of the Conseil more sensitive to the practical problems of government and more responsive to the needs of efficient administration.[80]

The French version of administrative justice makes demands on the political awareness of the judges, not only in considering the problems of the executive arm, but also in relation to the purposes of the legislature. To some extent the two sets of considerations tend to counter-balance one another—at any rate they sometimes point in opposite directions. On the one hand the administrative judges are supposed to take account of the practical needs of the administrators in running the day-to-day government of the country; on the other hand, it is their duty to act as the guardians of the long-term *intention* of the legislators. The executive is ever present and articulate; the original makers of a law are usually silent, and if they happen to speak they do not have to be listened to. Having made the law, their personal function is at an end. However, it is part of the duty of the administrative judge to ensure that an ill or ambiguously drafted law does not produce consequences which the legislature failed to foresee, and which it would have tried to prevent if it had done so. In order to decide the matter, the judge will go

---

[79] See for example *Études et Documents, Conseil d'État, 1961*, pp. 63–64, for an account of the way in which the Conseil has tried to limit the arbitrary employment of the government's power to make laws (*Ordonnances*) without consulting parliament. This legislative power, with which de Gaulle's Government had been endowed, was being used to reverse retrospectively the Conseil's own annulments of administrative acts. This meant that the normal effect of an annulment, to make the administrative order illegal from the moment when it was promulgated, was being avoided. The proposed answer of the Conseil was to award large amounts of damages to people who claimed to have been harmed by the Government's retrospective legislation. (The Gaullist *Ordonnance* is formally a legislative act, and therefore escapes the normal control exercised by the Conseil over government decrees.)

[80] See *Le Monde*, 1 Aug. 1963, the statement on behalf of the Government by J. Foyer. The aim of the reform, he said, was to have an institution which did not see itself in the role of 'juge de l'administration' but as 'seulement sa conscience intérieure'. The distinction between the two roles, in view of the well established and open judicial procedures of the Conseil d'État, is more subtle than the artificial clarity of the French language might seem to imply. It points to a desired shift of emphasis, not a change of principle.

behind the literal meaning of the words, back to the recorded views of those responsible for making the law, and will interpret its significance in the light of these '*travaux préparatoires*'.

The separation of powers therefore breaks down at both ends; not only are the judges acting as the allies of the executive arm, they are also doing part of the work of the legislative arm. By contrast, the British judicial reaction, when faced with an inadequately drafted law which distorts the intention of those who made it, is that it is up to parliament to make a new and better law. In the meanwhile the existing law must be applied as it stands; and judges, in interpreting it, will conscientiously stick to the meaning of the words in which the law happens to be expressed. They refuse to go beyond those words and look at independent evidence of what those who made the law were trying to achieve. This whole approach, as Bertrand de Jouvenel has pointed out,[81] is characteristic of a certain kind of traditional society—a 'nomocracy', where 'the Law, made independently of the active Power, prescribed and circumscribed its operations'. The law was supposed to be absolutely explicit about all the details of its application and to foresee all the circumstances in which it might have to be applied. De Jouvenel contrasts this political system with the 'telocracies', where 'the active Power, pursuing objectives in changing circumstances, demands from the legislature *ad hoc* rules as required to implement policies'. He argues that 'if there are important goals of government which should be achieved, and if the ways to achieve them cannot be boiled down to routines prescribed by the legislative to the executive, then the law is consequently devalued and the executive upgraded'. In practice 'the faster the pace of change, the more difficult it becomes to provide the executive magistrates with a complete set of instructions for their future operations'.[82] The argument of the earlier chapters of this book may be summed up as being that the efficient and humane modern state is a 'telocracy', taking an increasingly long view of its purposes.

Emphasis on Procedure

What is characteristic of a would-be 'nomocracy' like Britain is an overwhelming emphasis on legal procedure. Again, this has in the past helped to secure some large gains in individual liberty. It still gives an Englishman more protection against arbitrary imprisonment, for example, than a Frenchman has. But procedural guarantees, however elaborate, are a feeble weapon against a determined official who knows how to stick to the formalities and to use them to get his own way. They then appear as a ceremonial hoax, the more obnoxious for the pretence of having something to do with human rights. In the summer of 1962 Dr Soblen, a refugee from the United States

[81] 'Forms of government', *Futuribles Studies*.   [82] Ibid., p. 94.

with an American prison sentence for espionage standing against him, landed in Britain. Although there was great pressure from the United States to get him back, there was no question of extradition. But Soblen found, when he was refused permission to stay on British soil, that an official expulsion order could be readily used to achieve the same practical purpose. British courts do not allow the Home Secretary, when expelling someone, to specify to which country he is to go. On the other hand the law gives him complete discretion to determine on which aeroplane or ship the expellee is to be made to depart. The one chosen for Soblen was a non-stop BOAC morning flight from London to New York. The only thing that ruined the plot was that Soblen then committed suicide. But by intention at least this was a gross case of *détournement de pouvoir*, and the British courts were powerless to do anything about it.[83]

The exclusive concern with judicial ritual is itself a reflection of the myth that the law, when properly made, is fixed, transparent and unequivocal. The only problem then is to provide a legal procedure which will ensure that the facts of any case are sufficiently established to attract the relevant bit of the law to its judgement. The procedural approach is of course a convenient one; it is politically attractive; about all, it saves fuss, involving as it does no more interference than that of a referee whom the players like to have about in order to ensure that they all stick to the rules of the game. It was the principle adopted once again, when the British came to look, during the 1950s, at the problem of tightening the control over certain powers of the civil service which affect the welfare and property rights of individual members of the public. The outcome of an independent inquiry[84] into the methods used by the bureaucracy to settle disputed cases led to the establishment of the Council on Tribunals—a body made up of rather more than a dozen notable persons, working unpaid and charged with a watching brief over the behaviour of some 2,000 administrative tribunals. In the few years that it has been in operation the Council has unobtrusively brought about some useful improvements in the ways in which administrative decisions of an overtly judicial character are arrived at. Above all, it has insisted, wherever it has had the opportunity, that a reasoned explanation for decisions should be given.[85] Previously the bare announcement of the finding of the administrative tribunal was deemed to be sufficient.

But the Council is kept severely at arm's length from the substance of any act of administrative discretion: its concern is with the form in which complaints and queries and arguments from the public are heard and judged. Moreover, its rights of inspection are confined to the overtly judicial acts of

[83] See Paul O'Higgins, 'Deportation and Extradition', *New Society*, 25 Feb. 1965.
[84] The Committee on Administrative Tribunals and Inquiries (under the chairmanship of Lord Franks). See its Report, Cmnd 218, 1957.
[85] See, for example, *Annual Report of the Council on Tribunals*, 1963, para. 73.

government. Thus it may not, for example, look into 'inquiries' held on the initiative of a minister. However weighty their consequences may be for members of the public, they are treated as non-judicial, because they are covered by the theory that the minister is merely trying to inform himself as a preliminary to an administrative decision for which he alone is responsible.[86] Equally the important discretionary powers exercised by local authorities, sitting in judgement on the relative needs and rights of individual members of the public (notably in matters of housing), escape from its purview. These decisions, made under the aegis of the elected representatives of local government, are not regarded as belonging to the conventional judicial category.[87]

The Ombudsman

The expedients employed by the British in trying to adjust the methods of a traditional legal philosophy to the realities of modern government seem to offer little promise. On the other hand the French system, for all the flexibility and vigour of the Conseil d'État at its centre, is still deficient in certain qualities required for the civilized conduct of public business in a modern capitalist society. The Conseil is a wonderful curb on arbitrary or irrational behaviour by the bureaucracy, once this gives rise to complaints. But it does little about the more commonplace problem of the merely inconsiderate—the acts of officials who are thoughtless and lacking in sympathy for the people they are appointed to administer. This is not a matter of designing a negative check on some bureaucratic vice; the problem is rather to secure a positive effort of imagination and kindness from public officials in their treatment of private persons. The familiar symbol of this kind of preoccupation, which is in this century the characteristic mark of Scandinavian society, is the Ombudsman.

[86] Ibid. It is interesting to find that the same somewhat artificial distinction was used in the *Wednesbury Borough Council* case (see above, p. 413) by Lord Justice Denning to justify the decision *not* to insist on the production of official documents in the reports of the Ministry's Inspectors' reports. 'If', he said, 'the inspectors' inquiry partook of the nature of a judicial inquiry so that the rules of natural justice ought to be observed, then it would be wrong for a Minister to issue a brief or instructions to the inspector behind the backs of the parties. . . . In such a case full disclosure should be given. But if the inquiry was a mere channel for providing information to the Minister, it was a different matter altogether'. He concluded that the purpose of the inquiry in question 'was not judicial or even quasi-judicial, but merely to inform the mind of the Minister when he came to make his decision' (*The Times Law Report*, 4 Dec. 1964).

[87] See *The Citizen and the Administration*, a report by Justice (London, Stevens, 1961), p. 87. Anyone coming unprepared on the work of the Council on Tribunals as reflected in its series of Annual Reports from 1959 onwards would be driven to the conclusion that it had been deliberately under-equipped for a mock contest with the Administration. Members of the Council are part-time, they are unpaid, and their role is purely advisory. They have no executive power whatever—not even the power to enforce their right to be present while the deliberations of certain tribunals are in progress. The Council pleaded for five years for permission to be present as

The original inventors of this device, and they used it for more than 100 years before anyone else began to take any notice of it, were the Swedes. During the present century it has been adopted, with modifications, by a few other countries, among whom the most recent is New Zealand. In this discussion of its possible wider uses in modern Western society, I shall draw chiefly on the experience of Sweden, not only because its experience is the longest, but also because there the Ombudsman is buttressed by other arrangements—of which I have already referred to one, the automatic publicity of official documents—which make him peculiarly effective. It is of interest that the institution of the Swedish Ombudsman owed its development, in part, to certain weaknesses in the system of parliamentary control. (The analogy with the Conseil d'État suggests itself.) In Sweden there is no effective system of parliamentary questions, and no ministerial responsibility for most administrative acts. The ministers are not the heads of the offices of government but are solely concerned with the formulation of policy. Their role is akin to that of 'councillors of state';[88] meanwhile the day-to-day work of government is done by a number of administrative 'boards' under the control of senior officials, whose responsibility for the work of their offices is direct to parliament rather than to any minister. The Ombudsman was set up in 1809 by parliament in order to provide it with a check on the performance of these officials. It was parliament's answer to the power of the Crown over the ministers; the 'boards' were its servants. Only gradually has the function of the Ombudsman become that of supervising the conduct of the administration in its widest sense.

The main task of the office is to curb acts of maladministration, where an official concerned has used the power conferred on him in a way not intended by the law. The notion of *détournement de pouvoir* is implicit in the action of the Ombudsman in, for instance, such a routine case as that of the prison

observers at certain private sessions of National Health Service tribunals in England (*Annual Report, 1963*, p. 2). They also asked that once they had been consulted on the drafting of any Statutory Instrument containing provision for the establishment of a tribunal, their views should, whenever they were not reflected in the wording of the proposed law, be included with the printed document of its text laid before parliament. This was turned down out of hand; the Council was told that it must organize its own means of publicity for its views (see *Annual Report, 1959*, p. 24, for the proposal). Finally, it is dependent on the goodwill of individual government departments who are asked to pass on those complaints about administrative tribunals from the public which are not made direct to the Council; the 'two-way traffic' with government departments is apparently not always forthcoming (ibid.). That in spite of these disabilities the Council has managed to do useful work is due in part to the personal quality and determination of the people involved in the work—and more generally to the remarkable responsiveness of the British to even the feeblest kind of machinery for producing more fair play.

[88] See Justice report, *The Citizen and the Administration*. The exception is the Foreign Office, where the minister is in full charge of his department.

which had banned a certain magazine wanted by the inmates. The investigation showed that the reason for the ban was that the magazine had published a critical article on the prison authorities. This was not judged to be a sufficient reason for denying the prisoners the right to read it, and it was reinstated.[89]

It should be observed however that the Ombudsman in a case such as this has none of the power of enforcement possessed by the Conseil d'État. He can call evidence and demand explanations; but his means of pressure on a recalcitrant official are indirect: he can threaten to take him to court. That this threat is a very powerful weapon is suggested by the fact that only a tiny fraction of the cases investigated in any one year result in court actions— and in some of these no doubt it is the Ombudsman who wants to make sure that the law imposes a penalty on an erring official. His own direct powers are limited to giving an official a formal 'admonition'.[90]

Another important difference between the practice of the Swedish Ombudsman and the Conseil d'État is that the former is, in principle, exclusively concerned with acts of maladministration—i.e. where the complaint is that an official has failed to act in accordance with some specific law—and not with complaints about the exercise of administrative discretion. It is difficult to draw a precise line between the two in practice; the principle is that where an official has acted legally but has shown poor judgement which has hurt someone, this is not a case for the Ombudsman but for the administrative courts. In France, we have seen that the Conseil d'État is able to annul certain acts of discretion on the ground that the judgement of the facts by the official concerned was faulty. In Sweden this function is performed by the Supreme Administrative Tribunal. Appeals to it against administrative decisions are 'cheap and frequently used';[91] indeed the Swedish authorities claim that one of the reasons for the relatively small number of complaints submitted to the Ombudsman—about one thousand a year in the late 1950s—is that people often find this other remedy against the unfair exercise of administrative power more convenient for their purposes.[92]

As in the French system, the judicial and the administrative arms are closely intertwined in the Swedish court. Not only are the judges frequently members of the administrative service, but also the active officers of the court, the men responsible for bringing the cases forward and conducting the preliminary investigations, are in the employ of various government departments. Each of these 'ministerial secretaries' looks after the complaints of a particular ministry; it is his duty to take up any case brought against his department, to present the details to the Supreme Administrative Court, and

[89] See ibid., p. 52.   [90] Ibid., p. 51.
[91] N. Herlitz, 'The Rule of Law in the Northern Countries', *Annales de la Faculté de Droit d'Istanbul, 1959*, pp. 139 ff.
[92] See Justice report, p. 32.

also to prepare a draft decision for the judges to consider.[93]   These men are not called upon either to prosecute or to defend the department with which they are concerned; indeed there is no 'adversary' procedure in this court. Submissions are made in writing, and the whole approach is that of an administration rigorously investigating its own doings in the light of other people's complaints.   It is, Professor Herlitz says, 'exceptional that the state is represented by someone who plays the role of a party in opposition to the private party'.[94]

The formal powers with which the Swedish court is endowed are more far-reaching even than those of the Conseil d'État, for it not only has the right to annul acts of administrative discretion, it can also substitute its own decision for that of the official whose action is being judged.[95]   There are, it is true, certain limitations on the range of its authority and on the kind of redress which it can directly provide for administrative faults which have harmed somebody.   But its function has to be seen as a part of the general apparatus of the Swedish system of control—including the Ombudsman, the strong and independent civil courts, the publicity of official documents and, above all, the attitudes that go with an open system of administration.   The deliberate use of publicity as a constant means of pressure on the administration is perhaps the most striking feature of the Swedish method, and the one which most obviously lends itself to wider application elsewhere.   It is the chief weapon of the new generation of Ombudsman that has arisen since the war in countries like Denmark and New Zealand.

Indeed, the Danes rely on the effect of publicity for their Ombudsman (established in 1955) even more heavily than the Swedes.   Not that official acts are subject to freer public inspection than in Sweden; that is barely conceivable.   The difference is that the Swedish Ombudsman sees himself as having, in addition to the resources of journalism and moral pressure, a natural and easy recourse to the courts.   His whole approach, as Herlitz remarks, approximates to that of a judge.   'The Danish Ombudsman, on the other hand, adopts a more flexible approach to his intervention which some-

---

[93] Chapman, *The Profession of Government*, pp. 241 ff.

[94] 'Swedish Administrative Law', *International & Comparative Law Quarterly*, Apr. 1953, p. 234.

[95] See Justice report, p. 32, and Herlitz, 'Swedish Administrative Law'.   The court, the latter says, not only has the authority 'to decide whether there has been an excess or an abuse of a discretionary power'; it will also 'decide whether a discretionary power has been exercised unreasonably or generally in a way that it does not consider appropriate' (p. 231).   In view of this it is surprising that Chapman (*Profession of Government*, p. 245) describes the court as 'weak'.   Although certain administrative acts are excluded from its purview, e.g. decisions of ministers and of elected local governments, what is left over is still very extensive—and here, as Herlitz says, the administrative courts have 'the same power as a superior appellate authority, namely, to judge the case as comprehensively as the authority which made the initial decisions' ('Swedish Administrative Law', p. 227).

times takes the form of a persuasive opinion rather than a critical report.[96] The Swedes probably benefit from the fact that their system was developed before the full resources of modern publicity were available, when journalism alone, unsupported by the exercise of direct authority, was obviously inadequate; the result is that they can now call on an older and more varied institutional armoury.[97]

A Cult of Bureaucratic Humanity

There are, however, certain kinds of administrative power which are peculiarly sensitive to the threat of publicity. Especially when wielded by a body with the recognized function of securing fair play beyond the normal means of the courts, it is a uniquely effective form of pressure against the more elusive kind of bureaucratic abuse. There are the many cases where the administrators have not contravened any law or even been inefficient in any obvious way, but have merely been deficient in human touch. They can cause as much damage in that way as in any other. As was suggested earlier, the special virtue of the Ombudsman lies in the deliberate effort to impart more humanity—that is, greater concern for individual circumstances—into the behaviour of the administration. The essential point is the recognition that to be 'correct' is not enough. How does one induce busy officials, who instinctively think in terms of human aggregates, to take a sympathetic interest in the awkward individual case?

This type of problem, characteristically undramatic and very familiar indeed, can be illustrated by any one of dozens of cases which now come to the Ombudsman in those countries that have appointed one—and beforehand went to no one at all. Take this example out of the bag of the new Zealand Ombudsman during the first eighteen months of his operations.[98] A small farmer with two deaf sons had been trying to buy some land for them to work adjoining his own farm, so that he could be at hand to help them. He was in the middle of the negotiation, which had taken some time because of his difficulties in raising the money to finance the purchase price of the plot that he was after, when a government department stepped in with an offer to the owner, who promptly sold the land for cash. The purpose for which it was to be used was to form part of a training centre in forestry for delinquent boys; and the Ombudsman when he came to look at the farmer's complaint, had to weigh the needs of one public welfare service against those of a rather

---

[96] Justice report, p. 59.
[97] The Danish Ombudsman also has the right to start legal proceedings against an offending official, but the latter can stop him at any time by demanding that his case be transferred to the internal civil service authority charged with the investigation of disciplinary complaints (see S. Hurwitz, 'The Danish Parliamentary Commissioner', *Public Law*, 1958, p. 242).
[98] See the report of a lecture by Sir Guy Powles, the New Zealand Ombudsman, on his first eighteen months in office, in the *Guardian*, 14 May 1964.

smaller private one. There was no question that the public authorities had acted fully within their rights. But the farmer alleged, among other things, that they had been unduly rigid in their attitude towards his problem; they had, he said, refused even to consider an alternative suggestion to allow him to purchase from them a smaller parcel of land, also next door to his own property, which he asserted was in any case too good for forestry but was suitable for his two sons.

The end of the story was that the Ombudsman, in the course of his investigation of the case, discovered another piece of land in the vicinity, which was suitable only for forestry, and put it to the government department that they might buy this and release the parcel of land which was conveniently placed for the farmer. That was the arrangement to which the officials concerned eventually agreed. It is not recorded what it was which induced them to give way. But it is a safe bet that a highly persuasive influence in such a situation would have been the thought of a public report to parliament suggesting that public servants, although acting within their legal rights in pursuit of an acknowledged public interest, were doing so with insufficient humanity and friendliness.

This is a form of pressure which the French brand of administrative justice fails to supply. The French system is designed to provide a curb on bad behaviour rather than a spur to positively good. It may be that the exclusive emphasis on the negative check rather than the active nudge to the administration derives from an underlying philosophical optimism which seems to pervade many French institutions—essentially an eighteenth century, pre-Revolution optimism about the predominant goodness of the nature of man. Intervention by public authority is therefore deemed to be necessary only to check deviations from the path of virtue; for the rest the positive humanity of the state official may be relied upon to protect the individual in any conflict between public and private interest. One does not have to be a believer in a large dose of original sin in order to find this approach inappropriate to modern conditions in Western society.

A further important function which is fulfilled by the Swedish Ombudsman in particular[99] is to exercise personal initiative in seeking out cases of maladministration, without waiting for complaints to be brought to him. He makes systematic tours of inspection covering all district government offices above a certain size, giving each of them 48 hours notice of his impending arrival with his staff and then making a test check of the official files. He follows this up with the investigation of any doubtful cases.[100] According to Brian Chapman, the Ombudsman manages to cover the whole of the country in this way about once every eight years. A considerable number of the

[99] Though not by the Ombudsman in other countries, e.g. New Zealand and Denmark.
[100] See Justice report, and Chapman, *Profession of Government*, ch. xii.

complaints which he later subjects to investigation are turned up in this way. Indeed the Ombudsman dealing with army affairs (the *Militieombudsman*) finds that the overwhelming majority of the cases investigated by his office on grounds of maladministration emerge in the course of his personal tours of inspection.[101] The ordinary complaints procedure still apparently leaves a great many soldiers and some civilians feeling diffident about asserting their rights, unless prompted by the Ombudsman.

It may be argued that all this is simply an extension of the work of the inspectorate system, regularly employed in most Western countries by government departments which have direct dealings with the public. So it is. The advantage of the Ombudsman type of inspection, however, is that it is conducted by someone right outside the ministry concerned, who cannot be suspected of being in any sense judge in his own cause. It is a job done explicitly in order to buttress the private citizen, who is assumed to be in a position of relative weakness *vis-à-vis* the public official. An extra effort is made on behalf of persons over whom the public authorities have more than the usual amount of power. Thus, apart from the special function of the Ombudsman dealing with military affairs, exceptional arrangements are made, for example for people in prison, who may send a sealed letter to the Ombudsman without having its contents examined by the prison authorities.

It is worth making the point that in a system where so much light is let into the obscure corners of administrative practice, the civil servant must also have the benefit of an open judicial procedure to protect his rights. It is not only that his reputation needs to be defended against the insinuations of informers. The informers, too, when they come from inside the service—as they often must if the information is to be worth having—stand in especial need of protection. A young prison officer, for example, or a teacher in his first job is immensely dependent on the goodwill of his superiors in pursuing his further career; a malicious posting or an unfair testimonial can at this stage blight it. Just as the courts should have the right to require reasons from officials for any decisions affecting the public, so they should be able, in case of need, to demand a reasoned explanation of the treatment meted out by one official or another. Administrative courts are a necessary element in any system using the Ombudsman technique to achieve a more open style of administration. The Ombudsman is not a substitute for a system of administrative law; he is a powerful supplement to it—pushing the modern administration beyond mere justice, towards the recognition of a duty of active kindness in a society which grows increasingly dependent on the initiative and the sensibility of its public officials.

---

[101] Chapman, p. 251. The *Militieombudsman* is able to make more frequent tours of inspection that the *Justieombudsman* (concerned with civilian affairs), and covers the whole country about once every five years.

APPENDIX I

THE INDUSTRIAL COUNTRIES AS A MARKET FOR CAPITAL GOODS

THE table traces the growth of world trade in capital goods from 1899 and its changing distribution. As the first column shows, the markets of the industrial and the non-industrial countries were at the end of the nineteenth century roughly equal in importance. During the subsequent four decades, up to 1937, there was a large increase in international sales of capital goods, but it was absorbed overwhelmingly by the non-industrial countries (see first column under 'Increment of Imports at end of period as percentage of total increase in world imports of capital goods').

The trend was reversed in the 1950s, when imports of capital goods into the industrial countries grew faster than imports into the non-industrial countries. The former absorbed slightly over half of the total increase in world trade in capital goods during this period. The sharpest rise was in exports to the big four industrial countries (US, UK, Germany, and France), which took one-quarter of the increase in the volume of capital goods entering into world trade, compared with only 6 per cent of the increase that occurred between 1899 and 1937.

World Trade in Capital[1] Goods, 1899–1959

| | Value of Imports in $ Million F.O.B. at 1955 Prices | | | | | Increment of Imports at End of Period as Percentage: | | | | | | | |
| | | | | | | Of Imports at Beginning of Period | | | | Of Total Increase in World Imports of Capital Goods | | | |
	1899	1937	1950	1955	1959	1899–1937	1950–5	1955–9	1950–9	1899–1937	1950–5	1955–9	1950–9
Selected industrial countries													
UK, France, Germany[2]	340	507	555	965	1,450	49	74	50	162	5	13	17	15
Other Western Europe[3]	200	552	1,256	1,815	2,300	176	45	27	84	11	17	17	17
USA	20	48	160	383	760	140	140	98	375	1	7	14	10
All industrial countries[4]	620	1,529	2,800	4,596	6,080	146	64	32	117	27	56	53	55
All others	600	3,042	5,212	6,651	7,950	407	28	15	52	73	44	47	45
Total imports	1,220	4,571	8,012	11,247	14,030	276	41	24	74	100	100	100	100

Source: Maizels, Industrial Growth and World Trade (Tables 10.6, A6, A8, A10, A12, A15–23, A25).

Notes

1 Machinery and transport equipment other than road passenger vehicles.
2 For 1899 and 1937 German figures cover pre-1939 territory.
3 Belgium, Luxemburg, Netherlands, Italy, Switzerland, Norway, Sweden.
4 Including Canada and Japan.

APPENDIX II

TRADE IN SYNTHETIC PRODUCTS

AT first sight, my assertion about the effect of the increased rate of innovation on postwar international trade in new chemical products may appear to be at variance with the detailed analysis by G. C. Hufbauer, *Synthetic Materials and the Theory of International Trade* (London, Duckworth, 1966). Hufbauer's analysis of trade in 56 synthetic products over the period 1910–60 shows that there is a remarkable consistency about the average 'age' of the products in this group entering into international trade. (The 'age' is simply the time since the product was first produced in significant amounts.) If the age of each product is weighted by its relative importance in the international trade of this group of synthetics—consisting of plastics, man-made fibres and synthetic rubbers—the average works out at 30 years in 1910 and at about the same figure in 1960. Of course, world trade in synthetics in 1910 was tiny compared with 1960 and consisted to the extent of 72 per cent of one product, celluloid (first brought into production in 1870). But it is striking how steady the 30-year average figure remains throughout the period between the two world wars and again in the 1950s.

One might have expected that if the increased rate of innovation were responsible for the expansion in trade among industrial countries, it would be reflected in a diminishing average age of the synthetic products being traded. Indeed, Hufbauer shows that the 'imitation lag'—i.e. the time from first production of a synthetic in the innovating country to its manufacture elsewhere—has come down sharply in the past half century in Italy and Japan, and he comments that the advanced countries will have to discover 'new products at an ever-increasing tempo to prevent less advanced regions from partially closing the technological gap'. But perhaps this is to put altogether too much emphasis on the relatively simple phenomenon of a 'new product'. E.g. the fact that high pressure polyethylene was produced for the first time in Britain in 1937 is not necessarily of much significance. After the initial appearance of a novelty of this kind, the product and the process of production itself undergo very rapid development.

As C. Freeman points out in his study, 'The Plastics Industry' (NIESR, *Econ. R.*, Nov. 1963), even 20–25 years after the appearance of a new product, the original innovator is still able to maintain his grip on old markets and to open up fresh ones by the constant introduction of 'new and improved qualities in the old materials'. 'This is happening,' he comments, 'with all the three major thermoplastic materials—PVC, polystyrene and polythene'. It is to be observed that these three products, which were responsible according to Hufbauer for 50 per cent of international trade in synthetics in 1960, were at that date 20–30 years old. Polystyrene and PVC were brought into commercial production respectively in 1930 and 1931 by I. G. Farben in Germany and polythene in 1937 by ICI in England.

The advanced nations also develop sub-specialities of a particular product and exchange these among themselves. That has always been a feature of trade in advanced chemicals. Sometimes the innovating concern, which in the synthetic materials industry is usually very big and equipped with advanced research facilities, manages to keep a move ahead simply because it is able to cheapen the process of production. Thus in an example cited by Hufbauer, British Xylonite installed a polystyrene polymerization plant in 1952 with a rated annual capacity of 2,000 tons and was able to boost the capacity of the same plant, with only minor modifications, to 16,000 tons in the course of the following ten years. This was essentially the result of improvements in process control which speeded up production—using the same space for a much larger throughput. The final effect was that 'to earn the same profit on invested capital in 1962 as in 1952, British Xylonite only had to earn one-eighth as much profit per kilogram of output.'

Hufbauer's detailed account of the history of innovation and imitation in synthetic products[1] is effectively used by him to support his thesis that the flow of international trade is determined over a certain range of goods by the 'technological gap' between countries, rather than by the relative costs of factors of production. 'As a synthetic material grows older, its technology is more or less perfected. International price differences then depend more on unit factor cost and static scale economy differences than on differences in the level of technology. But when this happens, the discovery of new and better products may serve to bring technological differences once again to the fore'. If it is accepted that, as I argue, the pace of technological innovation has been significantly speeded up—i.e. more innovations appear over a given period of time— the scope for this kind of trade would be increased, even though the 'imitation lag' between countries had shortened. In fact the average 'imitation lag' over the whole range of these synthetics in 1960 (weighted by the relative importance of the products in international trade in that year) was nearly 12 years in France and 14½ years in Italy. In Sweden and the Netherlands it was 19 and 20 years respectively.

Even when faced with shorter imitation lags in Britain (9·9 years) and Germany (5·4 years), the innovator has scope for the development of a significant export trade over the period of time during which his early technological lead continues to give him an advantage in quality, product variety or price. (Note that the British postwar 'lag' is inflated as a result of the long drawn out refusal to embark on the production of synthetic rubber, out of deference to the interest of natural rubber producers.) C. Freeman concludes that 'for standard grades [of plastics], new producers with cost advantages may after 15–30 years eventually challenge the innovating firms'.

---

[1] These are not the same as the group of new chemical products analysed by Maizels referred to in the text. E.g. Maizels includes synthetic detergents, but not man-made fibres which bulk large in Hufbauer's analysis.

GROWTH OF PUBLIC INVESTMENT: GERMANY AND GREAT BRITAIN COMPARED

Category of investment expenditure[1]	Germany (DM billion)			Great Britain (£ million)		
	1958/9	1963	% change (4½ years)[2]	1958/9	1963/4[3]	% change (5 years)
A. Housing	4·5	5·9	+ 31	271	398	+ 47
B. Education, cultural activities, science	1·6	3·8	+138	135	224	+ 66
C. Social services	·9	1·7	+ 89	31	80	+158
D. Communal institutions and facilities	1·1	2·5	+127	97	202	+108
E. Transport and communications	3·1	7·9	+155	352[4]	565	+ 61
F. Economic development:						
i. Trade and industry	·8	·6	− 25	2	8	+300
ii. Agriculture, forestry, fisheries	1·1	2·6	+136	13	25	+ 92
iii. Other development aid	—	·5	—	15	37	+147
G. Government administrative buildings, etc.	·6	1·0	+ 67	10	17	+ 70
Total public expenditure	13·7	26·5	+ 93	926	1,556	+ 68
£ m. sterling[5]	1,170	2,370				

Sources: Germany: 'Public Authorities' Capital Expenditure in the Years 1959 to 1963', Deutsche Bundesbank, *Monthly Report,* Aug. 1964.

       Britain: White Papers on *Public Investment in Great Britain,* 1958/9 figures from Cmnd 1203 (Nov. 1960); 1963/4 figures from Cmnd 2177 (Nov. 1963).

Notes

[1] For purposes of comparison, most of the British public investment figures (other than housing, Category A) have had to be reclassified to conform as closely as possible with the broader categories used in the German analysis. On p. 433 is a list of the White Paper items reclassified under each heading.

Note [1] (*cont.*)

Category	White Paper heading
A. Housing	Housing
B. Education, cultural activities, science	Education University Grants Committee DSIR Grant aided bodies (research)
C. Social services	Hospital services Local Authority health and welfare services (But some Scottish Department of Health expenditure included under D.)
D. Communal institutions and facilities	Water and sewerage Prisons Civil defence Police and fire services Markets Miscellaneous Home Office and Scottish Home and Health Departments' investment General services' investment by Local Authorities

(German figures in this category include expenditure on street lighting; British investment in street lighting is included under the heading of 'Roads and lighting' in E.)

E. Transport and communications	British Transport Commission Air corporations Post Office BBC and ITV Road programme and local authority expenditure on roads and lighting Civil airports and air traffic Harbours Oil distribution Other expenditure by local authorities on road passenger transport, car parks, municipal aerodromes, docks and harbours
F. Economic development: i. Trade and industry	Central Government investment in factory building
ii. Agriculture, forestry, and fisheries	Central and Local Government investment in agriculture, fishing, forestry Local Government investment in arterial drainage, sea defence, coast protection, etc.
iii. Other development aid	Investment under the Town and Country Planning Acts New towns (excluding housing, water, sewerage)
G. Government administrative buildings, etc.	Central Government expenditure on government buildings.

(This is the German 'Other purposes' category, the bulk of which is stated to be expenditure on administrative buildings.)

Note ¹ *(cont.)*
    General :

Investment in nationalized industries (other than transport) has been excluded from the analysis because of the different fields covered by the British and German nationalized sectors. As the German Government Printing Office is classified among the nationalized industries, the corresponding British figures for investment in the Stationery Office have also been omitted. Armed forces and defence investment has been omitted throughout; so has investment in Ministry of Aviation civil research and development.

² The German financial year was changed to a calendar year basis (previously March to March) in 1960 ; so that the 5-year period is reduced by one calendar quarter.

³ Estimates (Cmnd 2177) at March 1963 prices.

⁴ Investment by the transport undertakings (British Transport Commission), which accounted for some 40 per cent of the British investment in transport and communications during this period, was calculated on a calendar year basis.

⁵ DM converted at 11·75 to £ before the 1961 revaluation, at 11·2 to £ after 1961.

APPENDIX IV

DISCRIMINATORY SUBSIDIES AND TAX CONCESSIONS IN GERMANY AND BRITAIN

GERMAN data are derived from two elaborate calculations by the Ministry of Finance, published in the *Bulletin* of July 1959 and the *Finanzbericht* 1962. The latter provides detailed information of actual expenditure and estimates of tax revenue forgone through special allowances in the year 1961. The listing of individual items where a discriminatory tax or subsidy measure was in operation runs to 17 pages. For several of them it was found to be impossible to make an estimate of the amount of tax revenue lost as the result of the concessions made; so that the total, which includes the value of only those items that could be measured, is known to be an underestimate.

The Finance Ministry's analysis covers not only direct concessions to particular groups of persons but also any fiscal arrangement which is designed 'to promote the development of the economy by an alteration of the factors of production, leading indirectly to an improvement in the profitability of selected areas of economic activity' (1959 *Bulletin*, para. 3). Social welfare payments are excluded, even though the recipients may be a restricted group, e.g. old people; so are all payments directly connected with national defence and with the regular public investment programme, e.g. road building. Fiscal concessions which benefit industry are included only where the concession is not uniformly applied; thus, ordinary investment and depreciation allowances are left out, but special allowances for particular purposes, e.g. investment in shipbuilding, are included. (The allowances and subsidies for research and development were excluded from the German analysis and have also been omitted from the British figures.)

The total value of the German concessions in 1961 is given as DM 12·3 billion.[1] The figure includes the capital value of interest-free loans granted by the state in the course of the year (rather than the value of the interest forgone on the loans outstanding). If concessions which are primarily of benefit to the nationalized undertakings (land and air transport) and a number of other doubtful items are excluded from the German list,[2] the total is reduced to DM 10,799 million.

---

[1] This figure excludes the subsidy paid by the state to the Social Insurance Fund, which figures in the grand total given by the Finance Ministry.

[2] Some of the items are excluded in order to make possible a fair comparison with Britain. This applies in particular to all the concessions to transport undertakings, other than shipping. These amounted to DM 1,516 m. Other excluded items are:

DM million

Subsidies

Farmers' old-age pensions	70
School milk	10
Support for Social Insurance Fund	6,506

Tax concessions

Charitable, religious, and similar bodies	53
Pension funds	5
Health insurance schemes	170

435

The value of these subsidies and tax concessions was equal to 23 per cent of the central Government's budget. The DM 10,799 m. was divided as follows:

	DM million	Per cent
Subsidies	*4,758*	*44*
of which: Grants	3,275	30
Loans	1,483	14
Tax concessions	*6,041*	*56*

The following were the main beneficiaries in order of importance:

Beneficiaries	*DM million*	*Percent*
Agriculture, forestry, fisheries	3,497	33
Industry and trade	3,055	28
Housing	2,568	24
Professional and self-employed persons	144	1
Other	1,535	14

Comparison with Britain

There are two major complications in any attempt to put the British and the German figures on a comparable basis. First of all, the role of the central Government in the finance of public expenditure is very different in the two countries. It is much larger in Britain (where it accounts for about 80 per cent of the total) than in Germany (where it is only a little over half). The *Länder* and the local authorities are responsible for a substantial amount of expenditure—some of it involving the payment of subsidies, not listed above—which in Britain is done by the central Government.

The second problem is the difference in the structure of indirect taxation in the two countries. In Germany there is a uniform sales tax which applies in principle to everything ; discrimination in favour of any particular product is therefore immediately apparent and, once the turnover of the product is known, measurable. But in Britain, where the purchase tax has always been levied at widely differing rates, there is no level of tax which can be regarded as the norm. Moreover, the variations in the rates cannot be realistically regarded as pieces of deliberately thought-out tax discrimination, in the German sense—any more than the difference between the tax levied on a gallon of petrol and a gallon of beer. These differences are the outcome of long-standing custom or modern prejudice ; they apply in Germany, too, to certain items, like alcohol, where the tax-collector traditionally assumes that he has special rights.

It seems reasonable to omit those taxes which are guided either (*a*) by considerations of social equity—e.g. that drinkers and smokers should pay a kind of penalty for their pleasures which is escaped by others with more innocent tastes ; or (*b*) by sumptuary motives—so that the gradations of the indirect tax are regarded as being in essence an extension of the progressive income tax principle, with consumers of expensive goods, like furs and jewelry, paying more than those who buy ordinary clothes, or the purchasers of cars paying a higher rate than cyclists. The special rebates applied to the German sales tax on certain goods are generally prompted by quite different motives. Their aim is to assist certain producers, rather than to mete out justice among consumers. The criterion that has been used for the comparison with Britain is that discriminatory tax concessions must be *deliberately producer-oriented*.

There are in fact very few British tax allowances of this type. Indeed, British fiscal discrimination has until recently been overwhelmingly in the form of direct subsidies, either grants or loans ; it is the traditional aim of the British fiscal authorities to make the tax system non-discriminatory. Exceptions have been occurring with increasing frequency in the 1960s, but there is no liking for them.

The result is apparent in the following table showing the value of discriminatory tax concessions and subsidy payments in the financial year 1961/2. There has been no official inquiry in Britain comparable to the German one ; the data on which the table is based have been obtained with the assistance of officials in the Treasury, the Inland Revenue, and the Customs and Excise. It is unlikely that any major item has been overlooked, though it is possible that certain minor concessions may have been omitted.

	£ m.	Per cent
Total discriminatory subsidies and tax concessions	617	
Subsidies	*554*	*90*
of which: Grants	468	76
Loans[3]	86	14
Tax Concessions	*63*	*10*
of which: Inland Revenue	53	9
Customs and Excise	10[4]	1

Subsidies, in the form of grants and loans, were distributed as follows:

	Grants £ m.	Loans £ m.
Agriculture, fisheries, forestry	348·0	2·9
Industry and trade	24·7	39·4
of which: Promotion of local employment	(12·7)	(19·4)
Housing	95·3	43·4

Source : Estimates 1963–4, Memo. by the Financial Secretary to the Treasury (Cmnd 1965). Figures of 'actual expenditure' in 1961–62. Housing figure direct from Treasury.

Tax Concessions, Inland Revenue : The figures which follow are either the tax remissions which accrued during the year or actual tax repayments. In some cases insufficient profit was earned during the year to use up the tax allowances which accrued in the period.

Tax Concessions, Inland Revenue :	£ m.
Additional investment allowance on ships[5]	7
Overseas Trading Corporation's income relieved of tax	11
Preferential treatment of building and co-operative societies for profits tax	20
Small business exemptions and abatements of profits tax[6] ...	15
100 per cent depreciation allowance in development districts ...	—[7]

Tax Concessions, Customs and Excise : Producer-oriented remissions of purchase tax cannot always be identified with certainty, and their value is impossible to calculate with any precision. Only those cases are included in the following table which were clearly intended to assist a particular industry or handicraft.

[3] Net of repayments.

[4] This is a maximum estimate for the tax lost on the items identified. The order of magnitude of the figure, based on the best available indications of the volume of sales of the items concerned (where the official statistics did not conform to the classification of the goods exempted), was £8–10m.

[5] Over normal investment and initial allowances on new plant.

[6] No profits tax charged on incomes below £2,000, and abatements up to £12,000.

[7] This concession did not operate until after 1961.

	£ m.
Tax Concessions, Customs and Excise :	*(estimates)*
Handknitted and crocheted articles	under 0·5
Keyboard instruments	0·1 — 0·5
Cane and wicker baskets	under 0·1
Racing cars and cycles	under 0·1
Textile piece-goods, non-wool, over 12″ in width ...	7·0 — 8·0[8]

In the following table an attempt is made to divide up the total of British subsidies and tax concessions in broad categories of benefits, comparable, as far as possible, with the German table above.

Beneficiaries :	£ m.	Per cent
Agriculture,[9] forestry, fisheries	351	57
Industry and trade	74	12
Housing	139	22
Small business	15	3
Other	38	6
	617	100

The main difference between the British and the German case which emerges from the last table is the relatively small value of British concessions made under the heading of Industry and Trade. German subsidies etc. to Agriculture are roughly of the same order of magnitude in monetary terms as the British. But the German concessions to industry and trade are vastly greater. It is here that the German policy of public intervention in the private sector of the economy shows up most clearly. The *relative* weight of total subsidy payments and tax concessions in the Government's budget is very much greater in Germany than in Britain. The German total is the equivalent of 23 per cent of the central Government's budget of some DM 47 billion, while the corresponding British figure is 9 per cent of a budget of nearly £7,000 million.

---

[8] This is a very approximate figure. It is based on an estimate, by the trade, of all piece-goods sold retail; this was reduced by one-third (allowing for the estimated retail mark-up) to arrive at the wholesale value; and the purchase tax lost was calculated at 10 per cent on this figure. 10 per cent is the rate applicable to textiles which have been made up into ready-made clothing. This is the only purchase tax concession of any serious industrial significance.

[9] There are some additional benefits which British agriculture receives in its tax treatment, e.g. the basis of income tax assessment is believed to be more favourable for farmers' incomes than for others; but it is impossible to put even an approximate figure to this kind of gain.

APPENDIX V

THE CONTROL OF THE UNITED STATES OIL MARKET

THE way in which 'allowables' are actually laid down provides an instructive insight into the oblique methods employed by US government when it invades the private sector. The end product is a closely supervised control over the output of all the oilfields of any significance in the country. Moreover, the combined effect of the restriction of domestic oil production well below capacity and of the ceiling imposed on imports is to set the price of oil at some point above where it would stand in a free market. But the level of prices is never officially discussed by the controllers; it is treated as given.

What happens is that once a month each of the great oil companies which refine and market petroleum products submits a bid to the authorities of the leading oil-producing state, Texas, for the amount of crude oil that it needs in order to meet its estimated sales to customers. This figure is translated into a calculation of the 'allowable' production—i.e. the number of days working at full capacity in the course of the month—that would be needed by the company's crude oil suppliers (including the wells which it owns itself) to reach the target output. This is, of course, another way of expressing the proportion of their capacity that the oil producers are expected to use; the important point is that any restrictions are supposed to apply equally to all of them—with some minor exceptions to allow for new sources of production. Again, the companies assume (but never state) that the price will stay at the existing level; they would clearly come up with different answers about the amount which the market would absorb if they allowed for the possibility of a change of price.

The Texas Railroad Commissioners then give the companies, who by this time know the size of each other's bids, an opportunity to argue their case before them. What the Texas Railroad Commission does in practice is to search for some kind of consensus among the forward estimates of what is likely to be sold a month ahead at a stated price. It almost always chooses some compromise between the various figures submitted by the companies. Once it has decided and fixed the percentage rate at which the Texans may operate their wells, the other states fix their 'allowables' in relationship to this. They are not compelled to do so— and there are exceptions, the biggest being California, where the official rationing system does not apply—but all the states know that if they stepped seriously out of line and produced more than their 'fair share', Texas with its overwhelming oil capacity would be able to retaliate by swamping their markets.

It is, indeed, the textbook case of organized oligopoly, in which the producer with the largest potential acts as policeman for the cartel. All these bargains are covert; no one openly threatens anyone else or fixes a price. But an essential bulwark of the system is provided by the Federal Government which bans the use of inter-state transport facilities for 'hot oil', i.e. oil produced outside the network of restrictions. The government also fixes the volume of imports from month to month—a weapon which is available for use as an ultimate resort to discipline any group of American oil producers who might be tempted to rebel against the system of 'orderly marketing'. It has never had to be used.

439

INDEX

441